D1068707

HIS GRACE, THE FIRST DUKE OF RICHMOND
(1672-1723)
By Sir Godfrey Kneller

MARRIAGES

OF

RICHMOND COUNTY

VIRGINIA

1668 - 1853

Compiled and Published

By

George H.S. King

SOUTHERN HISTORICAL PRESS, INC.
P.O. Box 738
Easley, South Carolina 29641-0738

ISBN 0-89308-579-0

IN MEMORIUM

ELLIS CARTER DELANO

1892 - 1951

DEPUTY CLERK OF THE COURT OF RICHMOND COUNTY

1921 - 1951

CLERK'S OFFICE OF RICHMOND COUNTY - 1748

CONTENTS

PREFACE   ix

PLAQUES ON THE COURTROOM WALL   xv

SEGMENT OF A SURVEY OF THE NORTHERN NECK OF VIRGINIA   xvii

BOND AND MARRIAGE LICENSE FORMS   xx

KEY TO ABBREVIATIONS OF TITLES AND SYMBOLS   xxi

MARRIAGES OF RICHMOND COUNTY, VIRGINIA 1668-1853   1

GENEALOGICAL CHARTS   241

INDEX   271

COLOPHON   369

ILLUSTRATIONS

FRONTISPIECE   HIS GRACE, THE FIRST DUKE OF RICHMOND

CLERK'S OFFICE, RICHMOND COUNTY, VIRGINIA, BUILT 1748   vi

A SEGMENT OF THE 1737 SURVEY OF THE
                         NORTHERN NECK OF VIRGINIA   xviii

MARRIAGE BOND OF BENJAMIN EDWARDS, 1750   xix

PREFACE

RICHMOND COUNTY was formed by an act of the House of Burgesses in April 1692 at which time the county of Rappahannock became defunct. Though the life of Rappahannock County was of relatively short duration [1652-1692], its domain was very extensive. It covered all that territory on both sides of the Rappahannock River which was drained by that long estuary which forms the southern boundry of the Northern Neck of Virginia.

Since the time of Captain John Smith Englishmen had plyed the Rappahannock River to its falls at Fredericksburg and the fertility of the soil had attracted many settlers. After 1650 land patents for large acreages issued in great numbers and the gentlemen in lower Tidewater established "quarters" and were gradually pressing the Indians out of the territory so long cherished by them. The population of Rappahannock County expanded rapidly westward.

By 1692 a separation of the immense territory called Rappahannock County, into two counties, was deemed expedient and in the fourth year of the reign of their Majesties King William and Queen Mary of England it was enacted that Rappahannock County be divided into two distinct counties "so that Rappahannock river divides the same, and that that part which is now on the north side be called and known by the name of Richmond county, and that that part which is now on the south side thereof be called and known by the name of Essex county." ... "That the records belonging to the county court of Rappahannock before this division be kept in Essex county, that belonging wholly to their Majesties and the other to the proprietors of the Northern Neck."

Things moved slowly in those days and it was some weeks later that a copy of the act dissolving Rappahannock County reached that then outpost of civilization. It was apparently known that the county was to be divided as on 4-5 May 1692 the first court order book opens with these lines: "At a court held for the North Side of Rappahannock County," but it was not until the 12th of May 1692 that the name of the new county was mentioned in the county court records.

> "Att a Meeting of their Maj^{ties} Justices
> of the Peace for the late County of Rappa-
> hannock att the Court House of the said
> County on the North side of Rappahannock
> River the 12th day of May An^{o} Dom: 1692:
>   "The Laws made at the last sessions of Assembly were Read
> Publickly, Wherein by the 6th Act of the s^{d} Assembly Entitled
> An Act for deviding Rappahannock County, It is Provided, that
> the North side of the County shall be called and knowne by the
> name of Richmond County. And for as much as a Commission of
> the Peace for the said county of Richmond was then openly read
> with a Dodimus for administering oaths to the Gentlemen in the
> said Commission named to be Justices of the Peace for the said
> County, In Pursuance thereof Colonel John Stone and Captain

ix

George Taylor, to whom with others the said Dominus was
directed, did administer the Oaths enjoyed by Act of Par-
liament instead of the Oaths of Alligiance and Supremacy
together with the oaths of a Justice of the Peace for the
County of Richmond unto Mr. James Harrison, Capt. Alexander
Swan, Mr. William Underwood, Mr. Thomas Glascock, And the
said Gentlemen after having taken the oaths aforesaid did
administer the same unto the said Colonel John Stone and
Captain George Taylor."

At this same court Colonel John Stone was sworn sheriff; Mr. William Colston, clerk of the court and Mr. John Deane, a justice. On 1 June 1692 three
other gentlemen were sworn justices, viz: Captain William Barber, Mr. James
Scott and Mr. Alexander Doniphan; thus the quorum of the newly formed county
of Richmond was completed.

These two newly formed counties were long and narrow. Essex County, on
the south side of the Rappahannock River, extended from the Middlesex County
line up the river to the westward and included all the territory drained by the
Rappahannock River. Likewise Richmond County, on the north side, extended from
the Lancaster County line up the river to the westward and included all the
territory drained by the Rappahannock River. The 1692 bounds of Richmond County
included the present county of Richmond and the Rappahannock River watershead of
the present counties of Westmoreland, King George, Stafford and Fauquier. So,
until King George County was formed from the upper portions of Richmond County
in 1721, its territory was immense and stretched westward into vast unsettled
areas.

In 1691 King and Queen County had been named for King William and Queen Mary
of England. At this time there were two gentlemen in great favor at their court
and in their honor Essex and Richmond counties were named.

Algernon Capel, Esquire, (1670-1710), Second Earl of Essex, was Gentleman
of the Bedchamber to King William III in 1691 and served with him in all of his
campaigns. Furthermore, he married on February 28, 1692, Mary the daughter of
Hans William Bentinck, Earl of Portland, also a particular favorite of the King.

Richmond County was named in honor of the Duke of Richmond and for this
reason I wish to include a more detailed account of him than the Earl of Essex.

Charles Lennox, Esquire, (29 July 1672-27 May 1723), was the natural son of
King Charles II of England by Louise Renee de Keroualle, Duchess of Portsmouth
and Aubigny (1649-1734); she was maid of honor to Queen Catherine in 1670 and
shortly thereafter she was established as mistress en titre to King Charles II.
On the 9th of August 1675 the King greatly favored his three year old illegitimate son by creating him Baron of Settrington, Yorkshire, Earl of March and Duke
of Richmond, Yorkshire, in the peerage of England and on the 9th of September
1675 Baron Methuen of Tarbolton, Earl of Darnley and Duke of Lennox, in the peerage of Scotland. The two dukedoms had reverted to King Charles II as nearest
heir male of Charles Stuart (1640-1672), Duke of Richmond and Lennox, who had
died without issue. King Louis XIV of France also gave young Charles Lennox the

the dignity of Duke of Aubigny in remainder to his mother. In 1684 John Evelyn (1620-1706) described Charles as "a very pretty boy" and other contemporaries stated he was an extremely handsome young man and bore a striking resemblance to his royal father.

The following diagram will illustrate the close connection of the Duke of Richmond to the reigning monarchs of Great Britain.

<pre>
                           King Charles I
                            (1600-1649)
                                :
        _____:_____
        :   :   :   :
Prince William II -m- Princess Mary   King James II   King Charles II
  of Orange   :   (1631-1660)   (1633-1688)   (1630-1685)
                  :   :   By his mistress, the
_____: :   Duchess of Portsmouth
:   :   :   :
King William III -m,cousin- Queen Mary   Queen Anne   Charles Lennox, Esqʳ.
  (1650-1702)   (1662-94)   (1664-1714)   Duke of Richmond
                                                          (1672-1723)
</pre>

King Charles II (1630-1685) died without legitimate issue; he was succeeded by his brother, King James II (1633-1688). King James hated the Duchess of Portsmouth and in August 1685 she left the English court and took her son to France where she held property. They were received at the French court and young Charles served as aide-de-camp to the Duke of Orleans. In 1690 King Louis gave him a company in the royal regiment of horse. He was not, however, satisfied with his position and soon secretly left the court and went to England where he made peace with his cousins, King William and Queen Mary. His actions displeased his mother a great deal; she thought h▒m out of his senses.

In England the Duke of Richmond found it convenient to change both his politics and religion and on Whitsunday, May 15, 1692, he was received again into the Church of England. On November 14, 1693 he took his seat in the House of Lords and thereafter was much in favor at court. At the corornation of his cousin, Queen Anne, on April 23, 1702, the Duke of Richmond bore the sceptre and the dove and remained in her particular favor. Shortly after the accession of King George I in 1714, he was made lord of his bedchamber and on August 5, 1715 privy councillor of Ireland. He died at Goodwood, Sussex, on the 27th of May 1723. His portrait, by Kneller, is at Goodwood.

Shortly after his return to England he married Anne, widow of Henry, son of John, Lord Bellasis, and daughter of Francis, Lord Brundenell. They had three children, viz: (1) Louise (1694-1717) who married James, third earl of Berkeley; (2) Charles Lennox (1701-1750), second Duke of Richmond, Lennox and Aubigny; and (3) Anne (1703-1722) who married William Anne Keppel, second earl of Albemarle.

Persons interested in further detail in regard to the Duke of Richmond are referred to H. Forneron's, Louise de Keroualle, Duchesse de Portsmouth (Paris, 1886); there is an English translation of this excellent biography by Mrs. Crawford published in 1888. There are extended biographical accounts of the Duke of

Richmond and Mademoiselle de Keroualle in The Dictionary of National Biography.

Save for the unexplained loss of Richmond County Will Book #1 [1692-1699], most of the record books of the county are well preserved. Unfortunately I am forced to observe that the deed books are very poorly indexed; particularly is this true for the colonial period. Here were not only recorded deeds for real estate, most of which instruments are carried in the general index to deeds, but also a wide variety of bonds, conveyances of Negroes and other chattels, bills of exchange, the mark of stock, depositions and the like, all of which are of prime genealogical import, but, for the most part, are not carried in the general indecies to the deed books. Thus, the records abound with a wealth of interesting material which, I dare say, has been overlooked by many who have placed too much confidence in the existing indecies to the records.

The marriage bonds prior to 1824 were never recorded in a bound volume; they were filed with the loose papers. As there is no index to them they have been virtually inaccessible and being very fragile have not been available to the public. In 1917 the late Ellis Carter Delano, Esquire, (1892-1951), made a list of the marriage bonds for his personal use. Mr. Delano, deputy clerk of Richmond County court 1921-1951, was interested in genealogy and assisted many persons professionally. Some of his papers are in the Virginia Historical Society and in these he observes when he attempted to copy some of the marriage bonds in 1930 he found the bundle for 1760-1770 had been completely destroyed by worms. He immediately set about making handwritten copies of the earliest marriage bonds which had survived and for the next several years, during his spare time, made verbatim copies of many bonds prior to 1800. Thus Mr. Delano has preserved considerable which otherwise would have been lost.

These vermin did not confine their activity to the 1760-1770 bundle of marriage bonds, but to a lesser extent mutilated other bundles until all of the marriage bonds ante 1824 are in dire need of restoration.

As all the marriage bonds prior to 1750 are now missing as well as those for the years 1760-1770, I have relied upon Mr. Delano's 1917 transcriptions for these years. In making this arrangement from the existing marriage bonds, I find that some of the marriage bonds noted by Mr. Delano have mysteriously disappeared from the files. For instance, under his court seal of 7 April 1931, Mr. Delano certified a verbatim transcription of the marriage bond of John France, 1794, but this document is now missing from the bundle. There are other bonds which are not to be found in their proper place.

The marriage licenses for 1709-1716, recorded in Deed Book #6, page 275, have been included in this arrangement. They were published by Mr. Delano in the Daughters of the American Revolution Magazine, Volume LVII, Number 11, pages 675-676; this is the November 1923 issue.

In the clerk's office is a Register of Marriages 1802-1842, kepted by the Reverend William Forrester, performed in Richmond, Lancaster and Westmoreland counties. There are about 800 unindexed entries; I have checked all of these marriages, noted by him "RC" [Richmond County], against the existing marriage bonds and if the bond itself was not found, included the marriage in the present arrangement.

From Lancaster County Marriage Register #1 [1715-1852], I have included in this arrangement all parties shewn to be of Richmond County prior to 1800. There was much intercourse between residents of Richmond and Lancaster counties and some may find these entries helpful.

Two unpublished parish registers are available in the Archives Division, Virginia State Library. Lunenburg Parish Register 1790-1800 contains no marriage entries; North Farnham Parish Register 1668-1800 contains 224 marriage entries and these have been included in this arrangement. The pages noted are to the original register; there is also a transcript in the clerk's office which was made in 1901. It is my intention to publish an arrangement of the North Farnham and Lunenburg Parish registers in the not too distant future.

The marriages by inference which are cited in this arrangement are but a few of those which are of record in the many record books of Richmond County. Perhaps I should not include a sampling as some may think this volume is a complete coverage of the existing records. Please let all be informed that this arrangement includes but a small portion of the many inferred marriages in Richmond County; a full coverage would require years of intense research and fill several volumes the size of this book. I am fearful we cannot hope to see this accomplished in our time.

In 1896 Doctor Lyon G. Tyler published in the William and Mary College Quarterly, First Series, Volume 5, pages 19-20, a selected group of Richmond County marriage bonds which someone undoubtedly submitted to him. Not all of these marriage bonds are now in the files, yet I feel we should have confidence in these published excerpts and they have been included in the present arrangement. I have taken the liberty to make such corrections as I deemed proper. As no Luggitt family inhabited Richmond County, I have altered the surname to Suggitt in this arrangement. It is well known that Billington McCarty's name was not Bellingham McCarty and as the marriage bond of Isaac Degge, 1772, is in the file, this gives evidence that the published date, 1792, was a typographical error.

The many references to Richmond County and its inhabitants in Swem's Virginia Historical Index will be evident to most researchers, but I should like to call attention to the Richmond County material in the late Beverley Fleet's series, Colonial Virginia Abstracts, Volumes 16 and 17. Mr. Fleet is incorrect in stating that Richmond County Deed Book #3 is "lost;" it is in the clerk's office.

The rent rolls of Richmond County for the colonial period are often helpful. Preserved in the Archives Division of the Virginia State Library are lists for the various parishes for the years 1721, 1744, 1746, 1751, 1765, 1766, 1768 and 1770. As county lines and rivers did not act as determents, many persons owned property in more than one county and thus we must be mindful that the rent rolls, county records and other manuscript material available for other counties, particularly those adjoining, are helpful in genealogical and historical studies.

Bishop William Meade in his masterly work, Old Churches and Families of Virginia, Volume II, pages 172-182, has recorded some facts in regard to Richmond

PREFACE

County and its two parishes which many may find of interest. A later ecclesiati-
cal historiographer, George Carrington Mason, Esquire, has left us a definitive
study of "The Colonial Churches of Essex and Richmond Counties" in The Virginia
Magazine of History and Biography, Volume 53, pages 3-20. Also, the late Henry
Ragland Eubank, Esquire, has left us some interesting lore in regard to the old
homes, churches and families of Richmond County in his work, Historic Northern
Neck of Virginia (Richmond, 1934), pages 82-89.

The County Court Note Book, Volume IV, pages 14, 21, 39, and 47 contains
citations to the probates and administrations in Richmond County 1692-1699 as
taken from the court order books by the late Ellis Carter Delano; this is an ex-
cellent attempt to bridge the gap left by the loss of Will Book #1. In July 1924,
Mrs. Milnor Ljungstedt, editor of The County Court Note Book, announced in Volume
III, Number 4, page 31: "VALUABLE PUBLICATION: A list of the Marriage License
Bonds of Richmond County, Virginia, from 1740, is about to be published by Mr. E.
Carter Delano, of Warsaw, Virginia." The proposed volume was never published.

The history of Richmond County and the genealogy of many of its families
has yet to be published. It is hoped that the facts under this cover may make
those tasks a triffle easier.

I am very much indebted to Hundley Balderson, Esquire, Clerk of the Court
of Richmond County, and to his deputies, Mrs. Ruth (Peyton) Balderson and Mrs.
Gertrude (Payne) Sanford Delano, for the many courtsies extended to me on my
frequent visits to their office. Each was patient with my interest and project,
although the current duties of their offices precludes an interest in genealogical research.

John Melville Jennings, Esquire, director of the Virginia Historical Society
and his curators there, and John W. Dudley, Esquire, assistant archivist at the
Virginia State Library, have extended me courtsies for which I am grateful.

I wish to take this opportunity to express my sincere appreciation to those
persons who have purchased my genealogical publications. Their interest has en-
couraged me to present this arrangement of the MARRIAGES OF RICHMOND COUNTY, VIR-
GINIA, in order to preserve many marriage records the original recordings being
destroyed.

George Harrison Sanford King

1301 Prince Edward Street
Fredericksburg, Virginia
Eastertide, 1964

1692 -   RICHMOND   COUNTY   - 1908

When "Old Rappahannock County" was extinguished in
1692, Richmond and Essex were formed from it. The
Prosecuting Attorneys have been,

COUNTY

Dennis McCarty, "Attorney for their Majesties"	1692-1693
John Gardener, " " " "	1693-1704
Daniel McCarty and George Eskridge, "Attorneys for Our Sovereigne, The Queen	1704-1711
Daniel McCarty, Queen's Attorney (King's Attorney, 1714)	1711-1724
John Tarpley, Jun., King's Attorney	1724-1736
William Robinson " "	1736-1742
Charles Beale " "	1742-1759
Richard Parker " " (Commonwealth's Attorney, 1777)	1759-1788
Alexander Campbell, Commonwealth's Attorney	1788-
Order Books Nos. 21, 22 & 23 Missing*	1789-1816
Foushee G. Tebbs Commonwealth's Attorney	-1818
William Y. Sturman " " (resigned)	1818-1819
John Campbell " "	1819-1828
William Y. Sturman " "	1828-1848
George W. Crittenden " "	1848-1849

The following were ex officio
Commonwealth's Attorneys for the Circuit Court:

Thomas Jones, Jr. Commonwealth's Attorney	1849-1869
Wm. R. Brownlee " " (military appointee)	1869-1870
Thomas Jones, Jr. " "	1870-1871
Wm. R. Brownlee " " (elected)	1871-1873
T. C. Chinn " "(elected and resigned)	1873-1873
W. A. Jones " "	1873-1883
John D. Garland " "	1883-1891
J.W. Chinn, Jr. " " (incumbent)	1891-19

Superior and Circuit Superior Courts:

Stokley Towles Commonwealth's Attorney	1808-1812
" " (office vacant)	1812-1816
Ellyson Currie " " (resigned)	1816-1816
John Campbell " "	1816-1828
Augustine Neale " " (resigned)	1828-1845
Presley Thornton Lomax " "	1845-1852

Donated through the Circuit Court to Richmond County, Virginia, by
O.J. Hamwell Company, Pleasantville, New Jersey

---

* Court Order Book No.21 [1789-1794] was overlooked; page 68, August 3, 1790,
notes the qualification of John Monroe, Gent. "to act as Commonwealth's Attorney
in this County," (q.v.), pages 134-135.

PLAQUES ON THE COURTROOM WALL

1692 -   RICHMOND COUNTY   - 1908

When "Old Rappahannock County" was extinguished
in 1692, Richmond and Essex were formed from it.

The clerks have been

1.	William Colston	1692-1701
2.	James Sherlock	1701-1709
3.	Sir Marmaduke Beckwith, Baronet	1709-1780
4.	Leroy Peachy	1780-1793
5.	Bartholomew McCarty	1793-1815
6.	George Saunders	1815-1838
7.	John F.B. Jeffries	1838-1848
8.	Isaac S. Jeffries	1848-1849
9.	Joseph R. Jeffries pro. tem.	1849-1849
10.	Francis W. Pendleton	1849-1865
11.	Robert Hall	1865-1868
12.	L.D. Warner	1868-1870
13.	William A. Brockenbrough	1870-1871
14.	L.D. Warner	1871-1901
15.	J.B. Rains (incumbent)	1901-19

DONATED THROUGH THE CIRCUIT COURT OF RICHMOND COUNTY
BY THE GENEROSITY OF CITIZENS AND FRIENDS

*****

The following letter from the Honorable Edmund Jenings, President of the Council of Virginia, to the Justices of Richmond County, is of record in DB#5,p.68.

April ye 25th 1709

Gentlemen

    I have yours recommending Mr. Joseph Tayloe to succeed Mr. Sherlock in the Clerkship of your County, but before it came to my hand I had disposed of that Office to Mr. Beckwith a near relation of my owne who had bin bred up in the Secretary's Office under Mr. Thacker above these three years and I doubt not both in respect of his Capacity and dilligence will merritt your good opinion.

    If on any other occassion I can serve Mr. Tayloe wch tis like may be againe in my power, I shall readily do it and believe he does not doubt of my good will. I am particularly obliged to you for the kind expressions of your Letter. Assureing you I shall take all opportunities to manifest to you that I am

                                        Gentlemen
                                    Your most humble Servt
                                        E. Jenings

Mr. Beckwith has given security for the due
keeping of the records, which I desire the
Court would order to have perused and that
the oaths be administered to Mr. Beckwith.

To/The Worshipful her Maj^{ties} Justices
    of the peace for Richmond County

SEGMENT OF A SURVEY OF THE NORTHERN NECK OF VIRGINIA

ON THE REVERSE of this page is a segment of the 1737 survey of the Northern Neck of Virginia, made at the insistence of My Lord Thomas Fairfax, showing colonial Richmond County and adjacent areas. The present lower Richmond County line on the Rappahannock River is at Morattico Creek [now called Lancaster Creek] and the upper Richmond County line is at Charles' Beaver Dam [now called Brockenbrough Creek].

Downing Bridge crosses the Rappahannock River at Tappahannock and Warsaw, the county seat of Richmond County, is seven miles northeast. The first plantation to our left is Crondall, seat of Colonel Moore Fauntleroy (1680-1739), and immediately in view (when the trees are leafless), on an eminence overlooking the Rappahannock Valley, is handsome Mount Airy, the well known seat of the Tayloe family, which was built in 1758 by Colonel John Tayloe (1721-1779).

Above Rappahannock Creek [now called Cat Point Creek] is Naylor's Hole, once an important port of entry and the seat of the immigrant, Colonel Moore Fauntleroy, which he purchased from the Rappahannock Indians by a written conveyance dated the 4th of April 1651. In 1927 Fauntleroy descendants erected a handsome monument here with a large bronze plaque outlining the history of their distinguished family but no vestage of it now remains. There is a photograph of the monument and a copy of the inscription on the plaque in the Virginia Magazine of History and Biography, Volume 35, pages 204-205.

Just above Pepeticker [Perpetoc] Creek and below Leedstown are the tombs of John Birkett (16??-1719) and his wife nee Ann Mills (16??-1691), daughter of William Mills (16??-1661),the original patentee. The will of William Mills was proved in Rappahannock County and the will of John Birkett in Richmond County. In 1721, upon the formation of King George County, this area fell into that county and so remained until 1777, when, by an alteration of the county lines, it fell into Westmoreland County. Margaret Birkett (16??-1749), daughter of John and Ann (Mills) Birkett, married John Pratt (16??-1724) and they succeeded to the aforementioned plantation and their wills were proved in King George County, but by the time of the death of their daughter, Ann (Pratt) Hungerford (1718-1800), who succeeded to the plantation, the area had fallen into Westmoreland County. Thus in four successive generations on the same plantation, their wills were proven in four counties.

A thorough knowledge of the formation of the counties and the frequent alterations in the boundry lines is essential to historical and genealogical research. Two publications are particularly helpful in the study of Virginia counties, viz: Morgan P. Robinson, Virginia Counties, Bulletin of the Virginia State Library, Volume 9, Numbers 1,2,3 (1916) and Martha W. Hiden, How Justice Grew: Virginia Counties: An Abstract of Their Formation, Historical Booklet Number 19, published by the Virginia 350th Anniversary Celebration Corporation (1957). Related information will be found in those sources mentioned by Mrs. Hiden in her bibliography on page 79.

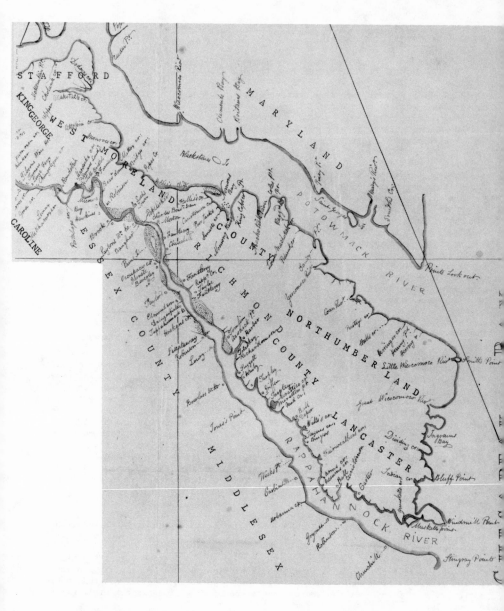

A SEGMENT OF THE 1737 SURVEY OF THE NORTHERN NECK OF VIRGINIA

xviii

Know all men by these Presents that we Benjamin Edwards and John French
eeeeeeeeeeeee are held & firmly bound unto our Sovereign
Lord George the Second by the Grace of God of Greatt Brittain france & Ireland
King Defender of the faith &c: in £50 Curr^t. Money to be paid to our s^d. Lord the
King his heirs and Successors to the wch. Payment well & Truly to be made we bind
our Selves our heirs, Ex^{rs}. & Adm^{rs}. Joyntly & severally firmly by these Presents
Sealed with our Seals Dated this 3rd Day of May 1750.

Whereas there is a Marriage suddenly Intended to be solemnized between the
above Bound Benjamin Edwards & Jean Gray Spinster of the County of Richmond
The Condition of this present Obligation is such that if there be no Lawfull cause
to Obstruct the same; then this Obligation to be void else to remain in full force.

Seal^d and Deliver^d
in presents of   Benjamin Edwards

Travers Tarpley D.Cl.   John French

xix

BOND AND MARRIAGE LICENSE FORMS

Know all Men by these Presents that We AB & CD are held and firmly bound unto our Sovereign Lord George the Second by the Grace of God of Great Britain &c. in Fifty Pounds Current Money to be paid to our said Lord the King his Heirs and Successors; To the which Payment well and truly to be made we bind ourselves our Heirs Ex^{rs} and Adm^{rs} jointly and severally firmly by these Presents Sealed with our Seals Dated this __ Day of _____ 1739.
Whereas there is a Marriage suddenly intended to be solemnized between the above bound AB and PR Spinster/Widow, The Condition of this Present Obligation is such that if there be no Lawful Cause to obstruct the same, then this Obligation to be void else to remain in full force.

Sealed and Delivered)
  in Presence of   )

    A.B.   [L.S.]
    C.D.   [L.S.]

James City County Ss/
            These are to Licence and Permit you to join together in the Holy State of Matrimony according to the Rites and Ceremonies of the Church of England FE and PR, spinster, Daughter of MR both of the County aforesaid and for so doing this shall be your sufficient Warrant. Given under my hand this __ Day of _____ 1739.
To the Rev^{d} _____ or any other Orthodox)
  Minister of the Church of England   )

Whereas there is a Marriage suddenly intended to be solemnized between FE and PR Spinster both of the County aforesaid, I do hereby Certifie that MR, father of the said P (She being under the Age of 21 Years), Personally appeared before me this Day and declared his free Consent to the said intended Marriage and at the same time the said FE with WM his Security intred into Bond in my Office in £50 Current Money Payable to the King with Condition that there is no lawful cause to obstruct the said Marriage. Given under my hand &c.
To _____ Gen^{t}., first Justice in the)   J.E.
  Comission of the Peace for the County afores^{d})
                                        Cl:Cur:

    The above forms were adopted by "Act of the General Assembly made in the Eighth Year of the Reign of King George the Second" [1734] and continued in use until the establishment of the Commonwealth of Virginia. There are various acts in Hening, The Statutes at Large...of Virginia, in regard to the solemnization of marriages, the returns of the officiating clergymen to the clerks of the county courts and the manner the clerks were to keep the marriage records. It appears there was flagrant disregard for many of these laws and regulations. In 1748 it was enacted that "if either of the parties intending to marry shall be under the age of one and twenty years, and not heretofore married, the consent of the father, or guardian, of every such infant, shall be personally given before the said clerk or certified under the hand and seal of such father or guardian, attested by two witnesses" and this remains in force now. [6H81-84]

KEY TO ABBREVIATIONS OF TITLES AND SYMBOLS

* - The asterisk, placed after the bride's name in the marriage bonds, pages 1-239, indicates the bride gave her consent to the court clerk for the bond or license to issue. This symbol does not necessarily mean that the said consent was written in her own handwriting as most often it was not.

* - The asterisk, placed before a name on the genealogical charts, pages 242-269, indicates the party died testate, however, it does not necessarily mean that the last wills and Testaments of all these parties now remain of record.

AB# - Account Book Number[1]

ABC Book - Alexander - Brown - Chapman And Associated Families by Sigismunda Mary Frances Chapman (Richmond, Va., 1946).

A.P.& P. - Adventurers of Purse and Person, Virginia, 1607-1625 by Annie Lash Jester and Martha Woodroof Hiden (Princeton, N.J., 1956).

(b) - bondsman or security on the marriage bond or license.

Beale - The Genealogy of the Beale Family 1399-1956 by Frances Beal Smith Hodges (Ann Arbor, Michigan, 1956).

c. - circa - about

C&P - Cavaliers And Pioneers, Abstracts of Virginia Land Patents and Grants, [Volume I (1623-1666)] by Nell Marion Nugent (Richmond, Va., 1934).

CCPR - The Parish Register of Christ Church, Middlesex County, Va., 1653 to 1812 (Richmond, Va., 1897).

COB# - Court Order Book Number[1]

d.s.p. — died without issue or died without surviving issue

DB# - Deed Book Number[1]

DB#6,p.275 - Richmond County Deed Book Number Six, page 275. Here are recorded seventy two marriage licenses issued by Marmaduke Beckwith, Esquire, clerk of the court, between 19 January 1709/10 and 7 May 1716.

ECD - Ellis Carter Delano (1892-1951) and/or the papers of Ellis Carter Delano, deputy clerk of Richmond County 1921-1951 in the Virginia Historical Society.

---

1 - AB#, COB#, DB# and WB# refer to volumes by numbers of Richmond County Court records; references to the court records of other counties are so designated.

xxi

Eubank - The Authentic Guide Book of Historic Northern Neck of Virginia by H. Ragland Eubank (Colonial Beach, Va., 1934).

FDC - Fredericksburg District Court, Fredericksburg, Virginia. The loose suit papers of this court, now defunct, are in numbered files in the office of the clerk of the court of the City of Fredericksburg.

Fauntleroy - Colonel Moore Fauntleroy, His Ancestors and Descendants, a two volume typescript, by Miss Juliet Fauntleroy (1936), Virginia State Library [CS:71. F:264].

Graham - General George Mason Graham of Tyrone Plantation And His People by Dr. George Mason Graham Stafford (New Orleans, La., 1947).

Hayden - Virginia Genealogies by the Rev. Horace Edwin Hayden (Wilkes-Barre, Pa., 1891).

LCMR - Lancaster County, Virginia, Marriage Register Number One (1715-1852), a manuscript volume in the Archives Division, Virginia State Library.

Lee - Abstracts Lancaster County, Virginia, Wills 1653-1800 by Ida Johnson Lee (Richmond, Va., 1959).

MBB - Richmond County Marriage Bond Book (1824-1850), paged.

MRB - Richmond County Miscellaneous Record Book (1699-1724).

Meade - Old Churches, Ministers and Families of Virginia, in two volumes, by the Rt. Rev. William Meade, Bishop of P.E.C. of Virginia (Philadelphia, Pa., 1889).

n.f.r. - no further record

n.p. - not paged

NFPR - North Farnham Parish Register (1668-1800), paged, Richmond County, Va.

OPR - The Register of Overwharton Parish, Stafford County, Virginia, 1723-1758, compiled by George H.S. King (Ann Arbor, Michigan, 1961).

p. - page or pages

PB - Patent Book; the manuscript volumes are in VSL:AD.

Payne - The Paynes of Virginia by Colonel Brooke Payne (Richmond, Va., 1937).

(q.v.) - quod vide - which see

SPR - The Register of Saint Paul's Parish 1715-1798, Stafford County, Virginia, 1715-1776; King George County, Virginia, 1777-1798 by George H.S. King (Ann Arbor, Michigan, 1960).

Sweeny - Wills of Rappahannock County, Virginia, 1656-1692 by William Montgomery Sweeny (Lynchburg, Va., 1947).

T - Tyler's Quarterley Historical and Genealogical Magazine, citing the
volume ante and the page post, T.

VCA - Virginia Colonial Abstracts, in thirty four volumes, by Beverley Fleet,
Esquire, (Richmond, Va.).

VHS - Virginia Historical Society, Richmond, Virginia.

VSL:AD - Virginia State Library, Archives Division, Richmond, Virginia.

V - Virginia Magazine of History and Biography, citing the volume ante and
and the page post, V.

(w) - witness to marriage bond, license and/or consent filed.

W - William and Mary College Quarterly Historical Magazine, series one and
two, citing volume, series and page, viz: 1W(2)3 - volume one, second
series, page three.

WB# - Will Book Number[1]

WFMR - Reverend William Forrester's Marriage Register [1802-1842], not paged;
a manuscript volume in the clerk's office of Richmond County, Virginia.

```
        * * * * *
         * * * *
          * * *
           * *
            *
```

"I cannot tell how the truth may be;
I say the tale as 't was said to me."

[Sir Walter Scott: The Lay of the Last Minstrel]

A

ABSHONE, WILLIAM married Eleanor Starks, 15 October 1729.   NFPR.,p.77
    [She was the daughter of Henry and Jane Todd and widow of James Starks
    (16??-1726), q.v.]

ADAMS, JAMES and Elizabeth C. Stonum, bond 7 February 1815. Consent by William
    Stonum, father of the bride. Samuel Dunaway (b); Hiram Stonum (w).

ADAMS, JAMES J. and Mary Sisson, bond 2 July 1846. Consent by Susan Sisson
    (widow of James Sisson), mother of the bride. William P. Harper (b);
    John E. Sanford (w).   MBB.,p.278

ADAMS, RICHARD and Elizabeth Griffin, bond 10 April 1755. John Tarpley (b).

ALDERSON, GEORGE N. and Lucy B. Darby, bond 18 January 1840. Consent by T.L.
    Darby, father of the bride. Bartholomew Bell (b).   MBB.,p.190

ALDERSON, JAMES and Catherine Scurlock*, bond 5 May 1813. James Adams (b).

ALDERSON, JAMES and Mary Ann Brown, license 29 December 1852. Richard Fones
    (w) and Thomas B. Fones (w). Married 23 January 1853 by Rev. E.L. Will-
    iams.

ALDERSON, JELOFF JR. [also rendered TELIFF ALVERSON] married 171? Rebecca Hat-
    ton; her cousin Daniel Sullivant [Swillevan] of Northumberland County by
    will dated 29 August 1704 bequeathed her land in Richmond County. Jeloff
    Alderson Jr., died testate 1719 and his widow m(2) 17 February 1728 Peter
    Oldham, q.v. AB#1,p.144; DB#3,p.16; DB#4,p.62; DB#10,p.351; DB#12,p.517,
    541,719; DB#13,p.206; WB#4,p.79; WB#5,p.265; WB#6,p.91.

ALDERSON, JEREMIAH and Barbara B. Northen, bond 5 February 1805. Edward J.
    Northen (b).

ALDERSON, JERY and Caty Alloway*, bond 17 May 1791. Consent by Isaac Alloway,
    father of the bride. Griffin G. Berrick (b).

ALDERSON, JOHN married Jane Starks, 4 July 1729.   NFPR.,p.77
    [She was the daughter of James and Eleanor (Todd) Starks. COB#10.,p.544.]

ALDERSON, JOHN of Richmond County married Rachel Davenport of Lancaster County,
    31 January 1787. Thaddeus Pope of Richmond County (b).   LCMR#1,p.62

ALDERSON, JOHN and Elizabeth Scrimger*, bond 26 December 1812. Thomas S. Davis
    (b); Samuel B. Kelsick (w).

ALDERSON, WILLIAM and Elizabeth Baker, bond 29 April 1789. Consent by Sarah
    Ann Alderson, mother of the groom. John Baker (b).

ALDERSON, WILLIAM and Ann M. Tapscott (widow)*, bond 20 February 1805. Edward
    Saunders (b).

1

ALDERSON, WILLIAM and Ann Webb*, bond 2 July 1816. Thomas T. Reynolds (b);
    Isaac Webb (w).

ALVERSON, TELIFF married by 1 August 1737 Eleanor Starks, daughter of James
    and Eleanor (Todd) Starks, (q.v.),p.194.   COB#10,p.544

ALVERSON, TELIFF JR. See JELOFF ALDERSON, JR., Page 1

ALEXANDER, EUEL of Northumberland County and Dewanna Smither*, bond 18 January
    1792. Launce L. Smither (b); John Dawson (w).

ALEXANDER, JOHN married Elizabeth Barnes in May 1761; she was the daughter of
    Captain Richard and Penelope (Manly) Barnes, q.v.[Colonel John Alexander
    (1739/40-post 1806) was the son of John Alexander,Sr., Gentleman, (1711-
    1763) of Boyd's Hole, Saint Paul's Parish, Stafford County, and his wife
    nee Susanna Pearson (1717-1788). Colonel and Mrs. Alexander settled in
    Loudoun County and those records contain considerable information in re-
    gard to their family. DB#12,p.303; FDC#15, Alexander vs Beckwith; ABC
    Book, p.57,79,67,281-283.]

ALEXANDER, JOSEPH and Ellen Barnes (widow), bond 30 January 1807. Thomas
    Bryant (b).

ALEXANDER, PHILIP THORNTON and Lucy Brockenbrough, bond 23 September 1782.
    Moore Fauntleroy (b). [Philip Thornton Alexander (1760-1783) was the son
    of John Alexander, Gentleman, (1735-1775) of Salisbury, Saint Paul's Par-
    ish, Stafford County, and his wife nee Lucy Thornton (17??-1781) of King
    George County. He m(1) Jane Willis, daughter of Colonel Lewis Willis
    (1734-1813) of Fredericksburg, Va. He was killed in a duel by Lawrence
    Washington (c.1760-1809) of Waterloo, King George County; he had a son by
    each wife. Lucy (Brockenbrough) Alexander, second wife and widow of Philip
    Thornton Alexander, m(2) 20 October 1784, William P. Quarles. 3 Calendar
    of Virginia State Papers 534; SPR.,p.110; 20W(2)318.]

ALEXANDER, THOMAS B. and Alice Pursell, bond 19 May 1845. Samuel Pursell (b);
    V.R. Pursell (w).   MBB.,p.260

ALGAR, THOMAS married by 3 January 1692 Alitia Kennedy [Kenney, Kennida, Canni-
    da &c:], daughter of John Kennedy, deceased, of Rappahannock County.
    DB#1,p.53; DB#3,p.13; DB#16,p.240; Sweeny,p.51.

ALLARD, HENRY married Grace Davis, 15 February 1730/1.   NFPR.,p.77

ALLEN, FRANK and Rachel Gibson*, "a slave purchased by the said Allen of Thomas
    ap C. Jones of Richmond County," bond 22 June 1833. Lindsey Rich (b);
    E.E. Buckner (w) and Winney Allen (w).

ALLEN, JOHN married Catherine Major, 15 November 1678.   NFPR.,p.75

ALLEN, THOMAS and Jane Newman "free people of color," bond 28 November 1849.
    Consent by John Newman; no relationship stated. Frederick Newman (b);
    Bartholomew Bell (w). Married 6 December 1849 by Rev. William N. Ward.
                                                                  MBB.,p.328

ALLGOOD, WILLIAM married by 1761 Elizabeth Pursell, born 2 November 1730, daughter of Tobias Pursell (1691-1761) and Margaret, his wife. William Allgood and wife were living in 1764.   COB#15,p.313; WB#6,p.201

ALLISON, HENRY and Bathsheby Lawson, bond 28 September 1761. Stanley Gower (b).

ALLISON, WILLIAM and Margaret Ann Jones, bond 1 May 1850. James Jones (b).
                                                          MBB.,p.336

ALLOWAY, GABRIEL married by 2 October 1695 Elizabeth Hinds, daughter of Richard
Hinds, deceased, whose widow Judith Hinds married Captain Alexander Swan,
q.v.,p.200.   COB#2,p.76,91
[NFPR records the deaths of Gabriel Alloway on 31 January 1745/6 and of
Elizabeth Alloway on 8 November 1747.]

ALLOWAY, HENRY and Alice Rust*, bond 16 March 1831. Thomas Lewis (b). MBB.,p.75
[Ales Russ writes her own consent for her marriage to Henry Halloway.]

ALLOWAY, ISAAC and Mary Ann Hammond (spinster)*, bond 29 July 1797. Martin
Sisson (b); Patty Sisson (w).

ALLOWAY, JOHN and Elizabeth Stott*, bond 15 March 1797. Newby Barrick (b).

ALLOWAY, JOHN and Elizabeth Jenkins*, bond 4 March 1818. John Jenkins (b).

ALLOWAY, JOHN and Sally Stephens (spinster), bond 21 June 1830. Samuel Alloway (b); R. Woody (w) and Samuel Hallaway (w). Judy Steavens (sic) consents for the marriage of her daughter Sally to John Hallaway. MBB.,p.65

ALLOWAY, SAMUEL and Lucy Habron*, bond 11 January 1836. Joseph Clarke (b);
George R. Thrift (w).   MBB.,p.141
#
AMBROSE, ELIJAH and Nelly Jenkins, bond 7 July 1806. James Jenkins (b).

AMBROSE, ELIJAH and Caroline Pratt*, 20 August 1849. William R. Balderson
(b); John F. Morris (w) and R.B. Ambrose (w). Married 20 August 1849 by
the Rev. William Balderson.   MBB.,p.326

AMBROSE, REDMAN B. and Apphia C. Gutridge, bond 20 April 1832. Consent given
by Reuben Gutridge and Elizabeth Gutridge. William Carter (b). MBB.,p.89

AMBROSE, WILLIAM and Elizabeth Hinson, bond 3 August 1801. Consent given by
Jonas and Haney Hinson, parents of the bride. James Marks (b) and James
Hinson (b).

AMORY, THOMAS C. of Gloucester County and Isabella K. Weathers, bond 8 October
1818. John Weathers (b). On 3 October 1818 before James C. Wiatt, a
justice of the peace for Gloucester County, Virginia, William Robins made
oath that Thomas C. Amory "is not under the age of 21 years."

ANDERSON, EDWARD married Margaret Conor, 18 October 1725.   NFPR.,p.77

ALVERSON : SEE ALDERSON : ALVERSON   PAGE 1-2

ANDERSON, WALTER married by 5 April 1715 Susanna Prou, daughter of Cyprian Prou
(16??-1712) who died testate in Richmond County. Walter Anderson (16??-
1733) died in King George County and those records contain information in
regard to his family. DB#3,p.137; DB#7,p.47; WB#3,p.110. Also see King
George County DB#4,p.610 and DB#5,p.626.

ANDERSON, WALTER of Cople Parish, Westmoreland County, married Ann Thornton,
one of the daughters of Thomas Thornton (1688-1729) and his wife nee Susannah Smith, to whom Henry Burditt (16??-1725) bequeathed land. Ann
(Thornton) Anderson died prior to 1762; she was survived by her husband,
Walter Anderson, and heir-at-law, John Anderson. DB#12,p.361,422; WB#4,
p.265; WB#5,p.146; WB#6,p.203.

ANSWORTH, JOHN and Sarah Bridger, 15 July 1678.   NFPR.,p.75

ANTHONY, JAMES and Haney [Haynie] Hinson*, bond 21 December 1840. James S. Sanders (b); George W. Sanders (w). Married 21 December 1840 by the Rev.
John M. Waddey.   MBB.,p202

ANTHONY, THOMAS and Nancy Jenkins*, bond 6 September 1837. James C. Sanders (b);
Rheuben Jenkins (w).   MBB.,p.158

ANTON, JOHN of Westmoreland County and Hannah Self*, bond 3 February 1818.
Robert Anton (b).

APLEBY, RICHARD married Anne Arnolds, 4 July 1680.   NFPR.,p.75

APPLEBY, RICHARD married Elizabeth Pression, 17 November 1728..   NFPR.,p.77

ARMISTEAD, HENRY and Winifred Peachey, bond 14 October 1774. William Peachey,
father of the bride, (b). [Henry Armistead (c.1752-1787), son of Robert
Armistead (17??-1767), clerk of the court of King George County 1752-1761
and clerk of the court of Caroline County 1761-1767, and his wife Elizabeth
(Burgess) Ball, was first clerk of the Hustings Court of the town of Fredericksburg 1782-1787, dying in office. Henry Armistead was the only half-
brother of Colonel Burgess Ball (1749-1800) of Traveller's Rest, Stafford
County, who sold that valuable estate and removed to Springwood, Loudoun
County. Fredericksburg District Court Deed Book "E", p.213 and Fredericksburg Will Book A-1,p.48. Hayden,p.100,111.]

ARMISTEAD, JOHN of Richmond, Westmoreland and Cumberland counties, married by
1741 Hannah Harrison, daughter of William Harrison (16??-1726) of Westmoreland County. John Armistead (1718-1769) was the only son of Francis Armistead (16??-1719) who removed from Gloucester County to Richmond County
where he died testate; his widow Sarah Armistead m(2) by 8 November 1722
Joseph Russell,Jr.,q.v. COB#9,p.78; DB#6,p.260; WB#4,p.104. Also see Cumberland County WB#1,p.411 and other records there; Westmoreland County COB
1739-1743,p.88 and D&W#12,p.195. 26T308; 7V52.

ARMSTRONG, BENJAMIN and Mary Pope, bond 26 December 1844. Consent by Leroy Pope,
father of the bride. Joseph W. Bryant (b); Richard M. Efford (w). Married
27 December 1844 by Rev. E.L. Williams.   MBB.,p.252

ASBURY, HENRY and Sally Maulden Kelly, bond 17 February 1792. James Kelly, Seig^r., consents to the marriage of his daughter. John Kelly (b). [Henry Asbury (17??-1813) m(1) Ann Lyne, born 15 February 1751, daughter of Thomas and Mary Lyne; m(2) 1792 Sally Maulden Kelly; m(3) 9 April 1796 Sally Moxley of Westmoreland County. See Dr. B.C. Holtzclaw's manuscript genealogy of The Asbury Family of Virginia, Virginia State Library, Microfilm #327.]

ASBURY, JOHN G. and Penelope Pope, bond 4 June 1787. Edward Wright (b).

ASBURY, THOMAS and Jane Lyne, bond 21 September 1784. James Lyne (b); Bartholomew McCarty (w). [Thomas Asbury (1757-1825), son of Thomas Asbury (1725-1766) and Ann Read, his wife, m(1) Jane Lyne, daughter of Thomas Lyne (17??-1765) and Mary, his wife; and m(2) in Augusta County, Sarah Finley. See Dr. B.C. Holtzclaw's manuscript genealogy of The Asbury Family of Virginia, Virginia State Library, Microfilm #327.]

ASBURY, THOMAS and Molly Kelly, bond 18 February 1794. Consent by James Kelly, father of the bride. William Bragg (b); John How, Jr. (w).

ASCOUGH, THOMAS (16??-1701) married before 3 June 1701 Elizabeth Ingo (16??-1748), daughter of John Ingo, Sr. (16??-1701); she m(2) c.1702, Leonard Dozier, Jr. (16??-1733). WB#2,p.27,32; WB#5,p.207,558.

ASHBURN, THOMAS of Northumberland County and Rachel Headley, bond 23 December 1795. Henry Headley (b).

ASKINS, BENJAMIN W. and Frances R. Downman, bond 13 November 1839. Consent by Elizabeth Downman, mother of the bride. Jefferson Stephens (b); John D. Glascock (w).   MBB.,p.186

ASKINS, YOUELL (bachelor) and Ann Weathers (Spinster), bond 29 November 1828. Robert L. Montgomery (b) who made oath bride is of full age. MBB.,p.46

ASKINS, WILLIAM married Elizabeth Morgan, 23 December 1729.   NFPR.,p.77

ASTIN, LAWRENCE of Westmoreland County and Polly Sallard (widow), bond 15 November 1815. Name of bondsman is mutilated; Griffin G. Berrick (w).

ATWELL [ATWILL], THOMAS L. of Westmoreland County and Elizabeth S. Tapscott (widow), bond 15 November 1830. John A. Lyell (b).   MBB.,p.69

ATWELL, THOMAS L. and Dewanna Sydnor* (spinster), bond 15 September 1834. Albert G. McCarty (b); John W. Wollard (w) and Elizabeth Wollard (w).
                                                          MBB.,p.124

AUSTIN, CHAPMAN and Sally Hammack, bond 11 February 1808. Richard Woollard (b); John Dudley (w). Consent by William Hammack, father of the bride.

AUSTIN, JOHN and Lucy Thrift*, bond 15 September 1847. Benjamin Tucker (b); Thomas B. Berrick (w) and George R. Thrift (w).   MBB.,p.298

AVERY, YEO and Elizabeth Harbin, license June 1710.   DB#6,p.275

AYRS, WILLIAM and Margaret Etmon*, bond 4 June 1788. Allen Cambron (b).

                                    B

      BAILEY : BALEY : BAYLEY

BAILEY, CHARLES and Mary Plummer, bond 1 January 1783. Thomas Smith (b).

BAILEY, JEREMIAH GARLAND and Susannah Sydnor, bond 13 August 1774. John Syd-
      nor (b). [See p.201 under John Sydnor (1736/7-1808)]

BAILEY, JOHN of Westmoreland County and Julia L. Mitchell* of Grove Mount in
      Richmond County, bond 10 December 1817. Richard B. Hutt (b).

BAYLY, SAMUEL and Eliz.^{a} Baker, license July 1713.   DB#6,p.275

BAILEY, SAMUEL married Elizabeth Metcalfe, 2 December 1725.   NFPR.,p.189
      [She was the daughter of Richard Metcalfe (16??-1699) and his second
      wife nee Anne Stone (c.1672-1728),q.v.]

BAYLEY, SAMUEL and Catherine Hammond (spinster), bond 1 June 1752. Thomas
      Freshwater (b).

BALEY [BAYLEY], WILLIAM and Charity McMillion [MackMellion], license October
      1710.   DB#6,p.275
      [William Bayley (16??-1729) married Charity MackMellion (McMillion),
      daughter of John MackMellion who died testate in 1706 and Frances, his
      wife, who died testate in 1747, being then the widow of George Hopkins
      who died testate in 1721. WB#2,p.90; WB#4,p.170; WB#5,p.127,530.]

BAILEY, WILLIAM H. and Barbara English*, bond 6 July 1840. William English (b).
                                                                     MBB.,p.195

BAKER, JOHN and Sary Ann Stone (widow), bond 26 December 1786. James Alderson
      (b).
      [She was the widow of Thomas Stone (q.v.) and daughter of James Alderson
      (17??-1785). WB#7,p.472; WB#9,p.383.]

BAKER, WILLIAM and Betty Stanfield, bond 7 April 1746. Henry Miskell (b).
      [She was born in North Farnham Parish on 9 October 1723, only daughter
      of Thomas and Mary (Dalton) Stanfield (q.v.).]

BAKER, WILLIAM and Ann Dobbyns, bond __ May 1749. Charles Dobbyns (b).

BALDERSON, EDWARD T. and Louisa Jones, bond 19 January 1847. Consent given by
      Clinton Jones; no relationship stated. James R. Carter (b); James Jones
      (w). Married 21 January 1847 by Rev. John Pullen.   MBB.,p.288

BALDERSON, GILBERT H. and Elizabeth Pope, bond 12 April 1834. James M. Morris
   (b).   MBB.,p.118

BALDERSON, HENRY and Frances Balderson*, bond 18 December 1838. Theoderick N.
   Balderson (b); David Balderson (w).   MBB.,p.178

BALDERSON, JAMES P. and Elizabeth Evans (widow)*, bond 21 January 1818. Thomas
   S. Davis (b); John Garland (w).

BALDERSON, JOHN and Lucy Tune*, bond 1 January 1831. Thomas S. Davis (b);
   John Garland (w).   MBB.,p.71

BALDERSON, JOHN and Hannah Dameron*, bond 2 January 1839. Elias S. Burton (b);
   Thomas P. Lewis (w).   MBB.,p.180

BALDERSON, LEONARD and Mahala Ambrose*, bond 22 March 1842. Robert Sanders (b);
   William J. Reamy (w). Married by the Rev. William Balderson. MBB.,p.221

BALDERSON, MALBOROUGH B. and Susannah D. Olliffe, bond 11 November 1846. Consent by William S. Olliffe, father of the bride. Theoderick N. Balderson
   (b); William D. Olliffe (w).   MBB.,p.282

BALDERSON, RANSDEL and Maria Sanders*, license 10 February 1851. John Bartlett
   (w) and S. Weadon (w). Married 13 February 1851 by the Rev. John Pullen.

BALDERSON, RICHARD and Elizabeth Sanders, bond 19 July 1832. Consent by Thomas
   Saunders, father of the bride. John F. Morris (b); Elizabeth Sanders (w)
   and Josiah Newman (w).   MBB.,p.91

BALDERSON, SALATHIEL G. and Elizabeth M. Oliff*, bond 27 September 1847. William Carter (b); William S. Oliffe (w). Married 29 September 1847 by the
   Rev. John Pullen.   MBB.,p.298

BALDERSON, URIAH and Delila Balderson*, bond 15 February 1836. Henry Balderson
   (b).   MBB.,p.144

BALDERSON, WILLIAM JR. and Amelia Ambrose, bond 5 February 1833. Consent by
   Elijah Ambrose; no relationship stated. James B. Balderson (b). MBB.,p.101

BALDERSON, WILLIAM SR. and Mary Ann Sandy*, license 18 August 1852. T.N. Balderson (w). Married 18 August 1852 by the Rev. John Pullen.

BALDERSON, WILLIAM O. and Frances A. Sanders, bond 9 December 1846. Consent by
   Henry V. Sanders, father of the bride. Theoderick N. Balderson (b); Henry
   Sandy (w).   MBB.,p.284

BALDERSON, WILLIAM O. and Julia Ann Sanders, bond 5 September 1849. Henry V.
   Sanders (b). Married 11 September 1849 by Rev.William N. Ward. MBB.,p.327

BALEY   SEE : BAILEY : BALEY : BAYLEY PAGE 6

BALL, CHANEY and Catharine Bunyan, bond 9 January 1805. Richard Benneham (b).

BALL, JOHN B. [M.D.] and Julia E.Y. McCarty*, bond 18 January 1843. Isaac S.
Jeffries (b); B.C. Chinn (w). Married 26 January 1843 by Rev. William N.
Ward.   MBB.,p.232

BALL, THOMAS and Mildred Downman, bond 3 April 1766. Raleigh Downman (b).
[She was born in North Farnham Parish, 6 March 1749, the daughter of
Captain Robert Downman (1720-1769) and his wife nee Elizabeth Porteus.
Thomas and Mildred Ball moved to Amelia County, Virginia, and appear
frequently on those records. AB#2,p.4; WB#7, p.40,48.]

BALL, THOMAS P. of Lancaster County and Elizabeth B. Garland, bond 9 March 1811.
Jeremiah Garland (b).

BALL, CAPTAIN WILLIAM JR. of Lancaster County married by 11 November 1672 Margaret Williamson, only child of James Williamson, Gentleman, (16??-1656)
of Rappahannock County to leave issue. Captain William Ball, Jr. (1641-
1694) and his wife nee Margaret Williamson, died in Lancaster County and
certain land in Richmond County descended to their eldest son Captain William Ball, Jr. who conveyed it by deed 7 December 1709. This deed confirms
what Hayden,p.53 was dubious about. DB#5,p.212; Sweeny,p.5-6; 30T80-86;
30T259-271; 39V276; 18W(2)89; 20W(2)551; Lee,p.6, will of Margaret Ball.

BALL, WILLIAMSON and Ann Beale (spinster), bond 23 November 1762. Thomas Beale
(b). See note below.

BALL, WILLIAMSON and Priscilla Glascock, bond 24 March 1763. Richard Glascock
(b). See note below.

[The two marriages just above concern two men who were first cousins. As
Hayden has erred in regard to them, I will attempt to clarify the facts.
Colonel William[3] Ball (167?-1745) of Millenbeck, Lancaster County, eldest
son of Captain William[2] Ball, Jr. and his wife nee Margaret Williamson, is
mentioned by Hayden as #6,p.61. He married Hannah Beale, daughter of Capt-
ain Thomas Beale, Jr. (1647-1679) of Richmond County (see Beale,p.23-25).
Among their children were:
   I. Captain William[4] Ball, Jr., who predeceased his father having married
      on 17 February 1723/4 his first cousin, Margaret Ball (170?-1783). He
      is detailed by Hayden as #25,p.83 and the will of his wife, Margaret
      (Ball) Ball, proved in Lancaster County, is informative. Their son,
      i. Williamson[5] Ball (17??-1765) married 24 March 1763 Priscilla Glas-
         cock, daughter of William Glascock, Gentleman, who died testate in
         Richmond County in 1784. Priscilla (Glascock) Ball m(2) 18 August
         1769 in Lancaster County, Mungo Harvey (q.v.). The only child of
         Williamson[5] and Priscilla (Glascock) Ball was:
         a. Alice[6] Ball, born c.1764, married 12 June 1786 per bond in Rich-
            mond County, John Smith (q.v.). Hayden,p.84 and p.105 assigns
            both Williamson[5] Balls as her father. Alice (Ball) Smith d.s.p.
  II. George[4] Ball, Gentleman, designated by Hayden as #26,p.84, married 10
      October 1735 Judith Payne (see Payne,p.488-489) and their eldest son

was:
i. Captain Williamson[5] Ball (1736-1793); he resided in both Lancaster
    and Richmond counties at various periods but died testate in Rich-
    mond County. He m(1) a daughter of William Glascock, Gent., who
    died testate in Richmond County in 1784, and they had two daughters;
    m(2) 23 November 1762 Ann Beale who d.s.p. 20 May 1764 [Beale,p.55];
    m(3) circa 1765 Priscilla (Churchill) Spann, childless widow of his
    cousin Richard Spann (1738-1764) [Hayden,#30,p.245] and daughter of
    Colonel Armistead Churchill (1704-1763) and his wife nee Hannah Har-
    rison (1706-1776) of Bushy Park, Middlesex County, by whom he had
    four daughters and one son. Captain Williamson[5] Ball is detailed by
    Hayden #105,p.104. The two daughters of Captain Williamson[5] Ball and
    his first wife nee Glascock, were:
    a. Mildred ("Milly")[6] Ball married Epaphroditus Sydnor, (q.v.),p.201
    b. Elizabeth[6] Ball married Townshend Dade,(q.v.),p.47
    The five children of Captain Williamson[5] and Priscilla (Churchill)
    Ball,were:
    c. Priscilla[6] Ball married Colonel Walker Tomlin, (q.v.),p.218
    d. Judith[6] Ball married John Short, Gentleman, (q.v.),p.186
    e. Lucy Harrison[6] Ball married Newman B. Barnes, (q.v.),p.10
    f. Margaret Williamson[6] Ball married John W. Tomlin, (q.v.),p.216
    g. Harrison[6] Ball of whom there is some detail in Hayden,#161,p.104
    AB#3,p.211; DB#12,p.579; WB#7,p.459; WB#8,p.166; Lancaster WB#22,p.3-4.]

BARBER, CHARLES [COLONEL] (1676-1727) married c.1700 Frances Glascock, daughter
    of Thomas and Ann Glascock. COB#6,p.297,365; WB#3,p.163; WB#5,p.26; 35V
    416-418; J.B. Boddie, Historical Southern Families (1960), Vol.IV,p.44-47;
    54V79-80.

BARBER, JAMES R. and Mary Mothershead, bond 27 December 1843. Consent by George
    Mothershead; father of the bride. Richard H. Mothershead (b); Benjamin D.
    Rust (w). Married by Rev. Nathan Healy.   MBB.,p.244

BARBER, SAMUEL married Ann Foster, 30 November 1727.   NFPR.,p.189
    [Samuel Barber, Gentleman, (17??-1735) was the only son of Captain William
    and Joyce (Bayley) Barber (q.v.),p.9; Ann Foster was the only child of John
    Foster (16??-1711) of Essex County and his wife Susannah Cammack (168?-1747)
    who m(2) Gilbert Metcalfe (16??-1737), (q.v.),p.131. Ann (Foster) Barber m(2)
    by 1753, William Jordan, Gentleman, who died intestate in 1757, (q.v.),p.110.
    WB#4,p.476; WB#5,p.272; WB#6,p.339; Essex County W&D#13,p.411 & W&D#19,p.61.]

BARBER, THOMAS married Ann Nash, 28 January 1729/30.   NFPR.,p.189

BARBER, WILLIAM JR. [CAPTAIN] (1679-1721) married by 2 August 1694 Joyce Bayley,
    born 17 January 1677, only child of Samuel and Joyce (Robinson) Bayley. COB
    #1,p.201; COB#2,p.19 et seq; Sweeny,p.78; 35V416-418; birth dates, NFPR!

BARBER, WILLIAM married by 1767 Elizabeth Jones, daughter of Edward Jones (17??-
    1759) and Barbary, his wife, and niece of Isaac Jones (17??-1764). AB#1,p.
    546; AB#3,p.48; WB#6,p.148,350.

BARCROFT, WILLIAM of Northumberland County and Winnefred Rock (widow)*, bond
    27 January 1806. Edward R. Jeffries (b).

BARKER, LAWRENCE (16??-1716) married by 1714 Mary Skelderman one of the three
   daughters of Herman Skelderman who died testate in Rappahannock County in
   1684, leaving land,which he had patented 11 July 1666, to his children.
   Lawrence and Mary (Skelderman) Barker had two children, viz: Lawrence Barker,Jr. and Elias Barker. DB#7,p.35; DB#9,p.210; DB#12,p.142; WB#3,p.244;
   Sweeny,p.108. She married (2) Thomas Grimstone (q.v.), p.82.

BARNES, CHARLES and Molly Nash (widow)*, bond 24 September 1800. Luke Hanks (b).

BARNES, NEWMAN BROCKENBROUGH married between 1786-1800 Lucy Harrison Ball, daughter of Captain Williamson Ball (1736-1793) and his third wife nee Priscilla Churchill (q.v.). AB#3,p.211; WB#8,p.166.

BARNES, PETER and Winifred Tune, bond 29 December 1787. James Tune (b).

BARNES, PETER M. of Northumberland County and Mrs. Lucy Brown, bond 29 October
   1822. Alexander Dodson (b); John F.B.Jeffries (w).

BARNES, CAPTAIN RICHARD (16??-30 September 1760) m(1) c.1720, Frances Ingo, daughter of James and Frances (Moss) Ingo (q.v.); their only child to survive
   infancy was Thomas Barnes (c.1723-1767) (q.v.) Captain Richard Barnes m(2)
   172?, Penelope Manly (17??-22 May 1768), daughter of William and Penelope
   (Higgins) Manly of Westmoreland County; they had six daughters. The wills
   of both Captain Richard Barnes (proved at Richmond County Court) and his
   widow, Mrs. Penelope (Manly) Barnes (proved at the General Court of Virginia), were contested and litigation extended over many years. AB#1,p.488;
   WB#4,p.255; WB#6,p.212. Also see Westmoreland County D&W#6,p.43 and D&W
   #8,p.39; FDC#15, Alexander vs Beckwith; Richard Barnes Papers, Duke University Library; 20W(2)551.

BARNES, SAMUEL and Elizabeth Stott, bond 6 October 1786. Consent by John Stott,
   father of the bride. LeRoy Stott (b).

BARNES, SAMUEL and Elinor Hanks*, bond 21 March 1792. John Nash (b).

BARNES, SAMUEL and Sally Hanks*, bond 7 February 1827. Ewell Hanks (b).MBB.,p.29

BARNES, THOMAS (c.1723-1767), only child of Captain Richard and Frances (Ingo)
   Barnes (q.v.),m(1) 1745, Winifred Brockenbrough, daughter of Newman Brockenbrough, Gentleman, who died testate 1742; m(2) 176?, Molly Beckwith Morton, daughter of Joseph and Margaret (Beckwith) Morton and granddaughter
   of Sir Marmaduke Beckwith. AB#2,p.198; COB#16,p.385,401; DB#10,p.350;
   DB#12,p.87,153,642; DB#13,p.27; WB#5, p.401, 490, DB#13,p.120.

BARNES, TRAVERS [TRAVIS] and Clarkey Watts, bond 3 January 1816. Edmund R. Jeffries (b).

BARNES, WILLIAM F. and Catharine B. English*, bond 19 November 1844. William
   English (b); Thomas English (w).   MBB.,p.251

   BARRICK   SEE: BERRICK

BARROTT, JAMES and Amelia Wafel, bond 25 May 1850. Consent by Mariah Wafel, mother of the bride. Richard McGinnis (b); John Bowen (w). MBB.,p.338

BARROW, EDWARD [GENTLEMAN] (16??-1721) married c.1700 Anne (Stone) Metcalfe (c.1672-post 1728), widow of Richard Metcalfe, Gentleman, (q.v.)p.131 and daughter of Colonel John Stone (q.v.). DB#3,p.37; DB#7,p.230;DB#6,p.134.

BARROW, EDWARD [GENTLEMAN] (170?-1733), son of Edward and Anne (Stone) Barrow (q.v.), married Elizabeth Minor, daughter of Nicholas Minor, Gentleman, who died testate in Westmoreland County in 1744. Elizabeth (Minor) Barrow m(2) _____ Wherret, probably of Maryland. AB#1,p.209; DB#6,p.134; WB#4,p.200; WB#5,p.199. See also Westmoreland County D&W#10,p.24,332; 35V297; 22W(1)272.

BARROW, JOHN (1729/30-1810), son of Edward and Elizabeth (Minor) Barrow, removed from Richmond County to Culpeper County circa 1751 where he shortly married Margaret Ball, daughter of Samuel and Anna Catherine (Tayloe) Ball. John and Margaret (Ball) Barrow left no surviving child. Culpeper County DB "A",p.282; DB "B",p.385; DB "D",p.478; WB "A",p.60-61; WB "D",p.321,385; WB "F",p.144. Hayden,p.55.

BARTLETT, ELISHA and Leah Scates, bond 9 February 1791. Consent by Joseph and Sarah Scates, parents of the bride. John Bartlett (b).

BARTLETT, ELISHA SR. (widower) and Elizabeth Jones (widow)*, bond 6 August 1798. John Fawcett (b).

BARTLETT, ISAAC and Winifred Crask, bond 5 November 1798. Consent by John Crask, father of the bride. John Fawcett (b); Elishea Bartlett,Sr. (w).

BARTLETT, JAMES of Westmoreland County and Sarah Ann Sacra, bond 18 December 1837. Consent by Charles C. Sacra, father of bride. Richard Asbury (b).
MBB.,p.163

BARTLETT, JOHN and Elizabeth Mothershead, bond 13 January 1819. Consent by John Mothershead, father of the bride, directed to "the Clerk of the County Court of Westmoreland." William Kendall (b).

BARTLETT, JOHN and Lawienda Balderson, bond 10 February 1836. James Hall (b).
MBB.,p.144

BARTLETT, JOSEPH and Ellin Crask, bond 1 November 1802. Consent by John Crask, father of the bride. Daniel Marmaduke (b).

BARTLETT, SAMUEL and Mahala Carter, bond 26 September 1832. Consent by Daniel Carter, father of the bride. John S. Carter (b); Joshua Reamy (w).
MBB.,p.94

BATES, EDWARD and Jane Peck married 16 January 1729/30.   NFPR.,p.189

BATTEN [BATTIN], JOHN (16??-1712) married Elizabeth _____. She m(2) by

license, July 1712, John Williams (q.v.) and m(3) by 7 March 1716 William
Stokes of Essex County (q.v.). DB#6,p.139; DB#7,p.100; WB#3,p.109,205.

BAYLEY   SEE : BAILEY : BALEY : BAYLEY   PAGE 6

BAYLIS, ROBERT and Ellin McCarty by license, November 1711.   DB#6,p.275
    [Robert Baylis(s) (1681-1725), son of Thomas and Catherine (Samford) Baylis
    (q.v.), was born and died in North Farnham Parish. His wife Ellin (Ellen,
    Eleanor) McCarty died 9 November 1721; she was the daughter of Dennis and
    Elizabeth (Billington) McCarty (q.v.) DB#6,p.152; DB#7,p.211,483; WB#4,
    p.267.]

BAYLIS, THOMAS (16??-1699) m(1) c.1680, Catherine Samford, daughter of James
    Samford (c.1624-1704), by whom he had six children; m(2) c.1697 Sarah
    (Edgcomb) Suggitt (16??-1703), widow of John Suggitt (16??-1690) (q.v.),
    by whom he had no issue. Thomas Baylis was the son of Robert Baylis, Sr.
    (16??-1692) whose will is in lost WB#1. COB#1,p.87,88; DB#3,p.87; MRB.,
    p.8 et seq.; WB#2,p.2,61; Sweeny,p.128.
    N.B. Dr. and Mrs. William Blum, Sr., in their genealogy, The Baylis Family
    of Virginia, Washington, D.C. (1958), touch very lightly on the Baylis fam-
    ily of Richmond County and the data given on pages 20-21 is not entirely
correct as the aforementioned referenced statements will testify.

BEALE, ALFRED and Susanna F. Tomlin, bond 2 March 1805. Townshend D. Peyton (b).

BEALE, GEORGE of Richmond County and Miss Susan Brooke, daughter of Captain
    William Brooke of Culpeper County, were married 18 September 1817 by the
    Rev.Mr. Connor in Culpeper County. The marriage was announced in the
    Fredericksburg Virginia Herald 27 September 1817. Her death on 7 January
    1826 at Chestnut Hill, Richmond County, was announced in the Fredericks-
    burg Virginia Herald 25 January 1826. For further information relative to
    George Beale (1794-1822) and his wife, who was his first cousin, see Beale,
    p.46,62.

BEALE, REUBEN and Frances Robinson, bond 9 March 1749. Daniel Hornby (b). See
    Beale, p.170.

BEALE, ROBERT [MAJOR] of Madison County and Martha Filecia Turberville of Rich-
    mond County, bond 1 August 1802. Thomas Chilton, guardian of the bride,
    consents to the marriage of his ward. Jesse Ewell (b); William B. Hamil-
    ton (w). [The Fredericksburg Virginia Herald of 20 August 1802 announced
    the marriage "lately in Westmoreland County of Mr. Robert Beale to Miss
    Martha Turberville, both of the said county." See Beale, p.66, 269.]

BEALE, THOMAS married Sarah McCarty, 27 April 1728.   NFPR.,p.189
    [She was the daughter of Captain Daniel and Elizabeth (Pope) McCarty (q.v.)
    of Westmoreland County. See Beale, p.35-36; Payne, p.223-226.]

BEALE, WILLIAM married Harwear Haruear [!], 29 April 1729.   NFPR.,p.189
    [Beale,p.37,40,237, and court records makes it certain this is an error
    and her name was Ann Harwar.]

BEACHAM and BEAGES : SEE PAGE 13

BEALE, WILLIAM of Westmoreland County and Lucy Brann, bond 28 December 1807.
Consent by Daniel Jackson, guardian of the bride. Edward J. Northen (w);
Daniel Flinn (b).

BEACHAM, JOHN and Betsy Wroe*, bond 23 April 1795. Roger Dameron (b); Thomas
Dugliss (w).

BEACHAM, SAMUEL L. and Caty Morris, bond 6 May 1830. Jere: Middleton (b).
MBB.,p.64

BEAGES, WILLIAM married Katherine Hopper, 5 May 1728.   NFPR.,p.189

BEAN, LEVY married Frances E. Connolly, 30 January 1851; minister's return of
Rev. Cyrus Doggett. No license found.

BEARCAFF, JOHN and Elizabeth Pullen, bond 22 December 1810. Consent by James
Pullin, father of the bride, who states his daughter is "free." Peter
Shearley (b); John Todd (w) and Henry P. Todd (w).

BEARD, GEORGE of Westmoreland County married by 1762, Marina Williams (who is
under 21 years of age in 1762), daughter of Francis Williams of Westmoreland County (who is living in 1762) and his wife nee Rachel Thornton of
Richmond County (who is deceased in 1762), daughter of Thomas and Susannah
(Smith) Thornton (q.v.). DB#12,p.361,422.

BEAZLEY, WILLIAM and Sarah Jane Brann, license 7 November 1852. Consent by
Frances Brann, mother of the bride. William English (w). Married 18
January 1853 by Rev. Elijah L. Williams, Baptist Minister.

BECKWITH, JENNINGS and Catherine Miskell, bond 2 April 1787. William Miskell
(b). [See, John Bennett Boddie: Historical Southern Families, Volume III
(1959), p.28-29 for Miskell ancestry. The bride was the daughter of William and Elizabeth (Samford) Miskell (q.v.).]

BECKWITH, SIR JONATHAN, son of Sir Marmaduke and Elizabeth (Brockenbrough) Beckwith, married 27 May 1753 Rebecca Barnes, daughter of Captain Richard and
Penelope (Manly) Barnes (q.v.). FDC#15, Alexander vs Barnes; Richard Barnes Papers, Duke University Library. [Sir Jonathan Beckwith was born in North Farnham Parish, 14 November 1720. The Fredericksburg Virginia Herald
of 13 December 1796 said: "Died: In Richmond County, on Tuesday last in an
advanced age, Sir Jonathan Beckwith."]

BECKWITH, SIR MARMADUKE (1687-1780), son of Sir Roger and Elizabeth (Jenings)
Beckwith of Yorkshire, England, married c.1716 Elizabeth (Brockenbrough)
Dickenson, daughter of William and Mary (Newman) Brockenbrough (q.v.) and
young widow of Thomas Dickenson, Gentleman, (16??-1714/15) who served as
deputy clerk of the court under James Sherlock, Gentleman, (16??-1709).
Marmaduke Beckwith served as clerk of Richmond County court 1709-1780. He
became a baronet in 1743 upon the death of his elder brother, Sir Roger
Beckwith (1682-1743), who died without issue, and he in turn was succeeded
in 1780 by his son Sir Jonathan Beckwith (1720-1796). COB#5,p.1,24; COB#6,

p.268; COB#18,p.157; DB#5,p.68; <u>The Beckwiths</u>, by Paul Beckwith, Albany, N.Y., 1891.

BECKWITH, RICHARD M. of Richmond County married Elizabeth Scott Buchanan of Clear View, Falmouth, Stafford County and the marriage was announced in the Fredericksburg <u>Virginia Herald</u> of 17 February 1798. The bride was the daughter of Major Andrew Buchanan (17??-1804), attorney at law, of Clear View, and his first wife,nee Miss Hewitt, daughter of James Hewitt (17??-1763) and his wife nee Susanna Crump (1723-1797) variously of King George and Stafford counties. Oddly, the second wife of Major Andrew Buchanan was his first wife's niece, Anne Hooe, daughter of Harris Hooe, Gentleman, (1736-c.1790) of Stafford County and his wife nee Hewitt daughter of the aforementioned James and Susanna (Crump) Hewitt. The Fredericksburg <u>Virginia Herald</u> of 3 September 1834 announced the death of Mrs. Elizabeth Scott (Buchanan) Beckwith "aged about 54 years," on 30 August 1834 in Fredericksburg. Fredericksburg District Court WB "A",p.80,220; <u>Graham</u>,p.267.

BECKWITH, ROGER and Winifred Miskell, bond 6 January 1762. Travers Tarpley (b).

BEDDER, LAURENCE and Ann Sanders, bond 20 December 1786. William Harris (b).

BEDDOO, JOHN JR. (bachelor) and Mary Balderson (spinster), bond 13 October 1828. John Beddoo (b) made oath the bride was of full age.   MBB.,p.42

BEDDOO, LAURENCE and Elizabeth Balderson, bond 2 April 1792. Consent by Frances [? Francis] Balderson for the bride's marriage and this is also signed by Elizabeth Balderson. Gerard McKinny (b).

BEDDOWS, JOHN married by 22 November 1815 Nancy Balderson, daughter of Gilbert Balderson, then deceased. DB#20,p.75.

BEEN, MATHEW and Mary Lemon, license July 1710.   DB#6,p.275

BELFIELD, JOHN [CAPTAIN] (23 June 1725-19 August 1801) married 5 April 1744 Ruth Sydnor (15 March 1727-8 March 1802). He was the eldest child of Captain Thomas Wright and Mary (Meriwether) Belfield (q.v.) and she was the daughter Anthony Sydnor (1682/3-1759) and his wife nee Elizabeth Dew (1694-1778) (q.v.). See Bible record in, L.H.Jones: <u>Captain Roger Jones of London and Virginia</u> (1911), p.182-184; WB#6,p.164; WB#7.p.304; WB#9,p.158; 12T141-145.

BELFIELD, JOHN [MAJOR] (1751-1792) and Mary Beckwith, bond 5 December 1785. Thomas Smith (b). [He was the son of Captain John and Ruth (Sydnor) Belfield (q.v.); she was the daughter of Sir Jonathan and Rebecca (Barnes) Beckwith (q.v.). Their only child, Alice C. Belfield married Peter R. Garland (q.v.). WB#8,p.156 records inventory of Major John Belfield, Jr., 11 October 1792.]

BELFIELD, JOHN D. and Elizabeth Belfield*, bond 22 December 1845. Richard C. Belfield (b).   MBB.,p.269

BELFIELD, JOHN W. JR. and Mary E. Payton, bond 13 August 1849. Consent by Eliza-

beth Payton, mother of the bride. William Broocke (b). Married 16 August
1849 by the Rev. John Pullen.   MBB.,p.325

BELFIELD, JOSEPH [DOCTOR] (16??-1738) married (1) c.1704, Frances Wright (1686-
    c.1706), daughter of Mottrom Wright, Gentleman, (16??-1701) and his wife
    nee Ruth Griggs, of Lancaster County; married (2) per marriage contract
    dated 27 May 1707, Mary (Lane) Mountjoy Wilson, daughter of William Lane of
    Rappahannock County and widow successively of Alvin Mountjoy, Gentleman, who
    died testate in 1700 and of Elias Wilson, who died testate in 1707; married
    (3) Elizabeth Dozier, who was many years his junior, daughter of Richard
    Dozier who died testate in Westmoreland County in 1751. Elizabeth (Dozier)
    Belfield, widow, married (2) James Wilson who died testate in Richmond Coun-
    ty in 1743, and she married (3) Jehu Glass and left issue by each of her
    said three husbands. COB#8,p.125,198; COB#7,p.208; DB#4,p.108a; DB#7,p.83-
    85; WB#2,p.18,106; Eubank,p.72-73; L.H.Jones, Captain Roger Jones of London
    and Virginia (1911), p.63,182-184; 12T141-145; Lee,p.101,236.

BELFIELD, JOSEPH and Jane Jones, bond 7 January 1811. Reuben Beale, guardian of
    the bride, gives his consent stating she is the orphan of the late Thomas
    Jones of Essex County. Charles R. Thompson (b). [See, L.H.Jones, Captain
    Roger Jones (opere citato), p.63,182-184, for further details.]

BELFIELD, RICHARD C. and Mary Frances Harwood, bond 30 March 1847. Consent by
    R.H. Harwood, father of the bride. Richard T.A. Gresham (b); George W.
    Sydnor (w). Married 31 March 1847 by the Rev. John Pullen.   MBB.,p.292

BELFIELD, SYDNOR (1758-1841) of Richmond County married 28 November 1782 Ann
    Young of Essex County agreeable to a recording in CCPR,p.203. Sydnor Bel-
    field (12 September 1758-22 February 1841) was the son of Captain John and
    Ruth (Sydnor) Belfield (q.v.),p.14. Ann Young was the daughter of Colonel
    William Young (19 November 1729-5 March 1783) and his wife nee Elizabeth
    Smith (25 December 1737-10 January 1792) of Essex County; their interesting
    Bible record is preserved [VSL:AD #20270; 12W(2)41]. ECD Papers, Belfield
    Folder, reference is made to a Bible record from which we observe:
        Sydnor Belfield died 22 February 1841 in the 83rd year of his age.
        His will remains of record in WB#10,p.349. Among the children of
        Sydnor and Ann (Young) Belfield were the two mentioned below.

John Belfield	Anna Maria Belfield
(17??-19 March 1829)	(22 February 1788-28 May 1816)
m. 6 February 1807, Peggy Crox-	m. 8 February 1810, George Saunders
: ton of Essex County, Va.[Ess-	: (9 October 1786-25 January 1843)
: ex Co.WB#10,p.349;WB#13,p.374]	: m(2) 18 Feb.1819, Mary S. Neale

Maria Belfield - married, 8 May 1833 -Edward Sydnor Saunders
(18 December 1813-   (30 October 1810-   )
   21 April 1877)   Jones
[L.H.Jones, Captain Roger / (opere citato),p.182-184; 12W(2)41-42.]

BELFIELD, THOMAS and Ann Harwar Beale, bond 25 October 1780.   William Travers

Peachey (b); Eliza G. Peachey (w). [For ancestry of contracting parties see, L.H. Jones: Captain Roger Jones of London and Virginia (1911),p.182-184 and Beale,p.42,208. The widow of Thomas Belfield (1745-1804) survived him many years and his estate was not divided among their children until 1824 after her death. AB#4,p.123; WB#9,p.280.]

BELFIELD, THOMAS WRIGHT [CAPTAIN] (1 January 1704/5-7 December 1743), son of Doctor Joseph and Frances (Wright) Belfield (q.v.), married 9 March 1723/4 Mary (Meriwether) Colston (170?-6 October 1750), widow of William Colston, Gentleman, (16??-1721) and daughter of Francis and Mary (Bathurst) Meriwether. The inventory of the very handsome estate of Captain Thomas Wright Belfield, and the wills of himself and wife, are interesting documents. WB#5,p.430,481,652; L.H. Jones, Captain Roger Jones of London and Virginia (1911) p.182-184; 12 T 141-145; Lewises, Meriwethers and Their Kin (1938), p.144 et seq.

BELL, CHARLES and Betsy Garland (widow)*, bond 5 January 1807. Peter Moore (b); George Pursell (w) and Sarah Pursell (w).[See William Garland (q.v.),p.75.]

BELL, LEMUEL G. (bachelor) and Ann Morris (spinster), bond 27 January 1829. William Bryant made oath both parties were over 21 years of age. Richard Clarke (b).   MBB.,p.52

BELL, RICHARD V. and Ann G. Richardson*, bond 17 January 1842. William Bell (b); George S. Richardson (w) and Elizabeth P. Richardson (w).   MBB.,p.219

BELL, THOMAS of Northumberland County and Nancy Foster (widow)*, bond 2 November 1803. George Dameron (b); Thomas Oldham (w).

BELL, WILLIAM and Frances G. Littrell*, bond 17 January 1842. Richard V. Bell (b); John P. Littrell (w).   MBB.,p.218

BENNEHAM, DOMINIC and Mary S. Bramham, bond 13 June 1826. George Saunders (b).
                                                                    MBB.,p.21
[Benneham, Benniham, Bennehan, &c: is an ancient name in Richmond County. One Dominic(k) Benniham died testate in 1716. WB#3,p.281.]

BENNEHAN, RICHARD and Catharine Oldham, bond 12 January 1796. David Williams (b). [She was the daughter of William Oldham (1728-17) and granddaughter of William and Priscilla (McLaughlin) Oldham (q.v.).]

BENNETT, CHARLES and Ann Rout, bond 28 December 1762. John Sydnor (b).

BENSON, ROBERT (16??-1757) of Richmond and King George counties married c.1713 Frances Prou, daughter of Cyprian Prou (16??-1712) of Richmond County. DB#3,p.137; DB#7,p.47; WB#3,p.110. See also King George County DB#5,p.626; WB#2,p.57.

BERRICK : BARRICK

BERRICK, CHARLES and Elizabeth Clarke, bond 26 January 1795. Daniel Brown (b).

BARRICK, CHARLES and Margaret C. Newgent, bond 28 February 1844. Consent by
  Sarah Pope, mother of the bride. Leroy Pope (b); B. Armstrong (w).
                                                          MBB.,p.246

BERRICK, GEORGE JR., and Esabell Thornton, bond 24 January 1781. Elijah Isaacs
  (b).

BERRICK, GEORGE JR., and Elizabeth Barecraft, bond 22 December 1790. Thomas
  Jesper, Jr. (b).

BERRICK, GEORGE B. (bachelor) and Rebecah D. Davis (spinster), bond 29 December
  1828. John Davis (b).   MBB.,p.50

BERRICK, GRIFFIN (bachelor) and Mary Elmore (spinster), bond 30 July 1828. Consent by Thomas Elmore, father of the bride; Mary Ann Elmore signs under
  his name. John Littrell (b); Thomas Scrimger (w).   MBB.,p.41

BERRICK, JAMES and Mary P. Hammack*, bond 5 March 1827. Bartholomew Bell (b)
  and William Weathers (b).   MBB.,p.30

BERRICK, NEWBY and Nancy Gupten, bond 19 January 1795. David Berrick (b).

BERRICK, REUBEN and Alice Dunaway (widow), bond 19 October 1814. Thomas Sydnor
  (b).

BERRICK, THOMAS B. and Maria Thrift*, bond 28 October 1845. Benjamin Tucker
  (b); George R. Thrift (w). Married 29 October 1845 by Rev. William N.
  Ward.   MBB.,p.265

BARRICK, THORNTON F. and Elizabeth Lewis, bond 23 May 1838. Consent by Edward
  Lewis, father of the bride. Joseph Clarke (b).   MBB.,p.172

BERRY, HENRY JR. (16??-1696) married Sarah Harper, only sister and heir at law
  of William Harper of Essex County who died intestate in 1714. The will of
  Henry Berry, Jr. was recorded in now lost Richmond County WB#1. Sarah (Harper) Berry, widow, m(2) John Spiller. COB#2,p.165. See also Essex County
  Wills &c:#3,p.226 and D&W#14,p.266,294; The Virginia Genealogist,Vol.1,p.7.

BERRY, WILLIAM (16??-1721) of Rappahannock, Richmond and King George counties,
  married long before 1686 Margaret Doughty, daughter of Enoch Doughty, Gentleman. See The Virginia Genealogist,Vol.1,p.5-17 for an account of William Berry and his family.

BERTRAND, WILLIAM and Susanna Foushee, license November 1713.   DB#6,p.275
  [William Bertrand (c.1687-1761) of Belleisle, Lancaster County, was the son
  of the Rev. John and Charlotte (de Jolie) Bertrand, Huguenots, who settled
  in Lancaster County where he was a minister in the Prostestant Episcopal
  Church. His wife, Susanna(h) Foushee, was born in Richmond County the 12th
  December 1695, daughter of James Foushee (16??-1729/30), a Frenchman, whose
  interesting naturalization paper remains of record (MRB.,p.68; 6 February
  1711/12). Fauntleroy,p.438 et seq; Hayden,p.334; Ida J. Lee, Abstracts

from Will Books of Lancaster County, Virginia,(Richmond,1959),p.15,16,88,
89.]

BETTS, ROYSTON of Northumberland County and Fanny H. Pittman (spinster), bond
6 March 1802. Consent by Molley Pitman for the marriage of her daughter.
Henry Hazard (b).

BEVERLEY, ROBERT of Essex County and Miss Maria Carter, daughter of Colonel
Landon Carter of Sabine Hall, bond 1 February 1763. Robert Wormeley Carter
(b). [The family of Robert Beverley, Esq. (1740-1800) and Maria Carter
(1745-1817), his wife, is detailed in John McGill, The Beverley Family of
Virginia,(Columbia,S.C.,1956),p.535 et seq. The obituary of Robert Beverley, Esq. of Blandfield, Essex County, appeared in the Fredericksburg Virginia Herald, 18 April 1800, and a very intresting portrayal of the Blandfield Beverleys appeared in Virginia Cavalcade, Volume XI, Number 4, p.18-
27.]

BEVERLEY, ROBERT JR. of Essex County and Jane Tayloe, bond 23 May 1791. Byrd
Beverley (b). Consent by Francis Lightfoot Lee, guardian of the bride.
[See, John McGill, The Beverley Family of Virginia, (Columbia,S.C.,1956),
pg.549 et seq. for further genealogical detail. Robert Beverley, Jr.
(1769-1843) of Blandfield was the son of Robert and Maria (Carter) Beverley (q.v.); his wife was the daughter of Colonel John and Rebecca (Plater)
Tayloe of Mount Airy, Richmond County.]

BEVINGTON, FRANCIS and Mary Mozingo, bond 13 October 1780; Gerrard McKenny (b).

BEVERTON, HENRY and Fidelia Ann Drake*, bond 27 December 1847. William Bowen
(b). Married by Rev. John Pullen on 28 December 1847.   MBB.,p.303

BIRD, PHILEMAN married Mary Mackgyar, 25 February 1727/8.   NFPR.,p.189
[Phileman (Philemon) Bird married the half-sister of John Glew (1688-1721)
who d.s.p. and by will bequeathed his half-sisters Mary and Elizabeth Mack-
guyer (MacGivier) certain land; the latter married Job Tillery (q.v.),p.216.
DB#9,p.525,657; WB#4,p.184; WB#5,p.686; WB#6,p.269; AB#1,p.437.]

BIRKETT, JOHN married prior to 1676 Ann Mills (16??-1691), elder of the two
daughters of William and Joane Mills of Rappahannock County. Near Leedstown, now in Westmoreland County, are two unique tombstones:
               "Heere lyes the wife   "Heere lyes the
                of John Birkett   Body of John Birkett
               who Departed this life   who Departed this life"
               the 16 Day of Sept 1691"   [Death date is not inscribed]
Payne,p.119-120 errs in quoting from these tombstones; they are correctly
quoted by C.A. Hoppin in his Washington-Wheelwright and Allied Families,p.222
which source, quoting from the Pratt Bible record, states John Birkett
"departed this life the 26 October 1719." His will was dated 10 December
1718 and admitted to probate at Richmond County court 3 February 1719/20.
John Birkett's plantation fell into King George County in 1721 and upon
an alteration of the boundries of King George and Westmoreland counties in
1777, it fell into Westmoreland County. Richmond County COB#1,p.75; COB#2,

p.396; Rappahannock County DB#6,p.53,78; WB#4,p.138; King George County
COB#1,p.36 and DB#1,p.51; Sweeny,p.43; Land Patent Book #6,p.656.

BISPHAM, ROBERT and Nancy Asbury, bond 11 May 1804. Consent by James Smock,
  guardian of the groom; consent by Henry Asbury, father of the bride.
  [Robert Bispham (c.1784-1810) came to Richmond County from England when he
  was not more than 14 years of age at the insistence of his bachelor uncle,
  John Fawcett (17??-1802), who settled in Richmond County prior to the Revolutionary War. Robert Bispham died without becoming a naturalized citizen
  of the United States and his landed estate escheated to the Commonwealth of
  Virginia. He left two only children, Maria and Ann Bispham, and by their
  petitions to the Virginia Legislature dated 4 December 1812 and 15 November
  1816 petitioned that the land in Richmond County, formerly held by their
  deceased father, might vest in them. William Bispham, younger brother of
  Robert Bispham, and their sister Margaret Bispham, came to Richmond County
  in 1802 and they took the oath of allegiance in 1816. Margaret Bispham
  was married 13 May 1813 by Rev. Samuel Templeman to Thomas Moore Bragg per
  bond dated 3 May 1813. WB#9,p.164,373; Richmond County, Petitions to the
  Legislature of 4 December 1812 and 15 November 1816 in VSL:AD.]

BISPHAM, WILLIAM and Mary Asbury (widow)*, bond 19 July 1820. Joseph Belfield
  (b); Richard N. Mariner (w).

BLACKERBY, THOMAS of Northumberland County and Chloe Craine*, bond 25 January
  1796. The bride writes her own consent, signing her name Cloway Crain.
  Job Thomas (b); Job Thomas (w) and Mary Thomas (w).

BLACKERBY, WILLIAM of Northumberland County and Sally S. Davenport*, bond 4
  December 1826. Edwin Brown (b); Linsey O. Davenport (w) and Elizabeth H.
  Davenport (w).   MBB.,p.25

BLACKLEY, GEORGE D. and Sarah S. Pursell, bond 16 January 1838. Moore F.
  Brockenbrough (b).   MBB.,p.165

BLACKMORE, GEORGE married Christian Shaw, 13 September 1729.   NFPR.,p.189

BLAND, WILLIAM married by 6 February 1716/17 Catherine Kay [Key], daughter of
  James and Mary (Pannell) Kay (q.v.). William Bland lived in Overwharton
  Parish, Stafford County, and his land fell into Hamilton Parish, Prince
  William County, upon the formation of the latter from a portion of the
  former in 1731. COB#7,p.80; DB#4,p.109; Prince William County DB "A",p.81;
  Stafford County DB 1722-1728,p.144,146,404, and Book "Z",p.108,110,460.

BLEWFORD, GEORGE married Janey Palmer, 26 January 1730/1.   NFPR.,p.175,189.

BLOMFIELD [BROOMFIELD], SAMUEL of Rappahannock County married by 1683 Elizabeth Jones, daughter and sole heir of Thomas Jones who possessed 1,100 acres
  of land which fell into Richmond County in 1692. Frances Blomfield (168?-
  1737), only child of Captain Samuel and Elizabeth (Jones) Blomfield, married
  by 1699, Colonel William Robinson (16??-1742) (q.v.). Elizabeth (Jones)
  Blomfield, widow, married (2) Captain Arthur Spicer (16??-1700) (q.v.).
  COB#5,p.133; DB#1,p.94; WB#2,p.14; 17W(1)78.

BLUEFORD, ROBERT G. and Alice Hudson*, bond 1 April 1850.   William C. Haynes (b);
    William E. Hill (w) and K.R. Cralle (w).   MBB.,p.334

BLUFORD, GEORGE married by 22 August 1699 Mary Kennedy [Kenney, Kennida, Cannida
    &c:, daughter of John Kennedy, deceased, of Richmond County.   George Blu-
    ford died intestate in 1723.   DB#1,p.53; DB#3,p.40; DB#4,p.67; WB#4,p.216;
    Sweeny,p.51. See: THOMAS ALGAR, p.2.

BOGGES, BENNETT married Elizabeth Samford, 27 December 1727.   NFPR.,p.189

    BOING : BOWING   SEE : BOWEN PAGE 21 - 22

BOWING, JAMES and Martha Bowing, bond 18 December 1833. Consent by Thomas and
    Mary Bowing, parents of the bride. Kelly H. Bowing (b); John Pullin (w)
                                                                    MBB.,p.113

BOING, JOHN and Meley McKenney*, bond 4 January 1802. Meley [? Milley ?] Mc-
    Kenney writes her own consent stating she is twenty one years of age.
    Daniel Connallee (b).

BOWING, JOHN and Catherine Pullen, bond 8 October 1832. Katherine Pullin, Senior,
    gives her consent for her daughter's marriage. John Pullin (b); William
    Bowing (w).   MBB.,p.94

BOWING, JONATHAN W. and Sarah Barrot* [Barrett], bond 20 May 1825. John Barrett
    (b).   MBB.,p.11

BOING, JONATHAN W. and Julia [Julylee] McKenney*, bond 4 February 1833. Nicholas
    Quesenbury (b).   MBB.,p.101

BOWING, JOSEPH and Sarah A. Marshall*, bond 26 December 1838. Robert Yeatman
    (b); John Bowing (w). Married 26 December 1838 by Rev. Lovell Marders.
                                                                    MBB.,p.179

BOING, JOSHUA and Mary Sanders, bond 1 December 1803. Consent by Pattey Sanders,
    mother of the bride. Benjamin Rennolds (b).

BOWING, RICHARD and Deliley Scates, bond 29 December 1836. Consent by Susan
    Scates, mother of the bride. James Bowing (b); John Pullin (w). MBB.,p.152

BOWING, RICHARD and Mary Wilson*, bond 24 April 1839. James Bowing (b); John
    Pullin (w).   MBB.,p.181

BOWING, WILLIAM H. and Rebecca Bowing, bond 18 December 1832. Consent by Thomas
    and Mary Bowing,parents of the bride. John F. Morris (b).   MBB.,p.97

BONTZ, VALENTINE and Mary Sisson, bond 19 September 1792. Richard Sisson (b).

BOOKER, GEORGE of Maryland and Mary W. Davis, bond 29 June 1836. Everett R.
    Pullen (b).   MBB.,p.147

BOOTH, ANDREW J. and Elizabeth Northen*, bond 7 June 1847. Richard Clarke, Sr.,
    (b).   MBB.,p.294

BOOTH, JAMES and Frances Dale married 5 November 1727.   NFPR.,p.189

BOOTH, JAMES and Caty Draper, bond 15 May 1787. Consent by Leannah Draper,
    mother of the bride. John Lewis (b); John Lewis (w).

BOSTON, ROBERT married Margaret Thornton, 14 September 1727.   NFPR.,p.189

BOUGHTON, ANDERSON and Anne C.B. Belfield, bond 2 October 1821. Consent by Ann
    H. Belfield, mother of the bride, was written from Belmount on 3 August
    1821. William R. Jeffries (b). [The bride was the daughter of Thomas and
    Ann Harwar (Beale) Belfield. AB#4,p.123.]

BOUGHTON, BENJAMIN and Rebecca H. Hipkins*, bond 29 November 1832. Feriol Lem-
    oine,Jr. (b); Vincent Bramham (w).   MBB.,p.96
    [In the Fredericksburg Virginia Herald of 24 August 1836, Benjamin Bough-
    ton advertised for sale his mansion house, Menokin in Richmond County,...
    "built of stone such as was used for Mt. Airy" and gives a full descript-
    ion of the mansion and outbuildings. Menokin was the residence of the Hon.
    Francis Lightfoot Lee (q.v.). Eubank, p.86.]

BOWCOCK, EDWARD and Mary Mitchell (spinster), bond 20 June 1755. Henry Weather-
    burn (b). [In 1756 Edward Bowcock was a resident of James City County.
    DB#11,p.435.]

BOWDOIN, PETER and Margaret Smith, bond 4 October 1783. Consent by Isaac Smith,
    father of the bride. Littleton Eyre (b). [The Richmond County records
    reflect a considerable intercourse with various areas, particularly the
    Eastern Shore of Virginia. John Bowdoin (17??-1775) of Northampton Coun-
    ty by will mentions his business partnerships with Littleton Eyre, de-
    ceased, Isaac Smith and his brother Presson Bowdoin. John Bowdoin, Jr.
    died testate at Morattico Hall, Richmond County, 3 April 1786. WB#7,p.
    533; Northampton County Record Book #25,p.455.]

    BOWEN   SEE: BOING : BOWING   PAGE 20

BOWEN, JAMES K. and Ann Sanders*, bond 26 March 1844. James C. Sanders (b);
    John Sanders (w). Married 27 March 1844 by Rev. John Pullen. MBB.,p.248

BOWEN, JOHN and Hannah Waphul*, bond 29 January 1849. Joseph Bowen (b); George
    W. Sanders (w). Married 7 February 1849 by Rev. John Pullen. MBB.,p.320

BOWEN, KELLY H. and Julia Ann Morriss*, license 15 December 1851. Zachariah
    Sanders (w) and William Mothershead (w). Married 17 December 1851 by
    Rev. John Pullen.

BOWEN, MARTIN V. and Martha Sanders*, bond 1 October 1845. John France, Jr.
    (b). Married 3 October 1845 by Rev. John Pullen.   MBB.,p.263

BOWEN, WILLIAM and Ann Figit*, bond 3 September 1827. George T. Spilman (b).
    BOWING   SEE: BOING : BOWING PAGE 20   MBB.,p.31

BOYLE [BOILE], JOHN and Elizabeth O'harrow*, bond 24 January 1839. Thomas
    Scott, Jr. (b); Edwin J. Reynolds (w).   MBB.,p.180

BOYLE, JOHN and Sarah M. Clarke*, bond 26 September 1842. William Lambard (b);
    William Clark (w).   MBB.,p.226

BRAGG, CHARLES married Elizabeth Packet, 11 June 1728.   NFPR.,p.189

BRAGG, ISHMAEL of Westmoreland County and Hannah Gawen*, bond 25 May 1838.
    Matthew M. Yeatman (b); Matthew V. Yeatman (w). Married by Rev. Thomas
    M. Washington; no date given on his returns.   MBB.,p.172

BRAGG, ISHMAEL and Mary L. Harford*, bond 18 March 1840. William Burgess (b);
    Charles C. Sacra (w).   MBB.,p.194

BRAGG, JAMES and Ann Jones, bond 10 January 1788. Thomas Stowers (b); John
    Kelly (b). No witness.

BRAGG, JAMES and Eliza Jesper*, bond 6 March 1821. Henry Harford (b); Henry
    Harford, Jr. (w).

BRAGG, JOHN and Rachel Fones*, bond 1 October 1798. John Fones (b).

BRAGG, JOSEPH and Nancy Dye*, bond 6 July 1801. Daniel Marmaduke (b).

BRAGG, JOSEPH JUN.^{R} and Mary Suttle, license April 1716.   DB#6,p.275
    [ECD notes a suit in chancery styled Elizabeth Bruce, widow, vs John
    Bragg & Others, instigated in 1765, which probably relates to the con-
    tracting parties. The suit papers say Joseph Bragg, Sr. died testate in
    1747 (WB#5,p.525) leaving twelve children by two wives; his widow Eliza-
    beth Bragg died in 1757. By his unnamed first wife he had issue: (1)
    Joseph; (2) Thomas; (3) Mary m. by 1758 Gaton Settle of Prince William
    County; (4) Catherine m. Benjamin Burras; (5) Elizabeth m. Mr. Bruce and
    now (1765) a widow; she is the complaintant in his cause. By his second
    wife, Elizabeth, who survived her husband about ten years, Joseph Bragg,
    Sr. had issue: (6) William; (7) John; (8) Benjamin; (9) Moore; (10) New-
    man; (11) Joseph, Jr. and (12) Reuben Bragg. The following persons, who
    state their approximate age, made depositions in this cause on 25 July
    1764: John Edison, age 47 and upwards; Henry Sisson, age 54 and upwards;
    John Redman, age 36 and upwards.]

BRAGG, THOMAS MOORE and Margaret Bispham*, bond 3 May 1813. Foushee G. Tebbs
    (b); Ann Bispham (w). Married 13 May 1813 by Rev. Samuel Templeman.
    [See data under the bride's brother, Robert Bispham, on page nineteen.]

BRAGG, WILLIAM K. and Elizabeth Hart, bond 16 November 1808. Henry Sisson con-
    sents to the marriage of his granddaughter, Elizabeth Hart, now "under my
    protection." Enoch Finch (b); Fanny Edwards (w).

BRAMHAM : BRANHAM

BRAMHAM, BENJAMIN and Elizabeth Beale, bond 25 May 1792. Bartholomew McCarty (b).

BRAMHAM, BENJAMIN JR. and Jemima Sanford Moxley of Westmoreland County, bond 7 March 1797. Consent by Joseph Moxley, father of the bride. Bartholomew McCarty (b); Daniel Moxley (w) and Thomas Butler (w).

BRANHAM, JOHN and Ann Green (widow), license October 1714.   DB#6,p.275
    [She was nee Ann Hobbs and widow of Richard Green (q.v.),p.81.]

BRANHAM, JOHN married Rachel Gower, 16 March 1726/7.   NFPR.,p.189
    [The bride was the widow of Francis Gower who died testate in Richmond County in 1726. John Branham [Bramham] died testate in Orange County in 1761. WB#5,p.29; DB#9,p.633; Orange County WB#2,p.315.]

BRAMHAM, VINCENT of Richmond County married 28 December 1793 in Westmoreland County, Hannah Bushrod Smith, daughter of Philip and Elizabeth (Bushrod) Smith. Stratton Nottingham, The Marriage License Bonds of Westmoreland County, Virginia, 1786-1850 (1928), p.8; Westmoreland County D&W#19,p.19.

BRAMHAM, VICNENT JR. [DOCTOR] and Mary S. Benneham*, bond 8 October 1832. Richard O. Jeffries (b); T.W.M. Shearman (w).   MBB.,p.95

BRANAN, SPENCER and Caty Martin (spinster)*, bond 22 December 1794. The consent, written by Caty Martin and addressed to Bartholomew McCarty, Clerk of Richmond County Court, is signed by her and also by Hannah Martin under her name. Leroy Stott (b) and Samuel Dew (b); William Dogett (w) and Samuel Dew (w).

BRANN, ANDREW and Frances Asbury, bond 30 October 1783. Gerard McKenny (b).

BRANN, CORBIN and Mary Lewis, bond 21 January 1847. Consent by Thomas Lewis, father of the bride. Jeremiah Lewis (b); William P.Middleton (w). MBB.,p.289

BRANN, REUBEN G. and Frances D. Efford*, bond 5 May 1830. Samuel A. Efford (b).
                MBB.,p.64

BRANN, VINCENT and Susanna Teague, bond 1 July 1794. Bartholomew McCarty (b).

BRANSON, VINCENT T. of Westmoreland County and Mary C. Middleton*, bond 22 September 1815. Thomas Barber (b).

BRASSER, RICHARD and Elizabeth How[r] [? Haw ?] married 7 July 1678. NFPR.,p.85

BRAXTON, THOMAS and Mary Plummer, bond 29 November 1837. Consent by Ann Plummer, mother of the bride. George Saunders (b); Alice Smith (w) and Maria G. Braxton (w). Married 30 November 1837 by Rev. Lovell Marders. Also filed is the consent of Thomas C. Braxton, father of the groom, which is witnessed by Ebenezer Jeffries and Benjamin D. Rust. [The Rev. Thomas Corbin Braxton (17??-1846), father of the groom, was the son of Carter Braxton (1764-1809) of Williamsburg and his wife nee Sarah Scandrett Moore (1766-1833) of Essex County, and grandson of the Honorable Carter Braxton (1736-1797) a signer of

the Declaration of Independence and his second wife nee Elizabeth Tayloe
Corbin. Maria G. (Davis) Braxton, mother of the groom and one of the witnesses to the marriage bond, was the daughter of Staige Davis who died
testate in Middlesex County in 1813 and his wife nee Elizabeth Macon Gard-
ner, daughter of John Gardner of King and Queen County. Obituaries of the
Rev. Thomas Corbin Braxton and his widow appeared in the Fredericksburg
Weekly Recorder of 24 July 1846 and the Fredericksburg News of 1 October
1858. As the Rev. Mr. Braxton was pastor of the Fredericksburg Baptist
Church in 1842 there is a biographical sketch of him in Oscar H. Darter,
The History of Fredericksburg Baptist Church (Richmond, 1959), p.71-72.]

BRENT, HUGH and Alice Martin, bond 30 November 1799. George Brent (b). [See
Chester Horton Brent, The Descendants of Hugh Brent (Rutland, Vermont,
1936), p. 110,238.]

BRENT, WILLIAM B. of Lancaster County and Susan Pope*, bond 4 February 1822.
William Gresham (b); A.J. P[mutilated]#(w).[The (w)# was Ann J. Priddy.]

BRETT, WILLIAM married by 1 February 1699 Diana Howell, widow of George Howell.
COB#2,p.365.

BRICKEY, JERARD and Fanny Richards, bond 19 July 1802. Peter Moore (b).

BRICKEY, JARRARD and Nancy Pugh [Pew], bond 8 May 1804. Peter Moore (b).

BRICKEY, WILLIAM JR. and Elizabeth Ashburn*, bond 3 January 1820. James S.
Smith (b); Polley Smith (w).

BRISSEE, JAMES married by 1735 Elinor Gallop, one of the four daughters of
Robert Gallop who died 20 May 1720 leaving a nuncupative will which failed
to apply to his landed estate. WB#4,p.161; King George County DB#2,p.1.

BRIZENDINE, EWEN of Essex County and Betsey Johnston, bond 3 June 1811. David
Barrick (b).

BROCK, THOMAS (16??-1722) of Richmond and King George counties, married (1) by
1709 Cecely [Cicily] Barrow, daughter of John Barrow (16??-1685); they had
one child; married (2) by 1719 Mary (Birkett) Jones (16??-1745), daughter
of John and Ann (Mills) Birkett (q.v.), p.18 and widow of Nebuchadnezzar
Jones (q.v.), p.109, by whom Thomas Brock had no issue. DB#5,p.142; King
George County DB#1,p.96,509; Sweeny,p.115; Richmond County DB#5,p.142,145.

BROCKENBROUGH, AUSTIN and Mary Metcalfe, license August 1714.   DB#6,p.275
[She was the daughter of Richard and Anne (Stone) Metcalfe, (q.v.). Austin
Brockenbrough (1685-1717) was the son of William and Mary (Newman) Brockenbrough (q.v.). Mary (Metcalfe) Brockenbrough m(2) John Spicer, Gentleman,
(16??-1727), only son of Capt. Arthur Spicer (q.v.). Fauntleroy,p.151,261.]

BROCKENBROUGH, AUSTIN [DOCTOR] and Lettice Lee Fauntleroy, bond 4 May 1808. Consent by Judith Fauntleroy, mother of the bride. Moore F. Brockenbrough (b).
[This was Doctor Austin Brockenbrough's first marriage; see 18W(2)98-99
for a full biographical account of him.]

BROCKENBROUGH, JOHN F. of Essex County and Frances Ann Carter, bond 2 May 1833.
Consent by James K. Ball, guardian of the bride, who states she is his niece.
Edward S. Saunders (b); E.E. Buckner (w) and William D. McCarty (w).
MBB.,p.105

BROCKENBROUGH, LITTLETON and Lucy C. Shackleford married 19 August 1851. Minister's returns of Rev. Henry F. Greene. [See, 18W(2)100.]

BROCKENBROUGH, COLONEL MOORE FAUNTLEROY of Richmond County married 12 November
1823 at the residence of Robert Weir, Esq., in Tappahannock, Essex County,
Miss Sarah Smith of the town of Tappahannock. The marriage was announced
in the Fredericksburg Virginia Herald of 13 December 1823.

BROCKENBROUGH, NEWMAN of Richmond County married Sarah Heale (21 years of age),
24 October 1715. Witnesses and security on the marriage bond were Austin
Brockenbrough, William Brockenbrough and Charles Taylor.   LCMR#1,p.1

BROCKENBROUGH, WILLIAM (c.1650-1702) married 168? Mary Newman (16??-1734), sister
of Anne (Newman) Deen Austin (16??-1713) who d.s.p. Mary (Newman) Brockenbrough m(2) by 6 May 1702, John Dalton, and died testate in North Farnham
Parish 12 December 1734 leaving issue by both husbands. COB#3,p.165; COB#4,
p.83; WB#2,p.102; WB#3,p.122; WB#5,p.219,249.

BROOCKE, WILLIAM and Nancy Belfield, bond 7 September 1846. Consent by Joseph
Belfield, father of the bride. Isaac S. Jeffries (b).   MBB.,p.280

BROOCKE, WILLIAM H. and Violett Bryant, bond 1 January 1808. Joseph Bryant (b).

BROOKE, GEORGE and Hannah S. Davis, bond 17 June 1818. Consent by Martin Sisson,
guardian of the bride. Whitfield Brooke (b); Elias Northen (w) and George
Northen (w).

BROOKE, SAMUEL and Ann Harrison*, bond 31 January 1837. William Harrison (b).
MBB.,p.154

BROOKS, RICHARD and Mary Harrison, bond 15 December 1834. Consent by Matthew
Harrison, father of the bride. William Harrison (b).   MBB.,p.127

BROOMFIELD   SEE: BLOMFIELD

BROWN,CHARLES EDEN [Reverend] and Frances Catherine Tapscott*, bond 4 February
1840. Daniel Atwill (b).   MBB.,p.192

BROWN, CHRISTOPHER and Susanna McKenney*, bond 30 December 1817. William Brown
(b); Joseph Fones (w).

BROWN, DANIEL and Elizabeth Jones (widow)*, bond 14 January 1800. Mark Stevens
(b).

BROWN, DANIEL married by 6 April 1801 Lucy Jones, daughter of Edward Jones
(17??-1759) and Barbary, his wife, and niece of Isaac Jones (17??-1764).
AB#1,p.546; AB#3,p.48; WB#6,p.148,350.

BROWN, DANIEL and Hannah Jenkins (widow), bond 9 September 1785. Almon Sanders (b).

BROWN, EDWARD and Lucy Dobyns, bond 22 August 1798. Luke Jackson (b).

BROWN, EDWARD and Nancy Ruick [Reuick]*, bond 31 December 1808. George Jesper (b).

BROWN, GEORGE and Winney Dodson, bond 19 December 1808. Consent by Alexander Dodson; no relationship to the bride stated. Susannah Dodson (w) and Ailcey Dodson (w).

BROWN, HUDSON and Polly France, bond 1 November 1813. John France (b). [The bride was born 11 July 1793, daughter of John and Catherine (Fones) France (q.v.). The groom was the son of Thomas and Ann (Morris) Brown (q.v.).]

BROWN, JOHN and Fanny Jenkins, bond 20 January 1817. Consent by Marthy Jenkins, mother of the bride. William Brown (b).

BROWN, JOHN R. and Cleopatra Reynolds, bond 7 January 1850. Consent by Sally E. Reynolds, mother of the bride. Richard Clarke, Jr.,(b); James Marks (w).
                                                                    MBB.,p.331

BROWN, NEWMAN (17??-1751) of King George County married 173? Martha Slaughter, only child of Francis Slaughter (1657-1718) and his second wife Ann Hudson, (q.v.) of Richmond County. The eldest child of this couple was William Brown (1740-1832) of King George County, who was the father of Solomon James Slaughter Brown (1782-1862), clerk of the court of King George County, 1838-1845. S.J.S.Brown was the father of William Saunders Brown (1820-1898), also clerk of the court of King George County, 1845-1887 and 1892-1898. The home of the latter was Waverley; it was subsequently the home of his granddaughter and her late well-known husband, the Honorable Thomas Lomax Hunter, poet laureate of Virginia, attorney at law, newspaper columnist, and an aristocratic Virginia gentleman. King George County DB#2,p.389-390; Eubank,p.24; 33V89-90.

BROWN, SIMON and Fanny Howe, bond 6 September 1820. Consent by George Mothershead, guardian of the bride. George Mothershead (b); John Yeatman (w).

BROWN, THOMAS SR. married 174? Katherine Oldham, born 11 September 1730 in North Farnham Parish, only child of Peter Oldham and Rebecca (Hatton) Alverson [Alderson](q.v.). AB#1,p.144; DB#12,p.517,541,719; DB#13,p.206; WB#4,p.79; WB#5,p.265.

BROWN, THOMAS and Nancey Morris, bond 6 January 1789. Consent by "William Morris and Mary An his wife;" no relationship stated. William Harris (b).

BROWN, THOMAS and Sally France*, bond 2 January 1827. Hudson Brown (b); John France, Sr. (w) and Kitty France (w).   MBB.,p.28
[The bride was born 17 May 1801, daughter of John and Catherine (Fones) France (q.v.). The groom was the son of Thomas and Ann (Morris) Brown (q.v.).]

BROWN, WILLIAM (16??-1699) married by 7 December 1693 Frances Moss, elder daughter of William Moss, Sr. (1632-1685) of Rappahannock County; she m(2) James Ingo (1680-1725) (q.v.). The will of William Brown, proved 7 June 1699, was recorded in now missing WB#1. William Brown was the eldest of the three sons of William Brown, Sr. who died testate in Rappahannock County in 1677; his land on Chingateaque Creek in Sittenburn Parish (now King George County) was devised to his sons William, John and Maxfield Brown. COB#2,p.409; COB#6,p.112; DB#2,p.1-2; WB#2,p.9; Sweeny,p.57,117.

BROWN, WILLIAM married by 1 April 1719 Mary Mathews, daughter of Giles Mathews who died testate in 1710. COB#8,p.89; WB#3,p.5.

BROWN, WILLIAM of Westmoreland County married by 1762 Susannah Williams, daughter of Francis and Rachel (Thornton) Williams and granddaughter of Thomas and Susannah (Smith) Thornton (q.v.). DB#12,p.361,422.

BROWN, WILLIAM and Martha H. Yeatman, bond 16 December 1816. Consent by Thomas Yeatman, father of the bride. James Reynolds (b); Christopher Brown (w).

BROWN, WILLIAM M. and Elizabeth D. Dodson, bond 26 December 1820. Thomas W. Bryant (b).

BROWNE, WILLIAM W.H. and Mary Reynolds*, bond 22 January 1838. George Mothershead (b). Married by Rev. Thomas M. Washington.   MBB.,p.167

BRUCE, ANDREW and Rebecca Bragg*, bond 5 February 1798. Daniel Marmaduke (b).

BRUCE, GEORGE and Elizabeth Bayne*, bond 7 September 1807. William Brinham (b); Reuben Bruce (w).

BRUCE, HENRY JR. (169?-1720) married by 5 February 1718 Susanna Stewart, daughter of William Stewart [Steuart], late of Richmond County, deceased; she m(2) Michael Winder (q.v.) and they were very tardy in returning an inventory of the estate of Henry Bruce, Jr. He was the son of Henry Bruce, Sr. (1664-1727) and Mary Morton, his wife, daughter of Andrew Morton of Northumberland County. Henry Bruce, Sr. and George Bruce (1650-1715) both died testate in Richmond County and both gave rise to a numerous progeny now widely dispursed. DB#7,p.264; DB#8,p.149; WB#4,p.7,213; see also Westmoreland County D&W#3,p.299.

BRUCE, HENRY and Salley Sutton, bond 12 August 1786. Benjamin Bruce (b).

BRUCE, JOSEPH married Katherine Taylor, 30 April 1728.   NFPR.,p.189
[He was the son of Henry and Mary (Morton) Bruce. WB#5,p.72.]

BRUCE, THOMAS married between 1752-1759 Sarah Bird, daughter of Phileman and Mary (Mackgyar) Bird (q.v.). AB#1,p.437,510; WB#5,p.686; WB#6,p.269,343.

BRYAN, DANIEL married by 3 September 1713 Susanna [also called Hannah] Peorey [also called Peers], then the widow of Samuel Steele (q.v.). COB#6,p.146; DB#3,p.82; DB#7,p.341. Samuel Steel(e) (16??-1706/7) and Daniel Bryan resided in Lancaster County, Virginia.

BRYANT, ALEXANDER and Lucy Clarke (widow)*, bond 17 December 1816. Edmund North-
    en (b).

BRYANT, ALEXANDER and Catharine Jasper, bond 9 November 1819. Consent by George
    Miskell, guardian of the bride, who states she is the orphan of William
    Jasper, deceased. George Saunders (b).

BRYANT, ALEXANDER and Margaret J. Northen*, bond 29 November 1837. Richard
    Clarke (b); Lucy D. Northen (w).   MBB.,p.161

BRYANT, ALEXANDER and Maria F. Clarkson (widow)*, bond 12 December 1846. Consent
    by R.H. Lyell, guardian of the groom. Edward J. Northen (b); Virginia Ann
    Bennehan (w).   MBB.,p.284

BRYANT, ALEXANDER and Jane M. Burch*, bond 19 October 1847. Carlos Cox (b);
    Richard Clark (w).   MBB.,p.299

BRYANT, CHARLES married Margaret Jeffrey, 30 November 1738.   NFPR.,p.190

BRYANT, EDWARD married Frances Smith, 6 April 1727.   NFPR.,p.189

BRYANT, HENRY married 31 October 1825, Nancy Elmore.   WFMR.,n.p.

BRYANT, JESSE and Melia [Milley] Ashburn*, bond 12 August 1793. William Feagans
    (b). This certificate is filed with the marriage bond: "Milley Ashburn,
    Daughter of Thomas Ashburn and Hannah, his wife, was born June 9, 1771. Ex-
    tract from St.Stephen's Parish Register in Northumberland County. Thomas
    Coelman, Clerk."

BRYANT, JESSE G. and Martha L. Booth*, bond 27 March 1844. William J. Jenkins
    (b). Married 28 March 1844 by Rev. William N. Ward.   MBB.,p.248

BRYANT, JOHN married Mary Hinds, 3 August 1726.   NFPR.,p.189

BRYANT, JOHN and Frances Montague*, bond 13 January 1796. Joseph Bryant (b).
    Patsey Sadler certifies that Frances Montague, daughter of Nancy Montague,
    is over the age of 21 years. John Montague (w).

BRYANT, JOHN and Elizabeth Deacon, bond 24 July 1797. John Muse (b). Consent
    by Nancy Deacon, mother of the bride. Benjamin Hail (w).

BRYANT, JOHN and Elizabeth Hunt, bond 24 November 1814. John Hunt (b).

BRYANT, JOSEPH and Elizabeth Jackson*, bond 25 February 1793. Thaddeus Jackson
    (b); Christopher Jackson (w) and Patty Brown (w).

BRYANT, RAWLEIGH D. and Winny B. Haydon*, bond 22 January 1849. John Haydon (b);
    George Haydon (w).   MBB.,p.319

BRYANT, REUBEN and Ann Thrift, bond 27 July 1804. Consent by Jonathan Bryant for
    the marriage of Reuben Bryant who is under age. Consent by John Thrift for
    the marriage of Ann Thrift who is of full age. John Bryant (b).

BRYANT, REUBEN and Mary Thrift*, bond 16 December 1845. Benjamin Tucker (b);
Thomas B. Herrick (w) and George R. Thrift (w). Married 18 December 1845
by Rev. E.L. Williams.   MBB.,p.268

BRYANT, RICHARD P. and Alice C. Brown, bond 1 February 1847. Thomas W. Bryant
(b). [He was son of Thomas and Frances (Dodson) Bryant (q.v.).] MBB.,p.290

BRYANT, SAMUEL and Sally Stott, bond 26 December 1815. Epp.ª Stott (b).

BRYANT, SAMUEL and Olivia N. Elmore, bond 9 April 1823. Thomas W. Bryant (b).

BRYANT, THADDUS and Ann Phillips (widow), bond 21 December 1809. Richard Bennehan (b).

BRYANT, THADDEUS and Courtney Loury, bond 7 September 1818. Warner L. Tapscott
(b).

BRYANT, THOMAS (styled "the younger") of North Farnham Parish married between
18 April 1714 and 8 April 1718, Margaret Jeffries, daughter of Edward and
Elizabeth Jeffries [Geffrys]. DB#7,p.215; WB#3,p.190.

BRYANT, THOMAS married Elizabeth Fowler, 27 June 1729.   NFPR.,p.189

BRYANT, THOMAS and Fanny Dodson, bond 23 September 1803. James B. Dodson (b).
[ECD: Bible Record of Thomas Bryant (1 July 1783-4 January 1853) and his
wife Frances Dodson (30 October 1785-1 December 1857) who were married 25
September 1803 in Richmond County. Issue: (1) Robert, born 13 February
1805; (2) Henry, born 13 September 1806; (3) Thomas F., born 19 April 1808;
(4) Fedelia D., born 27 June 1810; (5) Catherine, born 15 September 1812;
(6) Elizabeth, born 2 December 1814 and died 20 December 1814; (7) Lucinda,
born 9 March 1816; (8) James M., born 19 February 1818 and died 17 March
1837; (9) Rachel,born 23 January 1821 and died 22 June 1842; (10) Frances,
born 23 January 1822 and died 25 August 1823; Richard P., born 30 August
1824 and (12) Rawleigh Bryant, born 19 April 1827.]

BRYANT, THOMAS L. and Susanna Pope*, bond 7 February 1815. Alexander Bryant (b).

BRYANT, WILLIAM of Northumberland County and Hannah Efford*, bond 7 January 1792.
Charles Jones (b).

BRYANT, WILLIAM and Jane Wroe*, bond 30 December 1800. Rawleigh Bryant (b);
George Nash (w) and William Bryant (w).

BRYANT, WILLIAM C. and Martha Ann Garland Lewis, bond 18 October 1845. Valentine Lewis (b). Married 20 October 1845 by Rev. E.L. Williams. MBB.,p.264

BRYANT, WILLIAM E. and Mary Ann Jeffries*, bond 30 January 1840. John Wesley
Douglas (b); Lucy Douglas (w).   MBB.,p.191

BUCKLEY, REUBEN and Mary White, bond 30 May 1787. Consent by Zechariah White,
father of the bride. Edward Marks (b).

BUCKNER, ELIAS E. [DOCTOR] and Maria H. Smith, bond 6 October 1818. Harrison
    Ball (b). Consent by Catharine Smith, mother of the bride. Sarah T.
    Snead (w). [Doctor Elias Edmonds Buckner (14 February 1792-11 January
    1865) practiced medicine in Richmond County for some years after his mar-
    riage on 14 October 1818 to Maria Henrietta Smith (1793-31 March 1875) of
    Moratico Hall, before they moved to Missouri. He was the son of Major
    Richard Buckner (c.1750-1798) of Caroline County and his wife nee Judith
    Edmonds, daughter of Elias Edmonds, Gentleman, (1726-1784) of Fauquier
    County. W.A. Crozier, The Buckners of Virginia and the Allied Families of
    Strother and Ashby (New York,1907),p.39; Chester Horton Brent, The Descend-
    ants of Hugh Brent (Rutland, Vermont, 1936), p.224-225.]

BULGER, EDMUND married by 2 August 1748 Jane Wright, widow of John Wright who
    died intestate in 1736; she died testate in 1790. COB#10,p.398; COB#12,
    p.158; DB#11,p.286,375; WB#5,p.285; WB#8,p.65; see Thomas Wright,p.236.

BULGER, JOHN and Julia Ann Hinson*, bond 21 January 1850. Richard McGinnis (b);
    Joseph Scates (w). Married 24 January 1850 by Rev. John Pullen. MBB.,p.332

BULGER, JOHN JR. and Susanna Smith*, bond 7 December 1807. William Smith (b);
    Jeames Smith (w).

BULGER, WILLIAM and Lucy Nash, bond 5 April 1813. Consent by Ann Nash, mother
    of the bride. James S. Smith (b).

BULGER, WILLIAM S. and Eliza Reynolds, bond 18 May 1831. Consent by Frances
    Reynolds; no relationship stated. John McGuier (b); William H. Sisson (w).
                                                                    MBB.,p.78

BURCH, GILSON B. and Susan S. Northen, bond 17 December 1833. Consent by Mary
    Northen; no relationship stated. Richard G. Northen (b).   MBB.,p.113

BURCH, JILSON B. and Lucy Morgan (spinster), bond 4 September 1797. Winifred
    Morgan, mother of the bride, consents. Benjamin Morgan (b).

BURGESS, JAMES H. and Elizabeth Brown*, bond 20 December 1842. William H. Mor-
    ris (b); Ann Brown (w). Married 23 December 1842 by Rev. R.N. Herndon.
                                                                    MBB.,p.230

BURKE, JOHN of Westmoreland County and Matilda F. Levy, bond 27 June 1815. Con-
    sent by Dr. John Y. Chinn, guardian of the bride, who states he was so ap-
    pointed by the will of her father, Ezekiel Levy of Richmond County, deceas-
    ed. Bartholomew McCarty (b).

    BURKETT   SEE: BIRKETT PAGE 18

BURN, CHRISTOPHER married Alice Gwien, 2 August 1728.   NFPR.,p.189

BURN, JOSEPH married Eleanor Flowers, 3 April 1728.   NFPR.,p.189

BURRELL, THOMAS and Judah Weldon "free blacks of the County of Richmond," bond
    21 May 1849. Consent by Sampson Weldon, father of the bride. William

Ball (b). Married 24 May 1850 by Rev. William N. Ward.   MBB.,p.323

BURT, DAVID married Mary Read, 19 October 1673.   NFPR.,p.85

BURTON, THOMAS and Molly White, bond 14 May 1791. Consent by George White,
    father of the bride. George White (b); James Pullen (w) and Leroy Luttrell
    (w).

BURWELL, GEORGE and Mary Wells* "free persons of colour," bond 9 February 1836.
    Mary Wells writes her consent with her own hand. Robert Rich "a free man
    of colour" (b).   MBB.,p.143

BURWELL, NATHANIEL of York County and Elizabeth Smith, bond 19 April 1786. Con-
    sent by John Smith, Jr., father of the bride. John Smith (b); Samuel Kel-
    sick (w) and Mary Kelsick (w). See the will of bride's father, John Smith,
    Jr., proved 5 June 1797 and recorded in WB#9,p.72.

BURWELL, THOMAS and Elizabeth Newman "both free persons of color," bond 6 Janu-
    ary 1820. Daniel Hardwick (b).

BUSH, URBANE and Ann Haynie*, bond 20 January 1847. Yarret Haynie (b); Joseph
    Haynie (w).   MBB.,p.288

BUTLER, ISAAC O. and Cornelia A. Stiff, bond 12 February 1844. Consent by J.M.
    Stiff, father of the bride. John W. Collins (b). Married 15 February
    1844 by Rev. William N. Ward.   MBB.,p.245

BUTLER, LAWRENCE of Westmoreland County married circa 1750, Mary Beckwith, who
    was born in North Farnham Parish 12 June 1727, daughter of Sir Marmaduke
    and Elizabeth (Brockenbrough) Beckwith (q.v.). They lived at Bleak Hall,
    Westmoreland County, where there is a tombstone difficult to decipher:
    "Here lyeth interred the body of Mrs. Mary Butler, the wife of Lawrence
    Butler and daughter of Mr. Marmaduke Beckwith, Baronet, who departed this
    life the 3rd day of December 1755 in the 27th year of her age. She had
    three children, Beckwith, Peggy and Lawrence." On 4 June 1764 Roger Beck-
    with gave bond in Richmond County as guardian of Beckwith Butler, orphan of
    Lawrence Butler, deceased and on 4 May 1761 Sir Marmaduke Beckwith made a
    deed of gift of a Negro to his grandson Beckwith Butler (DB#12,p.75). The
    informative will of Lawrence Butler [Jr.] (175?-1811) is of record in Fred-
    erick County, Virginia, WB#9,p.44. Eubank,p.34, sketch of Bleak Hall.

BUTLER, LAWRENCE and Hannah Litterell, bond 6 December 1804. Jarrard Brickey (b).

BUTLER, SAMUEL C.F. and Lucinda Nash, bond 17 January 1840. Consent by Catherine
    Nash, mother of the bride. Reuben Hinson (b); Frances T. Butler (w).
                                                                MBB.,p.190

BUXSTON, JOHN married Anne Hais, 18 February 1730/1.   NFPR.,p.189

C

CALLAHAN, JAMES and Margaret F. Dobyns, bond 26 December 1840. Consent by Fran-
    ces L. Dobyns, mother of the bride. Benjamin Pursell (b); William Bryant
    (w). Married 23 December 1840 by Rev. John M. Waddey.   MBB.,p.203

CALLIS, ROBERT (17??-1785) married Elizabeth Neale, daughter of Richard and
    Catherine (Fauntleroy) Neale (q.v.) WB#7,p.482; references cited, R.Neale.

CAMBELL, ALEXANDER married by 3 November 1708 Mary Marshall, daughter of Abraham
    Marshall (16??-1709) and Thomasin, his wife. WB#2,p.131. Difficult to
    understand is the recording in NFPR of the birth of Mary Marshall, daughter
    of Abraham and Thomasin Marshall, on 7 January 1699.

CAMBROM, ALLEN and HannahEskridge*, bond 2 June 1788. Daniel Connally (b).
    In writing her own consent, the bride signs her name "Hannah Esquig."

CAMMELL, GEORGE and Betty Stonum, bond 16 March 1779. George Scurlock (b).

CAMPBELL, ARCHIBALD and Hannah Mackay, bond 23 July 1760. William Mackay (b).
    [Rev. Archibald Campbell (17??-1775) was rector of Washington Parish, West-
    moreland County, 1745-1775. His first wife was Rebecca Rallings (c.1734-
    1754). His second wife was the only child to leave issue of the Rev. Mr.
    William Mackay (McKay, McCoy &c:), rector of Hanover Parish, King George
    County and of North Farnham Parish, Richmond County, from 1754 until the
    time of his death, circa 1774, and his wife nee Barbara Fitzhugh (q.v.).
    The will of the Rev. Mr. Archibald Campbell was proved at Westmoreland
    County court 25 April 1775, but oddly enough, is recorded in a XIX Century
    volume, viz: D&W#22,p.385. Hannah (Mackay) Campbell m(2) Richard Hipkins
    (17??-1786), widower, of Westmoreland County. Eubank,p.34; Edward Lewis
    Goodwin, The Colonial Church in Virginia (1927), p.258; Meade, II,p.158-
    162 (which account contains several errors); SPR.,p.xxix,lll.]

CAMPBELL, JOHN and Polly Fauntleroy, bond 28 January 1800. Consent of Ann Faunt-
    leroy, mother of the bride, was written from Mars Hill and witnessed by B.
    Fauntleroy and Joseph Fauntleroy. Bartholomew McCarty (w). [Judge John
    Campbell was the youngest son of the Rev. Archibald and Hannah (Mackay)
    Campbell (q.v.). This was his first marriage; his second wife was Eliza
    Ferguson Murphy per bond dated 7 December 1808, Westmoreland County.
    Eubank,p.62,63; Meade, II,p.161; Stratton Nottingham, The Marriage Licen-
    se Bonds of Westmoreland County, Va. 1786-1850, p.11.]

CAMRON, DENNIS married Ann Preseon, 1 December 1728.   NFPR.,p.91

    CANNAN   SEE :   KENNAN

CANNAN, WILLIAM and Betsey Linton Harrison (widow), bond 1 October 1787. Samuel
    Cralle (b). [The court clerk renders the name William Kennan, but the groom
    signs his name, William Cannan. The bride was the widow of Captain George
    Harrison (17??-1784); by him she had two children, viz: Alice Griffin Harri-
    son and Betty George Harrison. AB#2,p.175,181; WB#7,p.454.]

CARILL, DANIEL and Ann Lase, married 26 February 1726/7.   NFPR.,p.88

CARPENTER, ELI C. and Mary Carter, license 28 December 1852. Consent by Daniel
    Carter, father of the bride. William A. Gutridge (w) and Robert A. Fones
    (w). Married 30 December 1852 by Rev. James W. Hunnicutt.

CARPENTER, JOHN married Frances Brown, 9 June 1729.   NFPR.,p.91

CARPENTER, OVERTON of Lancaster County and Ann Bennehan, bond 13 December 1815.
    Catherine Bennehan writes her consent to the marriage of her daughter and
    this is witnessed by Emma D. Glascock. James Shepherd (b).

CARPENTER, WILLIAM and Sarah Ann Pope (spinster), bond 29 January 1780. John
    Pope (b).

CARTER, CHARLES· and Margaret N. Jesper*, bond 14 February 1838. Septimus M.
    Clarke (b).   MBB.,p.169

CARTER, CHARLES B. and Ann Beale Carter, bond 5 April 1796. Robert Wormeley
    Carter (b). [Charles B. Carter (1766-1807) was the son of Charles Carter,
    Esq. of Shirley and his first wife (who was his first cousin) Mary Walker
    Carter of Cleve. His wife was the daughter of Robert Wormeley and Winifred
    (Beale) Carter and granddaughter of Colonel Landon Carter (1710-1778) the
    builder of Sabine Hall. Mr. and Mrs. Charles B. Carter lived at Mt. Atlas,
    near Haymarket, Prince William County; in the family cemetery near the house
    stands his handsome tombstone. The obituary of Charles B. Carter, Esq.,
    appeared in the Fredericksburg Virginia Herald of 4 December 1807. Beale,
    49-51; Prince William: The Story of Its People and Its Places, Richmond
    (1941),p.183, records an interesting account of Mt.Atlas and its inhabitants.]

CARTER, DANIEL SR. and Mrs. Elizabeth Balderson*, license 29 March 1853. M.A.
    Carter (w) and William Carter (w). Married 29 March 1853 by Rev. John Pullen.

CARTER, FENNER and Rebeckah Sanders, bond 14 December 1825. Joshua Reamy (b).
                                                                           MBB.,p.16

CARTER, GEORGE of Westmoreland County and Lettice Stowers, bond 5 January 1792.
    Consent by Ann Coalman, mother of the bride. Thomas Asbury (b).

CARTER, JAMES R. and Susan Coats, bond 31 April 1834. Consent by James Coats,
    Sr.; no relationship to either party stated. William Carter (b). MBB.,p.120

CARTER, JOHN and Susanna Reamy, bond 2 June 1788. Consent by Mary Carter, mother
    of the groom and Joshua Reamy, father of the bride - "all parents and partys
    have agreed" to the marriage, says a quaint note. Gerrard McKenny (b).

CARTER, JOHN C. and Apphia Fauntleroy, bond 4 February 1782. Thomas Brockenbrough
    (b). [John Champe Carter was the son of Colonel Edward Carter (1733-1792) of
    Blenheim, Albemarle County. The bride was the youngest child of Colonel Will-
    iam Fauntleroy (1713-1793) of Naylor's Hole, Richmond County, and Margaret
    Murdock, his wife. Colonel George S. Wallace, The Carters of Blenheim (1955),
    p.18; Fauntleroy.]

CARTER, JOHN S. and Ann Morris*, bond 29 December 1840. Robert Sanders (b).
    Married 29 December 1840 by Rev. John M. Waddey.   MBB.,p.204

CARTER, JOSEPH and Nancy Christian, bond 14 December 1782. John Woollard (b).

CARTER, LANDON and Elizabeth Thornton (widow), bond 14 March 1782. Henry Armis-
    tead (b); George Carter (w). [Colonel Landon Carter (1751-1811) of Cleve,
    King George County, m(1) 15 February 1772, Mildred Willis, daughter of Col-
    onel Lewis and Mary (Champe) Willis of Willis Hill, Fredericksburg, Va.; he
    m(2) 16 March 1782, his cousin, Elizabeth (Carter) Thornton, daughter of
    Robert Wormeley Carter, Esq: of Sabine Hall, Richmond County, and childless
    widow of Peter Presley Thornton, Esq: (1750-1780) (q.v.). The unusual and
    interesting Bible record of Colonel Landon Carter of Cleve is preserved in
    the Virginia Historical Society (Mss.5:9c:2462:1). For an incomplete and
    somewhat imperfect account of Colonel Landon Carter of Cleve and his family
    see Miss Stella Pickett Hardy, Colonial Families of the Southern States of
    America (New York,1911),p.119-120.]

CARTER, LANDON JR. and Catherine Tayloe, bond 3 February 1780. John Mackay (b).
    [For the lineage of Colonel Landon Carter of Sabine Hall and his Lady, see
    Beale,p.49,264.]

CARTER, WILLIAM (bachelor) and Elizabeth Gutridge (spinster), bond 21 December
    1829. Consent by Reuben Gutridge; no relationship stated. Samuel Cralle,Jr.,
    (b).   MBB.,p.58

CARTER, WILLIAM and Mary Ann Scrimger, bond 24 April 1834. Consent by James
    Scrimger; no relationship stated. Thomas B. Coats (b).   MBB.,p.119

CASH, JOHN and Polly Yeatman, bond 3 May 1826. William Richards (b) and William
    P. Brinnon (b).   MBB.,p.21

CASH, WILLIAM and Fillishsha France*, bond 7 January 1828. John Cash (b). John
    France, Sr. (w) and Kitty France (w).   MBB.,p.33
    [The Bible record of the bride's parents, John and Catherine (Fones) France,
    records the birth of their daughter Felishehe France on 20 June 1810, (q.v.).]

CEARRON, WILLIAM married Ann Dammurell, 27 August 1730.   NFPR.,p.91

CHAMBERLAIN, JOHN and Rachel Alderson*, bond 16 December 1791. The bride writes
    her own consent and her mother, Mary Alderson, also gives her consent. Jery
    Alderson (b).

CHAMBERLAIN, JOHN L. (bachelor) and Elizabeth Elmore (spinster)*, bond 23 July
    1828. Henry Sisson (b); he made oath both parties "are above the age of
    twenty one years."   MBB.,p.39

CHANDLER, FRANCIS married Margaret Mozingo, 18 July 1731.   NFPR.,p.91

CHANLER, JOHN married Sarah Mozingo, 25 August 1729.   NFPR.,p.91

CHAPMAN, JOSEPH of Gloucester County and Jane Foard (widow)*, bond 7 January
1788. John Robins (b). [The bride was the widow of William Ford who died
intestate in 1783; family tradition says she was nee Thornton. The suit
papers, Thompson vs Ford (1818), in FDC#281, indicate William and Jane Ford
had five children, viz: (1) George Ford who died shortly after his father;
(2) Thomas Ford and (3) William Ford, both of whom died in 1787 without issue; (4) Mathew Thornton Ford (born 28 May 1783), who sold 426 acres of land
in Richmond County, inherited from his father, in 1806 and is said to be a
resident of North Carolina in 1818 when the aforesaid suit in chancery was
instigated; (5) Elizabeth Ford who married 27 August 1794 in King George
County, John Thompson; he died 9 January 1832 and in 1840 was living in
Richmond County. Elizabeth (Ford) Thompson contended her only surviving
brother had no right to sell the land of their father; she claimed an equal
right. The indications in the suit papers are that Elizabeth Ford was born
circa 1772 and in 1841 was living in Augusta County, Virginia; at the same
date her son, William F. Thompson, was a resident of Westmoreland County and
is drawn into this controversy. Jane Ford, widow, was baptized 15 April 1787
and became a member of the Nominy Baptist Church. William Ford was the eldest son of John Ford, who died testate in 1764; grandson of John Ford, Jr.,
who died intestate in 1714; and great-grandson of John Ford who died testate
in 1699. AB#1,p.509; DB#3,p.24,117; DB#4,p.78a,92a,131a; DB#10,p.87,188,250,
330,332,391,429; DB#11,p.124; DB#12,p.9,526,779; DB#14,p.470; WB#2,p.12; WB#3,
p.179; WB#4,p.53; WB#6,p.342-343; WB#7,p.426,434; COB#6,p.201,314; MRB,p.103.]

CHAPMAN, PHILIP P. and Elizabeth Oldham, bond 4 November 1830. Robert Scott (b).
                                                               MBB.,p.69

CHEAZUM, WILLIAM and Judah Packet*, bond 22 April 1801. Eppa: Weathers (b).

CHILTON, JOHN STEWART married by 1762 Mary Samford; she was born in North Farnham
Parish, 5 May 1739, daughter of Thomas Samford (1688-1762) and Frances _____
(17??-1750), his wife. AB#1,p.507; WB#6,p.315.

CHILTON, MARK and Sarah Keys, license January 1710/11.   DB#6,p.275
[The bride was the daughter of James and Mary (Pannell) Kay (q.v.). COB#7,
80.]

CHILTON, RALPH H. and Susan F.C. Glascock*, bond 23 July 1838. Richard M. Glascock (b).   MBB.,p.174

CHINAULT, CHRISTOPHER and Catherine Barnes*, bond 13 December 1791. Thaddeus
Forrester (b).

CHINN, BARTHOLOMEW C. and Cordelia B. McCarty, bond 6 March 1838. George Saund-
ers (b).   MBB.,p.171
[This was the second marriage of Bartholomew Carter Chinn; for details see
Hayden,p.120.]

CHINN, CHICHESTER (171?-1747) of Lancaster and Richmond counties [son of Rawleigh
and Esther (Ball) Chinn] married 26 October 1739 in Lancaster County, Agatha
Thornton, daughter of Doctor Thomas Thornton (16??-1741) and Agatha Curtis
(1692-1755), his wife, who were married 25 July 1708 in Christ Church Parish,

Middlesex County. Chichester Chinn died intestate in Richmond County; his widow moved to Prince William County with her infant children and her eldest son, Thomas Chinn (c.1740-1773) appears on the records with his mother and mention is made in 1767 of the orphans of Chichester Chinn, deceased, to whom the said Thomas Chinn was then guardian. Unfortunately the names of these orphan children are not mentioned in this record, but as the family of Chichester Chinn (171?-1747) was the only one known to be in Prince William County in pre-Revolutionary War times, no doubt is left that Rawleigh Chinn of Prince William County (see below) was the son of Chichester and Agatha (Thornton) Chinn. LCMR.,p.17; COB#12,p.91,100; WB#5,p.537; Kathrine Cox Gottschalk and A. May Osler, Withers Family of the County of Lancaster, England, and of Stafford County, Virginia, (Richmond, 1947) p.159-166.

CHINN, JOSEPH W. and Marianna Smith, bond 7 January 1822. Consent by Catherine Smith, mother of the bride. John R. Matthews (b).

CHINN, JOSEPH of Lancaster County and Elizabeth Griffin, bond 18 July 1792. Consent by John Fauntleroy; no relationship to either party stated. Thomas Sydnor (b). [The bride was born 18 August 1773, daughter of Major LeRoy Griffin and Judith Ball (1753-1817), his wife, who m(2) John Fauntleroy. For further information regarding Joseph Chinn (1768-1803) see, Hayden, p. 120; also AB#2,p.232,238; WB#7,p.211.]

CHINN, RAWLEIGH of Prince William County and Judith Glascock, bond 2 February 1768. James Sherman (b). [The groom was the son of Chichester and Agatha (Thornton) Chinn (q.v.), p.35-36.]

CHINN, RA(W)LEIGH and Fanny Tarpley, bond 30 January 1775. Charles McCarty (b). [Ra(w)leigh Chinn (17??-1816) of Loudoun County m(1) Fanny Tarpley, daughter of Major Travers Tarpley who died testate in Richmond County in 1768. He m(2) 8 February 1797, his cousin, Elizabeth Shearman, daughter of Martin and Ann (Chinn) Shearman of Lancaster County. Rawleigh Chinn was the son of Thomas Chinn of Lancaster County who was married there on 12 November 1735 to Sarah Mitchell (1717-1752), daughter of Robert Mitchell, Gentleman, (1684-1748). WB#7,p.11; Loudoun County WB "M",p.45 (will of Rawleigh Chinn,1816); Middlesex County WB "G",p.30 (will of Lucy Tarpley Jones); LCMR.,p.14,92; VSL:AD #25212 (Bible record of Robert Mitchell, Gentleman, (1684-1748).]

CHINN, ROBERT and Elizabeth Belfield, bond 15 May 1764. Richard Mitchell (b). [The groom was the son of Thomas Chinn (17??-1768) and his first wife nee Sarah Mitchell (1717-1752) of Lancaster County; the bride was born 9 January 1747, the daughter of John and Ruth (Sydnor) Belfield (q.v.). WB#9,p.158.]

CHINN, ROBERT and Elizabeth Belfield, bond 11 July 1804. Consent by Sydnor Belfield for the marriage of his daughter. Peter R. Garland (b); William Lee Beale (w).

CHRISTIAN, FRANCIS HUMPHREY (17??-1788) of Lancaster, Richmond and Frederick counties, m(1) 6 July 1756 Catherine Chinn, elder of the two daughters of Rawleig Chinn who died intestate in Lancaster County in 1756 and Ann, his wife, who also died intestate in Lancaster County in 1784. He m(2) 16 December 1768

Ann Shearman, daughter of Martin and Ann (Chinn) Shearman of Lancaster County; she was a first cousin of his first wife, Catherine Chinn. Francis Humphrey Christian, Gentleman, and his second wife, moved to Frederick County, Virginia, circa 1785 and he died testate there in 1788. DB#12, p.298; DB#15,p.213; LCMR.,p.26,37; Frederick County WB#5,p.185,266.

CHRISTIE, ROBERT married Elizabeth Lambeart, 23 April 1731.   NFPR.,p.91

CHRISTOPHER, WILLIAM and Catharine D. Davenport, bond 1 June 1839. Consent by Lucy T. Davenport, mother and guardian of the bride. George Christopher (b); William Davenport (w). Married 11 June 1839 by Rev. Addison Hall.
MBB.,p.182

CHRISTOPHER, WILLIAM and Jane H. Miskell, license 7 March 1853. Consent by William H. Miskell, father of the bride. Married 9 March 1853 by the Rev. John Godwin.

CHURCHILL, SAMUEL and Sally Weymoth, bond 2 May 1798. Thomas Weymoth (b).

CHURCHWELL, SAMUEL and Jane Day* "both free persons of colour," bond 8 April 1819. John Ferguson (b).

CHURCHWELL, SIMON married Darks Starks, 4 March 1730/1.   NFPR.,p.91
[Darcus Starks was a daughter of James and Eleanor (Todd) Starks, (q.v.), p.194. COB#10,p.544.]

CLAPMAN, WILLIAM (c.1654-1696) married by 1683 Mary Thatcher (166?-1727), daughter of Sylvester Thatcher (16??-1667); she m(2) by 7 October 1696, Thomas Richardson (16??-1719). COB#2,p.121,167,350,474,500; DB#1,p.41, WB#4,p.132. See also King George County COB#1,p.359; Inventory Book #1, p.100; Sweeny, p.60,106, Payne,p.51-52. The name appears often as CLAPHAM.

CLARK : CLARKE

CLARKE, ATTERSON and Caroline McClananhan*, bond 20 May 1837. Peter T. Duff (b)
MBB.,p.156
[The bride was the daughter of Jeremiah and Apphia (Northen) Webb (q.v.),p. 226 and widow of Vincent M. McClanahan (q.v.),p.125. AB#11,p.346.]

CLARKE, CHARLES and Betty Deatney (widow)*, bond 16 July 1792. Lancelot L. Smither (b); Lancelot L. Smither (w) and Nancy Smither (w).

CLARKE, DAVID and Fanny Proctor*, bond 29 September 1801. William Proctor (b).

CLARKE, DAVID and Drucilla R. Woollard, bond 14 June 1816. Lemuel L. Woollard (b).

CLARKE, EDWARD and Rebecca M. Dobyns*, bond 26 June 1844. Thomas Saunders (b).
Married 27 June 1844 by the Rev. William N. Ward.   MBB.,p.250

CLARKE, HIRAM and Ann Lewis, license 16 February 1852. Consent by Thomas P. Lewis, father of the bride. John C. Brann and Benjamin Tuckner, witnesses. Married 18 February 1852 by Rev. Elijah L. Williams.

CLARKE, JAMES of Westmoreland County and Margaret Walker Cain, bond 16 April 1792. Consent by Ann Welch, mother of the bride. Thomas Taite (b); George Carter (w).

CLARK, JOHN and Rebecca Rimer, (spinster), bond 3 November 1750. Lamberth Morgan (b).

CLARKE, JOHN and Almira L. Walker, bond 28 January 1823. Miskell Saunders (b).

CLARK, JOHN and Sally Daniel*, bond 29 December 1824. Shadrach Clark (b); Darius G. Cralle (w).   MBB.,p.7

CLARKE, JOHN H. and Hannah Todd, bond 11 July 1832. Consent by Maliady Edwars, guardian of the bride. John W. Doggett (b).   MBB.,p.91

CLARKE, JOHN H. and Lucy Bryant, bond 24 February 1835. Thomas W. Bryant (b).
                                                          MBB.,p.131

CLARKE, JOHN R. and Alice Clarke*, bond 9 December 1847. The bride writes her own consent and consent is also given by Nancy Heifford (sic) [? Efford ?]; no relationship to either party indicated. Henry O. Hudson (b); Benjamin Tucker (w).   MBB.,p.302

CLARKE, JOHN R. and Sarah Kent*, license 21 October 1852. Robert Sydnor (w), Benjamin Tucker (w), and William King (w). Married 21 October 1852 by Rev. William C. Haynes.

CLARK, MESHACK and Elizabeth B. Clark, bond 2 January 1824. Consent by Nancy Clark, mother and guardian of the bride. John Hudson (b); John Darby (w).

CLARKE, PRESLEY and Winifred Self, bond 8 August 1787. Consent by Samuel A. Self, father of the bride. Jeremiah Self (b); John Clarke (w) and Vincent Clarke (w).

CLARK, PRESLEY and Sally Smith*, bond 4 September 1792. Vincent Clark (b).

CLARKE, PRESLEY and Winney Wroe (widow)*, bond 9 February 1821. Thomas O. Lewis (b); John King (w).

CLARKE, PRESLEY S. and Nancy Brown*, bond 11 February 1840. Lindsey Headley (b); William B. Hale (w). Married by Rev. Nathan Healy.   MBB.,p.192

CLARK, RANDALL and Mary Stephens Messer, bond 27 November 1799. Consent by Hannah Messer, mother of the bride. Merridith Hudson (b); Mary Stephens (w).

CLARKE, REUBEN and Lucy Warner*, bond 5 December 1803. Newby Berrick (b).

CLARKE, RICHARD and Sarah Northen, bond 25 February 1832. Consent by Edward J. Northen, father of the bride. Daniel Garland (b); Eppa Clarke (w).
MBB.,p.88

CLARKE, RICHARD JUN.^R and Susan N. Clarke*, bond 17 November 1840. The bride in her consent says she is "to be twenty one years of age the 17th day of Nov. 1840." Thomas L. Darby (b); Seth Rockwell (w).   MBB.,p.199

CLARKE, SAMUEL and Hannah Lane Lewis*, bond 6 May 1799. George Lewis (b).

CLARK, SHADRACH and Elizabeth Samford (spinster), bond 22 December 1828. Consent by Mary Efford, mother and guardian of the bride. John L. Clark (b).
MBB.,p.49

CLARKE, THOMAS and Patcy Dozier*, bond 23 July 1821. George Saunders (b); Thomas Tune (w).

CLARKE, THORNTON and Elizabeth T. Evans (widow), bond 1 May 1829. Henry A. Montague (b).   MBB.,p.54

CLARK, VINCENT and Hannah L. Self (widow)*, bond 16 October 1788. Presley Clark (b); Isaac Lewis (w) and Rubin Lewis (w).

CLARKE, VINCENT and Polly Sidney Brickey, bond 7 February 1814. William Brickey consents to the marriage; no relationship stated. William Morgan (b); James G. Moore (w) and Betsy Brickey (w).

CLARKE, VINCENT and Nancy Brann*, bond 2 January 1816. Consent by Reubin Brann; no relationship stated. William Hammack (b); Samuel Brann (w) and Jeremiah Brann (w).

CLARKE, WALKER of King George County and Milly Scott*, bond 1 February 1813. Conoway Dozier (b); John Bayne (w).

CLARKE, WILLIAM and Elizabeth Brann, bond 15 September 1824. Shadrich Clarke (b) states both parties are of age.   MBB.,p.1

CLARKE, WILLIAM JR. and Rebecca Dozier*, bond 29 March 1808. David Clarke (b). In writing her consent, the bride says she is 23 years of age and acts for herself.

CLARKSON, RICHARD H. and Maria F. Jeffries, bond 11 March 1843. Consent by Thomas Oldham, guardian to the bride; consent by John Mayo, guardian to the groom. John F.B. Jeffries (b). Married 16 March 1843 by Rev. R. N. Herndon.   MBB.,p.236

CLAUGHTON, JOHN and Frances S. Downman, bond 20 February 1790. John Wroe (b).

CLAUGHTON, JOHN of Northumberland County and Sarah S. Smith*, bond 10 April 1807. Thomas P. Smith (b); William C. Smith (w).

CLAUGHTON, RICHARD and Nancy Hunton*, bond 5 March 1795. Thaddeus Pope (b);
    Betsy H. Pope (w).

CLAYTON, THOMAS and Mary Butler, license January 1710/11.   DB#6,p.275

CLAYTOR, RICHARD and Ann B. Bragg (widow)*, bond 7 October 1793. James Scates
    (b).

CLEAVE(S), EMANUELL [GENTLEMAN] married by 5 April 1707 Patience Naylor, relict
    and executrix of Avery Naylor (16??-1705) and formerly the widow and execu-
    trix of John Ford, Sr. (16??-1699). DB#3,p.24,117; DB#4,p.78a,92a,105;
    MRB.,p.42,81; WB#2,p.12,76; WB#3,p.179; see Joseph Chapman, p.35.

CLEMENTS, WILLIAM and Lucy Smith, bond 9 April 1788. Consent by John Smith, Jr.,
    father of the bride. James Burwell of Essex County (b); Molly Smith (w).

COATS, CHARLES L. and Sarah Ann Hinson*, bond 7 February 1848. John Hinson (b);
    G. White (w).   MBB.,p.305

COATS, HENRY and Elizabeth R. Woollard, bond 8 December 1831. Richard Woollard
    gives his consent; no relationship stated. Thomas B. Coats (b); John W.
    Woollard (w) and Elizabeth Woollard (w).   MBB.,p.82

COATS, JAMES and Lucy Jones*, bond 3 March 1792. Luke Jackson (b).

COATS, JAMES and Mahalah Gutridge*, bond 9 January 1836. John Peed (b).
                                                                 MBB.,p.140

COATS, MISKELL and Elizabeth Hall*, bond 20 November 1848. Redman B. Ambrose
    (b); Blaton Hall (w) and James H. Jenkins (w).   MBB.,p.315

COATS, THOMAS and Mary Fones, bond 12 February 1788. Laurence Beddoo (b).

COATS, THOMAS B. and Frances R. Scrimger, bond 8 December 1831. Henry Coats (b);
    William S. Towles (w). Consent by James Scrimger; no relationship stated.
                                                                 MBB.,p.81

COATS, ZACHARIAH and Mary Woollard*, bond 6 June 1846. Samuel B. Roe (b); John
    Roe (w).   MBB.,p.278

COBURN, JOHN and Bridgett Taylor (widow), license August 1712.   DB#6,p.275

COCKE, JOHN C. and Winifred Thornton (spinster), bond 28 August 1772. Consent
    by John Tayloe and Francis Thornton, guardians of the bride, who state she
    is the daughter of the Honorable Presley Thornton, deceased. Hudson Muse
    (b); John Thornton (w); W. Thornton (w). [Deed dated 4 August 1783 and re-
    corded at the General Court of Virginia, 17 October 1783: John Catesby
    Cocke, Gentleman, of Northumberland County and Winifred, his wife, parties
    of the first part; Daniel McCarty of Westmoreland County and Presley Thorn-
    ton of Northumberland County, parties of the second part; Catesby, Elizabeth,
    Presley Thornton, Alice Thornton, Peter Presley and Catherine Cocke, children
    of the said John Catesby Cocke and Winifred, his wife, parties of the third

part: "Whereas an unhappy difference has arisen between John Catesby Cocke and Winifred Cocke, his wife, which has induced them to separate from each other" ... this is a trust marriage settlement putting certain property in the hands of the parties of the second part as trustees for the children mentioned. It appears Mr. and Mrs. Cocke were reconciled and moved to Culpeper County where they appear jointly on those records. They also had a youngest daughter Lucy Cocke, not mentioned in the 1783 deed, and born after their reconciliation. The will of the Honorable Presley Thornton (2 March 1721/2 - 7 December 1769) of Northumberland House, Northumberland County, was involved in extensive litigation in the first quarter of the XIX Century and the children of his daughter Winifred (Thornton) Cocke (c.1752- c. 1816) are mentioned as follows: (1) Elizabeth wife of William Fitzhugh; (2) Alice T., wife of Elias Edmonds; (3) Kitty wife of Joshua Tennison; (4) Thornton Cocke; (5) Peter T. Cocke and (6) Lucy Cocke. John Catesby Cocke was found dead on the banks of the Rappahannock River near Port Royal in Caroline County on 17 April 1808; the Fredericksburg Virginia Herald of 22 April 1808 stated the facts and added: "His relatives, who are thought to be in Culpeper, are hereby informed." The inventory of the estate of Winifred (Thornton) Cocke was recorded in now lost Culpeper County Will Book "G" (1813-1817), p.404. There is considerable about this Cocke family in the Culpeper County records. See also, Thornton vs Cocke FDC#282.]

COELMAN, THOMAS and Ann Stowers, bond 13 July 1790. Thomas Sydnor (b). [Thomas Coelman (or Coleman) had nine children born in North Farnham Parish; he mentions all of them in his will proved in 1810 (WB#9,p.369). By his first wife Betty _____ he had issue: (1) Lucy, born 1 March 1759, married 4 February 1779, William Faulks; (2) Richard, born 22 April 1761; (3) Betty, born 26 January 1763, married Mr. Rout; (4) Thomas, born 30 June 1770; (5) Robert, born 15 August 1772; (6) Sarah, born 19 May 1775, married 27 April 1793, Thomas Walker; (7) James, born 4 January 1778; and (8) Molly, born 23 April 1780, married 28 January 1797, Oliver Stott. By his second wife Ann Stowers, he had issue only (9) Thaddeus Coelman (Coleman), born 21 May 1791. She was the widow of Samuel Stowers who died testate, 1786.WB#7,p.525.]

COLEMAN, WILSON and Elizabeth Richards*, bond 26 February 1846. Autumn Connellee (b); Hamilton Thrift (w).   MBB.,p.273
[The bride, Elizabeth C. (Thrift) Richards, was the widow of Reuben S. Richards, deceased, (q.v.).]

COLLEE, THOMAS married Anne Fann, 13 July 1673.   NFPR.,p.89

COLLINS, JOHN W. [CAPTAIN] and Mary Sophia Stiff, bond 7 October 1843. Consent by J.M. Stiff, father of the bride. Isaac S. Jeffries (b); George W. Goldsby (w) and Isaac O. Butler (w). Married 12 October 1843 by Rev. William N. Ward.   MBB.,p.242

COLLINS, JOHN W. of Richmond County and Mrs. Mary S. McKildoe of Fredericksburg were married 24 June 1847 by the Rev. Edward C. McGuire, rector of Saint George's Church. Fredericksburg Weekly Recorder, 2 July 1847; Fredericksburg Marriage Register No.1,p.10. [The bride was the widow of James McKildoe whose handsome tombstone in the Fredericksburg Cemetery states he was

"A native of the Northern Neck of Virginia who at an early age settled in the City of Richmond where he was much respected. He died at Auburn, Spottsylvania County, June 18th 1846, aged 58 years."

COLLINS, RICHARD and Drusilla Collins, bond 21 November 1817. William R. Jeffries (b).

COLLINS, RICHARD and Mary M. Jones, bond 27 January 1834. James Jones (b).
                                                                    MBB.,p.115

COLLINS, THOMAS and Mary Smith*, bond 22 December 1802. In writing her consent (which is mutilated), the bride says she "is of full age, about 2?, and have no friends in these parts." Samuel Gilbert (b).

COLLINSWORTH, JOHN and Hannah White (spinster), bond February 4, 1750. Edmund Collinsworth (b).

COLSTON, CHARLES and Rebecca Taverner (widow), license May 1713.   DB#6,p.275
[Captain Charles Colston (1691-1724) married Rebecca (Travers) Taverner (169?-1727), childless widow of John Taverner (1683-1711) and daughter of Captain Samuel and Frances (Allerton) Travers. They had five children. COB#6,p.214; WB#3,p.65; WB#4,p.248, WB#5,p.28; A.P.& P.,p.361; Beale, p. 213,263; Hayden,p.300.]

COLSTON, WILLIAM (c.1660-1701), first clerk of the court (1692-1701) of Richmond County, married by 1681 Ann (Gooch) Beale, widow of Captain Thomas Beale. They had two sons, viz: William Colston (168?-1721) who married Mary Meriwether and left two only children, viz: (a) Mary Colston who married John Smith, Gentleman; and (b) Frances Colston who married Joseph Morton, Gentleman; and Captain Charles Colston (1691-1724) (q.v.). WB#4,p.198; Beale, p.23,213,232.

COLSTON, WILLIAM and Lucy Carter, bond 19 October 1775. LeRoy Peachy (b).
[The bride was the daughter of Colonel Landon Carter (1710-1778) and his third wife nee Elizabeth Beale. William Colston (1744-1780) died testate in Richmond County and his widow moved to Alexandria and was living there, a widow, in 1820. Their children were: (1) William T. Colston, born 25 July 1776; from 1804-1807 he was a partner in business with his brother in law James Turner and in 1807 moved to near Battletown in Frederick County where his widow, Elizabeth B. Colston, was living in 1820; (2) Susanna (Susan) Colston, born 1778, married in 1805 James Turner who died about 1810; (3) Elizabeth Colston, born 1780, married in 1802 Benjamin Harrison Hall; they moved to Kentucky in 1817. FDC#272, Turner vs Carter (1817); Beale,p.213-214; see diary of Colonel Landon Carter 15W(1) and 16W(1).]

COLSTON, WILLIAM TRAVERS and Elizabeth Burgess Armistead, bond 10 July 1802. Bartholomew McCarty (b). [The bride was the daughter of Henry and Winifred (Peachey) Armistead (q.v.); the groom was the son of William and Lucy (Carter) Colston (q.v.). Fredericksburg District Court DB "E",p.213.]

CONNELL, DAVIS and Suckey Hammond, bond 7 March 1757. John Hammond (b).

CONNELL, MICHAEL married Mary Jesper, 8 September 1727. NFPR.,p.88
[Mary Jesper was born in North Farnham Parish in 1708, the daughter of Thomas and Anne (Lewis) Jesper (q.v.). WB#5,p.562,685.]

CONNELLEE : CONNELLY : CONOLY

CONNELLEE, AUTUMN and Juliann Mazuro, bond 23 July 1842. Consent by Louis Mazuro, father of the bride. Jesse G. Bryant (b); William Gilbert (w).
MBB.,p.225

CONNELLEE, DANIEL and Jane Newman*, bond 8 April 1791. The bride writes her own consent and it is witnessed by Hannah Marks "grandmother to the fores? Girl." Edward Marks (b); Edward Marks (w).

CONNELLY, DAVID and Lucy S. Burch, license 30 March 1852. Consent by Susan S. Burch, mother of the bride. James W. Brown (w). Married 30 March 1852 by Rev. E.L. Williams.

CONOLY, GEORGE and Sally Morris, bond 2 November 1789. William Morris (b).

CONNOLLY, GEORGE K. and Frances A. Rice, license 15 March 1853. Peter W. Rice (w). Married 17 March 1853 by Rev. John Godwin.

CONNOLLY, JAMES S. and Elizabeth Harrison, bond 2 August 1841. Consent by Matthew Harrison, father of the bride. William Harrison (b); John Harrison (w).
MBB.,p.211

CONNELLY, JOHN married Margaret Oldham, 26 February 1729/30. NFPR.,p.91

CONNELLY, PATRICK married Mary Widdilow, 28 July 1728. NFPR.,p.91

CONNELLY, RICHARD H. and Rebecca M. Clarke*, bond 30 December 1850. M.P. McCarty (w). Married 30 December 1850 by Rev. Elijah L. Williams.

CONNELLY, WASHINGTON T. and Elizabeth G. Hundley (widow)*, bond 17 December 1833. John D. Glascock (b). MBB.,p.112

CONNELLEE, WILLIAM and Mary Ramey, bond 2 September 1799. Daniel Connellee (b).

CONNELLEE, WILLIAM H. and Catharine Fallen* (widow of Samuel E. Fallen, deceased), bond 30 December 1846. John W. Woollard (b); Joseph H. Fallen (w).
MBB.,p.285

CONSERVE, EMANUEL married Elizabeth Killingsby, 22 January 1675. NFPR.,p.89

COOK, ANTHONY and Ann Clark, bond 8 March 1762. James Clark (b).

CONWAY, EDWIN [GENTLEMAN] (c.1640-1698) married (1) Sarah Walker (c.1663-1695), daughter of Colonel John Walker (16??-1668/9) by whom he had two children; m(2) 21 May 1695 Elizabeth Thornton (1674-1732/3), daughter of Francis and Alice (Savage) Thornton (q.v.), by whom he had an only child. Elizabeth (Thornton) Conway, widow, m(2) by 3 March 1698/9 Jonathan Gibson, Gentleman,

(16??-1729) and left issue by him. This last marriage is confirmed by COB #2,p.331,396,442, and other records. Hayden,p.231 favors us with a copy of the will of Edwin Conway, Gentleman, once of record in now lost WB#1, but errs in the surnames of both of his wives. The Rev. Mr. Hayden also fails to recognize the second marriage of the widow Conway to Jonathan Gibson, Gentleman, and her issue by him. If this marriage had been known to the Honorable T. Elliott Campbell, this fact would have explained considerable in regard to Jonathan Gibson and his family, so often mentioned by him in his Colonial Caroline (Richmond,1954). President James Madison (1751-1836), born upon his maternal ancestral lands at Port Conway, King George County, indicates in a genealogical diagram that his mother, Eleanor Rose ("Nellie") Conway (1731-1829),was the daughter of Francis and Rebecca (Catlett) Conway and granddaughter of Edwin and Elizabeth (Thornton) Conway. (Madison Papers, Volume I, p.211). Bible record of Francis Thornton, Senior, Gentleman, (1651-1726) in the Virginia Historical Society. There is an imperfect account of the Jonathan Gibson family by Olive Nelson Gibson in her Descendants of John Nelson,Sr. - Mary Toby, Stafford County, Virginia, 1740-1959 with Related Families (Redlands,California, 1961), p.222 et seq.

CORBIN, RICHARD (1714-1790) "eldest son of Col. Gawin Corbin, was lately married to Miss Betty Tayloe, daughter of Hon. John Tayloe (of Richmond County), one of his Majesty's Council of this Colony," said the Virginia Gazette of 29 July 1737. Beverley Fleet, Virginia Colonial Abstracts, Volume 4, p.63-66; and Return Jonathan Meigs, The Corbins of Virginia (Westfield, N.J., 1940), p.11.

CORDERE, HENRY and Elizabeth Peachy Hillyer, bond 2 January 1804. Joseph Jones Monroe (b).

CORNISH, WILLIAM and Ruth Dodson*, bond 17 September 1791. Thomas Weymouth, Jr. (b); Charles Dodson (w).

CORNWELL, JOHN of Prince William County and Mary Garland*, bond 4 August 1791. Consent by Anne Garland, mother of the bride. William Garland (b). [A Bible record says Mary (Garland) Cornwell m(2) Samuel Anderson and "departed this life in September 1832, aged 63 years." Her children by John Cornwell: (1) William Garland Cornwell, born 28 May 1792; (2) Artemisa Griffith Cornwell (30 April 1794-15 September 1873) married Joshua Taylor (20 August 1793-17 March 1873) of Prince William County; (3) Ann Cordelia Cornwell, born 20 April 1796; (4) John Burrell Cornwell, born 12 October 1798; and (5) Louisa Valentine Cornwell, born 30 April 1800. The issue of Samuel and Mary (Garland) Anderson are not entered in this Bible record.]

CORSON, ALFRED and Mary Ann M. Jones, bond 1 November 1847. James Jones (b). Married 4 November 1847 by Rev. William N. Ward.   MBB.,p.300

COURTNEY, HENRY and Elizabeth Brann, license 3 February 1853. Consent by William Ingram,Sr., guardian of the bride. J. Harriss and William Courtney, witnesses. Married 3 February 1853 by Rev. William N. Ward

COURTNEY, JEREMIAH and Ann Alderson*, bond 7 December 1848. William H. Packett(b). Married 7 December 1848 by Rev. William N. Ward.   MBB.,p.316

COURTNEY, JOHN and Nancy Moore*, bond 25 April 1816. John Harris (b).

COURTNEY, JOHN and Eliza A. Potter*, bond 8 January 1845. John Packett (b);
William Courtney (w). Married 8 January 1845 by Rev. William N. Ward.
MBB.,p.253

COURTNEY, LEONARD and Mary Alderson, bond 4 November 1812. Thomas S. Davis (b).

COURTNEY, WILLIAM and Lucy Ann Brizendine*, bond 26 January 1843. Joseph G.
Moore (b); William L. Lee (w) and Joseph Moore (w). MBB.,p.234

COURTNEY, WILLIAM and Mary Brann, bond 1 September 1847. Consent by William
Ingram; no relationship stated. Lemuel G. Bell (b); Joseph R. Jeffries
(w). MBB.,p.297

COVERT, MORRIS and Nancy Pursell, bond 20 March 1819. Consent by Sarah Purcell;
no relationship stated. William Y. Sturman (b).

COWARD, JAMES married by 3 January 1693 Mary Collidge, widow of Hezechia Collidge. COB#1,p.155; Milnor Ljungstedt, The County Court Note-Book, Volume
IV, p.42, for this and other Marriages by inference in Virginia Records..

COX, JOHN married 28 December 1826 at Alborough, Westmoreland County, Miss Mary
W. Hipkins, eldest daughter of Robert S. Hipkins, Esq. John Cox, Esq., is
said to be of Richmond County in this announcement in the Fredericksburg
Virginia Herald of 13 January 1827.

COX, PRESLEY of Westmoreland County and Sophia F. Mitchell*, bond 11 January
1810. John Turberville (b).

COX, THOMAS M. and Elizabeth C. Hardwick, bond 23 July 1821. Consent by John
Hardwick; no relationship stated. Darius G. Cralle (b); Thomas C. Beacham
(b).

COX, WILLIAM P. of Northumberland County and Eliza Clarke*, bond 15 April 1835.
Daniel C. Harrison (b); William R. Pridham (w). MBB.,p.133

CRABB, BENEDICT M. and Jane Crabb, bond 2 January 1804. Robert Clarke (b).

CRABB, WILLIAM M.M. of Westmoreland County and Ann T. Peck*, bond 17 February
1838. John C. Mitchell (b). Married 22 February 1838 by Rev. Lovell Marders. MBB.,p.169

CRAINE, JAMES [CAPTAIN] and Elizabeth McCarty, bond 13 January 1784. Consent by
Thaddeus McCarty for the marriage of his daughter Elizabeth, to Captain James Craine. Charles McCarty (b).

CRALLE, DARIUS G. and Jane Redman Hardwick, bond 3 February 1820. Consent by
John Hardwick, father of the bride. Peter P.C. Straughan (b).

CRALLE, DARIUS G. of Northumberland County and Maria G.Gordon*, bond 22 December
1826. Walter Self (b); Frances A. Gordon (w). MBB.,p.27

CRALLE, KENNER of Northumberland County and Susan M. Street, bond 14 May 1832.
    Consent by Elizabeth Street, mother of the bride. William C. Haynes (b);
    Mary Henderson (w).   MBB.,p.89

CRALLE, SAMUEL JR. and Frances M. Belfield, bond 10 September 1832. Consent
    by Joseph Belfield, father of the bride. Feriol Lemoine,Jr.(b).MBB.,p.93

CRANSTON, ANDREW and Jane Polly, bond 18 January 1762. Younger Kelsick (b).

CRASK, GEORGE and Rebecca Güttridge, bond 7 August 1820. William Settle (b).

CRASK, JAMES and Felicia Hardwick, bond 4 December 1833. Consent by John Hard-
    wick, Sr., father of the bride. John Hardwick, Jr. (b).   MBB.,p.112

CRASK, JESSE and Peggy Frary*, bond 5 December 1791. William Yates (b); James
    Frary (w).

CRASK(E), JOHN [CAPTAIN] (16??-1706) married by 7 December 1693 Elizabeth Moss
    (16??-1710), younger daughter of William Moss, Sr. (1632-1685) who had a
    land patent 10 September 1663 which descended to his two daughters as co-
    heirs upon the death of their only brother, William Moss, Jr. Elizabeth
    (Moss) Crask(e), widow, m(2) circa 1708 James Lockhart. COB#4,p.148; DB#2,
    p.1-2; DB#5,p.102-109; WB#2,p.120,126; WB#3,p.33; Sweeny,p.117.

CRASK, VINCENT and Sarah M. Willson, bond 30 April 1785. Consent by Sarah Crask,
    mother of the groom, who says he is "at liberty to act for himself"... and
    "am perfectly agreed to the match;" also, consent by Joseph Willson, father
    of the bride, assuring the court clerk "that it is now agreeable to their
    own desires." Edward Marks (b); Daniel Willson (w).

CRASK, WILLIAM (1???-1744) married by 30 November 1726 Rebecca Thornton, daughter
    of Mathew and Elizabeth (Hopkins) Thornton (q.v.). DB#5,p.99-102 (29 March
    1709) where William Craske is dubbed the son of Captain John Crask(e) (q.v.).
    DB#9,p.500; WB#5,p.57,462.

CRASK, WILLIAM of Westmoreland County and Bethiah Sanford (widow)*, bond 6 Febru-
    ary 1797. Daniel Willson (b). [She was the widow of Richard Sanford, (q.v.).]

CRAWLEY, WILLIAM married Jane Coear, 30 November 1728.   NFPR.,p.91

CREEL, WILLIAM married Ales Dodson, 25 November 1729.   NFPR.,p.91
    [Alice Dodson was the daughter of Thomas and Mary (Durham) Dodson (q.v.).
    WB#5,p.378.]

CRESWELL, WILLIAM married Anne Allin, 18 June 1677.   NFPR.,p.89

CREWDSON, HENRY and Sophia Carter Garland, bond 26 March 1799. Consent by Vin-
    cent Garland; no relationship stated. Peter Temple (b). [The Fredericksburg
    Virginia Herald of 24 March 1824 announced the death in Fredericksburg on
    Saturday last of Mrs. Sophia Crewdson, relict of the late Mr. Henry Crewdson
    of Richmond County, aged 43 years.]

CREWDSON, WILLIAM [CAPTAIN] and Ellen Robins* (spinster), bond 17 September 1794.
    John Cannaday (b). John Cannaday (w) and John Robins (w). [Ellen Robins
    was the daughter of William and Ellen (Thornton) Robins (q.v.) DB#17,p.29.]

CROLORIR, THOMAS and Alice King married 13 October 1729.   NFPR.,p.91

CROOKHORN, THOMAS and Hannah Mezingo, bond 17 February 1793. John Mezingo (b).

CROOKHORN, THOMAS and Margaret Bruce (widow), bond 27 May 1800. John How (b).

CROSWELL, GILBERT and Eleanor Hill married 9 December 1728.   NFPR.,p.91

CROW, WILLIAM of Culpeper County and Ann Woollard, bond 17 February 1789. Con-
    sent by Mary Ann Woollard, mother of the bride. John Woollard (b).

CRUTCHER, GEORGE and Sally Hadon*, bond 18 January 1809. Joshua Stone (b).

CURRELL, ISAAC of Lancaster County and Frances Pursell*, bond 3 September 1818.
    Lawson Hathaway (b); Thomas Bell (w) and Elin Tapscott (w).

CURREN, DENNIS (bachelor) and Catharine A. Miskell (spinster)*, bond 26 May 1828.
    Peter S. Northen (b).   MBB.,p.37

CURTIS, HENRY C. and Mary S. Dobbins*, bond 10 January 1843. William Jackson
    (b). Married by Rev. Nathan Healy; no date recorded.   M3B.,p.233

CURTIS, JOHN and Elizabeth Crawford, bond 30 September 1802. William Webster
    (b).

                                    D

DABNEY, JAMES married by 30 April 1690 Anne Sherwood, daughter of Philip Sher-
    wood of Rappahannock County whose land fell into Richmond County in 1692.
    23T116,207,278.

DADE, TOWNSHEND and Elizabeth Ball, bond 26 May 1784. Henry Washington (b).
    [The bride was the daughter of Captain Williamson[5] Ball (q.v.),p.9. See
    Hayden,p.104.]

DAINGERFIELD, WILLIAM and Apphia Fauntleroy, bond 14 April 1748. William Faunt-
    leroy, Jr. (b). [Apphia Fauntleroy (c.1722-1799), daughter of William and
    and Apphia (Bushrod) Fauntleroy of Richmond County,was the second wife of
    Colonel William Daingerfield (1710-1769) of Essex County where both of
    their wills remain of record. Colonel William Daingerfield m(1) c. 1732,
    Catherine Fauntleroy (1710-c.1747), daughter of Griffin and Ann (Bushrod)
    Fauntleroy of Northumberland County; his two wives were double cousins and
    he left issue by each. Colonel William Daingerfield (1710-1769) was the
    son of Colonel William Daingerfield (1680-1735) of Greenfield, Essex County,
    and his wife nee Elizabeth Bathurst.]

DAINGERFIELD, WILLIAM and Elizabeth M.B. Belfield, bond 20 December 1814. John W. Belfield (b).

DALE, JOSEPH and Elizabeth Williams, bond 1 January 1789. Bartholomew McCarty (b); Thomas Lightfoot (w).

DALE, JOSEPH and Chloe Palmer*, bond 6 November 1809. Cyrus Chilton (b).

DALE, WILLIAM of Woodford County and Elizabeth Booth, bond 27 July 1789. LeRoy Howard (b); Thaddeus Williams (w).

DAMERON, GEORGE and Mary Bryant*, bond 10 March 1797. Roger Dameron (b).

DAMERON, JOHN C. and Esther Shelly*, bond 7 April 1837. William Harper (b); Robert Damerl [? Dameron ?] (w).   MBB.,p.155

DAMERON, JOHN C. JR. and Lucy Jane Hall*; bond 8 January 1842. Robert H. Dameron (b). Married 12 January 1842 by Rev. William N. Ward. MBB.,p.218

DAMERON, RICHARD and Sarah J. Thrift*, bond 23 March 1844. George L. Winstead (b); John Thrift (w).   MBB.,p.247

DAMERON, ROGER and Leanah Jones, bond 15 August 1775. John Saunders (b).

DAMERON, SAMUEL L. and Milly Doggitt (spinster), bond 28 December 1809. William Dameron,Jr. (b).

DAMERON, WILLIAM JR. and Milly Jones (spinster)*, bond 10 April 1809. Leroy Luttrell (b); Leroy Luttrell (w) and Thomas Stott (w).

DANIEL, BEVERLEY of Middlesex County and Milley Tarpley, bond 5 August 1775. George Daniel (b). [The bride was the daughter of Major Travers Tarpley who died testate in Richmond County in 1768 (WB#7,p.11). See will of the bride's sister, Lucy (Tarpley) Jones, 1788, in Middlesex County WB "G",p.30. For data regarding Beverley Daniel (1752-1782) and his family see Robert Neville Mann and Cathrine Cleek Mann, Middlesex, Virginia Daniel Descendants (1959),p.39,153.]

DARBY, WILLIAM B. and Judah Newgent*, bond 24 December 1807. Consent by Rawleigh Newgent; no relationship stated. Luke Hanks (b).

DARRACOTT, WILLIAM P. (bachelor) and Eliza M. Shackleford (spinster), bond 9 April 1829. Consent by Moore F. Brockenbrough, guardian of the bride. Richard T. Darracott (b).   MBB.,p.53

DASEY, WILLIAM married Mary Mills, 8 January 1727/8.   NFPR.,p.100

DAUGHITY, JAMES of Northumberland County and Winney Humphris*, bond 30 May 1809. Thomas Coelman (b); Faney Davis (w).

DAUGHITY, JAMES and Fanny Dawson*, bond 28 March 1826. Ewell Webb (b); William Headly (w).   MBB.,p.20

DAVENPORT, GEORGE and Mildred Dobyns, bond 17 December 1788. Daniel Dobyns (b).
[The bride was the daughter of Thomas Dobyns (17??-1788) of North Farnham
Parish. AB#2,p.162; WB#8,p.36.]

DAVENPORT, GEORGE W. and Nancy O. Norris*, bond 16 December 1836. Thomas S.
Dunaway (b).   MBB.,p.151

DAVENPORT, JOSEPH and Frances Dobyns, bond 2 September 1782. Abner Dobyns (b).

DAVENPORT, JOSEPH H. and Elizabeth O. Edwards*, bond 3 June 1833. Thaddus C.
Stott (b).   MBB.,p.107

DAVENPORT, JOSEPH P. of Richmond County married 10 December 1817 Miss Lucy Simmonds of Lancaster County. Announcement in the Fredericksburg newspaper,
Virginia Herald, 20 December 1817.

DAVENPORT, LINSEY O. and Judith Smither*, bond 16 August 1816. Richard Smither
(b).

DAVENPORT, LINSEY O. and Maria S. Davis, license 18 August 1851. Consent by
Robert H. Davis, father of the bride. W.B. McCarty (w). Married 20 August
1851 by Rev. John Godwin.

DAVENPORT, OPIE and Nancy Forrester (spinster), bond 13 December 1781. George
Sherlock (b), so signs but court clerk renders his name George Scurlock.

DAVENPORT, THOMAS D. and Lucy Davenport, bond 31 December 1825. William Hathaway (b). Married 4 January 1826 by Rev. Jeremiah B. Jeter.   MBB.,p.17

DAVENPORT, WILLIAM married Elizabeth Heale, 26 November 1728.   NFPR.,p.100

DAVENPORT, WILLIAM E. and Frances A. Palmer, daughter of Mary M. Palmer, license
27 November 1852. William Christopher (w). Married 2 December 1852 by Rev.
Thomas H. Ball.

DAVENPORT, WILLIAM H. and Elizabeth P. Davenport (spinster)*, bond 15 April
1809. George Davenport (b).

DAVIS, ALFRED and Sally B. Self*, bond 27 January 1841. Moses Self (b). Married
27 January 1841 by Rev. William N. Ward.   MBB.,p.206

DAVIS, BARTLEY and Fanny Humphries (widow)*, bond 5 November 1795. William Humphries (b); William Humphries (w) and Winneyfred Humphries (w).

DAVIS, CHARLES and Sally A. Shackleford, bond 23 December 1846. William S. North-
en (b).   MBB.,p.285

DAVIS, EDWARD married Mary Paxen, 15 November 1677.   NFPR.,p.95

DAVIS, EDWARD and Polley Barnes, bond 28 December 1797. Consent by Charles Barnes, father of the bride. Humphrey Davis (b).

DAVIS, GEORGE of Richmond, King George and Goochland counties married between
4 December 1724 and 7 June 1728 Patience Brock, only child of Thomas and
Cicily (Barrow) Brock (q.v.) King George County COB#1,p.229; DB#1,p.96,
509; DB#2,p.44. [Although King George County DB#1,p.96 indicates Cicily
(Barrow) Brock d.s.p. and her landed estate vested in Honour Richardson,
this seems to an error as other records name Patience (Brock) Davis as the
only child and heir of Cicily (Barrow) Brock.]

DAVIS, GEORGE and Elizabeth Toone (spinster), bond 20 January 1759. Almorein
Bryant (b).

DAVIS, GEORGE and Elizabeth Wright, bond [blank] May 1795. Vincent Bramham (b).

DAVIS, JESSE and Priscilla Downman, bond 14 December 1789. Bartholomew McCarty
(b).

DAVIS, JOHN married Susanna Hammond, 25 December 1727.   NFPR.,p.100

DAVIS, JOHN and Joanna Jackson, bond 15 May 1804. Consent by Luke Jackson,
father of the bride. William Dobyns (b); Edward Brown (w).

DAVIS, JOHN and Nancy Smith, bond 12 July 1808. Consent by Catharine Smith,
mother of the bride. Edward J. Northen (b).

DAVIS, JOHN and Sally Robertson*, bond 2 February 1819. Reuben Davis (b).

DAVIS, JOHN L. [or S.] and Mrs. Ann Stephens*, bond 4 July 1849. Joseph Newman
(b); Ward Richards (w). Married 4 July 1849 by Rev. William N. Ward.
MBB.,p.324

DAVIS, JOSEPH S. and Elizabeth A. Newsom*, bond 18 November 1845. Richard H.
Lyell (b); Robert B. Neasom (w). Married 22 November 1845 by Rev. E.L.
Williams.   MBB.,p.266

DAVIS, JOSEPH S. and Elizabeth W. Ball*, bond 18 December 1850. William Webb
(b); Peter S. Northen (w). Married 18 December 1850 by Rev. E.L. Williams.

DAVIS, LUCIUS [Esq:] "late of Texas" and Elizabeth H. Peck, bond 8 January 1841.
Consent by H. Peck for the marriage of his ward, Miss Elizabeth H. Peck.
William A. Brockenbrough (b).   MBB.,p.204

DAVIS, LUKE W. and Mrs. Mahalah B. Kennan*, bond 13 April 1843. William J. Jenkins (b). Married 13 April 1843 by Rev. William N. Ward.   MBB.,p.237

DAVIS, RICHARD and Mary Berrick, license February 1715/16.   DB#6,p.275
[Richard Davis (1687-1719) was the younger of the two sons of William and
Elizabeth (Thrift) Davis (q.v.)· He had an only child Elizabeth Davis who
married Thomas Thornton (q.v.). Mary (Berrick) Davis, widow, m(2) Robert
Thornton (16??-1737). WB#4,p.119; WB#5,p.323.]

DAVIS, RICHARD W. and Elizabeth Woollard*, bond 17 December 1838. John W. Woollard (b); Sydnor Davis (w).   MBB.,p.177

DAVIS, ROBERT (c.1680-1735/6), elder of the two sons of William and Elizabeth (Thrift) Davis (q.v.), married by 1 September 1708 Susanna Jacobus, daughter of Angell and Elizabeth (Clarke) Jacobus (q.v.). Susanna (Jacobus) Davis, widow, m(2) John Dozier (q.v.). AB#1,p.364; COB#4,p.387; COB#12,p.102; DB#4,p.155; DB#5,p.96; DB#8,p.498; DB#12,p.641; WB#5,p.272,541,558.

DAVIS, ROBERT H. (bachelor) and Mary Pope (spinster), bond 27 November 1828. Thomas Bryant (b); he made oath both parties are of full age. MBB.,p.46

DAVIS, ROBERT H. and Juliet Clarke*, license 29 September 1851. Thomas Sanders (w). Married 30 September 1851 by Rev. E.L. Williams.

DAVIS, RODHAM and Patty Sisson, bond 11 August 1798. Consent by George Sisson, father of the bride. Samuel Cralle (b); Mary Sisson (w).

DAVIS, RODHAM and Betsy English, bond 2 January 1805. Consent by Caty English, mother of the bride. Ezekiel Cookman (b).

DAVIS, SYDNOR and Mary Woollard*, bond 17 January 1840. Robert G. Lewis (b).
                                                                    MBB.,p.189

DAVIS, THOMAS SM [?] and Jane Alloway (spinster), bond 5 May 1798. Consent by Isaac Alloway, father of the bride. John Woollard (b). [This bond is signed Thomas Sm (? Sen ?) Davis; maybe intended to be Thomas Davis, Sr.]

DAVIS, THOMAS and Tillize Roles*, bond 4 March 1826. William Richards (b); Thomas T. Reynolds (w).   MBB.,p.20

DAVIS, THOMAS S. and Lucy Balderson, bond 7 October 1816. Consent by E. Balderson for daughter's marriage. Vincent Jones (b).

DAVIS, WALTER married by 3 November 1719 Martha Jenkins, daughter of William and Elizabeth (Skelderman) Jenkins (q.v.). They were both deceased ante 28 February 1740 when Edward Davis of Richmond County, as sole heir of his late mother, deeded fifty acres of land, part of the original land patent of his great-grandfather, Herman Skelderman, to his maternal uncle, Mansfield Jenkins. DB#7,p.454; DB#9,p.646; WB#4,p.159; WB#5,p.348.

DAVIS, WILLIAM married Elizabeth Thrift, 23 April 1677.   NFPR.,p.95
[William Davis (16??-1698) died testate, but his will in lost WB#1 is recited in part in DB#12,p.641 and in a suit in chancery styled Thornton & wife vs Dozier & Davis instigated in 1746 for a division of his landed estate. William Davis devised 300 acres to be equally divided between his two sons, viz: Robert Davis (q.v.) and Richard Davis (q.v.). At the time the suit was instigated (1746), Robert Davis was deceased and his widow Susanna married to John Dozier and his son and heir Robert Davis was living, but d.s.p. in 1748, leaving his three sisters as his co-heiress. Richard Davis, the younger son, died leaving an only daughter Elizabeth, wife of Thomas Thornton and they were the plaintiffs in this suit brought for a division of the aforesaid 300 acres. COB#2,p.275 and other references under Robert and Richard Davis.]

DAVIS, WILLIAM of Westmoreland County married by 4 June 1733 Eleanor (Short)
Threlkeld, widow of Henry Threlkeld (c.1700-1731) (q.v.). COB#10,p.82;
WB#5,p.539.

DAVIS, WILLIAM and Haney Reynolds, bond 21 January 1791. Consent by Sarah Reynolds, mother of the bride. Abner Howe (b).

DAVIS, WILLIAM and Sarah Dameron*, bond 24 April 1849. John C. Dameron (b);
John Graham, Jr. (w).   MBB.,p.323

DAVIS, WILLIAM F. of Essex County and Elenor Ficklin, bond 29 January 1810.
Famous Ficklin (b). [Elenor (Eleanor,Ellen) Ficklin was the daughter of
Famous Ficklin who died intestate in Richmond County in 1816. See Ficklin
vs Ficklin, FDC#103.]

DAVIS, WILLIAM F. and Letty R. Pursell*, bond 23 March 1818. John Cauthorn (b);
George R. Pursell (w).

DAVIS, WILSON and Nancy Bustle, bond 10 May 1810. Consent by Hannor Bustle,
mother of the bride, who says her daughter is of legal age. Joseph Alexander (b); John Shehan (w).

DAWKINS, JOHN and Ann Churchwill (spinster), bond 3 January 1759. James Churchwill (b).

DAWSON, GEORGE L. of Northumberland County and Frances D. Lightfoot*, bond 11
December 1817. Richard Knott (b) and Presley Hudson (b).

DAWSON, JEREMIAH of Northumberland County and Betsy Lewis, bond 24 January 1804.
Consent by Hannah Lewis, mother of the bride, who says her daughter is of
legal age. James Wall (b); Epaphaditus Dawson (w) and Hannah Feagines (w).

DAWSON, LINDSEY O. and Rebecca Lewis, bond 13 July 1846. Jeremiah Lewis (b); he
is the bride's father.   MBB.,p.279

DAWSON, LINDSEY T. and Polly Shearley (widow)*, bond 23 February 1815. Jeremiah
Stephens (b).

DAWSON, RICHARD and Mary Douglas*, bond 26 November 1838. John W. Doggett (b).
                                                                   MBB.,p.176

DAWSON, RICHARD and Jane E. Jackson*, license 23 October 1853. George W. Burton
(w).

DAWSON, WILLIAM married between 1704-1711 Elizabeth Stone, daughter of William
Stone (16??-1704) and Sarah_____(16??-1717). DB#6,p.15,16; WB#2,p.114;
WB#3,p.323.

DAWSON, WILLIAM and Elizabeth Hill*, bond 3 January 1807. John Maley (b); John
Maley (w) and Sally Maley (w).

DEAN, CHARLES and Eliz.^{a} Jordan, license April 1716.   DB#6,p.275

DEANE, CHARLES married by 1720 Anne Jones, daughter of Nebuchadnezzar and Mary
(Birkett) Jones (q.v.) and sister of John Jones (16??-1719) who d.s.p.
DB#8,p.3; WB#4,p.91; King George County DB#1,p.3.

DEANE, JOHN [GENTLEMAN] (circa 1648-1712) married (1) by 1683 Jane Walker, daughter of Colonel John Walker (16??-1668/9); married (2) Elizabeth Thatcher,
daughter of Sylvester Thatcher (16??-1667). DB#1,p.41; MRB.,p.41; WB#2,
p.108; WB#3,p.92; Payne,p.55-56; Sweeny,p.89, 161-163.

DEATLEY, WILLIAM and Betsy Smither, bond 14 January 1788. Famous Ficklin (b).

DEATLEY, WILLIAM and Charlotte P. Tarpley*, bond 26 July 1822. Robert Scott
(b); Frances Ann Tarpley (w).

DEEKE, JOSEPH (16??-1718) married before 8 March 1704/5 Katherine Lewis, one of
the five daughters and coheiress of Edward Lewis, deceased. DB#3,p.178;
DB#6,p.115; DB#9,p.186; WB#4,p.45.

DEGGE, ISAAC and Mary Degge, bond 31 December 1772. Younger Kelsick (b). [This
bond is incorrectly given in 5W(1)20 as the 31st December 1792 and the
bondsman's name is incorrectly given as Younger Belsick.]

DEGGES, ROBERT and Betty Lawson, bond 9 December 1766. George Reynolds (b).

DELANO, JOSEPH and Lucinda Self, bond 25 August 1847. Consent by Moses Self,
father of the bride. Samuel W. English (b); Augustus Delano (w).MBB.,p.297

DEMERITT, BENJAMIN and Mary Dobyns, bond 14 August 1797. David Williams (b).

DEMERITT, JOHN and Alice Bramham, bond 10 February 1767. Benjamin Bramham (b);
he is the father of the bride.

DEMERITT, LUKE married Judith Win, 13 February 1728/9.   NFPR.,p.100

DENBY, JOHN and Alice Forester, bond 14 December 1841. Consent by William Forester; no relationship stated. Richard P. Forester (b); Eliza G. Forester (w).
MBB.,p.215

DENTON, WILLIAM and Mary Samford (widow), bond 10 March 1753. Richard Woollard
(b). [Mary (Barber) Samford was the widow of James Samford (c.1690-1742)
(q.v.) and daughter of Colonel Charles and Frances (Glascock) Barber (q.v.).]

DESCHAMPS, JOSEPH and Delia Griffin Haynie, bond 20 December 1809. Consent by
Wilalmira W. Haynie, mother of the bride. James D. Sydnor (b); Harriott
Montague (w). [The bride was the daughter of Captain Holland and Wilalmira
(Webb) Haynie (q.v.)]

DESHIELDS, JOSEPH [CAPTAIN] of Northumberland County and Matilda B. Waide, bond
6 December 1814. Consent by Thomas Plummer, guardian of the bride. Martin
Sisson (b).

DESHIELDS, JOSEPH (widower), and Emily C. Crewdson (spinster), bond 6 April 1829. Daniel Garland (b).   MBB.,p.53

DEW, SAMUEL and Betty Lewis*, bond 31 January 1766. LeRoy Peachey (b).

DEWBRE, JOHN of Lancaster County and Mary F. Connolly*, bond 16 January 1838. Washington T. Connolly (b).   MBB.,p.166

DICKSON, JAMES and Julia H. Deatley*, bond 17 January 1846. Lindsey Headley (b); William Deatley (w). Married 22 January 1846 by Rev. E.L. Williams.
                                                                       MBB.,p.271

DIDIER, HENRY and Lucy F. Alderson, license 6 October 1851. Consent by William Webb, guardian to the bride. Lyne Shackleford (w). Married 7 October 1851 by Rev. John Godwin.

DISKIN, JOHN and Agathy Nash, bond 14 November 1763. John Hill (b).

DOBYNS, ABNER and [not entered], bond 5 January 1783. Charles McCarty (b).

DOBYNS, ABNER, JR. and Winifred Northen, bond 14 November 1798. William Dobyns (b). [The bride was the daughter of George and Margaret (Jones) Northen (q.v.). AB#3,p.48,49; WB#9,p.29,107.]

DOBYNS, AUGUSTINE W. (bachelor) and Sarah J. Hale (spinster), license 4 February 1853. Consent by Thomas R. Hale and Peggy Hale, parents of the bride. James A. Hale (w). Married 8 February 1853 by Rev. Elijah L. Williams.

DOBYNS, CHARLES and Lucy Elder, bond 19 August 1762. George Davis (b).

DOBYNS, CHARLES and Sarah L. Dobyns, bond 5 February 1806. Consent by L.R. Dobyns, father of the bride. LeRoy Dobyns, Jr. (b).

DOBYNS, CHICHESTER and Fanny L. Bryant, bond 25 December 1811. Alexander Bryant (b).

DOBYNS, DANIEL and Elizabeth Sydnor, bond 26 February 1765. Griffin Peart (b).

DOBYNS, DANIEL and Frances Sisson Thornton, bond 17 December 1788. Consent by Rebekah Dobyns, mother of the bride. [The bride, born circa 1770, was the daughter of Thomas and Rebecca Sisson (Lawson) Thornton (q.v.). Thomas Thornton Dobyns and Rebecca Sisson Dobyns, twin children of Daniel and Frances Sisson (Thornton) Dobyns, were born 21 March 1796. (NFPR.,p.205)]

DOBYNS, DANIEL JR. and Caty Palmer, bond 31 May 1800. Consent by William Palmer, father of the bride. Bartholomew McCarty (b).

DOBYNS, EDWARD and Amony Forrister (widow), bond 31 October 1769. William Baker (b).

DOBYNS, EDWARD and Sally Mott*, bond 26 December 1797. William Alderson (b); Frederick Dobyns (w) and Nancy Mott (w).

DOBYNS, FREDERICK and Barbara Baker, bond 21 February 1792. Consent by Ammy Dobyns, mother of the groom. John Baker (b); John Baker (w).

DOBYNS, HENRY and Sarah Freshwater, bond 16 November 1770. Thomas Dobyns (b). [The bride was the daughter of Thomas and Elizabeth (Jesper) Freshwater (q.v.). WB#6,p.82.]

DOBYNS, HENRY M. of Caroline County and Betsy P. Dobyns, bond 23 August 1802. Daniel Dobyns (b); Consent by John Alde [mutilated].

DOBYNS, HENRY M. and Sarah Saunders, bond 20 April 1819. George Saunders (b).

DOBYNS, JESSE and Polly S. Miskell, bond 29 July 1807. George T. Garland (b).

DOBYNS, JOHN L. and Mary S. Deschamp, bond 22 January 1838. Thomas Oldham (b); John Roe (w).   MBB.,b.166

DOBYNS, JOSEPH A. and Elizabeth M. Gordon*, bond 20 December 1839. Bartholomew Miskell (b); Septimes M. Clarke (w).   MBB.,p.187

DOBYNS, JOSEPH A. and Sarah Davis*, license 18 December 1852. William D. Miskell (w) and H.C. Curtis (w). Married 23 December 1852 by Rev. E.L. Williams.

DOBYNS, LEROY and Lucy Lawson, bond 16 September 1782. Robert Neason (b). [LeRoy Dobnys left a will dated 29 October 1820 and it was admitted to probate 6 August 1821 and recorded in WB#9,p.708. He mentioned only his son William Dobyns and grandson John Lawson Dobyns by name and gave the residue of his estate to his daughters and grandchildren in proportions as his executor, Warner L. Tapscott, deemed proper. Such a testament was seemingly designed to provoke litigation and in 1829 the suit Dobyns vs Dudley was instigated (FDC#80). These papers stated that LeRoy Dobyns at his death left two sons and three daughters living, also seven grandchildren living but others were born after his death, viz: (1) Christopher L. Dobyns died prior to 1829, leaving issue: (a) Edwin Dobyns and (b) Matilda C. Dobyns; (2) William Dobyns also died prior to 1829, leaving issue: (a) John Lawson Dobyns, (b) Sarah L. Dobyns, (c) William Dobyns and (d) Rebecca Dobyns; (3) Sarah L. Smith (widow, 1829) who had issue by her first husband, Charles Dobyns, (a) Sydnor L.R. Dobyns; (4) Rebecca M. Dobyns married Edmund N. Northen and died prior to 1829; and (5) Alice Dobyns wife of Griffin G. Dudley in 1829.]

DOBYNS, LEROY JR. and Polly Northen, bond 19 December 1808. Consent by Edward J. Northern, guardian of the bride. Edmund Northen (b).

DOBYNS, THOMAS and Rachel Miskell (spinster), bond 2 December 1758.

DOBYNS, THOMAS and Rebecca Hammond, bond 24 March 1781. James Hillyer (b). [Rebecca Sisson Lawson m(1) 1769 Thomas Thornton (q.v); m(2) 177? Thomas Hammond (q.v.); m(3) 1781 Thomas Dobyns (17??-1788), widower.

DOBYNS, THOMAS and Betsy Lawson, bond 5 November 1811. Consent by Daniel Lawson, Sr., father of the bride. Bartholomew McCarty (b).

DOBYNS, THOMAS and Elizabeth Palmer*, bond 10 December 1816. George Saunders (b).

DOBYNS, THOMAS W. and Ann C.T. Durrett, bond 7 October 1833. Richard Durrett (b).   MBB.,p.110

DOBYNS, WASHINGTON and Priscilla Glascock*, bond 18 November 1812. Henry M. Dobyns (b).

DOBYNS, WILLIAM married by 31 October 1760 Rebecca Miskell, daughter of Henry and Winifred (Dalton) Miskell (q.v.); the bride was born 20 January 1724/5 in North Farnham Parish. WB#6,p.197.

DOBYNS, WILLIAM and Susanna Davis, bond 11 December 1790. George Miskell (b).

DOBYNS, WILLIAM and Caty L. Neasom, bond 5 December 1807. Consent by L.R.Dobyns for the marriage of his ward, Caty L. Neasom. Charles Dobyns (b).

DOBYNS, WILLIAM and Catherine Austin*, license 7 January 1852. Cyrus Clarke (w). Married 8 January 1852 by Rev. E.L. Williams.

DOBYNS, WILLIAM FORRESTER and Betty Hale Davenport (spinster), bond 22 May 1782. Abner Dobyns (b).

DODSON, ALEXANDER and Lucinda Dodson*, bond 14 October 1840. Thomas W. Bryant (b); Charles Dodson (w) and Susan Dodson (w).   MBB.,p.198

DODSON, ALEXANDER and Catharine Bryant married 3 February 1848, by Rev. Bartholomew Dodson. No bond found in Richmond County; this from the Rev. Mr. Dodson's "returns."

DODSON, ALFRED and Margaret Conley*, bond 6 November 1847. James S. Conley (b).   MBB.,p.300

DODSON, CHARLES and Elizabeth C. Churchwell*, bond 18 December 1805. Edmund R. Jeffries (b); Elender Harris (w).

DODSON, EDWARD L. and Martha Ann Pope*, license 16 February 1852. Joseph W. Bryant (w) and William Christopher (w). Married 18 February 1852 by Rev. Bartholomew Dodson.

DODSON, FORTUNATUS married Ellis Goad, 9 September 1726.   NFPR.,p.100

DODSON, GEORGE married Margaret Dagod, 30 April 1726.   NFPR.,p.100
[The surname(s) Dagod, Doged, Dogged, Doget, Dogget &c: seem to interchange in the North Farnham Parish Register recordings.]

DODSON, George and Catharine Weymoth, bond 28 July 1802. John Weymoth (b).

DODSON, JAMES B. and Winifred Bryant, bond 1 January 1795. Joseph Bryant (b).

DODSON, RAWLEIGH and Lettice Bryant*, bond 26 June 1795. William Cornish (b).

DODSON, RAWLEIGH JUNIOR and Charlotte Tillery, bond 16 August 1800. William Dodson (b).

DODSON, REUBEN B. and Lucy Elmore*, bond 22 December 1832. Henry Elmore (b); Charles Dodson (w). MBB.,p.99

DODSON, RICHARD and Millian Keiser, license 14 October 1851. William Walker (w) and John Keiser (w). Married 15 October 1851 by the Rev. John Godwin.

DODSON, THOMAS (1681-1740) married between 2 August 1700 and 29 August 1701, Mary Durham (born 1686), only daughter of Thomas Durham (circa 1660-1714) and Dorothy, his wife. DB#3,p.57; WB#3,p.210,270; WB#5,p.378; see also Lancaster County WB#8,p.106 and Silas Emmett Lucas, Jr., Genealogy of the Dodson (Dotson), Lucas, Pyles, Rochester, and Allied Families (Birmingham, Alabama, 1959).

DODSON, THOMAS and Frances Weymouth, bond 4 January 1815. Samuel Pritchett (b).

DODSON, WILLIAM and Milley Nash*, bond 25 September 1798. Richard Nash (b); Molley Nash (w).

DOGGETT, COLEMAN of Lancaster County and Patty Morgan (widow)*, bond 13 October 1812. Thomas P. Smith (b).

DOGGETT, ISAAC and Elizabeth Churchwell married, 11 December 1729. NFPR.,p.100 [The children of this couple are dubbed with the surname of DOGED in the recordings of their births in the North Farnham Parish Register.]

DOGGETT, JOHN and Elizabeth Brown*, bond 29 April 1831. Thomas A. Sorrell (b); Elizabeth M. Miskell (w). MBB.,p.77

DONAHOE, EDMUND [or EDWARD] (16??-1748) married Ann Tippett, daughter of Thomas Tippett (16??-1710). Her sister, Abigail Tippett, married in 1714 John Green (q.v.); neither were named in the will of their father, Thomas Tippett, which was dated 15 February 1699 and proved 6 December 1710. Apparently their brother, William Tippett, d.s.p. and his aforementioned two sisters inherited their father's land in Richmond County which fell into King George County in 1721. WB#3,p.27; King George County DB#3,p.278.

DONIPHAN, ALEXANDER [CAPTAIN, GENTLEMAN] (circa 1653-1717), widower, married (2) by 2 November 1691 Margaret Mott, second daughter of George Mott, Gentleman, of Rappahannock County, patentee of thousands of acres of land in the Northern Neck of Virginia. Margaret (Mott) Doniphan died prior to 23 March 1709. DB#1,p.8; see also Essex County DB#13,p.320 and 26T275-285, 28T226-238.

DONNAHAN, RICHARD H. and A. Cloudis, bond 14 October 1845. William N. Ward (b). Married 14 October 1845 by the Rev. William N. Ward. MBB.,p.264

DOUGLAS : DOUGLASS : DOUGLISS

DOUGLASS, EDWARD and Hannah B. Hogans*, bond 25 May 1807. Consent by Thomas
   Hogans and Nancey Hogans for the marriage of their daughter. Edmund R.
   Jeffries (b).

DOUGLISS, JOHN and Catherine Dodson (widow), bond 31 March 1800; William Elmore
   (b).

DOUGLISS, JOHN and Judah Bryant (spinster), bond 23 December 1801. Consent by
   Jonathan Bryant, father of the bride. John Bryant (b).

DOUGLASS, JOHN C. and Sarah Ann French*, license 3 January 1853. John Harrison
   (w). Married 4 January 1853 by Rev. E.L. Williams.

DOUGLASS, SAMUEL H. and Lucy Ann Doggett, bond 1 June 1850. Francis W. Pendleton (b) [Clerk of the Court]. Married 1 June 1850 by Rev. John Godwin.
                                                                  MBB.,p.339

DOUGLISS, THOMAS and Hannah Harper (widow), bond 31 March 1801. John Dougliss
   (b).

DOUGLASS, THOMAS and Fanny Watts, bond 18 August 1813. Spencer Watts (b).

DOUGLASS, THOMAS married 21 November 1824, Elizabeth Sherley.   WFMR.,n.p.

DOUGLASS, THOMAS H. and Malindy Douglass, bond 1 April 1845. Consent by Ann
   Douglass, mother of the bride. James Douglass (b); J.C. Stott (w). Married
   4 April 1845 by Rev. E.L. Williams.   MBB.,p.257

DOUGLAS, THOMAS H.L. and Rachel Bryant, bond 17 December 1838. Thomas W. Bryant
   (b); he is father of the bride.   MBB.,p.178

DOUGLAS, WILLIAM married 17 October 1805, Nancy Lewis.   WFMR.,n.p.

DOUGLASS, WILLIAM G. and Elizabeth F. Lewis*, license 27 January 1852. Fleet W.
   Lewis (w) and Thomas Douglass (w). Married 28 January 1852 by Rev. E.L.
   Williams.

DOWNING, GEORGE of Northumberland County and Louisa H. McCarty*, bond 4 December
   1815. George Saunders (b); Alice B. Redman (w).

DOWNING, ROBERT E. (bachelor) and Eliza Bell (spinster), bond 2 November 1829.
   Consent by Betsy Bell, mother of the bride. S.A.M. Leland (b); James L.Bell
   (w).   MBB.,p.57

DOWNMAN, JAMES and Lucy Sydnor, bond 15 February 1749. Travers Tarpley (b).

DOWNMAN, JOSEPH H. (bachelor) and Elizabeth Sophia Chinn (spinster), bond 8 November 1828. S.A.M. Leland, deputy clerk of Richmond County court, (b).
                                                                  MBB.,p.44

[Doctor Joseph Henry Downman (23 June 1805 - 24 December 1830) of Lancaster
County sojourned in Tallahassee, Florida, for his health and died at the
Planter's Hotel there. His tombstone, in the Episcopal Cemetery there, is
inscribed: "Here lieth the body of JOSEPH H. DOWNMAN, M.D., late of Lancaster County, Va. Died December 24, 1830 aged 25 years and 6 months, leaving a
widow and infant son to lament his loss." The informative obituary of Doctor
Joseph Henry Downman appeared in the Fredericksburg Virginia Herald of 2 February 1831 and there is further detail in Hayden,p.126.]

DOWNMAN, RAWLEIGH married long before 5 February 1784 Elizabeth Glascock, daughter of William Glascock who died testate in 1785. WB#7,p.459.

DOWNMAN, RICHARD and Winnefred Ball Glascock*, bond 21 January 1806. Milton
Glascock (b).

DOWNMAN, RICHARD and Elizabeth Bryant (widow)*, bond 4 May 1816. William Downman (b).

DOWNMAN, ROBERT P. and Elizabeth Sydnor, bond 9 July 1770. John Sydnor (b).
[Robert Porteus Downman (1744-1774) was the son of Captain Robert Downman
(1720-1769) and Elizabeth Porteus, his wife. Elizabeth Sydnor was the daughter of Anthony Sydnor, Jr. (1724-1755). AB#1,p.582; WB#7,p.40,48,164.]

DOWNMAN, WILLIAM and Fanny Sydnor, bond 11 August 1798. Consent by Epa: Sydnor,
father of the bride. Richard Downman (b).

DOZIER, CONOWAY and Lucy Gill (spinster), bond 3 November 1806. Daniel Jackson (b).

DOZIER, JAMES and Mary Randall*, bond 4 May 1789. William Packett (b). John Kelly
certifies that Mary Randall "is of full age to act for herself."

DOZIER, JAMES M. and Elizabeth M.A. Spence, bond 27 February 1844. Consent by
W.G. Walker, guardian of the bride. R.W. Yeatman (b); Joseph S. Lyell (w).
MBB.,p.246

DOZIER, JOHN (16??-1748) married Susannah (Jacobus) Davis, widow of Robert Davis
(q.v.) and daughter of Angell and Elizabeth (Clarke) Jacobus (q.v.). John
Dozier died intestate in Richmond County in 1748.

DOZIER, LEONARD (16??-1733) married circa 1702 Elizabeth (Ingo) Ascough (16??-
1748), widow of Thomas Ascough (16??-1701) and daughter of John Ingo, Sr.
(16??-1701). Leonard Dozier was the son of the immigrant Frenchman, Leonard
Dozier (16??-1693), who settled in Westmoreland County; his naturalization
certificate dated 28 January 1684 is of record in Westmoreland County Record
Book 1723-1746,p.147. Richmond County WB#2,p.27,32; WB#5,p.207,558.

DOZIER, MARTIN P. of Westmoreland County and Nancy Jones*, bond 11 August 1826.
Richard Mothershead (b).   MBB.,p.23

DOZIER, RICHARD married by 5 October 1699 Elizabeth Hudson, daughter of Bryan
and Mary Hudson [Hodgson], deceased. DB#3,p.37; Sweeny,p.5.

DRAKE, HENRY married by 3 April 1706 Mary Richardson, widow of John Richardson.
COB#4,p.149

DRAKE, JOHN J. and Duley Marlton*, bond 3 January 1833. Corbin Drake (b).
                                                                    MBB.,p.99

DRAPER, RICHARD married Elizabeth Man, 12 September 1680.   NFPR.,p.95

DUDLEY, ALEXANDER and [blank], bond 1 March 1762. John Hammond (b).

DUDLEY, GRIFFIN and Alice Dobyns, bond 8 July 1815. Consent by L.R. Dobyns and
    John Dudley "that the license be issued." Christopher L. Dobyns (b). [The
    bride was the daughter of LeRoy and Lucy (Lawson) Dobyns (q.v.),p.55.]

DUDLEY, GRIFFIN G. and Henrietta Palmer, bond 3 September 1832. Albert G. Plum-
    mer (b).   MBB.,p.92

DUDLEY, GRIFFIN G. and Apphia R. Mothershead, bond 4 July 1842. Consent by Eliza-
    beth T. Mothershead, mother of the bride. Thomas Oldham (b); James T.
    Mothershead (w).   MBB.,p.225

DUDLEY, JOHN [CAPTAIN] and Mary Griffin Garland, bond 14 January 1793. Consent
    by Griffin Garland, father of the bride. Bartholomew McCarty (b); Benjamin
    N. Garland (w).

DUDLEY, THOMAS and Eliza Pitman Spooner (spinster), bond 3 May 1756. Richard
    Brown (b).

DUDLEY, THOMAS of Lancaster County and Elizabeth Hathaway, bond 7 June 1830.
    Morean Lemoine (b).   MBB.,p.65

DUFF, PETER and Jane Goldsby, bond 12 May 1767. Robert Ferguson (b).

DUFF, PETER and Patty Berreck, bond 11 October 1778. James Hillyer (b).

DULANY, HENRY R. [MAJOR] was married in April 1827 by the Rev. Mr. Edward C. Mc-
    Guire, rector of St. George's Church in Fredericksburg, "to Miss Fanny A.
    Carter, daughter of the late Landon Carter, Esq: of Richmond County," said
    the Fredericksburg Virginia Herald of 7 April 1827. The bond for their mar-
    riage was dated 3 April 1827; John Minor (b). See Catherine Lindsay Knorr,
    Marriage Bonds and Ministers' Returns of Fredericksburg, Virginia, 1782-1850
    also Tombstone Inscriptions from St.George's Cemetery 1752-1920, (Pine Bluff,
    Arkansas, 1954),p.14. See her obituary in the Virginia Herald, 13 May 1835.

DUNAWAY, CHARLES and Jane Smith, bond 20 March 1784. Robert Forester (b).

DUNAWAY, JOHN and Sally S. Allgood, bond 24 December 1794. Consent by Elizabeth
    Allgood, mother of the bride, who calls the groom "Mr. John Donoway." John
    Muse (b); John Muse (w), Elizabeth Muse (w) and Jane Muse (w).

DUNAWAY, JOHN G. and Martha A. Sebra*, bond 30 September 1850. Joseph W. Bryant
    (w) and William Christopher (w). Married 9 Oct. 1850 by Rev.Bartholomew Dodson.

DUNAWAY, JOHN J. and Ann S. Bryant*, bond 12 January 1838. Jefferson Stephens
    (b); Sarah Bryant (w).   MBB.,p.165

DUNAWAY, MALACHI and Elizabeth Nell married 23 January 1726/7.   NFPR.,p.100

DUNAWAY, PRESLEY and Alice Dobyns*, bond 25 December 1811. John Haywood (b);
    Thaddeus Pope (w) and John Pope (w).

DUNAWAY, RAWLEIGH W. and Amanda Critcher*, bond 5 January 1842.   Walter N. Booth
    (b); George Sampson (w).   MBB.,p.217

DUNAWAY, THOMAS and Eleanor Woollard, bond 23 July 1789. John Woollard (b).
    Consent by Mary Ann Woollard, mother of the bride.

DUNAWAY, WILLIAM of Lancaster County and Fanny T. Davenport*, bond 7 September
    .1811. William H. Davenport (b); William Hathaway (w).

DUNCAN, COLEMAN married 17 March 1769 Mary Lyne (spinster), daughter of Thomas
    Lyne (17??-1765) and Mary_____(17??-1785), his wife, both of whom died
    testate in Richmond County. Coleman Duncan was the son of Henry Duncan
    [Dunkin] who died testate in Richmond County in 1772 leaving his estate to
    several sons but failing to mention his son Coleman Duncan and confirm a
    verbal deed of gift of certain Negroes to him made at the time of his afore-
    mentioned marriage. The neglect of Henry Duncan to do this prompted Coleman
    Duncan to instigate the suit in chancery styled Duncan vs Duncan in which
    these facts are detailed. AB#2,p.98; WB#6,p.386; WB#7,p105,503; see Doctor
    B.C. Holtzclaw's manuscript genealogy of The Asbury Family of Virginia,
    Virginia State Library, Microfilm #327.

DUNCAN, HENRY and Charity Mitchell, bond 29 October 1766. Coleman Duncan (b).
    [This is the second marriage of Henry Duncan (17??-1772); see references
    above under his son by his first marriage, Coleman Duncan.]

DUNCAN, ROBERT married by 1735 Ann Gallop, one of the four daughters of Robert
    Gallop who died 20 May 1720 leaving a nuncupative will which failed to take
    effect as to his landed estate. WB#4,p.161; King George County DB#2,p.1.

DURHAM, THOMAS married 168? Dorothy _____ (born circa 1663), probably a re-
    lative of William Smoot, Sr. (16??-1716) who, "for love and affection," deed-
    ed her land 2 August 1700 with reversion to her children Thomas, John and
    Mary Durham. Thomas Durham (circa 1660-1714) died testate but before his
    last will was admitted to record his widow had married Jeremiah Greenham
    (q.v.). DB#3,p.57; DB#4,p.111; DB#7,p.63; DB#10,p.474; MRB.,p.27; WB#3,p.
    210,270; WB#5,p.718.

DURHAN, THOMAS JR. (27 June 1690-3 December 1734) was born and died in North
    Farnham Parish; he was the eldest child of Thomas and Dorothy Durham (q.v.).
    He married circa 1710 Mary Smoot (7 April 1693-8 May 1750), daughter of Will-
    iam Smoot, Sr. (16??-1716) and Jane _____(16??-1726), his wife; they had a
    large family. DB#10,p.474; WB#3,p.270; WB#5,p.258; see Harry Wright Newman,
    The Smoots of Maryland and Virginia, (Washington,D.C.,1936),p.5-6.

DYE, AVERY SR. (16??-1757) married by 17 August 1719 Katherine MackMellion, daughter of John MackMellion who died testate in 1706, and Frances _____,
his wife, who died testate in 1747, being then the widow of George Hopkins
who died testate in 1721. WB#2,p.90; WB#4,p.170; WB#5,p.530; WB#6,p.98.

E

EDISON, JAMES and Molly Morris, bond 7 December 1789. Consent by William Morris
who says "all parties is agreed that James Edison and Molly Morris shall be
married." George Connally (b).

EDMONDS, CORNELIUS (16??-1722) of Richmond and King George counties married by
13 September 1712 Ann Birkett (16??-1745), daughter of John and Ann (Mills)
Birkett (q.v.) p.18-19. DB#6,p.72; WB#4,p.138; see also King George County
COB#1,p.24,36,72; COB#2,p.334,463; DB#1,p.51.

EDMONDS, VINCENT married by 22 November 1815 Frances Balderson, daughter of
Gilbert Balderson then deceased. DB#20,p.75.

EDMONDSON, JAMES and Ann Webb, bond 30 May 1774. James Webb (b).

EDMONDSON, JAMES JR. and Ann McCarty Singleton, bond 19 April 1775. Robert
Singleton (b). [The surname of the bride was omitted in the published
"Marriage Bonds ... of Richmond County," in 5W(1)19; she was the daughter
of Joshua and Ann (Samford) Singleton. James Edmondson,Jr. d.s.p. in Essex
County in 1779 and his widow married (2) Eppa: Hubert (q.v.). AB#2,p.2;
WB#7,p.150; Essex County WB#13,p.262.]

EDWARDS, BENJAMIN and Jean Gray (spinster), bond 3 May 1750. John French (b).
[Benjamin Edwards was the son of William Edwards who purchased 200 acres of
land in Washington Parish, Westmoreland County, in 1708 and in 1746 made a
deed of gift to his two sons Haden Edwards (1716-1803) and Benjamin Edwards
for for various chattels and to his son Benjamin Edwards 100 acres of the
aforementioned purchase being the plantation "whereon the said William now
lives." Benjamin Edwards and Jean (Jane), his wife, moved to Loudoun County and in 1758,1759, and 1760 acquired property there; he was an ordinary
keeper in Leesburg. In 1760 he was joined by his wife Jane in conveying
the 100 acres in Westmoreland County which he had by deed of gift from his
father in 1746. Benjamin Edwards died testate in Loudoun County in March
1789 but circumstances caused the court to pronounce the document nul and
void and declare his four children to be his heirs-at-law, viz: (1) Benjamin
Edwards of Loudoun County; (2) Mary Smith Powell, wife of William Powell of
Prince William County; (3) Jane Gray Moss, widow, of Prince William County;
and (4) Sarah Edwards, an infant under the age of 21 years in 1789. In 1799,
after she attained legal age, Sarah Edwards made a deed to her brother Benjamin Edwards for her one fourth interest in certain landed estate of which
their father Benjamin Edwards (17??-1789) had died seized. She is believed
to be the Sarah Edwards who married 13 August 1805 in Loudoun County, Gidion
Cummings (MR#1,p.24). Jean (Jane) (Gray) Edwards predeceased her husband;
she was born in Richmond County, the only child mentioned in the records of

Samuel and Susanna (Smith) Gray (q.v.), p.80. Westmoreland County D&W
#4, p.160; D&W#10, p.270-273; D&W#13, p.292; Loudoun County DB "A", p.
64,308; DB "B", p.9; DB "R", p.239; DB "Z", p.445; WB "G", p.166,450;
COB "L", p.201; OPR, p.127,131; "The Edwards Family" by George Harrison
Sanford King in The Register of the Kentucky State Historical Society,
Volume 32, p.357-364, where there are some errors. See page xix for
photograph of the marriage bond of Benjamin Edwards (17??-1789).]

EDWARDS, RICHARD and Ann Hamilton, bond 14 March 1764. Charles Bell (b).

EDWARDS, SAMUEL of Caroline County married between 14 January 1723 and 3 May
    1735 Eleanor Brown(e), one of the two daughters of William Brown(e) of
    Richmond County who died testate in 1724. WB#4,p.233; DB#9,p.139.

EDWARDS, WILLIAM·married Mary Peace, 16 December 1725.   NFPR.,p.102

EDWARDS, WILLIAM LEE of Northumberland County and Elizabeth Garland, bond 30
    October 1830. Consent by Moore F. Brockenbrough, guardian of the bride.
    Samuel A.M. Leland (b).   MBB.,p.68

EFFORD, GEORGE W. and Elizabeth W. Thrift*, bond 24 December 1836. Samuel B.
    Thrift (b); John Thrift (w).   MBB.,p.151

EFFORD, JOHN and Frances Polly (widow), bond 15 January 1745. Charles Jones (b).

EFFORD, JOHN and Alice Reuick*, bond 31 October 1810. Edward Brown (b).

EFFORD, JOHN and Nancy Reuick*, bond 6 October 1837. George R. Thrift (b);
    James H. Rust (w).   MBB.,p.160

EFFORD, JOHN D. and Elizabeth Barrack*, bond 19 April 1819. John Davis (b).

EFFORD, JOHN D. and Nancy Clarke (widow), bond 22 December 1831. William Hud-
    son (b).   MBB.,p.85

EFFORD, RICHARD and Frances F. Glascock (widow), bond 6 February 1821. George
    Saunders (b).

EFFORD, SAMUEL A. and Frances Brann, bond 14 April 1830. Reuben Brann (b).
                                                                     MBB.,p.62

EFFORD, WILLIAM of Northumberland County and Anney Rice, bond 1 April 1795. Con-
    sent by Richard Rice,Jr., father of the bride. Charles Rice (b); Richard
    Rice Sr. (w).

EFFORD, WILLIAM and Ann Jesper, bond 4 May 1796. Charles T. McCarty (b).

EFFORD, WILLIAMSON and Nancy Hammack (spinster), bond 26 January 1802. Consent.
    by William Hammack, father of the bride. Richard Jesper (b).

EFFORD, WILLIAMSON and Ann Jesper, bond 2 September 1824. John Minter (b); he
    makes oath both parties are 21 years of age.   MBB.,p.1

EFFORD, ZACHARIAH and Polly Samford*, bond 1 August 1815. William Reuick (b).

EFFORD, ZACHARIAH and Margaret Roberts, bond 3 February 1843. Consent by Thomas
     Roberts, father of the bride. Richard Maley (b).   MBB.,p.235

ELIASON, WILLIAM ALEXANDER married 27 June 1825 by the Rev. Edward C. McGuire,
     rector of St.George's Church in Fredericksburg, Mary L. Carter, daughter
     of the late Landon Carter, Esq: of Sabine Hall, Richmond County. The mar-
     riage was announced in the Fredericksburg Virginia Herald of 29 June 1825
     which says the groom is "of Corps of Engineers of U.S." The bond for the
     marriage was secured on 27 June 1825 in Fredericksburg; John Minor (b) made
     oath the bride was of legal age. Catherine Lindsay Knorr, Marriage Bonds
     and Ministers' Returns of Fredericksburg, Virginia 1782-1850 also Tombstone
     Inscriptions from St. George's Cemetery 1752-1920 (Pine Bluff, Arkansas,
     1954),p.15.

     ELIFF   SEE : OLIFF PAGE 151

ELIFF, GEORGE and Franky Harris*, bond 31 October 1801. Franky Harris, aged 23,
     writes her own consent and William Bragg certifies "Franky Harris lives with
     me as housekeeper and has dun for eight years past." Isaac Hall (b).

ELKINS, RICHARD married by 12 January 1695 Mary Williams, daughter of Evan and
     Christian Williams; they have a son James Elkins, a minor, who is to be ed-
     ucated. DB#2,p.87; DB#6,p.37.

ELKINS, RICHARD of King George County married by 1735 Mary Gallop, one of the
     four daughters of Robert Gallop who died 20 May 1720 leaving a nuncupative
     will which failed to take effect as to his landed estate. WB#4,p.161; King
     George County DB#2,p.1.

ELLISTON, ROBERT SR. (17??-1785) of King George and Stafford counties married
     circa 1722 Ellinor (Eleanor) Miller, daughter of Simon Miller (16??-1720)
     who died testate in Richmond County and whose landed estate fell into King
     George County in 1721. WB#4,p.151; King George County DB A-1,p.1 and COB
     #1,p.123,126,134,173,180; OPR.,p.79.

ELMORE, CHARLES married Sarah Barton, 11 October 1728.   NFPR.,p.102

ELMORE, CHARLES and Alice Douglass*, bond 5 July 1815. John Brown (b).

ELMORE, FRANCIS married Anne Allen, 2 December 1677.   NFPR.,p.101

ELMORE, FRANCIS married Mary Hammock, 23 February 1738.   NFPR.,p.102

ELMORE, GEORGE WASHINGTON and Nancy Hazard*, bond 2 June 1814. Royston Thomas,
     alias Austin Thomas, (b), makes oath the bride is about 25 years of age.

ELMORE, GEORGE W. and Polly Brown*, bond 11 December 1815. William Elmore (b).

ELMORE, HENRY (bachelor) and Charlotte Dodson (spinster), bond 29 October 1828.
     Charles Dodson (b) made oath the bride is of full age.   MBB.,p.43

ELMORE, JAMES and and Susan S. Headley, bond 12 July 1830. Consent by Griffin
Headley and Martha Hale [or Hall], his wife; no relationship stated. William B. Hale (b).   MBB.,p.66

ELMORE, JOHN married Ann Raynolds, 29 November 1728.   NFPR.,p.102

ELMORE, JOHN WILLIAM and Winnefred Jackson, bond 22 May 1833. Consent by Thomas
Elmore, father of the groom. Gilson B. Burch (b); John Littrell (w) and
William Flinn (w).   MBB.,p.106

ELMORE, JOHN W. and Virginia Ann Hill, bond 27 October 1846. Consent by William
H. Hill, father of the bride. Robert F. Northen (b); R.C. Hammack (w).
                                                                    MBB.,p.281

ELMORE, JOSEPH and Elizabeth Elmore, bond 16 January 1836. George W. Elmore (b)
is the father of the bride.   MBB.,p.142

ELMORE, RAWLEIGH and Catharine Bryant, bond 24 February 1835. Thomas W. Bryant
(b).   MBB.,p.131

ELMORE, RICHARD and Catherine Dodson (spinster), bond 17 December 1794. John
O. Stott (b).

ELMORE, THADDEUS married Nancy D. McClanahan of Richmond County on 19 December
1822. No marriage bond found in Richmond County.   WFMR.,n.p.

ELMORE, THOMAS and Polly Ashburn, bond 4 April 1825. Charles Elmore (b).
                                                                    MBB.,p.9

ELMORE, WILLIAM and Frances Clarke*, bond 9 April 1793. William Alloway (b);
Ann Hudson (w), William Alloway (w) and Elizabeth Alloway (w).

ELMORE, WILLIAM and Frances W. Jones, bond 29 November 1841. Consent by Violet
Jones, mother of the bride. Joseph Elmore (b); Thomas D. Jones (w).
                                                                    MBB.,p.214

ENGLISH, JAMES and Jane King, bond 10 December 1803. Samuel King (b).

ENGLISH, JOHN and Catharine Brown, bond 22 December 1807. Edward J. Northen (b).

ENGLISH, THOMAS and Matilda Corey*, bond 5 December 1831. Robert Woody, guardian
of the bride, states she is about 24 years of age. Robert Scott (b).
                                                                    MBB.,p.81

ENGLISH, WILLIAM and Emily C. Lathom, bond 13 February 1847. Consent by H. Lathom,
parent of the bride. Edwin C. Edwards (b); J. Mayo (w).   MBB.,p.291

ERSKING, WILLIAM and Penilopy Barns were married 27 May 1726.   NFPR.,p.102

EUSTACE, JOHN married Alice Corbin Peachey, 6 October 1743.   NFPR.,p.102
[John Eustace (circa 1721-1786) was the son of William Eustace of Northum-

berland County and Ann Lee, his wife, daughter of Hancock and Sarah (Allerton) Lee of Ditchley, Northumberland County. Alice Corbin Peachey was the
eldest daughter of Captain Samuel and Winifred (Griffin) Peachey (q.v.).
Beale,p.221 errs in stating John and Alice Corbin (Peachey) Eustace "had
issue;" they did not. John Eustace, by his will proved in Northumberland
County in 1786, entailed his estate upon a nephew but that young man died
intestate and without issue shortly after his uncle and this provoked length
litigation. Alice Corbin (Peachey) Eustace wrote two wills in both of which
she bewailed having been plagued for many years with suits concerning the
will and estate of her late husband. Her last will and Testament, dated 10
July 1799 was proved at Northumberland County court 8 September 1800 and in
it she mentions many relatives. Her brother,Samuel Peachey (1732/3-1784),
of Essex County had issue, among others, Elizabeth Peachey (1762-1837), wife
of James Pendleton (1754-1815) of King and Queen County; and Catherine Peach
ey (1776-1858), wife of Josiah Ryland (1767-1850), also of King and Queen Cou
ty, and these two couples were ancestors of Charles Hill Ryland, Esq. of War
saw, prominent attorney-at-law of Richmond County.] [See references, p.155-6

EVANS, FRANCIS and Elizabeth Garland, bond 12 November 1803. William Garland (b)
John Garland (w); Joseph Elgin (w).

EVANS, JOHN T. and Elizabeth Ann Walker, bond 1 November 1824. Consent by Fleet
B. Plummer, guardian of the bride, who certifies she is a resident of Richmond County. John B. Garland (b).   MBB.,p.2

EVANS, KEMP and Catherine Lawson (widow)*, bond 5 January 1815. Richard Efford
(b); Catherine Williams (w) and Elizabeth C. Roy (w).

EVANS, SOLOMON and Susanna Davenport*, bond 8 June 1815. Joseph P. Davenport (b)
he certifies Susanna Davenport is his sister and "she is of the age of 24
years."

EVANS, WILLIAM and Augusta W. Plummer, bond 16 February 1843. Elizabeth Plummer
writes her consent to the marriage; no relationship stated. Moore F. Garland (b); L. Shackleford (w).   MBB.,p.236

EVERITT, CHARLES and Sarah Webb, bond 2 April 1821. Consent by Thomas Everitt;
no relationship stated. Thomas Everitt (b); Mary Thurston (w) and William
Harford (w).

EVERITT, THOMAS and Fanny Harford*, bond 7 July 1817. William A. Packett (b);
Henry Harford (w).

EWELL, JESSE and Mildred Beale*, bond 12 November 1799. The bride wrote her own
consent on 10 November 1799 from the family seat, Chestnut Hill. Robert T.
[or Robert S.] Hipkins (b). [For the lineage of the groom see Hayden,p.331-
347; for the lineage of the bride see Beale,p.12-45. These sources also
give data concerning the issue of Jesse and Mildred (Beale) Ewell of Edge
Hill, Prince William County, where their tombstones are to be seen in the
family cemetery. Prince William: The Story of Its People and Its Places
(Richmond,1941),p.194-195; Alice Maude Ewell, A Virginia Scene, Or Life in
Old Prince William (Lynchburg,1931),p.12 et seq.]

F

FALLIN, DENNIS and Ann Dawson (widow), license June 1711.   DB#6,p.275

FALLIN, JEREMIAH and Ann Dameron*, bond 27 January 1834. Thomas P. Lewis (b);
    Darius G. Cralle (w).   MBB.,p.114

FALLIN, SAMUEL E. and Elizabeth Hendley*, bond 18 March 1823. Robert Clarke (b).

FALLIN, SAMUEL E. and Catharine Woollard*, bond 4 October 1836. John W. Woollard
    (b).   MBB.,p.149

FALLIN, THOMAS of Lancaster County and Nancy Opie Davenport (spinster), bond 1
    July 1803. William Forester (b).

FALLIN, THOMAS of Northumberland County and Peggy Harris*, bond 15 June 1808.
    Martin Sisson (b).

FALLIN, THOMAS and Hannah Hendley (widow)*, bond 13 January 1818. George North-
    en (b); Eppa: Sydnor (w).

FANN, WILLIAM and Alicia Samford were married 23 January 1675.   NFPR.,p.105

FARRELL, EDWARD L. and Pinkston Laycock, bond 25 November 1816. Horace Wellford
    (b).

FARRELL, JOHN W. and Lucy Newman (widow)*, bond 24 February 1817. William C.
    Quesenbury (b).

FAULKNER, JESSE and Ann Watts, bond 9 April 1773. William Watts (b).

FAULKS, WILLIAM and Lucy Coleman, bond 4 February 1779. Thomas Coelman (b); he
    is father of the bride and so signs his name but the court clerk renders
    the name Coleman. The surname of the groom is given as Faulks and Fulks.
    [The bride was the daughter of Thomas and Betty Coleman (Coelman), (q.v.),
    p.41.]

N.B.- FAUNTLEROY: In 1936 my late friend, Miss Juliet Fauntleroy, placed in the
    Virginia State Library a copy of her two volume typescript entitled, Colonel
    Moore Fauntleroy, His Ancestors and Descendants [CS:71.F:264]. These volumes
    are a great source of accurate information not only in regard to the Fauntle-
    roy family but the many families with whom they became allied and consequent-
    ly frequently cited by me as Fauntleroy. This excellent work of Miss Juliet
    Fauntleroy should be published and thereby made available to libraries and
    individuals throughout the United States; few of the gentry of Richmond Coun-
    ty are not mentioned! Miss Julia's deep affection for the late Mrs. James
    Claiborne Pollard (nee Mary Blount Hall), assistant archivist of the Virginia
    State Library, moved her to contribute liberally toward the restoration of a
    large number of manuscripts in that repository. As Miss Fauntleroy's volumes
    contain a full and accurate account of the Fauntleroy family of Richmond and
    adjacent counties, very few notes will follow in this volume.

FAUNTLEROY, GEORGE and Sally Fauntleroy (spinster), bond 8 March 1768. Robert
    Tomlin (b). [Doctor George Heale Fauntleroy d.s.p. but testate in 1770; his
    wife (who was his first cousin) was the daughter of John and Judith (Little-
    page) Fauntleroy; she married (2) Colonel Walker Tomlin (q.v.).]

FAUNTLEROY, GRIFFIN MURDOCK married circa 1770 Anne Belfield (born 17 November
    1754) daughter of John and Ruth (Sydnor) Belfield (q.v.),p.14. He was the
    son of William Fauntleroy, Gentleman, (1713-1793) and his wife nee Margaret
    Murdock. See Fauntleroy for details.

FAUNTLEROY, JOHN and Judith Griffin (widow), bond 8 February 1781. Griffin
    Fauntleroy (b). [Judith (Ball) Griffin (1753-1817) was the widow of Major
    LeRoy Griffin (q.v.). John Fauntleroy (17??-1798) and his wife nee Judith
    Ball had three children, viz: (a) William Henry Fauntleroy; (b) Louisa
    Fauntleroy and (c) Lettice Lee Fauntleroy who became the first wife of Dr.
    Austin Brockenbrough (q.v.) p.24. AB#2,p.232,238,247; WB#7,p.211; WB#9,p.
    89; Hayden,p.110.]

FAUNTLEROY, JOSEPH and Elizabeth Fauntleroy, bond 24 January 1787. Robert Tomlin
    (b).

FAUNTLEROY, MOORE [MAJOR] (1680-1739) married circa 1715 Margaret Micou, daughter
    of Doctor Paul Micou (1658-1736) and his wife nee Margaret Cammack (168?-174(
    both of whom died testate in Essex County. AB#1,p.184; COB#11,p.269; MRB.,p.
    91b,97; WB#5,p.346; Fauntleroy,p.230,232.

FAUNTLEROY, MOORE [COLONEL] of Lunenburg Parish, Richmond County, married [(1)]
    Ann Heale of St. Mary's White Chappel Parish, Lancaster County, 20 Decemeber
    1736. William Fauntleroy, father of Moore Fauntleroy (1716-1791), gives his
    consent and the bondsman and witnesses are: Joseph Heale, Lindsay Opie, Will-
    iam Fauntleroy, Jr., and Jane Weathersbee.   DB#9,p.453   LCMR#1,p.15

FAUNTLEROY, MOORE [COLONEL] (1716-1791), married (2) by 1748 Elizabeth Mitchell
    (28 September 1726-26 December 1785), daughter of Robert Mitchell, Gentleman,
    (1684-1748) who held property in Richmond and Lancaster counties. Lee,p.157;
    VSL:AD #25212 (Bible record of Robert Mitchell, Gentleman); Fauntleroy,p.663.

FAUNTLEROY, MOORE JR. [GENTLEMAN] and Susannah Armistead, 2 October 1749. Landor
    Carter (b).

FAVER , JOHN and Susanna Meads (widow), license June 1713.   DB#6,p.275

FAVER, WILLIAM of Culpeper County and Ann Walker (spinster), bond 9 February 1767.
    John Suggitt (b).

FAWCETT, SAMUEL and Levina Maden, bond 2 January 1821. George Maiden (b).

FEAGINS, WILLIAM and Jane Winstead*, bond 21 January 1793. Thomas Hogans (b).

FENTON, SAMUEL and Polly White*, bond 19 June 1838. Reuben Marks (b). MBB.,p.173

FERGUSON, ROBERT and Sarah Morgan*, bond 5 December 1786. William Garland (b).

FERGUSSON, ROBERT and Joanna Jesper*, bond 31 May 1796. William Everitt (b).

FERGUSSON, WILLIAM and Sarah Kirk, bond 2 April 1787. Consent by John Kirk; no relationship stated. John Kirk (b); Sarah Kirk (w).

FERGUSSON, WILLIAM R. and Elizabeth Robertson, bond 12 January 1818. Consent by W. Fergusson, father of the groom. John Davis (b); Nancy Fergusson (w).

FICKLIN, CHRISTOPHER and Louisa Franklin*, bond 19 April 1821. Richard Sydnor (b).

FICKLIN, CHRISTOPHER D. and Mary A.F. Wright*, bond 20 July 1843. John F.B. Jeffries (b); William C. Oldham (w). Married 3 August 1843 by the Rev. William N. Ward.   MBB.,p.239
[Famous Ficklin seems to have died intestate in Richmond County circa 1816 leaving a widow and six children, viz: (1) John D. Ficklin; (2) LeRoy D. Ficklin; (3) Christopher D. Ficklin; (4) Ellen Ficklin who predeceased her husband William F. Davis (q.v.),p.52; (5) Sally Ficklin and (6) Nancy Ficklin d.s.p.. FDC#103, Ficklin vs Ficklin]

FICKLIN, JOHN D. and Elizabeth Hutson*, bond 11 September 1800. Thomas Hazard (b). The mutilated consent of Elizabeth Hudson certifies that ..."parents is also willing to the marriage as witness - Famous Ficklin, Elizabeth Ficklin, Frinefrid Hudson, 11 September 1800."

FICKLIN, WILLIAM W. and Mary B. Rockwell married 8 November 1853 by the Rev. John Godwin. [Ministers' Returns]

FINCH, GRIFFIN of Fauquier County and Elizabeth White, bond 30 December 1796. Consent by Zechariah White, father of the bride. John White (b).

FINDLEY, JOHN and Eliz.^{a} Whaley (widow), bond 2 September 1754. John Tayloe, Esquire (b).

FISHER, JOHN and Elizabeth Barker*, bond 18 January 1792. Elizabeth Barker writes her own consent stating she was born in 1767 and desires a license to issue for her marriage and John Fisher, Tailor, of Richmond County. Daniel Connellee (b).

FITZHUGH, THOMAS [GENTLEMAN] (circa 1689-1719) married circa 1716 Anne Fowke (Mason) Darrell, widow; they had no child to survive infancy. MRB.,p.56, 114; WB#4,p.120,146; OPR.,p.226.

FLEET, HENRY (circa 16??-1733) of Rappahannock and Lancaster counties, married by 14 December 1683 Elizabeth Wildey, daughter of William and Jane Wildey of Lancaster County. DB#4,p.131a (re-recorded deed,1708); Beverley Fleet, Virginia Colonial Abstracts, Volume 20, p.105; A.P. & P.,p.174.

FLEMING, ALEXANDER [CAPTAIN] (16??-1668) of Rappahannock County was thrice married; he must not be confused with Alexander Fleming (16??-1711), planter, of Richmond County (q.v.), nor were they father and son. My late friend, Mrs. Lenora (Higginbotham) Sweeny, has left us an excellent account of

Captain Alexander Fleming of Westfalia, Rappahannock County, and his wives
in her article in the Americana, Volume 33, p.1-31. She errs, however, in
suggesting Alexander Fleming, planter, may have been a son of Captain Alexander Fleming as Rowland Thornton, grandson of the Captain, is dubbed his
heir-at-law and he would not have been if Captain Alexander Fleming (16??-
1668) had left male issue. Sweeny,p.3-4; see Rowland Thornton,p.211-212.

FLEMING, ALEXANDER (16??-1711), planter, married by 3 January 1692 Sarah Kennedy
[Kenney, Kennida, Cannida &c:], daughter of John Kennedy, deceased, and
niece of William Kennedy, deceased, both of Rappahannock County. DB#1,p.53;
DB#3,p.13,121; DB#7,p.260,343; DB#16,p.240; WB#3,p.60; Sweeny,p.51. These
citations will correct Mrs. Sweeny's statement in the Americana, Volume 33,
p.31, that Alexander Fleming married Sarah, "daughter of William Kenny;"
a careful reading of the cited document (DB#1,p.53) makes it certain the
said Sarah was the daughter of John Kennedy and the niece of William Kennedy, both deceased, of Rappahannock County.

FLINN, DANIEL and Polly M. Alderson, bond 9 May 1808. James Alderson (b).

FOGG, LEWIS B. of Essex County and Maria Louisa Headley, bond 22 March 1836.
Alexander Bryant (b).   MBB.,p.145

FONES, JOHN H. (bachelor) and Eliz_ Hall (spinster), bond 11 December 1829.
Williamson Hall (b) who makes oath the bride is over 21.   MBB.,p.58

FONES, JOSEPH and Jane Drake, bond 7 April 1794. William Harris (b).

FONES, JOSEPH S. and Elizabeth A. Nash*, bond 7 December 1840. William T. Fones
(b). Married 7 December 1840 by the Rev. John M. Waddey.   MBB.,p.200

FONES, RICHARD and Lucy Efford*, bond 20 August 1849. Barnes B. Mozingo (b);
T.W. Walker (w).   MBB.,p.326

FONES, THOMAS B. and Nancy Richards, bond 9 February 1826. Consent by Susanna
Richards, mother of the bride. Jesse D. Reynolds (b); William Richards (w).
MBB.,p.19

FONES, WILLIAM T. and Ann C. White*, bond 25 December 1821. William Settle (b);
Joseph Fones (w).

FORBES, WILLIAM and Frances T. Mitchell, bond 29 October 1803. Consent by the
bride's father, R.Mitchell, was written from Grove Mount on 26 October 1803.
Peter Temple (b).

FORD, JOHN married Jane Deane, widow of John Deane who died testate in 1742; said
Ford administered upon Deane's estate. In June 1761 John Newman and Elizabeth, his wife, filed their bill in chancery vs John Dean(e), in which they
say John Deane died testate, 1742 (WB#5,p.402) leaving five children, viz:
(1) John Deane (an officer in the army when his three sisters died, 1756);
(2) Elizabeth Deane who married circa_1744 John Newman; (3) Aseneath; (4)
Agatha and (5) Susanna Deane all d.s.p.1756 and their sister Elizabeth
(Deane) Newman died prior to August 1763 when this suit abated. See suit

Newman vs Dean(e), Richmond County Loose Papers.

FORESTER : FORRESTER

FORRESTER, WILLIAM of Richmond County married 13 July 1715 Frances Bryant, dau-
ghter of Thomas Bryant of Lancaster County. Bondsman and witness: Richard
Lee and John Callehan.   LCMR#1,p.1
[William Forrester was murdered 5 November 1723 by Thomas Glascock. There
is considerable detail in the volume called Fines, Examination of Criminals,
Tryals of Slaves &c: 1710-1754, page 67 et seq. Gregory Glascock, son of
Thomas Glascock, was named as an accessory in this crime and the matter was
heard before the General Court of Virginia sitting in Williamsburg. In his
last will and Testament, Colonel Robert Carter (1663-1732) of Corotoman,
Lancaster County, refers to the land of Thomas Glascock of Richmond County.]

FORRESTER, WILLIAM and Penelope Ersbien (spinster), bond 11 August 1750. James
Forrester (b). [Ersbien-Erskein-Erskin-Ersking &c: seem to interchange. On
2 April 1750 administration on the estate of William Erskein was granted
to Penelope Erskein and an inventory of his estate remains of record. See
William Ersking (q.v.), p.65. COB#12,p.227; WB#5,p.60.]

FORRESTER, WILLIAM and Sarah Stonum, bond 23 September 1761. Consent by William
Stonum, father of the bride. Samuel Dobyns (b).

FORESTER, WILLIAM and Bridgett Forrister (spinster), bond 28 August 1784. Robert
Forester (b). [The groom signs the bond, William Forester but the clerk
spells the name of both parties, Forrister. This is the Reverend Mr. Will-
iam Forrester whose register of marriages performed by him in Richmond,
Lancaster and Westmoreland counties 1802-1842 is preserved in the Richmond
County clerk's office.]

FORESTER, WILLIAM W. and Emma D. Glascock*, bond 3 December 1816. James Bland
(w); George Saunders (b).

FOSSAKER, JOHN [GENTLEMAN] married by 28 March 1692 Elizabeth Mott (166?-1712),
eldest of the four daughters of George Mott (16??-1674), who with his brother John Mott (16??-1677), in 1670 patented in one tract 15,654 acres of
land on Muddy Creek in present King George and Stafford counties. John Fossaker was living 1 March 1705/6 but died prior to 23 March 1709 leaving Richard
Fossaker his only son. The latter's only child, Elizabeth Fossaker married
Francis Strother (q.v.). DB#1,p.23,36; DB#4,p.27a; COB# 6, p. 11; Essex
County DB#13,p.320; Sweeny,p.17,27,28,62,63.

FOSTER, EDWARD B. and Nancy Northen, bond 21 May 1822. Edward J. Northen (b).

FOSTER, EZEKIEL and Nancy Thrift, bond 29 January 1787. Benjamin Purcell (b).

FOSTER, EZEKIEL and Ann E. Bryan, bond 20 October 1794. Consent by Alicia Bryan,
mother of the bride. Alexander Bryan (b); Stephen Gupton 69 (sic) (w).

FOUSHEE, FRANCIS and Fanny Beale, bond 19 October 1798. Harrison Ball (b).
[The Fredericksburg Virginia Herald of 26 October 1798 announced the mar-

riage on 21 October 1798 of "Mr. Francis Foushee of Northumberland County
to Miss Fanny Beale, daughter of Mr. Thomas Beale of Richmond County."
See Beale,p.46.]

FOUSHEE, JOHN married Elizabeth, daughter of Winifred Williams. On 2 August
1734 Winifred Williams of Richmond County made a deed of gift to her two
grandchildren James and Elizabeth Foushee, son and daughter of John and
Elizabeth Foushee of Richmond County. AB#1,p.74.

FOWLER, TIMOTHY and Sally Shackleford, bond 7 December 1807. Richard L. Shackelford (b).

FOWLES, GEORGE and Nancy Morse, bond 8 October 1792. Consent by Moley Sisson;
no relationship stated. Daniel Jackson (b). [Two Richmond County Petitions to the Legislature are contradictory, viz: 16 December 1819 and 22
January 1845. The former states Thomas Morse, an alien with property in
Richmond County, d.s.p. 6 August 1792. The latter states Thomas Morse and
his wife nee Ann Sisson (who died in 1815) had an only child, Sinah Morse,
who married Richard Reynolds (q.v.). The marriage bond of Thomas Morse
and Ann Sisson, dated 21 June 1792, remains of record in Westmoreland
County and the inventory of his estate is recorded in Richmond County WB
#9,p.7. The marriage bond of George Fowles and Ann ("Nancy") (Sisson)
Morse, widow, is cited above and the inventory of the estate of George
Fowles (17??-1796) is recorded in Richmond County WB#9,p.44. It appears
Sinah is acknowledged to be the only child of Ann ("Nancy") (Sisson) Morse
Fowles but as her mother had two husbands within two months, there is con-
siderable doubt as to her paternity. She was married to Richard Reynolds
under the name of Sinah Fowles (q.v.).]

FOXHALL, THOMAS married by 4 April 1716 Elizabeth Innis, daughter of Doctor
James Innis of Richmond County who died testate in 1710 possessed of land
near the falls of the Rappahannock River (now in Stafford County) which
had been granted to him by patent 21 December 1709 by the proprietor of
the Northern Neck of Virginia. DB#7,p.116; WB#3,p.31; King George County
DB#1-A,p.251.

FRANCE, JOHN of Richmond County married Catharine Fones per bond dated 7 February 1788 of record in King George County Marriage Register #1,p.6, but the
name of the groom is incorrectly entered as John Francis. This fact is
mentioned in John France's Revolutionary War pension file #W-7327 which
details his service in that war. ECD cites the Bible record of John France,
Sr. (circa 1762-26 December 1842) and his wife nee Catharine ("Caty") Fones
who died 7 February 1845; their children were: (1) Nancy France, born 2 October 1788, married 1807 John Sanders; (2) Polly France, born 11 July 1793,
married 1 November 1813 Hudson Brown; (3) Fanny France, born 2 October 1796,
married 12 January 1819 Reuben Marks; (4) Betsy France, born 25 January
1799, died 2 May 1838, married 26 January 1818, James Jennings; (5) Sally
France, born 17 May 1801, married 2 January 1827 Thomas Brown; (6) John
France, Jr., born 28 November 1803, married 21 December 1824 Mary Elizabeth
Hall; (7) Kitty France, born 5 April 1806; (8) Felishshe France, born 20
June 1810, married 31 December 1827 William Cash; and (9) Bathsheba France,
born 24 October 1813 and died 2 October 1818. John France, Sr. died testate

in Richmond County; his will is recorded in WB#10,p.445.

FRANCE, JOHN and Frances Clarke; bond 1 February 1794. Frankie Clark, of full age, writes her own consent. Vincent Clarke (b); John Howe, Jr. (w), Catey Clarke (w), William Clark (w) and Elijah Moore (w). [ECD says this John France died intestate circa 1812 and there is a record in COB#24,p.53,124 in regard to the sale of the real estate of the four orphan children of John France, deceased, viz: Elizabeth, Thomas, Rodham and John T. France.]

FRANCE, JOHN (widower) and Elizabeth Hall (spinster), bond 16 May 1829. John Saunders (b).   MBB.,p.55

FRANCE, JOHN JR. and Mary Hall; bond 21 December 1824. John France, Sr. (b).
                                                                    MBB.,p.5

FRANCE, JOSEPH and Mary Hale, bond 11 October 1834. Thomas Hale (b).MBB.,p.125

FRANCE, JOSEPH and Mary Jones, daughter of Clinton Jones, license 15 March 1853. Shelton Weadon (w). Married 17 March 1853 by Rev. John Pullen.

FRANCE, SAMUEL and Elizabeth Hadon*, bond 6 January 1824. John Hammack (b); Shadrach Clark (w).

FRANCES, JOHN of Westmoreland County and Sarah Crane*, bond 4 February 1817. The bride signs her name to the consent, Sarah Craine. Richard Knott (b).

FRANKLIN, JAMES of Westmoreland County and Mary Ann Woollard*, bond 27 December 1836. Elijah V. Yeatman (b); Benjamin N. Garland (w).   MBB.,p.152

FRANKLIN, JOHN married long before 8 June 1714 Elizabeth Erwin, daughter of Thomas Erwin (c.1629-1676) of Rappahannock County. DB#6,p.249; Sweeny,p.32, 40.

FRANKLIN, SAMUEL R. and Susan S. Sisson, bond 24 February 1841. Consent by William H. Sisson; no relationship stated. James Johnson (b); John T. Sisson (w) and Elburton H. Sisson (w).   MBB.,p.207

FRANKLIN, STEWARD and Mary Buckley*, bond 1 December 1794. Thomas Moore (b); Abraham White (w).

FRANKLIN, STEWARD and Patty Scates (widow), bond 1 June 1818. William Mothershead (b).

FRANKLIN, THOMAS (16??-1721) married by 2 May 1711 Katherine Stewart [Steuart], daughter of William Stewart [Steuart] then of Nominy, Cople Parish, Westmoreland County, who died intestate in Richmond County in 1717. On 5 July 1721 Catherine Franklin gave her bond as administratrix of Thomas Franklin, deceased. COB#8,p.69; DB#5,p.329; DB#8,p.9,54,59; WB#4,p.7,191; also Westmoreland County COB 1705-1721,p.284,325; D&W#3,p.299.

FRANKLIN, WILLIAM A. and Elizabeth Rock*, bond 17 February 1848. Griffin Rock (b); John Davis (w).   MBB.,p.306

[The bride was the daughter of John and Catherine (Flanagan) Rock; she m(2) 6 May 1860 in King George County, Benjamin F. Jones. For details see, George Harrison Sanford King, The Family Tree of Caroline Jackson Lee (1864-1947), (Ann Arbor, Michigan, 1954), p.xx,51.]

FRENCH, HUGH of Richmond County married in 1736 Margaret Gervase [Jarvis], a legatee of Daniel Field, Jr. who died testate in Westmoreland County in 1733. French vs Hazell, suit in chancery, 1748; Westmoreland County COB 1739-1743,p.76a; Westmoreland County D&W#9,p.289.

FRENCH, JAMES of Northumberland County and Sarah France*, bond 9 January 1826. John Littrell (b).   MBB.,p.18

FRENCH, JOHN and Nancy Thornton, bond 17 May 1808. Jeremiah Brown (b).

FRESHWATER, JOHN married by 5 August 1746 Elizabeth Pridham, widow of Christopher Pridham, Jr., who died testate in 1739. COB#12,p.16; WB#5,p.336.

FRESHWATER, THOMAS (16??-1726) married by 3 October 1699 Mary Hudson [Hodgson] (16??-1744/5), daughter of Bryan and Mary Hudson [Hodgson], deceased; she m(2) 1730 William Linton (16??-1734) of Westmoreland County (q.v.). DB#3, p.37; DB#9,p.85; WB#5,p.15; Westmoreland County D&W#8,p.236 and Westmoreland Record Book 1723-1746,p.306,319.

FRESHWATER, THOMAS (c.1700-1755), son of Thomas and Mary (Hudson) Freshwater (q.v.), married (1) 172? Ann Pridham (1705-173?), daughter of Christopher and Mary (Lewis) Pridham (q.v.); married (2) 173? Elizabeth Jesper (1712-1772), daughter of Thomas and Sarah (Taylor) Jesper (q.v.). AB#1,p.327; WB#5,p.126,164,562,658; WB#6,p.82; WB#7,p.146; NFPR.

FRIER, SAMUEL and Nancy Ennis*, bond 1 September 1810. Rodham Pritchett (b).

FRISTOW, ROBERT and Jane Sherman were married 1 August 1675.   NFPR.,p.105

G

GAINES, BERNARD (16??-1747) married (1) before 1706 Martha Tayler, daughter of George Tayler who mentions them and two of their children in his will proved in 1706; married (2) Elizabeth _____ who survived him. AB#1,p345-348; COB#13,p.159; WB#2,p.100; WB#5,p.569. It appears the will of Bernard Gaines was recorded about two years after his death. He mentioned property in Albemarle County and there is an inventory of his personal estate of record in that county. 24 T 301-303.

GAINES, DANIEL, ordinary keeper, variously of Richmond and Essex counties, married circa 1721 Mary Doyle, widow and executrix of John Doyle (16??-1718) by whom she had two sons, viz: (1) John Doyle by 1734 of North Carolina, and (2) James Doyle. DB#7,p.343,344,260; DB#8,p.34; DB#9,p.127,308; WB#4, p.52; 24T301-303.

GALBRATH, ROBERT married Mary Dodson, 29 September 1743.   NFPR.,p.113

GALLIGO, JAMES and Lucy Croder*, bond 11 July 1850. Samuel L. Beacham (b);
    Kasper Albreckt (w). Married 11 July 1850 by Rev. William N. Ward.
                                                                 MBB.,p.340

GARDNER, RICHARD of St. Mary's County, Maryland, married by 1685 Elizabeth Weire,
    daughter and heiress of Major John Weire of Rappahannock County who bequeath-
    ed her a handsome landed estate in Richmond County. DB#3,p.5; Sweeny,p.7,8,
    120.

GARLAND, DANIEL and Frances A. Shackleford*, bond 20 January 1813. Richard L.
    Shackleford (b).

GARLAND, GEORGE and Mary Wright, bond 27 October 1796. Benjamin Bramham (b).

GARLAND, GEORGE T. and Sarah Miskell, bond 29 October 1803. Consent by Winifred
    Miskell, mother of the bride. Luke Jackson (b).

GARLAND, GRIFFIN and Mary Colston Smith, bond 27 July 1781. Consent by William
    Smith, father of the bride. LeRoy Peachey (b); Thomas Plummer (w), John
    Smith (w) and W. Webb (w). [See will of William Smith, Gent., WB#7,p.528.]

GARLAND, GRIFFIN and Sarah Plummer, 11 September 1785. James Cox (b).

GARLAND, JAMES V. and Juliet F.J. Lyell*, bond 3 February 1834. Samuel M. Lyell
    (b); Richard H. Lyell (w).   MBB.,p.115

GARLAND, JESSE and Ann Degges, bond 2 August 1773. William Smith (b).

GARLAND, JOHN and Henrietta Garland, bond 22 December 1803. William Palmer, Jr.
    (b).

GARLAND, JOHN and Sophia Garland, bond 21 December 1810. George T. Garland (b).

GARLAND, MOORE F. and Elizabeth P. Cooke*, bond 15 November 1841. Consent by
    Mary Garland, mother of the groom. Isaac S. Jeffries (b); William D. Gar-
    land (w); William E. Garland (w).   MBB.,p.213

GARLAND, PETER R. and Alice C. Belfield, bond 9 August 1806. Consent by Ann H.
    Belfield, guardian of the bride. James D. Sydnor (b); Sydnor Belfield (w).
    [The bride was the daughter of Major John and Mary (Beckwith) Belfield (q.v.);
    the suit papers Walker vs Jones in FDC#288, state she was their only child.
    Fauntleroy,p.56, indicates the groom was the son of Griffin and Mary (Rust)
    Garland.]

GARLAND, VINCENT and Betsey Jackson, bond 4 January 1808. Clement Shackleford (b).

GARLAND, WILLIAM and Betsy Lewis, bond 22 February 1796. James Lewis (b). [The
    bride was the daughter of James and Alice (Forrester) Lewis (q.v.) and was
    born 14 February 1775. Elizabeth ("Betsy") (Lewis) Garland, widow, m(2)
    5 January 1807 Rev. Charles Bell (q.v.) p.16.]

GARLAND, WILLIAM G. and Mary Leckie, bond 18 December 1816. Consent by Mary
     Leckie, mother of the bride. William R. Jeffries (b).

GARNER, JESSE and Lucy Pasquitt, bond 17 April 1805. Humphrey Pope (b).

GARNER, RICHARD and Ann Garland, (spinster), bond 14 November 1770. George Gar-
     land (b).

GARNETT, HENRY and Margaret Neale, bond 17 September 1765. Richard Neale (b).
     [Captain Henry Garnett (17??-1811) of Farmer's Hall, Essex County, was a
     Revolutionary War officer, and son of John and Elizabeth (Evans) Garnett;
     his lineage is detailed in 42V74 et seq. Margaret Neale was the daughter
     of Richard and Catherine (Fauntleroy) Neale (q.v.). DB#16,p.211; WB#9,p.
     141; Essex County WB#16,p.103 and DB#33,p.345.]

GARNETT, THOMAS and Peggy Miskell, bond 16 October 1783. Samuel P. Menzies (b).
     [Margaret ("Peggy") Miskell was the daughter of William and Elizabeth (Sam-
     ford) Miskell (q.v.). Thomas Garnett, Esquire, (17??-1798) married (1) a
     daughter of Charles Tilden of Kent County, Maryland, who died testate there
     in 1787; by her he had an only child, Anne Tilden Garnett (c.1780-1822),who
     m(1) in 1797 Richard Richards, son of Captain William and Martha (Loury)
     Richards of King and Queen County, and m(2) in 1810 Richard Baylor, Esquire,
     (1750-1822), son of Major Gregory and Mary (Whiting) Baylor of King and Queen
     County. Richard and Anne Tilden (Garnett) Baylor moved to Jefferson County
     and their tombstones are in Zion Episcopal Church Cemetery, Charlestown, West
     Virginia. Shortly after his second marriage to Margaret ("Peggy") Miskell,
     Thomas Garnett established himself as a merchant in Fredericksburg and, about
     the same time, James Monroe established himself as an attorney-at-law in the
     same town. On 7 June 1790 James Monroe wrote from Fredericksburg a letter of
     introduction to Thomas Jefferson for his friend, Thomas Garnett: "This will
     be presented to you by Mr. Garnett, a merchant of character and merit in
     this town. Whilst a resident here he was kind and attentive to me and as
     proof of my regard, I have taken the liberty to make him known to you."
     In 1790 Colonel Burgess Ball advertised his estate called Traveller's Rest
     in Stafford County for sale and Thomas Garnett became the purchaser per
     deeds recorded in Fredericksburg District Court DB "A",p.381,387. This
     most desirable plantation of 1030 acres had a three story brick house there-
     on overlooking the Rappahannock River about four miles below Fredericksburg
     and is described in Colonel Ball's advertisement in the Virginia Herald of
     15 April 1790. The Fredericksburg Virginia Herald of 6 June 1798 said:
     "Died: In Fauquier county on Saturday last, Mr. Thomas Garnett of Traveller's
     Rest, Stafford county, formerly a respectable merchant of this town." Mar-
     garet (Miskell) Garnett m(2) 20 April 1800 Richard J. Tutt and same was
     announced in the Virginia Herald of 29 April 1800. The obituary of Mrs.
     Margaret (Miskell) Garnett Tutt appeared in the Virginia Herald of 4 Febru-
     ary 1824; it said she died suddenly in Fredericksburg and described her as
     "a lady of piety and esteemed character." She left issue by both husbands.
     Thomas Garnett, Esquire, (17??-1798) died testate and his estate under went
     litigation. Traveller's Rest, the estate of Thomas Garnett, deceased, was
     advertised for sale in the Fredericksburg Virginia Herald of 6 November 1807.
     See suit papers, Tutt vs Garnett, FDC#280 and Rachel (a Negro) vs Stevenson,
     FDC#448.]

GASKINS, DAVID and Grace Fawcett, bond 7 February 1804. Daniel Attwell (b).
There seems to be some uncertainty about the bride's surname; this note
is appended: "Jeneway the 15 Day 1804. Grasie Smith living in Richmond
County are agreeable to join in wedlock with David Gaskin.   X
William Thomas
Thomas Mozingo"

GASKINS, DAVID and Keziah Bragg, bond 30 May 1831, George Henry (b). MBB.,p.79

GASKINS, DAVID and Kesiah Bragg "a woman of colour," bond 30 June 1831. George
Saunders (b).   MBB.,p.80

GATHINGS, COBHAM married Judith Millner, 26 February 1726/7.   NFPR.,p.112

GEORGE, MARTIN and Salley Hunton*, bond 26 January 1795. Alexander Hunton (b);
Robert Hunton (w) and Nancey Hunton (w).

GIBBINS, PATRICK and Margaret Coushee, license April 1711.   DB#6,p.275

GIBBS, JOHN C. and Harriet Ann Pare were married 13 February 1851 by Rev. George
Northam, L.M.G. [Minister's Returns]

GIBERNE, REVEREND ISAAC WILLIAM married Mary (Fauntleroy) Beale (1725-1820),
daughter of Major Moore and Margaret (Micou) Fauntleroy (q.v.) and widow of
Charles Beale. Her obituary, in the Fredericksburg Virginia Herald of 22
April 1820, said she died 31 March 1820 at Belle-ville, Richmond County,
aged 95 years. Beale,p.68,224-225; Fauntleroy,p.232; Meade II,p.179-180.

GIBSON, JOHN married Elizabeth Call, 7 August 1729.   NFPR.,p.112

GIBSON, JONATHAN [GENTLEMAN] (16??-1729) of Richmond and King George counties,
married by 3 March 1698/9 Elizabeth (Thornton) Conway (1674-1732/3), daughter of Francis and Alice (Savage) Thornton (q.v.) and widow of Edwin
Conway, Gentleman, (c.1640-1698) of Richmond County (q.v.). COB#2,p.331,
396,442; see references cited under Edwin Conway, p.43-44.

GIBSON, ROBERT married Elizabeth Draper, 26 January 1730/1.   NFPR.,p.112

GILBERT, JOHN married by 1717 Sarah Underwood, daughter of Major William Underwood (1649-1717). WB#3,p.344; King George County DB#1-A,p.152, and DB#2,
p.511; Spotsylvania County WB#"B",p.58; 39V273.

GILBERT, SAMUEL of Westmoreland County and Frances Dozier*, bond 7 January 1814.
Frances Dosher (sic) writes her own consent; she states she is 23 years of
age and her father has no objections to her marriage. Thomas Tune (b).

GILBERT, WILLIAM of Westmoreland County and Mary Habron*, bond 24 January 1837.
Benjamin Tucker (b); Frances Louis (w) and William Trosee (w). MBB.,p.153

GILL, EDWARD married by 5 December 1710 Mary Marcey, sister and heir-at-law of
John Marcey, then deceased, who purchased land of Angell Jacobus, 6 April
1697. DB#2,p.229; DB#5,p.308.

GLASCOCK :   GLASSCOCK

GLASCOCK, ALDEA A. and Mary B. Smith, bond 8 October 1822. Consent by John Y.
Chinn, guardian of the bride. Samuel Williams (b).

GLASCOCK, GEORGE of Richmond County and Mrs. Judith Ball, daughter of William
Ball of Lancaster County, bond 13 April 1726.   LCMR#1,p.7
[Maiden ladies were oftentimes addressed in colonial times as "mistress"
or madam. The bride was the daughter of Colonel William and Hannah (Beale)
Ball. See Beale,p.25-29 and Hayden,p.61.]

GLASCOCK, GEORGE of Richmond County and Judith Mitchell, bond 13 January 1748.
Solomon Ewell, security. (The date is 1748/9).   LCMR#1,p.22
[Judith Mitchell (19 March 1732/3-2 January 1791) was the daughter of Robert
Mitchell, Sr. (1684-1748) who died testate in Lancaster County. Her birth
and death are entered in his family Bible of which there is a photostat
copy in VSL:AD #25212.]

GLASCOCK, GREGORY married Elizabeth Elder, 29 January 1730/1.   NFPR.,p.112

GLASCOCK, JOHN and Mary Hendren, bond 28 November 1759. William Hendren (b).
[The bride was the daughter of William Hendren (Hendron), Sr., a weaver,
who died testate in Richmond County in 1768. WB#7,p.9.]

GLASCOCK, JOHN and Susanna Mitchell (spinster), bond 28 June 1770. Rawleigh
Downman (b). [The bride was the daughter of Robert and Hannah (Ball) Mitchell (q.v.). AB#1,p.569; WB#6,p.129.]

GLASCOCK, MILTON SYMS and Sally Meredith Yerby*, bond 10 November 1790. Bartholomew McCarty (b); Thomas Yerby (w) and Dennis McCarty (w).

GLASCOCK, PETER and Elizabeth Hinds (spinster), bond 16 January 1770. Samuel
Woollard (b). [Bond 5 May 1760 of Samuel Woollard as guardian of John,
Mary and Betty Hinds, orphans of James Hinds, deceased. James Hinds died
testate in 1755. AB#1,p.571; WB#6,p.64 prove his daughter Elizabeth ("Betty") Hinds married Peter Glascock.]

GLASCOCK, RAWLEIGH D. and Sarah L. Dobyns*, bond 25 July 1837. William B. Mitchell of Lancaster County, guardian of the groom, gives his consent. William H. Miskell (b); John D. Glascock (w).   MBB.,p.157

GLASSCOCK, RICHARD and Hannah Chichester (spinster), bond 29 April 1761. Williamson Ball (b).

GLASCOCK, THOMAS M. and Ann M. Downman, bond 8 January 1812. Consent by Rawleigh
Downman, father of the bride. William Downman (b).

GLASCOCK, WASHINGTON and Elizabeth Downman (spinster), bond 18 December 1805.
Consent by Rawleigh Downman, father of the bride. Charles Dobyns (b).

GLASCOCK, WILLIAM of Richmond County and Mrs. Esther (Easter) Ball of St. Mary's
White Chappel Parish, Lancaster County. Bondsman and witness: Thomas Edwards

and John Selden. The marriage bond was dated 10 April 1728. LCMR#1,p.9 [Esther Ball was the daughter of Captain Richard and Sarah (Young) Ball. Hayden,p.62-63. On 8 September 1770 William Glascock, aged 66, made a deposition in Richmond County court and on 28 September 1771 Esther Glascock, aged 59, made a deposition in the same suit. Thomas Taff vs John Yerby, VSL:AD #25391.]

GLASSCOCK, WILLIAM and Ann Sallard (spinster), bond 11 February 1755. LeRoy Hammond (b).

GLASCOCK, WILLIAM and Sally Keyser*, bond 18 March 1790. James Singleton of Frederick County (b); John Morris (w).

GLENDENING, JOHN [CAPTAIN, GENTLEMAN] married by 3 October 1692 Ann Mott (1671-1740), third daughter of George Mott (16??-1674). Captain John Glendening (16??-1712) died intestate in Richmond County and his wife died testate in King George County but her will is in lost WB#1. DB#1,p.34; DB#3,p.122; King George County COB#2,p.227; DB#1,p.113,221,226,230,234,287; DB#1-A,175, 230; DB#3,p.85; Sweeny,p.17,27,28,62,63; see John Fossaker (q.v.),p.71.

GOLDSBY, DAVID and Winifred Harford, bond 1 October 1786. James Webb (b). [Bond 3 August 1767 of John Goldsby as guardian of David Goldsby, orphan of Edward Goldsby, deceased; Richard Neale (b).]

GOLDSBY, DAVID and Ann Reynolds*, bond 10 September 1791. Thomas Reynolds (b). [The bride was the daughter of Thomas and Elizabeth (Davis) Thornton (q.v.) and widow of William Reynolds (1755-1784) (q.v.).]

GOLDSBY, GEORGE W. and Mary A. Mariner*, bond 8 December 1842. John B. Tiffey (b). Married 25 December 1842 by Rev. William N. Ward.   MBB.,p.229

GOODLETT, ADAM and Frances Balderson, bond [blank] September 17[blank]. Gilbert Balderson (b). [This is an incomplete bond; the form would indicate it was executed prior to 1776 but it is in the 1796 bundle.]

GORDON, JAMES and Susanna Warner*, bond 1 January 1794. James Alderson (b); Bartholomew McCarty (w).

GORDON, JOHN and Elizabeth Tune, bond 8 July 1795. Consent by Caster [? Carter ?] Tune, father of the bride. William W. Appleby (b).

GORDON, JOHN of Middlesex County and Jane Walker*, bond 22 March 1799. James Alderson (b).

GORDON, JOHN and Jane Stonum, bond 28 July 1800. John Alderson (b).

GORDON, JOHN and Sally A. Bryant (spinster), bond 28 February 1809. Joseph Bryant (b).

GOWER, PEIRCE (16??-1714) of Westmoreland County married by 5 March 1711/12 Frances Carpenter, daughter of John Carpenter. COB#6,p.3. See, Silas Emmett Lucas, Jr., Genealogy of the Dodson (Dotson), Lucas, Pyles, Rochester,

and Allied Families (Birmingham, Alabama, 1959), p.226-229, for data regarding the Gower family of Richmond County and environs.]

GOWER, STANLEY of Westmoreland County and Winifred Spencer (widow), license
     June 1714.   DB#6,p.275
     [The bride was the daughter of Richard and Ann (Hobbs) Green (q.v.) and
     widow of Edward Spencer (q.v.). WB#4,p.67.]

GOWER, STANLEY and Nancy Crawley, bond 6 July 1760. Walker Tomlin (b). [In 1777
     Standley Gower and Ann, his wife, sold their land in Richmond County and
     moved to Bedford County where he died testate in 1782. DB#14,p.451.]

GRANT, DANIEL (1711-1755) of Richmond, King George and Caroline counties, mar-
     ried before 28 January 1742 Mary Pannell, daughter of William and Frances
     (Sterne) Pannell of Richmond County (q.v.),p.154. They had five daughters;
     he died in Caroline County. King George County DB#2,p.393,395; DB#3,p.147;
     Caroline County COB#4,p.133,139. He was the youngest of the three sons of
     William and Elizabeth Grant of Richmond and King George counties, Virginia.

GRANT, WILLIAM and Judith Neale, bond 29 September 1755. John Beale (b).

GRAY, SAMUEL married by 3 May 1736 Susanna (Smith) Thornton (1???-1762), daughter
     of William Smith (16??-1717) and widow of Thomas Thornton (1688-1729) (q.v.)
     p.213-214. Samuel Gray died intestate in 1756 and his widow died testate in
     1762. COB#7,p.221; COB#8,p.31; COB#10,p.396; COB#14,p.19,33; WB#4,p.1; WB#6,
     p.85,203.

GRAY, THOMAS married Marthew (sic) [Martha] Peck, 10 July 1726.   NFPR.,p.112

GREEN, GEORGE and Anne Bodkin had a son Isaac Green born 12 August 1688.
                                                                   NFPR.,p.109

GREEN, GEORGE married by 7 March 1699/1700 Elizabeth Clapman [Clapham], one of
     the two daughters of William and Mary (Thatcher) Clapman (q.v.),p.37. In
     1689 William Clapman purchased 300 acres of land in what was to be Essex
     County in 1692 and in 1705 his daughter Elizabeth Green, widow, of St. Ann's
     Parish, Essex County, conveyed 150 acres of this same land to Philip Lake.
     21W(2)400 indicates Elizabeth (Clapman) Green m(2) Richard West; he died in-
     testate in Essex County in 1711 and she died testate in Essex County in 1722.
     COB#3,p.3; see also Essex County D&c.#7,p.32 and D&c.#12,p.271.

GREEN, JOHN married 24 August 1673 Dorothy Benjamin.   NFPR.,p.109

GREEN, JOHN and Abigall Tippett, license August 1714.   DB#6,p.275
     [The bride was the daughter of Thomas Tippett who died testate in 1710. The
     groom was the eldest son of George Green who died testate in 1719. He be-
     queathed one shilling to his son Robert Green and his plantation of 885 acres,
     which fell into King George County in 1721, equally to his other children,viz:
     John, Thomas, George, Joseph, William, Samuel, Daniel, Isaac, Elizabeth and
     Grace Green. John and Abigall [Abigail] (Tippett) Green moved to Overwharton
     Parish, Stafford County. WB#3,p.27; WB#4,p.131; King George County DB#1,p.
     77; DB#3,p.40-44; DB#4,p.447; OPR,p.43-44.]

GREEN, NATHANIEL of Westmoreland County and Sally E.G. Reynolds*, bond 17 January 1828. Benjamin Reynolds (b).   MBB.,p.34

GREEN, RICHARD (16??-1705) married Ann Hobbs, only child of Richard Hobbs (1644-
1683) and his wife nee Mary Meade, only child of Thomas Meade [Mead] who
owned 700 acres of land in Rappahannock County in 1662 which fell into Richmond County in 1692. Ann (Hobbs) Green m(2) John Branham (q.v.),p.23, 1714
and died prior to 1734 when John Branham [Bramham, Bramhan &c:] was yet living. There are numerous records in regard to the landed estate of Ann (Hobbs)
Green Branham but a deed dated 6 November 1752 (DB#11,p.155) indicates she
then had only two living heirs, viz: her grandson Edward Spencer, Gentleman,
(1710-1753) of Orange County and her great-granddaughter Ann the wife of John
White, also of Orange County. AB#1,p.79; COB#4,p.74; COB#6,p.258; DB#7,p.13,
14,60,492,545,547; DB#8,p.55; DB#9,p.100,388,633; DB#10,p.40,366,368; DB#11,
p.152,155; MRB.,p.118; WB#2,p.87; WB#4,p.67; WB#5,p.20,29; Sweeny,p.84.

GREENHAM, JEREMIAH and Dorothy Durham (widow), license February 1714/15.
                                                    DB#6,p.275
[Dorothy Durham was the widow of Thomas Durham of North Farnham Parish; his
will dated 4 August 1711 was proved 1 June 1715 after the marriage of his
widow to Jeremiah Greenham (16??-1753). Jeremiah Greenham m(2) Mary ___[?]
but died without issue; his will was proved in Richmond County, 1753. DB#7,
p.63; WB#3,p.210,270; WB#5,p.718; Stafford County DB "J", p.340-346.]

GREENLAW, DAVID of Westmoreland County and Alice B. Godfrey, bond 8 June 1811.
William Settle (b). [David Greenlaw was the son of William and Mary (Oldham)
Greenlaw (q.v.). In 1826 he became entangled with James V. Berrick, counter-
feiter of bank notes, and in order to avoid prosecution absconded, leaving
his wife Alice B. (Godfrey) Greenlaw with six infant children ranging in age
from about 15 years to 1 year, viz: (1) John Oliver; (2) William Bowden; (3)
Anders G; (4) Mary Agnes; (5) Lucy Ann; and (6) Donald Greenlaw. David Greenlaw was possessed of Islington on the Rappahannock River, about 20 slaves and
other valuable personal property. There is considerable detail in many petitions to the Legislature 1828-1834. Westmoreland County D&W#22,p.180 and D&W
#25,p.303,314.]

GREENLAW, WILLIAM SR. (17??-1811) of Westmoreland County married by 1778 Mary
Oldham (17??-1825), daughter of William Oldham (1728-17??) and granddaughter
of William and Priscilla (McLaughlin) Oldham (q.v.). AB#2,p.170; WB#5,p.115;
WB#7,p.424; Westmoreland County D&W#22,p.180; D&W#25,p.303,314; suit in chancery, Greenlaw vs Wheldon (1813), cited by ECD in his Papers, Box #13, VHS.]

GREGORY, James and Lorinday Weaver*, bond 30 March 1842. William Jackson (b);
Hopeful Weaver (w).   MBB.,p.221

GRESHAM, GEORGE of Mecklenburg County and Elizabeth Rust, bond 27 June 1792.
Thomas Williams (b).

GRIFFIN, LEROY of Richmond County and Mrs. Mary Ann Bertrand of St.Mary's White
Chappel Parish, Lancaster County, daughter of William Bertrand, bond dated
5 October 1734. Bondsman and witnesses: Thomas Edwards, Thomas Broom, William George.   LCMR#1,p.13
[The name of the bride is usually given as Marianne Bertrand; daughter of

William and Susanna (Foushee) Bertrand (q.v.). LeRoy Griffin (9 January
1711-0 July 1750) was the son of Thomas and Elizabeth Griffin of Richmond
County where he was born and died. The seventh child of LeRoy and Marianne
(Bertrand) Griffin was the distinguished Judge Cyrus Griffin (16 July 1748-
14 December 1810), president of Congress, United States District Judge 1789-
1810, &c: He was educated in England where he met and subsequently married
Lady Christina Stuart, daughter of John Stuart, Ninth Earl of Traquair in
Scotland, and a lady of most distinguished ancestry.]

GRIFFIN, LEROY of North Farnham Parish, Richmond County, and Alice Currie of
Christ Church Parish, Lancaster County, daughter of Rev. David Currie, bond
28 July 1764. William Griffin (b).   LCMR#1.p.33
[This was the first marriage of Major LeRoy Griffin (1738-1775), son of
LeRoy and Marianne (Bertrand) Griffin (q.v.); their only child, Ann Corbin
Griffin, was born 19 September 1765 in North Farnham Parish and was married
19 June 1784 to Thomas Pinkard of Lancaster County - the ceremony was performed by the bride's grandfather, the Rev. David Currie. Thomas Pinkard
(1786-1814) was the son of Thomas and Ann Corbin (Griffin) Pinkard; he died
testate in Westmoreland County and this document provoked litigation. AB#2,
p.232,238; WB#7,p.211; Westmoreland County D&W#23,p.26; FDC#241, Seward vs
McKenney.]

GRIFFIN, LEROY of Richmond County and Judith Ball of Lancaster County, daughter
of Colonel James Ball, bond 3 November 1772.   LCMR#1,p.42
[This was the second marriage of Major LeRoy Griffin (1738-1775) (q.v.). She
was the daughter of Colonel James and Lettice (Lee) Ball of Bewdley, Lancaster County; by her Major Griffin had two daughters, viz: (1) Elizabeth Griffin
who married 18 July 1792 Joseph Chinn (q.v.) p.36; and (2) Judith Griffin
(1775-1794) d.s.p. Judith Ball (30 May 1753-30 January 1817), widow of Major
Griffin, m(2) 8 February 1781, John Fauntleroy (q.v.),p.68. See references
cited above under Major LeRoy Griffin's first marriage; also WB#9,p.1 and
Hayden,p.95-96,110-111.]

GRIFFIN, WILLIAM and Ann Burgar, license March 1713/14.   DB#6,p.275

GRIGSBY, THOMAS (16??-1745) of Stafford County married by 4 May 1715 Rose Newton,
one of the two daughters of Gerrard Newton of Little Falls Plantation, Richmond County, who died intestate there in 1706. Thomas Grigsby d.s.p. in 1745;
his will was proved at Stafford County court. Rose (Newton) Grigsby m(2) 12
December 1745, Townshend Dade. See references, Gerrard Newton; also SPR,p.59;
Richmond County COB#6,p.278; King George County DB#1,p.618.

GRIMSTONE, THOMAS married Mary (Skelderman) Barker, widow of Lawrence Barker who
died testate in 1716 and daughter of Herman Skelderman who died testate in
Rappahannock County in 1684. They had two daughters, viz: Mary and Sarah
Grimstone. DB#9,p.210; DB#12,p.142; WB#3,p.244; Sweeny, p.108.

GUI[L]BERT, MATHEW of Maryland married by 1718 Elizabeth Newton, one of the two
daughters of Gerrard Newton of Little Falls Plantation, Richmond County, who
died intestate there in 1706. COB#8,p.50; King George County DB#1,p.618; and
see references under Gerrard Newton and Thomas Grigsby who married the other
daughter of the said Gerrard Newton (16??-1706).

GUPTON, STEPHEN married Margaret Coward, 23 January 1728/9.   NFPR.,p.112

GUTTRIDGE, HENRY R. of Westmoreland County and Lucinda Yeatman, bond 14 January
    1833. Consent by John H. Yeatman, father of the bride. Joshua Reamy (b).
                                                                    MBB.,p.100

GUTRIDGE, NEWTON and Harriet Scates*, bond 10 July 1833. William Balderson (b).
                                                                    MBB.,p.109

                                    H

HABRON, BENJAMIN and Rany Sanford*, bond 14 September 1832. Rany Samford writes
    her own consent. Samuel Wroe (b).   MBB.,p.93

HABRON, CHARLES and Molly Hammack, bond 20 December 1797. Benedict Hammack (b).

HABRON, WILLIAM and Ann Hudson*, bond 15 March 1844. Henry O. Hudson (b).
                                                                    MBB.,p.247

    HAIL : HAILE   SEE: HALE

    HAL[L]AWAY   SEE: ALLOWAY

    HALE : HAIL : HAILE

HAIL, BENJAMIN JR. of Northumberland County and Peggy Bryant (spinster), bond
    31 August 1795. Consent by John Hail, father of the groom; consent by Lydia
    Bryant, mother of the bride. John Beacham Jr. of Northumberland County (b)
    and John Bryant of Richmond County (b).

HALE, JOHN and Frances Northern married 16 November 1847. No bound found in
    Richmond County; this from the marriage returns of the Rev. Bartholomew
    Dodson sent to the clerk of Richmond County on 3 February 1848.

HAILE, MOSES and Nancy Sydnor, bond 17 December 1838. William Sydnor (b).[The
    surname is also rendered HALE in this bond.]   MBB.,p.177

HALE, RICHARD and Louisa Thrift*, bond 17 July 1850. Benjamin Tucker (w) and
    Harriet Tucker (w). Married 18 July 1850 by the Rev. Elijah L. Williams;
    he renders the name Richard Hail on his returns to the county clerk.

HALE, SAMUEL and Judith A. Levaine (spinster), license 29 December 1852. Con-
    sent by William Levaine, father of the bride. Benedict B. King (w) and Will-
    iam Levaine (w). Married 31 December 1852 by the Rev. John Godwin.

HALE, THOMAS and Elizabeth Bryant, bond 22 December 1808. William Hail and
    Johnathan Bryant jointly consent to the marriage; no relationship stated.
    John Bryant (b); John Douglis (w). The name is also rendered HAIL.

HALE, THOMAS and Margaret Haydon, bond 16 August 1830. Charles Hammock (b).
                                                                    MBB.,p.67

HALE, THOMAS R. and Elizabeth Hogans*, bond 26 September 1815. Jessey Thrift (b); Jeremiah Thrift (w).

HALE, THOMAS W. and Jane Wilkins*, license 24 January 1853. Benjamin Tucker (w) and Reubin Bryant (w). Married 26 January 1853 by the Rev. William C. Haynes.

HALE, WILLIAM S. and Furdelia Bisky King*, bond 28 January 1837. Henry P.F. King (b).   MBB.,p.154

HALL, BENJAMIN HARRISON of Fredericksburg, Virginia, and Elizabeth Landon Carter Colston, bond 10 March 1802. William T. Colston (b). [The bride was the daughter of William and Lucy (Carter) Colston (q.v.) p.42. The groom was the son of Doctor Elisha Hall (c.1752-1814), physician of Fredericksburg, and his wife nee Carolianna Carter (c.1756/7-1799), youngest child of Colonel Charles Carter (1707-1764) of Cleve, King George County, and his second wife nee Ann Byrd (1725-1757), daughter of Colonel William Byrd (1674-1744) of Westover. Needless to say, the bride and groom were cousins and of aristocratic ancestry. Patton vs Hall, FDC#220; 22W(1)135,145,151; 23W (1),p.46,47.]

HALL, BLADEN and Frances Morris, bond 6 February 1849. Consent by John Morris, father of the bride. Robert Sanders (b); Thomas Vickers (w). Married 8 February 1849 by the Rev. John Pullin.   MBB.,p.321

HALL, GRIFFIN D. and Alice Dodson, bond 27 July 1848. Consent by Alfred Dodson, father of the bride. Thomas H. Douglass (b); Joseph Bryant (w). MBB.,p.312

HALL, ISAAC and Jane Harris*, bond 27 January 1792. Williamson Hall (b).

HALL, JAMES and Ann Bartlett, bond 9 April 1834. John Bartlett (b); he certifies both parties are of full age.   MBB.,p.118

HALL, JOHN and Elizabeth Wall, bond 20 January 1802. Consent by Betsy Wall; no relationship stated. Edward Barns (b); Richard Littrell (w).

HALL, JOHN and Catharine P. Butler*, bond 13 January 1841. Richard McGinnis (b). Married 13 January 1841 by the Rev. John M. Waddey.   MBB.,p.205

HALL, JOSEPH and Elizabeth Morgan married 21 April 1729.   NFPR.,p.211

HALL, NEWMAN and Susanna Millians [or Williams] Guttridge, bond 3 April 1820. Consent by Reubin Guttridge; no relationship stated. William Bispham (b).

HALL, REUBEN and Sarah Fones, bond 16 March 1824. Consent by Elizabeth Fones; no relationship stated. William Smith (b); William H. Sisson (w).

HALL, RICHARD and Peggy Connolly, bond 4 October 1789. Jesse Pullin (b); Richard Literal (w).

HALL, RICHARD of Westmoreland County and Eliza A. Yeatman, bond 29 December 1830. William Burgess (b).   MBB.,p.71

HALL, RICHARD L. married Susan J. Elmore, 27 May 1827. No bond found in Richmond County; this record from the marriage returns of the Rev. Bartholomew Dodson made to the clerk of Richmond County, 3 February 1848.

HALL, ROBERT SANDY and Mrs. Louisa W. Balderson*, license 8 November 1853. James R. Carter (w) and Daniel Sanford (w). Married 9 November 1853 by the Rev. William Balderson.

HALL, STEPHEN (bachelor) and Mary Ann Hall (spinster), bond 5 October 1829. Williamson Hall (b).   MBB.,p.56

HALL, THOMAS of Northumberland County and Sally Brown, bond 13 January 1794.

HALL, WILLIAM of Northumberland County and Louisa Dodson, bond 21 December 1815. Alexander Dodson (b).

HALL, WILLIAM and Susan Carter, license 1 June 1853. Consent by Daniel Carter, Jr., father of the bride. T.N. Balderson (w); Robert G. Reamy (w). Married 2 June 1853 by the Rev. William Balderson.

HALL, WILLIAMSON and Susanna Harris*, bond 14 June 1788. Jesse Pullin (b).

HALL, WILLIAMSON and Mary Bragg, bond 26 March 1825. William Burgess (b).
                                                                MBB.,p.8

HALL, WILLIAMSON and Ann Crask, bond 3 February 1831. Consent by Richard Crask; no relationship stated. William Burgess (b); Thomas Brown (w). MBB.,p.74

HAMES, WILLIAM married Winifred Fann, 26 November 1730.   NFPR.,p.211

HAMILTON, GILBERT married Ann Beale, 4 November 1732.   NFPR.,p.211

HAMILTON, WILLIAM B. and Maria Beale, 9 July 1803. Consent by Sinah Beale, mother of the bride. Jesse B. Beale (b).

HAMMACK : HAMMOCK

HAMMACK, BENEDICT and Ellen B. Polk, bond 23 December 1834. Consent by A.G. Plummer, guardian of the bride. Thomas Oldham (b); Ann M. Polk (w).
                                                                MBB.,p.128

HAMMACK, BENJAMIN JR. and Molly Scott, bond 18 December 1786. Samford Jones (b).

HAMMACK, CHARLES and Alice G. Davis*, bond 31 May 1816. William Hammack (b); William Reuick (w).

HAMMOCK, CHARLES and Charlotte P. Deatley, bond 16 August 1830. Thomas Hale (b).
                                                                MBB.,p.67

HAMMOCK, JOHN married Mildred Lambert, 26 August 1741.   NFPR.,p.212

HAMMACK, JOHN and Anna Beale, bond 26 June 1799. Consent by Samuel Beale, father of the bride.

HAMMACK, JOHN W. and Winefred Demeritt, bond 10 July 1815. Consent by Molly Demeritt, mother of the bride. Miskell Saunders (b); Emma D. Glascock (w).

HAMMACK, LEWIS and Lucy Clarke*, bond 26 December 1811. John Hammack (b); John Beale (w).

HAMMACK, LEWIS and Elizabeth Leader*, bond 18 December 1844. Rodham C. Hammack (b); John L. Chamberlain (w).   MBB.,p.251

HAMMACK, ROBERT and Ann Beale Ruick*, bond 8 August 1816. Edward Brown (b); Nancy Brown (w).

HAMMACK, WILLIAM and Judith Sydnor (widow)*, bond 20 December 1815. John Sydnor, Jr. (b).

HAMMOND : HAMMON : HAMON

HAMMOND, JOB JR. (16??-1758) married by 1 September 1703 Amadine Baylis, born 18 January 1684 in North Farnham Parish, daughter of Thomas and Catherine (Samford) Baylis (q.v.) p.12. COB#3,p.275,277,287,299,354; DB#9,p.384; WB#2,p.2; WB#6,p.140.

HAMON, JOHN and Catherine Dobbins, license December 1712.   DB#6.,p.275

HAMMOND, JOHN married Judith Yeates, 21 February 1725/6.   NFPR.,p.120

HAMMOND, JOHN married by 6 March 1747 Elizabeth Davis, daughter of Robert and Susanna (Jacobus) Davis (q.v.),p.51. DB#12,p.641; WB#5,p.272,558.

HAMMOND, THOMAS married Ann Morris, 9 June 1726.   NFPR.,p.211

HAMMOND, THOMAS married Mary Bryant, 23 September 1728.   NFPR.,p.211

HAMMOND, THOMAS (17??-1777) married Rebecca Sisson (Lawson) Thornton, widow of Thomas Thornton (q.v.); they had two daughters, viz: Elizabeth Hammond and Lucy Hammond. Rebecca Sisson (Lawson) Thornton Hammond, twice a widow, m(3) per bond 24 March 1781, Thomas Dobyns (q.v.). ECD notes a suit in the chancery court detailing these marriages.

HAMMOND, THOMAS and Mary Berrick*, bond 31 December 1796. Thomas Elmore (b).

HAMMOND, WILLIAM and Sarah Dobyns (widow), bond 26 June 1804. William Dobyns (b).

HAMMOND, WILLIAM (the younger) and Catherine Nash (spinster), bond 9 April 1751. William Nash (b).

HAND, LAWRENCE and Delline [surname omitted], married 14 January 1727/8. NFPR.,p.21

HANKS, EWELL and Sally C. Stott, bond 4 January 1814. Consent by Mary Stott, mother of the bride. Eppa: Stott (b).

HANKS, EWELL and Judith P. Downman, bond 6 February 1834. Thaddus C. Stott (b).
                                                                          MBB.,p.116

HANKS, JOHN E. and Catharine Ann Webb, bond 23 January 1849. Ewell Webb (b).
MBB.,p.319

HANKS, JOSEPH T. and Judith P. Hanks (widow)*, bond 12 September 1837. Consent
by Elizabeth Hanks, guardian of the groom, "he being under age." Edward
Douglass (b); William H. Miskell (w).   MBB.,p.159

HANKS, LUKE and Levina Stott, bond 4 January 1792. Consent by John Stott, father of the bride; this is also signed by LeRoy Stott. LeRoy Stott (b); John
Nash (w).

HANKS, LUKE S. and Lucy Armstrong*, bond 14 November 1842. Benjamin Armstrong
(b); Edwin L. Dodson (w).   MBB.,p.228

HANKS, TURNER and Maria Hammack*, bond 4 December 1823. Rodham Clarke (b);
Lucy Hammack (w).

HANKS, TURNER and Catherine Wroe (spinster), bond 11 April 1836. Consent by
Winneyfrit Clark, mother and guardian of the bride. William Thornton (b);
Shadrack Clark (w).   MBB.,p.146

HANKS, TURNER and Jane Lowery*, bond 3 July 1839. John L. Clark (b); Shadrack
Clark (w).   MBB.,p.183

HANKS, WILLIAM and Esther Mills, license July 1711.   DB#6,p.275
[William Hanks (16??-1705) died intestate and administration on his estate
was granted to his son William Hanks. Shortly Sarah Hanks petitioned for
a division of his estate and it was divided 20 November 1705 into four
parts among (1) Richard White; (2) William Hanks; (3) John Hanks and (4)
Luke Hanks. COB#4,p.39,59; WB#2,p.78,88.]

HANKS, WILLIAM married Sarah Durham, 26 January 1738.   NFPR.,p.212
[The bride was the daughter of Thomas and Mary (Smoot) Durham (q.v.). DB#3,
p.57; DB#9,p.577-582; WB#3,p.210,270.]

HARBURN, DAVID married Sarah Peirce, 21 April 1729.   NFPR.,p.211

HARDING, JAMES and Ann Glascock, bond 13 May 1794. Joseph Mott (b). Consent
by George Glascock, guardian to the groom. In his note to Bartholomew Mc-
Carty, Esq., clerk of the court, George Glascock agrees to the marriage of
his ward and Miss Ann Glascock, and adds: "I will settle with you for the
license. May 1, 1794."

HARDING, WILLIAM married Sarah Bale [? Ball ?], 14 February 1730/1. NFPR.,p.211

HARDING, WILLIAM married before 3 February 1784 Milly Glascock, daughter of William Glascock who died testate in 1785 and whose will mentions his deceased
daughter Milly and her children by William Harding. AB#2,p.56; WB#7,p.459.

HARDWICK, AARON and Ann Goldsby (spinster), bond 7 September 1753. Edward Goldsby (b). [Bond 3 August 1767 of Griffin Garland guardian to William Hardwick,
orphan of Aaron Hardwick, deceased. ECD notes a suit instigated in 1759 by

Aaron Hardwick in right of his wife Ann, daughter of Edward Goosby (Goldsby), deceased, who died testate in 1758; Jane Goosby (Goldsby) was his executrix. The suit abated by June 1762 due to the death of the plaintiff, Aaron Hardwick. In 1769 when the estate of Edward Goldsby, deceased, was divided per order of court 7 March 1769, a portion was awarded to David Goldsby, John Goldsby, William Goldsby and Griffin Garland guardian to William Hardwick, the heir of Ann (Goldsby) Hardwick. AB#1,p.555; WB#6,p.119; suit in chancery Hardwick vs Goosby (1759).]

HARDWICK, SAMUEL R. and Rebecca Marmaduke, bond 15 June 1843. Consent by James B. Marmaduke, father of the bride, was dated 13 May 1843 and written from Shelby County, Missouri. Isaac S. Jeffries (b).   MBB.,p.238

HARFORD, HENRY and Frances Thornton*, bond 6 May 1795. William Webster (b). [The bride was the widow of Robert Thornton (q.v.) AB#2,p.293; WB#9,p.20.]

HARFORD, HENRY SENIOR and Susan English*, bond 3 June 1822. William A. Packett (b); Mary Ann Alloway (w) and William Scrimger (w).

HARFORD, WILLIAM and Sarah R. Kirk, bond 4 June 1792. John Kirk (b).

HARNSBERGER, STEPHEN M. and Sally Anne Fauntleroy, license 1 April 1852. Consent by Henry Fauntleroy, father of the bride. Robert B. Fauntleroy (w).

HARPER, ABRAHAM married Katherine Camel, 8 January 1729/30.   NFPR.,p.211

HARPER, BENEDICT and Elizabeth Weathers, bond 23 August 1845. Joseph G. Moore (b). Married 23 August 1845 by the Rev. Elijah L. Williams. MBB.,p.262

HARPER, DOWNING and Elizabeth Bryant*, license 8 January 1852. R.C. Pendleton (w). Married 8 January 1852 by Rev. William N. Ward.

HARPER, JOHN C. and Susan Sisson*, bond 2 September 1839. Consent by John Harper, guardian of the bride. William P. Harper (b); Richard Harper (w) and F. Lemoine (w).   MBB.,p.184

HARRINGTON, JOHN and Elizabeth Lewis, bond 24 December 1747. [No bondsman]

HARRIS, HENRY M. and Frances Mealey (spinster), bond 6 June 1835. Samuel Mealey (b); he certifies the bride is of age.   MBB.,p.134

HARRIS, HUGH and Patience Miller, license January 1711/12.   DB#6,p.275

HARRIS, HUGH and Flora Dew, license September 1714.   DB#6,p.275

HARRIS, HUGH and Sally Hall (widow)*, bond 23 February 1785. Thomas Dobyns (b).

HARRIS, JAMES M. and Amanda J. Quay, daughter of Sarah Ann Harris, license 25 November 1851. R.M. Harris (w). Married 27 November 1851 by Rev. Alfred Wiles.

HARRIS, JOHN and Mahala M. Berrick*, bond 27 April 1811. Consent by Caty Berrick, mother of the bride. Thomas S. Davis (b); he made oath the bride
was of lawful age.

HARRIS, WILLIAM and Molly Jinkins, bond 5 October 1789. Consent by Hanner
Brown of Lunenburg Parish for the marriage of "my daughter Molley Jinkins
and William Harris." Daniel Brown (b); William Jinkins (w).

HARRISON, DANIEL and Elizabeth Short, bond 31 December 1819. Daniel Hardwick
(b); W.Y. Sturman (w).

HARRISON, JAMES (16??-1712) married circa 1674 Elizabeth Mott, widow and executrix of George Mott, deceased; she died before 27 March 1697. Their only
child was Jael Harrison (167?-1733); she m(1) William Williams who died
intestate in Essex County in 1712 and (2) Richard Johnson with whom she
lived in Spotsylvania County on the Rappahannock River immediately opposite
Ferry Farm, home of George Washington's parents. Richard Johnson died intestate in 1726 and Jael (Harrison) Williams Johnson died testate in Spotsylvania County in 1733. The plantation where she lived passed to her son
James Williams and the 1737 survey of the Northern Neck of Virginia made
for Thomas, Lord Fairfax, designates the estate as "Williams" and immediately opposite the Strother plantation which was purchased and occupied by
Captain Augustine Washington in 1738. In 1745 a ferry was established from
the Williams plantation across Rappahannock River to the Washington plantation and this continued to be a well accustomed passage for many years.
Richmond County DB#3,p.3; Rappahannock County COB#2,p.253; Essex County COB
1708-1714,p.444,450; DB#13,p.320; D&W#14,p.61; Virginia Gazette 2 May 1745;
6 Hening 15.

HARRISON, JAMES and Ann Tomlin, bond 30 October 1823. Consent by Polly Kirtley,
mother of the bride. William Gilbert (b); Polley N. Kirtley (w).

HARRISON, JEREMIAH and Jane Moore*, bond 16 February 1790. Thomas Moore (b);
Thomas H. Moore (w) and James G. Moore (w).

HARRISON, MATHEW and Elizabeth Webb, bond 2 April 1774. John Webb (b). [6 April
1774: Marriage Contract between Mathew Harrison of Prince William County and
Elizabeth Webb of Richmond County with John Webb of Fauquier County, her trus-
tee. The bride was the daughter of Isaac and Frances (Barber) Webb (q.v.) and
a legatee of her childless brother James Webb who died in 1775. DB#14,p.296;
WB#6,p.187; WB#7,p.200,450.]

HARRISON, RICHARD H. and Rebecca B. Dameron*, license 21 March 1853. Robert
Hudson (w).

HARRISON, ROBERT (16??-1720) married by 2 October 1696 Elizabeth Woffendall, daughter of Adam Woffendall (16??-1704) of Richmond County who made her a deed ·
of gift for land. Robert Harrison mentions his second wife Mary and several
children in his will of 1720. DB#2,p.200; DB#3,p.59; WB#2,p.70; WB#4,p.148.

HARRISON, SAMUEL of Westmoreland County and Judy Weldon "both free persons of colour," bond 15 December 1825. Consent by Rebeckah Weldon, mother of the bride.
Simon Reid (b) and George Weldon (b).   MBB.,p.16

HARRISON, SAMUEL and Eliza Hudson*, bond 2 January 1832. Jeremiah Cookman (b).
                                                                    MBB.,p.86

HARRISON, THOMAS and Susanna Lewis, bond 31 December 1795. Jeremiah Lewis (b).

HARRISON, WILLIAM and Ann Moore, Junior, bond 16 February 1790. Consent by Ann
     Moore, Senior; no relationship stated. Thomas Moore (b); Thomas H. Moore
     (w) and James G. Moore (w).

HARRISON, WILLIAM and Polly Weathers, bond 13 May 1823. Daniel Harrison (b).

HARRISON, WILLIAM and Elizabeth Davis*, bond 3 August 1840. William Sydnor (b).
     Married by the Rev. Nathan Healy.   MBB.,p.196

HARRISON, WILLIAM and Lucinda Connolley*, bond 21 December 1841. Jesse G.
     Bryant (b); James S. Connolley (w).   MBB.,p.215

HART, FIELDING and Frances T. Carlton*, license 1 March 1852. Richard Marshall
     (w). Married 11 March 1852 by the Rev. G.H. Northam.

HART, JOHN and Patty Newman, bond 6 June 1785. Zechariah White (b).

HARVEY, MARCIUS C. and Ann Bispham, bond 4 November 1822. Consent by John W.
     Belfield for the marriage of the bride. John Spence (b). [The bride was
     the daughter of Robert and Ann (Asbury) Bispham (q.v.),p.19.]

HARVEY, MUNGO and Priscilla Ball, bond 18 August 1769.   LCMR#1,p.37
     [The bride was the daughter of William Glascock, Gentleman, who died testate
     in Richmond County in 1785 and widow of Williamson Ball (q.v.) p.8. Mungo
     Harvey, a native of North Britain, died in Westmoreland County on his 60th
     birthday, 21 March 1794; his obituary appeared in the Fredericksburg Virginia
     Herald of 27 March 1794. Richmond County WB#7,p.459; AB#2,p.56; Lancaster
     County WB#17,p.134; WB#22,p.3-4,47-49; Westmoreland County D&W#18,p.368; see
     Hayden,p.83-84 where he errs as to dates and renders the surname HENRY in-
     stead of HARVEY.]

HASTIE, WILLIAM married Ann Roberson, 17 September 1730.   NFPR.,p.211

HATCH, JOSEPH of the City of Richmond and Eliza Tarpley*, bond 25 June 1811.
     Joseph Deschamps (b); Anna Maria Garland (w). [The bride was the daughter
     of Thomas Tarpley who died testate in 1815. WB#9,p.491.]

HATHAWAY, WILLIAM and Rachel M. Davenport*, bond 11 November 1811. William H.
     Davenport (b) who states the bride is "of the age of 21 years" and is a
     daughter of George Davenport, deceased.

HAWES, HENRY (16??-1717) married Ann Skelderman one of the three daughters of
     Herman Skelderman who died testate in Rappahannock County in 1684. He had
     a land patent 11 July 1666 and bequeathed his real estate to his children.
     Henry Hawes died testate in 1717 and in 1740 Henry Hawes [Hause] of St.Mark's
     Parish, Orange County, son and heir of Henry and Ann (Skelderman) Hawes, sold
     a portion of the land which descended to him from his grandfather Skelderman.
     DB#7,p.35,59; DB#9,p.210,607,646,680; DB#12,p.142; WB#3,p.324; Sweeny,p.108.

HAYDON, JOHN and Winifred Davis, bond 21 November 1794. Thomas Thomas (b).

HAYNES, AUSTIN B. and Catharine Street*, bond 10 February 1838. George Henderson (b). Married 28 February 1838 by Rev. Addison Hall.   MBB.,p.168

HAYNES, JOHN R. and Susan Ann Bagby*, bond 19 February 1840. Richard H. Harwood
(b); Richard A.T. Gresham (w).   MBB.,p.193

HAYNES, WILLIAM C. and Maria Street, bond 14 May 1832. Consent by Elizabeth
Street, mother of the bride. Kenner Cralle (b); Mary Henderson (w).
                                                              MBB.,p.90

HAYNES, WILLIAM C. and Louisa R. Harwood*, bond 28 March 1848. Richard A.T.
Gresham (b); R.H. Harwood (w). Married 30 March 1848 by Rev. George Northam.   MBB.,p.308

HAYNIE, HOLLAND [CAPTAIN] married 17 September 1781 Wilalmira Webb. Middlesex
County Marriage Register #1,p.25. [Wilalmira Webb (1765-1822) was the only
child of William and Winifred Griffin (Tarpley) Webb of Richmond County; the
said Winifred married (2) Captain James Montague (1741-1781/2) of Middlesex
County (q.v.). Mrs. Haynie had a considerable interest in Richmond County
which those records reflect. AB#1,p.567-569,691; AB#2,p.25; DB#9,p.824; DB
#12,p.69,237; WB#6,p.391; WB#7,p.8; WB#9,p.291; WB#10,p.8.]

    HAZARD : HAZZARD

HAZZARD, HENRY and Olivia Stott*, bond 7 June 1834. George C. Newgent (b).
                                                              MBB.,p.121

HAZARD, JAMES and Ellen Stonum, bond 25 December 1800. Consent by William Stonum, father of the bride. Daniel Scurlock (b).

HAZARD, JOHN and Rosey Hendren*, bond 22 December 1795. John Keyser (b).

HAZARD, JOSEPH and Elizabeth Austin, bond 28 February 1833. Consent by Chapman
Austin, father of the bride. James F. Minor (b).   MBB.,p.102

HAZARD, RAWLEIGH and Sally Pullen*, bond 4 January 1797. Jonathan Pullen (b);
Jeduthum Pullen (w).

HAZARD, RAWLEIGH and Elizabeth R. Purssell*, bond 15 March 1817. Richard Smither
(b).

HAZARD, THOMAS and Polly Keyser, bond 22 January 1795. John Keyser (b).

HAZARD, WILLIAM and Hannah S. Clarke*, bond 28 July 1847. Consent by John L.
Clark, father of the bride. Charles Barrock (b); W. Christopher (w).
                                                              MBB.,p.296

HAZELL, JOHN married by 1740 Mary Field, widow of Daniel Field, Jr. who died
testate in Westmoreland County in 1733. French vs Hazell, suit in chancery,
1748; Westmoreland County COB 1739-1743,p.76a and D&W#9,p.289; Hugh French
of Richmond County (q.v.), p.74.

HEABERD, JOHN [CAPTAIN] (16??-1690) of Stafford County married 167? Ann Freake
    (Frack), daughter of William Freake who died testate in Rappahannock County
    in 1685 leaving his entire estate to his wife Martha Freake. He held land
    on Poutridges Creek which fell into Richmond County in 1692 and is now in
    King George County. William Heaberd (1678-circa 1720), son and heir of Ann
    (Freake) Heaberd (Haybered), recites some of these facts in a suit filed in
    Richmond County court 6 March 1700/1 vs John Hawksford. COB#3,p.82; King
    George County DB#1,p.607; Sweeny,p.113; 47V23,248; 22 Maryland Historical
    Magazine 139; Boddie, Virginia Historical Genealogies (1954),p.83-85.

HEAD, HENRY (16??-1772) of Richmond, King George and Spotsylvania counties, mar-
    ried by 1714 Frances Spence, daughter of Doctor Alexander and Elizabeth
    (Brown) Spence (q.v.). They had several children including Alexander Spence
    Head, born circa 1715 per his deposition in Spotsylvania County in 1747.
    Henry Head died testate in Spotsylvania County in 1772. King George County
    DB#2,p.523; Spotsylvania County COB 1749-1755,p.16 et seq., and WB "D",p.
    404.

HEADLEY, HENRY and Letty Dodson (widow), bond 30 September 1803. William Lewis
    (b).

HEADLEY, HENRY W. and Anna Maria Garland*, bond 1 January 1818. George Saunders
    (b).

HEADLEY, HENRY W. and Catharine M. Thrift, bond 25 January 1849. Rodham C. Ham-
    mack (b); Catherine M. Hammack (w).   MBB.,p.320

HEADLEY, HENRY WIATT of Northumberland County and Rebecca Willoughby Plummer*,
    bond 17 April 1794. Peter Davis (b); John How, Jr. (w).

HEADLEY, JOHN T. and Nancy Dodson, bond 15 December 1831. Ransdell P. Headley
    (b).   MBB.,p.83

HEADLEY, PAUL of Northumberland County and Sarah Oldham, bond 7 February 1794.
    John Wheldon (b). [The bride was the daughter of William Oldham (1728-17??)
    and granddaughter of William and Priscilla (McLaughlin) Oldham (q.v.).]

HEADLEY, RANDALL and Elizabeth Jones, bond 31 December 1799. Consent by John
    Jones and Hanner Jones, parents of the bride and also by the bride herself.
    John Jones, Jr. (b).

HEADLEY, RANSDELL P. and Elizabeth M. Wright*, bond 7 December 1835. George
    Crutcher (b); G.M. Wright (w).   MBB.,p.137

HEADLEY, ROBERT P. and Priscilla Chinn*, bond 19 April 1825. Thomas H. Headley
    (b) and Albert G. McCarty (b); Sarah F. Chinn (w).   MBB.,p.10

HEADLEY, THOMAS H. and Erretto A. White*, bond 6 January 1823. Consent by Rich-
    ard B. Plummer, guardian of the groom. Robert P. Headley (b); M. Saunders
    (w).

HEADLEY, WILLIAM of Northumberland County and Nancy Jones*, bond 16 January 1805.
    James Wall (b).

HEATH, JOHN and Judith Glascock, bond 2 July 1768. William Glascock (b).

HEFFORD   SEE : EFFORD

HELFORD, ZACHARIAS married Elizabeth Lewis, 21 February 1727/8.   NFPR.,p.211

HENDERSON, JAMES married by 3 March 1714 Mellinor [Millinder] Williams, daughter
of Francis Williams who made them a deed of gift for 100 acres of land. By
28 April 1733 she is a widow and conveys this land to John Chinn, Gentleman,
of St. Mary's White Chappel Parish, Lancaster County. The will of John Henderson, 1730, mentions some of the children of James and Mellinor Henderson.
DB#6,p.203; DB#8,p.649; DB#10,p.46; WB#5,p.161.

HENDERSON, WILLIAM and Magdalene Miskell, bond 25 July 1809. George Miskell (b).

HENDREN, WILLIAM [JUNIOR] married circa 1768 Priscilla Oldham, daughter of Will-
iam Oldham (1728-17??) and granddaughter of William and Priscilla (McLaughlin)
Oldham (q.v.). He was the son of William Hendren (Hendron) Sr., a weaver of
North Farnham Parish, who died testate in 1768. William Hendren, Jr. followed
in his father's trade and in 1778 appears on the account book of Colonel John
Tayloe (1721-1779) of Mount Airy as a weaver at his Landsdown Plantation in
Richmond County; at that time he had a wife and three children. AB#2,p.170;
DB#14,p.260; WB#5,p.115; WB#7,p.9,424; Account Book 1776-1786 of Colonel John
Tayloe of Mount Airy in VHS.

HENRY, FREDERICK and Eliza Webb*, bond 14 March 1846. Thomas Allen (b); J. Croxton (w). Married 14 March 1846 by Rev. Elijah L. Williams.   MBB.,p.274

HENRY, JAMES and Ann Rich, bond 9 January 1845. Harry Henry (b); William S.
Northen (w). Married 12 January 1845 by Rev. Elijah L. Williams. MBB.,p.254

HIGHTOWER, CHARNEL and Sarah Glascock, married 16 January 1727/8. NFPR.,p.211

HIGHTOWER, WILLIAM and Susanna Hanks, married 12 October 1743.   NFPR.,p.213

HILL, GEORGE and Mary Clark, married 20 October 1726.   NFPR.,p.211

HILL, GEORGE and Jane Hammond, married 20 December 1728.   NFPR.,p.211

HILL, GEORGE and Anne Randall, bond 28 December 1768. Francis Randall (b).

HILL, JOHN and Margaret Port, license July 1715.   DB#6,p.275

HILL, JOHN and Elizabeth Suggett, married 19 July 1728.   NFPR.,p.211

HILL, JOHN and Betty Hammond, married 13 August 1739.   NFPR.,p.212

HILL, MARTIN and Mary Jesper, bond [blank] December 1823. George Saunders (b).

HILL, WILLIAM of Northumberland County married by 13 April.1695 Ann Chissell,
granddaughter of Hezekiah Turner (16??-1678) of Rappahannock County. DB#2,
p.103; Swenny,p.65; see John Powell,p.161.

HILL, WILLIAM and Sarah Suggitt, married 3 March 1726/7.   NFPR.,p.211

HILL, WILLIAM E. and Virginia A. Benneham*, license 4 February 1851. Joseph H.
    Taylor (w). Married 5 February 1851 by Rev. Elijah L. Williams.

HILL, WILLIAM H. (widower) and Harriet A. Moss (spinster), bond 8 March 1828.
    Lyne Shackleford (b).   MBB.,p.36

HILLMAN, RICHARD and Ann Thomas, married 10 July 1729.   NFPR.,p.211

HILLYER, JAMES and Isabella Peebles, bond 27 December 1780. LeRoy Peachey (b).

HINDS, BENJAMIN married by 1700 Mary Fuller, daughter of Thomas Fuller, deceas-
    ed, who bought land 4 January 1683 from Walter Pavey. COB#3,p.12; DB#7,p.29.

HINDS, CHARLES and Mary Green, married 9 November 1727.   NFPR.,p.211

HINDS, JAMES and Ann Singleton, married 23 September 1739.   NFPR.,p.212

HINDS, THOMAS and Ann Grigrye, married 19 April 1731.   NFPR.,p.211

HINDS, THOMAS and Sarah Warner, bond 3 May 1779. Thomas Stone (b).

HINKLEY, EDWARD and Elizabeth Pridham, married 10 July 1726.   NFPR.,p.211
    [The bride was born in North Farnham Parish in 1710, the daughter of Chris-
    topher and Mary (Lewis) Pridham (q.v.); she m(2) Moses Hopwood (q.v.).]

HINSON, ANDREW J. and Mariah Ann Oliff*, license 20 January 1851. Daniel Car-
    ter (w) and William Gutridge (w). Married 22 January 1851 by the Rev. Will-
    iam Balderson.

HINSON, DANIEL and Sophia Newman*, bond 20 January 1840. Theoderick N. Balder-
    son (b).   MBB.,p.191

HINSON, GEORGE W. and Catherine Hinson, license 8 November 1852. The groom was
    the son of Mahaly Hinson and the bride was the daughter of Madrith Hinson;
    they both give their consent for the license to issue. Joseph R. Gutridge
    (w), William A. Gutridge (w) and Robert W. Carter, Jr. (w). Married 11
    November 1852 by the Rev. William Balderson.

HINSON, JAMES and Molly Ambrose, bond 3 August 1801. Consent by Molley Ambers
    (sic), mother of the bride. James Marks (b) and William Ambrose (b).

HINSON, SALATHIEL S. (bachelor) and Elizabeth M. Morrison (spinster), bond 24
    December 1829. David Goldsborough (b) made oath the bride was over 21 years
    of age; he so signs but the court clerk writes his name Goldsby. MBB.,p.59

HINSON, WILLIAM and Alice Carter*, bond 4 November 1799. James Marks (b).

HINSON, WILLIAM SENIOR and Mary Ball*, bond 24 December 1824. Moore F. Brocken-
    brough (b); Carter Ball (w) and Peggey Marks (w).   MBB.,p.7

HINSON, WILLIAM JUNIOR and Haney Waple, bond 4 February 1828. Jo^S [? Ja^S ?]
Reamy (b).   MBB.,p.35

HINSON, WILLIAM W. and Maria Scates, bond 4 March 1850. Consent by Joseph
Scates, father of the bride. Richard McGinnis (b); Bartlet Scates (w).
Married 13 March 1850 by the Rev. William Balderson.   MBB.,p.333

HIPKINS, JOHN of Middlesex County and Mary Glascock, license February 1712/13.
                                                                  DB#6,p.275
[She was the daughter of Thomas and Ann Glascock. COB#6,p.297,365; WB#3,
p.163.]

HIPKINS, ROBERT S. (bachelor) and Gertrude G. Chinn (spinster), bond 15 July
1847. Consent by Marianna Chinn, mother of the bride. James Roy Micou (b);
Benjamin W. Brockenbrough (w).   MBB.,p.295

HIPKINS, SAMUEL W. and Catharine Jackson (widow)*, bond 8 September 1797.
Daniel Tebbs (b).

HIPKINS, SAMUEL WILLIAM and Jane Sallard*, bond 25 July 1796. Vincent Bramham (b).

HOBBS, JOHN G. and Ann H. Priddy*, bond 27 December 1839. Consent by A.J.
Priddy; no relationship stated. George G. Palmer (b); Mary M. Palmer (w).
                                                                  MBB.,p.189

    HOGAN : HOGANS

HOGANS, CHRISTOPHER D. and Elizabeth Jackson (spinster), bond 24 April 1810.
Consent by Travis Hogans, father of the groom; consent by Elizabeth Jackson,
grandmother and legal guardian of the bride. Rawleigh Bryant (b); Samuel
Wroe (w), Jeduthan Hogans (w), and Elizabeth Bryant (w).

HOGAN, CHRISTOPHER D. and Polly L. Hogan, bond 7 January 1813. Consent by Thomas
and Ann Hogan; no relationship to either party stated. Richard H. Hogan (b).

HOGANS, JAMES and Winney Thrift, bond 6 October 1792. Nathaniel Thrift (b).

HOGAN, JAMES and Haney Lewis, bond 7 March 1799. Jeremiah Lewis (b).

HOGANS, JEDUTHAN and Nancy Vanlandingham, bond 14 December 1805. Consent by
Nancy Vanlandingham, mother of the bride. George Jones (b); Judah Walmoth
(w).

HOGANS, THOMAS and Elizabeth Thrift, bond 5 October 1808. Samuel Mealey (b).

HOGANS, THOMAS (bachelor) and Frances Hale (spinster), bond 4 January 1830.
William Kennan (b); he states the father of the bride consents to the marriage.   MBB.,p.60

HOGAN, TRAVERSE and Sally Deathey, bond 17 June 1786. Consent by Christopher
Deathey, father of the bride. Thomas Hogan (b).

HOLLAND, THOMAS and Joyce Johnson, married 2 August 1675.   NFPR.,p.115

HOLMES, WILLIAM WILSON married by May 1732 Mary Ingo, daughter of James and
Frances (Moss) Ingo (q.v.). British Colonial Office 5/1389, ff 62-63; microfilm, VSL:AD. [This is an act to break the entail on 200 acres of land in
Richmond County, devised by the last will and Testament of James Ingo (1680-
1725) to his daughter Mary Ingo with reversion to the issue of his other daughter Frances, wife of Captain Richard Barnes (q.v.), if the said Mary Ingo
should die without issue. By May 1732 Frances (Ingo) Barnes is deceased
leaving Thomas Barnes (q.v.) her only living child. This complex act was
designed to vest the 200 acres devised by James Ingo in Thomas Barnes and
his father, Captain Richard Barnes, agrees to convey to William Wilson Holmes
and Mary, his wife, 250 acres of land in Spotsylvania County - part of 1,200
acres purchased 6 April 1724 by the said Richard Barnes of William Skrine of
King George County who patented it 17 August 1720 with Reuben Welch and William Winston both of Essex County. A William Wilson Hollmes witnessed a deed
recorded in Spotsylvania County in 1736 and a William Wilson Holmes died intestate in Halifax County in 1775.]

HOLT, SIMON and Sarah Hinds, bond 6 July 1763. Samuel Williams (b).

HOOE, GERARD and Sarah Barnes, bond 9 January 1761. Thomas Barnes (b). [Colonel
Gerard Hooe (1733-1785) and Sarah Barnes (1742-1805) were married 11 January
1761 and resided at Barnesfield, Saint Paul's Parish, now in King George
County. She was the daughter of Captain Richard and Penelope (Manly) Barnes
(q.v.),p.10. He was the son of Captain John Hooe (1704-1766) and his wife
nee Ann Alexander; the Hooe lineage is detailed in A.P.& P.,p.211-213. See
also ABC Book, p.281-283, and 48V368-372 gives the inscription from the Hooe
memorial monument erected in the family cemetery at Barnesfield in 1852 and
since moved to Saint Paul's Churchyard. There are some errors in the last
mentioned account and I will here give the correct inscription on the handsome sarcophagus of Captain John Hooe: "Here lies interred the Body of CAPT:
JOHN HOOE, son to Col. Rice Hooe and Frances his wife Daughter to Robert
Townshend, Esq. He was born the 1 day of September Anno Domni 1704 and Departed this life the 18 day of April 1766 in the 62nd year of his age. He
was a kind affectionate husband, A Tender Parent & Sincere friend. --- This
was Erected to his Memory by ANN his wife Daughter of Major Robert Alexander."

HOOE, RICE [IV] (circa 1692-1748) of Stafford County, Va., only child of Colonel
Rice[3] Hooe (c.1660-1726) and his first wife nee Mary Dade (1661-1694) of Saint
Paul's Parish, was twice married, viz: (1) circa 1724 to Catherine Taliaferro
(1706-1731), daughter of Colonel Richard and Sarah Taliaferro of Richmond Coun
ty and (2) circa 1737 to Tabitha, traditionally nee Harrison of Charles County
Maryland, who was granted administration on his estate by the Stafford County
court. COB#5,p.229; King George County DB#1,p.332 and DB#1-A,p.48; Stafford
County Book "O",p.70,122,153. The ancestry of Rice[4] Hooe is detailed in A.P.
& P.,p.211-213, but errs p.336 in stating his mother was nee Frances Townshend
the mother of Rice[4] Hooe was nee Mary Dade, p.88-89. There is an account of
Rice[4] Hooe (circa 1692-1748) and some of his descendants in Graham,p.239 et
seq.
Colonel Rice[3] Hooe (c.1660-1726) m(1) Mary Dade (1661-1694), daughter of Captain Francis and Beheathland (Bernard) Dade (A.P.& P.,p.88-89) and widow of

Captain Robert Massey (16??-1689) by whom she had four sons, viz: (a) Robert
Massey; (b) Captain Dade Massey (1679-1735); (c) Benjamin Massey and (d)
Thomas Massey. The only child of Colonel Rice[3] and Mary (Dade) Hooe was
Rice[4] Hooe (c.1692-1748) (q.v.). Colonel Rice[3] m(2) 1695 Anne Howson, dau-
ghter of Robert Howson, Gentleman, deceased, by whom he had an only child,
Howson[4] Hooe (1696-1780) who is detailed in Graham,p.242 et seq.   Colonel
Rice[3] Hooe m(3) 1699 his first wife's sister-in-law, Frances (Townshend)
Dade Withers (c.1665-8 - 1726), daughter of Robert and Mary (Langhorne)
Townshend of Albion in Saint Paul's Parish and widow of Francis Dade, Jr.
(1659-1694) and Captain John Withers (16??-1698); by her he had two children, viz: (1) Captain John[4] Hooe (1704-1766), see Graham,p.269 et seq., and
(2) Sarah[4] Hooe (1708-1758) who married 11 November 1726 Captain Philip
Alexander (1704-1753) of Salisbury, Saint Paul's Parish, where their tombstones now are.

HOOE, ROBERT H. of Stafford County and Catharine Marshall*, bond 5 September
1792. William Fauntleroy (b). [Robert Howson Hooe (c.1772-c.1843) is detailed very poorly by Graham,p.250 et seq. His wife was the widow of George
Marshall (q.v.) and the bondsman, William Fauntleroy, was the bride's brother; he d.s.p. 1797, having married 17 October 1792 Elizabeth Hooe of King
George County. In spite of the fact published accounts state Catherine
(Fauntleroy) Marshall Hooe d.s.p., it is known she had at least one child,
viz: Apphia Bushrod Hooe (c.1800-1868) who married c.1825 Doctor George Hill
of Stafford County. This is revealed in the suit papers Hill vs Hooe, FDC
#138, and the Fredericksburg Ledger of 11 September 1868 announced the death
on 25 August 1868 at White Hall, near Opelousas, St. Landry, Louisiana, "the
residence of her husband, Dr. George Hill,"... of "Apphia Bushrod Hooe, daughter of Robert H. Hooe and Catherine Fauntleroy of Stafford County, Va., in
the 68th year of her age."]

HOOPER, THOMAS of Lancaster County and Sarah Price, widow, license July 1710.
DB#6,p.275

HOPKINS, GEORGE and Frances Wilson, widow, license October 1710. DB#6,p.275
[Frances___[?]___ m(1) John MackMellion (16??-1706); m(2) by 30 July 1707,
John Willson (16??-1709); m(3) in October 1710, George Hopkins (16??-1721).
Frances and her three husbands died testate in Richmond County. MRB.,p.111;
WB#2,p.90; WB#3,p.1; WB#4,p.170; WB#5,p.530.]

HOPKINS, JOHN married 171? Ann Hinson (born circa 1695), daughter of Mary Hinson
who seems to have resided in Pennsylvania, Richmond and Stafford counties as
well as upon the James River in Virginia. Ann Hinson heired 100 acres of
land in Richmond County from her uncle, William Wood (16??-1706), of Stafford
County and with her husband John Hopkins sold it to William Lampton. Ann
(Hinson) Hopkins seems to have been a relative of John Rowley (16??-1704) of
Richmond County but by some means escaped being murdered in 1704 when the
other members of John Rowley's household were murdered by the Indians - of
which incident there is considerable account. COB#3,p.361-384; King George
County DB#1,p.271,314 and DB#1-A,p.110; Stafford County Book "Z",p.347.

HOPWOOD, MOSES and Elizabeth Hinkley married 10 April 1727.   NFPR.,p.211
[She was the widow of Edward Hinkley (q.v.). DB#8,p.454; DB#5,p.55; also
Westmoreland County D&W#8,p.89.]

HORE, ELIAS and Isabell Triplett, license April 1711.   DB#6,p.275
[The bride was the daughter of William and Isabella (Miller) Triplett; her
name is rendered both Isabell and Isabella. OPR.,p.54-55; genealogical chart
of the Triplett family of Virginia, VSL:AD #22634.]

HORGIN, JAMES and Ann Hammontree, married 17 July 1742.   NFPR.,p.212

HORNBY, DANIEL and Winifred Traverse, married 28 November 1741.   NFPR.,p.212
[The bride was the daughter of Captain Samuel and Frances (Allerton) Travers.
The groom was a wealthy merchant; his plantation is noted on the 1737 Survey
of the Northern Neck of Virginia. Winifred (Travers) Hornby died 10 August
1749 and Daniel Hornby died 14 February 1749/50. They had no issue and his
will remains of record in WB#5,p.592. A.P.& P.,p.361; NFPR.,p.214; DB#8,p.
537.]

HOW : HOWE

HOW, DOZIER and Catharine Scrimger*, bond 14 May 1816. William Alderson (b);
Jeremiah Webb (w).

HOW, GEORGE and Nancy Packett (spinster), bond 15 February 1779. Benjamin Bramham (b).

HOW, THOMAS and Ann Oldham, bond 20 December 1785. James How (b). [She was the
daughter of William Oldham (1728-17??) and granddaughter of William and Priscilla (McLaughlin) Oldham (q.v.).]

HOW, THOMAS and Ann M. Sandy*, bond 1 January 1796. Thomas Sandy (b); John How,
Jr. (w). [The bride was the daughter of John Sandy (17??-1770) of Lunenburg
Parish; she was called Nanny Murfey Sandy in her father's will. The bondsman
was the bride's brother. DB#18,p.435; WB#7,p.73.]

HOWE, THOMAS and Sally Tune*, bond 22 December 1821. Lemuel G. Sandy (b); Samuel
Lyell (w) and Peggy S. Lyell (w).

HOWE, WILLIAM T. and Alice Richards*, license 15 January 1851. R.H. Mothershead
(w). Married 15 January 1851 by the Rev. John Pullen.

HOWARD, JEREBOAM and Ellen Stott, bond 25 December 1781. James Howard (b).

HOWARD, LEROY and Ellen Oliver (widow), bond 20 March 1781. James Howard (b).

HOWARTH, JOHN H. and Martha A.R. Wooddy, bond 9 August 1834. Robert Wooddy (b);
he is the father of the bride.   MBB.,p.122

HOWE   SEE :   HOW : HOWE

HOWEND, JAMES and Mary Scurlock, married 7 November 1729.   NFPR.,p.211
[Their children are dubbed HOWARD in NFPR.]

HUBARD, JAMES [GENTLEMAN] married 1760 Frances Morton, only child of Joseph and
Frances (Colston) Morton (q.v.).WB#5,p.652; King George County COB#3,p.1200

et seq; King George County DB#5,p.1226.]

HUBERT, EPPA: married 178? Ann McCarty (Singleton) Edmondson, daughter of Joshua
Singleton, Gentleman, (17??-1773) of Richmond County and widow of James Ed-
mondson, Jr. (177??-1779) of Essex County (q.v.). AB#2,p.2; WB#7,p.150; also
Essex County WB#13,p.262 and Hubert vs Miskell, suit in chancery filed by the
Honorable John Marshall - see the latter's legal papers in the Manuscript
Division, Alderman Library, University of Virginia, #1106.]

HUDSON, CHAROLOUS B. and Patsey Headley*, bond 23 March 1833. William Hale (b).
MBB.,p.104

HUDSON, HENRY O. and Kitty S.J. Gordon*, bond 14 June 1822. William Reuick (b).

HUDSON, HENRY O. and Mary Pew, bond 7 February 1848. Consent by Martin Pew,
father of the bride. Richard H. Harrison (b); John H. Cox (w). MBB.,p.306

HUDSON, JOHN and Betsy Brown*, bond 20 January 1795. Thomas Hogan (b). Nancy
Hogan (w), Thomas Hogan (w), Hugh Harris (w) and Nancy Harris (w).

HUDSON, MEREDITH and Elizabeth Richards*, bond 23 February 1815. William Alderson (b); Henry O. Hudson (w).

HUDSON, MEREDITH and Elizabeth F. Lewis, license 10 March 1852. Consent by
Thomas P. Lewis, father of the bride. Jeremiah S. Lewis (w) and R.H. Harrison (w). Married 10 March 1852 by the Rev. John Godwin.

HUDSON, PRESLEY and Catherine S. Jackson, bond 18 March 1812. Meredith Hudson
(b). Consent by Daniel Jackson; no relationship stated.

HUDSON, PRESLEY of Northumberland County and Eliza W. Alderson, bond 30 January
1818. Consent by Luke Jackson, guardian of the bride. Daniel Flinn (b).
[The Fredericksburg Virginia Herald of 7 March 1818 announced the marriage
on the 4th of February 1818 "in Richmond County, Va., by the Rev. Mr. Charles
Bell, [of] Presley Hudson, Esq. of Northumberland County to Miss Eliza W.
Alderson of Richmond County."]

HUDSON, RAWLEIGH and Hannah Norwood, bond 3 January 1778. Consent by Ann Norwood, mother of the bride; the bride also signs the consent. Thaddeus Jackson (b).

HUDSON, ROBERT H. and Elizabeth Self, bond 15 June 1848. Consent by Moses Self,
father of the bride. Joseph P. Delano (b).   MBB.,p.310

HUDSON, SAMUEL and Nancy Lewis*, bond 9 August 1825. William Hale (b); Fanny
Lewis (w).   MBB.,p.12

HUDSON, WILLIAM and Sarah Brann*, bond 12 December 1831. Samuel A. Efford (b);
John Roe (w).   MBB.,p.82

HUDSON, WILLIAM R. (bachelor) and Catharine Davis (spinster), bond 18 December
1828. Consent by Martha Hudson, mother and guardian of the groom; also con-

sent by Caty Alderson, mother and guardian of the bride. George Delano (b);
John Wroe (w) and Hiram S. King (w).   MBB.,p.48

HUGHES, JOHN and Sally Hammack*, bond 28 August 1805. John Hammack (b).

HUGHES, THOMAS (16??-1766) of Richmond, King George and Orange counties, married
    (1) by 4 April 1717 Frances (Sterne) Pannell, widow of William Pannell (circa
    1670-1716) (q.v.); married (2) by 1748 Elizabeth   [?]   , who survived
    him. By will dated 2 August 1765 and proved 26 June 1766, Thomas Hughes
    mentions his children by both of his aforementioned wives. He must not be
    confused with Thomas Hughes who died intestate in King George County in 1759
    [King George County COB#3,p.875,877 - 6 September 1759].   Richmond County
    COB#7,p.106; DB#7,p.335; King George County DB#A-1,p.311; DB#3,p.261;
    Orange County WB#2,p.362.

HUMPHRIES, ELIAS and Fanny Forrester*, bond 12 August 1783. Maximillion Haynie
    (b); Bridgett Forester (w) and Robert Forester (w).

HUNDLEY, JOHN of Essex County and Elizabeth G. McTier [Mactier]*, bond 17 Decem-
    ber 1823. Washington Glascock (b).

HUNDLEY, WILLIAM L. and Eliza Ann Forester*, bond 16 March 1846. Richard P.
    Forester (b); William W. Forester (w).   MBB.,p.274

HUNT, GEORGE married Elizabeth Barber, 5 June 1730.   NFPR.,p.211
    [The bride was the daughter of Colonel Charles and Frances (Glascock) Bar-
    ber (q.v.) p.9. He died testate in Northumberland County in 1745 and his
    will is of record in Northumberland County Record Book 1743-1749,p.79a.]

HUNT, GEORGE and Judith Glascock, bond 19 September 1778. George Glascock, Jr.
    (b).

HUNTER, JOHN [CAPTAIN] of Westmoreland County and Sally Davis*, bond 24 October
    1809. John Wright (b).

HUNTER, JOHN of Westmoreland County and Sally T. Reynolds, bond 20 December 1826.
    Edwin Waller (b).   MBB.,p.26

HUNTON, JAMES of Fauquier County and Hannah Lee Brown, bond 4 February 1786.
    Consent by Elen Brown, mother of the bride. Daniel Brown (b).

HUNTON, ROBERT and Eleanor Brown (spinster), bond 25 February 1782. Consent
    by Elen Brown, Sen. and Elenor Brown for Mr. Robert Hunton to obtain license
    to wed the said Eleanor Brown. Daniel Brown (b); William Whealey (w).

HUNTON, WILLIAM W. of Fauquier County and Sally Cannan*, bond 17 September 1805.
    Bryant Phillips (b); Ludwell A. Hunton (w) and Rawleigh Hazard (w).

HUTT, GERARD and Elenor Demeritt, bond 12 December 1804. James Rice (b).

HUTT, RICHARD B. of Westmoreland County and Evelina S. Glascock, bond 21 January
    1819. Consent by Ann T. Glascock, mother of the bride. Horace Wellford (b).

HUTT, STEPTOE D. of Alabama and Nancy N. Moxley*, bond 20 October 1836. Steptoe
    T. Rice (b) of Westmoreland County.   MBB.,p.149

                                    I

INGO, JAMES (26 April 1680-1725) married by 2 February 1704 Frances (Moss) Brown,
    elder daughter of William Moss, Sr. (1632-1685) of Rappahannock County and
    widow of William Brown (16??-1699) (q.v.). James Ingo was the elder of the
    two sons of John Ingo, Sr. (16??-1701) who died testate in Richmond County,
    and Mary, his wife. James Ingo died testate in Richmond County in 1725.
    DB#2,p.1-2; DB#3,p.168-170; DB#7,p.373; MRB.,p.27-37; WB#2,p.27; WB#4,p.255.

ISLES, ABSOLOM and Betty Palmer (widow), bond 22 February 1786. James Keasar (b).

IVES, WILLIAM and Lucy Guilliams, bond 5 May 1764. John Hammock (b).

                                    J

JACKSON, DANIEL and Sarah Jesper, bond 8 December 1785. Consent by Cathren (sic)
    Jesper, mother of the bride. William Sadler (b).

JACKSON, DANIEL and Mary Dozier, bond 12 February 1803. Richard Dozier (b).

JACKSON, DANIEL and Lucy Burch (widow)*, bond 9 December 1806. George Jesper
    (b); Richard Dozier (w).

JACKSON, DANIEL and Ann Bricky (widow), bond 20 August 1814. Meredith Hudson
    (b).

JACKSON, LUKE and Rebecca Dobyns, bond 18 February 1786. Consent by William
    Dobyns, father of the bride, she "being under the age of 21 years." Thomas
    Jesper (b); Lucy Morris (w).

JACKSON, LUKE and Ann Dobyns (spinster)*, bond 28 February 1794. Bartholomew
    McCarty (b); Charles Bailey (w). Charles Bailey writes Mr. Bartholomew
    McCarty, clerk of the court, he will be security for Mr. Luke Jackson on
    his marriage bond and authorizes Mr. McCarty to sign his name on the said
    bond; this note is dated 24 December 1794.

JACKSON, LUKE and Sally Alderson*, bond 3 June 1815. Samford Jones (b).

JACKSON, NATHANIEL and Ann Berrick, license April 1715.   DB#6,p.275

JACKSON, NATHANIEL and Hannah Redman, bond 8 March 1785. John Smith (b).

JACKSON, VINCENT and Ann Hutt, bond 1 September 1766. Benjamin Bramham (b).

JACKSON, WILLIAM and Catharine Allison, bond 7 May 1792. Daniel Lawson (b).

JACOBS, JOHN married Mary Cary, 8 November 1680.   NFPR.,p.121

JACOBS, WILLIAM and Mary Bridges (spinster), bond 23 April 1753. Thomas Barber,
    Jr. (b).

JACOBUS, ANGELL (16??-1698) appears on the records of Rappahannock, Richmond
    and Middlesex counties; he had several land patents. He married (1) by
    1688 Elizabeth Clark(e), daughter of Henry and Joan Clark(e) of Rappahan-
    nock County; and (2) 12 July 1694 Ann Vallott, widow of Claud Vallott who
    died 29 January 1693 in Christ Church Parish, Middlesex County. Angell
    Jacobus is described as a cooper of North Farnham Parish; his will was ad-
    mitted to probate 2 November 1698 but was recorded in now lost Richmond
    County WB#1. COB#2,p.345; DB#1,p.1; DB#2,p.157,229; Rappahannock County
    DB#7,p.543 and DB#8,p.4; The Parish Register of Christ Church, Middlesex
    County, Va. (Richmond, 1897), p.53; Middlesex County, Miscellaneous Deeds
    1687-1750,p.31.

JAMES, FRANCIS (16??-1721) of Richmond, Westmoreland and King George counties,
    married (1) by 8 February 1685 Mary Sherwood, eldest of the four daughters
    of Philip Sherwood, deceased, whose land fell into Richmond County in 1692;
    m(2) by 24 October 1717 Margaret ___[?]___ who is mentioned in his will of
    this date. The will of Francis James is of record in King George County
    Deed (sic) Book #1,p.6. Richmond County COB#2,p.313, DB#2,p.133; 23T116,
    207,278. See David Ross(i)er, p.173.

JAMES, JOHN married prior to 1 December 1727 Anne Trent, daughter of James Trent
    (16??-1707) of Richmond County. WB#2,p.113; King George County DB#1,p.469.

JAMES, THOMAS married long before 1715 Mary Willis, daughter of John Willis, Sr.
    (16??-1715) of Richmond County; he bequeathed them land which fell into King
    George County. Thomas and Mary (Willis) James separated and she sued for
    alimony for the support of herself and children; he was placed under a peace
    bond for £50 Sterling. Richmond County WB#3,p.214-217; King George County
    COB#1,p.16,125 and DB#2,p.398.

JAMES, THOMAS and Grace Kirkham (widow), license December 1714. DB#6,p.275
    [Thomas James died testate in North Farnham Parish in 1727. WB#5,p.78.]

JARRETT, SHERVELL and Winifred Davis, bond 24 December 1746. John Doren (b).
    [The bride was the daughter of Robert and Susanna (Jacobus) Davis (q.v.),
    p.51; she was mentioned in the will of her only brother, Robert Davis, Jr.,
    who d.s.p. in 1748. WB#5,p.558.]

JARRETT, SHERVILL and Elizabeth Hammond (spinster), bond 13 January 1751. Henry
    Williams (b).

        JASPER   SEE :   JESPER : JASPER

JEFFRIES, EBENEZER and Susan Ann Belfield, bond 22 April 1834. Pearson Cauthorn
    (b).   MBB.,p.119

JEFFRIES, EBENEZER and Ann A. Jeffries, license 11 June 1853. Consent by Eben:
    Jeffries, father of the bride. Married 14 June 1853 by Rev. Penfield Doll.

JEFFRIES, EDMUND R. of Westmoreland County and Nancy H. Brown*, bond 26 March 1798. Thomas Hogan (b); Nancy Hogins (w), Sally Hall (w), and Hannah B. Hogan (w). "I have no objection. (signed) Hugh France."

JEFFRIES, GRIFFIN of Westmoreland County and Elizabeth Douglass, bond 17 May 1814. Edmund R. Jeffries (b).

JEFFRIES, JOSEPH R. and Myrenda Hutt, license 23 January 1851. Consent by S.S. Hutt, parent of the bride. J.V. Garland (w). Married 23 January 1851 by the Rev. Alfred Wiles.

JEFFRIES, RICHARD O. and Emily Rockwell, bond 16 October 1838. Consent by Seth Rockwell, father of the bride. Thomas L. Darby (b); Thomas Oldham (w).
MBB.,p.175

JEFFRIES, RICHARD ORLANDO and Eleanor Ann Bramham, bond 16 December 1824. Ellzey Atchison (b). MBB.,p.4

JEFFRIES, ROBERT and Elizabeth Chinn*, bond 7 March 1796. Thomas Belfield (b).

JEFFRIES, ROBERT G. and Sally Hall (widow)*, bond 1 January 1799. Thomas Hogins (b); Nancy Hogins (w) and Nancy Jeffries (w).

JEFFRIES, THOMAS (17??-1833) of Richmond County married by 1804 Ann Adams Smith (born 25 November 1772), eldest child of Colonel William and Mary (Belfield) Smith of Essex County (q.v.). Essex County WB#36,p.380; WB#13,p.454.

JEFFRIES, THOMAS H. and Clementina Webb, bond 16 April 1831. William S. Belfield (b). MBB.,p.76
[Clementina Webb (21 October 1810-26 July 1870), daughter of Jeremiah and Apphia (Northen) Webb (q.v.), m(1) 16 April 1831 Thomas H. Jeffries and m(2) 2 December 1841, William Young Sturman (7 February 1788-8 July 1848). AB#11, p.346, division of the estate of Jeremiah Webb in 1860. 17W(2)105-106; ECD Papers in VHS Box #24.]

JEFFRIES, WILLIAM R. and Eleanor Weathers, bond 24 December 1818. Consent by John Weathers, father of the bride. William Y. Sturman (b); Thomas C. Amory (w). [See notes under the bride's father, John Weathers (1763-1822), p.225.]

JENIFER, JAMES C. and Louisa R. Tayloe were married 4 December 1850 by the Rev. Mr. William N. Ward, Minister of the Gospel in the Protestant Episcopal Church. No license found; this from Rev.Mr. Ward's minister's returns.

JENKINS, BLADEN and Elizabeth Sandford*, bond 18 December 1849. James A.B. Sanders (b); Joseph M. Crask (w). MBB.,p.329
Married 19 December 1849 by the Rev. Mr. John Pullen.

JENKINS, HENRY and Selina Crask*, bond 27 March 1845. John F. Morris (b).
Married 28 March 1845 by the Rev.Mr. William Balderson. MBB.,p.257

JENKINS, JAMES and Frances Marks, license 6 January 1851. Consent by John B. Scates, guardian of the bride. George Jenkins (w) and Joseph F. Sanders (w). Married 9 January 1851 by the Rev. Mr. John Pullen; R.B. Ambrose (w).

JENKINS, JAMES and Ann Hall*, license 22 January 1851. James A.B. Sanders (w) and Daniel Sanford (w). Married 23 January 1851 by Rev. William Balderson.

JENKINS, JAMES and Ann Jenkins*, license 28 March 1853. William H. Morris (w); Bladen Jenkins (w) and Elizabeth Jenkins (w). Married 31 March 1853 by Rev. John Pullen.

JENKINS, JAMES H. and Mary Sanders*, license 20 October 1851. Bladen Hall (w) and T.N. Balderson (w). Married 23 October 1851 by Rev. William Balderson.

JENKIN[G]S, JOEL R. and Margaret Smith*, bond 5 March 1827. James Jones (b); Elizabeth Smith (w).   MBB.,p.29

JENKINS, JOHN and Judith Brown (widow)*, bond 25 February 1818. John Alloway (b).

JENKINS, JOHN and Martha Jenkins*, bond 4 December 1848. John Sanders (b); Henry Jenkins (w), William H. Morris (w) and John Sanders, Sr. (w). Married 6 December 1848 by Rev. John Pullen.   MBB.,p.316

JENKINS, MATTHEW and Eliza Richards*, bond 8 December 1840. John Pullin (b); Matthew Bartlett (w). Married 8 December 1840 by Rev. John M. Waddey.
                                                                    MBB.,p.200

JENKINS, MATTHEW JR. and Emmaline Susan Harper*, bond 20 November 1849. William L. Lee (b); Joseph Moore (w). Married 28 November 1849 by Rev. William N. Ward.   MBB.,p.328

JENKINS, PETER and Rebecca Thompson*, bond 28 December 1818. The contracting parties are described as "free persons of colour;" Hanamore Thompson also consents to the marriage but no relationship is stated. Henry Thompson (b); William Brickey,Sr., (w) and Moriah Williams (w).

JENKINS, ROBERT and Sally Bragg, bond 4 August 1800. Consent by Charles Bragg, father of the bride. William Morris (b).

JENKINS, ROBERT A. and Ann Bryant, bond 3 January 1842. Consent by Jesse Bryant, father of the bride. Jesse G. Bryant (b); William Harrison (w). MBB.,p.217

JENKINS, TASCOE C. and Wilalmira Clarke*, bond 25 December 1834. Richard Jenkins (b); John W. Jenkins (w).   MBB.,p.128

JENKINS, THOMAS and Eliz.ª Porter, license July 1714.   DB#6,p.275

JENKINS, THOMAS and Julia Saunders, bond 11 April 1838. Consent by Sally Saunders; no relationship stated. Married by Rev. Thomas M. Washington. Bladen Jenkins (b).   MBB.,p.171

JENKINS, THOMAS A. and Martha Carter*, license 1 December 1851. T.N. Balderson (w). Married 29 January 1852 by Rev. William Balderson.

JENKINS, WILLIAM (16??-1720) married Elizabeth Skelderman, one of the three dau-

ghters of Herman Skelderman who died testate in Rappahannock County in 1684
leaving land, which he had patented 11 July 1666, to his children. William
Jenkins died intestate in 1720 and his widow Elizabeth (Skelderman) Jenkins
died testate in 1739. They had several childen. DB#7,p.454; DB#9,p.210,
607,646; DB#12,p.142; WB#4,p.159; WB#5,p.348; Sweeny,p.108.

JENKINS, WILLIAM and Nancy Deately (spinster), bond 10 June 1778. Edmond Mitchell (b). The bond is signed William Jinkins and the bride's name is also
rendered Deatley.

JENKINS, WILLIAM and Priscilla Woollard, bond 27 November 1779. Edmond Mitchell
(b).

JENKINS, WILLIAM and Sarah Hinson, bond 25 March 1793. Consent by William and
Anna Hinson, parents of the bride. Richard Hall (b).

JENKINS, WILLIAM and Eliza Jenkins, bond 6 November 1848. William H. Morris (b).
MBB.,p.314

JENKINS, WILLIAM and Maria Jenkins*, bond 15 September 1850. Daniel Jenkins (w)
and James A.B. Sanders (w). Married 16 September 1850 by Rev.John Pullen.

JENNINGS, JAMES and Betsy France*, bond 26 January 1818. Samuel McGinnis (b);
John France (w). [Betsy France (25 January 1799-2 May 1838) was the daughter of John and Catharine (Fones) France (q.v.), p.72.]

JENNINGS, JAMES and Juley Beder*, bond 11 February 1845. John France (b); Joseph
Scates (w). Married 12 February 1845 by Rev. William Balderson. MBB.,p.255
[The bride's surname is rendered Bedow in the minister's returns.]

JENNINGS, JOHN and Elizabeth Kelly, bond 11 November 1824. John France (b).
MBB.,p.3

JESPER : JASPER

JESPER, GEORGE and Elizabeth Dunaway, bond 29 January 1795. Samuel Dunaway (b).

JESPER, GEORGE and Hannah Cookman, bond 3 January 1811. Newman Miskell (b).

JESPER, GEORGE and Peggy Wall*, bond 21 July 1813. Newman Miskell (b).

JASPER, RICHARD and Elizabeth Stonum, bond 30 December 1793. Consent by William
Stonum, guardian of the bride; she is the orphan of George Stonum, deceased.
Ezekiel Levy (b); Joseph Redman (w).

JESPER, ROBERT and Betty B. Harford, bond 15 January 1781. John Harford (b).

JESPER, SAMUEL B. and Elizabeth Flinn, bond 10 March 1814. Daniel Flinn (b).

JESPER, SAMUEL B. and Lucy Beale, bond 24 January 1816. Consent by Alice Beale,
mother of the bride, who states the bride is of age. John Hammack (b); John
Beale (w).

JESPER, THOMAS (16??-1748) married (1) circa 1700 Anne Lewis, one of the five
daughters and coheiresses of Edward Lewis, deceased; m(2) 1711 Sarah Taylor (see below).

JESPER, THOMAS and Sarah Taylor, license March 1710/11.   DB#6,p.275
[Sarah Taylor was born in North Farnham Parish 28 September 1692; she was
the daughter of Simon and Elizabeth (Lewis) Taylor (q.v.) and a niece of
Anne Lewis, first wife of the said Thomas Jesper. AB#1,p.327; DB#3,p.178;
DB#6,p.115; DB#9,p.186; WB#5,p.126,562,685,722.]

JESPER, THOMAS married Elizabeth Hammond, 12 November 1730.   NFPR.,p.123
[Thomas Jesper (1705-1760) was the son of Thomas and Anne (Lewis) Jesper
(q.v.), p.106.]

JASPER, THOMAS and [blank], bond 6 February 1760. LeRoy Peachey (b).
[This is probably the second marriage of Thomas Jesper (Jasper), Sr. (1705-
1760) as by will dated 20 October 1759 he mentions no wife, but when his
will was admitted to record 5 May 1760 (as well as subsequent records) the
indications are he was survived by a widow, Elizabeth Jesper. AB#1,p.442;
COB#14,p.358; WB#6,p.176.]

JESPER, THOMAS and Margaret N. Dobyns*, bond 24 December 1827. Joseph B. Kelsick (b).   MBB.,p.32

JESPER, THOMAS H. and Fanny Cadeen*, bond 30 May 1817. Chapman Austin (b);
Charles Palmer (w).

JESPER, WILLIAM and Haney Gupton, bond 25 December 1798. George Miskell (b).

JESPER, WILLIAM and Rutha Knott (spinster)*, bond 12 July 1794. Matthew Partridge (b); Matthew Partridge (w) and Elizabeth Bathan Partridge (w).

JESSE, THOMAS and Polly Greenwood Jesse (spinster)*, bond 4 July 1797. Consent
by John Jesse, guardian of the groom. The bride writes her own consent
stating she is 22 years of age. Richard Jesse (b); Thomas Mullins (w),
Benjamin Mullins (w) and John Rocherson (w).

JETT, PETER and Margaret James were cited for living in adultry on 8 March 1715.
It appears they later married. The wills of Peter Jett and his wife Margar-
et Jett were both admitted to probate on 27 November 1739 at Westmoreland
County court. [COB#6,p.408; Westmoreland County D&W#9,p.31.]

JETT, WILLIAM (16??-1698) married by 14 April 1681 Elizabeth (Hoskins) Wood (c.
1655-1699), widow of Cornelius Wood (16??-1677) and daughter of Anthony
Hoskins, Gentleman, (c.1613-1665) of Accomac County, and Joyce Jones, his
wife. William Jett was the son of the immigrant, Peter Jett (16??-1688)
a tailor, who with his wife Mary and children Peter Jett, Jr., William Jett,
Martha Jett and Mary Jett were "headrights" of Francis Triplett (16??-1701)
in 1666. John Washington, Gentleman, (1671-1719) of Stafford County, [only
child of Captain Lawrence Washington (1635-1677) and his second wife Joyce
(Jones) Hoskins Fleming] stated in a letter dated 22 June 1699 to his paternal half-sister Mary (Washington) Gibson then in England the following facts:

"My Mother had three Daughters when my Father married her, one died last winter and left four or five children, the other two are alive & married and have had several children." John Washington refers to the death of his maternal half-sister, Elizabeth (Hoskins) Wood Jett, in the winter of 1699; administration on her estate was granted to her daughter Mary Jett on 7 June 1699. COB#2,p.331,408,434-435; Accomac County W&D 1676-1690,p. 263; Patent Book #6,p.29 (29 January 1666); A.P.& P.,p.336-337; Americana, Volume 33,p.1-31; New Haven Genealogical Magazine, Volume 9, p.143 et seq.

JETT, WILLIAM N. [DOCTOR] and Virginia J. Mitchell*, license 29 November 1853. J.B. Jett (w). Married 1 December 1853 by Rev. G.M. Northam.

JOBSON, WILLIAM (16??-1717) married by 1715 Bridgett McLaughlin, eldest daughter of Manus and Elizabeth (Woodbridge) McLaughlin (q.v.). DB#7,p.40; DB#10,p. 42; WB#3,p.13,273; WB#4,p.3; WB#5,p.516; WB#6,p.93.

JOHNSON, JOHN and Nancy Clarke*, bond 22 March 1822. William Hammack (b).

JONES, BENJAMIN of North Wales, Great Britian, married long before 1731 Elizabeth Pugh, daughter of David Pugh of South Wales and sister of Lewis Pugh who settled in Richmond County by 1704. Benjamin and Elizabeth (Pugh) Jones were living in North Wales in 1731. AB#1,p.157-160.

JONES, CHARLES married Mary Hammock, 22 August 1727.   NFPR.,p.123

JONES, CLINTON and Catharine Brown, bond 19 June 1847. Consent by Thomas Brown, father of the bride. John France (b); T.N. Balderson (w).   Married 23 June 1847 by Rev. John Pullen.   MBB.,p.294

JONES, DAVID and Caty Baker*, bond 7 November 1781. John Amis Samford (b). In writing her own consent, the bride states that "I am of age and a right to act for myself."

JONES, EDWARD married Alicia Lunn, 27 August 1679.   NFPR.,p.121
[Alicia Lunn was probably the widow of William Lunn. The North Farnham Parish Register records the birth of Roger, son of William and Alicia Lun, on 28 February 1676 and also the birth of Mary, daughter of William and Alicia Lun, on 12 September 1673.]

JONES, EDWARD married Elizabeth Gower, 26 September 1728.   NFPR.,p.123

JONES, EDWARD and Jane Williams, bond X[ber] the 7th 1747; no bondsman. [The bride was the daughter of John Williams, Sr. who died testate in 1751. WB#5,p.659.]

JONES, EDWARD and Barbary Baker, bond 21 July 1750. Isaac Jones (b).

JONES, EDWARD JUNIOR and Margaret White (widow), license December 1714.
                                                             DB#6,p.275

JONES, EDWARD [REVEREND] and Hannah Suggitt, bond 27 May 1775. LeRoy Peachey (b).

JONES, EPAPHRODITUS and Sally Lewis Claughton, bond 14 December 1798. Consent
by Richard Claughton, father of the bride. James Pullen (b); Thomas Dugliss (w).

JONES, FRANCIS D. of Gloucester County and Lucy Jones Peck, bond 10 August 1832.
Harriot Peck (b).   MBB.,p.92

JONES, GEORGE and Milly Hogans, bond 1 January 1805. Jeduthan Hogans (b).

JONES, GEORGE and Alice Woollard*, bond 9 December 1845. Robert G. Lewis (b).
Married 11 December 1845 by Rev. Elijah L. Williams.   MBB.,p.267

JONES, GEORGE LEWIS of Northumberland County and Polly Sydnor Cookman, bond 16
January 1818. Consent by Ann Cookman; no relationship stated. Willis
Jones (b); Priscilla L. Jones (w).

JONES, GRIFFIN and Mary C. Stott (widow)*, bond 24 June 1816. John Garland (b).

JONES, JAMES and Alice Mothershead, bond 20 December 1825. Consent by Thomas
Jones, father of the groom. Newby Berrick (b).   MBB.,p.17

JONES, JAMES and Mary Hall*, bond 1 March 1847. Joseph N. Jones (b). Married
10 March 1847 by Rev. John Pullen.   MBB.,p.292

JONES, JEREMIAH NASH and Betty Connolly*, bond 7 September 1795. In writing her
own consent, Betty Connolly states "I am thirty years of age." George Connolly (b).

JONES, JESSE and Apphia Lewis, bond 25 April 1837. Consent by Affire Lewis;
no relationship stated. Ezekiel Headley (b); J.C. Tellis (w). MBB.,p.156

JONES, JOHN (16??-1716) married by 7 July 1703 Elizabeth (Fleming) Thornton,
widow of Rowland Thornton (16??-1701) (q.v.). COB#3,p.96,264; DB#7,p.118,
120.

JONES, JOHN married Sarah Mountjoy, 30 November 1725.   NFPR.,p.123
[The bride was the daughter of John and Ann (Thornton) Mountjoy (q.v.) and
a legatee of Henry Burdett who died testate in 1725. DB#8,p.295; DB#9,p.76,
WB#4,p.265; WB#5,p.6.]

JONES, JOHN of Essex County married by 28 November 1730 Elizabeth, daughter of
Jane wife of Edmund McLynch; he died testate in 1718 and mentioned her in
his will. DB#8,p.553; WB#4,p.48.

JONES, JOHN and Alice French*, bond 11 January 1836. Joseph Clarke (b); George
R. Thrift (w).   MBB.,p.141

JONES, JOSEPH N. and Patsy Weedon, bond 20 December 1831. Consent by Thomas
and Elizabeth Weedon; no relationship stated. Samuel Morris (b). MBB.,p.84

JONES, LODOWICK of Christ Church Parish, Middlesex County, married 6 May 1775
Lucy Tarpley, daughter of Major Travers Tarpley who died intestate in Rich-

mond county in 1768. Their only child, Elizabeth Travers Jones, died in infancy. The Parish Register of Christ Church, Middlesex County, Va. 1663-1812 (Richmond,1897), p.201; Middlesex County WB "G",p.30 and Middlesex County Miscelleanous Wills 1675-1798,p.406.

JONES, NEBUCHADNEZZAR married Mary Birkett (16??-1745), daughter of John and Ann (Mills) Birkett (q.v.) p.18. Their only son, John Jones (16??-1719) d.s.p., but testate in Richmond County and their daughter Ann Jones married Charles Deane (q.v.) p.53. Mary (Birkett) Jones, widow, m(2) by 1719, Thomas Brock (q.v.) p.24. COB#8,p.142,162,189; DB#8,p.3; WB#2,p.9.

JONES, OWIN married Jane Wilkerson, 19 January 1730/1.   NFPR.,p.123

JONES, RICHARD and Elizabeth Dameron*, bond 19 January 1831. Edward K. Tune
    (b).   MBB.,p.73

JONES, RICHARD H. married 21 January 1819 Polly Walker.   WFMR.

JONES, ROBERT and Lucy Ann Carter, bond 29 December 1847. Consent by Rebecca
    Carter; no relationship stated. Daniel Carter, Jr. (b); William Carter
    (w).   MBB.,p.303

JONES, SAMFORD and Elizabeth Stephens*, bond 6 March 1790. Daniel Ruelk (b).

JONES, SANFORD and Rebecca Beacham Self, bond 15 August 1798. Consent by Vincent Clarke and Hannah, his wife, mother of Rebecca Beckham Self. William Jesper (b).

JONES, THOMAS and Rachel Scates, bond 3 September 1798. Consent by Sarah Scates, mother of the bride. John Fawcett (b).

JONES, THOMAS ap of Essex County and Elizabeth Fauntleroy, bond 8 May 1810. Joseph Fauntleroy (b). [See Judge Lewis H. Jones, Captain Roger Jones of London and Virginia (1911), p.57 et seq.]

JONES, THOMAS and Violett Broocke (widow), bond 20 February 1821. John Gordon
    (b).

JONES, THOMAS JR. and Margaret Northen*, bond 23 December 1848. Aldwin Northen
    (b); James L. Lamkin (w).   MBB.,p.318
    From Pleasant Hill on 23 December 1848 James L. Lamkin writes the court
    clerk that it is inconvient for him to come to the office. He states that
    the contracting parties have been living with him some year or two and he
    certifies the groom is of full age and the bride about 26 or 27 years old.
    Aldwin Northen (b), brother of the bride, is going on 23 years of age.

JONES, THOMAS D. and Elizabeth Weymoth, bond 4 May 1808. Rodham Pritchett (b).

JONES, VINCENT and Sally Scates, bond 22 December 1792. Consent by Joseph and Sarah Scates, parents of the bride. James Jennings (b).

JONES, VINCENT and Rebecca Sanders (spinster), bond 3 July 1797. Consent by
William Sanders, father of the bride, who states she is of full age. John
Eidson (b).

JONES, VINCENT and Mary Morris (spinster), bond 17 January 1829. John A. Payton (b).   MBB.,p.51

JONES, WILLIAM married Katherine Smith, 16 February 1725/6.   NFPR.,p.123

JONES, WILLIAM and Elinor Jeffries, bond 20 May 1749. Jeremiah Brown (b).

JONES, WILLIAM of Northumberland Court House, married 14 January 1819 at Northumberland Court House, Miss Kitty Elmore of Richmond County. They were
married by the Rev. Mr. Forester. The marriage was announced in the Fredericksburg Virginia Herald of 13 February 1819.

JONES, WILLIAMSON P. and Judith L. Tomlin, bond 11 January 1804. Bartholomew
McCarty (b). [The bride was the daughter of Colonel Walker Tomlin (17??-
1802) (q.v.). AB#3,p.80,629,635; WB#9,p.165.]

JORDAN, WILLIAM [GENTLEMAN] married (1) by 1733 Mary (Mountjoy) Morton, widow of
John Morton, Jr. (q.v.) who died intestate in 1728; the rich merchant, John
Morton Jordan, Gentleman, (173?-1771), of King George County was their only
child; married (2) by 1753 Ann (Foster) Barber, widow of Samuel Barber (q.v.)
who died testate in 1735. William Jordan, Gentleman, died intestate in 1757.
COB#10,p.83; COB#14,p.95; DB#9,p.677; DB#10,p.352; DB#11,p.186; WB#5,p.272;
WB#6,p.102.

JORDAN, RICHARD married by 4 March 1694/5 Cecely [Cisley] Barrow, daughter of
John Barrow who died testate in 1685. She m(2) Thomas Brock (q.v.),p.24.
DB#2,p.113-115; DB#5,p.142-145.

JORDAN, ROBERT married by 7 May 1707 Ann Jacobus, daughter of Angell and Eliza-
(Clarke) Jacobus (q.v.),p.102. DB#4,p.104,155; DB#5,p.96.

JOY, JOSEPH and Sarah Efford*, bond 1 May 1815. Samford Jones (b).

                                    K

KAY, JAMES (16??-1698) married circa 1687 Mary Pannell, daughter of Thomas Pannell
(16??-1677) of Rappahannock County. She married (2) circa 1700, Francis
Stone (16??-1716) (q.v.). COB#2,p.330; COB#3,p.22,30,50; WB#2,p.30; Essex
County DB#9,p.32,34,270; King George County DB#1,p.344,367; 20T171-180;
21T243-250.

KELLEY, EDWARD married Mary Goulding, 18 April 1726.   NFPR.,p.127

KELLY, ALEXANDER (17??-1754) married Elizabeth Willson, daughter of Henry Willson
(16??-1737). Their son James Kelly (1737-1802) married his cousin Susan Willson; she was born 4 October 1741. WB#5,p.303; WB#6,p.48; Payne 86-88; 15W(1)

129-131; 17W(1)27; Richmond County, Petition to the Legislature 20 December 1804, regarding the heirs of James Kelly,Sr. (1737-1802) of Richmond County.

KELLY, BECKHAM and Susanna McGinnis*, bond 9 January 1797. James Kelly,Jr. (b). In writing her own consent, the bride states she was born 3 August 1774.

KELLY, JAMES [CAPTAIN] and Winifred Eidson*, bond 6 August 1798. William Morris (b).

KELLY, JAMES JR. and Mary Dye*, bond 6 August 1792. William Bragg (b). In writing her own consent, the bride states she was born 11 April 1771 the daughter of Fauntleroy and Anne Dye.

KELLY, JOHN JR. and Ann B. Claytor*, bond 2 March 1801. Vincent Kelly (b).

KELLY, REUBEN and Nancy Crabb (widow), bond 5 December 1803. George Gill (b).

KELLY, REUBEN and Elizabeth Sanders*, bond 16 January 1847. Elijah Scates, Jr. (b); Zachariah Sanders (w). Married 20 January 1847 by the Rev. John Pullen.   MBB., p.287

KELLY, RICHARD H. and Sarah Bragg*, bond 1 January 1827. John Spence (w).
                                                                           MBB.,p. 27

KELLY, THADDEUS and Dinah Moore Gaskins "both free persons of colour," bond 21 October 1819. Consent by David Gaskins, father of the bride. Henry "a free person of colour," (b); Henry Beah (w).

KELLY, VINCENT and Susanna Eidson, bond 2 June 1800. Consent by Winnefred Kelly, mother of the bride. John Morris (b).

KELLY, WILLIAM and Patty Gill, bond 3 December 1798. George Gill (b).

KELSICK, JOSEPH B. and Parthenia Dobyns*, bond 18 December 1824. Edward J. Northen, Jr. (b); Edward J. Northen (w).   MBB.,p.5

KELSICK, SAMUEL and Mary Smith, bond 25 December 1781. Daniel Jackson (b). [4 May 1761: William Brockenbrough gives bond as guardian to Samuel Kelsick, son of Younger Kelsick with Landon Carter his security.]

KELSICK, SAMUEL B. and Jane C. Belfield, bond 13 May 1800. Consent by Thomas Belfield, father of the bride. Barnes Beckwith (b). [The bride was the daughter of Thomas and Ann Harwar (Beale) Belfield (q.v.),p.15-16. AB#4, p.123.]

KELSICK, YOUNGER [CAPTAIN], son of Richard and Eleanor (Younger) Kelsick of Whitehaven, Cumberland, England, married circa 1752 Mary Barnes (17??-1793), daughter of Richard and Penelope (Manly) Barnes (q.v.),p.10. Captain Younger Kelsick was a mariner. His marriage to Mary ("Molly") Barnes provoked a distasteful family controversy. In excluding the Kelsicks from participating in her estate, Mrs. Penelope (Manly) Barnes in her last will and Testament made derogatory remarks concerning Captain Younger Kelsick. Mary (Barnes)

Kelsick died testate in Richmond County in 1793. WB#9,p.5; see references under Captain Richard Barnes (q.v.),p.10.

KEM, WILLIAM T. and Mahala Hazard*, bond 5 December 1825. John Jenkins (b). Miskell Saunders (w); H.M. Dobyns (w).   MBB.,p.15

KENNAN   SEE : CANNAN

KENNAN, JOHN of Frederick County and Fanny Harris, bond 19 February 1798. George Miskell (b).

KENNAN, WILLIAM and Mahalah B. Hazard, bond 3 December 1832. Consent by William Hazard, father of the bride. Joseph Hazard (b).   MBB.,p.96

KENNEDY, JOHN [GENTLEMAN] of Saint Mary's County, Maryland, married by 2 July 1738 Catherine Heale, daughter of George Heale, Gentleman, deceased, of Lancaster County. DB#9,p.453; Lancaster County WB#13,p.45; 54V71-72.

KENNEDY, THOMAS A. and Sarah Pursell*, bond 6 October 1825. LeRoy Pursell (b). [ECD Papers, VHS Box #11, are notes in regard to this couple. These indicate Thomas Allen Kennedy was born 22 July 1796 at Falmouth, Stafford County, Virginia, and died 31 July 1871 at Lyells, Richmond County, Virginia. He married Sarah Davis Pursell (14 August 1802-7 April 1875), daughter of George and Sarah Pursell (Purcell) of Richmond County. WB#23,p.453.]

KENNER, RODHAM GRIFFIN and Elizabeth Clarke, bond 16 July 1792. John Smith (b).

KENNER, WILLIAM and Lucy Robbins, bond 17 March 1795. Consent by James Robbins, father of the bride. Jonathan Abbay (b).

KENNON, LEFEVRE (bachelor) and Elizabeth Miskell (spinster), bond 25 June 1828. Samuel Miskell (b).   MBB.,p.38

KESER, JAMES and Nancy Nickerson*, bond 2 December 1847. George S. Richardson (b).   MBB.,p.302

KEY   SEE : KAY

KEY, HENRY GREENFIELD SOTHORON of Maryland and Henrietta Hill Tayloe, bond 19 June 1815. Consent by John Tayloe of Mount Airy, father of the bride. Robert W. Carter.

KEYSER, WALTER and Lucinda Sebree, bond 7 July 1834. Gilbert Sebree (b).
                                                                      MBB.,p.121

KILPATRICK, SAMUEL and Mary A. Luckham, license 11 August 1851. Fleet W. Lewis (w) and B. Dodson (w). Married 12 August 1851 by Rev. Bartholomew Dodson.

KING, HENRY P.F. (bachelor) and Juliet Ann Dobyns (spinster)*, bond 15 May 1839. In writing her own consent the bride states she is 24 years of age. William S. Hale (b); John King (w).   MBB.,p.182

KING, HIRAM S. and Hannah Harrison*, bond 1 July 1822. Consent by Sally R. King, mother of the groom. William Brickey, Sr. (b); Ann Brickey (w).

KING, JAMES of Westmoreland County and Ann O. Brown, bond 3 August 1812. Consent by John Hughes, guardian of the bride and by William King, guardian of the groom. John King of Richmond County (b).

KING, JOHN married Elizabeth Dozier, 29 August 1727.   NFPR.,p.123

KING, JOHN and Katherine Hammond, bond 19 July 1765. LeRoy Peachey (b).

KING, RICHARD married by 20 April 1693 the widow of John Cannada [Kennedy], deceased. DB#3,p.121.

KING, SAMUEL of Westmoreland County and Sarah Rowe (spinster), bond 9 March 1802. Consent by Sary Rus Wroe, a guardian of the bride. John Potter (b); William King (w) and Jane Street (w).

KING, WILLIAM married by 3 September 1713 the widow of James Willson, deceased. COB#6,p.149.

KING, WILLIAM married Mary Piarse, 14 June 1727.   NFPR.,p.123

KING, WILLIAM and Martha Ann Kent, bond 6 August 1842. Consent by Lucy Sydnor, mother of the bride. William P. Middleton (b); Robert Sydnor (w) and James King (w).   MBB.,p.226

KIRCUM, JAMES of Northumberland County and Frances Mitchell of Lunenburg Parish, Richmond County, bond 16 November 1778. William Kircum (b). The court clerk renders the surname KIRKHAM in the body of the bond but both men sign KIRCUM.

KIRK, JOHN and Abigail Harrison*, bond 1 October 1792. Thomas Franklin (b); W. Ferguson (w).

KIRK, RANDALL R. of Northumberland County and Jane L. Straughan, bond 1 December 1810. John C. Straughan (b); he is guardian of the bride. Betsy S. Straughan (w) and Jane Beacham (w).

KIRK, THOMAS and Ellender T. Yeatman, bond 20 January 1823. Levi Yeatman (b); he makes oath both parties are of full age. William Smart (w).

KIRK, THOMAS and Lucinda Allen, bond 19 April 1845. Consent by Rachel Allen, mother of the bride. John W. Jones (b); James H. Rust (w). Married 22 April 1845 by the Rev. Elijah L. Williams.   MBB.,p.258

KIRK, WILLIAM of King George County and Frances Mitchell, bond 17 June 1788. Consent by Charity Dunkan; no relationship to either party stated. Richard Littrell (b).

KIRKMIRE, FREDERICK and Sally Stonum*, bond 23 December 1805. Daniel Scurlock (b).

KNIGHT, JOHN of Stafford County and Katherine Phillips, license June 1715.
                                                          DB#6,p.275
[Katherine (Catherine) Phillips was the only child of James and Isabella
(Pannell) Phillips (q.v.) and as such on 24 March 1715/16 the said John
Knight and Catherine, his wife, sold certain land in Richmond County which
descended to her as the only heir of her mother Isabella (Pannell) Phillips,
to Francis Thornton and Anthony Thornton, Gentlemen. The deed is not re-
corded in Richmond County; it was probably recorded at the General Court of
Virginia, which records were destroyed in 1865. Barton's Virginia Colonial
Decisions, Volume I,p.R31, states that Isabella Pannell married "Rich'd
Phillips;" this is an error.]

                                    L

LAMBERT, JAMES and Elizabeth Clarke*, bond 9 January 1810. Randall Clarke (b);
    William Clarke (w).

LAMBERT, WILLIAM and Ann Baley (widow), license May 1715.   DB#6,p.275

LAMBERT, WILLIAM and Frances Clarke, bond 16 February 1846. Consent by Meshac
    Clarke, father of the bride. Samuel R. Hardwick (b); John H. Cox (w).
                                                          MBB.,p.273

LAMPTON, WILLIAM and Frances White (widow), license November 1715. DB#6,p.275
    [William Lampton (16??-1723) of Richmond and King George counties is de-
    scribed as a "planter" and "Gentleman," in contemporary records. By patent
    and purchase he acquired a considerable landed estate which he bequeathed
    to his children by his last will and Testament dated 21 October 1722. This
    document was admitted to probate 1 February 1722/23 but was recorded in now
    lost King George County WB#1 (1721-1752); his widow Esther (Hester) Lampton
    qualified as administratrix with the will annexed. William Lampton married
    (1) unknown by whom he had issue (a) William Lampton (c.1706-1760) of Spot-
    sylvania County who became the great-great-grandfather of Samuel Langhorne
    Clemens ("Mark Twain"); (b) Ann Lampton who married c.1730 John Grigsby, Jr.
    of Stafford County and removed to Fauquier County where he died c.1771; and
    (c) Samuel Lampton who d.s.p., under age, prior to 1730. William Lampton
    married (2) per license November 1715, Frances White childless widow of
    Thomas White who died testate earlier this same year; he had no issue by
    her and she died testate in 1716. William Lampton married (3) in 1717 Hest-
    er (Esther) Davis (169?-c.1762), daughter of Joshua Davis, Gentleman, (16??-
    1710), prominent attorney at law of Richmond County, and had an only child,
    (d) Joshua Lampton who appears on the records of Prince William and Culpeper
    counties. Hester (Davis) Lampton, widow, married (2) James Jones (16??-1744)
    of Hanover Parish, King George County; he owned considerable real estate in
    King George, Orange, Culpeper, Prince William and Fauquier counties. The will
    of James Jones was recorded in now lost King George County WB#1; he was a
    architect and master-builder and the inventory of his handsome personal estate
    remains of record in King George County Inventory Book #1,p.306. James and
    Hester (Davis) Jones had three children, viz: (a) Honorable Joseph Jones
    (1727-1805), member of Congress, judge of the General Court of Virginia and

gentleman of affairs in Virginia; (b) Elizabeth Jones married in 1752 Spence
Monroe, Gentleman, (1727-1774) of Westmoreland County - they were the parents
of President James Monroe (1758-1831); (c) Esther Jones (173?-1778) married
by 1755 William Tyler, Gentleman, (17??-1772) of Westmoreland County and had
several children named in her will and also that of the Honorable Joseph Jones. COB#6,p.452,517; DB#7,p.143,145-155,311; WB#3,p.280; King George County
COB#1,p.67,109,280; DB#1-A,p.110; DB#3,p.320 and other indexed Lampton-Jones
instruments; Clayton Keith, Sketch of the Lampton Family in America 1740-1914
(CS71:L236).]

LANDMAN, VINCENT and Jane Shirley, bond 1 September 1810. Mary More gives her
   consent for the marriage, but there is no relationship stated. Rodham Pritchett (b).

LANDMAN, VINCENT and Elizabeth Stephens*, bond 24 October 1814. George Harris
   (b); John Garland (w).

LANDRUM, JOHN married Elizabeth Landrum in Richmond County, 1 May 1763, by the
   Rev. Mr. William Douglas. William Macfarlane Jones, The Douglas Register
   (Richmond,1928),p.30.

LANDON, GEORGE H. and Mary A. Spillman*, bond 13 May 1850. William Evans (b).
                                                              MBB.,p.337

LANE, WILLIAM and Ann Willson, bond 1 May 1754. John Willson (b).

LANKFORD, HENRY LOINS of Gloucester County married between 25 August 1781 and 18
   March 1795 Isabel Robins, daughter of William and Ellen (Thornton) Robins
   (q.v.). DB#17,p.100; WB#7,p.403.

LATHAM, ROBERT W. of Goochland County and Matilda Howe, bond 11 November 1835.
   Peter T. Duff (b).   MBB.,p.136

LAURENCE, WILLIAM married 16 X^embr 1683 Johannah Sydnor, both of Lancaster County. The Parish Register of Christ Church, Middlesex County,Va. 1653-1812
   (Richmond,1897),p.22.

LAWSON, DANIEL JUNIOR and Mary Garland, bond 25 June 1783. George Garland (b).

LAWSON, DANIEL JUNIOR and Catherine Williams, bond 9 January 1809. Consent by
   Catherine Williams, mother of the bride. John Redman, Sr. (b). [The bride
   was born in North Farnham Parish, 8 September 1790, the daughter of Thaddeus
   and Catherine (Corrie) Williams (q.v.).]

LAWSON, JOHN and Mary Dew, license January 1715/16.   DB#6,p.275

LAWSON, RICHARD and Mary Harris, married 22 September 1727.   NFPR.,p.134

LAWSON, RICHARD and Isabella Barber Kelsick, bond 31 August 1792. Samuel Kelsick (b). [The bride was the daughter of Captain Younger and Mary (Barnes)
   Kelsick (q.v.). AB#3,p.137,198; WB#9,p.5.]

LAWSON, ROWLAND of Lancaster County (16??-1716) married Jane (Jean) Glascock, daughter of Thomas and Ann Glascock. COB#6,p.297,365; WB#3,p.163; Lancaster County WB#10,p.189,201.

LAWSON, WILLIAM married by 22 August 1699 Isabel Kenney [Kennedy, Kennida, Cannida &c:], daughter of John Kenney, deceased. DB#1,p.53; Sweeny,p.51.

LAWSON, WILLIAM and Ann Harrison Rust, bond 24 October 1772. Stanley Gower (b).

LAWSON, WILLIAM and Melissa Glascock, bond 25 December 1810. Consent by Milton S. Glascock, who states the bride is of lawful age. Thomas M. Glascock (b).

LEACOCK, DANIEL and Nancy Thrift, bond 5 August 1789. Consent by Amey P. George, mother of the bride. Thomas Franklin (b). Thomas Pritchett (w).

LEADER, RICHARD and Elizabeth Littrell*, bond 25 October 1837. John Littrell (b).   MBB.,p.159

LEE, FRANCIS LIGHTFOOT married 25 May 1769 Rebecca Plater Tayloe, daughter of the Honorable John and Rebecca (Plater) Tayloe of Mount Airy. On 31 May 1769 Philip Ludwell Lee of Stratford wrote his brother William Lee in London a very newy letter of "This ... marrying year," in which in mentions thirteen marriages, including: "Our brother Franc: Lee was married to Miss Rebec: Tayloe last Thursday."   Francis Lightfoot Lee (1734-1797) and his wife nee Rebecca Plater Tayloe (1752-1797) resided at Menokin in Richmond County; they died there in the winter of 1797 with a month of each other. Her obituary appeared in the Fredericksburg Republican Citizen of 11 January 1797 and his in the Fredericksburg Republican Citizen of 15 February 1797 and the Fredericksburg Virginia Herald of 14 February 1797. Edmund Jennings Lee, Lee of Virginia, 1642-1892 (Philadelphia,1895),p.167; Ethel Armes, Stratford Hall, The Great House of the Lees (Richmond,1936), p.108-112 et seq; Eubank, p.86; 6W(1)153.

LEE, HENRY married 1 December 1753 in James City Parish, James City County, Va., by the Rev. Mr. William Preston, Lucy Grymes, daughter of Charles Grymes, Esq., deceased, of Richmond County, Va. New York Public Library, Manuscript Division, Virginia Box, contains the original certificate. The ancestry of Lucy (Grymes) Lee is recited in Richmond County DB#12,p.680, and Ethel Armes, Stratford Hall, The Great House of the Lees (Richmond,1936).p.225-229,527, imparts interesting facts. See also 22W(2)151-154.

LEE, RICHARD C. married 26 February 1852 Margaret M. Garrett, by the Rev. Mr. Elijah L. Williams. [Minister's returns; no license found.]

LEE, THOMAS LUDWELL and Fanny Carter, bond 6 December 1785. LeRoy Peachey (b). [Colonel Thomas Ludwell Lee was the son of Thomas Ludwell Lee (1730-1778) of Belleview, Stafford County, Va. and Mary Aylett, his wife, daughter of Colonel William Aylett of Westmoreland County. Colonel Lee removed to Coton in Loudoun County and with his wife Fanny sold the handsome Belleview estate on 10 June 1799 to William Alexander, Esq. of Stafford County. Fanny (Carter) Lee was the daughter of Robert Wormeley Carter of Sabine Hall. Chester Horton Brent, The Descendants of Coll. Giles Brent, Cap. George Brent

and Robert Brent, Gent., (Rutland, Vermont, 1946),p.154; Beale,p.50,243.
Shortly after the marriage of Thomas Ludwell and Frances (Carter) Lee he
is mentioned in the following letter; it was written from Green Spring in
James City County to the Honorable Robert Carter at Nomony Hall in Westmoreland County:

                                              Green Spring
                                              March 9th 1787
      Sir
         I am much concerned at learning that nothing has been yet done
      towards liquidating my debt to you. Colonel Thomas Ludwell Lee of
      Belleview, who is now here, tells me that at your request he did in-
      form your agent Mr. Carr what balance was due to you which is all
      that I am able to do myself as the late confused times occassioned
      my Books and papers to be dispersed over various parts of Europe.
      Col. Lee promises me that he will wait on you in a few days after
      his return to Sabine Hall, and as there are some considerable debts
      due to me in your neighbourhood, he will in all probability settle
      your demand very speedily and to your satisfaction.
         I am with very great respect and esteem,
                                        Sir,
                                           Your Most Ob.^{t} Humble Servt
                                              W.Lee
      [Addressed]
            The Hon. Robert Carter
            Nomony Hall

LEMOINE, FERIOL JR. and Ann Maria Saunders, bond 5 February 1833. George Saun-
      ders (b).   MBB.,p.102

LEVY, EZEKIEL and Frances Sydnor, bond 28 September 1787. Consent by John Syd-
      nor; no relationship stated. Epaphroditus Lawson (b).

LEWIS, GEORGE JR. and Hannah Walker*, bond 26 February 1816. Meredith Hudson
      (b); Henry O. Hudson (w).

LEWIS, GEORGE JR. and Nancy Harris, bond 17 February 1819. Consent by William
      Harris, father of the bride. John Davis (b); Rebecah Jones (w).

LEWIS, GEORGE H. and Elizabeth H. Efford*, bond 14 December 1843. Robert G.
      Lewis (b). Married by the Rev. Nathan Healy.   MBB.,p.243

LEWIS, GRIFFIN and Lucy Suggitt, bond 18 September 1760. John Suggitt (b).
      [The bride was the daughter of Edgcomb Suggitt who died testate in Richmond
      County in 1753. In 1763 Griffin Lewis and Lucy, his wife, were residing in
      Amelia County, Virginia. DB#12,p.550; WB#6,p.6.]

LEWIS, HENRY and Jane Hammack*, bond 2 January 1818. John Sydnor, Jr. (b);
      Frances Hammack (w).

LEWIS, HIRAM B. married circa 1832 Nancy Winstead. He died 2 May 1851 and she
      3 August 1851. For issue see Mitchell Bible record, VSL:AD #25212.

LEWIS, ISAAC and Nancy Rice*, bond 29 March 1790. Consent by Charles Rice, father of the bride. Presley Clarke (b). Vincent Clarke (w) and George Shearly (w).

LEWIS, JAMES and Susanna Clarke, bond 7 February 1810. Consent by Lucy Clarke; no relationship stated. Lewis Hammack (b).

LEWIS, JAMES JUNIOR and Alice Forester (spinster), bond 25 August 1772. Robert Forester (b). [ECD's notes contain considerable date in regard to his couple. They indicate he was the son of Peter and Hannah (Nelms) Lewis of Northumberland County; James Lewis, Jr. died testate in Fleming County, Kentucky, in 1820. The children of James and Alice (For(r)ester) Lewis were: (a) Charles Nelms Lewis, born 26 June 1773, who married in 1801 in Fleming County, Kentucky, Betsy Bragg; (b) Elizabeth Lewis, born 14 February 1775, m(1) William Garland and (2) Charles Bell (q.v.),p.16,75; (c) Bridgett Lovelace Lewis, born 5 March 1777, married Mr. Gault; (d) Alice Lewis, born 4 September 1779, married Mr. Hawkins; (e) Hannah Lewis, born 22 January 1782, died in infancy; (f) Frances Lewis, born 12 October 1784, married Mr. Goddard; (g) James Lewis, born 31 May 1787; (h) Peter B. Lewis born in 1789, married Catherine Ringo; (i) Robert G. Lewis; (j) Nancy Lewis married in 1815 in Fleming County, Kentucky, John Ringo; and (k) William D. Lewis.]

LEWIS, JEREMIAH and Alice Hogans, bond 21 February 1809. Consent by Thomas Hogans and Alice Hogans; no relationship stated. Richard Hogans (b).

LEWIS, JEREMIAH and Keterah Thrift*, bond 27 April 1847. Richard H. Harrison (b); John Harrison (w).   MBB.,p.293

LEWIS, JOHN and Ann Greenlaw, bond 14 August 1786. Thomas Collins (b).

LEWIS, JOHN JR. of Northumberland County and Nancy Hogan*, bond 20 November 1809. Consent by Travers Hogan, father of the bride. Jeduthan Hogan (b).

LEWIS, JOSEPH B. of Northumberland County and Louisa M. Stott*, bond 11 December 1817. Thomas W. Bryant (b).

LEWIS, RICHARD married Mary Hix, on 3 March 1738.   NFPR.,p.134

LEWIS, RICHARD and Alice Alderson*, bond 28 February 1814. William Alderson (b).

LEWIS, ROBERT and Matilda Woollard*, bond 27 April 1835. Samuel B. Thrift (b); Mary Woollard (w) and Lemima Woollard (w).   MBB.,p.133

LEWIS, THOMAS and Joyce Hammon, license July 1712.   DB#6,p.275

LEWIS, THOMAS P. and Elizabeth Dameron, bond 23 October 1822. Matthew Harrison (b).

LEWIS, WILLIAM married by 5 April 1742 Ann Barber, daughter of Captain William and Joyce (Bayley) Barber (q.v.)p.9. DB#11,p.390.

LEWIS, WILLIAM of Northumberland County and Elizabeth Stuckey*, bond 20 May 1799.
In writing her own consent, Elizabeth Stuckky says she is "fully the age of
25 years." William Stuckey (b) and Richard Dawson (b); George Shearley (w)
and Mary Beachum Stuckky (w).

LEWIS, WILLIAM of Northumberland County and Fanny Bryant, bond 23 August 1809.
Joseph Bryant (b).

LEWIS, WILLIAM and Elizabeth Pearce, bond 1 April 1842. Orange Lowry (b);
Willia L. Winstead (w).   MBB.,p.222

LIGHTFOOT, DANIEL (17??-1755) married circa 1740 Alitia [Alicia, Elicca, Lisha,
Licia &c:] Algar; she was born 7 June 1724 in North Farnham Parish the daughter of Samuel and Mary Algar and granddaughter of Thomas and Alitia (Kennedy) Algar (q.v.) p.2. Their children were: (a) Ann Lightfoot, born 8 May
1743; (b) William Lightfoot, born 21 July 1745; (c) Betty Lightfoot, born
5 May 1750, married John Ames Samford (q.v.); (d) Samuel Lightfoot, born
1 November 1752 and (e) Thomas Lightfoot, born 31 March 1755, married Milly
Miskell; also Daniel Lightfoot (Jr.), whose birth is not recorded in NFPR,
next below. DB#12,p.126; DB#16,p.240; DB#18,p.434; WB#6,p.80,313; WB#5,p.602.

LIGHTFOOT, DANIEL and [not entered], bond 2 April 1771. William Smith (b).
[Daniel Lightfoot, son of Daniel and Alitia (Algar) Lightfoot (q.v.), married Mary Hinds, daughter of James Hinds who died testate in Richmond County in 1755. AB#1,p.571; WB#6,p.64.]

LIGHTFOOT, THOMAS and Milly Miskell, bond 28 September 1789. Thaddeus Williams
(b). [Thomas Lightfoot was born 31 March 1755, son of Daniel and Alitia
(Algar) Lightfoot (q.v.). The marriage of Thomas Lightfoot to Million
Miskell on 2 October 1789 is recorded in NFPR.,p.136.]

LIGHTFOOT, WILLIAM [GENTLEMAN] of Richmond and Orange counties, Virginia, and
Jefferson County, Kentucky,/per marriage contract dated 5 March 1746/7 of
record in Westmoreland County, Elizabeth Barrow, daughter of Edward and
Elizabeth (Minor) Barrow (q.v.) p.11. William Lightfoot (17??-1805) was
the son of Colonel Goodrich Lightfoot of Orange County. Westmoreland County D&W#10,p.332; Lightfoot Papers, College of William and Mary Library.

LINTON, WILLIAM (16??-1734) of Nomany, Westmoreland County, married (1) by 8
March 1704/5 Johanna Lewis, daughter of Edward Lewis of Richmond County;
their son and heir was Anthony Linton of Overwharton Parish, Stafford County. William Linton died testate in Westmoreland County in 1734; he married
(2) Mary (Hudson) Freshwater (see below), by whom he had no issue.

LINTON, WILLIAM married Mary Freshwater, 31 March 1730.   NFPR.,p.134
[She was the widow of Thomas Freshwater (16??-1726) (q.v.), p.74; Mary
(Hudson) Freshwater Linton died intestate in Westmoreland County in 1744/5.
DB#3,p.178; DB#6,p.115; DB#9,p.85,177,186; OPR.,p.69.]

LISLE, JOHN and Sophia Jackson, bond 16 November 17??. Daniel Jackson (b).
[The wording of the document indicates it was written ante 1776, but it is
filed in the 1796 bundle of marriage bonds.]

LITTMAN, WILLIAM and Frances Bowen, license February 1709/10.   DB#6,p.275
  [The bride was the daughter of Samuel Bowen (16??-1708) who died intestate
  in Richmond County. On 4 May 1737 William Letman and Frances, his wife,
  of Hanover Parish, King George County, conveyed land in that county which
  had been purchased 17 April 1677 by her father, Samuel Bowen, deceased, of
  Francis Triplett, the original patentee.King George County DB#2,p.104-107.]

  LITTRALL : LITTRELL : LITTRILL : LUTTRELL : LUTTRILL

LITTRALL, ALFRED and Jane Thrift*, license 8 January 1852. Thomas S. Nothen (w).
  Married 9 January 1852 by the Rev. Elijah L. Williams.

LITTRELL, JOHN and Elizabeth Gordon* (spinster), bond 29 March 1813. In writing
  her own consent, the bride states she is of "full age" and she is joined by
  her mother, Susannah Gordon, who also gives her consent. John Wroe (b).

LUTTRELL, JOHN P. and Ann H. Davenport*, bond 7 August 1826. Hiram Claughton
  (b).   MBB.,p.23

LUTTRILL, LEROY and Betsey H. Pope, bond 24 June 1795. John Pope (b).

LUTTRELL, RICHARD and Sarah Yeatman (spinster), bond 21 December 1752. William
  Thomas (b).

LUTTRELL, WILLIAM and Mary McGuire, bond not dated. Richard Packett (b).
  [The phraseology of the bond indicates it was written post 1776. It is filed in the 1796/with a number of other undated bonds.]

LITTRELL, WILLIAM and Sarah Jones*, bond 4 January 1844. James Scrimger (b).
  Married 4 January 1844 by the Rev. William N. Ward.   MBB.,p.244

LLOYD, EDWARD [ESQUIRE] of Maryland married on 19 November 1767 Miss Elizabeth
  Tayloe, daughter of the Honorable John Tayloe, Esquire, of Mount Airy in
  Richmond County. The marriage was announced in the Williamsburg Virginia
  Gazette of 26 November 1767. See Stella Pickett Hardy, Colonial Families
  of the Southern States of America (New York,1911), p.499-501; 6W(1)153.

LLOYD, JOHN [ESQUIRE] married 169? Elizabeth Carter (16??-1694) only daughter of
  Colonel John Carter (16??-1690) who died testate in Lancaster County. COB#1,
  p.168; COB#3,p.200,272; ECD Papers, VHS, Boxes #29 and #30.

LOCKHART, JAMES married circa 1708 Elizabeth (Moss) Crask(e) (16??-1710), daughter of William Moss, Sr. (1632-1685) and widow of Captain John Crask(e) (q.v.)
  p.46. DB#2,p.1-2; DB#3,p.162; DB#5,p.62,99-102; WB#2,p.120,126; WB#3,p.33.

LONGWITH, BURGESS and Jane Fergerson*, bond 16 October 1795. John Haw (b).
  Griffin G. Berrick (w).

LONGWITH, WILLIAM and Betsey Nash, bond 7 July 1788. Consent by Mary Nash, mother of the bride. George Berrick (b).

LONGWORTH, BURGIS and Polly C. Harrison, bond 20 October 1807. The bride writes her own consent and she is joined by her guardian, Jane Harrison. Daniel Harrison of Westmoreland County (b).

LONGWORTH, JOHN married by 7 May 1753 Catherine Pridham, youngest child of Christopher and Mary (Lewis) Pridham (q.v.); she was born in 1730. DB#11, p.250; WB#5,p.164.

LOVELACE, CHARLES (1696-1755) married by 1741 Bridgett (McLaughlin) Jobson, eldest daughter of Manus and Elizabeth (Woodbridge) McLaughlin (q.v.) and widow of William Jobson (q.v.). DB#7,p.40; DB#10,p.42; WB#3,p.13,273; WB#4,p. 3; WB#5,p.516; WB#6,p.93.

LOWRY, STOKELY D. and Ann Oldham, bond 31 October 1842. Consent by Mary Oldham, mother of the bride. Benjamin Armstrong (b); John L. Clark (w). MBB.,p.227

LOWRY, STOAKLEY D. and Josephine Dewbre*, bond 19 May 1846. William Christopher (b); Fayall Hanks (w). Married 21 May 1846 by the Rev. Elijah L. Williams.
MBB.,p.276

LUCAS, FRANCIS and Ann Smith, license May 1711.   DB#6,p.275
[Francis Lucas died intestate in Prince William County in 1739. DB#8,p.570; DB#10,p.28,266; Prince William County WB "C",p.167-168,190-193,251-252.]

LUCKHAM, JOHN and Lucy E. Jones, license 22 December 1851. Richard Scates (w) and Hiram M. Jones (w). Consent by James Jones, father of the bride. Married 23 December 1851 by the Rev. Elijah L. Williams.

LUCKHAM, WILLIAM and Mahala Hazard, bond 6 February 1816. Elias Hazard (b).

LUCKUM, JOSEPH and Lucinda S. Harrison*, bond 18 December 1849. Lyne Shackleford (b); William F. Tebbs (w).[He is also called Joseph Luckam.]MBB.,p.329

    LUTTRELL : LUTTRILL   SEE : LITTRALL : LITTRELL : LITTRILL &C: PAGE 120

LYELL, HENRY and Fanny L. Pitts, license 22 November 1852. Consent by R.L.Pitts, father of the bride. Henry B. Scott (w). Married 25 November 1852 by the Rev. William N. Ward.

LYELL, JOHN and Catherine Dobyns*, bond 27 April 1825. Samuel McPherson (b); Elizabeth Tapscott (w).   MBB.,p.10

LYELL, JONATHAN married Mary Stanfield, 16 October 1729.   NFPR.,p.134
[The bride was the daughter of John and Mary (Newman) Dalton and widow of Thomas Stanfield (q.v.). In 1753 Jonathan Lyell and Mary, his wife, were residing in Dinwiddie County, Virginia. DB#11,p.163-164.]

LYELL, JOSEPH and Lucy Appleby, bond 28 March 1796. Richard Appelay (b).

LYELL, JOSEPH and Nancy Dale, bond 12 May 1798. Richard Webb (b).

LYELL, RICHARD H. and Frances L.M. Belfield, bond 28 November 1837. Consent by
John W. Belfield, father of the bride; consent by John Lyell, father of the
groom. Thomas R. Barnes (b).   MBB.,p.160

LYELL, RICHARD H. and Elizabeth T. Tapscott, bond 5 October 1840. James V. Garland (b).   MBB.,p.197

LYELL, ROBERT and Mary E. Plummer, bond 8 January 1835. George Mothershead (b).
                                                                 MBB.,p.130

LYELL, SAMUEL M. and Felicia Ann Garland, bond 9 July 1833. The bond states the
bride is the orphan of Vincent Garland, Jr., deceased. James V. Garland
(b).   MBB.,p.109

LYELL, WILLIAM M. and Judith F. Page*, bond 5 July 1828. John B. Bramham (b);
Frances Neasome (w) and Thomas T. Page (w).   MBB.,p.38

                                    Mc

MC CALL, ARCHIBALD and Katherine Flood, bond 12 May 1761. Adam Menzies (b).
[The bride was the daughter of Doctor Nicholas Flood (1715-1768) and Eliza-
beth Peachey (17??-1792), his wife. In the churchyard of North Farnham
Church is a large tombstone: "Beneath this stone lie the remains of Kath-
arine, The wife of Arch^d. McCall, Merch^t. in Tap^a., and only daughter of Dr.
Nicholas & Eliz^a. Flood, who departed this life on the 5th January 1767 in
the 25th year of her age, leaving issue two daughters, Eliz^a & Kath: Flood."
WB#7,p.310; WB#8,p.141; Richmond County Petitions to the Legislature of 17
May 1779 and 5 December 1783 in VSL:AD; 11W(1)128.]

MC CALLEY, JOHN and Elizabeth Samford, bond 4 January 1763. John Stewart Chilton (b). [Bond 7 December 1762 of John Stewart Chilton (q.v.),p.35 as
guardian of Elizabeth Samford, orphan of Thomas Samford, deceased, with
Thomas Samford and James Samford his securities. Elizabeth Samford was
born in North Farnham Parish 26 November 1743, the daughter of Thomas Samford (1688-1762) and Frances ____[?]____ (17??-1750), his wife. John Mc-
Calley was born in North Farnham Parish 28 March 1740, the son of Charles
and Ann McCalley. AB#1,p.507; WB#6,p.315.]

MC CAN, JOHN and Judith B. Mactear were married 23 November 1827. WFMR.,n.p.

MC CARTY, BARTHOLOMEW and Elizabeth Tomlin, bond 28 April 1788. Thomas Sydnor
(b); Chichester Tapscott (w). [Bartholomew McCarty (circa 1763-1815) served
as clerk of Richmond County court 1793-1815; his obituary appeared in the
Fredericksburg Virginia Herald of 14 October 1815. He was the son of Major
Charles Barber and Winifred (Tarpley) McCarty (q.v.). Elizabeth Tomlin was
the daughter of Robert and Susanna (Fauntleroy) Tomlin (q.v.). AB#2,p.309;
WB#9,p.11,19.]

MC CARTY, BILLINGTON married Ann Barber, 16 June 1732.   NFPR.,p.141
[Billington McCarty, Gentleman, (170?-1745) was the son of Captain Daniel

and Elizabeth (Pope) McCarty (q.v.); Ann(e) Barber was the daughter of
Colonel Charles and Frances (Glascock) Barber (q.v.) p.9. AB#1,p.141,416;
WB#5,p.480. Anne (Barber) McCarty (1709-1753) was named in the will of
her maternal grandmother, Mrs. Anne Glascock, in 1714. WB#3,p.163.]

MC CARTY, BILLINGTON and Elizabeth Downman, bond 18 October 1756. William Glascock, Sr. (b). [Billington McCarty (1736-1771) was the son of Billington
and Anne (Barber) McCarty; he died testate in 1771. Hayden,p.87-88 misidentifies Billington McCarty (1736-1771) as he did not take into consid-
eration the will of his father, Billington McCarty (170?-1745), and thus
a considerable part of the Rev. Mr. Hayden's "Excurus - McCarty Family" is
out of focus.]

MC CARTY, CHARLES BARBER (1741-1785) married circa 1760 Winifred Tarpley, daughter of Major Travers and Betty (Sydnor) Tarpley (q.v.). Major Charles
Barber McCarty was the son of Billington and Anne (Barber) McCarty (q.v.);
he died testate in Richmond County in 1785. WB#7,p.11,284,452.

MC CARTY, CHARLES TRAVERS and Apphia Fauntleroy Tomlin, bond 12 January 1796.
Bartholomew McCarty (b). [He was the son of Major Charles Barber and Winifred (Tarpley) McCarty (q.v.) and she was the daughter of Robert and Susanna (Fauntleroy) Tomlin (q.v.) AB#2,p.309; WB#9,p.19.]

MC CARTY, CHRAIN married Mary Mozingo, 30 December 1729.   NFPR.,p.141
[There were McCartys in Richmond and adjacent counties who cannot be identified with the family of Dennis McCarty, Gentleman, (16??-1694) and Elizabeth Billington, his wife.]

MC CARTY, DANIEL [CAPTAIN] (1679-1724) of Richmond and Westmoreland counties,
son of Dennis and Elizabeth (Billington) McCarty, married (1) 19 October
1698 Elizabeth (Pope) Payne (1667-1716), widow of William Payne, Gentleman,
of Westmoreland County; married (2) by 27 May 1719 Ann (Lee) Fitzhugh (1683-
1732), daughter of the Honorable Richard Lee and widow of Colonel William
Fitzhugh of Eagle's Nest where her tombstone now is. Captain McCarty acquired considerable land in the Northern Neck of Virginia which he devised
by will of record in Westmoreland County. There are some errors in regard
to Captain Daniel McCarty and his family in Hayden,p.86-87. Westmoreland
County COB 1705-1721,p.368a; D&W#8,p.17,169; OPR,p.225-226; Payne,p.226.

MC CARTY, DANIEL L. and Ann B. Yerby, bond 26 August 1806. Consent by William
Gibson, guardian of the bride. George Saunders (b); John Redman (w).

MC CARTY, DENNIS [GENTLEMAN] (16??-1694) of Rappahannock and Richmond counties
married Elizabeth Billington, daughter of Luke and Barbara Billington of
Rappahannock County. He acquired considerable landed estate and died testate
in Richmond County but his last will was recorded in now lost WB#1. COB#1,
p.174; Hayden,p.84A,84B,85-86, Payne,p.226, Sweeny,p.16,17,29,127-128.

MC CARTY, DENNIS and Elizabeth Yerby, bond 3 December 1790. Charles Travers Mc-
Carty (b). [Elizabeth Woodbridge Yerby was the daughter of John Yerby who
died testate in Richmond County in 1775. WB#7,p.205.]

MC CARTY, GEORGE B.A. and Jane Ann Smith, bond 6 February 1847. Consent by John
B. Bramham, guardian of the groom; consent by Charles W. Smith, father of
the bride. William F. Tebbs (b); Frances R. McCarty (w). Married 9 February 1847 by the Rev. William N. Ward.   MBB.,p.290

MC CARTY, GEORGE Y. and Apphia F. Yerby, bond 13 June 1815. William D. McCarty
(b).

MC CARTY, GEORGE Y. and Frances E. Bramham, bond 12 November 1823. Augustine
Neale (b).

MC CARTY, JOHN and Susan Stonum*, bond 17 December 1822. Hiram Stonum (b);
James Adams (w) and Robert Clarke (w).

MC CARTY, MADISON P. and Olivia Ann Mitchell, bond 10 January 1838. Consent by
Robert B. Mitchell, father of the bride. Lyne Shackleford (b). MBB.,p.164

MC CARTY, ROBERT W. and Winifred T. Smith (widow)*, bond 1 April 1816. George
Saunders (b); Fanny P. McCarty (w) and John McCarty (w).

MC CARTY, ROBERT W. and Frances Ann Smith*, bond 25 September 1822. John Mc-
Carty (b).

MC CARTY, SYDNOR and Elizabeth W. Hunton*, bond 27 September 1809. George Saunders (b); William D. McCarty (w). The bride addresses her written consent to
Mr. Bartholomew McCarty, clerk of Richmond County, and requests him to issue
a license for her marriage to "your brother Mr. Sydnor McCarty."

MC CARTY, TARPLEY and Catharine Tomlin, bond 30 March 1803. Bartholomew McCarty
(b).[She was the daughter of Robert and Susanna (Fauntleroy) Tomlin (q.v.).]

MC CARTY, THADDEUS [COLONEL] of Richmond County married 19 May 1758 Ann Chinn;
William Glascock, Jr. (b).   LCMR#1,p.27
[Colonel Thaddeus McCarty (1739-1787), son of Billington and Anne (Barber)
McCarty, moved to Lancaster County shortly after his marriage and appears
prominently on those records. Ann (Chinn) McCarty was the younger of the
two daughters of Rawleigh Chinn who died intestate in Lancaster County in
1756 and Ann, his wife, who also died intestate in Lancaster County in 1784.
Hayden,p.87-89 incorrectly identifies the parentage of both Colonel Thaddeus
McCarty and his wife, but the biographical data in regard to Colonel McCarty
appears to be accurate. His will is of record in Lancaster County WB#22,p.
159. Richmond County DB#10,p.46,517; DB#12,p.298.]

MC CARTY, WILLIAM and Judith Yerby, bond 24 December 1798. Charles Smith (b).

MC CARTY, WILLIAM and Lucinda Moss (widow), bond 20 September 1820. Consent by
Judith G. McCarty, mother of the groom. Warner L. Tapscott (b). [The bride
was the widow of John A. Moss (q.v.) Beale,p.64.]

MC CARTY, WILLIAM B. and Virginia A. McCarty*, bond 4 May 1846. Consent by Lucinda McCarty, mother of the groom. George Payne (b). Married 7 May 1846
by Rev. William N. Ward.   MBB.,p.275

MC CARTY, WILLIAM D. and Margaret F. Yerby, bond 7 December 1813. Daniel L. McCarty (b).

MC CLANAHAN, PETER of Northumberland County and Fanny Claughton*, bond 3 September 1803. Eppa: Jones (b); Sally Jones (w).

MC CLANAHAN, VINCENT M. of Westmoreland County and Caroline Webb, bond 4 December 1827. Jeremiah Webb (b)   MBB.,p.32
    [Caroline Webb was born 16 October 1808, daughter of Jeremiah and Apphia (Northen) Webb (q.v.). She married (1) 6 December 1827 Vincent M. McClanahan and had two children, viz: (a) Augusta Marmaduke McClanahan, born 14 October 1828 and (b) Meredith Miles McClanahan, born 7 December 1829; she married (2) 20 May 1837, Atterson Clarke (q.v.),p.37. See Bible record in ECD Papers, VHS, Box 24.]

MC GLATHLIN [or MAC GLATHLIN], MANUS - See : Manus McLaughlin

MC GUIER, WILLIAM of Westmoreland County and Martha C. Smith, bond 14 February 1805. Consent by Winnefred Smith, mother of the bride. James Reynolds (b); William Smith (w).

MC GUIRE, WILLIAM and Susan Hudson*, bond 13 April 1849. Richard Harrison (b); Richard Hudson (w) and Samuel Hudson (w).   MBB.,p.322

MC INDREE [or MC KINDREE], JAMES married by 2 July 1753 Mary (Meeks) Milner, widow of Luke Mil(1)ner who died testate in 1746 and daughter of Richard and Ann Meeks. AB#1,p.418; DB#11,p.229,303; WB#5,p.152,511; WB#6,p.195.

MC KAY, WILLIAM [REVEREND] and Barbara Fitzhugh were married 6 February 1738/9. "We hear that on 6th ulto., the Rev. Mr. Mackay, Rector of Hanover Parish in King George County was married to Miss Barbara Fitzhugh, daughter to Major John Fitzhugh of Stafford County, deceased, a young Lady of great Beauty and Merit." The bride was the daughter of Major John Fitzhugh (169?-1733) of Marmion, Saint Paul's Parish, Stafford [now King George] County and his wife nee Anna Barbara McCarty, daughter of Captain Daniel and Elizabeth (Pope) McCarty (q.v.) p.123. Reverend Mr. William McKay was rector of North Farnham Parish, Richmond County, 1754-circa 1774. His widow, Barbara (Fitzhugh) McKay, moved to Westmoreland County and died testate in 1787. Meade, Volume II,p.160-161,173-174; OPR.,p.226-227; SPR.,p.88; Westmoreland County D&W#16,p.257,331; marriage announcement in the Virginia Gazette 2 March 1738/9.

    MC KENNEY : MC KENNY

MC KENNEY, BENJAMIN and Mary Keyser (widow), bond 24 February 1804. James Gregory (b).

MC KENNEY, CORNELIUS and Frances Scutt, bond 3 November 1814. Consent by Charles Scutt, father of the bride. Robert Anton (b).

MC KENNEY, VINCENT B. of Westmoreland County and Maria F. Reamy, bond 20 November 1834. Consent by James McKenney, father of the groom, and by Joshua Reamy, father of the bride; both say their children are under age. John A. Peyton (b); Presley McKenney (w).

MC KENNEY, WILLIAM M. of Westmoreland County and Catherine P. McKenney*, bond
1 February 1836. Baldwin Bell McKenney (b).   MBB.,p.142

MC KENNY, WILLIAM R. of Westmoreland County and Elizabeth K. Webb, bond 24 January 1838. Consent by Ann Reynolds, guardian of the bride. Robert L. Montgomery (b). Married by the Rev. Thomas M. Washington.   MBB.,p.167

MC KILDOE, ROBERT and Elizabeth Shackleford*, (widow), bond 8 January 1799.
William Bragg (b); George Eliff (w).

MC KILDOE, ROBERT D. and Mary A. Askin, license 10 March 1853. Consent by Nancy
Askin, mother of the bride. William McGawley (w). Married 10 March 1853
by Rev. Penfield Doll.

    MC KINDREE ; MACKINDREE   SEE : MC INDREE   PAGE 125

MC LANE, JAMES SYLVANUS and Apphia F. McCarty, bond 21 June 1800. Joseph Fox,
Jr. (b).

MC LAUGHLIN, MANUS (16??-1710), otherwise MANUS MAC GLATHLIN, married by 3 January 1694 Elizabeth Woodbridge (16??-1746), daughter of Paul Woodbridge
(1631-1691) of Rappahannock County. Manus McLaughlin died testate in Richmond in 1710; his will mentions five daughters all under eighteen years of
age. Elizabeth (Woodbridge) McLaughlin, widow, married secondly Peter Taff
(q.v.). COB#1,p.157; WB#3,p.13,273; WB#5,p.516; suit in chancery styled
Thomas Taff vs John Yerby, VSL:AD #25391; Sweeny,p.50,151.

MC NAMARA, JOHN and Katherine Dolphin, married 30 April 1730.   NFPR.,p.141

MC NEIL, HUGH and Ann Younger Kelsick*, bond 7 July 1795. Vincent Redman, guardian of the bride, writes his consent from Totusky on 7 July 1795. John
Brockenbrough (b); Mary Kelsick (w).

MC PHERSON, JAMES and Harriet Brooke, bond 8 December 1824. Reuben Brooke (b);
he makes oath both parties are over twenty one.   MBB.,p.3
[Their marriage was announced in the Fredericksburg Virginia Herald of 18
December 1824 and her death in the same newspaper on 25 January 1826. She
was the daughter of Captain William and Mary (Beale) Brooke; she died at
the Beale ancestral seat in Richmond County, Chestnut Hill. Beale,p.58-63.]

MC TYRE, WILLIAM C. and Alice Pope (spinster)*, bond 13 February 1798. George D.
Pope (b).

                                M

MACCAY, HENRY married Elizabeth Gibbs, 19 March 1729/30.   NFPR.,p.141

MAIDEN [MADEN], JOSEPH and Elizabeth Maiden (Maden) "free coulord,", bond 6 November 1849. Consent by Maria Ma(i)den, mother of the bride. John Maiden

(b); James C. Saunders (w).

MALEY   SEE : MEALEY : MEALY PAGE 130

MALEY, LUNSFORD and Elizabeth Ann Downman*, bond 3 August 1836. George G. Palmer (b).   MBB.,p.148

MALONE, JOHN and Lucy Flinn*, bond 21 December 1820. Thomas J. Scrimger (b).

MALONE, JOHN WHITFIELD and Mary Ann Efford*, bond 9 May 1846. William Dobyns
(b); W.D. Miskell (w) and Lucy Miskell (w). Married 4 June 1846 by the
Rev. Elijah L. Williams.   MBB.,p.276

MANIRE, WILLIAM of Raleigh Parish, Amelia County, married by 1748 Ann Stone,
daughter of William Stone, formerly of Richmond County, who died testate
in Amelia County, Virginia, in 1749. DB#10,p.505; Amelia County WB#1,p.
55. [William Stone (16??-1749) and Elizabeth, his wife, had a large family of children whose births are recorded in the North Farnham Parish Register; their daughter Ann(e) (Stone) Manire was born 5 March 1713. William
Stone was the son of William Stone (16??-1704) and Sarah ___[?]___ (16??-
1717), his wife, who settled in what is now Richmond County when it was
yet a part of Rappahannock County; they both died testate in Richmond County and those records contain many instruments in regard to them and their
numerous progeny. WB#2,p.114; WB#3,p.323.]

MARDERS, LOVELL and Sarah F. Chinn*, bond 7 September 1835. Joseph F. Harvey
(b); Walter J. Peck (w).   MBB.,p.136
[Lovell Marders was an elder in the Baptist Church and was active in Rich-
mond and Westmoreland counties. He was born 16 March 1798, the son of
James and Mildred (White) Marders and named for his maternal grandfather
Lovell White (circa 1725-1801) of King George County. Sarah Fairfax Chinn
was the daughter of Dr. John Yates and Sarah Fairfax (Carter) Chinn; see
Hayden,p.120. Lovell Marders and Sarah Fairfax Chinn were married by the
Rev. Thomas Corbin Braxton and same was announced in the Religious Herald
of 25 September 1835 and the same paper of 31 March 1837 carried her obituary. Rev. Lovell Marders married (2) Eliza McCance and same was announced
in the Religious Herald of 21 November 1839 and same paper of 28 June 1849
carried her obituary. Rev. Lovell Marders married (3) Catharine J. Rogers
and same was announced in the Religious Herald of 23 October 1851.]

MARKES : MARKS

MARKS, JAMES and Sarah Buckley, bond 12 September 1791. Daniel Connellee (b)
and also Edward Marks (b).

MARKS, JAMES and Frances Hinson*, bond 3 September 1798. Elias Willson (b);
William Hinson (w).

MARKS, JAMES and Ann Bowen*, license 22 February 1853. James Sanders (w),
Lemuel Marks (w) and Martin Bowen (w). Married 24 February 1853 by the
Rev. John Pullen.

MARKS, REUBEN and Fanny France*, bond 12 January 1819. In writing her own consent to the court clerk, Fanny France says she is "aged 22 years." William
Sanders (b); John France (w). [Fanny France was born 2 October 1796, the
daughter of John and Catherine (Fones) France (q.v.), p.72.]

MARKS, SAMUEL and Frances Hinson*, bond 6 March 1838. James L. Sanders (b).
Married by the Rev. Thomas M. Washington; date not stated.   MBB.,p.170

MARKS, THORNTON and Jane Hinson, bond 30 April 1836. Consent by Mary Hinson; no
relationship stated. Meredith Hinson (b).   MBB.,p.146

MARKS, VINCENT and Susan France*, bond 20 January 1847. Consent by John France;
no relationship stated. Samuel Marks (b); James Barrott (w). Married 21
January 1847 by the Rev. John Pullen.   MBB.,p.289

MARKS, VINCENT and Mary France, bond 9 May 1850. Consent by John France; no relationship stated. Martin V. Bowen (b); L. [or S.] Weadon (w).MBB.,p.336

MARKS, WILLIAM and Julia Hall*, bond 16 February 1847. Samuel Marks (b); James
M. Morris (w); Molley Hall (w). Married 17 February 1847 by the Rev. John
Pullen.   MBB.,p.291

MARKES, WILLIAM B. and Mary Weadon*, bond 4 February 1850. James Weadon (b).
Married 6 February 1850 by the Rev. John Pullen.   MBB.,p.332

MARMADUKE, DANIEL and Rebecca Bragg*, bond 17 December 1791. William Bragg (b).

MARMADUKE, JAMES B. and Catharine Pursell, bond 24 March 1824. Tobias Pursell
(b).

MARMADUKE, JAMES B. and Lucinda Lyell, bond 29 May 1827. Consent by John Lyell,
father of the bride. Benjamin D. Rust (b). [Bond in loose papers only.]

MARSH, ROBERT M. of Northumberland County and Ann Carter*, bond 22 October 1805.
Rodham Booth (b).

MARSHALL, GEORGE and Catherine Fauntleroy, bond 25 December 1786. Robert Tomlin
(b). [She was the daughter of Captain Moore and Elizabeth (Mitchell) Fauntleroy (q.v.) p.68 and m(2) Robert H. Hooe (q.v.),p.97. George Marshall (Jr.),
son of George and Ann Marshall of King George County, died without issue in
King George County in 1788 and his widow promptly denounced the provisions
made for her in his last will and Testament. King George County COB#5A,p.
194,240; King George County WB#2,p.107,111; Fauntleroy,p.664.]

MARSHALL, JOHN (circa 1682-1752) of Westmoreland County married by 5 January 1721/2
Elizabeth Markham (1704-1779), daughter of Lewis Markham, Gentleman, (16??-
1713) of Westmoreland County and sister of James Markham of Richmond, King
George and Stafford counties who was her curate. The inventory of the estate
of James Markham, Gentleman, deceased, was taken in 1741 in Stafford County.
King George County COB#1,p.18,35; Stafford County Book "M",p.316; Westmoreland County D&W#5,p.176. John and Elizabeth (Markham) Marshall were the grand
parents of the Honorable John Marshall (1755-1835); his will was admitted to

probate in Westmoreland County in 1752 and hers in Culpeper County in 1779.
Westmoreland County D&W#11,p.419; Culpeper County Will Book "B",p.287.

MARSHALL, RICHARD and Elizabeth McClanahan, bond 28 March 1848. James Grant
   (b); he is the legal guardian of the bride. Married 30 March 1848 by the
   Rev. George Northam.   MBB.,p.308

MARSHALL, THOMAS (16??-1704) of Rappahannock and Westmoreland counties, married
   before 8 February 1685 Martha Sherwood, daughter of Philip Sherwood of Rappahannock County whose lands fell into Richmond County upon its formation in
   1692. Martha (Sherwood) Marshall married (2) by 25 July 1705 Alexander
   Thomson of Westmoreland County. Thomas and Martha (Sherwood) Marshall were
   the parents of John Marshall (q.v.), p.128-129; he died testate in Westmoreland County in 1704 bequeathing his plantation to his son William Marshall. The latter moved to King and Queen County and conveyed the plantation in Washington Parish, Westmoreland County, to his brother, John Marshall (q.v.) p.128-129. Westmoreland County COB 1698-1705,p.268a; D&W#3,
   p.232; D&W#8,p.93; 23T116,207,278.

MARSY, JOHN married Anne Canes, 11 July 1680.   NFPR.,p.137

MARTIN, JOHN and Lucy A. Nash, bond 17 March 1845. George M. Nash (b). Married
   20 March 1845 by the Rev. Elijah L. Williams.   MBB.,p.256

MARTIN, NICHOLAS married Frances Petty, 15 November 1728.   NFPR.,p.140

MARTIN, WILLIAM of Lancaster County and Katharine Branham, bond 28 December 1786.
   Thomas Thomas (b).

MASLIN, WILLIAM and Julia Ann Newcomb, bond 29 September 1847. Consent by Catherine Newcomb, mother of the bride. William T. Murrin (b); Samuel G. Taylor (w) and John J. Crump (w).

MASON, ELIAS and Heathy Eaton, bond 11 March 1789. Consent by Ann Easton, mother
   of the bride. Winder Nash (b); Thomas Wroe (w) and Charles T. McCarty (w).

MASSEY, LEROY and Syntha Matthews*, bond 4 March 1811. The bride writes her own
   consent and this she signs Prissey Matthews. John Price (b).

MATHEWS, SAMUEL $^{(4)}$ [CAPTAIN] (16??-1719) of King and Queen, Essex and Richmond
   counties was thrice married; his ancestry is detailed in A.P.& P.,p.244-248
   but this source errs in regard to his first marriage. Captain Samuel[4] Mathews married (1) a Miss Paullin, daughter of Colonel Thomas and Elizabeth
   Paullin of King and Queen County; her sister married Colonel George Braxton
   (1677-1748) of Newington, King and Queen County, and thus Captain Mathews
   refers to "Brother Braxton" in his will. By his first wife Captain Samuel[4]
   Mathews had two daughters mentioned in the will of their maternal grandfather, Colonel Thomas Paullin, which is recited in Essex County DB#17,p.105-106,
   and also mentioned in his will, viz: (a) Elizabeth Mathews who m(1) Robert
   Taliaferro, Gentleman, (16??-1728) of Spotsylvania County, and m(2) 22 October 1728 Moseley Battaley, Gentleman, (1???-1758) of Spotsylvania County; (b)
   Mary Mathews who d.s.p. post 1718. Captain Samuel[4] Mathews married (2) 10

August 1706, while he "was very much in drink," Katherine Tunstall, daughter of Edmund Tunstall, Gentleman, of King & Queen County, by whom he had two sons, viz: (c) John Mathews d.s.p., testate, in 1729 in King George County and (d) Baldwin Mathews who d.s.p., post 1731. Captain Samuel[4] Mathews married (3) Margaret (surname unknown), who survived him, and was named as executrix in his last will and Testament which was dated 16 November 1718 and proved 4 March 1718/19 at Richmond County court; by her he had two children, viz: (e) Francis Mathews and (f) a posthumously born child both of whom died in infancy. Margaret (?   ) Mathews, widow, married (2) William Skrine (16??-1729) by whom she had two children, viz: (a) Anne Skrine who d.s.p., and (b) Elizabeth Skrine (172?-1810) who married William Bunbury (1727-1767) of St. Paul's Parish, Stafford County; they d.s.p., testate, in the said parish and their wills were recorded in King George and Stafford counties respectively. Margaret (?   ) Mathews Skrine, twice a widow, married (3) Robert Richards who died testate in King George County in 1735; by him she had an only child, viz: (a) Frances Richards who married 5 October 1749 in St. Paul's Parish, Horatio Dade, Gentleman, and left issue. Margaret (?   ) Mathews Skrine Richards died testate in King George County in 1748 but her will and those of her last two husbands were recorded in now lost King George County Will Book #1 (1721-1752), however, the surviving records contain considerable genealogical information concerning this entire connection. The large land holdings of Captain Samuel[4] Mathews, lying on the Rappahannock River in present King George County, which had descended to him from his grandfather, Lieutenant Colonel Samuel[2] Mathews (who patented the said land 7 September 1654), were sold in 1731 by Baldwin[5] Mathews to Colonel John Champe and in 1754 Moseley Battaley [whose first wife was Elizabeth[5] Mathews, then deceased, the only child of Captain Samuel[4] Mathews to leave issue] was joined by their eldest son and heir, Samuel Battaley of Spotsylvania County, in a deed of surrender by which genealogically informative instrument Colonel John Champe (16??-1763) of Lamb's Creek, King George County, was placed in unquestionable legal possession of the Mathews estate in that county. Richmond County WB#4,p.80; King George County COB#1,p.332,368; DB#1,p.396; DB#1-A,p.177; DB#4,p.140; other indexed records in Essex, King George, Richmond and Spotsylvania counties; 21T240-243; Whit Morris, The First Tunstalls in Virginia and Some of Their Descendants (San Antonio, Texas, 1950),p.5-6.

MATTHEWS, RICHARD E. (mariner) and Eliza Glascock, bond 8 April 1811.   Joseph Glascock (b).

MAXWELL, HERBERT and Ann Alverson, married 7 October 1729.   NFPR.,p.141

MEALEY   :   MEALY   SEE :   MALEY   PAGE 127

MEALEY, JESSE and Sarah B. Harris*, bond 20 February 1844.   Henry M. Harris (b); Robert Harris (w).   Married 22 February 1844 by the Rev. William N. Ward.
MBB.,p.245

MEALEY, JOHN and Lucy Gordon*, bond 16 December 1822.   Edmund Northen (b); Susan Gordon (w).

MEALEY, JOHN of Lancaster County and Fanny Littrell*, bond 18 June 1836. Richard O. Jeffries (b); John L. Chamberlain (w).   MBB.,p.147

MEALY, RICHARD B. and Jane Roberts*, bond 3 February 1843. Zachariah Efford
(b); John Roberts (w).   MBB.,p.235

MEALEY, SAMUEL and Massey Thrift, bond 10 February 1798. John Thrift (b).

MEALY, SAMUEL (bachelor) and Matilda Jones (spinster), bond 7 November 1828.
Consent by Rebecca Jones, guardian of the bride. Shadrack Clark (b);
George R. Thrift (w).   MBB.,p.44

MENZIES, ADAM and Phebe Peachey (spinster), bond 6 August 1752. John Tarpley
(b). [11 August 1752: marriage contract between the aforementioned parties in which he is described as of Culpeper County, Virginia; this is recorded in Richmond County DB#11,p.157. The bride was the daughter of
Captain Samuel and Winifred (Griffin) Peachey (q.v.). The will of Adam
Menzies was recorded in Northumberland County in 1767 and the inventory of
the estate of Phebe (Peachey) Menzies was recorded in Northumberland County in 1780.]

MENZIES, SAMUEL PEACHEY and Frances Miskell (spinster), bond 24 June 1782. Le-
Roy Peachey (b). William Miskell writes his consent to the marriage of
his daughter Frances Miskell but indicates his consent is quite insignifi-
cant as she is already "of lawful age to dispose of herself." [The bride
was the daughter of William and Elizabeth (Samford) Miskell (q.v.); the
groom was the son of Adam and Phebe (Peachey) Menzies (q.v.). Samuel Peachey and Frances (Miskell) Menzies moved to Frederick County, Virginia. DB#17,
p.17,102,129; John Bennett Boddie, Historical Southern Families, Volume IV,
(Redwood City, California, 1960), p.48.]

MESSICK, WILLIAM J. and Alice Efford*, bond 29 May 1841. John Woollard (b);
Thomas Oldham (w).   MBB.,p.210

METCALFE, GILBERT (168?-1737) married by 1716 Susannah (Cammack) Foster (168?-
1747), widow of John Foster (16??-1711) of Essex County and daughter of
Warwick and Margaret Cammack of Rappahannock and Richmond counties. The
groom was the son of Richard and Elizabeth (Fauntleroy) Metcalfe (q.v.),
p.131. Gilbert and Susannah (Cammack) Metcalf(e) left no issue; both died
testate in Richmond County. COB#7,p.117; DB#7,p.130,200; DB#9,p.519; WB#5,
p.307,524; MRB.,p.95; also Essex County D&W#13,p.411 and D&W#15,p.50.

METCALFE, HENRY (16??-1767) married by 20 January 1718 Precilla Shippy, daughter
of Richard Shippy [Shippie, Shippe &c:], Sr. of Richmond County who died
testate in 1698; they resided in Northumberland County. Precilla (Shippy)
Metcalfe, widow, married (2) George Harrison. COB#2,p.299; DB#3,p.21,56;
DB#7,p.262; see also Northumberland County Record Book 1766-70,p.90,504.

METCALFE, RICHARD (16??-1699) married (1) 1685 Elizabeth Fauntleroy, daughter of
Colonel Moore Fauntleroy, and had issue, viz: (a) Gilbert Metcalfe (168?-
1737) (q.v.),p.131; (b) Jane Metcalfe, spinster; she did not marry one Wat-
ralfe [!?!] as stated 54V72 - this is obviously an error for Metcalfe; (c)
Ann Metcalfe married in March 1713/14 Captain John Opie (q.v.). Richard
Metcalfe married (2) Ann Stone, daughter of Colonel John Stone, and had
issue, viz: (d) Mary Metcalfe m(1) in August 1714, Austin Brockenbrough

(q.v.),p.24 and (2) John Spicer, Gentleman; (e) Elizabeth Metcalfe m(1)
2 December 1725 Samuel Bayley (Bailey) (q.v.),p.6 and m(2) by 1741 William
Bridges of Westmoreland County; (f) Sarah Metcalfe married circa 1724 Benj-
min Rust (170?-1754); and (g) John Metcalfe d.s.p., testate, in Richmond
County in 1728. Ann(e) (Stone) Metcalfe (c.1672-post 1728), widow, married
(2) circa 1700 Captain Edward Barrow, Gentleman, (q.v.),p.11 and left issue
by him, viz: (a) Edward Barrow (q.v.),p.11; (b) Anne Barrow and (c) Margaret
Barrow - all born ante 1713 per deed of gift to them recorded in DB#6,p.134.
Richard Metcalfe (16??-1699) was the son of Gilbert Metcalfe of London, England, whose estate became involved in extensive litigation in Richmond County beginning in 1709; COB#5,p.91-92 et seq. contains many entries of genealogical import as does MRB.,p.70; WB#5,p.307,524; 5W(1)10-13; 20W(2)557; and
Fauntleroy,p.151.

MICKELBOROUGH, RICHARD S. (bachelor) and Mary G. Palmer (spinster), bond 20 Dec-
    ember 1828. Consent by William Palmer; no relationship stated. George G.
    Palmer (b); Henrietta Palmer (w).   MBB.,p.48

MIDDLETON, BENJAMIN S. [DOCTOR] and Sarah Ann Cox, bond 5 July 1847. Consent by
    Mary W. Smith, mother of the bride. Joseph William Shearman (b); James W.
    Hipkins (w). Married 27 July 1847 by the Rev. William N. Ward. MBB.,p.295

MIDDLETON, JEREMIAH of Westmoreland County and Nancy S. Harrison (spinster) of
    Richmond County, bond 28 May 1808. Consent by Samuel Harrison, father of
    the bride. John Withers (b); Richard Johnson (w).

MIDDLETON, ROBERT R. and Mary M. Pridham*, bond 15 November 1850. H.M. Pursell
    (w) and Richard T. Oldham (w). Married 18 November 1850 by the Rev. Elijah
    L. Williams.

MIDDLETON, WILLIAM of Westmoreland County and Maria C. Redman, bond 7 April 1813.
    Thomas Plummer (b).

MILES, GEORGE and Hannah How, bond 24 April 1817. Horace Wellford (b).

MILLER, RICHARD of Westmoreland County and Lucinda Guttridge*, bond 9 October
    1833. Henry H. Hazard (b); he certified that the bride "had been once marr-
    ied." Adeline Reamy (w).   MBB.,p.110

MILLER, SIMON (16??-1720) of Hanover Parish, Richmond County, was the son of the
    well known Captain Simon Miller of Rappahannock County; he married (name
    unknown) who married (2) William Smith (carpenter) who was boarding in the
    house of Simon Miller when he wrote his will 1 December 1719. The landed
    estate of Simon Miller fell into King George County the year following his
    death and those records hold data in regard to his family which has been
    detailed in OPR.,p.79. COB#2,p.15; DB#2,p.2; WB#4,p.151; also King George
    County COB#1,p.123,124,125,173; 12 T237-243; Sweeny,p.92,93.

    MILLNER : MILNER

MILLNER, BENJAMIN married Frances Glascock, 13 July 1730.   NFPR.,p.141
    [Benjamin Mil(1)ner (1710-1733) was born and died in North Farnham Parish.

He married there, 13 July 1730, Frances Glascock, sister of Gregory Glascock.
Their only child, Benjamin Mil(l)ner, Jr., was mentioned in the will of his
paternal grandfather, John Mil(l)ner (16??-1744), proved in Richmond County.
AB#1,p.65,418; WB#5,p.188,466,467,511.]

MILLNER, LUKE married Mary Meeks, 19 August 1731.   NFPR.,p.141
  [Luke Mil(l)ner (1708-1746) was born, married and died in North Farnham Parish; his widow, Mary (Meeks) Millner married (2) by 1753 James McIndree
  (q.v.),p.125. She was the daughter of Richard and Ann Meeks. AB#1,p.418;
  WB#5,p.152,188,466,467,511; WB#6,p.15,195.]

MINTER, JOHN and Caty Woollard*, bond 1 January 1789. Alexander Bryant (b).

MISKELL, BARTHOLOMEW M. and Ann E. Miskell*, bond 17 January 1846. William D.
  Miskell (b); G.H. Miskell (w).   MBB.,p.271

MISKELL, DANIEL and Ann Williams (spinster), bond 7 October 1756. John Williams
  (b). [The bride was the daughter of John Williams who died testate in Richmond County in 1762. WB#6,p.293.]

MISKELL, GEORGE and Sarah Saunders, bond 29 April 1783. John Hammond (b).

MISKELL, HENRY (1???-1761) married 172? Winifred Dalton (170?-1766), daughter of
  John and Mary (Newman) Dalton. The births of some of their children are recorded in the North Farnham Parish Register. DB#8,p.358; DB#11,p.164; WB#5,
  p.249; WB#6,p.197.

MISKELL, HENRY and Hannah Bryant, bond 12 September 1798. Consent by Alexander
  Bryant, father of the bride. William Alderson (b).

MISKELL, JOHN AUSTIN (bachelor) and Elizabeth G. Franklin (spinster), bond 29
  December 1828. Robert Scott (b).   MBB.,p.49

MISKELL, NEWMAN and Jane Beacham, bond 17 December 1811. Thomas Beacham (b).

MISKELL, SAMUEL and Nancy Dameron, bond 23 January 1808. Consent by Roger Dameron; no relationship stated. George Saunders (b); William Dameron, Jr.(w).

MISKELL, THOMAS A. and Elizabeth M. Pursley, bond 28 July 1828. Joseph Dale (b);
  he seems to be guardian to one of the parties and consents. MBB.,p.40

MISKELL, WILLIAM (1729-1789) married circa 1755 Elizabeth ("Betty") Samford, dau-
  ghter of James and Mary(Barber) Samford (q.v.). He died intestate in Richmond
  County and there was litigation concerning his estate. DB#17,p.71,102,129;
  WB#5,p.414; Beckwith vs Garnett's Executors, FDC#560, Bundle "C" 236-257;
  John B. Boddie, Historical Southern Families (1959), Volume III,p.28-29.

MISKELL, WILLIAM and Fanny Hogan, bond 4 August 1813. Richard Street (b).

MISKELL, WILLIAM D. and Lucy English*, bond 31 March 1836. William English (b);
  George H. Miskell (w).   MBB.,p.145

MISKELL, WILLIAM H. and Frances E. Downman*, bond 23 March 1832. Thomas M.
    Glascock (b); John D. Glascock (w).   MBB.,p.88

MITCHELL, JAMES and Lucy Rout, bond 14 December 1770. Gabriel Smither,(b).

MITCHELL, JOHN C. and Sally E. Chinn, bond 1 May 1841. John L. Chinn (b). Mar-
    ried 4 May 1841 by the Rev. William N. Ward.   MBB.,p.209

MITCHELL, LITTLETON DOWNMAN and Lavinia A. McCarty, bond 19 September 1850.
    Consent by Frances R. McCarty, mother of the bride. James B. McCarty (w).
    Married 24 September 1850 by the Rev. William N. Ward.

MITCHELL, RICHARD and Ann Sydnor, bond 24 August 1752. Anthony Sydnor, Sr.(b).
    [The bride was the daughter of Anthony and Elizabeth (Dew) Sydnor (q.v.).
    Richard Mitchell (1728-1781) and his wife nee Ann Sydnor (1728-1793) died
    childless; his will was proved in Lancaster County and hers in Richmond
    County. He was the son of Robert Mitchell, Gentleman, (1684-1748), of Lan-
    caster County whose will is of record and Bible record in VSL:AD#25212.
    WB#8,p.163; Lee,158; Hayden,p.92n, quoting letter 11 October 1752.]

MITCHELL, ROBERT [THE YOUNGER] of Richmond County married Hannah Ball, 7 Sept-
    ember 1746.   LCMR#1,p.20
    [The groom was the son of Robert Mitchell, Gentleman, (1684-1748), above
    mentioned; Robert Mitchell (1724-1758) is styled both "the younger" and
    "junior" in various records. He died testate in Richmond County and his
    wife nee Hannah Ball (172?-1769), survived him. She was the daughter of
    Colonel William Ball, identified by Hayden,p.48,62. AB#1,p.569; WB#6,p.129.]

MITCHELL, THOMAS and Sally M. Bailey (widow)*, bond 23 December 1806. Samuel
    Oldham (b); Thomas Brown (w).

MITCHELL, WILLIAM C. of Northumberland County and Alice F. Bell, bond 7 January
    1828. Consent by Thomas S. Sydnor for the marriage "between my ward Mr.
    William C. Mitchell and Miss Alice F. Bell." Charles L. Bell (b); Cyrus
    Harding (w).   MBB.,p.34

MITCHELL, WILLIAM D. of Gloucester County and Judith McTier, bond 7 April 1823.
    Washington Glascock (b).

MONROE, JOHN [JUDGE] married 13 January 1777 in Northumberland County, Jane
    Jones. 47V47. [Judge John Monroe (circa 1758-1814) resided at Cone Place
    in Northumberland County, Foulis in Richmond County, and after the death of
    his wife, Jane (Jones) Monroe (1760-1795), moved to Scott County, Kentucky.
    He was the only son of Captain John Monroe of Westmoreland County who married
    in 1754 Catherine Waughope of Northumberland County; they both came of unique
    and distinguished ancestry. His wife was the daughter of Colonel Thomas and
    Sally (Skelton) Jones; her ancestry is detailed by Judge Lewis H. Jones in
    Captain Roger Jones of London and Virginia (1911), p.40,56. On 3 August
    1790 John Monroe, Gentleman, took the oath of office as Commonwealth's Attor-
    ney of Richmond County. About the time of his wife's death financial diffi-
    culties overtook him and he made a deed of trust on estate, Foulis, in Rich-
    mond County, and in the Virginia Herald of 9 December 1796 advertised it for

sale in considerable detail. Before removing to Kentucky, Judge Monroe resided a few years in Augusta County and its environs. The Reporter, published in Lexington, Kentucky, 9 April 1814, announced the death "in Scott
County [of] John Monroe, Esq., Attorney and Counsellor at Law, formerly one
of the Judges of the Circuit Court." As the issue of Judge John and Jane
(Jones) Monroe are either inaccurately or incompletely accounted for in
various printed accounts, I will name their issue known to me, viz: (a)
Sally Skelton Monroe married 1796 Edwin Bathurst Smith (q.v.),p.189; (b)
Lucy Monroe; (c) Catherine Monroe married Mr. Vance; (d) Dr. Thomas Jekyll
Catesby Monroe (17??-1839) married Elizabeth Conkling; he served in the
War of 1812 and his widow received a pension (#OWW-12,512, National Arch-
ives); and (e) Jane Jones Monroe married 11 November 1802 in Bath County,
Virginia, John Banks Lewis. COB#21,p.68; DB#17,p.104; Monroe vs Lewis,
Augusta County chancery paper file #9 and Smith vs Lewis, and Lee's Admin-
istrators vs Monroe, both in Augusta County chancery paper file #17; Scott
County, Kentucky, WB "B",p.180; Chalkley, Augusta County Records, Volume
II,p.21,68,87; 13W(2)236 contains many errors regarding Judge Monroe and
his family, but his paternal ancestry is correctly given in the same article, 13W(2)234-235, viz: Judge John[5] Monroe; Captain John[4] Monroe (17??-
1767); Colonel Andrew[3] Monroe (c.1696-1770); Colonel Andrew[2] Monroe (1664-
1714); Major Andrew[1] Monroe (c.1625-1668), all of Westmoreland County.]

MONTAGUE, EDWARD married by 4 November 1698 Johanna Brown.   COB#2,p.356

MONTAGUE, HENRY A. and Elizabeth F. Shackleford, bond 29 December 1835. Peter
    S. Northen, guardian, consents to the marriage but it is not definitely
    stated to which party he was acting. Thomas Oldham (b); William B. Slaugh-
    ter (w).   MBB.,p. 139
    [Henry Albert Montague was the son of Thomas Tarpley and Elizabeth (Monta-
    gue) Montague, (q.v.),p.136. G.W. Montague, History and Genealogy of Peter
    Montague of Nansemond and Lancaster Counties, Virginia, 1621-1894, (Amherst,
    Mass., 1894),p.421.]

MONTAGUE, JAMES [CAPTAIN] of Middlesex County and Winifred Webb (widow)*, bond 20
    November 1771. Peter Montague (b). [The bride was the widow of William Webb,
    Gentleman, who died testate in 1765, (q.v.),p.226-227. Captain James Montague
    (1741-1781/2) married (1) 20 June 1760 Mary Eliza Chinn, daughter of Joseph
    Chinn of Lancaster County. Captain Montague served in the House of Burgesses
    in 1774 and held other offices of importance in his native county of Middle-
    sex where he died testate; his widow returned to her native county of Rich-
    mond and died testate there in 1806. The chancery cause, styled Montague vs
    Webb, which pended in Richmond County court in 1786, states the said Winifred
    m(1) William Webb, only son of John Spann Webb, Gentleman, who died intestate
    in 1756, and whose brother, Isaac Webb and Frances, his wife, (q.v.),p.226,
    were concerned in the administration of the estate of the said John Spann
    Webb, Gentleman, deceased; and further that the said Winifred Webb, widow,
    m(2) Captain James Montague, late of the county of Middlesex, deceased. The
    above cited Montague genealogy, pages 84 and 411, is inaccurate in regard to
    the family of Captain James Montague as it fails to recognize his two mar-
    riages and assigns his second wife to a certain Thomas Montague, thereby per-
    petrating multiple omissions and errors. WB#6,p.391; WB#9,p.291; Middlesex
    County WB "F",p.213; other indexed records in Middlesex and Richmond counties.]

MONTAGUE, THOMAS TARPLEY married 27 October 1801 in Middlesex County, his cousin, Elizabeth Montague. Middlesex County Marriage Register #1, p. 63, 154. [Thomas Tarpley Montague was the son of Captain James and Winifred Griffin (Tarpley) Montague (q.v.), p.135.]

MONTEITH, THOMAS [GENTLEMAN] (circa 1694-1746/7) married by 1737 Phillis [Telis] Gallop, daughter of Robert Gallop who died testate in Richmond County in 1720. On 30 July 1714 Thomas Monteith, Merchant of Glasgow, gave a power of attorney to Thomas White of Hanover Parish, Richmond County, authorizing him to recover certain debts due to him and transact other business. Thomas Monteith, Gentleman, appears frequently on the King George County records from 1721 until the time of his death in 1746/7. He died testate but his will is in now lost King George County WB#1 (1721-1752), however, the surviving records show he left four infant children at the time of his death, viz: (a) Magdaline Monteith who m(1) Anderson Doniphan [they were ancestors of President Harry Shipp Truman] and m(2) Jonathan Finnall of Stafford County; (b) Elizabeth Monteith; (c) James Monteith and (d) John Monteith. Phillis (Gallop)Monteith, widow, married (2) Benjamin Elkins by 1755. WB#4,p.161; MRB, p.84; also King George County COB#2,p.508; COB#3,p.535,555,560; DB#3,p.146 [deposition 9 May 1746 of Thomas Monteith, aged about 52 years - other records indicate he was older!]; DB#2,p.1,138-139; 26T283-285; 28T238.

MONTGOMERY, ROBERT G. "late of Westmoreland County," and Frances E. McCarty (widow)*, bond 28 November 1835. George Saunders (b).   MBB.,p.137

MONTGOMERY, ROBERT L. of Westmoreland County and Elizabeth T. Reynolds*, bond 16 August 1825. Williamson Webb (b); Thomas T. Reynolds (w).   MBB.,p.13

MOODY, WILLIAM married Jane Griffin, 23 November 1725.   NFPR.,p.140

MOORE, ELIJAH and Nancy Clarke, bond 8 March 1786. Vincent Clarke (b). [Bond dated only 1763: Richard Parker, guardian of Elijah Moore, son of William Moore, who has a legacy due to him from the estate of his maternal grandfather, Richard Lawson, deceased. Richard Lawson seems to have died testate in Richmond County in 1761. WB#6,p.249.]

MOORE, FRANCIS (1660-1718) married 170? Ann, probably nee Harbin; this surname appears inconspicuously on the Richmond County records. Francis Moore, merchant of Dublin, Ireland, and owner of the Dublin Merchant, imported many indented servants into Virginia beginning in 1681. He appears frequently on the records of Rappahannock, Essex and Richmond counties and in 1703-1706 in Essex County was granted certificates for thousands of acres of land for the transportation of hundreds of indebted servants into Rappahannock River. On 10 May 1705, stating his age to be "45 or thereabouts," he made a deposition in Essex County in regard to certain "servants ... he brought into this Colony ... in the ship called the Dublin Merchant ..." in March 1699. In 1701 he acquired a plantation in Essex County and dying intestate in 1718, this descended to his eldest son and heir, Francis Moore (1711-1796); he sold it in 1739. Francis and Ann Moore had four children, viz: (a) Colonel Francis Moore (1711-1796) who appears prominently on the records of Orange County; (b) Harbin Moore (171?-1802) who died testate in Culpeper County; (c) a daughter who married Thomas Pattey, Jr. of Orange County and removed to Lunen-

burg County; (d) Martha Moore who married, as his second wife, Captain David
Bronough (17??-1774) of King George County. Ann Moore, widow, married (2)
circa 1719, John Naylor, Gentleman, of Richmond and King George counties
(q.v.),p.143, and she died testate in Orange County in 1744. COB#3,p.368;
MRB.,p.4; also Essex County COB#3,p.54,164,232,233; DB#10,p.96; DB#22,p.60;
W&D#12,p.92; WB#3,p.34; COB#5,p.133; Orange County WB#1,p.317.

MOORE, JAMES G. and Ann Jones*, bond 17 December 1791. Reubin Moore (b); William
Brickey (w), Elener Brickey (w) and Elener Rochester (w).

MOORE, JOSEPH and Elizabeth Delanoe*, bond 28 May 1840. Eppa: Weathers (b).
MBB.,p.195

MOORE, JOSEPH G. and Ellen Weathers*, bond 13 July 1848. Joseph Weathers (b);
Fanny Weathers (w). Married 13 July 1848 by the Rev. William N. Ward.
MBB.,p.311

MOORE, PETER and Elinor Brickey*, bond 15 October 1796. Reuben Moore (b) and
Samuel Fleming (b).

MOORE, SAMPSON married Mary Anne Pridham, daughter of Edward Pridham who died
testate in Richmond County in 1774. WB#7,p.183.

MOORE, THOMAS of "the County [blank]" and Katherine Fauntleroy "of this county,"
bond 21 January 1783. Walker Tomlin (b).

MOORE, WALKER and Martha Willson, bond 22 July 1786. Consent by Joseph Willson,
father of the bride, who states his daughter is "of age." Reubin Moore (b);
Henry Bruce (w) and Martha Willson (w).

MORGAN, ANDREW married Sarah Dawson, 13 November 1730.   NFPR.,p.141

MORGAN, ANDREW married circa 1771 Winifred Pursell Murray alias Pursell [Purcell],
daughter of Tobias Purcell and Mary Ann Murray [Murrah, Murrow &c.]. COB#15,
p.313; COB#17,p.268; WB#6,p.201. See notes under TOBIAS PURCELL, p.164.

MORGAN, ANTHONY and Ann Dunkin, license July 1711.   DB#6,p.275
[Martha W. Hiden in her account of Anthony[1] Morgan of Old Rappahannock Coun-
ty in 25T270 fails to fully account for the many Morgan - Morgin records in
Rappahannock and Richmond counties. COB#10,p.394; WB#5,p.598; and others.]

MORGAN, BENJAMIN and Nancy Garland*, bond 15 February 1797. William Garland (b).

MORGAN, DAVID and Hannah Sisson, bond 27 February 1802. George Sisson (b).

MORGAN, EVAN (16??-1684) married circa 1677 Elizabeth Brown, widow of William
Brown (16??-1677); they had no issue but Evan Morgan mentioned several of
his step-children in his will. William and Elizabeth Brown had three sons,
viz: (a) William Brown; (b) John Brown and (c) Maxfield Brown (167?-1745).
COB#2,p.232; COB#6,p.112; Sweeny,p.57,106.

MORGAN, JOHN married Elizabeth Hammock, 21 August 1729.   NFPR.,p.140

MORGAN, JOSIAH of Gloucester County and Malvina Weathers, bond 28 July 1828. Consent by Rebecca Weathers, mother of the bride. William Morgan (b).
MBB.,p.40

MORGAN, PETER and Fanny Morgan*, bond 1 November 1809. William Morgan (b).

MORGAN, THOMAS married by 4 March 1718/19 Sarah Pannell, widow and executrix of Thomas Pannell (1677-1719) (q.v.).   COB#8,p.81.

MORGAN, WILLIAM and Nancy Morgan (spinster), bond 9 April 1801. David Morgan (b).

MORGAN, WILLIAM married by 1806 Isabella Barber (Kelsick) Lawson, widow of Richard Lawson (q.v.), p.115 and daughter of Captain Younger and Mary (Barnes) Kelsick (q.v.), p.111-112.   AB#3,p.137,198

MORGAN, WILLIAM and Patty Pully*, bond 11 February 1807. Edward J. Northen (b).

MORRIS, EDWARD and Elizabeth Hammond, married 25 May 1727.   NFPR.,p.140

MORRIS, HUDSON and Sally Nash, bond 4 August 1806. Consent by Mary Pratt, mother of the bride. John Morris (b).

MORRIS, JAMES M. and Parmela Newman*, bond 11 October 1834.   Joseph Newman (b); Samuel M. Newman (w).   MBB.,p.124

MORRIS, JOHN and Caty Stott (spinster)*, bond 1 July 1798. The bride, in writing her own consent, states she is "twenty years of age and act for myself." William Morris (b); John Fawcett (w).

MORRIS, JOHN and Mahala Kelly, bond 6 August 1798. Consent by John Kelly, father of the bride. Reuben Kelly (b); John Fawcett (w).

MORRIS, SIMON and Susannah Lyne, bond 7 September 1789. Ann Lyne and Susannah Lyne write their consent for the license to issue. William Packett (b).

MORRIS, WILLIAM and Alice Mothershead, bond 7 September 1801. Nathaniel Mothershead (b).

MORRISON, JOSEPH married Margaret Scurlock, 9 December 1739.   NFPR.,p.141

MORRISON, JOSEPH of Northumberland County and Hannah Morrison (widow), bond 14 April 1802. William Morrison, Sr. (b).

MORRISON, WILLIAM and Hannah Woollard, bond 7 January 1796. Consent by Mary Woollard, mother of the bride. William Miskell (b).

MORROW, ANDREW married Deborah Sherlock, 11 October 1728.   NFPR.,p.140
[The name is rendered Morrow, Murrow, Murrah, Murray &c: 20 February 1733 Andrew Murrow, bricklayer, and Deborah, his wife, daughter and heir of John Sherlock, deceased, conveyed 80 acres of land in Lunenburg Parish whereon they then lived. DB#8,p.684; WB#5,p.371.]

MORSE, THOMAS (17??-1792)   SEE : GEORGE FOWLES   PAGE 72

MORTON, JAMES (17??-1760) married prior to 2 December 1745, Elizabeth (Snead)
    Keith, widow, daughter of Charles Snead (16??-1724) who died testate in
    Richmond County. DB#10,p.343; WB#4,p.240; WB#6,p.191.

MORTON, JOHN JUNIOR and Mary Mountjoy, license July 1714.   DB#6,p.275
    [The bride was the daughter of Alvin and Mary (Lane) Mountjoy (q.v.). She
    married (2) by 1733 William Jordan, Gentleman, and the rich merchant, John
    Morton Jordan, Gentleman, (173?-1771) of King George County, was their only
    child. John Morton, Jr. (16??-1728) died intestate in Richmond County.
    There is a considerable account of the Morton family in Dr. Daniel Morton's
    two volume typescript, The Mortons and Their Kin (1920), in the Library of
    Congress (CS71.M89). COB#8,p.125,198; DB#7,p.83-85; 17V312; OPR.,p.84,134.]

MORTON, JOSEPH [GENTLEMAN] (1715-1759) of James City County, son of Captain John
    and Mary (Mountjoy) Morton (q.v.) p.139, married (1) by 1738 Frances Colston,
    younger of the two daughters of William and Mary (Meriwether) Colston (q.v.),
    p.42,by whom he had an only child, viz: Frances Morton who married James Hub-
    ard, Gentleman, (q.v.),p.98; married (2) Margaret Beckwith, born 29 July 1725
    in North Farnham Parish, daughter of Sir Marmaduke and Elizabeth (Brocken-
    brough) Beckwith (q.v.),p.13 and left issue several children. Joseph Morton
    represented James City County in the House of Burgesses 1756-1758; he died
    testate in that county but his will is recorded in a volume now lost. How-
    ever, there is a copy of it in King George County COB#3,p.1202 et seq., and
    here too is considerable genealogical fact. WB#4,p.198; WB#5,p.652; 17V321;
    12T142-145.

MOSELEY, EDWARD [MAJOR] (16??-1727) of Essex County married by 2 March 1698 Eliza-
    beth Willson, daughter of Elias Willson, the elder, (16??-1699) of Richmond
    County. COB#3,p.331; WB#2,p.9; Essex County Wills &c:#4,p.204.

MOSS, JOHN A. of Northumberland County and Lucinda Beale, bond 5 October 1808.
    Consent by Richard Beale, father of the bride. Alfred Beale (b). [Lucinda
    (Beale) Moss m(2) William McCarty (q.v.),p.124. Beale,p.64.]

MOSS, WILLIAM and Rose Ann Cash, license 19 January 1852. Consent by Felisha
    Cash, mother of the bride. Samuel Marks (w) and Richard Scates (w). Mar-
    ried 21 January 1852 by the Rev. John Pullen. [The bride was the daughter
    of William and Fillisha (France) Cash (q.v.),p.34.]

MOTHERSHEAD, GEORGE M. and Lucy Bartlett*, bond 26 October 1848. George Mothers-
    head (b); Samuel T. Reamy (w) and Henry Pare (w). Married 26 October 1848
    by Rev. John Pullen.   MBB.,p.313

MOTHERSHEAD, JAMES S. and Martha Ann Lathom, bond 23 May 1846. Consent by H.
    Lathom, parent of the bride. Edwin C. Edwards (b); Samuel Mothershead (w).
    Married 28 May 1846 by the Rev. Elijah L. Williams.   MBB.,p.277

MOTHERSHEAD, JOHN and Milly Connolly, bond 5 December 1785. Nicholas Stowers
    (b).

MOTHERSHEAD, RICHARD H. and Frances S. McKenney*, bond 1 January 1846. Samuel
McKenney (b); Daniel Atwill (w). Married 1 January 1846 by the Rev. John
Pullen.   MBB.,p.269

MOTHERSHEAD, SAMUEL and Elizabeth Asbury*, bond 7 February 1803. William Bragg
(b).

MOTHERSHEAD, SAMUEL D. and Mary A.F. Ficklin*, bond 14 May 1850. Richard H.
Lyell (b); Henry Lyell (w).   MBB.,p.338

MOTHERSHEAD, WILLIAM and Sally Morris (widow)*, bond 9 March 1821. Thomas
Bartlett (b); Richard Mothershead (w).

MOTHERSHEAD, WILLIAM H. and Rebecca Pullen, daughter of John and Henretta Pullen, license 1 March 1852. Joseph Bowen (w). Married 10 March 1852 by
the Rev. John Pullen.

MOTHERSHEAD, WILLIAM R. and Ann Mothershead*, bond 23 January 1834. William H.
Morris (b); Mary Morris (w).   MBB.,p.114

MOTT, JAMES of Northumberland County and Ellen Pullen*, bond 18 January 1791.
Jeduthum Pullen (b); Moses Pullen (w).

MOTT, JOSEPH and Tabitha Dobyns, bond 28 May 1794. Consent by Amney Dobyns,
mother of the bride. Joseph Tapscott (b); John How, Jr. (w).

MOUNTJOY, ALVIN [GENTLEMAN] (16??-1700) married circa 1690 Mary Lane, daughter
of William Lane who had large land patents in the Rappahannock watershead.
She married (2) Elias Wilson who died testate in 1706/7 and (3) per marriage
contract 27 May 1707, Dr. Joseph Belfield (16??-1738), widower of Frances
Wright (q.v.),p.15. Alvin and Mary (Lane) Mountjoy had four children, viz:
(a) Sebella Mountjoy; (b) Thomas Mountjoy d.s.p.; (c) Mary Mountjoy married
in July 1714, Captain John Morton, Jr. (q.v.),p.139; and (d) Alvin Mountjoy
(Jr.),(1700-1760) (q.v.). C&P.,p.391 patent 1662 to William Lane, recited
in DB#7,p.83-85 to be the father of Mary (Lane) Mountjoy Willson Belfield.
COB#8,p.125,198; DB#7,p.83-85; WB#2,p.18; 20W(2)556; Louis des Cognets, Jr.,
in his Governor Garrard of Kentucky (1962) gives some account of the Mountjoy family of the Northern Neck of Virginia.

MOUNTJOY, ALVIN and Ellen Thornton, married 3 May 1728.   NFPR.,p.140
[Captain Alvin Mountjoy (1700-1760) was the posthumously born son of Alvin
and Mary (Lane) Mountjoy. His wife appears on the records as Ellen, Ellin
and Eleanor; she was the daughter of Captain John and Elizabeth (Moss)
Crask(e) (q.v.),p.46 and widow of Mathew Thornton (16??-1727). Captain Alvin
Mountjoy died intestate in 1760 and his widow died testate in 1776, both in
Richmond County; their only child was Mary Mountjoy who married in 1753
William Peirce of Westmoreland County (q.v.). COB#8,p.125,198; COB#9,p.410;
DB#8,p.83-85; DB#9,p.216; DB#10,p.343; DB#15,p.61,116; WB#5,p.57; WB#6,p.266;
WB#7,p.79,220.]

MOUNTJOY, JOHN married long before 1725 Ann Thornton, daughter of Luke Thornton,
Sr. who died testate in 1726, however, a deed of gift dated 5 October 1725

is more genealogically informative than the will of Luke Thornton, Sr. as
the latter seems to have been drawn to confirm the former. By the aforementioned deed of gift, Luke Thornton, Sr. mentioned his daughter, Ann wife
of John Mountjoy, and their daughter Sarah Mountjoy, but by his will dated
29 January 1725/6 he refers to his said granddaughter as Sarah Jones. Sarah
Mountjoy married 30 November 1725 John Jones (q.v.),p.108. DB#8,p.295;
WB#5,p.6.

MOXLEY, JAMES B. and Mary B. Deatley*, bond 2 December 1833. Archibald Sisson
     (b); Margaret N. Jesper (w).   MBB.,p.111

MOXLEY, JAMES B. and Margaret B. Lusby*, bond 7 January 1845. Daniel Hardwick
     (b). Married 7 January 1845 by the Rev. Elijah L. Williams.   MBB.,p.253

MOXLEY, RICHARD JR. and Betty Muse, bond 3 September 1753. Daniel Muse (b).

MOXLEY, THOMAS married by 26 March 1741 Ann Smith, daughter of John Smith, saw-
     yer, (16??-1718). DB#11,p.124; WB#4,p.21. [6 April 1752: Deed from the
     executors of Thomas Wright Belfield, Gentleman, deceased, to William Ford
     for certain land, reciting same was purchased 26 March 1741 by the said
     Belfield from Thomas Moxley who married Ann Smith, daughter of John Smith,
     sawyer, deceased, per a deed of record in the Secretary's Office. Unfor-
     tunately the many important documents of record in this repository and in
     the General Court of Virginia, were destroyed in 1865 when Richmond, Va.,
     was burned. However, hidden references such as this, which give an insight
     to the documents once of record in these repositories, are frequent in the
     surviving records of the counties whose records have been preserved.]

MOZINGO, ALFRED S. and Mary M. Coles*, bond 18 September 1839. Edwin J. Rey-
     nolds (b); John Boyle (w). Married by the Rev. Nathan Healy.   MBB.,p.185

MOZINGO, BARNES B. and Adeline Yeatman*, license 14 August 1851. John E. Sandy
     (w) and Miskell Mozingo (w). Married 14 August 1851 by the Rev. George M.
     Northam.

MOZINGO, CHRISTOPHER B. and Fanny Barnes, bond 2 January 1821. Peirce Mozingo
     (b).

MOZINGO, JAMES F. and Anne Maskill (spinster)*, bond 3 February 1806. Consent
     by Edward and Elizabeth Mozingo, parents of the groom. John Wright (b).

MOZINGO, JONATHAN B. and Matildy Efford*, bond 8 May 1847. Charles C. Carter
     (b).   MBB.,p.293

MOZINGO, JOSEPH and Elizabeth Brenham, bond 14 June 1831. Jonathan W. Bowen (b).
                                                                 MBB.,p.79

MOZINGO, THOMAS C. and Rebecca Jones, bond 1 February 1813. William Thomas (b).

MOZINGO, WILLIAM and Elizabeth Barrett, license 12 April 1851. Consent by Mary
     Barrett, mother of the bride. James Barrett (w). Married 24 April 1851 by
     the Rev. George Northam.

MULLINS, JAMES of Westmoreland County and Jemima Sisson (spinster)*, bond 5 October 1820. Consent by William M. Walker, guardian of the bride. John M. Luttrell (b); Frances Thomas (w).

MULLINS, JOHN married long before 31 October 1774 Sarah Brickey, daughter of John Brickey who died intestate in 1733. By 31 October 1774 the said Sarah (Brickey) Mullins is deceased, leaving Thomas Mullins, a minor, her heir-at-law. DB#14,p.335; WB#5,p.189,208.

MUNDAY, HENRY and Alice Shackleford, bond 12 September 1839. Daniel Garland (b).   MBB.,p.185

MURRAH : MURRAY : MURROW   SEE : ANDREW MORROW, PAGE 138

MURREN, WILLIAM T. of Richmond County was married on 19 January 1826 by the Rev. Henry Slicer, to Miss Mary McPherson of Fredericksburg. The marriage was announced in the Fredericksburg Virginia Herald of 25 January 1826. Fredericksburg Marriage Register No.1,p.38: 19 January 1826, marriage bond of William Thompson Murren and Mary McPherson, ward of Benjamin Clark who is the bondsman.

MUSE, NICHOLAS and Eliz.^{a} Asbury, bond 26 November 1749. Daniel Muse (b). [The Muse family, appearing in the records of Richmond County, had their origin in the adjoining county of Westmoreland. The late Madams West and Fauntleroy deposited a genealogical account of the Muse Family of Virginia in VSL:AD #21498; see also 53V132-138,221-227,312-323.]

MUSE, REUBIN and Livinia Fossett, bond 7 November 1848. John B. Tiffey (b); William Henry Settle (w). Married 4 February 1849 by the Rev. John Pullen.
                                                                    MBB.,p.315

MUSE, THOMAS and Sarah Chattin, bond 22 May 1751. Richard Taylor Jesper (b). Oddly, the bride is described as both a widow and a spinster!

MUSE, THOMAS and Elizabeth Lawson, bond 20 November 1765. John Lawson (b).

                                         N

NASH, GEORGE of Westmoreland County and Ann Smith, bond 2 June 1788. Consent by Winefred Smith, mother of the bride. James How (b).

NASH, GEORGE and Frances Newgent*, bond 12 December 1822. John Hanks (b).

NASH, NEWMAN and Molly Burgess*, bond 7 September 1789. James Nash (b); Gilbert Balderson (w).

NASH, RICHARD married Hannah Nash, 30 October 1743.   NFPR.,p.144

NASH, RICHARD and Fanny Stonum, bond 24 December 1799. Consent by William Stonum, father of the bride. Richard Bennehan (b).

NASH, THOMAS and Lucy Lawson, bond 21 November 1761. Christopher Lawson (b).

NASH, WILLIAM married Margaret Brian, 30 May 1729.   NFPR.,p.77,144

NASH, WILLIAM and Judith Meeks, bond 13 May 1749. Daniel Hornby (b).

NASH, ZACHARIAH and Mary Marks, bond 12 March 1833. Consent by James Marks; no
     relationship stated. John F. Morris (b).   MBB.,p.103

NAYLOR, JOHN and Mary Rogers, license February 1711/12   DB#6,p.275
[John Naylor, Gentleman, (16??-1735) of Richmond and King George counties,
married (1) in February 1711/12, Mary Rogers who died 16 September 1717
leaving two daughters, viz: (a) Elizabeth Naylor, born in North Farnham Parish 25 September 1712, married in Saint Paul's Parish, Stafford (now King
George) County, 6 August 1735 John Simpson of Overwharton Parish, Stafford
County; and (b) Hannah Naylor, born in North Farnham Parish, 4 February 1715,
married in 1735 Captain David Bronough (17??-1774) of King George County as
his first wife, and died circa 1737 leaving an only child, (i) Mary Bronough
(circa 1736-1799) who m(1) Joseph Waugh, Gentleman, and m(2) Colonel Elijah
Threlkeld, both of Stafford County (21T265-266). Captain David Bronough,
Gentleman, married (2) Martha Moore, step-sister of his first wife and daughter of Francis and Ann Moore (q.v.),p.136, by whom he had issue; married
(3) Elizabeth Bruce, daughter of Charles Bruce who died testate in King
George County in 1754 and his wife nee Elizabeth Pannell, daughter of William
and Frances (Sterne) Pannell (q.v.) of Richmond County. Captain David Bron-
ough was the son of Jeremiah Bronough, Sr. (1672-circa 1749) and grandson of
David Bronough who purchased land in 1671 in what is now King George County.
The title to the Bronough land on Lamb's Creek is found in Richmond County
DB#1,p.10 and DB#3,p.50-52; also King George County DB#3,p.122 and other records there. John Naylor, Gentleman, married (2) circa 1719 Ann Moore, widow of Francis Moore (1660-1718) (q.v.),p.136, by whom he had two daughters,
Anne and Joyce, who died in infancy. John Naylor died testate on 8 June 1735
in King George County and by his last will and Testament bequeathed his landed estate in that county to his younger daughter Hannah, and John Simpson, the
husband of the elder daughter, Elizabeth, strongly contested the validity of
the document and sought to prevent its probate. This action caused various
depositions to be taken in 1735, and the court "on hearing the arguments and
having taken the depositions" of sundry persons "are of opinion the said will
shall be established." But this action, coupled with other legal factors,
threw a cloud upon the title of the Naylor land and for this we are grateful
genealogically as it caused the deposition of aged William Chadwell (1728-
1813) to be taken in King George County on 27 April 1808; he had married in
1758 Ann Moore Bronough, daughter of Captain David and Martha (Moore) Bronough,
and stated in detail the entire Moore-Naylor genealogy. From this deposition
and other records, Robert Hening (1771-1828), attorney at law, drew a genealogical chart clearly outlining the descendants of John Naylor for six generations. DB#6,p.139; DB#7,p.100,217; MRB.,p.47; King George County COB#2,p.44;
Hening vs Fitzhugh, FDC#575,in which is a copy of the will of John Naylor,
Gentleman, (16??-1735), and the various depositions taken at the time it was
offered for probate, which said documents were recorded in now lost King George
County WB#1 (1721-1752); SPR.,p.124; 21T265-266.]

NEALE, AUGUSTINE and Juliet Ann McCarty, bond 21 December 1815. Consent by
Elizabeth McCarty, mother and guardian of the bride. George Saunders (b).
[The marriage was announced in the Fredericksburg Virginia Herald of 3 January 1816; it states both parties were of Richmond County and that they were
married on 21st December 1815 by the Rev. Mr. Seward.]

NEALE, AUGUSTINE and Lucy S. Bramham*, bond 24 June 1845. Augustine N. Saunders
  (b).   MBB.,p.260

NEALE, RICHARD (171?-1800), son of Major Richard Neale (1682-1729) and his wife
nee Judith Shapleigh (1692-circa 1725) of Northumberland County, was twice
married in Richmond County. First, between 1742-1744 to Catherine Fauntleroy, daughter of Major Moore Fauntleroy (1680-1739) (q.v.) p.68, by whom he
had five daughters. As the wife of Richard Neale was not properly recogniz-
ed in the usually authorative work of Miss Fauntleroy and she has been incorrectly dubbed in other accounts, I wish to point out that Catherine Fauntleroy, infant, was allotted 200 acres upon certain division of a tract of
land belonging to her father per the terms of his will, in 1742. In 1744
the rent roll of Lunenburg Parish carries this line: "Catherine Fauntleroy
200 acres - to Richard Neale," and the rent rolls of 1751 and 1765 carry
the said Richard Neale with 200 acres of land. In 1791 Richard Neale was
joined by his five daughters and their spouses in conveying the land in Lunenburg Parish of which his first wife, Catherine Neale, then deceased, was
vested but reserved to himself and his "present wife Ann" a life estate in
the said land. The five daughters of Richard Neale, Gentleman, and Catherine Fauntleroy, his first wife, were: (a) Margaret Neale married Captain
Henry Garnett (q.v.),p.76; (b) Judith Neale married Edward Matthews of Essex
County; (c) Susanna Neale m(1) William Miller and (2) Andrew Boulware, both
of Essex County; (d) Elizabeth Neale married Robert Callis (q.v.),p.32; and
(e) Hannah Shapleigh Neale, spinster, of Essex County, in 1801 when the estate of her father was divided. AB#1,p.184; COB#11,p.269; DB#11,p.269; DB#12,
p.59,60,354,357; DB#14,p.287; DB#16,p.211; WB#9,p.141; Rent Rolls of Lunenburg Parish 1742,1746,1751,1765 in VSL:AD; also Essex County DB#33,p.345; WB
#16, p.103. In the Carter Papers, College of William and Mary, is an agree-
ment dated 8 November 1786 between Richard Neale, his aforementioned five
daughters and the spouses of those then living, with Robert Wormeley Carter,
Esq. of Sabine Hall, obligating them to convey to the said Carter two tracts
of land, viz: 200 acres the said five ladies "claim as tenants in common and
heirs to Catherine Neale, the first wife of Richard Neale and same being the
land whereon the said Richard Neale now lives," and also 60 acres of land
purchased by the said Neale of William Garland, reserving to the said Neale
a life estate in said 260 acres. The deed conveying this property was dated
11 July 1791 and recorded in DB#16,p.211. Richard Neale, Gentleman, was
married secondly to Ann Reynolds (q.v.).

NEALE, RICHARD and Ann Reynolds (widow), bond 4 March 1762. George Reynolds (b).
[The bride was the widow of John Reynolds (17??-1761). Their marriage con- '
tract was dated 6 March 1762. DB#12,p.354,357; WB#6,p.262; WB#9,p.141.]

NEALE, WILLIAM and Eliza T. Smith, bond 14 January 1817. Consent by Catherine
Smith for the bride's marriage; no relationship stated. Harrison Ball (b);
Sarah T. Snead (w).

NEASOM : NEASOME : NEASUM   SEE :   NEWSOM PAGE 146

NEASOM, EPP.^A L. and Fanny Palmer*, bond 7 June 1813. Fouchee G. Tebbs (b).

NEASOM, ROBERT and Polly Glascock, bond 1 September 1798. Edward Saunders (b).

NEASOM, SAMUEL W. married Nancy Baker, 12 September 1811.   WFMR.,n.p.

NEASUM, WILLIAM and Winifred Dobyns (widow)*, bond 6 February 1818. Vincent
    Shackleford (b); George H. Dobyns (w).

NEASOME, WILLIAM J. and Emily M. Wright*, bond 26 April 1845. A.M. Wright (b).
                                                                  MBB.,p.259

NELMS, JOSHUA married Sarah Northen, 12 February 1728/9.   NFPR.,p.144

NELSON, ALEXANDER married Prudence Pettey, 8 January 1729/30.   NFPR.,p.144

NEWBY, CYRUS of Lancaster County and Nancy Hunton*, bond 21 May 1796. Oswald
    Newby of Lancaster County (b); Oswald Newby (w) and Susannah Hunton (w).

NEWBY, WILLIAM of Lancaster County and Betty Hunton*, bond 22 April 1791.
    Thomas Hunton (b).

NEWCOMB, EDWARD and Elizabeth Miller*, bond 8 November 1786. James Nash (b).

NEWGENT, DOMINICK and Ann Smith (widow), license April 1711.   DB#6,p.275

NEWGENT, DOMINICK married Margaret Durham, 2 December 1729.   NFPR.,p.144
    [The bride was the daughter of Thomas and Mary (Smoot) Durham, (q.v.),p.61.
    DB#3,p.57; DB#9,p.577-582; WB#3,p.210,270; 8 September 1770, Dominick New-
    gent, aged about 61, made a deposition in the suit, Taff vs Yerby, which
    pended in Richmond County chancery court. VSL:AD #25391.]

NEWGENT, GEORGE and Sarah Nash*, bond 21 December 1824.LeRoy Pope (b). MBB.,p.6

NEWMAN, FREDERICK and Jane Taylor*, bond 3 August 1818. Robert Thompson (b).
    The bride's consent was dated 12 May 1818: ..."if God speare my life and
    his, I have promised Frederick Newman to be his wedded wife on August next."

NEWMAN, GEORGE and Ann Marks, bond 21 January 1763. John Eidson (b).

NEWMAN, HENRY and Sarah Brann, bond 22 October 1840. Consent by Mary Brann,
    mother of the bride. Eppa: Weathers (b); Joseph Newman (w). Married by
    the Rev. Nathan Healy.   MBB.,p.198

NEWMAN, JOHN married circa 1744 Elizabeth Deane, daughter of John and Jane Deane
    (q.v.),p.70-71.

NEWMAN, JOHN and Susanna Jinkins, bond 3 September 1792. Consent by James and
    Martha Jinkins, parents of the bride. James Jinkins (b).

NEWMAN, JOHN JR. and Millicent Newton "free persons of colour of Richmond County," bond 20 May 1829. William Settle (b).   MBB.,p.55

NEWMAN, JOSEPH (bachelor) and Sophia Hinson (spinster), bond 1 February 1830. William Hinson (b); he is the bride's father.   MBB.,p.61

NEWMAN, JOSEPH and Winifred B. Weathers*, bond 24 December 1839. Youell F.P. Askins (b).   MBB.,p.188

NEWMAN, SAMUEL M. and Susan Sanders*, bond 22 April 1833. Samuel Cralle, Jr. (b).   MBB.,p.105

NEWMAN, SEPHENS and Easter Belfield, bond 26 September 1846. Consent by Jane Belfield; no relationship stated. Thomas Kirk (b).   MBB.,p.197

NEWMAN, THOMAS married by 1699 Bridgett Willson, daughter of Elias Willson the elder (16??-1699). The groom was the son of Thomas Newman, who lived upon Rappahannock Creek, and seemingly a kinsman of Captain Alexander Newman (16??-1698) who left the said Thomas Newman (Jr.) his landed estate. On 30 December 1700 Thomas Newman conveyed to Captain John Tarpley the land bequeathed to him by Captain Alexander Newman, deceased. The last will and Testament of Captain Alexander Newman was proved in court 1 June 1698; it was recorded in now lost Richmond County WB#1 (1692-1699). In 1711 various depositions were taken in regard to the will of Captain Alexander Newman as it appears there was some contention as to which of the several Thomas Newmans the said Captain bequeathed his land. COB#2,p.299; DB#3,p. 61; WB#2,p.9,55; WB#3,p.58. There is a sketch of the Newman family in William Fletcher Boogher, Gleanings of Virginia History (Washington, 1903), p.236 et seq.

NEWMAN, THOMAS and Catherine Dye, bond 3 February 1746. Avery Dye, Jr. (b).

NEWSOM   SEE : NEASOM : NEASOME : NEASUM PAGE 145

NEWSOM, WILLIAM and Barbara Williams*, bond 4 December 1786. William Williams (b).   In her note of consent for the license to issue, the bride assures Colonel Peachey that "I am of age;" he was clerk of the court.

NEWTON, GERRARD [GARRARD] (16??-1706) married by October 1694 Rebecca (surname unknown); she married secondly by 11 November 1707 Thomas Walters (q.v.). John Newton (16??-1697) of Westmoreland County by will bequeathed to his son Gerrard Newton his Little Falls Plantation of 1000 acres - it was then in Richmond County, in 1721 in King George County and since 1777 in Stafford County. John Newton entailed this estate upon the male heirs of Gerrard Newton and Rebecca, his wife. Gerrard Newton died intestate prior to 6 March 1706 leaving three children, viz: (a) John Newton who died when 12-13 years of age; (b) Rose Newton who married (1) Thomas Grigsby and m(2) Townshend Dade (q.v.),p.82; and (c) Elizabeth Newton who married Mathew Guilbert (q.v.),p.82. As the only son and heir of Gerrard and Rebecca Newton died in his minority, the Little Falls Plantation reverted to Major William Newton and it became his well known pre-Revolutionary abode. COB#4,p.135;

WB#3,p.55; COB#5,p.264; Stafford County Record Book "Z",p.392; Westmoreland County W&D#2,p.104; Fredericksburg District Court DB "C",p.241,363;
title papers of Little Falls Plantation in the Tazewell Papers, Boxes 1,
2, and 26, VSL:AD; 23T222.

NEWTON, WILLIAM JR. married 177? his first cousin, Martha Rust, daughter of Captain Peter and Elizabeth (Newton) Rust and granddaughter of William and
Elizabeth (Berryman) Newton of Westmoreland County. William Newton, Jr.
was the son of Major William Newton (171?-1789) of Little Falls Plantation
and his wife nee Elizabeth Kenyon. Major Newton by will (23T222) bequeathed to his "absent" son William Newton, Jr. 250 acres of his Little Falls
Plantation and provided if "he never should return then it shall fall with
all its increase to his daughter Sarah Newton." In 1779, after the death
of his wife, William Newton, Jr. made a deed of gift to his daughter Sarah
Newton for 250 acres of land in Stafford County whereon he then lived (and
subsequently mentioned in his father's will), 8 Negro slaves, various chattels and household furniture. William Newton, Jr. joined the Revolutionary
Army and was never heard from again. About 1801, Robert Hening (a special
agent in regard to the status of certain British debtors) reported that William Newton, Jr. "was a drunk; a worthless man." He states Newton was sent to
South Carolina during the Revolutionary War, deserted the American Army and
joined the British Army and was never heard from again according to his in-
formants Isaac Newton, Thomas Newton, Nathaniel Fox and John Bell all of
Stafford County. Sarah Newton, only child of William and Martha (Rust)
Newton, was raised by her maternal relatives in Westmoreland County and married there per bond dated 8 January 1789, Robert Sanford. In 1798 the Stafford County Land Tax Book indicates the 250 acres of land in that county
possessed by Robert Sanford and wife was sold to Arthur Morson. Suit in
chancery, Robert Sanford vs Peter Rust, Richmond County court papers, bundle 1795; British Public Records Office, Special Agents Reports (Robert Hening), microfilm #121, Library of Congress; Stafford County Land Tax Books
1782-1798, VSL:AD; Ellsworth Marshall Rust, Rust of Virginia (1940, CS71-
R97),p.55-68; 23T222-236; Stratton Nottingham, The Marriage License Bonds
of Westmoreland County, Va. 1786-1850,p.62. (I make this detailed mention
of William Newton (Jr.), son of Major William and Elizabeth (Kenyon) Newton,
as he has been misidentified and issue assigned to him in error.)

NICHALS, WILLIAM and Nancy Todd*, bond 1 April 1844. George Jones (b). MBB.,p.249

NICHOLS, CHARLES married Ann Davis, 17 August 1727.   NFPR.,p.144

NICHOLS, JOHN married Mary Lillis, 5 March 1727/8.   NFPR.,p.144

NICHOLSON, JOHN of Henrico County and Susanna Peachey*, bond 24 April 1789.
Bartholomew McCarty (b); Charles T. McCarty (w). [The Fredericksburg Virginia Herald of 14 May 1789: "Married: On Sunday the 26th ulto., Mr. John Nicholson, of Baltimore, merchant, to Miss Susanna Peachey, daughter of Colonel
William Peachey of Milden Hall, Richmond county." The bride was the daughter of Colonel William Peachey (1729-1802) and his second wife nee Elizabeth
Griffin Colston (q.v.).]

NORRIS, EPAPHRODITUS of Lancaster County and Fanny Dobyns (spinster), bond 27
    August 1795. Consent by Abner Dobyns; no relationship stated. Robert Pal-
    mer (b); John Palmer (w). The bond is signed by the groom, "Eppy Norris."

NORRIS, WILLIAM of Northumberland County and Winney Headley*, bond 10 January
    1809. The bride writes her own consent and she is joined by her parents,
    James and Winney Headley. Griffin Headley (w).

NORTHEN, ALFRED G. and Harriet Jesper*, bond 22 October 1844. Archibald Sisson
    (b). Married 24 October 1844 by the Rev. William N. Ward.   MBB.,p.250

NORTHEN, EDMUND and Polly Street, bond 9 April 1811. Richard Street (b).

NORTHEN, EDMUND N. and Rebecca M. Dobyns, bond 28 January 1812. Consent by LeRoy
    Dobyns, father of the bride. Christopher L. Dobyns (b). [The bride was the
    daughter of LeRoy and Lucy (Lawson) Dobyns (q.v.),p.55. The groom was the
    son of Captain Peter and Jane (Alderson) Northen (q.v.),p.148. This was the
    groom's first marriage; his second is recorded next below.]

NORTHEN, EDMUND N. and Peggey Jesper*, bond 21 October 1822. Robert W. Carter
    (b).

NORTHEN, EDMUND N. and Frances Hogan (widow), bond 1 April 1835. Thomas R. Hale,
    father of the bride, gives his consent (q.v.),p.95. George Saunders (b);
    Robert Lewis (w) and Aphier Lewis (w).   MBB.,p.132

NORTHEN, EDWARD J. and Sarah Dobyns*, bond 5 December 1796. Samuel Baker (b).

NORTHEN, EDWARD J. JR. and Catharine M. Northen*, bond 7 December 1832. Peter S.
    Northen (b).   MBB.,p.97

NORTHEN, ELIAS and Sally Kennan, bond 11 June 1817. Consent by Richard Street,
    guardian of the bride. Richard Efford (b); Martin Sisson (w).

NORTHEN, GEORGE (17??-1795) married after 1767 Margaret Jones (17??-1799), dau-
    ghter of Edward Jones (17??-1759) and niece of Isaac Jones (17??-1764).
    AB#1,p.546; AB#3,p.59; WB#6,p.148,350; WB#9,p.29,107.

NORTHEN, GEORGE and Nancy W. Neasome, bond 13 December 1824. Alfred C. Askins
    (b); he makes oath both parties are 21 years of age.   MBB.,p.4

NORTHEN, GEORGE and Elizabeth H. Bryant, bond 17 February 1835. Richard O. Jeff-
    ries (b).   MBB.,p.130

NORTHEN, JAMES and Catharine Gwinn Smith, bond 22 December 1800. William C.
    Smith (b).

NORTHEN, PETER [CAPTAIN] (17??-1811) married 17?? Jane Alderson (1756-1832),
    daughter of James and Sarah Ann Alderson. ECD says they had issue: (a)
    James Northen, born 4 January 1774, married 22 December 1800 Catharine
    Gwinn Smith; (b) Sarah Ann Northen, born 20 December 1775, married 6 March

1797, Joseph Redman, Jr; (c) William Northen, born 16 June 1778, married
22 June 1801 in Westmoreland County, Lucy Robinson Yeatman; (d) Jeremiah
Northen, removed to Kentucky; (e) Edmund N. Northen married (1) 28 January
1812, Rebecca M. Dobyns and m(2) 21 October 1822, Peggy Jesper; (f) George
Northan married Margaret Jones; (g) Elias Northan married 11 June 1817
Sally Kennan; (h) Jane Northen married 11 January 1814, Richard L. Shackleford; (i) Peter Smith Northen, born 23 March 1785, married Harriet S. Montague. The dates of birth cited are taken from the North Farnham Parish
Register; the issue is not named in order - George Northan was probably
the eldest son. DB#23,p.496; WB#7,p.472; WB#9,p.383; ECD Papers, Box 17,
in VHS; Account Book of Colonel John Tayloe 1776-1786, p.96,146, in VHS,
carries the account of William Northen of North Carolina, 1779, and same
was settled with Colonel Tayloe's executors in 1780 by "your son Peter"
Northen.

NORTHEN, PETER S. and Harriet S. Montague*, bond 14 March 1833. George B. Ston-
    um (b).   MBB.,p.103
    [The bride was the daughter of Thomas Tarpley and Elizabeth (Montague) Mon-
    tague (q.v.),p.136.]

NORTHEN, PETER S. and Alice Smith*, bond 12 July 1848. Richard H. Lyell (b);
    L. Davenport (w).   MBB.,p.310

NORTHEN, ROBERT F. and Hannah H. Porter, bond 1 November 1842. William Porter
    (b).   MBB.,p.227

NORTHEN, SAMUEL and Sarah Ann Baker, bond 13 November 1815. Samuel Baker (b).

NORTHEN, SAMUEL and Frances C. Hunt*, bond 19 January 1831. Thomas M. Glascock
    (b); John D. Glascock (w).   MBB.,p.73

NORTHEN, WILLIAM S. and Sarah A. Davis, bond 20 December 1832. Albert G. Plum-
    mer (b); he is guardian of the bride and consents.   MBB.,p.98

NORWOOD, CHARLES and Ann Dale, bond 20 April 1781. Vincent Brown (b).

NORWOOD, JOHN SR. and Elizabeth Windsor*, bond 8 June 1814. Foushee G. Tebbs
    (b).

                                    O

OBEAR, WILLIAM and Sarah Ann Jones, bond 21 December 1840. Consent by Viley
    Jones; no relationship stated. Lindsey Headley (b); William B. Hale (w).
    Married by the Rev. Nathan Healy.   MBB.,p.201

O'HARROW, THOMAS and Jane Reynolds, bond 4 March 1805. Robert Reynolds (b).

OLDHAM, JAMES and Nancy How, bond 11 January 1804. Consent by John How, father
    of the bride. Eppa: Weathers (b). [The groom was the son of William and

Ann Oldham (q.v.) whose Bible record cited by ECD states James and Nancy
(How) Oldham had two children, viz: (a) William Howe Oldham (28 October
1804-25 July 1806) and (b) Samuel Butler Oldham (25 November 1806-1 September 1827).

OLDHAM, PETER married Rebecca Alverson, 17 February 1728/7 (sic).   NFPR.,p.149
[The bride, Rebecca (Hatton) Alverson (Alderson), was the widow of Jeloff
Alderson, Jr. (q.v.), p.1. Peter Oldham died intestate in Richmond County
in 1735 and John Oldham was his administrator and also guardian in 1739 of
his only child, Katherine Oldham, who married shortly after this date Thomas
Brown,Sr. (q.v.), p.26.]

OLDHAM, WILLIAM married circa 1727 Priscilla McLaughlin (170?-1783), youngest
daughter of Manus and Elizabeth (Woodbridge) McLaughlin (q.v.), p.126. He
died testate in Richmond County in 1728, leaving an only child, William
Oldham, born 3 November 1728 in North Farnham Parish. William Oldham, Jr.
married (unknown to me); he predeceased his mother and she mentions his
children in her will dated 6 May 1783 which was proved 2 June 1783 at Richmond County court. Priscilla (McLaughlin) Oldham, widow, married (2) 22
January 1730, Henry Williams (q.v.). AB#2,p.170; WB#5,p.115; WB#7,p.424.

OLDHAM, WILLIAM (13 May 1745-6 June 1799) married (1) 25 May 1765 Susannah Sydnor (17??-5 March 1766) per bond dated 14 May 1765 in Northumberland County
(47V44) and had an only child, Susannah Sydnor Oldham, born 26 February 1766.
He married (2) 24 January 1768, Ann (surname unknown) (17??-12 October 1803)
and had nine children, viz: (b) James Oldham (2 September 1768-28 January
1809), married 12 January 1804 Nancy How (q.v.),p.149-150; (c) John Oldham
(10 May 1772-12 July 1803); (d) Sally Oldham (18 September 1774-21 October
1790); (e) Jinny Oldham, born 21 June 1778; (f) Samuel Oldham (21 March 1781-
29 December 1801); (g) Thomas Oldham, born 28 January 1783; (h) Betsy Oldham
8 February 1785-22 November 1794); (i) Nancy Oldham, born 13 July 1787; (j)
Edward ("Neddy") Oldham, born 27 July 1790 and married 28 January 1812 Fanny
(surname not given). ECD Papers, Box 33 in VHS, cites above genealogy from
a record in Nancy Oldham Book in which there is a notation she moved to
Northumberland County, 9 January 1811. This record indicates that William
Oldham (1745-1799) was the son of James Oldham of Richmond County who died
20 February 1754, and his wife Tabitha, who died 20 January 1747. Their
only other child mentioned was Tabitha Oldham, born 12 January 1747. James
Oldham married (2) Leannah (surname unknown) and died testate in Richmond
County. Richmond County WB#6,p.29.

OLDHAM, WILLIAM of Northumberland County and Nancy Dobyns, bond 29 April 1786.
Consent by Thomas Dobyns, father of the bride. Hugh Harris (b). [The bride
was the daughter of Thomas Dobyns who died testate in Richmond County in 1788.
William Oldham died testate in Northumberland County in 1791. Nancy (Dobyns)
Oldham, widow, married (2) in Northumberland County on 23 August 1792, Merri-
man Payne, widower. AB#2,p.162,330; WB#8,p.36; Northumberland County Record
Book #14,p.424; Payne,p.504.]

OLDHAM, WILLIAM C. and Virginia Ficklin, bond 8 August 1843. Consent by C.D.
Ficklin, father of the bride. John F.B. Jeffries (b); Alexander M. Wright
(w). Married by the Rev. Nathan Healy.   MBB.,p.240

OLIFF   SEE : ELIFF   PAGE 64

OLIFF, THOMAS and Elizabeth Kelly (spinster), bond 4 November 1783. Benjamin
    Bramham (b); Robert Wormeley Carter (w).

OLIFF, WESLEY B. and Elizabeth Kelly*, license 1 December 1851. Frederick Bow-
    en (w), Zachariah Sanders (w) and W.D. Oliff (w). Married 16 December 1851
    by the Rev. John Pullen.

OLIFF, WILLIAM JR. and Sophia Carter*, bond 23 December 1835. John S. Carter
    (b); D.F. Ward (w).   MBB.,p.138

OLIFF, WILLIAM B. and Mary Sanders, bond 22 December 1842. Consent by Thomas
    Sanders, father of the bride. Griffin Sanders (b); John A. Payton (w).
    Married by the Rev. William Balderson.   MBB.,p.230

OLLIFF, WILLIAM D. and Mary Ann Bowen, bond 11 May 1850. Consent by William S.
    Bowen and Nancy Bowen, parents of the bride. Zachariah Sanders (b); Joseph
    Bowen (w). Married 15 May 1850 by the Rev. John Pullen.   MBB.,p.337

OLIVER, BENJAMIN JR. of Hanover County married by 1818 Lucy Harrison Tomlin,
    daughter of Colonel Walker and Priscilla (Ball) Tomlin of Richmond County
    (q.v.). AB#3,p.80,629,635; WB#9,p.165; Hayden,p.127; William Ronald Cocke
    III, Hanover County Chancery Wills And Notes (Columbia,Va.,1940),p.150,179.

OLIVER, DAVID married by 1794 Elizabeth Miskell, daughter of William and Eliza-
    beth (Samford) Miskell (q.v.), p.133. DB#17,p.17,102,129. Circa 1794
    David Oliver resided in Fredericksburg, Virginia.

OLIVER, THOMAS of Northumberland County and Alice Harrison, bond 19 November
    1788. Abraham Proctor (b).

OMOHUNDRO, WILLIAM H. and Eliza Ann Hutt, license 15 December 1851. John Graham
    (w). Consent by S.S.Hutt, father of the bride. Married 16 December 1851
    by the Rev. Alfred Wiles.

O'NEAL, DANIEL married Elizabeth Hading, 10 May 1674.   NFPR.,p.149

OPIE, JOHN of Northumberland County and Ann Metcalfe, license March 1713/14.
                                                                 DB#6,p.275
    [This was the second marriage of Captain John Opie (1675-1722) of Northum-
    berland County. There is an account of the Opie family in 54V68-76. The
    bride was the daughter of Richard and Elizabeth (Fauntleroy) Metcalfe,
    (q.v.), p.131.]

OPIE, LINDSAY (1715-1747) of Northumberland County married 18 February 1735
    Sarah Heale, daughter of George Heale, Gentleman, deceased, of Lancaster
    County. The groom was the eldest child of Captain John and Ann (Metcalfe)
    Opie (q.v.)p.151. Richmond County DB#9,p.453,519; 54V70-72.

ORNBAUN, LEWIS of Rockbridge County and Elizabeth Clarke, bond 1 January 1816.
    Robert Clarke (b). [In 1815 Lewis Orenbaum appears on the Rockbridge Coun-

ty personal property tax list and the same of 1816 renders the name Lewis
Orinbaun.]

OSBORNE, THOMAS married Frances Smith, 11 February 1726/7.   NFPR.,p.149

OWENS, JOHN of King George County married by 1735 Elinor Gallop, widow of Robert
    Gallop who died testate in Richmond County in 1720 and his landed estate
    fell into King George County upon its formation in 1721. MRB.,p.84; WB#4,
    p.161; also King George County DB#2,p.1 and DB#2,p.138-139.

                                      P

PACE [PACEY, PAICE, PAISE, PASIE &c.], THOMAS (16??-1725) of Rappahannock, Rich-
    mond and King George counties, also held property in Westmoreland and Staf-
    ford counties; he is described as a planter in the records of Rappahannock
    County and later as a gentleman. Thomas Pace was thrice married, but he
    appears to have died without issue. He married (1) by 1683 Alexia Fleming
    (circa 1662-circa 1687), only child of Captain Alexander Fleming (q.v.),p.
    69-70, and his second wife Elizabeth (Madestard) Lawson Clapman, widow suc-
    cessively of Epaphroditus Lawson and William Clapman, Jr., both of Lancast-
    er County. Alexia (Fleming) Pace d.s.p. leaving her only half-sister, Eliza-
    beth Fleming wife of Rowland Thornton (q.v.), her only heir. Thomas Pace
    married (2) by 25 February 1690, Jane (?   ) Bowcock White Harvey, widow
    successively of Thomas Bowcock, Thomas White and Thomas Harvey, all of West-
    moreland County. Jane had issue by her first two husbands, viz: (a) Thomas
    Bowcock (Jr.) who died testate in Westmoreland County in 1700, leaving issue;
    (b) Margaret Bowcock, wife of William Monroe, Gentleman, (1666-1737) of West-
    moreland County - the great-grandparents of President James Monroe (1758-1831)
    (c) Daniel White married Ann Sterne (q.v.); (d) George White married Elizabeth
    Birkett (q.v.); (e) Jane White married George Payne (q.v.). Thomas Pace mar-
    ried (3) by 31 January 1714/15, Mary Lilley, widow of John Lilley of Stafford
    County and step-daughter of John Pratt, Gentleman, (16??-1714) of Westmore-
    land County. On 3 December 1725 Mary Paise (Pace), widow and executrix of
    Thomas Paise (Pace), deceased, presented his will for probate before the
    King George County court and gave bond according to law; it was recorded in
    now lost King George County WB#1 (1721-1752). Mary Paise, widow, married
    in 1726 Major Thomas Vivion, widower of Frances Thacker (1696-1724); he sur-
    vived the said Mary, remarried and died testate in Westmoreland County in
    1761. DB#1,p.20; DB#3,p.30; MRB.,p.34; Westmoreland County COB 1690-1698,
    p.11,39,63; Westmoreland County W&D#2,p.78 and W&D#14,p.7; Northern Neck Land
    Grants #5,p.53,54,55; King George County COB#1,p.294; 46V361; Payne,p.369.

    PACKET : PACKETT

PACKET, HENRY and Nancy Scrimger*, bond 7 September 1807. James Scrimger (b);
    Charity Scrimger (w). [Henry Packett (27 February 1782-2 May 1842) married
    9 September 1807 Nancy Scrimger (1785-4 November 1870); see Bible record of
    his father William Packett (1736-1792) (q.v.),p.153.]

PACKETT, JAMES L. and Mary F.B. Walker*, bond 22 January 1833. W.R. Jeffries
certifies the bride is upwards of 21 years of age. Henry Packett certifies
the groom is 21 years of age. Thomas W. Walker (b).   MBB.,p.100

PACKETT, JAMES L. and Virginia Parr*, license 28 October 1852. William H. Packett (w). Married 28 October 1852 by the Rev. Elijah L. Williams.

PACKETT, JOHN and Maria Courtney*, bond 4 February 1841. William H. Packett (b);
Nancy Courtney (w). Married 4 February 1841 by the Rev. William N. Ward.
MBB.,p.206

PACKETT, RICHARD and Sarah Edwards*, bond 31 December 1788. William Packett (b).

PACKETT, WILLIAM and Mary Harford (spinster), bond 11 February 1778. William
Webster (b). [ECD Papers in VHS (1D3743b) cites the Bible record of William
Packett (4 April 1736- September 1792) married 13 February 1778 Mary Har-
ford (13 January 1754-6 May 1787), daughter of John and Elizabeth (Oldham)
Harford. William Packett died testate in Westmoreland County and his will
is of record in Westmoreland County W&D#18,p.227.]

PACKETT, WILLIAM and Polly Franklin*, bond 26 December 1807. James Northen (b);
Edmund Walker (w).

PALMER, ARMISTEAD J. of Lancaster County and Sally Palmer, bond 26 December 1808.
Consent by William Palmer, Sr., father of the bride. Thomas Dobyns (b).

PALMER, GEORGE G. (bachelor) and Mary Priddy (spinster), bond 4 April 1829. Consent by Ann J. Priddy, guardian of the bride. John Hundley (b). MBB.,p.52

PALMER, PARMENUS married Mary Ann Draper, 30 March 1741.   NFPR.,p.157

PALMER, RAWLEIGH and Nancy Dobyns, bond 9 February 1802. Daniel Dobyns, Jr. (b).

PALMER, ROBERT and Betty Hale Dobyns, bond 4 June 1792. John Alderson (b).

PALMER, TRUMAN married Ann Hanes, 31 October 1743.   NFPR.,p.157

PALMER, WILLIAM and Betty Dobyns, bond 22 November 1769. Daniel Dobyns (b).

PALMER, WILLIAM JR. and Melia Garland, bond 5 February 1798. Consent by George
Garland, father of the bride. Henry M. Dobyns (b).

PANNELL, THOMAS (16??-1677) married Katherine ____[?]____; she married (2) Thomas
Swinburne (q.v.). Thomas Pannell died testate in Rappahannock County in
1677 leaving four infant children, viz: (a) William Pannell (q.v.); (b) Isabella Pannell married James Phillips (q.v.); (c) Mary Pannell married (1)
James Kay (q.v.) and married (2) Francis Stone (q.v.); (d) Thomas Pannell
(q.v.). These four children gave rise to large families. Sweeny,p.59-60.

PANNELL, THOMAS [JUNIOR] (1677-1719), youngest child of Thomas and Katherine Pannell, was born after his father's will was written. He married (1) by 1705

Elizabeth ____[?]____, who was living in 1712; married (2) Sarah ___[?]___, who married (2) by 4 March 1718/19, Thomas Morgan. COB#8,p.81; DB#6,p.111, 112; WB#4,p.81; Essex County DB#12,p.195; Sweeny,p.59-60.

PANNELL, WILLIAM (circa 1670-1716), eldest child of Thomas and Katherine Pannell (q.v.),p.153, married by 1 June 1698 Frances Sterne, only child of David and Elizabeth (Mills) Sterne (q.v.); she married (2) Thomas Hughes who died testate in Orange County in 1766. Frances (Sterne) Pannell Hughes left issue by both marriages. COB#1,p.75; COB#2,p.396; DB#4,p.26; WB#3,p.278; Sweeny,p.88-89; for other references see Thomas Hughes, p.100.

PARKER, AUGUSTINE G. of Middlesex County and Amelia A.T. White*, bond 20 June 1826. Aldea Glascock (b); A.A. Glascock (w).   MBB.,p.22

PARKER, RICHARD [JUDGE] and Eliza Beale, bond 24 December 1751. William Beale (b). [The obituary of Judge Richard Parker (1729-1813) appeared in the Richmond Enquirer of 13 April 1813. Beale,p.47,251; Eubank, p.50.]

PARR, JAMES and Anne Packett*, daughter of Henry and Anne Packett, license 1 June 1853. William H. Packett (w).

PARTRIDGE, JOHN married Frances Creswell, 6 April 1678.   NFPR.,p.153

    PATTY   SEE PETTY PAGE 158

PATTY, THOMAS (16??-1750) of Richmond and Orange counties, married by 6 March 1701 Katherine Garton, daughter of John Garton, deceased. The will of John Garton was dated 17 June 1698; it was recorded in now lost WB#1 (1692-1699). In his said will he mentioned his wife Martha and five children, viz: (a) Richard Garton d.s.p. by 4 March 1702; (b) John Garton; (c) Mathew Garton; (d) Katherine Garton who married Thomas Patty; and (e) Ruth Garton. John Hughes qualified as executor of John Garton but he died intestate in 1700 and his widow Hannah (also called Ann(e) and Anna) Hughes took out administration on the estate of John Hughes, her husband, and by 6 March 1701 married Robert Port (q.v.). COB#3,p.85,140; DB#3,p.118; DB#8,p.429,622,624; WB#2,p.16; Orange County WB#2,p.144-145.

PAVEY, WALTER married circa 1680 Mary Webley, daughter of Richard Webley. Their son and heir was Webley Pavey. DB#6,p.272; DB#7,p.29.

PAYNE, GEORGE (circa 1660-1711) married Jane White, daughter of Thomas and Jane White of Westmoreland County (q.v.),p.152. Thomas White died testate at his home on Appomattox Creek in 1687, but his will is among the missing Westmoreland County records. George Payne died testate in Richmond County. Westmoreland County COB 1675-1689,p.564,677 and COB 1690-1698,p.11,39,63. Payne,p.367-369.

PAYNE, GEORGE and Sarah E. Stiff, bond 30 September 1846. Consent by J.M. Stiff, father of the bride. John W. Collins (b). Married 1 October 1846 by the Rev. William N. Ward.   MBB.,p.280
Payne, p.133.

PAYNE, MERRIMAN (circa 1763-1815) of Lancaster County married (1) in Fauquier County on 26 February 1786, Frances Johnson; married (2) in Northumberland County on 23 August 1792, Nancy (Dobyns) Oldham, daughter of Thomas Dobyns who died testate in Richmond County in 1788 and widow of William Oldham, (q.v.),p.150.   AB#2,p.162,330; WB#8,p.36; Payne,p.504.

PAYNE, RICHARD and [blank] Kelly, bond 1 March 1790. John Kelly (b). [Payne, p.86,89, makes it certain the bride's name was Susannah Kelly, daughter of James and Susan(nah) (Willson) Kelly (q.v.),p.110-111.]

PAYNE, RICHARD A. [DOCTOR] and Lucy P. McCarty, bond 24 June 1841. Consent by William McCarty of Woodford, father of the bride. James H. Payne (b). [See, Payne,p.132-133.]   MBB.,p.210

PAYNE, THOMAS E. and Louisa James Stiff, bond 20 May 1846. Consent by J.M. Stiff, father of the bride. John W. Collins (b). Married 21 May 1846 by the Rev. P. Rescoel. [See, Payne,p.134.]   MBB.,p.277

PAYNE, WILLIAM of Westmoreland County and Alicia Jones, license February 1712/13. [See, Payne,p.228-230.]   DB#6,p.275

PAYTON, CHARLES W. of Westmoreland County and Catharine Brinham, bond 25 September 1827. Consent by William Brinham, father of the bride. William T. Richardson of Westmoreland County (b). [In loose bonds only; not in MBB.]

PAYTON, JOHN A. (bachelor) of Westmoreland County and Elizabeth Morris (spinster)*, bond 11 November 1828. John Morris (b); Joshua Reamy (w).   MBB.,p.45

PEACHEY, LEROY and Betty Tarpley, bond 7 November 1759. [The bride was the daughter of Major Travers and Betty (Sydnor) Tarpley of North Farnham Parish. The groom was the youngest son of Captain Samuel and Winifred (Griffin) Peachey (q.v.).]

PEACHEY, SAMUEL [CAPTAIN] (1699-1750) of Milden Hall, son of William and Phoebe (Slaughter) Peachey, was twice married: (1) Winifred Griffin, daughter of Thomas Griffin, Gentleman, (1684-1730), who was the mother of all his children; (2) per marriage contract dated 16 February 1749/50, recorded in Northumberland County, to Judith (Steptoe) Lee, widow of Richard Lee, Gentleman, (1691-1740) of Ditchley, and evidently the daughter of John and Elizabeth (Pinkard) Steptoe of Northumberland County. Captain Samuel Peachey's will was dated 12 December 1748 and he died 2 October 1750 without altering it; it was admitted to probate in Richmond County court on 5 November 1750. There is considerable data in regard to the family of Captain Samuel Peachey in two lengthy chancery suits which pended before the Fredericksburg District Court, viz: Nicholson vs Eustace, FDC#205 and Nicholson vs Palmer, FDC #206, and the Richmond County records abound with data. WB#2,p.29; WB#3,p. 83,252; WB#5,p.639; Northumberland County Record Book 1749-1753,p.32; Eubank, P.79.

PEACHEY, WILLIAM [CAPTAIN] and Million Glascock, bond 31 May 1748. Samuel Peachey (b) and Travers Tarpley (b). [Captain, later Colonel, William Peachey (1729-1802) was the eldest son and heir of Captain Samuel and Winifred (Griffin) Peachey. Colonel Peachey resided at Milden Hall and died there on 7 June 1802; his obituary appeared in the Fredericksburg Virginia Herald of 14 June 1802. His will is very long, complex and involved. He gave directions as to the family vault and made other demands and remarks not usually found in wills. He identifies himself as the eldest son and heir entail of his father, but says he had rather given his manor estate to a second son (Samuel Peachey 1732/3-1784 of Essex County) but that the entailment placed on the estate by an honored ancestor prevented this act. Colonel Peachey goes on at great length in regard to the laws of entailment which were set aside when the Commonwealth was founded. He married (1) 31 May 1748, Million Glascock, daughter of William Glascock of Richmond County who died testate in 1784, and had an only child to survive infancy, viz: (a) Winifred Peachey who married Henry Armistead (q.v.)p.4. Colonel William Peachey married (2) in 1761, Elizabeth Griffin Colston, the daughter of Travers and Alice Corbin (Griffin) Colston; they had a large family of children. Milden Hall, so long the seat of the Peachey family, was advertised for sale in considerable detail in the Fredericksburg Virginia Herald of 1 May 1824; the advertisement was signed by John Nicholson as administrator of William Peachey, deceased. WB#9,p.186; Beale,p.214.]

PEACOCK, RICHARD [GENTLEMAN] of North Farnham Parish, Richmond County, on 31 November 1695 entered into a marriage contract stating that he has lately intermarried with Mary Glascock, the relict and administratrix of George Glascock, deceased, and he obligates himself to leave his estate to his said wife and her children. DB#2,p.150; John Bennett Boddie, Historical Southern Families, Volume IV, (Redwood City, California, 1960), p.46-47.

PEARSON, JESSEE [CAPTAIN] and Mary E. Newton*, license 14 January 1851. Lefever Kennan (w). Married 15 January 1851 by the Rev. Elijah L. Williams.

PEARSON, LAWSON T. [CAPTAIN] and Alice M. Saunders*, bond 26 November 1842. James Anderson (b); Ann C. Chilton (w).   MBB.,p.228

PECURARA, WILLIAM and Ann Denham, license September 1714.   DB#6,p.275

PEED, JOHN of Westmoreland County and Rebecca Coats (spinster)*, bond 20 April 1830. James Coats, Jr. (b).   MBB.,p.63

PEED, JOHN and Catharine R. Saunders*, bond 6 March 1848. Richard Saunders (b); J.B. Fones (w).   MBB.,p.307

    PEIRCE : PIERCE

PEIRCE, JOHN [GENTLEMAN] (16??-1698) married before 6 May 1691 Esther (Hester) (Walker) Tomlin, widow of Robert Tomlin, Jr. (16??-1689) and daughter of Colonel John Walker (16??-1668/9) and his second wife Sarah, formerly the wife of Captain Henry Fleet (circa 1600-1660). John Peirce died a young-man and his last will was presented for probate 1 June 1698 by his father, Colonel William Peirce of Westmoreland County; it was recorded in now lost Richmond County WB#1 (1692-1699). Colonel William Peirce patented and purchased large acreages in the Northern Neck of Virginia and died testate in

Westmoreland County in 1702; his will made his only grandson of his surname his principal legatee - William Peirce, Gentleman, (169?-1733). COB
#1,p.31; COB#2,p.295; DB#1,p.85; Westmoreland County D&W#3,p.2,50,243 and
D&W#5,p.184; NorthemNeck Patent Book #3,p.123, dated 25 January 1705/6,
in a patent to William Stewart of Richmond County, there is a long recita-
tion of title of the land and it is stated it was by the will of Colonel
John Walker bequeathed to his daughter Esther who married John Pearce and
they made sale of it 6 May 1691. Mr. Robert Page Henley, Jr. has rendered
an account of the Peirce family in the Northern Neck of Virginia Historical
Magazine, Volume VIII, p.744-749 and the original records abound with additional information. A.P.& P.,p.172-175.

PIERCE, JOHN of Westmoreland County and Betsy Muse Moxley, bond 25 December 1786.
Lovell Peirce (b).

PEIRCE, JOSEPH of Westmoreland County and Elizabeth Hall*, bond 24 December 1790.
William Yeatman (b); he procured the marriage bond through a letter of attorney from Joseph Peirce.

PIERCE, WILLIAM and Mary Mountjoy (spinster), bond 2 April 1753. Alvin Mountjoy
(b). [The bride was the daughter of Captain Alvin and Eleanor (Craske) Mountjoy (q.v.),p.140. The groom was the elder of the two sons of William Peirce,
Gentleman, (169?-1733) of Westmoreland County and Sibella, his wife, and
grandson of John and Hester (Walker) Peirce of Richmond County, (q.v.),p.156-
157. William Peirce married (2) Sarah ____[?]____ and died testate in Westmoreland County in February 1782. Westmoreland County W&D#16,p.163.]

PENLEY, THOMAS married Sarah Stone, 30 January 1728/9.   NFPR.,p.157

PENNY, JOHN and Sarah Hill, license March 1711.   DB#6,p.275

PETERS, OTHO married by 4 July 1748 Elizabeth Jones, widow and relict of Edward
Jones who died testate in 1739, leaving his mother, wife and six children
to be provided for. COB#12,p.131; WB#5,p.341. An inventory of the estate
of Otho Peters was filed in Frederick County, Virginia, in 1757.

PETTIT, JOHN and Ann Fauntleroy (spinster), bond 7 January 1755. John Orr (b)
and John M. Jordan (b). [Coupling the data in Fauntleroy,p.498 and that
found in the chancery suit Brooke vs Brooke, FDC#43, we see these facts:

```
        William Fauntleroy, Gentleman -m.circa 1712-Apphia Bushrod
        (1684-1757), Richmond County              :
                                                  :
:                                          :              1755
Mary Fauntleroy -m- Robert Brooke          Ann Fauntleroy -m- John Pettit
        :      of Essex County     She died c.1758 :
        :                                                  :
:                                          :
Robert ["Robin"] Brooke -married his first cousin- Lydia Bushrod Pettit
Born 21 January 1755     They had an only child
Died 1779, Essex County              :
                          Ann Pettit Brooke
                   m. by 1801  William  Chowning
```

Robert ["Robin"] Brooke (1755-1779) predeceased his parents; his will was
recorded in Essex County. By his wife nee Lydia Bushrod Pettit, who was
his first cousin, he left an only child, Ann Pettit Brooke. She is described as an infant in 1795 and by 1801 the wife of William Chowning.
John and Ann (Fauntleroy) Pettit had an only son, John Pettit; in 1801 he
was residing in Columbia County, Georgia, and in a deposition states the
family genealogy: "The circumstance of my intimacy arose from Robert Brooke
marrying into my grandfather Fauntleroy's family whose wife was sister of
my mother, and Robin Brooke, the son of Robert, married my sister Lydia
Bushrod Pettit."]

PETTY   SEE : PATTY PAGE 154

PETTY, THOMAS and Elizabeth Doon, married 24 August 1727.   NFPR.,p.157

PEW   SEE : PUGH PAGE 163

PEW, MARTIN and Nancy Habron, bond 26 February 1824. John Hammack (b). Married by the Rev. Charles Bell. [ECD Papers, box #4, identifies the groom
as Martin Lewis Pugh, son of Lewis and Nancy (Richards) Pugh (q.v.).]

PHILLIPS, BRYANT and Nancy Stonum (spinster), bond 22 December 1794. William
Stonum (b).

PHILLIPS, GEORGE (16??-1716) married between 12 January 1697/8 and 7 September
1698, Martha Swinburne, daughter and executrix of the last will and Testament of Thomas Swinburne, deceased. George Phillips died testate in Richmond County in 1716; his will mentions his wife Martha and five children.
COB#2,p.276,332; DB#3,p.101; DB#4,p.43; WB#3,p.259,267.

PHILLIPS, JAMES (16??-1716) married by 10 April 1696 Isabella Pannell, daughter
of Thomas and Katherine Pannell (q.v.),p.154. James Phillips married (2)
by 1 February 1704 Sarah   [?]   and she joined him in several conveyances. James Phillips died intestate in 1716 and on 5 December 1716
Sarah Phillips, widow and relict of James Phillips of Sittingburne Parish,
bound her son James Phillips (born 24 November 1707) to Sir Marmaduke Beckwith to serve him as an apprentice until he attained the age of 21 years.
James Phillips (16??-1716) and George Phillips (16??-1716) were brothers,
sons of James Phillips of Lancaster County who died testate in 1690 bequeathing them land in the area which became Richmond County in 1692.
DB#3,p.4,123,133,136,137; DB#4,p.16,18,47,49,54; DB#5,p.136; MRB.,p.89;
WB#3,p.276; Essex County DB#9,p.32,34,270; Lancaster County WB#8,p.2.

PHILLIPS, JEREMIAH married Anne Brooks, 3 June 1678.   NFPR.,p.153

PHILLIPS, JOHN W. and Mrs. Maria L. Fogg, bond 6 June 1842. John Garland (b).
Married 7 June 1842 by the Rev. William N. Ward.   MBB.,p.224

PHILLIPS, LEONARD and Eliz.ª Favor, license August 1713.   DB#6,p.275

PHILLIPS, WILLIAM married before 24 April 1687 Elizabeth Loyd, daughter of Lewis
Loyd who died testate in Rappahannock County in 1690 and Joan, his wife.

On 14 December 1692 Joan Loyd repatented 159 acres of land in North Farnham Parish, Richmond County, which was "surveyed and taken up by Lewis
Loyd, deceased," on 6 February 1681 and by his last will bequeathed to
his wife the aforementioned Joan Loyd. On 1 August 1695 Joan Loyd, widow,
made a deed of surrender for this 159 acres of land to William Phillips,
"excepting my widowhood;" i.e., reserving an interest during her widowhood.
DB#2,p.112; Sweeny,p.147.

PHILPOTT, BENJAMIN of Frederick County, Maryland, and Eliz.[a] Hackney of Richmond
County, Virginia, bond 25 October 1786. Benjamin Hackney (b).

PIERCE		SEE : PEIRCE PAGE 156 - 157

PINC[K]ARD, THOMAS married Elizabeth Downman, 22 April 1727.			NFPR.,p.157

PINCKARD [PINKARD], THOMAS married 19 June 1784 in Lancaster County, Ann Corbin
Griffin, daughter of Major LeRoy and Alice (Currie) Griffin (q.v.),p.82.
The marriage was performed by the Rev. Mr. David Currie, maternal grandfather of the bride; there is a certificate of it in Seward vs McKenney,
FDC#241. Thomas Pinckard died testate in Lancaster County in 1795, but
his last will does not seem to have been recorded in the record book of
the period but is preserved among a group of Lancaster County "loose wills"
in VSL:AD.

PITTS, REUBEN L. of Essex County and Maria L. Dobyns, bond 7 December 1830.
Joseph Palmer (b).								MBB.,p.70

PLUMMER, FLEET B. and Eliza B. Ball (widow)*, bond 6 September 1816. Consent
by Thomas Plummer, father of the groom. John Plummer (b).

PLUMMER, JOHN married Sarah Smith, 7 May 1756.				NFPR.,p.158
[Bond 5 May 1756 for the marriage of John Plummer and Sarah Smith, with
Charles Dobyns (b), also remains of record.]

PLUMMER, JOHN and Elizabeth Smith*, bond 28 January 1812. William Smith (b);
John Smith (w).

PLUMMER, JOHN [CAPTAIN] and Elizabeth Thrift, bond 22 September 1818. Consent
by Richard Efford for the marriage of his ward, Miss Elizabeth Thrift.
John G. White (b).

PLUMMER, JOHN and Elizabeth Garland (widow)*, bond 13 July 1819. Robert P.
Headley (b).

PLUMMER, RICHARD B. and Sarah L. Headley, bond 7 May 1821. Consent by Joseph
Palmer, guardian of the bride. John Plummer (b). A.W. Glascock (w) and
Horace Wellford (w).

PLUMMER, RICHARD B. (widower) and Julia Davis (spinster), bond 16 July 1828.
Robert H. Davis (b); he made oath the bride is 21 years of age and a resi-
dent of Richmond County. Margaret J. Northen (w).			MBB.,p.39

POLK, CHARLES PEALE of the City of Washington and Ellen B. Downman*, bond 23
    December 1816. William Downman (b); Thomas M. Glascock (w).

POLLEY, JOSEPH married Joanna Ken, 4 May 1677.   NFPR.,p.153

POLLING, SIMON married Jean Wade, 19 October 1673.   NFPR.,p.153

POOLEY, WILLIAM and Elizabeth Hammond, bond 13 September 1787. John Downey (b).

POOLEY, WILLIAM and Annaniah [? Amaniah ?] Thrift, bond 21 September 1789. George
    Miskell (b).

POPE, FORTUNATUS and Frances R. Purssell*, bond 8 December 1817. Rawleigh Haz-
    ard (b); William C. Wheeler (w). The groom signs the bond, Natuy Pope.

POPE, GEORGE and Frances MacTyre*, bond 22 March 1796. Benjamin Cundiff (b).

POPE, LEROY of Richmond County and Elizabeth Mitchell, married 24 April 1765.
    He was born 21 August 1742; she was aged 22. James Tapscott (b). LCMR#1,p.34

POPE, LEROY and Hannah Nash*, bond 21 December 1824. George Newgent (b); George
    Newgent (w).   MBB.,p.6

POPE, LEROY and Sarah Newgent*, bond 7 November 1838. Shadrach Clarke (b).
                                                                  MBB.,p.176

POPE, LEROY and Lucy A. Nash married 2 September 1847 by the Rev. Mr. Bartholo-
    mew Dodson according to his returns to the clerk of the court of Richmond
    County, 3 February 1848. No marriage bond found in Richmond County.

POPE, THADDEUS and Suckey Dobyns, bond 19 December 1789. Joseph Davenport (b).

POPE, THADDEUS and Ann ("Nancy") Palmer, bond 7 January 1795. Consent by William
    Palmer, father of the bride. William Palmer, Jr. (b).

POPE, WESLEY and Lucy T. Bryant*, bond 6 January 1823. Thomas Bryant (b).

PORT, ROBERT married by 6 March 1701 Hannah (sometimes called Ann(e) and Anna)
    ___[?]___ Harbin Taylor Hughes, seemingly thrice a widow. In 1698 as
    Hannah Taylor, widow, she apprenticed her son George Harbin. She married
    John Hughes who died testate in 1700 and by 6 March 1701 was the wife of
    Robert Port. COB#3,p.85,140; COB#5,p.6 et seq.; WB#2,p.16.

PORTER, SAMSON of Westmoreland County and Catharine Neasom*, bond 23 March 1827.
    Thomas A. Kennedy (b); Samuel W. Neasom (w).   MBB.,p.30

POTTER, JAMES and Catharine S. Courtney*, bond 26 October 1841. William L. Lee
    (b); Lennord Courtney (w). Married 28 October 1841 by the Rev. William N.
    Ward.   MBB.,p.212

POUND, JOHN (16??-1718) married circa 1708 Deborah Lewis (16??-1727), daughter
    of Thomas Lewis (16??-1709) of North Farnham Parish. DB#7,p.364; WB#2,p.

129; WB#4,p.92; WB#5,p.53.

POWELL, JOHN married by 9 January 1695 Michall Turner, only child of Hezechia Turner, deceased, of Rappahannock County. DB#2,p.101-104; Sweeny,p.65.

POWELL, THOMAS (16??-circa 1700) married by 30 September 1667 Mary Place (16??-1709), daughter of Francis Place who had a land patent for 300 acres of land 7 September 1654 and on 11 August 1655 made a deed for same to his daughter Mary Place. Place Powell, son of Thomas and Mary (Place) Powell, in 1710 (after his mother's death) made a lease for this land for 99 years and shortly departed out of Virginia for parts unknown. The land lay in "the fork of Lamb's Creek," dubbed in the 1654 patent the "dividing creek," and in 1721 fell into King George County. In 1750 Honorias Powell (16??-1752) of St. Mary's Parish, Caroline County, brother and heir-at-law of Place Powell, thought to be deceased, conveyed the fee simple interest in this land to Colonel John Champe. COB#6,p.108; King George County DB#3, p.353; Caroline County COB#3,p.312 indicates the will of Honorias Powell was proved in 1752; C&P.,p.293.

PRATT, JOHN [JUNIOR] (16??-1724) of Westmoreland, Richmond and King George counties, married circa 1709 Margaret Birkett (16??-1749), daughter of John and Ann (Mills) Birkett (q.v.),p.18-19; she married (2) Daniel French (16??-1736) and died 21 November 1749. The wills of John Pratt,Jr., Daniel French and Margaret (Birkett) Pratt French are in lost King George County WB#1, but the wills of John Pratt, Sr. of Westmoreland County (1714), his son John Pratt, Jr. of King George County (1724) and his son Thomas Pratt of St.Paul's Parish, Stafford County (1766), together with considerable genealogical detail,are preserved in the suit Hungerford vs Pratt of record in King George County COB 1766-1790,p.285-298. John Pratt, Jr. (16??-1724) married (1) Elizabeth Jones, daughter of Mrs. Mary Jones who died testate in Westmoreland County in 1708; by her he had an only child, viz: (a) Margaret Pratt (d.s.p.) who married William Tyler, Gentleman, (17??-1772) of Westmoreland County; he m(2) Esther Jones (173?-1778), daughter of James and Hester (Davis) Jones (q.v.),p.114-115, and left issue. John Pratt, Jr. (16??-1724) married (2) circa 1709 Margaret Birkett (16??-1749) and had issue four children, viz: (b) John Pratt (1710-1738) d.s.p.; (c) Birkett Pratt (1713-1760) d.s.p.; (d) Ann Pratt (1718-1800) married Colonel Thomas Hungerford (171?-1772) and left issue; and (e) Thomas Pratt, Gentleman, (1721-1766) of Eden, Saint Paul's Parish, Stafford (now King George) County. He married Margaret Vivion (1724-1818), daughter of Major Thomas and Frances (Thacker) Vivion, and had nine children. WB#4,p.138; King George County COB#2,p.54,62,74,650 and DB#1,p.51; Westmoreland County COB 1705-1721,p.84. The records of the counties of Westmoreland, Stafford, Richmond, and King George abound with records of the aforementioned Pratt family. John Pratt, Sr. (16??-1714), described as a gentleman and a merchant, seems to have confined his activities to the Northern Neck of Virginia and consequently should not be confused with John Pratt (1658-post 1728), also mentioned as a gentleman and a merchant, who came to York River in 1679 and became a man of affairs in the Glocester County - Yorktown - Williamsburg area. Shortly after the death of his nephew, William Pratt (circa 1692-1724) [who had married 4 September 1720 in Williamsburg, Elizabeth Cocke, daughter of the Honorable Doctor William Cocke,

Secretary of Virginia], John Pratt of New Aberdeen upon York River, returned to England and wrote several interesting letters to his said nephew's
widow, who shortly married secondly Colonel Thomas Jones. See John Pratt
letters 1725-1728, VSL:AD #24756; the Jones Family Papers in the Manuscript
Division, Library of Congress; and Judge Lewis H. Jones, Captain Roger Jones
of London and Virginia (Albany, N.Y.,1891).

PRATT, JOHN and Lydia Pugh*, bond 1 December 1788. Lewis Pugh (b); Abner Howe
(w).

PRICE, ARJALON (170?-1773) of Richmond and Orange counties, married 173? Joyce
Barber, born 9 June 1712 in North Farnham Parish, the daughter of William
and Joyce (Bayley) Barber (q.v.),p.9. He was the son of Richard and Mary
Price of St.Stephen's Parish, Northumberland County and is named in the
will of his mother probated there in 1726. Arjalon Price moved to Orange
County and appears on the records there as Colonel Arjalon Price. He died
testate in Orange County in 1773. DB#11,p.383,390; Orange County WB#2,p.
470.

PRICE, ARJALON (1738-   ) married in 1761 Katey Hill, born 26 February 1741 in
North Farnham Parish, the daughter of John and Betty (Hammond) Hill (q.v.)
p.93. This is taken from a small fragment of a marriage bond on which John
Hill, Jr. (b), appears. The North Farnham Parish Register records the birth
on 22 February 1762 of John Hill Price, son of the aforesaid couple. The
birth date of Arjalon Price, Jr., is taken from a deposition made by him in
King George County; he was the son of Arjalon and Joyce (Barber) Price.
King George County COB#3,p.922, 26 September 1760.

PRIDHAM, CHRISTOPHER married 167? Bridgett Bryer, only child of Captain George
Bryer whose will was admitted to probate at Rappahannock County court in
1665. Bridgett (Bryer) Pridham married (2), 168?, Lewis Richards and died
testate in Rappahannock County in 1685 leaving two children by each spouse.
COB#6,p.126; Rappahannock County Deeds &c:#6,p.70; Sweeny,p.116.

PRIDHAM, CHRISTOPHER (167?-1731) married circa 1700 Mary Lewis, one of the five
daughters and co-heirs of Edward Lewis, deceased. The groom was the only
son of Christopher and Bridgett (Bryer) Pridham (q.v.) DB#3,p.178; DB#6,
p.115; DB#8,p.409,459; DB#9,p.111,186; WB#5,p.164,336; NFPR., Sweeny,p.116.

PRIDHAM, CHRISTOPHER and Katharine Longworth, bond 19 May 1783. Burges Longworth (b).

PRIDHAM, JOHN and Malinda B. Harrison, bond 25 February 1823. Consent by James
Harrison, father of the bride; consent by Christopher Pridham, father of
the groom. Daniel Harrison (b); Walt: Self (w) and Lezebeth Proctor (w).

PRITCHETT, GEORGE F. and Elizabeth Ann Cox, bond 26 February 1849. Consent by
Carlos Cox, father of the bride. George B. Oldham (b).   MBB.,p.322

PRITCHETT, RODHAM and Dewanah Hall, bond 12 January 1775. James Lewis,Jr. (b).

PRITCHETT, RODHAM and Caty Thurston, bond 2 April 1808. Consent by Mary Thurston; no relationship stated. Samuel Efford (b).

PRITCHETT, SAMUEL C. and Elizabeth Dodson (widow)*, bond 12 December 1815. Griffin Jeffries (b).

PUGH   SEE :   PEW PAGE 158

PUGH, LEWIS (16??-173?), son of David Pugh of South Wales, married circa 1703,
Ann _____[?]_____ (1680-post 1740). In 1731 Lewis Pugh and his eldest
son, John Pugh, went from Richmond County to South Wales where the said
Lewis Pugh died. At this time, Lewis Pugh's sister Elizabeth, wife of
Benjamin Jones, was residing in North Wales. In 1740 Ann Pugh, widow of
Lewis Pugh, was residing in Richmond County and her second son, David
Pugh of Lancaster County, was about to journey to Wales and seek the recov-
ery of certain property there due to the Pugh family in Virginia. Several
depositions were taken in regard to this matter and considerable genealogical detail is recited in AB#1,p.157-160. From this source, the North Farnham Parish Register and other seemingly reliable sources, ECD gives the
following information in regard to the seven children of Lewis and Ann Pugh,
all born in North Farnham Parish, viz: (a) John Pugh, born 29 April 1704,
accompanied this father to South Wales in 1731; (b) David Pugh, born 25 December 1706, resided in Lancaster County in 1740 when he embarked for Wales;
(c) Elizabeth Pugh, born 19 March 1708, married William Landman; (d) Henry
Pugh, born 2 March 1710; died testate in Richmond County in 1766. It appears from the will of Mary Collier, also proved in Richmond County in 1766,
he married Sarah, daughter of Elizabeth Billens, and had a large family; (e)
Willoughby Pugh, born 3 May 1711; died testate in Charlotte County in 1790;
(f) Anne Pugh, born 14 November 1715, married Henry Headley; and (g) Lewis
Pugh, born circa 1717, married 2 February 1738 Margaret Harvey (q.v.),p.163.
WB#6,p.396; ECD Papers, Box#4, Virginia Historical Society.

PUGH, LEWIS married Margaret Harvey, 2 February 1738.   NFPR.,p.157

PUGH, LEWIS and Nancy Richards*, bond 15 November 1791. Benjamin Purcell (b);
Benjamin Purcell (w) and Elizabeth Richards (w). [ECD Papers, Box 4, indicate Lewis Pugh died circa 1809 and that Martin Lewis Pugh (1801-27 January 1866) who married 26 February 1824 Nancy Habron (q.v.),p.158, was the
son of Lewis and Nancy (Richards) Pugh.]

PULLEN : PULLIN

PULLEN, EVERARD and Catharine Bartlett*, bond 3 June 1793. The bride states in
her written consent, she is "in the 24th year of her age." Elisha Bartlett
(b).

PULLIN, JESSE and Peggy Fisher*, bond 1 December 1788. Everard Pullin (b).

PULLEN, JOHN and Molly Jones, bond 13 March 1788. William Webb (b).

PULLEN, JONATHAN of Richmond County and Betsey L. Cannon were married 17 January
1795 in Lancaster County. Jeduthun Pullen (b).   LCMR#1,p.85

PULLEN, JONATHAN and Hannah Redman*, bond 6 February 1797. Jeduthan Pullen (b); Joseph Redman (w) and John Redman (w).

PURCELL : PURSELL   SEE : PURSLEY PAGE 165

PURSELL, BENEDICT R. of Westmoreland County and Jane Efford*, bond 17 March 1834. William P. Cox (b); D.P. Gilbert (w).   MBB.,p.117

PURSELL, DAVID (16??-1693) married Belinda, probably daughter of Joshua Lawson. She married (2) by 6 November 1695, Thomas Parker. A court order of 6 April 1704 mentions Joshua Lawson as the grandfather of Frances Pursell, orphan. COB#1,p.155; COB#2,p.99; COB#3,p.98,331.

PURSELL, EDWARD M. and Letty Redman, bond 22 February 1781. John How (b); Will: How (w). [ECD Papers say Edward Minty Purcell married Letty Redman, daughter of Joseph Redman, Sr., who died testate in Richmond County in 1811.]

PURSELL, JOHN R. and Patsy Hundley, bond 17 December 1831. William H. Miskell (b).   MBB.,p.84

PURSELL, JOSEPH R. and Roxy Arms, bond 4 December 1820. John Rogers (b); W.R. Jeffries (w).

PURSELL, LEWIS (bachelor) and Sarah S. Lyell (spinster), bond 31 December 1828. LeRoy C. Pursell (b).   MBB.,p.50

PURSELL, REUBEN and Nancy Longwith, bond 6 October 1812. William Morgan (b) Consent by Burges Longworth, father of the bride.

PURSELL, SAMUEL and Mary E. McKenney, bond 21 July 1846. Gerard A. McKenney (b).
                                                                    MBB.,p.279

PURSELL, STEPHEN D. (bachelor) and Catharine Payton (widow)*, bond 20 May 1831. Joshua Reamy (b); John Morris (w).   MBB.,p.78

PURCELL, TOBIAS and Mary Ann Murrah (spinster), bond 16 July 1751. [mutilated] Anderson (b). [Tobias Purcell was born in North Farnham Parish 23 December 1691, the son of David and Belinda Purcell (Pursell) (q.v.),p.164. He married (1) Margaret ____[?]_____ and had children born in wedlock. On 16 July 1751 he obtained bond to wed Mary Ann Murrah (Morrow); she was born 22 April 1730 in North Farnham Parish, the daughter of Andrew and Deborah (Sherlock) Morrow (q.v.),p.138. The marriage does not seem to have been solemnized as John, Tobias, Winifred and Lucy, the children of Tobias Purcell and Mary Ann Murrah (Morrow, Murrow, Murray), are dubbed "Murray als Purcell" and Tobias Purcell (1691-1761) refers to them in his will as the children of Mary Ann Murray. About the time of her marriage to Richard Shackelford, Mary Ann Murrah is referred to in a court order as the "executrix and legatee of the last will and Testament of Tobias Pursell, deceased." COB#3,p.98,331; COB#15,p.313; COB#17,p.268; WB#6,p.201,406.]

PURCELL, TOBIAS and Rebecca Redman, bond 6 January 1784. Benjamin Bramham (b).

PURSELL, WILLIAM R. and Mary S. Sydnor*, license 17 January 1852. R.G. Hogan
    (w). Married 20 January 1852 by the Rev. Elijah L. Williams.

PURKINS, GABRIEL and Lucy Baber, bond 6 December 1790. Thomas Purkins (b).

PURSLEY   SEE : PURCELL : PURSELL PAGE 164

PURSLEY, JOHN and Polly Dale, bond 10 July 1802. Joseph Lyell (b). [The groom
    signs the bond "John Pursley," but the court clerk renders his surname in
    the body of the bond, "Pursell."]

                                    Q

QUESENBERRY, NICHOLAS and Martha Jones*, bond 25 July 1825. Joshua Reamy (b).
                                                              MBB.,p.12

QUESENBERRY, NICHOLAS (widower) and Ann L. Mothershead (spinster)*, bond 6
    January 1829. Samuel Morris (b).   MBB.,p.51

QUESENBURY, LEWIS W. and Sarah L.L. Crabb*, bond 8 August 1850. J.R. Jeffries
    (w). Married 8 August 1850 by the Rev. J.C. Garlick.

QUESENBURY, WILLIAM C. of Westmoreland County and Elizabeth Newman, bond 2 Oct-
    ober 1816. George Newman (b).

                                    R

RAINS, ALFRED J. (bachelor) and Elizabeth Webb (spinster), bond 12 January 1830.
    Joseph Dale (b).   MBB.,p.60

RAINS, WILLIAM of Northumberland County and Molly Jones*, bond 5 October 1791.
    The bride, in writing her own consent, states she is of age and the dau-
    ghter of John Jones. John Nash (b); Jeduthum Pullen (w) and Jonathan Pul-
    len (w).

RAMEY   SEE : REAMY : RAMEY PAGE 166

RANDALL, FRANCIS and Hannah Ann Ramey (widow), bond 22 September 1752. Samuel
    Barber (b). [The bride was the widow of Samuel Ramey (17??-1752) (q.v.).]

RANDALL, SAMUEL JR. of the City of Cork, merchant, married by 25 June 1716 Mary
    Pope, only child and heir-at-law of Thomas Pope, the younger, Esquire, late
    of the City of Bristol, merchant, and who was heir-at-law of his brother
    Charles Pope (d.s.p.). The will of Thomas Pope (1639-1684/5), grandfather
    of the bride, is recited in this unusal record in Richmond County DB#7,p.
    219, conveying land upon Pope's Creek, Washington Parish, Westmoreland

County; it appears the document should have been recorded in the county
where the land lay. Mary (Pope) Randall died without issue circa 1730
and there is considerable Pope genealogy recited in a deed dated 10 November 1758 from Elizabeth (Pope) Pope Wroe to her son Nathaniel Pope, recorded in Westmoreland County W&D#13,p.199. Thomas Pope (1639-1684/5) was the
eldest son of Colonel Nathaniel Pope who died testate in Westmoreland County in 1660. When a young man he settled in Bristol and married there on 20
October 1663 in St. Philips and St. Jacobs Church, Jane Dowle alias Gatly;
her name has been rendered Joanna Pope in some records. Richmond County
DB#5,p.116; 21T234-235.

RANDALL, THOMAS and Jane Davis, married 4 October 1728.   NFPR.,p.162
    [The bride was the daughter of Robert and Susanna (Jacobus) Davis (q.v.),
    p.51. DB#8,p.498; DB#12,p.641; WB#5,p.272,558.]

RANSDELL, WHARTON of Westmoreland County married by 3 December 1744 Margaret
    Barrow, elder of the two daughters of Edward and Elizabeth (Minor) Barrow
    (q.v.),p.11. AB#1,p.209; COB#11,p.424; WB#4,p.200; WB#5,p.199.

RAVEN, WILLIAM married Mary Nichols, 30 November 1738.   NFPR.,p.163

RAWLIN[G]S, THOMAS married Elizabeth Gibton, 2 March 1730/1.   NFPR.,p.163, 189

    RAYNOLDS   SEE : REYNOLDS : RAYNOLDS : RENNOLDS PAGES 167-169

    REAMY : RAMEY

REAMY, BERIMAN and Sally Jarvis Balderson*, bond 15 April 1791. Gilbert Balder-
    son (b); he consents in person for the marriage of his aforesaid daughter.
    DB#20,p.75. [The family Bible of Joshua Reamy (1 May 1792-6 November 1857)
    and Frances Morris, his wife, of Westmoreland and Stafford counties, is pre-
    served in the family of their son, the late William Daingerfield Reamy (1852-
    1939), for more than twenty five years treasurer of Stafford County. Joshua
    Reamy was the eldest child of Berryman and Sally Jarvis (Balderson) Reamy.]

RAMEY, DANIEL married long before 31 October 1774, Darcus Brickey, daughter of
    John Brickey who died intestate in Richmond County in 1733. By 31 October
    1774 Daniel Ramey is deceased and his widow is residing in Dunmore County.
    DB#14,p.335; WB#5,p.189,208.

REAMY, JAMES and Ailsey Saunders*, bond 9 January 1832. James B. Fones (b);
    Richard J. Fones (w).   MBB.,p.86

REAMY, JAMES O. and Mary Jane Morris, bond 14 September 1843. Consent by Fer-
    een [?] Morris; no relationship stated. Richard C. Gutridge (b); John
    Gutridge (w).   MBB.,p.240

REAMY, ROBERT G. and Maria L. Carter*, bond 26 December 1849. Robert N. Reamy
    (b); Samuel T. Reamy (w). Married 27 December 1849 by the Rev. John Pul-
    len.   MBB.,p.330

RAMEY, SAMUEL and Hannah Ann Dye, bond 2 June 1747. Richard Evins (b).

REDMAN, JOHN and Mary Lawson (spinster), bond 1 February 1750. Thomas Lawson (b).

REDMAN, JOHN JR. and Maria C. Smith, bond 9 March 1807. Consent by William Smith, guardian of the bride. Alfred Beale (b); Edwin C. Brann (w).

REDMAN, JOHN SR. and Alice B. McCarty*, bond 23 November 1809. George Saunders (b); Judith G. McCarty (w).

REDMAN, JOSEPH JR. and Sarah Ann Northen, bond 6 March 1797. Peter Northen (b).

REDMAN, RICHARD L. and Alice P. Armistead, bond 11 March 1803. John M. Yerby (b). [The bride was the daughter of Henry and Winifred (Peachey) Armistead (q.v.),p.4. Fredericksburg District Court DB "E",p.213.]

REDMAN, SOLOMON (16??-1749) married by 2 May 1711 Mary Stewart (Steuart), daughter of William Stewart then of Cople Parish, Westmoreland County, but who died intestate in Richmond County in 1717. COB#8,p.69; DB#5,p.327; DB#8, p.9,59; WB#4,p.7; WB#5,p.587; also Westmoreland County COB 1705-1721,p.284, 325 and W&D#3,p.299.

REED, ELY married Mary Randall, 20 August 1729.   NFPR.,p.162

REID, JOSEPH B. of Westmoreland County and Elizabeth Asbury, bond 18 December 1826. William Bispham (b).   MBB.,p.26

RENNOLDS   SEE : REYNOLDS : RAYNOLDS : RENNOLDS PAGE 167

REUICK   SEE : RUICK PAGE 174

REVEER : REVERE : RIVEER

RIVEER, JAMES of Lancaster County and Ann Alderson (spinster), bond 3 January 1806. John Alderson (b).

REVEER, WILLIAM of Lancaster County and Sally Brown*, bond 30 December 1811. John Bean of Northumberland County (b); Elizabeth Brown (w).

REYNOLDS : RAYNOLDS : RENNOLDS

REYNOLDS, EDWIN J. and Mary Mozingo*, bond 27 December 1842. John M. Sisson (b). Married 29 December 1842 by the Rev. William N. Ward.   MBB.,p.231

RAYNOLDS, GEORGE and Frances Barber (spinster), bond 12 February 1759. Thomas Barber (b).

RENNOLDS, JAMES and Elizabeth S. Sisson, bond 1 October 1804. Consent by Henry and Winnefried Sisson, parents of the bride. William Smith (b).

REYNOLDS, JAMES and Catharine Davis, bond 29 December 1834. Consent by John
     Davis, father of the bride. James Peg (b); Robert L. Montgomery (w).
                                                            MBB.,p.129

REYNOLDS, JAMES and Alice Davis, bond 11 January 1843. Consent by Lucy Ann
     Davis, mother of the bride. George W. Booker (b); W.N. Harris (w). Mar-
     ried 12 January 1843 by the Rev. William N. Ward.   MBB.,p.233

REYNOLDS, JAMES and Martha Efford*, bond 12 August 1848. Rodham C. Hammack (b);
     Robert A. Jenkins (w).   MBB., p.313

REYNOLDS, JOHN and Sarah Grimes, married 5 August 1674.   NFPR.,p.161

REYNOLDS, JOHN of Cople Parish, Westmoreland County, married long before 31 Oct-
     ober 1774, Betty Brickey, daughter of John Brickey who died intestate in
     Richmond County in 1733. DB#14,p.335; WB#5,p.189,208.

RAYNOLDS, JOHN and Jane Hammond, bond 2 May 1785. Thaddeus Williams (b).

REYNOLDS, JOHN J. and Jane P. Reynolds*, bond 2 February 1843. Robert L. Mont-
     gomery (b). Married by the Rev. Nathan Healy.   MBB.,p.234

REYNOLDS, RICHARD and Sinah Fowles [Fouls], bond 24 December 1808. Consent by
     Nancy Fouls [Fowles], mother of the bride. Jesse D. Reynolds (b); William
     Smith (w). [The parentage of the bride is uncertain; see George Fowles,p.
     72. A petition to the Legislature, dated 22 January 1845, says Richard and
     Sinah (Fowles) Reynolds had issue: (a) James Reynolds; (b) Betsy Reynolds
     wife of Washington Scates; (c) Nancy Reynolds wife of William Webb; (d)
     William Reynolds; (e) Thomas Reynolds; (f) Edward Reynolds. Richmond Coun-
     ty Petition to the Legislature dated 22 January 1845 in VSL:AD.]

REYNOLDS, RICHARD and Maria Webb*, bond 11 June 1835. John Webb (b); Mary Webb
     (w).   MBB.,p.135

REYNOLDS, THOMAS and Nancy Webb*, bond 24 December 1850. R.A. Belfield (w) and
     William S. Richards (w). Married 26 December 1850 by the Rev. William N.
     Ward, Minister of the Gospel in the Protestant Episcopal Church.

REYNOLDS, THOMAS T. and Ann Webb*, bond 2 May 1796. William Webster (b). [ECD
     Papers, Box 19, says Thomas Thornton Reynolds was born 24 December 1774 and
     died ante 1838. He married 7 May 1796, Ann Webb; she was born 28 April
     1762, daughter of James and Edith (Harford) Webb. Issue: (a) Sally Rey-
     nolds, born and died 14 March 1797; (b) Sally Reynolds born 16 August 1798;
     (c) Ann Webb Reynolds (1 February 1802-7 November 1888), married 10 August
     1833, Henry Austin Yeatman (1808-1896); (d) Betty Thornton Reynolds, born
     19 June 1805.]

REYNOLDS, VINCENT and Elizabeth Alloway*, bond 28 December 1803. David Goldsby
     (b). [See data under the groom's father, William Reynolds, next below.]

REYNOLDS, WILLIAM (3 October 1755-1784) married circa 1773 Ann Thornton, daughter of Thomas and Elizabeth ("Betsy") (Davis) Thornton (q.v.); she married (2) 10 September 1791, David Goldsby (q.v.),p.79. All of the children of William and Ann (Thornton) Reynolds were living in 1796 when she settled the estate of their father, viz: (a) Thomas Thornton Reynolds (q.v.),p.168; (b) William Reynolds, born 23 September 1776; (c) Vincent Reynolds, born 21 December 1778, (q.v.),p.168; (d) John Reynolds, born 12 October 1782; and (e) Betty Thornton Reynolds, born 12 October 1782, married 2 November 1799 Joseph Sterling (q.v.). COB#15,p.79; AB#2,p.301-302; WB#7,p.466; WB#8,p.130, 166; ECD Papers, Box 19.

REYNOLDS, WILLIAM and Hannah Wilcox*, bond 20 May 1841. George Mothershead (b).
MBB.,p.209

REYNOLDS, WILLIAM HENRY and Lucetta W. McKenney*, bond 2 December 1840. Daniel Atwill (b). Married by the Rev. Nathan Healy, Baptist Minister. MBB.,p.199

RIAN, DENNIS married Sarah Neives, 24 October 1729.   NFPR.,p.163

RICE, CHARLES of Northumberland County and Nancy Wall*, bond 14 December 1798. William Webb (b); Edward Wall (w).

RICE, JAMES of Westmoreland County and Mary Bramham Taylor (spinster)*, bond 27 August 1805. Robert Sanford (b); Mary L. Neale (w).

RICE, JOHN [CAPTAIN] (16??-1693) married 1679 Rebecca Travers, widow of Colonel William Travers, Gentleman, of Rappahannock County. Captain John Rice died without issue in Richmond County in 1693 and his will was recorded in now lost WB#1 (1692-1699) of Richmond County. Fortunately, there is a certified copy of it, made in 1700, in the Landon Carter Papers, Alderman Library, University of Virginia, and this makes us mindful of many errors in Hayden, p.84A,297-301. Colonel William and Rebecca Travers had three sons, viz: (a) Captain Samuel Travers who married Frances Allerton; (b) William Travers; and (c) Rawleigh Travers; there is data in regard to them in John Bennett Boddie, Historical Southern Families, Volume II (Redwood City, California, 1958), p.133-135. Rappahannock County Book 1677-1682,p.289; Westmoreland County COB 1675-1689,p.206; Sweeny,p.30,129.

RICE, JOHN and Hannah Stuckey*, bond 23 November 1809. The bride in writing her own consent states she is "the age of 29 years." George Shearley (b); William Lewce (w) and William Rice (w).

RICE, RICHARD of Northumberland County and Sally Dodson (spinster), bond 13 October 1801. James B. Dodson (b).

RICE, SAMUEL S. and Catharine M. Booth, bond 9 December 1850. Consent by William P. Booth, guardian of the bride. A. Judson Sydnor (w) and Robert Reade (w).

RICH, BEVERLY and Mary Luin*, bond 29 June 1850. Richard Rich (b); John W. Clements (w).   MBB.,p.339

RICH, CHARLES and Ellen Tate "both free persons of colour," bond 8 October 1823. Linsey Rich (b).

RICH, GEORGE and Elizabeth Rich, bond 27 December 1814. Consent by David Rich, father of the bride. Robert Rich (b).

RICH, GEORGE and Polly Rich*, "Free persons of colour of Richmond County," bond 5 February 1831. Bass Rich (b); Joseph Dale (w) and George N. Alderson (w).   MBB.,p.75

RICH, GRIFFIN and Judy Venie [Veney], "free persons of colour," bond 20 December 1832. *Jerre Vinie (b); Darky Veney (w). [*(?) Jesse Vinie]   MBB.,p.98

RICH, LINSEY and Eliza Tate, bond 1 May 1823. William R. Jeffries (b).

RICH, ROBERT and Juda Wells*, "free persons of colour," bond 9 February 1836. Juda Wells writes her consent with her own hand. George Burwell "a free man of colour," (b).   MBB.,p.143

RICH, ROBERT JR. and Nancy Rich, bond 23 December 1839. Lindsey Rich (b); Peter S. Northen (w) and Robert Rich, Sr. (w).   MBB.,p.188

RICHARDS, AUSTIN N. and Martha Drake*, bond 18 December 1845. Samuel T. Reamy (b); William H. Connellee (w). Married 18 December 1845 by the Rev. John Pullen.   MBB.,p.268

RICHARDS, JOHN and Mary Webb*, bond 5 March 1841. John Webb (b). Married by the Rev. William N. Ward.   MBB.,p.208

RICHARDS, LEWIS (16??-post 1713) married 168? Bridgett (Bryer) Pridham, widow of Christopher Pridham (q.v.),p.162, and only child of Captain George Bryer who died testate in Rappahannock County in 1665. Bridgett (Bryer) Pridham Richards d. testate in Rappahannock County in 1685, leaving two children by each spouse. COB#6,p.126; Rappahannock County Deeds &c:#6,p.70; Sweeny,p.116.

RICHARDS, REUBEN S. and Elizabeth C. Thrift, bond 5 February 1841. Consent by Jane Thrift, mother of the bride. John Richards (b); Lucindy Efford (w).
                                                                          MBB.,p.207

RICHARDS, WADE and Fanny Ellen Webb, license 19 December 1853. Consent by Francis T. Webb, father of the bride. John Webb (w).

RICHARDS, WILLIAM and Elizabeth Reynolds, bond 6 May 1811. Consent by Benjamin Reynolds, father of the bride. Benjamin Reynolds, Jr. (b).

RICHARDS, WILLIAM and Elizabeth Webb, bond 22 December 1830. James Webb (b).
                                                                          MBB.,p.70

RICHARDS, WILLIAM S. and Mrs. Mariah Reynolds*, bond 29 December 1841. John Richards (b). Married 30 December 1841 by the Rev. William N. Ward.
                                                                          MBB.,p.216

RICHARDSON, GEORGE S. and Mary J. Straughan*, bond 2 December 1847. James Keser (b); Mrs. Sally Straughan (w).   MBB.,p.301

RICHARDSON, THOMAS (16??-1719) married by 7 October 1696, Mary (Thatcher) Clapman (166?-1727), widow of William Clapman [Clapham] (c.1654-1696) (q.v.),p.
37 and daughter of Sylvester Thatcher (16??-1667), all of Richmond County
area. See references under William Clapman, p.37; Richmond Co. DB#3,p.143.

RICHARDSON, THOMAS A. of Northumberland County and Elizabeth P. Luttrell*, bond
10 January 1821. John P. Luttrell (b).

RICHARDSON, WILLIAM married by 25 March 1709 Honour Barrow (16??-1749), elder
of ·the two daughters of John Barrow (16??-1685) who died testate in Rappahannock County. On 25 March 1709 William Richardson and Thomas Brock [who
married Cicily Barrow, younger of the two daughters of the aforesaid John
Barrow] (q.v.),p.24, divided the land which became the property of their
wives upon the deaths of their three brothers without issue. Honour (Barrow) Richardson was a widow by 6 December 1722; she died intestate in King
George County in 1749. King George County COB#2,p.651; DB#1,p.96,509;
DB#1-A,p.341; Sweeny,p.115; see also references under Thomas Brock, p.24.

RIVEER   SEE :   REVEER : REVERE : RIVEER PAGE 167

ROBERTSON, ANDREW [DOCTOR] (17??-1785) of Lancaster County married (1) 27 November 1758, Ellen Chichester.   LCMR#1,p.28
Doctor Andrew Robertson married (2) by 5 February 1784, Ann Glascock, daughter of William Glascock of Richmond County who mentions her in his will
of this date. WB#7,p.459; AB#2,p.56; King George County DB#5,p.946; Lancaster County WB#22,p.307; Hayden,p.92; 21W(2)406.

ROBERTSON, JONATHAN P. and Barbara B. Alderson*, bond 21 December 1819. William
F. Davis (b). The marriage bond is signed by the groom "Jonathan P. Robinson."

ROBINS, WILLIAM married Ellen Thornton, daughter of Thomas and Susannah (Smith)
Thornton (q.v.),p.213-214. William Robins (17??-1782), an alien and Greenwich pensioner, died testate in Richmond County; his widow died intestate
circa 1793. DB#17,p.24,29,100; WB#5,p.146; WB#6,p.203; WB#7,p.403; Fredericksburg Virginia Herald 27 October 1795 carried a notice, signed by John
Robins, in regard to the estate of William Robins, deceased, of Richmond
County.

ROBINSON, BROWN and Sally Raynolds, bond 6 July 1789. Consent by Elizabeth Roy-
nolds, mother of the bride. Thomas Pritchett (b); Fanny Reynolds (w).

ROBINSON, EPAPHRODITUS of Lancaster County and Susannah Pope*, bond 30 July 1791.
John Brown (b); John Brown (w); Elizabeth Brown (w).

ROBINSON, JAMES married Margaret Connelly, 29 July 1739.   NFPR.,p.163

ROBINSON, JOHN and Augusta M. Hammock, bond 2 May 1842. Consent by Winnef. S.
Hammock, guardian of the bride. Samuel G. Brann (b); Augillia [?] Rockwell
(w).   MBB.,p.223
ROBINSON, JOHN and Charlotte T. Hall, bond 15 October 1846. Consent by Robert
Hall, father of the bride. Richard C. Belfield (b); Robert B. Sydnor (w).

Married 15 October 1846 by the Rev. P. Rescoel.   MBB.,p.281

ROBINSON, WILLIAM [COLONEL] of Richmond and King George counties, married by 16
    September 1699 Frances Blomfield [Broomfield] (168?-1737), only child of
    Captain Samuel and Elizabeth (Jones) Blomfield of Rappahannock County (q.v.),
    p.19. COB#5,p.133; DB#1,p.94, DB#3,p.152, WB#2,p.14; Eseex County D&c:#12,p.
    59 and DB#23,p.247; Sweeny.,p.63,75,76,103. Colonel William Robinson died
    20 September 1742 at his estate Bunker Hill, near Leedstown, then in King
    George [now Westmoreland] County and his last will and Testament was admitt-
    ed to probate 3 December 1742 and recorded in now missing King George County
    WB#1 (1721-1752) per entry in COB#2,p.316. Captain Maxmillian Robinson, only
    child of Colonel William and Frances (Blomfield) Robinson, succeeded his fath-
    er at Bunker Hill and died there in 1776. He became a gentleman justice in
    1740 when his father was yet on the bench. Colonel William Robinson was the
    ranking justice of King George County when that county was formed in 1721;
    the King George County records abound with instruments in regard to him and
    his family. There is a sketch of the family in 22V22-24.

ROCHESTER, NATHANIEL [COLONEL] (21 February 1752-27 May 1831), founder of Roch-
    ester, New York, where he died, was born in Westmoreland County, Virginia,
    the son of John Rochester (17??-1756) and his wife nee Hannah Trift (17??-
    1784), daughter of William Thrift who died testate in Richmond County in
    1776; Hannah (Thrift) Rochester, widow, married (2) Thomas Critcher (17??-
    1778) and moved to Granville County, North Carolina. Colonel Nathaniel Roch-
    ester married in 1788 Sophia Beatty (1768-1845). Rochester History, Vol.
    XXIV,No.1,p.1-23 [January,1962]; Silas Emmett Lucas, Genealogy of the Dodson
    (Dotson), Lucas, Pyles, Rochester, and Allied Families (Birmingham, Alabama,
    1959), p.195-223; Richmond County WB#7,p.213, will of William Thrift, 1776.

ROCHESTER, WILLIAM and Ellianor Jones, bond 26 June 1764. Jeremiah Brown (b).
    [William Rochester married (1) Mary Asbury; her mother Anne Asbury by will
    1755, recorded in Westmoreland County W&D#12,p.303, mentions her daughter
    Mary Rochester and names, among others, Nicholas and William Rochester as
    residuary legatees. William Rochester by will 1767, recorded in Richmond
    County WB#6,p.419, mentions his wife Eleanor and children. The settlement
    of his estate, recorded in Richmond County AB#1,p.553, mentions a legacy
    bequeathed "to your children" by Mrs. Ann(e) Asbury. The family of William
    Rochester (17??-1767) of Richmond County is inaccurately accounted for by
    Silas Emmett Lucas, Genealogy of the Dodson (Dotson), Lucas, Pyles, Rochest-
    er, and Allied Families (Birmingham, Alabama, 1959),p.198.]

ROCK, GRIFFIN and Juliet A. Davis*, license 28 October 1852. John Davis (w) and
    William A. Franklin (w). Married 28 October 1852 by Rev. E.L. Williams.

ROCK, JAMES of Northumberland County and Sarah Ann Hardwick, bond 5 January 1837.
    Consent by John Hardwick; no relationship stated. John Hardwick, Jr. (b);
    Juliet Hardwick (w).   MBB.,p.153

ROCK, JOHN and Elizabeth Dodson (widow)*, bond 5 June 1833. There is a note to
    the court clerk stating "there is no danger in granting John Rock lisons to
    marry this woman. Mrs. Elizabeth (X) Dodson." Charles Dodson (b); Ransdall
    P. Headley (w).   MBB.,p.107

ROCK, JOHN D. and Sophia Hammock*, bond 22 March 1841. John Powers (b); Mary P.
    Berrick (w).   MBB.,p.208

ROCK, THOMAS and Julia Wooddy*, bond 25 April 1842. Robert H. Davis (b).
                                                             MBB.,p.222

ROCK, THOMAS C. and Ann Fulks, bond 30 July 1838. Consent by Alexander Rock,
    father of the groom. John Fulks (b); Ransdall Headly (w).   MBB.,p.174

ROCK, WESLEY of Northumberland County and Mary Luttrell*, bond 26 December 1831.
    Francis Rock (b); John P. Luttrell (w).   MBB.,p.85

ROCK, WESLEY and Ann D. Thrift*, bond 29 November 1841. Samuel B. Thrift (b);
    George W. Efford (w).   MBB.,p.213

ROCK, WILLIAM and Elizabeth Ayres, bond 18 September 1800. Consent by Charles
    Dodson, guardian of William Rock who is "under age." Alexander Rock (b);
    John Rock (w) and Alexander Rock (w).

ROCKWELL, WILLIAM and Mary B. Jeffries, bond 20 April 1846. John F.B. Jeffries
    (b). Married 22 April 1846 by the Rev. Elijah L. Williams.   MBB.,p.275

    ROE   SEE : WROE PAGE 236

ROE, SAMUEL B. and Winnefred Woollard*, bond 29 March 1848. John W. Woollard
    (b).   MBB.,p.309

ROGERS, GRIGSBY and [blank], bond __ December 1749. Augustine Sanford (b).

ROGERS, NICHOLAS and Eliz.^a Ford (widow), license December 1714.   DB#6,p.275
    [Nicholas Ro(d)gers (16??-1718) married in December 1714 Elizabeth Ford,
    widow of John Ford, Jr. (16??-1714), son of John and Patience Ford. See
    Emanuell Cleave(s), Gentleman, p.40. COB#6,p.201,314,383; MRB.,p.103; WB#3,
    p.192; WB#4,p.53.]

ROLLS, WILLIAM and Margaret Reeves, married 8 June 1674.   NFPR.,p.161

ROSE, JAMES and Winney Sandy, bond 11 July 1798. Consent by Mason and Elizabeth
    Sandy; no relationship stated. Mason Sandy (b).

ROSS[I]ER, DAVID (16??-1698) married (1) by 24 November 1688, Sarah Sherwood, one
    of the four daughters of Philip Sherwood, deceased, of Rappahannock County
    whose land fell into Richmond County upon its formation in 1721. Their son
    and heir, David Rosser, conveyed his one fourth interest in the landed est-
    ate of his grandfather Sherwood in 1715 to Francis James (q.v.),p.102. COB#2,
    p.301,313; DB#7,p.38; 23T116,207,278. It appears very likely that Francis
    James married (2) Margaret (surname unknown), the widow of David Rosser and
    to whom administration was granted on his estate 1 June 1698.
    David Rosser married (1) Sarah Sherwood; married (2) Margaret _____ [#]
    Francis James married (1) Mary Sherwood; married (2) Margaret _____ [#]
    I believe the aforementioned Margarets# are identical.

ROUT, JOHN married Winifred Sydnor, 3 March 1731/2. [See p.200]   NFPR.,p.163

ROUTT, JOHN of Northumberland County and Sarah Dodson, bond 16 October 1820. Thomas W. Bryant (b).

ROWAN, MANUS and Fanny P. McCarty, bond 5 August 1816. John Darby (b).

ROWLEY, JOHN (16??-1704) married Catherine Williams (16??-1704), daughter of Hugh Williams who possessed 500 acres of land in Richmond County. This couple,and others of their family,were murdered by the Indians in 1704 and William Wood petitioned the office of the Proprietor of the Northern Neck of Virginia for a grant for 500 acres of land in Richmond County which escheated by the death of Catherine (Williams) Rowley, he being in possession of the land and "next of kin." There is a long account of the Rowley affair in COB#3,p.361-384 and further reference to the troubles with the Nanzatico Indians in August-September 1704 in MRB.,p.29 et seq. See also Northern Neck Patent Book #3,p.128 and King George County DB#1.p.271.

ROWZEE, EDWARD (16??-1720) of Essex County married by 1701 Mary Peirce (16??-1726), daughter of Colonel William Peirce (16??-1702) of Cople Parish, Westmoreland County, who had large land holdings in Richmond and Westmoreland counties. Mary (Peirce) Rowzee, widow, married (2) Dr. Henry Oswald (16??-1726) of Essex County. Essex County WB#4,p.146,276a; Westmoreland County W&D#3,p.2,50,243; Dr. and Mrs. William Carter Stubbs, A History of Two Virginia Families (1918, #CS71:C362),p.98-99.

ROY, JOHN CORRIE of King and Queen County and Elizabeth Corrie Williams, bond 29 November 1804. Consent by Beverley Roy, father of the groom, of King and Queen County, which is witnessed by William Bird, Jr. Consent by Catharine Williams, mother of the bride, who states Thaddeus Williams, father of the bride, is deceased. Wily Campbell of King and Queen County (b); Kitty T. Roy (w) and Wily Campbell (w). [The bride was the daughter of Thaddeus and Catharine (Corrie) Williams and the groom was the son of Beverley and Ann (Corrie) Roy; they were first cousins and grandchildren of John Corrie of Essex County who mentioned his daughters Ann Roy and Catherine Williams in his will of 1787. The bride, Elizabeth Corrie Williams, was born in North Farnham Parish, 22 June 1788; see reference under her father Thaddeus Williams (q.v.). Essex County WB#14,p.74; John McGill, The Beverley Family of Virginia-(Columbia,S.C.,1956),p.918-919; Helen Dearborn (Tyler) Williams, The Roy Genealogy (Richmond, Va.,1943), p.39; Beverley Fleet, Virginia Colonial Abstracts, Volume #4, p.87-88.]

RUICK : REUICK

RUICK, JAMES and Nancy Jesper, bond 12 February 1799. Daniel Ruick (b).

RUICK, JOHN and Frances Efford, bond 24 December 1794. Samford Jones (b). The groom signs the bond, "John Ruix."

REUICK, WILLIAM and Nancy Hudson*, bond 17 January 1820. Henry O. Hudson (b).

RUSH, BENJAMIN (16??-1766) of Westmoreland, King George, and Prince William
counties, Virginia, and Bute County, North Carolina, married in the Spring
of 1717 Amy (surname unknown), widow of James Elkins (16??-1717), son of
Richard and Mary (Williams) Elkins (q.v.),p.64. James Elkins' plantation
of 250 acres fell into King George County upon its formation in 1721. COB
#7,p.99,218; DB#2,p.87; DB#6,p.37; DB#7,p.191; WB#3,p.317; King George
County COB#1,p.78,350 and DB#1-A,p.225,294; OPR.,p.104

RUSSELL, JOHN married Alicia Billington, 11 September 1673.   NFPR.,p.161
[The bride was the daughter of Luke and Barbara Billington. Sweeny, p.16-
17,29.]

RUSSELL, JOSEPH JR. married by 8 November 1722 Sarah Armistead, widow and executrix of Francis Armistead (16??-1719). Joseph Russell, Jr. died testate
in Richmond County, 1749; his will was recorded in WB#5,p.572. COB#9,p.81;
see references under John Armistead,p.4.

RUSSELL, THOMAS married long before 31 October 1774, Sarah Brickey, widow of John
Brickey who died intestate in 1733. DB#14,p.335; WB#5,p.189,208.

RUST, GEORGE (170?-1775) of Overwharton Parish, Stafford County, married by 4
September 1730, Sarah Innis daughter of Doctor James Innis who died testate
in Richmond County in 1709. George Rust removed to Bedford County, North
Carolina. WB#3,p.31; King George County DB#A-1,p.75; Ellsworth Marshall
Rust, Rust of Virginia (1940, #CS71:R97),p.52.

RUST, JAMES B. of Fauquier County and Molly Purssell, bond 27 December 1806.
Tobias Purssell (b).

RUST, JAMES H. (bachelor) and Susan Churchwell (spinster)*, bond 15 October 1828.
George Lewis (b); he made oath the bride is of full age.   MBB.,p.43

RUST, JOHN married by 8 November 1743 Sarah Singleton, daughter of Joshua Singleton (died testate 1732) and Ann, his wife, (died testate 1734), at which
times the said Sarah Singleton was a minor and unmarried. COB#11,p.362;
WB#5,p.184,239.

RUST, JOHN and Patty Duff*, bond 19 March 1808. Samuel Rust (b).

RUST, SAMUEL and Hannah Rust (spinster), bond 10 June 1755. Peter Rust (b).
[The parties were cousins; he died testate in 1769 and she married (2) 1769
John Corrie, Gentleman, (17??-1787) of Essex County. Hannah (Rust) Rust
Corrie died testate in Richmond County, 1791. WB#7,p.30; WB#8,p.107; Essex
County WB#14,p.74; Ellsworth Marshall Rust, Rust of Virginia (1940,#CS71:
R97); E.J. Lee, Lee of Virginia, 1642-1892 (Philadelphia, 1895), p.167.]

RUST, SAMUEL and Nancy Hammond* (spinster), bond 3 January 1798. In writing her
own consent, the bride states "I am of the age of 27 years." John Woollard
(b); William Hammond (w).

RUST, WILLIAM and Mary Tillery, bond 18 January 1812. William Everitt (b).

RYALS, SAMUEL and Sally Mothershead, bond 1 September 1806. Consent by John
    Mothershead, father of the bride. Joseph Eidson (b); John Eidson (w).

RYALS, WILLIAM and Susanna Nash*, bond 4 February 1788. Jeliff Alverson (b).

RYMER, MARK JUNIOR and Margaret Prou, license February 1712/13.   DB#6,p.275
    [The bride was the daughter of Cyprian Prou (16??-1712) who died testate in
    Richmond County; the groom was the son of Mark Rymer, Sr. who was set levy
    free by the court 3 July 1717 on account of his great age and inability to
    work. After the death of Mark Rymer, Jr., his widow became the concubine
    of the Reverend Mr. John Prince, minister of Hanover Parish; this gentleman
    was very much given to drink and their activities are of record. John Prin-
    ce, Clerk, (16??-1726) died testate; by Margaret (Prou) Rymer he had a bast-
    ard son called John Prince alias Rymer [Rimer] who was living in Caroline
    County in 1752. Mark Rymer, Jr. and his wife nee Margaret Prou had two
    children, viz: (a) Katherine Rymer and (b) Richard Rymer (1717-1738) whose
    tombstone at Green Bank Farm, Stafford County, reads: "In Memory of Richard
    Rimer who died May the 10th 1738 aged 21 years." There is a biographical
    sketch of the Reverend Mr. John Prince in Goodwin, The Colonial Church in
    Virginia, p.300, but this account states he died in King George County circa
    1723, thereby depriving him of several years of gay and risque life in Han-
    over Parish and environs. COB#6,p.172; DB#7,p.180; WB#3,p.298; King George
    County COB#1,p.12,27,32,126,330,400; DB#1,p.313; DB#3,p.489; Inventory Book
    #1,p.101. The will of John Prince, Clerk, was proved 7 October 1726 and the
    inventory of his estate recorded 6 July 1727 at King George County court.]

                                    S

SACRA, CHARLES C. and Mary Harford, bond 1 September 1834. Consent by Martha
    Harford; no relationship stated. Peter T. Duff (b).   MBB.,p.123

SADLER, WILLIAM and Patty Jones (widow), bond 17 August 1783. Edmond Mitchell
    (b).

SALLARD, GEORGE and Polly Pretty [Purty]*, bond 17 January 1807. David Gaskins
    (b); William Yeatman (w).

SALLARD, WILLIAM and Ann Barber, bond 14 May 1761. Thomas Suggitt Hill (b).

    SAMFORD   SEE : SANFORD : SANDFORD PAGE 179 - 180

SAMFORD, JAMES married Mary Barber, 20 September 1728.   NFPR.,p.229
    [The groom was the son of Samuel and Elizabeth (Keene) Samford (q.v.), p.
    177; the bride was the daughter of Colonel Charles and Frances (Glascock)
    Barber (q.v.),p.9. James Samford (circa 1690-1742) died testate in Richmond
    County and Mary (Barber) Samford married (2) per bond dated 10 March 1753,
    William Denton (q.v.),p.53. James and Mary (Barber) Samford had no son but
    four daughters, viz: (a) Ann Samford, married Joshua Singleton;(b)Elizabeth
    ("Betty") Samford married William Miskell; (c) Frances Samford (d.s.p.) but
    married 1756 John Suggitt; and (d) Winifred Samford married Daniel Dobyns.
    WB#5,p.414; suit Singleton vs Samford, Richmond County chancery papers, &c.]

SAMFORD, JAMES married Rebecca McKenny, 3 April 1772.   NFPR.,p.232

SAMFORD, JAMES and Raney Hammond, bond 4 April 1782. Edmond Mitchell (b).

SAMFORD, JAMES and Elizabeth G. Lightfoot (spinster), bond 24 December 1804.
    Thomas Lightfoot (b). Marriage returns dub the groom JAMES SANFORD.

SAMFORD, JAMES and Mary S. White*, bond 6 January 1823. Thomas Bryant (b);
    Wilalmina L. Walker (w) and Frances A. Tarpley (w).

SAMFORD, JOHN AMES and Betty Lightfoot (spinster), bond 1 April 1771. James
    Samford (b). [The bride was born in North Farnham Parish, 5 May 1750, the
    daughter of Daniel and Alitia (Alger) Lightfoot (q.v.),p.119. The groom
    was born in North Farnham Parish, 16 September 1746, the son of Thomas Sam-
    ford (1688-1762) and Frances ____[?]____ (17??-1750), his wife. The name of
    the groom appears as John Amis Samford and John Ames Samford. AB#1,p.507;
    WB#6,p.315;_DB#16,p.180; DB#17,p.157; DB#19,p.62.]

SAMFORD, KEENE married Winny Dowden, 28 July 1742.   NFPR.,p.229
    [The groom's full name was William Keene Samford; he was born in North Farn-
    ham Parish, 13 February 1722/3, the son of William and Elizabeth (Langhee)
    Samford (q.v.),p.177. He removed to Brunswick County, Virginia, where he
    died testate in 1795. Brunswick County WB#5,p.620.]

SAMFORD, SAMUEL (1662-1736), son of James Samford (circa 1624-1704) and Mary,
    his wife, married (1) circa 1687 Elizabeth Keene (1669-circa 1706), daughter
    of William Keene, Gentleman, (1642-1685) of Northumberland County and his
    wife nee Elizabeth Rogers; they had seven children. Samuel Samford married
    (2) 21 November 1707 in Christ Church Parish, Middlesex County, Mrs. Isabel-
    la Langhee (16??-1725) by whom he had no issue. She was probably the widow
    of Patrick Langhee who died intestate in Richmond County in 1705 and after
    his death moved to Middlesex County where she held property. COB#4,p.60-61;
    WB#2,p.80; WB#5,p.5,292; DB#3,p.172; DB#4,p.94; Fairfax County Land Causes
    of Long Standing 1742-1770,p.342,357-368 et seq.; Stafford County Deed Book
    1722-1728,p.217; CCPR.,p.80.

SAMFORD, WILLIAM (1692-1763) married circa 1713, Elizabeth Langhee; she was his
    step-sister, the daughter of Mrs. Isabella Langhee Samford, above mentioned.
    William Samford was the son of Samuel and Elizabeth (Keene) Samford (q.v.)
    p.177. He removed to Brunswick County, Virginia, where he died testate in
    1763 and his will is recorded in WB#4,p.317.

SAMPSON, GEORGE and Susan Stonum*, bond 17 November 1836. Thomas Oldham (b).
                                                                        MBB.,p.150

SANDERS   **SEE** SAUNDERS PAGE 180 - 181

SANDERS, GEORGE married by 6 April 1736 Mary Williams, daughter of Thomas Williams
    who died intestate in Richmond County in 1718; his widow, Catherine Williams,
    married Samuel Steele (q.v.). COB#10,p.371; AB#1,p.156; COB#8,p.20; WB#4,p.
    39.

SANDERS, GEORGE and Sarah Brumbelow, bond 30 January 1756. Thomas Smith (b).
[The bride was the daughter of Edward Brumbelow who died intestate in Richmond County in 1717. On 18 July 1770 Sarah Saunders, aged 43*, made a deposition in the suit Tillery vs Lewis in which she mentioned certain land on Totusky Creek which was "near a piece of land taken up by her father, Edward
Brumbelow." WB#3,p.339. *Undoubtedly 53 or a year or so older!]

SANDERS, GEORGE W. and Charlotte Scates, license 26 March 1851. Consent by John
B. and Elizabeth Scates, parents of the bride. James A.B. Sanders (w) and
Thornton Marks (w). Married 27 March 1851 by the Rev. John Pullen.

SANDERS, GRIFFIN and Mariah A. Sanders*, bond 9 January 1843. James K. Spillman
(b); John A. Payton (w). Married 12 January 1843 by the Rev. R.N. Herndon.
                                                                    MBB.,p.232

SANDERS, HENRY and Maria Jones*, bond 19 December 1848. Samuel Marks (b); James
M. Morris (w), James Marks (w) and Jackson Marks (w). Married 22 December
1848 by the Rev. John Pullen.   MBB.,p.317

SANDERS, HENRY V. and Lucy Marks, bond 21 November 1821. Consent by James Marks;
no relationship stated. William Sanders (b).

SANDERS, HENRY V. and Mary Hall*, bond 2 February 1846. John France (b). Married
5 February 1846 by the Rev. John Pullen.   MBB.,p.272

SANDERS, JAMES and Elizabeth Balderson, bond 28 December 1837. Consent by William Balderson, father of the bride. William R. Balderson (b); John A. Peyton (w). Married by the Rev. Thomas M. Washington.   MBB.,p.163

SANDERS, JAMES A.B. and Susan Sanders, bond 22 December 1841. Consent by Henry V.
Sanders, father of the bride. T.N. Balderson (b); Thornton Marks (w). Married 23 December 1841 by the Rev. R.N. Herndon.   MBB.,p.216

SANDERS, JAMES C. and Nancy Hinson*, license 22 January 1851. Joseph F. Sanders
(w), John Sanders (w) and Daniel Hinson (w). Married 23 January 1851 by the
Rev. William Balderson.

SANDERS, JOHN and Frances Jenkins*, bond 10 January 1848. Redman B. Ambrose (b);
W.R. Balderson (w). Married 13 January 1848 by Rev. John Pullen. MBB.,p.305

SANDERS, JOSEPH F. and Mary M. Bowing*, bond 21 March 1842. James A.B. Sanders
(b); James C. Sanders (w).   MBB.,p.220

SANDERS, ROBERT and Mary A. Morris, bond 24 June 1843. Consent by John Morris,
father of the bride. T.N. Balderson (b); James R. Carter (w). MBB.,p.239
[See ECD Papers, VHS #Mms.6:4:Sa.564:1, Bible record of aforementioned Robert Sanders (1 June 1798-31 January 1851), giving issue by two wives. Here,
also, are notes on his ancestry which indicate he was the son of Alexander
Sanders (1760-1829) and his wife nee Ann Carpenter who were married 28 November 1782. The above bond is for the second marriage of Robert Sanders.]

SANDERS, THOMAS and Nancy Connally*, bond 6 December 1790. John Edison (b); Zechariah White (w).

SANDERS, THOMAS and Caty Jones*, bond 5 March 1792. Alex.^{r} (Aleck) Sanders (b).

SANDERS, THOMAS and Susannah Jones*, bond 22 September 1819. William Sanders (b).

SANDERS, THOMAS and Clara Deane*, bond 7 December 1837. John A. Payton (b); Carter Sanders (w). Married 15 December 1837 by the Rev. Lovell Marders.
MBB.,p.162

SANDERS, WILLIAM and Nancy Sydnor*, bond 1 November 1813. Moore F. Tomlin (b).

SANDERS, WILLIAM A.H. and Margaret Morris, bond 26 December 1842. Consent by John Morris, father of the bride. Theoderick N. Balderson (b); John A. Payton (w). Married 29 December 1842 by Rev. R.N. Herndon.   MBB.,p.231

SANDERS, WILLIAM O. and Mary Ann Brewer, license 11 March 1851. Daniel Carter (w) and Carter Hinson (w). Mary Brewer consents to the marriage; no relationship stated. Married 12 March 1851 by the Rev. John Pullen.

SANDFORD   SEE SAMFORD PAGE 176-177 AND SANFORD PAGE 179

SANDFORD, ALBERT and Martha Brewer, bond 20 December 1848. James R. Carter (b); John Morris (w). Married 22 December 1848 by Rev. John Pullen. MBB.,p.317

SANDFORD, JOHN and Catherine Ruic*, bond 3 December 1846. Lemuel G. Bell (b). Married 3 December 1846 by the Rev. Mr. William N. Ward.   MBB.,p.283

SANDFORD, ROBERT and Maria Hall*, bond 27 November 1846. James R. Carter (b); John Morris (w).   MBB.,p.283

SANDY, JOHN and Fanny R. Sandford, bond 27 October 1819. Consent by Edward Sandford; no relationship stated. Lemuel G. Sandy (b); Sally M. Sandford (w), Lucy Y. Sanford (w) and Susan W. Sandford (w).

SANDY, LEMUEL G. and Johannah Bartlett*, bond 8 February 1822. John Sandy (b); Joel Bartlett (w).

SANDY, SAMUEL and Elizabeth Pullen, bond 8 January 1822. Consent by Catherine Pullin; no relationship stated. Thomas Howe (b); John Pullin (w) and John Sandy (w).

SANDY, URIAH and Ann Murphey (spinster), bond 18 January 1755. John Newton (b).

SANDY, WILLIAM and Harriet Sanford*, license 26 November 1851. George Mothershead (w). Married 27 November 1851 by the Rev. G.M. Northam.

SANFORD   SEE SAMFORD PAGE 176-177 AND SANDFORD PAGE 179

SANFORD, DANIEL and Mary A. Hall*, license 1 January 1851. Joseph M. Crask (w) and James R. Carter (w). Married 2 January 1851 by the Rev. John Pullen.

SANFORD, GEORGE and Elizabeth Jones*, bond 3 February 1845. William Littrell
(b). Married 6 February 1845 by the Rev. Elijah L. Williams. MBB.,p.255

SANFORD, RICHARD and Bethiah Asbury, bond 28 December 1790. Consent by Henry
Asbury, father of the bride. Thomas Stowers (b); Thomas Stowers (w).

SANFORD, WILLIAM (1670-1748) married Jemima ___[?]___ (16??-1743). ECD Papers,
Box 20, copy of their Bible record, but parts now lost. The Bible appears
to have been printed in 1714; the will of William Sanford was proved in Westmoreland County in 1749. His son William Sanford (1704-1783) also died testate in Westmoreland County, but the will of his wife Barbara Sanford was admitted to probate in Richmond County in 1797. There are many Sanford connections between the family in Westmoreland and that in Richmond county.

SANFORD, WILLIAM and Mary Ruicks, bond 29 July 1806. John Fryer (b). The bond
is signed by the groom, William Sanford, but the court clerk writes Samford.

SANFORD, WILLIAM H. [COLONEL] and Mary Jane Sandy, bond 27 October 1846. Consent
by John Sandy, father of the bride. E.M. Sandy (b); John F.B. Jeffries (w).
Married 29 October 1846 by the Rev. P. Rescoel.   MBB.,p.282

SAUNDERS   SEE : SANDERS PAGE 177

SAUNDERS, AUGUSTINE N. [DOCTOR] and Mary Catharine Sands, bond 5 December 1845.
Consent by O.H. and Maria Sands, parents of the bride. Isaac S. Jeffries
(b); George B. McCarty (w) and William F. Tebbs (w).   MBB.,p.266

SAUNDERS, DANIEL and Mary Mothershead, bond 22 May 1819. Allen Saunders (b);
Billy Saunders (w).

SAUNDERS, EDWARD and Magdalene Miskell, bond 16 April 1782. LeRoy Peachey (b).

SAUNDERS, EDWARD JR. and Maria Bennehan, bond 5 December 1825. Richard Saunders
(b).   MBB.,p.15

SAUNDERS, EDWARD S. and Maria Belfield, bond 8 May 1833. Consent by Peggy Belfield, mother of the bride. George Saunders (b); Pearson Cauthorn (w).
                                                               MBB.,p.106

SAUNDERS, GEORGE and Anne Maria Belfield, bond 6 February 1810. Bartholomew Mc-
Carty (b). [The bondsman was clerk of Richmond County court and the groom
was deputy clerk. The bride was the daughter of Sydnor and Ann (Young) Belfield (q.v.),p.15.]

SAUNDERS, GEORGE and Mary S. Neale, bond 17 February 1819. Miskell Saunders (b).

SAUNDERS, HENRY S. and Margaret J. Alderson, bond 7 January 1828. Jonathan P.
Robinson (b).   MBB.,p.33·

SAUNDERS, JAMES and Sarah Jennings were married 13 January 1853 by the Rev. John
Pullen. James Jennings, father of the bride, gave this consent.

SAUNDERS, JOSEPH and Peggy Shackleford, bond 29 August 1789. Consent by R. Shackleford, father of the bride. Abner Dobyns (b). [The bride was the daughter
of Richard and Margaret(Landman) Shackleford (q.v.). This couple had an only
child, Peggy Shackleford Saunders, mentioned in the will of her maternal
grandfather, Richard Shackleford (17??-1794). WB#5,p.649; WB#9,p.15.]

SAUNDERS, MISKELL and Catharine Miskell, bond 18 January 1819. George Miskell (b).

SAUNDERS, RICHARD S. and Catherine Tune*, bond 14 November 1821. George Saunders
(b).

SAUNDERS, THOMAS and Mary Tune*, bond 1 November 1824. Robert Scott (b).MBB.,p.2

SCATES, BARTLETT and Susanna Jones*, bond 2 August 1802. Vincent Jones (b).

SCATES, ELIJAH and Louisa A. Bartlett, bond 5 February 1827. Consent by Matthew
Bartlett; no relationship stated. Samuel Bartlett (b).   MBB.,p.28

SCATES, JAMES and Peggy Jones*, bond 10 July 1792. James Bragg (b); John Fawcett
(w).

SCATES, JOHN B. (bachelor) and Betsy Marks (spinster), bond 10 March 1830. Newby
Berrick (b).   MBB.,p.61

SCATES, JOSEPH and Patty Hinson, bond 6 March 1797. Consent by James Hinson,
father of the bride. John Fawcett (b); Henry Hinson (w) and John Bowing (w).

SCATES, JOSEPH and Lucy Sanders, bond 15 February 1826. Fenner Carter (b).
                                                                   MBB.,p.19

SCATES, JOSEPH and Roberta W. Butler*, bond 3 March 1845. Elijah Scates (b);
Richard McGinnis (w) and Frances T. Butler (w).   MBB.,p.256

SCATES, RICHARD and Mary F. Brown, bond 1 April 1850. Consent by Mary F. Brown,
mother of the bride. William Broocke (b); John France (w). Married 10 April
1850 by the Rev. John Pullen.   MBB.,p.335

SCATES, THOMAS and Susan Sanders*, bond 5 February 1838. Henry V. Sanders (b);
Joseph Scates (w). Married by the Rev. Thomas M. Washington.   MBB.,p.168

SCHOFIELD, JOHN KENT and Elizabeth Haseard, bond 11 January 1795. Consent by
Joseph Heseard, father of the bride. Joseph Heseard (b).

   SCHRIMSHER   SEE : SCRIMIGER : SCRIMGER : SCHRIMSHER : SCRIMSHER

                       PAGE 182

   SCOTT   SEE : SCUTT PAGE 183

SCOTT, GEORGE and Ann Scott*, bond 25 January 1842. In writing her own consent,
the bride says she is of age and her "father and mother perfectly willing."
John Scott (b); Thomas Scott (w) and William H. Sisson (w).   MBB.,p.219

SCOTT, JAMES (16??-1718) married Elizabeth Micou, daughter of Doctor Paul Micou
    (1658-1736) of Essex County and his wife nee Margaret Cammack, daughter of
    Warwick and Margaret Cammack of Rappahannock and Richmond counties. Eliza-
    beth (Micou) Scott married (2) by 1719 Meriday Price; his estate was admin-
    istered upon in 1726 in King George County. COB#8,p.165; MRB.,p.103.

SCOTT, JAMES and Matilda A. Scott*, license 5 November 1853. R.T.A. Gresham
    (w). Married 6 November 1853 by the Rev. George Northam.

SCOTT, JAMES T. of Westmoreland County and Fanny Sandy*, bond 5 July 1820. John
    Davis (b).

SCOTT, JOHN and Susan Newcomb*, bond 26 October 1825. Consent by Fanny McKenney,
    mother of the groom. George Mothershead (b); Simon Brown (w). MBB.,p.14

SCOTT, ROBERT and Catherine Saunders, bond 7 February 1815. Consent by Hundley
    Saunders, father of the bride. John Scott (b); Richard Saunders (w).

SCOTT, ROBERT and Susan C. Oldham, bond 4 September 1826. Dominic Benneham (b).
                                                              MBB.,p.24

SCOTT, THOMAS and Elizabeth Conally [Conoley], bond 23 September 1789. Thomas
    Coats (b).

SCOTT, THOMAS and Mary Fisher, bond 9 November 1789. John Fisher (b).

SCOTT, THOMAS and Betsey Brann*, bond 25 June 1839. John Scutt (b); Mary Brann
    (w). The groom's name is also written Thomas Scutt. Married by the Rev.
    Nathan Healy.   MBB.,p.183

    SCRIMIGER : SCRIMGER : SCHRIMSHER : SCRIMSHER

SCRIMGER, GEORGE B. and Susan Ann Hill*, bond 15 November 1847. William H. Con-
    nellee (b). Married 15 November 1847 by the Rev. William N. Ward.MBB.,p.301

SCRIMSHER, JAMES and Sarah Fowler (widow)*, bond 7 January 1811. Peter N. Morgan
    (b).

SCRIMIGER, JAMES and Delia G. Deschamps (widow)*, bond 21 January 1831. Thomas
    J. Scrimiger (b); Virginia W. Deschamps (w).   MBB.,p.74

SCRIMGER, JAMES and Lilly A. Miskell*, bond 30 August 1837. Alexander Bryant
    (b); Mary Miskell (w).   MBB.,p.158

SCRIMGER, JAMES W. and Addaline Miskell*, bond 24 February 1848. James Scrimger
    (b).   MBB.,p.307

SCHRIMSHER, THOMAS and Alice Harford*, bond 6 November 1798. William Harford
    (b). The bride, in writing her own consent, calls her prospective spouse
    Mr. Thomas Chrimse.

SCHRIMSHER, THOMAS J. and Polly S. Flinn, bond 9 April 1812. Daniel Flinn (b).

SCRIMGER, WILLIAM G. and Mary J. Scrimger, bond 5 July 1830. Thomas J. Scrimg-
    er (b).   MBB.,p.66

SCURLOCK, GEORGE JR. and Susanna Hunton, bond 24 December 1790. George Daven-
    port (b).

SCURLOCK, THOMAS and Winnefred Nash (spinster)*, bond 1 January 1806. Richard
    Nash (b).

    SCUTT   SEE SCOTT PAGE 181 - 182

SCUTT, JOHN and Emily S. Rose*, bond 5 May 1842. James Scutt (b); James Rose
    (w) and Henry Mothershead (w).   MBB.,p.223

SCUTT, ZACHARIAH (widower) and Margaret Newcombs (spinster), bond 30 July 1829.
    George Mothershead (b).   MBB.,p.56

SEABRY, WARNER and Elizabeth Douglas*, bond 6 September 1839. William L. Jones
    (b); he makes oath the bride is the widow of Edward Douglas, deceased.
                                                                  MBB.,p.184

SEAGAR, HENRY (16??-1718) married Mary Hudson [Hodgson], widow of Bryan Hudson
    [Hodgson] whose nuncupative will was proved 23 March 1687/8 in Rappahannock
    County court. DB#9,p.85; WB#4,p.32; Sweeny,p.5.

SEAMONS, JOHN married Jane Hammock, 2 September 1727.   NFPR.,p.229

SEAMONS, JOHN married Katherine Foster, 17 July 1728.   NFPR.,p.229

SEAMONS, JOHN married Elizabeth Jones, 30 November 1729.   NFPR.,p.229

SEBREE, WILLIAM and Jenny Teague (widow)*, bond 25 February 1801. Rawleigh Taff
    (b); John Sebery (w). The groom's name is also rendered William Sebery.

SELF, GEORGE and Mary B. Davis*, license 1 March 1853. Thomas N. Straughan (w).
    Married 1 March 1853 by the Rev. George N. Northam.

SELF, JOHN of Northumberland County and Sally Harris, bond 6 September 1779.
    Hugh Harris (b).

SELF, JOHN of Northumberland County and Elizabeth Lewis, bond 4 October 1798.
    Jeremiah Lewis (b).

SELF, MOSES of Northumberland, Richmond and Westmoreland counties, married
    "about the first of October 1785," Nancy Smith. On 26 July 1819 before
    the Westmoreland County court, Moses Self, aged 60, made his declaration
    for pension for his Revolutionary War services. He states he was drafted
    in 1780 while residing in Northumberland County and details his services.
    Moses Self died 14 March 1835 and on 26 August 1839, Nancy (Smith) Self,
    his widow, made application for pension. Revolutionary Pension File W-19009.

SELF, SAMUEL A. and Milley Short (widow), bond 28 November 1797. Vincent Brann (b).

SELF, SAMUEL Z. and Elizabeth Brickey (widow)*, bond 24 March 1835. William Lambert (b); John L. Clark (w).   MBB.,p.132

SELF, SAMUEL Z. and Martha Luckham, bond 29 April 1845. Consent by William Luckham, father of the bride. James Oldham (b); Benjamin Armstrong (w). Married 29 April 1845 by the Rev. Elijah L. Williams.   MBB.,p.259

SELF, STEPHEN and Mary Ann Wilkins*, license 14 January 1853. Henry Bromley (w). Married 14 January 1853 by the Rev. John Godwin.

        SETTLE   SEE :   SUTTLE   PAGE 199

SETTLE, FRANCIS SR. (16??-1707/8) married (2) 1702 Mary Williams, widow of Rice Williams (16??-1701); both parties then had grandchildren. Previously the marriage next below had taken place. DB#3,p.96; WB#2,p.37,45,125; WB#4,p.261.

SETTLE, FRANCIS JR. married 169? Elizabeth Williams (16??-1725), daughter of Rice Williams (16??-1701). Francis Settle, Jr. (16??-1701/2) died before his father and his widow, Elizabeth (Williams) Settle married (2) 170? Stephen Wells (16??-1723). In 1738 Francis Settle [III] of Hamilton Parish, Prince William County and his half-brother, Stephen Wells of St. Mark's Parish, Orange County, sons of Elizabeth (Williams) Settle Wells, joined in a deed to convey certain land in Richmond County whereon Thomas Williams, lately deceased, resided. COB#3,p.131; AB#1,p.165; DB#3,p.96; DB#8,p.169; DB#9, p.471; WB#2,p.37,45,125; WB#4,p.227,261.

SETTLE, GATON of Prince William County married by 1758 Mary Bragg. [See notes, Joseph Bragg, Jr.,p.22; also his will, Fauquier County WB#2,p.127.]

SETTLE, REUBEN and Susannah Lyne, bond 8 July 1760. Richard Flynt (b). [Reuben Settle (1737-1803) and his wife nee Susannah Lyne (1744-1825), daughter of Thomas and Mary Lyne of Richmond County, removed to Loudoun County. There, in the 1780's, they made depositions in the suit in chancery involving the estate of Captain and Mrs. Richard Barnes (q.v.) p.10. Their wills are of record in Loudoun County WB "G",p.65 and WB "Q",p.23.]

SETTLE, WILLIAM and Ann Hendren, bond 3 January 1769. William Hendren (b). [The bride was the daughter of William Hendren (Hendron), Sr., a weaver of North Farnham Parish; he died testate in 1768. WB#7,p.9.]

SETTLE, WILLIAM and Mary Gibson, bond 7 January 1769. Thomas Dale (b).

        SHACKLEFORD : SHACKELFORD

SHACKLEFORD, CLEMENT and Mary Lawson Redman, bond 23 May 1798. Consent by Vincent Redman, father of the bride, who states she "has not yet arrived at the age of twenty years." William Shackleford (b).

SHACKLEFORD, LYNE and Margaret Bramham, bond 14 December 1831.   Vincent Bramham
    (b).   MBB.,p.83

SHACKLEFORD, LYNE and Juliet Ann Saunders*, bond 5 January 1847.   Robert B. Syd-
    nor (b); Augustine N. Saunders (w).   MBB.,p.286

SHACKELFORD, RICHARD married circa 1764 Mary Ann Murrah, executrix and legatee
    of Tobias Pursell [Purcell] (1691-1761) (q.v.), p.164.   COB#15,p.313; COB
    #17,p.268; WB#6, p.201,406.

SHACKELFORD, RICHARD and Margaret Landman, bond 17 January 1767. Griffin Gar-
    land (b). [3 November 1766: Bond of Griffin Garland as guardian of Margaret
    Landman, orphan of John Landman, deceased. The bride was the daughter of
    John Landman who died testate in 1750 and Richard Shackleford by will men-
    tions the land which "came by my wife Peggy Landman."   DB#13,p.432; WB#5,
    p.649; WB#9,p.15.]

SHACKELFORD, RICHARD and Elizabeth Redman, bond not dated. Tobias Pursell (b).
    [The phraseology of the bond indicates it was written after 1776. It is
    filed in the 1796/with other undated marriage bonds.]
                        bundle
SHACKLEFORD, RICHARD and Joanna Lawson, bond 29 February 1788. LeRoy Dobyns (b).

SHACKLEFORD, RICHARD L. and Jane Northen, bond 11 January 1814. Edmund N. North-
    en (b).

SHACKLEFORD, RICHARD L. and Elizabeth S. Carter, bond 4 June 1849.   Charles C.
    Carter (b).   MBB.,p.324

SHACKLEFORD, VINCENT and Lucy R. Brockenbrough,* bond 19 December 1806.   Thomas
    Brown (b). [See 18W(2)99]

SHACKELFORD, WILLIAM of Northumberland County and Miss Frances Redman of Rich-
    mond County, bond 26 January 1786. Tobias Pursell (b).

SHACKLEFORD, WILLIAM of Lancaster County and Sarah New, bond 18 January 1794.
    Richard Shackleford of Richmond County (b).

SHACKLEFORD, WILLIAM and Elizabeth B. Smith, bond 9 June 1801. William C. Smith
    (b).

SHACKLEFORD, WILLIAM R. and Fanny L. Davis, bond 19 November 1816. Consent by
    G. Davis, father of the bride, is directed to George Saunders, clerk of
    Richmond County court; to this he adds: "P.S. I request your brother Miskell
    to come down and sup with me on Thursday the 21 inst: G.D.". Daniel Garland
    (b).

SHARP, THOMAS and Eliz.^a Harrison, license August 1711.   DB#6,p.275

SHAW, WILLIAM married Margaret Holland, 22 November 1680.   NFPR.,p.165

SHEARLEY   SEE : SHIRLEY PAGE 186 AND SHURLEY PAGE 186-187

SHEARLEY, JOHN and Elizabeth O. Ashburn*, bond 16 April 1830. Bartholomew Dodson
    (b); Elizabeth N. Dodson (w).   MBB.,p.63

SHEARLEY, PETER and Susanna Douglass*, bond 10 May 1815. Thomas Douglass (b).

SHEARMAN, JOSEPH W. and Sarah E. Hipkins*, bond 2 October 1843. John Mayo [Doc-
    tor] (b).   MBB.,p.241

SHEARMAN, JOSEPH W.B. and Lucy S. Northen*, bond 24 January 1846. Thomas H.
    Northen (b); Mary Northen (w). Married 29 January 1846 by the Rev. Elijah
    L. Williams.   MBB.,p.272

SHEPHERD, JAMES and Betsey W. Wheldon, bond 21 July 1807. Consent by John and
    Amelia Wheldon, parents of the bride, who state she is "not yet of age."
    George Saunders (b); Louis Boimard (w).

SHIPPY, RICHARD (16??-1708) married 1691/2 Ellen Mott (circa 1673-1741), youngest
    daughter of Mr. George Mott of Rappahannock County. He died intestate in
    Richmond County in 1708; she died testate in King George County in 1741 but
    her last will and Testament is recorded in now lost King George County WB#1
    (1721-1752). COB#4,p.389; DB#3,p.122; WB#2,p.127; King George County COB#2
    p.247; 23W(2)85. Richard Shippy (16??-1708) must not be confused with Rich-
    ard Shippy (16??-1698), styled Senior, who died testate in Richmond County
    but whose will is in lost WB#1 (1692-1699); if they were father and son, I
    have no positive evidence. See Sweeny,p.,17 and 27.

SHIRLEY   SEE : SHEARLEY PAGE 186 AND SHURLEY PAGE 186 - 187

SHIRLEY, JAMES and Catherine J. Pearson were married 30 November 1852 by the Rev.
    Mr. John Godwin. [Minister's Returns; no bond or license found.]

SHIRLEY, JOHN of Northumberland County and Milly Ashburn, bond 29 January 1816.
    Rachel Ashburn, widow of Thomas Ashburn, deceased, mother and guardian of
    the bride, gives her consent for the marriage. James Littrell (b).

SHIRLEY, THADDEUS and Betsy R. Jeffries*, bond 15 April 1816. Edward Dougliss
    (b); Edmund R. Jeffries (w) and Nancey H. Jeffries (w).

SHORT, CLARK married Mary Pendle, 2 March 1730/1.   NFPR.,p.229

SHORT, JOHN and Judith Ball, bond 7 April 1785. Epp[a] Sydnor (b). [Judith
    (Ball) Short (c.1770-1843) was the daughter of Williamson and Priscilla
    (Churchill) Ball (q.v.), p.9; her will was proved in Culpeper County, Va.
    John Short (1763-1794), builder of Carlton overlooking Falmouth, Virginia,
    has been detailed in 32T206-225. His miniature is on exhibit at Kenmore in
    Fredericksburg. In a letter dated 21 May 1789 from Williamson Ball, Rich-
    mond County, to his son-in-law John Short, he closes: "My love to Judy and
    the children." AB#3,p.211; WB#8,p.166; Hayden,p.104.

SHURLEY   SEE : SHEARLEY PAGE 186 AND SHIRLEY PAGE 186

SHURLEY, JEREMIAH and Polly Haynie, bond 1 October 1803. William Haynie (b).

SILBY, WILLIAM and Frances A. White*, bond 23 December 1840. John F. Morris
(b); John S. Carter (w). Married 23 December 1840 by the Rev. Mr. John M.
Waddey.   MBB.,p.203

SIMPSON, JOSEPH [REVEREND] (circa 1722-1762) married 1749 Mary Skinker, born 19
April 1732, illegitimate daughter of Colonel Samuel Skinker (16??-1752) of
Richmond and King George counties, where the Reverend Mister Simpson served
as curate for an extended period. Richmond County, Fines, Examination of
Criminals, Tryalls of Slaves &c: 1710-1754, p.343; also King George County
DB#3,p.238,288,467; DB#4,p.514; WB#2,p.5; OPR.,p.229; 10T167. The Rev. Mr.
Joseph Simpson died intestate in 1762. 6 September 1762, guardian bond of
George Simpson as guardian of John, Joseph, Thomas and Elizabeth Simpson,
orphans of Joseph Simpson, Clerk, deceased, with John Smith and Samuel Rust
his securities.

SINGLETON, JOSHUA and [blank], bond 24 January 1749. William Barber (b).
[ECD says Joshua Singleton (17??-1773), son of Joshua and Ann Singleton of
Richmond County, married 1749 Ann Samford, daughter of James and Mary (Barber) Samford (q.v.), p.176. Joshua Singleton (16??-1732) seated a plantation in Richmond County which had been purchased in 1711 by his father, Robert Singleton (16??-1724), of Gloucester County and bequeathed to him by his
will. The Richmond County records confirm these statements. DB#6,p.25; WB#
5,p.184,239; WB#7,p.150; Bill in Chancery, Hubert vs Miskell, filed by the
Honorable John Marshall - see his legal papers in the Alderman Library, University of Virginia, #1106; 64V103-104.]

SIPES, ALEXANDER and Lucy A. Pope*, license 5 September 1853. William H. Davenport (w). Married 14 September 1853 by the Rev. Mr. John Godwin.

SISSON, ARCHIBALD and Virginia W. Deschamps, bond 6 February 1832. Consent by
Cordelia G. Deschamps, mother of the bride. James Scrimiger (b). MBB.,p.87

SISSON, DAVID and Catherine E. Yarrington, bond 21 December 1843. Landon Yarrington (b). Married 26 December 1843 by the Rev. John Godwin.   MBB.,p.243

SISSON, ELBURTON H. and Hannah Elizabeth Hardwick, bond 7 January 1850. Consent
by John Hardwick; no relationship stated. Austin N. Richards (b); Joseph
R. Jeffries (w). Married 9 January 1850 by Rev. George Northam. MBB.,p.331

SISSON, GEORGE and Elizabeth Sallard, bond 3 March 1763. Hugh Marshall (b).

SISSON, GEORGE and Elizabeth Allgood*, bond 23 January 1796. George Jesper (b).

SISSON, HENRY (circa 170?-1775) married by 29 January 1729, Ann Meeks, daughter
of Richard and Ann Meeks. 24 June 1764: Henry Sisson, aged 54 and upward,
made a deposition - see Joseph Bragg, Jr. (q.v.), p.22. WB#5,p.152; WB#6,
p.195; WB#7,p.182.

SISSON, HENRY and Winifred Smith, bond 5 February 1787. Consent by Winifred Smith,
mother of the bride. James How (b); Thomas How (w) and James How (w).

SISSON, HENRY (bachelor) and Sarah Chamberlane (spinster), bond 26 November 1828.
    John Luttrell (b); he made oath the bride is of full age.   MBB.,p.45

SISSON, HENRY and Sarah Churchwell*, bond 9 April 1845. William D. Miskell (b);
    Lucy Miskell (w). Married 13 April 1845 by the Rev. Elijah L. Williams.
                                                                    MBB.,p.258

SISSON, HENRY and Martha A. Samuel, bond 4 November 1848. Consent by Harriet
    Samuel, mother of the bride. Horace W. Parker (b); Phebe Gouldman (w)
    and Levinia Kay (w). Married 9 November 1848 by the Rev. John Pullen.
                                                                    MBB.,p.314

SISSON, HENRY and Levinia C. Northen*, license 3 October 1853. William E. Hill
    (w).

SISSON, HIEROME [HIRAM] and Sally Littrell*, bond 24 February 1840. John Litt-
    rell (b).   MBB.,p.194

SISSON, HIRAM and Elizabeth Jones, bond 28 March 1825. James P. Balderson (b).
    Thomas Davis certifies as to the legal age of the parties.   MBB.,p.9

SISSON, JAMES (bachelor) and Susan Crowder (spinster), bond 16 December 1828.
    James V. Berrick (b); he makes oath the bride is over 21.   MBB.,p.47

SISSON, JOHN B. and Mary Sandy*, bond 14 September 1812. James Reynolds (b);
    Mayson Sandy (w).

SISSON, JOHN M. and Mary F. Newsome, bond 15 July 1845. William J. Newsome (b).
    Married 17 July 1845 by the Rev. Mr. William N. Ward.   MBB.,p.261

SISSON, MARTIN and Nancy Sydnor (widow), bond 10 April 1802. Ezekiel Cookman
    (b).

SISSON, RANDALL (bachelor) and Frances A. Gordon (spinster)*, bond 30 December
    1829. William Kennan (b); Mary Ann Woolard (w).   MBB.,p.59

SISSON, RICHARD and Hannah Thornton (spinster), bond 25 January 1782. Thomas
    Franklin (b).

SISSON, ROBERT and Amanda Ann Sanders, bond 5 August 1847. Consent by William
    Carter, guardian of the bride. Horace W. Parker (b).   MBB.,p.296

SISSON, SOLOMON and Martha Harford*, bond 11 December 1835. Robert Hall (b);
    Thomas Everett (w).   MBB.,p.138

SISSON, WILLIAM married Frances Gower, 31 August 1727.   NFPR.,p.229

SISSON, WILLIAM HENRY and Isabella Willson, bond 29 June 1820. Consent by Henry
    Sisson, father of the groom. John B. Sisson (b); Richard Reynolds (w).

SISSON, WILLIAM H. and Lucy A. Latham, license 7 April 1853. William Ingram (w)
    and James A. McKnight (w). Married 7 April 1853 by the Rev. Wm. N. Ward.

SLAUGHTER, FRANCIS and Ann Hudson, license August 1711.   DB#6,p.275
    [This was the second marriage of Francis Slaughter (circa 1658-1718); their
    marriage contract was dated 11 July 1711 and recorded in DB#6,p.5. WB#4,p.77.]

SLAUGHTER, FRANCIS and Jennie Suggett (spinster), bond 2 March 1752. William
    Lightfoot (b). [Colonel Francis Slaughter (17??-1776), son of Robert and
    Mary (Smith) Slaughter of Culpeper County, served as a lieutenant in the
    French and Indian War, as a burgess from Dunmore County and as a colonel in
    the early part of the Revolutionary War. He died testate in Shenandoah
    County in 1776. He was a first cousin of Colonel John Slaughter (next below);
    their wives were half-sisters, daughters of Edgecomb Suggett who died testate
    in Richmond County in 1753. WB#6,p.6.]

SLAUGHTER, JOHN and Elizabeth Suggett (spinster), bond 18 December 1758. John
    Suggitt (b). [Colonel John Slaughter (17??-1796) was the son of Francis
    and Anne (Lightfoot) Slaughter; he was a first cousin of Colonel Francis
    Slaughter (next above) and their wives were half-sisters, as above stated.
    This was the groom's second marriage. DB#12,p.550; WB#6,p.6.]

SMALL, OLIVER married Isabell Ramze, 11 June 1730.   NFPR.,p.229

SMITH, BENJAMIN and Jane Alderson (widow), bond 3 November 1762. Benjamin Bram-
    han (b). [The bride was the widow of John Alderson who died intestate in
    1757. The marriage contract between Benjamin Smith of North Farnham Parish
    and Jane Alderson of Lunenburg Parish, both within the county of Richmond,
    was dated 30 October 1762 and recorded in DB#12,p.422. COB#14,p.98; WB#7,
    p.181.]

SMITH, CHARLES W. and Mrs. Mary W. Cox*, bond 4 November 1843. John Mayo (b).
    Married 7 November 1843 by the Rev. Mr. William N. Ward.   MBB.,p.242

SMITH, COLSTON and Mary Sydnor, bond 21 January 1786. Epa: Sydnor (b). John
    Sydnor, father of the bride, gives consent. [The groom was the son of John
    Smith whose will was proved 1 September 1794 and recorded in WB#9,p.5.]

SMITH, DAVID (16??-1711) married circa 1709 Ann Gethings [Gaythings], widow of
    John Gethings [Gaythings] (16??-1709). DB#5,p.316; WB#2,p.124; WB#3,p.45.

SMITH, EDWIN BATHURST of King William County and Sally Monroe, bond 19 November
    1796. Consent by John Monroe, father of the bride, was written from his
    seat, Foulis, in Richmond County. John Monroe (b). [The couple were cous-
    ins. He was born 20 September 1775, the son of Colonel Meriwether Smith
    (1730-1794) of Bathurst, Essex County, and his wife Elizabeth Daingerfield
    (1747-1793), who were married 29 September 1769. The bride was the daughter
    of Judge John and Jane (Jones) Monroe (q.v.), p.134-135; #25740, VSL:AD.]

SMITH, GEORGE H. and Sally Bryant*, bond 24 May 1824. George L. Dawson (b).

SMITH, ISAAC and Winifred T. McCarty (spinster), bond 27 October 1814. Consent
    by Robert S. Hipkins, guardian of the bride. Bartholomew McCarty (b).

SMITH, JAMES and Patsy Clarke*, license 16 January 1852. Benjamin Tucker (w) and Meshack Clarke (w). Married 21 January 1852 by the Rev.E.L. Williams.

SMITH, JAMES S. of Westmoreland County and Polly P. Hardwick, bond 30 December 1816. John Hardwick (b).

SMITH, JAMES S. and Mary B. Sisson*, bond 27 October 1830. William H. Sisson (b); Susan W. Sisson (w).   MBB.,p.68

SMITH, JOHN married Margaret Canterbery, 9 February 1725/6.   NFPR.,p.229

SMITH, JOHN [GENTLEMAN] married by 1738 Mary Colston, elder of the two daughters of William and Mary (Meriwether) Colston (q.v.), p.42. WB#4,p.198; WB#5,p. 652; King George County COB#3,p.1200 et seq.; 12T142-145; 25V279.

SMITH, JOHN and Elizabeth Woollard (spinster), bond 10 April 1781. Samuel Wool- lard (b).

SMITH, JOHN and Sally Redman, bond 7 June 1784. Thomas Dobyns (b).

SMITH, JOHN and Alice Ball, bond 12 June 1786. John Woodford (b). [The bride was the only child of Williamson and Priscilla (Glascock) Ball (q.v.), p.8. Hayden,p.84, identifies the bride correctly, but as she could not have two sets of parents, he misidentifies her on p.105; d.s.p.,1803,Westmoreland Co.]

SMITH, JOHN (bachelor) and Polly Norris (spinster), daughter of James Norris, bond 13 March 1828. James Norris (b); William Hathaway (w).   MBB.,p.37

SMITH, JOSEPH of Essex County and Sarah Gwyn, license May 1713.   DB#6,p.275

SMITH, JOSEPH of Westmoreland County and Alice Proctor*, bond 27 March 1800. In writing her own consent the bride says she is aged "[mutilated]ty too years." Samuel Gilbert of Westmoreland County (b).[ECD transcript says "22 years."]

SMITH, JOSEPH WOOLLARD and Katharine Dobyns, bond 9 January 1787. Daniel Dobyns (b). "1786 Dec.29th: This is to certify that I gave Mr. Joseph
            Smith leave to marry Caty Dobyns, as witness my hand
                                              Abner Dobyns"

SMITH, NICHOLAS [GENTLEMAN, COLONEL] (4 September 1666-18 March 1734) married (1) by 5 May 1692, Agatha ___[?]___, widow of David Sterne (1645-1692) (q.v.), by whom he had no issue; married (2) in 1722 Elizabeth ___[?]___, by whom he had a son and two daughters but of these only Elizabeth Smith (172?-1750) [who married Major Harry Turner (171?-1751) in 1743] left issue. Col. Nicho- las Smith acquired considerable property and resided at Smith's Mount near Leedstown where he died when that estate was a part of King George County. The dates cited are from his tombstone. Elizabeth Smith, widow, married (2) in 1735 Daniel McCarty, Gentleman, (170?-1744) of Westmoreland County, widow- er of Penelope Higgins (1713-1732), and son of Captain Daniel and Elizabeth (Pope) McCarty (q.v.), p.123; they had an only child, Daniel McCarty (173?- 1795) of Longwood, Westmoreland County. COB#1,p.3,18,30; DB#1,p.42; King George County COB#2,p.35,39,41,149,155,303; DB#1,p.571; Fiduciary Account

Book #3,p.70; suit in chancery Dixon vs Turner (1759), proceedings recorded
in COB#3,p.994-1012; 21V109; Sweeny,p.149-150; Eubank,p.36,43-44; Hayden,p.
87-88, where there are some errors. Colonel Daniel McCarty (170?-1744) had
no child to survive infancy by his first wife Penelope Higgins (1713-1732),
only child of Augustine Higgins, Gentleman, of Westmoreland county; this is
amply demonstrated by Westmoreland W&D#8,p.209 and Record Book 1723-1746,p.
155.

SMITH, PETER and Ann Short, married 15 May 1727.   NFPR.,p.229

SMITH, ROBERT and Ann Russell, bond 2 August 1768. Benjamin Bramham (b).

SMITH, THOMAS P. and Sarah L. Dobyns (widow)*, bond 15 November 1815. John N.
Rootes (b); John Plummer (w). [The bride was the widow of Charles Dobyns
(q.v.), p.54 and daughter of LeRoy and Lucy (Lawson) Dobyns (q.v.), p.55.]

SMITH, WILLIAM JUNIOR and Margaret Fleming, license November 1711. DB#6,p.275

SMITH, WILLIAM married Sarah Truman, 5 July 1731.   NFPR.,p.229

SMITH, WILLIAM married Agnes Baroh, 15 March 1731/2.   NFPR.,p.229

SMITH, WILLIAM [COLONEL] (17??-1785) of Essex County, married circa 1771 Mary
Belfield (1753-18??), daughter of John and Ruth (Sydnor) Belfield of Richmond County (q.v.), p.14. ECD cites their children from a Bible record,
viz: (a) Ann Adams Smith, born 25 November 1772, married Thomas Jeffries of
Richmond County (q.v.), p.103; (b) Francis Smith, born 1 December 1774; (c)
William Smith, born 16 May 1777; (d) Elizabeth Smith, born 15 October 1779,
married 1803 her cousin, Thomas Belfield Walker; (e) Alice Smith, born 16
January 1782; and (f) Maria Smith, born 4 May 1784 and died in 1785. WB#9,
p.158; Essex County WB#13,p.495; Walker vs Jones, FDC#288; ECD Papers, Box
#6, Virginia Historical Society.

SMITH, WILLIAM and Elizabeth Sandy, bond 30 April 1788. Consent by Mary Sandy,
mother of the bride, who states her daughter is "of full age." John How
(b). [The bride was the unborn child mentioned in the will of her father,
John Sandy of Lunenburg Parish, which was dated 19 August 1769 and admitted
to probate 4 September 1770. At the time of her marriage she was 18 years
of age - considered at this period by many persons to be of "full age" for
a female. DB#18,p.435; WB#7,p.73.]

SMITH, WILLIAM and Elizabeth Dobyns, bond 15 January 1800. Rawleigh Downman (b).

SMITH, WILLIAM JR. and Peggy A. Weathers, bond 22 December 1814. Consent by Mary
W. Weathers, mother of the bride. John Harris (w). [ECD indicates the couple
were cousins and cites a Bible record. William Smith, born 17 May 1794, son
of William and Elizabeth (Sandy) Smith, was married on 25 December 1814 to
Peggy A. Weathers, born 29 October 1794, daughter of George and Mary (Sandy)
Weathers (q.v) and had issue, viz: (a) George W. Smith, born 28 November 1815,
died 19 September 1892, married 8 September 1856, Frances Dameron; (b) Henry-
retta Smith, born 9 October 1817; (c) Margaret A. Smith, born 8 February 1820,
married William H. Donnahaw; (d) Mary E. Smith, born 12 August 1822; (e) Will-

iam Smith, born 26 November 1824; (f) James L. Smith, born 14 August 1827;
(g) Robert Smith, born 15 January 1830; (h) and (i) Benjamin and Elies
Smith, twin sons, born 12 January 1833; and (j) John Ogle Smith, born 9
January 1838. ECD Papers, Box 24, Weathers family.]

SMITH, WILLIAM G. and Betsey B. Settle, bond 18 February 1823. William Settle
(b). [Betsy Bailey Settle, daughter of William Settle (17??-1833) and
his wife nee Mary ("Polly") Greenlaw, was born 14 February 1806 and married
20 February 1823 to William G.Smith. She was the granddaughter of Lieutenant
Bailey Settle (1733-1813) and Anne ___[?]___ (17??-1813), his wife, and of
William and Mary (Oldham) Greenlaw (q.v.), p.81.]

SMITHER, LANCELOT and Nancy Pritchet, bond 8 February 1785. Rodham Pritchet (b).

SMITHER, RICHARD and Sarah Glascock*, bond 17 January 1793. Ezekiel Levy (b);
Catherine Glascock (w).

SMITHER, RICHARD and Elizabeth D. Tune*, bond 2 November 1815. George Tune (b).

SMITHER, THOMAS married by 15 April 1724, Susanna Singleton, daughter of Robert
Singleton (16??-1724) of Gloucester County who purchased land in Richmond
County in 1711. In 1751 Susanna (Singleton) Smither, widow, was residing
in Caroline County. DB#6,p.25; Fairfax County DB "A",p.164; Prince William
County DB "M",p.198; 64V103-104.

SMITHER, WINTER B. and Frances Ann Pew, license 19 March 1851. Consent by Martin and Frances A. Pew, parents of the bride. George W. Landon (w). Married 22 March 1851 by the Rev. Elijah L. Williams.

SMOOT, BENJAMIN F. and Lucy Mothershead, bond 4 May 1835. Stephen D. Pursell
(b).   MBB.,p.134

SMOOT, JOHN of Northumberland County and Milley Philips, bond 19 March 1790.
John Nash (b).

SNEAD, CHARLES of Northampton County and Sally T. Smith, bond 10 January 1810.
Consent by Charles Smith, father of the bride. Caleb B. Upshur (b); A.
Neale (w).

SNEAD, JAMES ALLANELIA and Mary Christopher, bond 17 July 1826. Richard Clarke
(b). Married 20 July 1826 by the Rev. Jacob Larkin.   MBB.,p.22

SOMMEVELL [SOMMERVILLE], JOHN married by 5 September 1705, Margaret French, widow of Hugh French (16??-1701) who died testate in Richmond County. This
was her fourth and last marriage; her former husbands were John Prosser
(16??-1677) and Captain Simon Miller (1642-1683), both of Rappahannock County. COB#4,p.69; WB#2,p.34.

SORRELL, THOMAS and Million Glascock, bond 20 October 1770. George Glascock
(b). [1763: Guardian bond of John Glascock as guardian of Million Glascock, orphan of Gregory Glascock, deceased.]

SORRELL, THOMAS A. and Elizabeth Street, bond 19 September 1831. Seth Rockwell
(b).   MBB.,p.80

SPARK, ALEXANDER and Elizabeth Lawson, bond 21 November 1765. Thomas Yeatman
(b).

SPENCE, ALEXANDER [DOCTOR] (16??-1716) married before 6 March 1694/5 Elizabeth
Brown (167?-1720), youngest daughter of William Brown (16??-1677) and Elizabeth, his wife. Elizabeth Brown, widow, married (2) Evan Morgan (16??-1684)
and (3) James Taylor. The excerpt cited 17W(1)74 regarding the marriage of
Dr. Alexander Spence is incorrect. Dr. Spence has been confused with Alexander Spence, Gentleman, (16??-1704) [son of Lieut. Patrick and Dorcas Spence of Westmoreland County] who was a member of the House of Burgesses from
Westmoreland County in 1701 and died testate in that county. His heirs are
detailed in Northumberland County Record Book 1710-1713,p.319. COB#2,p.42,
64,232; COB#6,p.112; WB#3,p.282; WB#4,p.151; Sweeny,p.57,106.

SPENCE, HENRY and Isabella Hillyer*, bond 17 October 1789. Luke Jackson (b).
The bride signs her own consent, Esabella Hillyer.

SPENCE, JOHN and Elizabeth Maria Bispham, bond 19 April 1822. Consent by John W.
Belfield, guardian of the bride. M.C. Harvey (b). [The bride was the daughter of Robert and Ann ("Nancy") (Asbury) Bispham (q.v.), p.19.]

SPENCE, THOMAS JR. of Westmoreland County and Ann M.B. Settle, bond 4 September
1820. William Settle (b). [Anne Maria Bailey Settle, daughter of William
and Mary (Greenlaw) Settle, was born 27 November 1802 and married on 14
September 1820 to Thomas Spence, Jr., according to a Settle Bible record.
See notes under William G. and Betsey B. (Settle) Smith (q.v.), p.192.]

SPENCER, EDWARD married circa 1709 Winifred Green (1693-171?), daughter of Richard and Ann (Hobbs) Green (q.v.), p.81. Their only child, Edward Spencer,
Gentleman, (1710-1753) was a prominent citizen of Orange County. Winifred
(Green) Spencer married (2) in 1714 Stanley Gower (16??-1718) (q.v.), p.80
and on 2 April 1719 John Branham was appointed guardian to Edward Spencer,
son of Edward Spencer and Winifred, his wife, late deceased. COB#8,p.93;
DB#11,p.155, other indexed records in Richmond and Orange counties.

SPENDERGRASS, JOHN married Elizabeth Cribin, 2 December 1728.   NFPR.,p.229

SPICER, ARTHUR [CAPTAIN] (16??-1700) married by 27 September 1693, Elizabeth
(Jones) Blomfield, daughter and sole heir of Thomas Jones who possessed
1,100 acres of land, and widow of Captain Samuel Blomfield (q.v.), p.19.
Their only child was John Spicer, Gentleman, (16??-1727), who appears on the
records of Richmond and King George counties; he married Mary (Metcalfe)
Brockenbrough, widow of Austin Brockenbrough (1685-1717) (q.v.), p.24. COB
#3,p.23,25; COB#5,p.133; DB#1,p.94; WB#2,p.14; 17W(1)78; 23T103-104.

SPILLER, JOHN of Richmond County married long before 1714 Sarah (Harper) Berry,
only sister and heir-at-law of William Harper of Essex County who died intestate in 1714, and widow of Henry Berry, Jr. (16??-1696). COB#2,p.165;
Essex County Wills &c:#3,p.226 and W&D#14,p.266,294.

SPILMAN, JAMES K. and Mary C. Sanders, bond 14 December 1839. Consent by Mary
    Sanders, mother of the bride. Robert Sanders (b).   MBB.,p.187

SPILLMAN, JAMES K. and Mary Ann Mothershead*, bond 27 January 1845. James S.
    Mothershead (b).

SPRAGG, JOHN married Mary Edwards, 2 February 1726/7.   NFPR.,p.229

STANDLEY, THOMAS and Ann Jones, bond 11 October 1780. Charles Jones (b).

STANFIELD, THOMAS (1???-1726) married circa 1722, Mary Dalton, daughter of John
    and Mary (Newman) Dalton. Mary (Dalton) Stanfield married (2) 1729, Jona-
    than Lyell (q.v.), p.121. DB#8,p.358; WB#5, p.36,249.

STARKS, JAMES (16??-1726) married circa 1704 Eleanor Todd, daughter of Henry and
    Jane Todd. James Starks died in North Farnham Parish 10 December 1726 and
    his widow married (2) 1729, William Abshone (q.v.), p.1. COB#5,p.26,290;
    COB#9,p.175-176; COB#10,p.544; WB#3,p.65; WB#4,p.242; WB#5,p.34.

STEEL, LEWIS P. (bachelor) and Martha Morris (spinster), bond 1 December 1828.
    Moore F. Brockenbrough (b).   MBB.,p.47

STEELE, SAMUEL married circa 1700 Susanna [also called Hannah] Peorey [or Peers]
    John Oakely [Ockely] by will dated 19 November 1697 and proved 2 March 1697/
    bequeathed 100 acres to Susanna Peorey who married (1) Samuel Steele and by
    deed 19 December 1701 they sold same to James Willson, whose widow married
    William King. Susanna [otherwise Hannah] (Peorey) Steele married (2) Daniel
    Bryan by 3 September 1713. COB#6,p.146; DB#7,p.341; DB#3,p.82.

STEELE, SAMUEL married by 1736 Catherine (Hammond) Williams, widow of Thomas Will
    iams who died intestate in 1718. COB#8,p.20; COB#10,p.371; George Sanders
    (q.v.) and Thomas Williams (q.v.), p.177,232.

STEPHEN, DANIEL married Lucy Tarpley, 20 October 1728.   NFPR.,p.229

STEPHENS, ELIAS and Mary Headley*, bond 25 October 1811. George Shearley (b);
    William Headley (w).

STEPHENS, JEFFERSON and Ann M. Askins*, bond 6 April 1843. John Gibbs (b); Will-
    iam H. Packett (w). Married 6 April 1843 by the Rev. Wm.N.Ward. MBB.,p.237

STEPHENS, JEREMIAH and Elizabeth Haynie*, bond 24 February 1816. Thomas Sydnor,
    Jr. (b).

STEPHENS, JOHN H. and Mary Hazzard*, bond 29 August 1837. Joseph Luckam (b);
    Thomas Hazard (w) and Polly Hazard (w).   MBB.,p.157

STEPHENS [STEVENS], MARK and Eleanor Jesper*, bond 28 January 1800. Daniel Brown
    (b).

STEPHENS, THOMAS and Mary Ann Jesper*, bond 17 December 1796. William Jesper
    (b); William Jesper (w) and Ann Williams (w).

STEPTOE, JOHN JUNIOR and Mary Sallard (spinster), bond 18 September 1752.
Charles Sallard (b).

STERLING, JOSEPH and Betsy Rennolds, bond 2 November 1799. Consent by Ann
Gouldsby [Goldsby], mother of the said Betsy Reynolds. David Goldsby (b).
[The bride was born 12 October 1782, daughter of William and Ann (Thornton)
Reynolds (q.v.), p.168-169; her mother married (2) 1791, David Goldsby (q.v.),
p.79.]

STERNE, DAVID (1645-1692) married circa 1678 Elizabeth Mills, younger of the two
daughters of William and Joane Mills of Rappahannock County; they had an
only child, Frances Sterne who married (1) William Pannell (q.v.), p.154
and (2) Thomas Hughes (q.v.), p.100. David Sterne married (2) Agatha [?]
and had an only child, Ann Sterne who married in 1712/13 Daniel White (q.v.).
Shortly after the death of David Sterne, his widow married Colonel Nicholas
Smith (1666-1734) (q.v.), p.190, but had no issue by him. Francis Sterne
(next below) and his brother David Sterne were certified as headrights of
Colonel Thomas Beale, Esquire, on 26 February 1665/6; the record is in York
County Record Book #4, p.51. DB#1,p.42; Rappahannock County DB#6,p.53,78;
Westmoreland County COB 1665-1677,p.115-116; Patent Book #6,p.656; Sweeny,
p.43,149.

STERNE, FRANCIS (circa 1638-1713) married circa 1699 Mary Cammack (16??-1743),
daughter of Warwick and Margaret Cammack of Rappahannock County. She married (2) Isaac Truck (16??-1739) and with her illegitimate son William Cammack and her sons Francis and David Sterne, they moved to Caroline County
where they both died testate; the three aforementioned sons of Mary (Cammack)
Truck [Trocq &c:] gave rise to considerable progeny. WB#3,p.122,234; Essex
County D&W#15,p.192,195,226; Caroline County COB#1,p.532 and COB#2,p.150;
Sweeny,p.24; note above under David Sterne; other indexed Richmond County
records.

STITH, GRIFFIN JUNIOR and Elizabeth Smith, daughter of Isaac Smith of Richmond
County, bond 28 September 1782. George Kendall of Northampton County (b).
[See note under Peter Bowdoin, p.21.]

STITH, WILLIAM and Sarah Smith, bond 18 March 1783. P. Bowdoin (b).

STOKES, WILLIAM of Essex County married by 7 March 1716 .Elizabeth (?   )
Batten Williams, widow of John Batten and John Williams. DB#6,p.139; DB#7,
p.100; WB#3,p.109,205. [John Batten (q.v.),p.11; John Williams (q.v.),p.231.]

STONE, FRANCIS (16??-1716) married (1) Elizabeth ____[?]____ and (2) circa 1700,
Mary (Pannell) Kay, widow of James Kay (q.v.), p.110. COB#6,p.504; DB#4,p.
109; DB#7,p.131; Essex County DB#13,p.17; King and Queen County deeds &c:
AD:VSL, #25094; Payne,p.70.

STONE, JOHN [COLONEL] (1631-1698) married circa 1670 Sarah (?) Fleet Walker,
widow of Captain Henry Fleet (circa 1600-1660) and of Colonel John Walker
(16??-1668/9). Colonel John Stone was the first gentleman justice of Richmond County upon its formation in 1692. It appears to me that Colonel John

Stone was married after the death of Sarah (?) Fleet Walker Stone to
Mary ____(?)____ as Captain John Rice,(q.v.), p.169, by will dated 6 October 1693 and proved in Richmond County court 6 December 1693, "bequeathed unto Madam Mary Stone my Diamond Ring, the wife of Col? John Stone."
He also appointed "my good & loving friends Col? John Stone and my son-in-
law Sam¹. Travers Executors of this my last Will & Testament," and they
qualified as such on 6 December 1693. The last will and Testament of Colonel John Stone was dated 27 April 1695 at which time his wife was living
but she predeceased him and on 2 June 1698 his son-in-law, Richard Metcalfe
(q.v.), p.131-132, is mentioned as "executor in his own wrong of Colonel
John Stone, deceased." Richard Metcalfe died the following year and on 7
June 1699 his widow, Mrs. Ann Metcalfe, the daughter of Colonel John Stone,
is mentioned as having been granted the executorship of the last will and
Testament of Colonel John Stone. At the same court, administration was
granted to Mrs. Ann Metcalfe on the estate of her husband, Mr. Richard Metcalfe, deceased, and his estate ordered to be appraised and the appraisers
were directed to set apart the estate of "Col. John Stone, late deceased,
now intermix^t with the estate of the said Richard Metcalfe." The will of
Colonel John Stone was recorded in now lost Richmond County WB#1 (1692-1699).
COB#2,p.289,306,405; DB#2,p.41; A.P.& P.,p.174; Sweeny,p.6,7,76; 20W(2)557;
Westmoreland County Record Book 1723-1746,p.262a, bond 29 September 1741 re-
citing a decree of the General Court of Virginia handed down 3 November 1736
in regard to "the estate of John Stone, Gent: late of Richmond County," makes
it appear Ann(e) (Stone) Metcalfe Barrow was the only child of Col.John Stone

STONE, JOSHUA married Wilmoth Bryant, 22 November 1738.   NFPR.,p.229
[The bride was the daughter of Thomas and Margaret (Jeffries) Bryant (q.v.)
p.29. The groom was a descendant of William and Sarah Stone (q.v.), p.127
under William Manire. The land of these Stones remained in Richmond County
while the land of Francis Stone (16??-1716) and his family fell into King
George County upon its formation in 1721. DB#7,p.215; DB#10,p.142,453; the
will of Joshua Stone of Richmond County is of record in WB#7,p.202.]

STONE, JOSHUA and Nancy Lambert Habron, bond 27 May 1799. Consent by Margaret
Habron, mother of the bride. John Donaway (b); James Lambert (w).

STONE, JOSHUA and Ann Tune (widow)*, bond 5 February 1805. Lewis Tune (b).

STONE, THOMAS and Betty Dobyns, bond 8 August 1773. Henry Dobyns (b).

STONE, THOMAS and Sarah Alderson, bond 20 June 1780. Consent by James Alderson,
father of the bride. James Alderson (b). [The bride was the daughter of
James Alderson (17??-1785); she married (2) 26 December 1786, John Baker
(qv.), p.6. WB#7,p.472; WB#9,p.383.]

STONE, WILLIAM married Ann Harrison, daughter of Samuel Harrison and sister of
Jeremiah Harrison. William Stone died testate in 1772 and his widow in
1774; their wills remain of record in Richmond County WB#7,p.123,161.

STONUM, GEORGE N. and Elizabeth Phillips (spinster), bond 23 December 1807.
Richard Nash (b).

STONUM, RICHARD of Lancaster County and Peggy Dobyns*, bond 24 September 1791. Fortunatus Davenport (b); Joseph Davenport (w).

STONUM, WILLIAM of Northumberland County and Sarah Davenport, license December 1713.   DB#6,p.275

STONUM, WILLIAM and Mary Scurlock*, bond 15 April 1791. James Booth Dodson (b); George Scurlock (w).

STOTT, JAMES and Hannah Hanks, bond 4 April 1795. Oliver Stott (b), says the body of the bond, but it is signed by LeRoy Stott.

STOTT, JAMES and Frances W. Warrick*, bond 26 December 1815. Eppa: Stott (b); Thomas S. Warrick (w).

STOTT, JOEL (bachelor) and Betsy Baker (spinster)*, bond 6 October 1828. Joseph H. Davenport (b); he made oath both parties are of full age. Samuel W. Neasom (w).   MBB.,p.42

STOTT, JOHN and Nancy Stephens, bond 6 April 1807. James Samford (b).

STOTT, JOHN OLIVER and Betsey Suggit Gipson*, bond 26 August 1789. Oliver Stott (b). The bride signs her consent Gipson, but the clerk writes the name Gibson.

STOTT, LeRoy and Peggy Newgent, bond 30 March 1796. Rawleigh Newgent (b).

STOTT, OLIVER and Sally Redman, bond 14 October 1790. Consent by Joseph and Sally Redman, parents of the bride. Jeroboam Howard (b).

STOTT, OLIVER and Mary Coelman, bond 28 January 1797. Thomas Coelman (b). [The bride was the daughter of Thomas and Betty Coelman (q.v.), p.41.]

STOTT, RICHARD and Caty S. Tignor, bond 28 July 1800. Robert Neasom (b).

STOTT, THADDUS C. and Elizabeth W. Dale, bond 31 May 1834. Ewell Webb (b).
                                                                    MBB.,p.120

STOTT, THOMAS H. and Susan Rust*, bond 5 December 1845. Samuel Z. Self (b); John L. Clark (w). Married 6 December 1845 by the Rev. Elijah L. Williams.
                                                                    MBB.,p.267

STOTT, VINCENT and Elizabeth Stott (widow)*, bond 2 January 1836. George C. Newgent (b).   MBB.,p.140

STRAUGHAN, JAMES of Westmoreland County and Kitty Boothe, bond 11 January 1838. Samuel Anton (w).   MBB.,p.164

STRAUGHAN, JOHN C. of Northumberland County and Sally Phillips*, bond 19 November 1806. Christopher Dameron (b); Eppy Norris (w), Jane Pullen (w) and William H. Brooke (w). [The name of the last mentioned witness was probably William H. Broocke (q.v.),p.25.]

STRAUGHAN, RICHARD of Northumberland County and Jane Williams*, bond 6 December
1806. William P. Cox (b); William P. Cox (w); Sally Williams (w). This
certificate is filed: "Jane Williams, daughter of Thomas Williams and Hannah Williams, was born July 11 Day 1784. A true copy. William P. Cox."

STREET, RICHARD and Jane Wroe [Roe]*, bond 19 July 1788. Bartholomew McCarty (b).
[The bride's name is rendered Jane Wroe by the court clerk in the body of
the bond, but she signs her consent "Jane Roe."]

STREET, RICHARD and Elizabeth Miskell, bond 14 September 1807. George Miskell (b).

STROTHER, BENJAMIN (16??-1752), son of William Strother, Sr. who died testate in
Richmond County in 1702 and Dorothy, his wife, married prior to 25 April
1703 Mary Woffendall, daughter of Adam Woffendall who died testate in Richmond County in 1704. The will of Adam Woffendall, dated 25 April 1703 and
proved 7 June 1704, bequeathed to each of his "sons" Harrison and Strother
150 acres of land; this phraseology is deceiving as subsequent records assure
us that the legatees were his two sons-in-law, Robert Harrison (q.v.),p.89
and Benjamin Strother (16??-1752) who was sheriff of Richmond County in 1717.
The land of Benjamin Strother fell into King George County in 1721 and those
records abound with genealogical material in regard to the Strother family.
Benjamin Strother died testate in King George County in 1752. COB#6,p.112;
COB#7,p.103; WB#2,p.70; King George County DB#3,p.476; DB#4,p.254; WB#2,p.
11; Payne, p.66; William C. Kozee, Early Families of Eastern and Southeastern
Kentucky and Their Descendants (1961), p.689-711.

STROTHER, FRANCIS of St. Mark's Parish, Orange [later Culpeper] County, married
between 7 July 1732 and 6 December 1735, Elizabeth Fossaker, only child of
Richard Fossaker, deceased, and granddaughter of John and Elizabeth (Mott)
Fossaker (q.v.), p.71. King George County COB#1,p.606; COB#2,p.43,48; DB#2,
p.183,384.

STURMAN, WILLIAM Y. and Catherine Weathers, bond 21 February 1821. Whitfield
Brooke (b). [She was a daughter of John Weathers (1763-1822) (q.v.),p.225.]

STURMAN, WILLIAM Y. and Mrs. Clementina Jeffries*, bond 1 December 1841. Isaac S.
Jeffries (b). Married 2 December 1841 by Rev. William N. Ward   MBB.,p.214
[The bride was the daughter of Jeremiah and Apphia (Northen) Webb (q.v.), p.
226 and widow of Thomas H. Jeffries (q.v.),p.103. Paternally, the groom was
a scion of the ancient family of Sturman of Westmoreland County; his ancestry
is detailed 17W(2)99-106.

```
                        Colonel William Young -m- Elizabeth Smith
                        (1729-1783) of Essex   :  (1737-1792); m.
                        County, (q.v.), p.15   :  30 November 1755
                                               :
Elliott Sturman of Westmoreland -m(2), 10 June 1782-  Mary Young (20 February
and Essex counties (27 November  Essex County, Va.    1764-22 April 1824);she
1749-11 December 1791); will re-             :         m(2) 11 September 1792
corded in Westmoreland County                :         Thomas Hutt (30 January
W&D#18,p.230.                                :         1768-2 September 1805)
                                               :
                        William Young Sturman (1788-1848)
```

The aforementioned Elliott and Mary (Young) Sturman were the parents of
William Young Sturman (7 February 1788-8 July 1848) who married (1) 27 February 1821 Catherine Weathers (2 January 1805-7 April 1836) and (2) 2 Dec.
1841, Clementina (Webb) Jeffries (1810-1870), widow of Thomas H. Jeffries
(q.v.), p.103. William Young Sturman (1788-1848) was twice Commonweaths
Attorney of Richmond County, viz: 1818-1819 (resigned); 1828-1848. See
12W(2)41-42; 17W(2)101-106.]

SUGGITT, JAMES (16??-1734) married by 2 June 1703 Frances Bayliss; she was born
in North Farnham Parish 23 September 1686 the daughter of Thomas Bayliss
(16??-1699) and his first wife nee Catherine Samford. Thomas Bayliss m(2)
Sarah Edgcomb (16??-1703), widow of John Suggitt (16??-1690). James Suggitt (16??-1734) was the son of John and Sarah (Edgcomb) Suggitt; thus,
James Suggitt and Frances Bayliss were step-brother and sister. The surname Bayliss has been incorrectly rendered Bayley at times - as in this
case, viz: DB#5,p.319. COB#3,p.244,311,312; DB#5,p.319; WB#5,p.246.

SUGGITT, JOHN (16??-1690) married circa 1670 Sarah Edgcomb (16??-1703), daughter
of John Edgcomb who purchased land (later in Richmond County) 6 October 1652.
John Suggitt died testate in Rappahannock County in 1690 and on 4 May 1694
Sarah (Edgcomb) Suggitt made a deed of gift to her four sons, viz: John,
James, Edgcomb and Thomas Suggitt - the last of whom was born in North Farn-
ham Parish, 17 March 1677. Sarah (Edgcomb) Suggitt married (2) circa 1697
Thomas Baylis (q.v.), p.12, and died testate in 1703 in Richmond County.
COB#2,p.492; DB#2,p.51; WB#2,p.2,61; Sweeny,p.145-146.

SUGGITT, JOHN and Frances Samford (spinster), bond 29 April 1756. Joshua Singleton (b). This name is rendered Luggit 5W(1)20, but there is no such name
in Richmond County. [The bride was the daughter of James and Mary (Barber)
Samford (q.v.),p.176. John and Frances (Samford) Suggitt left no issue.]

SULLINGER, PETER of Essex County married by 1699 Elizabeth (Clotworthy) Dixon,
daughter and heir-at-law of Roger Clotworthy, deceased, who bought land 9
August 1666 which fell into Richmond County, and widow of John Dixon also
deceased. A portion of the land acquired by her aforementioned father was
sold 26 March 1715 by Elizabeth Sullinger, widow, of Essex County. Richmond
County DB#7,p.45; Essex County D&W#10,p.12; see Roger Clatworth, C&P.,p.297.

SULLINGER, Peter and Eliza [mutilated], bond 1 January 1744. William Paterson
(b). [The surname is also rendered Sullenger in various recordings.]

SULLIVAN, JOHN of Westmoreland County and Ann Scurlock (spinster), bond 10 August 1805. Frederick Kirkmire (b).

SUTTLE   SEE : SETTLE 184

SUTTLE, STROTHER married by 6 April 1720 Elizabeth Taylor, daughter of William
Taylor (16??-1718). COB#8,p.176; WB#4,p.58.

SUTTON, EDWARD and Elizabeth Mozingo, bond 3 February 1806. Consent by John and
Eleanor Mozingo, parents of the bride. John Wright (b).

SUTTON, GEORGE and Lucy Churchill, bond 13 July 1768.   Richard Yates (b).

SUTTON, JOHN and Mary Rose*, bond 7 March 1842.   Richard P. Fones (b); Robert
Hall (w).   MBB.,p.220

SUTTON, JOHN and Martha Elizabeth Mothershead, bond 19 July 1848.   George Mothershead (b).   Married 19 July 1848 by the Rev. John Pullen.   MBB.,p.312

SUTTON, THOMAS and Patsey Moore*, bond 29 March 1823.   Consent by Fanny Sutton
for the marriage of the groom; no relationship stated.   George Mothershead
(b); L.G. Sandy (w) and William Sutton (w).

SUTTON, WILLIAM and Hannah Ramey*, bond 30 January 1790.   Mason Sandy (b).

SWAIN, WILLIAM and Fadelia B. Hale*, bond 29 April 1850.   Henry P.F. King (b).
                                                                  MBB.,p.335

SWAN, ALEXANDER and Judith Hinds, married 15 November 1678.   NFPR.,p.165
[An order in court 9 August 1695 states that Captain Alexander Swan married
Judith Hinds, widow and administratrix of Richard Hinds, deceased. COB#2,
p.76,91.]

SWINBURN[E], THOMAS (16??-1697/8) married circa 1678 Katherine Pannell, widow
of Thomas Pannell (16??-1677) (q.v.), p. 153.   Thomas Swinburne died testate
in Richmond County and on 12 January 1697/8 his last will and Testament was
presented to court by his daughter Martha Swinburne, the "surviving executrix;" by 7 September 1698 the said Martha married George Phillips (q.v.),
p.158.   There were two other children, viz: William Swinburne, who joined
his sister Martha and her husband George Phillips, to convey 100 acres of
land in 1702 in which he had a reversionary interest, and Catherine Swinburne (168?-post 1735) who married (1) William Stone (1679-circa 1712), son
of Francis and Elizabeth Stone (q.v.), p.195, and (2) circa 1713 John Plaile
(16??-1734) who died intestate in King George County in 1734.   Catherine
(Swinburne) Stone Plaile left issue by both husbands; their land fell into
King George County in 1721.   COB#1,p.171; COB#2,p.275,276,332; COB#2,p.68;
DB#3,p.101; Rappahannock County DB#7,p.16,280; King George County DB#1,p.
74,125; DB#1-A,p.184,337; DB#4,p.78.

SWOPE, ELIJAH and Brunetta W. Dobyns, bond 5 February 1828.   Consent by Thomas
Dobyns, guardian of the bride.   Joseph Swope (b).   MBB.,p.36

SYDNOR, ANTHONY and Eliz.ᵃ Dew, license May 1710.   DB#6,p.275
[ECD cites the Bible record of Anthony Sydnor (1682/3-1759) which indicates
he married (1) Winifred ____[?]____ and had issue (a) Anthony Sydnor born,
25 March 1708; married (2) in May 1710, Elizabeth Dew (1694-1778) daughter
of Thomas and Elizabeth (Barber) Dew and had issue (b) John Sydnor, born 21
January 1711; (c) Winifred, born 6 February 1713; (d) Epaphroditus Sydnor,
born 2 May 1715, died 15 March 1756; (e) Betty Sydnor, born 23 February 1716/
1717, married Major Travers Tarpley (q.v.); (f) Dewanna(h) Sydnor, born 9
January 1719; died testate and unmarried in Richmond County in 1789; (g) Lucy
Sydnor, born 3 February 1722/3, married James Downman (q.v.), p.58; (h) Anth-

ony Sydnor, born 25 December 1724, died intestate in 1755; (i) Ruth Sydnor,
born 15 March 1726/7, died 8 March 1802, married Captain John Belfield (q.v.)
p.14; (j) Anne Sydnor, born 24 June 1729, died testate in 1793, married Richard Mitchell (q.v.), p.134. Anthony Sydnor, Sr. (1682/3-1759) and his wife
nee Elizabeth Dew (1694-1778) both died testate; their wills with the final
division of his estate after her death coupled with the wills of their two
childless daughters, Dewanna and Anne, give considerable data of genealogical import. I might add that it is likely that Winifred, first wife of Anthony Sydnor (1682/3-1759), was the daughter of Thomas and Anne Glascock as
as the said Anne Glascock by will dated 6 February 1713/14 and proved 3 March
1713/14 bequeathed to her grandson Anthony Sydnor 150 acres of land and provided if he d.s.p., same to revert to her granddaughter, Anne Barber. It is
likely Mrs. Glascock refers to Anthony Sydnor, born 25 March 1708 (above mentioned) and he dying another son, styled Anthony Sydnor, Jr. (1724-1755) was
so named. AB#1,p.582,649; WB#3,p.163; WB#6,p.164; WB#7,p.304; WB#8,p.61,163;
John Bennett Boddie, Historical Southern Families, Volume IV (Redwood City,
California, 1960), p.44-45; ECD Papers, Bible records, in Belfield folder.]

SYDNOR, EPA: and Milly Ball, bond 9 June 17___ (blank); Robert Sydnor (b).
    [As the bond was drawn to the Commonwealth, it is certain that it was dated
    post 1776 and ante 5 February 1784 when the bride's maternal grandfather,
    William Glascock, mentions her in his will as "Milly Sydnor." The bride was
    the daughter of Captain Williamson[5] Ball (1736-1793) (q.v.), p.9. The nun-
    cupative will of Milly (Mildred) (Ball) Sydnor was proved in 1810 and there-
    in she mentioned a legacy given to her by the will of her father-in-law [John
    Sydnor (1736/7-1808) (q.v.)]. For unknown reason, this bond and others undat-
    ed and incomplete, are now to be found in the 1796 bundle but it is certain
    they do not belong there! WB#9,p.337,378.]

SYDNOR, GILES and Nancy Harris, bond 7 April 1795. Hugh Harris (b).

SYDNOR, HARRISON and Judy Clarke, bond 12 August 1813. Consent by William Clark,
    father of the bride. James Lambert (b); Samuel Sydnor (w). [Harrison Sydnor,
    son of Epaphroditus and Mildred (Ball) Sydnor, was born in North Farnham Par-
    ish, 31 May 1789.]

SYDNOR, JOHN married Elizabeth Heall, 27 May 1728.   NFPR.,p.229

SYDNOR, JOHN SR. (20 February 1736/7-1808) married circa 1760, Frances Mitchell
    (15 February 1730/1-post 1807), daughter of Robert Mitchell, Sr. (1684-1748)
    of Lancaster County. DB#12,p.795; WB#8,p.163; WB#9,p.337; Lee,p.157-158.
    It is likely John Sydnor, Sr. was a widower when he married Frances Mitchell
    as ECD Papers contain excerpts from a suit styled Sydnor vs Burke which in-
    dicate that John Sydnor, Jr. d.s.p. and intestate circa 1836 and his handsome
    estate by law reverted to the heirs of his two half-sisters, viz: Betsy Smith
    (deceased) and Susan Bailey and the heirs of his whole brother Epaphroditus
    Sydnor (deceased) and his whole sister Fanny, wife of Ezekiel Levy. There is
    further detail in ECD Papers, Box 22, Sydnor folder.

SYDNOR, JOHN and Ann Keiser*, bond 27 November 1850. Vincent French (w) and
    Benjamin Tucker (w). Married 29 November 1850 by the Rev. John Godwin.

SYDNOR, JOHN JR. and Nancy Green*, bond 10 May 1813. Meredith Hudson (b);
    Alcey Davis (w).

SYDNOR, RICHARD and Eliza Wright, bond 16 July 1821. George M. Wright (b).

SYDNOR, ROBERT and Lucy Kent*, bond 9 July 1838. William Trasce (b); Benjamin
    Tucker (w).   MBB.,p.173

SYDNOR, THOMAS and Jane Self*, bond 15 August 1834. John L. Clarke (b).
                                                                  MBB.,p.123

SYDNOR, WILLIAM of Lancaster County and Ellen Fauntleroy, bond 12 October 1763.
    John Woodbridge (b). [He died testate in Lancaster County in 1794. Lee,
    p.214.]

SYDNOR, WILLIAM and Judith Williams, bond 31 October 1763. Thomas Smith (b).
    [William Sydnor, son of Epaphroditus Sydnor (1715-1756) and Mary, his wife,
    was born in North Farnham Parish, 24 February 1738/9. Judith Williams,
    daughter of Henry and Ann Williams, was born 31 October 1743 also in North
    Farnham Parish. They removed to Halifax County, Virginia, where he died in
    1818, very wealthy. Judith (Williams) Sydnor was the granddaughter of Abra-
    ham Forrest, Sr., who died testate in Amelia County, Virginia, in 1759.]

SYDNOR, WILLIAM SR. and Mary Harrow*, bond 6 May 1839. James F. Minor (b).
                                                                  MBB.,p.181

SYDNOR, WILLIAM F. and Salley Chinn, bond 30 November 1785. Bartholomew McCarty
    (b); William Sydnor Jr. (w). [The bride was born 19 August 1767, daughter
    of Robert and Elizabeth (Belfield) Chinn (q.v.), p.36; her birth is recorded
    in the family Bible of her great-grandfather, Robert Mitchell Sr. (1684-1748),
    of which there is a photostat copy, AD:VSL #25212. The groom was the son of
    William and Ellen(Fauntleroy) Sydnor, (q.v.), p. 202. Lee, p.51.]

                                    T

TAFF, PETER (16??-1716) married 171? Elizabeth (Woodbridge) McLaughlin (16??-1746),
    daughter of Paul Woodbridge (1631-1691) of Rappahannock County and widow of
    Manus McLaughlin (16??-1710) (q.v.), p.126. They had two sons, Thomas Taff
    and John Taff. The surname has been rendered Taff, Taft and Toff. Also the
    surname McLaughlin appears as MacGlathlin and McCaulin. COB#1,p.157; WB#3,
    p.13,273; WB#5,p.516; Thomas Taff vs John Yerby, suit in chancery, VSL:AD
    #25391; Sweeny,p.50,151.

TALIAFERRO, LAURENCE [CAPTAIN] (1683-1726) of Essex County, eldest son of Colonel
    John and Sarah (Smith) Taliaferro, married by 31 August 1706, Sarah Thornton
    (1680-17??), daughter of Major Francis and Alice (Savage) Thornton of Rich-
    mond County (q.v.). Captain Laurence Taliaferro died testate in Essex County
    and his will mentions three sons and four daughters. Of his sons only his
    second son left issue, viz: Francis Taliaferro (170?-1758) of Epsom on Mass-

assaponax Creek in Spotsylvania County; he married in 1730 Elizabeth Hay,
daughter of Doctor John and Ann (Robinson) Hay. Francis Taliaferro, Gentleman, died testate in 1758 and his estate was divided among his children
in 1759. His Bible record is cited by Byrd Charles Willis and Richard Henry
Willis, in A Sketch of the Willis Family of Virginia (Richmond, n.d.), p.141
et seq., but it must be noted that the account of The Taliaferro Family here
given contains many errors, particularly on p.140. Richmond County DB#4,p.
66; Essex County WB#4,p.133-134; Spotsylvania County WB "B",p.343 and Orphans Account Book 1759-1771,p.113; suit papers Steptoe vs Taliaferro, VSL:AD
#19793; suit papers Taliaferro vs Taliaferro (1786), Brock Collection Box
#217, Henry E. Huntington Library and Art Gallery, San Marino 9, California.

TALIAFERRO, RICHARD [COLONEL] (16??-1715), son of the immigrant Robert Taliaferro,
Gentleman, of Rappahannock County, married 169? Sarah (surname uncertain)
(16??-1718), daughter of Madam Martha Win(g)field who died testate in Boston,
Massachusetts, on 23 July 1709 while a transient.Mrs. Winfield (Wingfield,
Winkfield, Windfield &c:) was very wealthy and had wide interests; her daughter Sarah Taliaferro in Virginia and her children were her only legatees. Colonel Richard Taliaferro died intestate and administration on his estate was
granted to Thomas Turner by the Richmond County court on 4 January 1715/16.
Sarah Taliaferro died testate in 1718; her will disposes of a very handsome
estate and made her only son, Richard Taliaferro, residuary heir to all of
her estate "be it here in Virginia, West Indies or New England." The children of Colonel Richard and Sarah Taliaferro were: (a) Martha Taliaferro who
married in 1714, Colonel Thomas Turner (q.v.); (b) Richard Taliaferro, Jr.
(1700-1721) d.s.p., King George County; (c) Catherine Taliaferro (1706-1731)
married Colonel Rice Hooe (q.v.), p.96; (d) Sarah Taliaferro, born 171?, married the aforementioned Colonel Thomas Turner as his second wife. COB#5,p.
229; COB#6,p.375; DB#5,p.312; WB#3,p.237; WB#4,p.51; MRB,p.100; Suffolk County, Massachusetts, probate docket #3213 (Martha Winfield) and the following
recordings in regard to her estate: #16,p.605; #17,p.316-319; New Series #4,
p.490.

TALLEY, MOSES of Northumberland County and Ellin Maith*, bond 10 November 1806.
Thomas Way (b) and Rodham Booth (b); William Way (w) and Felcy Conaway (w).

TAPSCOTT, CHICHESTER and Betsy Williams, bond 23 December 1793. Bartholomew Mc-
Carty (b).

TAPSCOTT, JOSEPH and Ann M. Chinn, bond 19 December 1793. Griffin M. Fauntleroy
gives his consent for the marriage of his ward, Miss Ann M. Chinn. Rawleigh
Downman (b).

TAPSCOTT, SAMUEL C. and Ann C. Moore, married 18 October 1826.   WFMR., n.p.

TAPSCOTT, WARNER L. of Lancaster County and Elizabeth S. Dobyns, bond 27 December
1817. Consent by Catherine Dobyns, mother of the bride. Thomas Dobyns (b);
Frances Neasom (w).

TARKINTON, JOHN married by 3 March 1699, Martha Starke, relict of Francis Starke.
Richmond County COB#2,p.392,457.

TARPLEY, JOHN married circa 10 August 1699 per a prenuptial agreement, Elizabeth
Newman, widow of Captain Alexander Newman (16??-1698) (q.v.), p.146. DB#3,
p.32.

TARPLEY, JOHN and Ann Glascock, license January 1712/13.   DB#6,p.275
[The bride was the daughter of Thomas and Anne Glascock. COB#6,p.297,365;
WB#3,p.163.]

TARPLEY, JOHN JR. (1695-1736) married circa 1720 Elizabeth Ripping, daughter of
Edward and Mary Ripping of Williamsburg both of whom died testate in York
County. They had five children mentioned in the records, viz: (a) Travers
Tarpley (eldest son and heir); (b) Edward Ripping Tarpley (1727-1763) d.s.p.
in York County; (c) James Tarpley; (d) John Tarpley, Jr.; (e) Tertius Quint-
us Tarpley who died circa 1745 at which time there was a division of his
father's estate. COB#11,p.493; AB#1,p.227; WB#5,p.299; York County Record
Books #18,p.138; #20,p.327,333,344,352; #21,p.147.

TARPLEY, THOMAS G. and Jane Miskell*, bond 22 November 1815. George M. Wright
(b). Married 23 November 1815; the minister's returns call the bride Jane
Miskell, widow.

TARPLEY, TRAVERS [MAJOR] (17??-1768) married Betty Sydnor (1717-1777), daughter
of Anthony and Elizabeth (Dew) Sydnor (q.v.), p.200. Major and Mrs. Travers
Tarpley both died testate in North Farnham Parish and their wills remain of
record in WB#7,p.11,284. The recorded copy of Major Travers Tarpley's will
mentions his "sons" William Travers Peachey and Bartholomew McCarty and as
he had daughters married to gentlemen of the surnames of Peachey and McCarty
it has been taken for granted by some the aforementioned gentlemen were actually his sons-in-law. The marriage bonds here presented prove this assump-
ion erroneous and I discovered the original will of Major Travers Tarpley in
the loose papers and found this document names William Travers Peachey and
Bartholomew McCarty as "grandsons" of the testator. Major Travers and Betty
(Sydnor) Tarpley had no surviving male child but six daughters, viz: (a)
Betty Tarpley married Colonel LeRoy Peachey (q.v.), p.155; (b) Winney Tarpley
married Charles Barber McCarty (q.v.), p.123; (c) Fanny Tarpley married Rawleigh Chinn (q.v.), p.36; (d) Lucy Tarpley married Lodowick Jones (q.v.), p.
108; (e) Milly Tarpley married Beverley Daniel (q.v.), p.48; and (f) Nancy
Tarpley probably married a Mr. Killingham - this I deduct from the will of
her maternal aunt, Ann (Sydnor) Mitchell (1729-1793), in WB#8, p.163. The
Richmond County records abound with data in regard to the Tarpley family
and their many connections.

TATE, JOSEPH and Elizabeth Rich*, "both free persons of colour," bond 1 November
1834. Bass Rich (b).   MBB.,p.125
[In 1691 James, Jane, Elizabeth and William Tate, mulatto children of James
Tate (a Negro slave of Mr. Patrick Spence) and his wife Hester Tate (an English woman servant of Mr. James Westcomb), were bound out as apprentices by
the Westmoreland County court. Westmoreland County COB 1691-1698, p.40,41.]

TATE, JOSEPH T. and Hannah Read*, bond 7 July 1845. Taliaferro Hunter (b). Married 10 July 1845 by the Rev. Elijah L. Williams.   MBB.,p.261

TATE, TASKER and Sally Nickins, bond 17 September 1828. Lindsey Rich (b); he
makes oath both parties are 21 years of age.   MBB.,p.41

TAYLER, FRANCIS married by 23 April 1693 Elizabeth Snead, only daughter of Charles Snead, Sr. of Rappahannock County, deceased. On this date her only surviving brother, Charles Snead, Jr., deeds the Taylers land in Richmond County. DB#1,p.67; Sweeny,p.104-105; 21T54-61.

TAYLOE, JOSEPH [GENTLEMAN] (16??-1716) of Lancaster County married Barbara Billington (16??-1727), youngest daughter of Luke Billington, Sr. (16??-1672)
and his wife, Barbara ___[?]___ (16??-1674), both of whom died testate in
Rappahannock County. Joseph Tayloe was the brother of Colonel William Tayloe (1645-1710) of Richmond County, next below. Joseph and Barbara (Billington) Tayloe both died testate in Lancaster County; her last will leaves no
doubt that she was greatly displeased with her only son-in-law, John Thornbury (q.v.,p.209). Joseph and Barbara (Billington) Tayloe had three children, viz: (a) Anne Tayloe, d.s.p. in 1716; (b) Joseph Tayloe, Jr., d.s.p.
1724-1726; and (c) Elizabeth Tayloe married by 10 December 1726, John Thornbury (q.v.,p.209). DB#8,p.291,412; Lancaster County Record Book #9,p.326;
#10,p.188,197,217,509,537; #12,p.114,115; also Richmond County DB#5,p.68,
193; Sweeny,p.16-17,29; Hayden,p.84B, but author errs as to date of Luke
Billington's land patent - it was dated 1669 not 1779 as Richmond County
DB#5,p.193 recites.

TAYLOE, WILLIAM [COLONEL, GENTLEMAN] (1645-1710) of Richmond County, married (1)
1685 Anne Corbin (9 February 1664/5-1694), daughter of Hon.Henry and Alice
(Eltonhead) Corbin of Middlesex County. The Corbin pedigree, filed at the
College of Arms in London in 1715, states that "Anne Corbin 4th dau^r of Henry
[Corbin] married to Wm Tayloe of London descended from Gloucestershire. She
died in Virg^a Anno 1694." Colonel William and Anne (Corbin) Tayloe had three
children, viz: (a) Elizabeth Tayloe, born 26 July 1686, married Griffin Fount-
leroy as his first wife; (b) Honorable John Tayloe (15 February 1687/8-1747)
married Elizabeth (Gwyn) Lyde (1692-1745); (c) Colonel William Tayloe (30
July 1694-8 January 1770) married [not ascertained] and had an only child,
Anne Tayloe, who married 10 January 1746 in Lancaster County, John Wormeley,
Gentleman, (1724-1785) as his first wife. The obituary of Colonel William
Tayloe appeared in the Virginia Gazette of 22 February 1770 and his last will
remains of record in Lancaster County WB#18,p.169. Colonel William Tayloe
(1645-1710) married (2) Anne ___[?]___ [who m(2) James Burne (16??-1721]
and by her had issue, viz: (d) Anna Catherine Tayloe who married 25 November
1717 in Lancaster County, Samuel Ball (1686-1751); they moved to Culpeper
county; and (e) Mary Tayloe m(1) 11 June 1724 in Lancaster County, John Lyell
who died intestate in 1726/7; m(2) 8 January 1727/8 in Lancaster County,
James Pendleton (1702-1763), eldest son of Henry and Mary (Taylor) Pendleton
of King and Queen County. Mrs. Mary (Tayloe) Lyell Pendleton died shortly
after her second marriage and James Pendleton (1702-1763) m(2) Elizabeth
Coleman (17??-1769), daughter of Thomas Coleman (16??-1748) of King and
Queen County and Mary, his wife, who I believe to have been the daughter of
Richard Lort of the said county. James and Elizabeth (Coleman) Pendleton had
four children named in their wills of record in Culpeper County WB "A",p.305-
308,493. Colonel William Tayloe (1645-1710) died intestate in Richmond County

and on 7 February 1710/11 administration on his estate was granted to his
son, Mr. John Tayloe; at the same court the said Mr. John Tayloe was sworn
as a justice of the peace. The records abound with Tayloe material, but I
am fearful the second marriage of Colonel William Tayloe (1645-1710) and
her subsequent marriage to James Burne (16??-1721), have been overlooked by
many. After the death of Colonel Tayloe, his widow seems to have taken up
residence in Lancaster County and cohabitated with James Burn(e) and her
brother-in-law, Joseph Tayloe, Gentleman, complained to the Lancaster County
court that they were "vehemently disposed of fornication and incontinency."
This was in October 1715; Mrs. Anne Tayloe, widow, seems to have married the
said James Burn(e) shortly thereafter and he died testate in Lancaster County in 1721. Mrs. Anne Tayloe-Burn(e) was living in 1724 when she gave consent for the marriage of her daughter, Mary Tayloe, and John Lyell. COB#5,
p.226; Lancaster County COB 1713-1721, p.114,165; Lancaster County WB#10,p.
188,197,217,311,312,320.

TAYLOR, JAMES married 168? Elizabeth (?   ), widow of William Brown (16??-1677)
and of Evan Morgan (16??-1684). By 6 March 1694/5 she is deceased and Taylor has removed from Richmond County to Westmoreland County and claims he is
not responsible for a legacy bequeathed to his late wife's daughter, Elizabeth
Brown [who married Doctor Alexander Spence (q.v.), p.193] by her step-father,
Evan Morgan. COB#2,p.42,64,232; COB#6,p.112; Sweeny, p.57,106.

TAYLOR, JOHN married between 3 February 1705 - 6 November 1718, Mary Slaughter,
daughter of Francis Slaughter (circa 1658-1718) and his first wife, Margaret.
DB#4,p.14; DB#7,p.435; WB#4,p.77.

TAYLOR, JOSEPH H. and Frances H. Street, bond 17 July 1841. Consent by Elizabeth
Street, mother of the bride. William C. Haynes (b); Elizabeth Henderson (w).
Married 22 July 1841 by the Rev. Addison Hall.   MBB.,p.211

TAYLOR, MOSES and Frances Bramham, bond 4 June 1781. Joseph Pope (b).

TAYLOR, SAMUEL G. and Ann S. Bramham*, bond 26 May 1842. Lyne Shackleford (b).
                                                                 MBB.,p.224

TAYLOR, SIMON (16??-1729) married circa 1690 Elizabeth Lewis (16??-1727), one of
the five daughters of Edward Lewis, late of Rappahannock County. There are
entries in regard to this couple and issue in the North Farnham Parish Register. DB#3,p.178; DB#6,p.115; DB#9,p.186; WB#5,p.126.

TAYLOR, WILLIAM married Elizabeth Hendorson, 8 October 1730.   NFPR.,p.175

TEAGUE, JONATHAN and Jane Wroe Hudson*, bond 21 February 1793. Luke Jackson (b);
Thomas Tignor (w).

TEAGUE, NEWMAN B. and Rose Minter*, bond 13 February 1799. John Minter (b); Richard Woollard (w).

TEBBS, DANIEL and Elizabeth Gower, bond 14 January 1763. Stanley Gower (b).

TEBBS, FOUSHEE G. married 17 January 1799 Ann Quarles. The Fredericksburg Virginia Herald of 25 January 1799 announced the marriage: "Married: On Thursday the 17th inst. by the Rev. Mr. Young, Foushee Tebbs, Esq. of Richmond County, to the amiable Miss Ann Quarles, daughter of Captain Henry Quarles of Paradise, Essex County." The bride is mentioned in the will of her father as Ann Howell Tebbs; she was the daughter of Captain Henry Quarles (17??-1810) and his wife nee Ann West, daughter of Francis and Susanna (Littlepage) West of King William County. Captain Henry Quarles died testate in Essex County and his will remains of record in WB#17,p.243; there is considerable information in regard to the family in the suit papers, Jones vs Tebbs, FDC #155. This was the first marriage of Captain Foushee G. Tebbs.

TEBBS, FOUSHEE G. [CAPTAIN] and Nancy Yerby, bond 11 July 1815. John R.F. Corbin (b).

TEBBS, HENRY WILLIAM of Essex County and Nancy Y. McCarty, bond 15 December 1821. Consent by Foushee G. Tebbs, father of the groom and Judith G. McCarty, mother of the bride. William Settle (b); William McCarty (w) and Everet R. Pullen (w).

TEBBS, SAMUEL and Elizabeth Tebbs, bond 3 November 1798. Foushee Tebbs (b).

TELLIS, RODHAM of Northumberland County and Betsy Jones, bond 22 May 1788. Consent by Izabel Harrison, mother of the bride. James Pullen (b); William Kane (w) and William Fox (w).

TEMPLE, PETER and Louisa Fauntleroy, bond 2 February 1800. Consent by Judith Fauntleroy; no relationship indicated. Bartholomew McCarty (b).

TERRY, GEORGE and Elizabeth Alderson, bond 15 October 1785. Garland Moore (b).

THATCHER, SYLVESTER JR. (16??-1718) married Elizabeth Underwood, daughter of Major William Underwood (1649-1717). He was the son of Sylvester Thatcher (16??-1667) and his wife Margaret ___[?]___ (16??-1715) who married (2) Warwick Cammack (1636-circa 1685). Elizabeth (Underwood) Thatcher married (2) Francis Jett (16??-1724), a widower, son of William and Elizabeth (Hoskins) Jett (q.v.), p.106, by whom she had no issue. Francis Jett died in 1724 and Elizabeth (Underwood) Thatcher Jett in 1726; their wills are in lost King George County WB#1 (1721-1752), but the surviving records abound with genealogical data. Sylvester and Elizabeth (Underwood) Thatcher had seven children. WB#3,p.344; WB#4,p.26,54; King George County COB#1,p.233, 305 and Inventory Book #1,p.38,61,89; Underwood genealogy, 38V267 et seq.; Jett genealogy, 9 New Haven Genealogical Magazine 143 et seq.

THATCHER, THOMAS (17??-1751), son of Sylvester and Elizabeth (Underwood) Thatcher (q.v.), p.207, married by 1730 Catherine Pannell, daughter of William and Frances (Sterne) Pannell (q.v.), p.154; she married (2) circa 1762 David Zwelling. King George County DB#1-A,p.29,208,285; DB#2,p.535; DB#3, p.133; DB#4,p.159; DB#6,p.75; Stafford County Book "P",p.75,205,207,212; 18T234, will of Thomas Thatcher, proved at King George County court 1751, recorded in now lost King George County WB#1 (1721-1752).

THATCHER, WILLIAM (16??-1698) of Lancaster County married Alice Mathews, daughter
of William Mathews who patented 1148 acres of land which was in Richmond County in 1746. The will of William Thatcher is preserved in the Lancaster County
Loose Wills file, VSL:AD; Lee,p.220, incorrectly renders his surname, Thacker,
but she is by no means alone in so doing. DB#10,p.373; PB#6,p.217 [1668].

THOM [a free man of colour] and Mary Jane [a slave, the property of Robert W. Carter, Esq., of Sabine Hall]; the marriage was solemnized 14 December 1847 in
the home of the said Carter by the Rev. William N. Ward, minister of the P.E.
Church. No marriage bond found; this from Mr. Ward's minister's returns.

THOMAS, BECKHAM and Mary Sutton, bond 30 December 1800. Thomas Dozier (b).

THOMAS, DANIEL J. and Alice Yeatman, bond 4 January 1831. Samuel Yeatman (b).
                                                              MBB.,p.72

THOMAS, GRIFFIN E. and Mary Newgent*, bond 23 December 1817. George Nash (b).

THOMAS, JAMES of Northumberland County and Elinor Hazard, bond 3 March 1788.
Joseph Hazard (b).

THOMAS, JOB of Lunenburg Parish, Richmond County, married long before 31 October
1774, Mary Brickey, daughter of John Brickey who died intestate in 1733.
She d.s.p. before 31 October 1774, but Job Thomas is yet living on this date.
DB#14,p.335; WB#5,p.189,208.

THOMAS, JOSEPH and Lucy Headley*, bond 3 April 1837. William W. Forester (b).
                                                              MBB.,p.155

THOMAS, WILLIAM of Northumberland County married by 1743 Mary Ann Wood, only
child of Thomas Wood of Richmond County who died testate in 1727. DB#11,
p.229; DB#16,p.6; WB#5,p.63.

THOMAS, WILLIAM and Elizabeth Davis*, bond 20 April 1796. Thomas Davis (b).

THOMAS, WILLIAM and Nancy Mozingo, bond 6 January 1800. Consent by John Mozingo,
father of the bride. John Mozingo (b).

THOMPSON, CHARLES R. and Ann Fauntleroy, bond 28 December 1797. Consent by Ann
Fauntleroy, mother of the bride, was written from Mars Hill on 27 December
1797. Charles Smith (b); Polly Fauntleroy (w).

THOMPSON, DANIEL and Hannah Newman*, bond 1 April 1848. Married 6 April 1848 by
the Rev. Mr. William N. Ward, minister of the Gospel in the Protestant
Episcopal Church, who states the contracting parties are "free people of
color." Frederick Newman (b); Jane Newman (w).   MBB.,p.309

THOMPSON, GEORGE married Katherine Phillips, 21 February 1725/6.   NFPR.,p.174

THOMPSON, HENRY and Alice Newman*, bond 2 March 1818. Consent by John Newman; no
relationship stated. Daniel Thompson (b) and Frederick Newman (b); Daniel
Thompson (w).

THOMPSON, JAMES F. and Mary Ann Kelsick, bond 30 April 1821. John Weathers (b).
Filed with this marriage bond is a letter dated 30 April 1821 from John W.
Belfield to George Saunders, clerk of Richmond County court, stating that
Samuel B. Kelsick, father of the bride, was at his house 8 or 10 days since
and left a note consenting to the marriage of his daughter Mary Ann Kelsick
and James F. Thompson, but the said writing has been lost. Samuel B. Kelsick
is absent at the present time and it is not known when he will return - and
to these facts he will make oath. Joseph Kelsick, brother of the bride, in
person assured the court clerk, his father gave his consent in writing for
the marriage but the authorization for the license to issue "has been from
some cause destroyed."

THOMPSON, JOHN JR. and Elizabeth McKie*, bond 31 December 1838. John Thompson,
Sr. (b).   MBB.,p.179

THOMPSON, MOSES and Peggy Thompson "free persons of colour," bond 3 January 1831.
Darcas Thompson, mother of the bride, gives her consent. Daniel Thompson
(b).   MBB.,p.72

THOMSON, RICHARD and Mary Cambrum, bond 30 November 1785. Almon Sanders (b).

THORNBURY, THORNBERRY OR THORNBURGH, JOHN of Maryland and Virginia, married by
10 December 1726 Elizabeth Tayloe, daughter of Joseph and Barbara (Billington) Tayloe of Lancaster County (q.v.), p.205. The groom was the eldest son
of Rowland Thornbury [Thornberry and Thornburgh] of Baltimore County, Maryland, who held a 900 acre plantation in that county upon Patapsco River near
Joneses Falls called Selsad [Selsed, Celsed]; this by will be devised to his
three only sons, John, Rowland and Francis Thornburgh - equally to be divided
among them. The will of Rowland Thornburgh, planter, of Back River, Baltimore
County, was dated 5 July 1695 with a codicil dated 21 December 1695; it was
offered for probate 23 June 1696 by the testator's widow, Ann Thornburgh, but
was not recorded until 3 March 1702/3 in Baltimore County Will Liber #1, p.81-
83. The Calvert Rent Rolls in the Maryland Historical Society note the land
holdings of Rowland Thornbury, with a notation 1703 that his orphan had "gone
into Virginia." Under the heading of Thornton, a contributor in 3W(1)71 said
the record in regard to Rowland Thornbury read his orphan "born into Virginia"
and in the next volume, 4W(1)282, another said the cited record should be Rowland Thornton not Rowland Thornbury. Actually the record concerns Rowland
Thornbury's son and heir, John Thornbury, who removed to Virginia, and Rowland
Thornton is in no way concerned. On 8 August 1711 John Thornbury of the Colony of Virginia, by an attorney, sold his part of the Selsad tract and the
deed was recorded in Baltimore County Land Records TR No.A, p.152-153. See references under Joseph Tayloe, Gentleman, p.205; particulary Richmond County DB
#8,p.412 and the will of Barbara (Billington) Tayloe recorded in Lancaster
County WB#10,p.509.
Rowland Thornburgh (16??-1696) entailed his land called Selsad upon his three
aforementioned sons but his will provided if they all d.s.p. then "the whole
Tract of land afores. to descend unto the next akin of the family of the
Thornburgh at Hampsfield in Lancashire in Old England to them and their heirs
lawfully begotten forever and failing this family aforesaid then the land to
descend to the next akin of the Thornburges at Selsad, near Kendale,

in Westmoreland in Old England afores.[d] to them and their heirs lawfully begotten forever."

THORNBERRY, ROWLAND and Marcy Baylis, license March 1715/16.   DB#6,p.275
[The bride was the daughter of Thomas and Catherine (Samford) Baylis (q.v.), p.12. Rowland Thornberry (Thornbury and Thornbrough) was the second son of Rowland Thornbrough (16??-1696) of Baltimore County, Maryland, (q.v.),p.209. Francis Thornberry, eldest child of Rowland and Marcy (Baylis) Thornberry, was born in North Farnham Parish on 23 September 1717. In 1763 as Francis Thornbury, planter, of Baltimore County, Maryland, and in 1765 as Francis Thornburgh, planter, of Baltimore County, Maryland, he sold portions of the Selsad tract, describing himself as "son and heir at law of his father, Rowland Thornbury of the County aforesaid deceased" ... who "was one of the sons and devisees of his father, Rowland Thornbury late of the County aforesaid deceased." From these recordings in Baltimore County, Maryland, Land Records B No.L,p.118-122 and B No.O,p.55-58, it appears that Rowland Thornbury (who married Marcy Baylis) removed from Richmond County, Virginia, to Baltimore County, Maryland, where he died ante 1763 and where their eldest son and heir, the said Francis Thornbury, was living in 1763 with his wife Mary Thornbury. Richmond County DB#8,p.27-29; WB#2,p.2; DB#9,p.229.]

THORNLEY, AARON (16??-1728) of Richmond and King George counties, married by 6 July 1720, Mary, heir of John Berry, deceased; this is recited in Richmond County DB#7,p.528. The records indicate the said Mary was the daughter of John[2] Berry mentioned in 1 The Virginia Genealogist 7. Aaron Thornley died in King George County in 1728 and his widow, Mary Thornley, administered on his estate. Their son, John Thornley, married Ann Woffendale, daughter of Francis Woffendale and granddaughter of Adam Woffendale, and there is considerable record of them and their progeny in the King George County records. Aaron Thornley (1750-1821) of White Plains near Port Conway in King George County, son of John and Ann (Woffendale) Thornley, was twice married and his Bible record and other genealogical data is presented in 22 National Genealogical Society Quarterly 96-101; WB#2,p.70;indexed King George Co. records.

THORNTON, ___[?]___ married between 1784-1806, Eleanor Barnes Kelsick, daughter of Captain Younger and Mary (Barnes) Kelsick (q.v.), p.111. Eleanor Barnes (Kelsick) Thornton was a widow by 1806. AB#3,p.137,198; WB#9,p.5.

THORNTON, FRANCIS [MAJOR] (1651-1726) of Richmond, Stafford and King George counties, married (1) 13 April 1674, Alice Savage, daughter of Captain Anthony Savage (16??-1695) of Richmond County; she was the mother of all his children. He married (2) circa 1701, Jane Harvey, widow of John Harvey of Stafford County, and (3) circa 1709, Ann ___[?]___ who survived him and proved his will in King George County in 1726. Rappahannock County DB#6,p.64; King George County COB#1,p.330,349 and DB#1,p.453; Stafford County Book "Z", p.55; Westmoreland County W&D#3,p.439; 12T65; 19T170-173; 20T114-119; Bible record of Major Francis Thornton (1651-1726) in Virginia Historical Society.

THORNTON, LUKE married Millisent Longworth, 2 January 1727/8.   NFPR.,p.175
[The bride was the daughter of Edward Ransdell who died testate in Westmoreland County in 1724 and the widow of William Longworth who died in the same

county in September 1724. The only child of William and Millicent (Ransdell) Longworth to survive infancy was Jemima Longworth; she was born the day after her father died and married John Thornton. Luke Thornton and John Thornton, together with their wives, moved to Orange County and in 1741 engaged in a suit styled Thornton vs Thornton in which the aforementioned genealogical facts are recited. There are other records in Orange County in regard to these people.]

THORNTON, MATHEW (16??-1727) married (1) by 13 May 1706 Elizabeth Hopkins, eldest daughter of Robert Hopkins, by whom he had, viz: (a) Hopkins Thornton who died intestate in 1742; (b) Mathew Thornton, born 1 March 1715 who was apprenticed to George Hunt, carpenter, on 4 June 1729; (c) Rebecca Thornton who married by 30 November 1726 William Craske (q.v.), p.46. Mathew Thornton married (2) Eleanor (Ellen) Craske (17??-1776), daughter of Captain John and Elizabeth (Moss) Craske (q.v.), p.46, and she married (2) 3 May 1728 Captain Alvin Mountjoy (1700-1760) (q.v.), p.140. Mathew and Eleanor (Craske) Thornton had two children, viz: (d) Crask Thornton who died testate in 1771 and (e) Ellen (Eleanor) Thornton who married in 1746, Thomas Yeatman (q.v.),p.237. COB#9,p.468; DB#4,p.51; DB#7,p.425; DB#9,p.216,500; WB#5,p.57,396,462; WB#6, p.266; WB#7,p.220.

THORNTON, PETER PRESLEY and Elizabeth Carter, bond 4 May 1778.
[Peter Presley Thornton, Esq. (1750-1780) was the only son of the Honorable Presley Thornton and Elizabeth ___[?]___, his first wife; Elizabeth Carter was the daughter of Robert Wormeley Carter, Esq. of Sabine Hall. Sally Carter, the only child of this couple, died shortly after her father and the landed estate of Peter Presley Thornton reverted to his only whole sister, Winifred Thornton, wife of John Catesby Cocke (q.v.), p.40-41. Elizabeth (Carter) Thornton, widow, married (2) 16 March 1782 her cousin, Landon Carter, Esq. (1751-1811) of Cleve in King George County (q.v.), p.34. See suit papers, Thornton vs Cocke, FDC#282.]

THORNTON, ROBERT and Frances Dudley, bond 5 April 1787. Rodham Clark (b).
"This is to sertify that licence may be granted Robert Thornton to marry Frances Dudley by liberty from her parents

George Sisson
Winneyfrid Sisson
April 4,1787

Mary Ann Hammond
Rodham Clark"
[Robert Thornton died intestate in 1794; his widow married (2) 6 May 1795 Henry Harford (q.v.), p.88. AB#2,p.293 indicates Robert Thornton left two orphans. The Lunenburg Parish Register records the birth of Sharlott (Charlotte) Thornton, daughter of Robert and Frances Thornton, on 29 November 1791.]

THORNTON, ROWLAND [GENTLEMAN] (165?-1701) married by 1 June 1691 Elizabeth Fleming, born circa 1668, only child of Captain Alexander Fleming and his third wife nee Joyce Jones (q.v.), p. 69-70, who married shortly after the death of Captain Fleming, Captain Lawrence Washington (1635-1677). Elizabeth (Fleming) Thornton married (2) by 7 July 1703, John Jones (q.v.), p.108. Rowland Thornton (165?-1701) was the son of William Thornton, Gentleman, who settled in

York County circa 1641 and lived successively in Gloucester County 1665-76;
Rappahannock County, 1679 and Richmond County, 1693. In his old age he moved to Saint Paul's Parish, Stafford County, where his son Major Francis Thornton (1651-1726) (q.v.), p.210, was living and there in 1708 confirmed and acknowledged a deed dated 16 July 1675 to his sons Francis[2] Thornton and Rowland[2]
Thornton for 2,000 acres of land on the north side of Muddy Creek which he had
purchased 27 September 1673 from John and George Mott, the patentees. The document, of record in Richmond County DB#5,p.49-51, states the land was then in
Richmond County; it fell into King George County in 1721 and into Stafford
County in 1777. The title to the upper 1,000 acres, the land of Rowland [2]
Thornton (165?-1701), fell into dispute early in the XIX Century, and these
suit papers coupled with the court records completely set aside the 1895
statement of the late Doctor Stanard in 4W(1)90 that "there is no evidence"
Rowland and Elizabeth (Fleming) Thornton "had issue." This statement was
repeated by others for years, but writers in 23T102-106 and 44V185 finally
realized Rowland[2] Thornton left progeny but both misidentified his issue.
One writer confused Rowland[3] [Rowland[2], William[1]] Thornton with his far
more conspicuous first cousin Rowland[3] Thornton, Gentleman, (1685-1742) of
Crow's in lower King George County [Francis[2] William[1]] while another writer
stated Francis[2] Thornton (1651-1726) was the son of Rowland[2] Thornton [his
brother!] who died in 1701. COB#3,p.96,264; DB#1,p.20; DB#2,p.21. DB#3,p.
30; WB#2,p.29; Essex County DB#14,p.335 and DB#15,p.186; Morson vs Fox, FDC
#575, Bundle "F" 330-347; see mention of Captain Alexander Fleming on p.69-
70,152; 23T102-106; 44V185; 19W(2)309-317; 33 Americana 1-31; other records.

Rowland[2] Thornton (165?-1701) -married- Elizabeth Fleming (c.1668-17??),only
By his father's deed of gift of   : child to leave issue of Capt.Alexand-
1675 he received 1,000 acres on   : er Fleming. She married (2), circa
Muddy Creek; this land descended   : 1703, John Jones (16??-1716); he
to his only known child,   : died intestate in Richmond County.
                                     :

Rowland[3] Thornton (169?-ante 1750),planter,of King George County. 1714 conveyed land in Essex County as the heir of his grandfather Fleming and in
1716 was guardian to John and Elizabeth Jones, probably his half-brother and
sister. 1723 and 1725 leased portions of his 1,000 acre Muddy Creek tract inherited from his father. The name of his wife is unknown; they had two sons,
                                     :

Rowland[4] Thornton (171?-1755)   Colonel William[4] Thornton (171?-1776)
m. Sarah Bruce (17??-1790)   m(1) [unknown], mother of John[5](below)
: m(2) Thomas Casson (17??-1788)   : m(2) Sarah Newton (17??-1816); she
: and had an only child Sarah,who   : was much his junior and m(2) Capt-
: m. William Alexander (1758-1804).   : ain Nathaniel Fox (1748-1819).
:   :
William[5] Thornton, only child of   John[5] Thornton, Gent. (c.1740-1780)
his parents, d.s.p., and the 1,000   possessed the 1,000 acre Muddy Creek
acre tract on Muddy Creek reverted   tract by descent. He moved to Loudoun
to his uncle,the above mentioned   County in 1779 and died there in 1780,
Col. William[4] Thornton. In 1758   testate. He was twice married and
Thomas Casson was guardian to Wm[5].   left two children by each wife, (q.v.),
Thornton.   p.213.

John[5] Thornton, Gentleman, (circa 1740-1780), son of Colonel William[4] Thornton and his unknown first wife, was possessed in fee simple of the 1,000 acre tract on Muddy Creek of which his great-grandfather, Rowland[2] Thornton (165?-1701), had died seized. Colonel William[4] Thornton (171?-1776), late in life, married as his second wife, Sarah Newton (17??-circa 1816), a girl yet in her teens, the daughter of Major William Newton of Little Falls Plantation. In 1775 Colonel William[4] Thornton sold a parcel of land in King George County but his wife was unable to enter into the deed and release her right of dower in the land "on account of her infancy." [King George County DB#5, p.1142-1143.] Colonel William[4] Thornton died in King George County in 1776, the year before his Muddy Creek plantation fell into Stafford County, and John Newton took out administration papers on his estate. [King George County Bond Book #5, p.229]. Sarah (Newton) Thornton, widow, was entitled to her dower interest and she promptly married Captain Nathaniel Fox (1748-1819) and survived her step-son, John[5] Thornton, more than 35 years. In the meantime John[5] Thornton's widow also remarried and as she too held a dower interest in this valuable tract of land on Muddy Creek, there is little wonder that a suit developed over the boundries and the lines of the parcels held in dower. John[5] Thornton, Gentleman, (circa 1740-1780), married (1) 13 December 1761 in Saint Paul's Parish, Beheathland Gilson Berryman, daughter of Gilson Berryman, Gentleman, who was born there 23 March 1743/4 and died circa 1774. By her he had two sons, viz: (a) Anthony Thornton who frequently appears on the Loudoun County records and (b) Benjamin Berryman Thornton (circa 1772-1832) who also appears on the Loudoun County records and died testate in Hampshire County, now West Virginia. The second marriage of "John Thornton, Esq. of Stafford County to Miss Catherine Yates, daughter of the Rev. Robert Yates of Gloucester County," was announced in the Virginia Gazette of 5 September 1777 and by her he had two children, viz: (c) William Thornton (1778-1803) who engaged in a duel with his distant cousin Francis F. Conway (1772-1803) of Mount Scion, Caroline County, in which both men were mortally wounded, over the affections of their distant cousin Miss Nelly Conway Madison of Orange County; and (d) Mary Randolph Thornton (1780-1851), wife of Doctor Charles Landon Carter (1774-1832) of Fredericksburg, d.s.p. Catherine (Yates) Thornton (1760-1831) married (2) 1 January 1781, Doctor Robert Wellford (1753-1823) of Fredericksburg and had several children by him. Georgia Dickinson Wardlaw in The Old and the Quaint in Virginia (Richmond, 1939), p. 274-277, gives an interesting account of the Thornton-Conway duel but errs in identifying John[5] Thornton as of "The Falls," near Fredericksburg; he was a distant cousin as the Thorntons of The Falls and Fall Hill were descendants of Major Francis[2] and Alice (Savage) Thornton (q.v.), p.210.

THORNTON, THOMAS (5 April 1688-1729), son of Luke[1] Thornton (16??-1726) and Ann, his wife, was born and died in North Farnham Parish; he married 171? Susannah Smith, daughter of William Smith (16??-1717) who died intestate in Richmond County. Susannah (Smith) Thornton married (2) by 1736, Samuel Gray (q.v.), p.80. Thomas Thornton died testate in Richmond County leaving his estate to his wife Susannah Thornton and by his last will and Testament oddly made no reference to his children. However, long recitations in DB#12,p.361,422, state that Henry Burditt of Lunenburg Parish by will dated 29 November 1723 bequeathed 90 acres of land to Thomas Thornton and Susanna, his wife, with reversion to their children, and that as the said Susanna(h) died circa 1762.

The children of Thomas and Susannah (Smith) Thornton were: (a) Rachel
Thornton married Francis Williams (q.v.); (b) Ann Thornton married Walter
Anderson (q.v.); and (c) Ellen Thornton married William Robins (q.v.).
COB#7,p.221; COB#8,p.31; COB#9,p.12; COB#10,p.396; COB#14,p.19,33; DB#12,
p.361,422; WB#4,p.1,265; WB#5,p.146; WB#6,p.85,203.

THORNTON, THOMAS (17??-1763) married circa 1731 Elizabeth Davis (circa 1717-1793),
only child of Richard and Mary (Berrick) Davis (q.v.), p.50. This is recited
in the chancery suit papers styled Thomas Thornton and Elizabeth, his wife,
vs Dozier and Davis, instigated in 1746 seeking a division of the landed
estate of William Davis (q.v.), p.51, grandfather of the said Elizabeth, who
died testate in Richmond County leaving a will dated 21 January 1697 and recorded 12 January 1698 in now lost Richmond County WB#1 (1692-1699). COB#2,
p.275; COB#15,p.78,79; WB#4,p.119; WB#8,p.130,166.

THORNTON, THOMAS and Rebecca Sisson Lawson, bond 11 February 1769. Daniel Lawson
(b). [Thomas Thornton died testate in 1771 leaving two daughters, viz: (a)
Frances Sisson Thornton who married in 1788 Daniel Dobyns (q.v.), p.54 and
(b) Elizabeth Thornton who d.s.p. ante 1777. Rebecca Sisson (Lawson) Thornton married (2) 177?, Thomas Hammond (q.v.), p.86, who died testate in 1777,
and she married (3) 1781, Thomas Dobyns (q.v.), p. 55, a widower, who died
testate in 1788. Rebecca Sisson (Lawson) Thornton Hammond Dobyns acted as
executrix of her last husband and was living in 1792 when his estate was
divided. ECD cites a suit in regard to the estate of Thomas Hammond (17??-
1777) which indicates the three marriages of Rebecca Sisson Lawson. AB#2,p.
162; WB#7,p.99,293; WB#8,p.36.]

THORNTON, WILLIAM married Elizabeth Talburt, 10 August 1727.   NFPR.,p.174

THORNTON, WILLIAM and Frances Clarke*, bond 10 January 1832. John L. Clarke (b);
he made oath both parties are "21 years of age." William Brickey (w).MBB.,p.
87

THRELKELD, HENRY married Eleanor Short, 15 July 1728.   NFPR.,p.175
[Henry Threlkeld (circa 1700-1731) died testate; his only son George Threlkeld (1730-1748) died testate bequeathing his estate to William Davis and
Elizabeth Davis, his half-brother and sister. Because he was not of legal
age to make a will, it was contested by William Threlkeld, the heir-at-law.
Eleanor (Short) Threlkeld married (2) by 4 June 1733, William Davis of Westmoreland County (q.v.), p.52. AB#1,p.386; WB#5,p.164,539.]

THRIFT, ABSALOM and Mary Bramham, bond 11 January 1772. John Demervill (b).

THRIFT, GEORGE and Elizabeth McKenny, bond 7 January 1788. Thomas Smith (b).

THRIFT, GEORGE and Polly Jones*, bond __ August 1815. Edward Brown (b).

THRIFT, GEORGE and Jane Neasom*, bond 21 December 1821. William R. Jeffries (b);
Mary Scrimger (w) and Lucy D. Northen (w).

THRIFT, GEORGE W. and Mary A. Sisson, bond 1 January 1849. Consent by Hiram
Sisson, father of the bride. John L. Chamberlain (b).   MBB.,p.318

THRIFT, JERY and Priscilla Bryant, bond 15 January 1817. Consent by Sarah Hall, mother of the bride. Thomas Hale (b); Thomas Fallin (w).

THRIFT, JESSE and Ellen Stephens (widow)*, bond 14 October 1807. George Jesper (b); Edward Brown (w).

THRIFT, JOHN and Alice Barnes, bond 19 August 1790. Rodham Pritchett (b).

THRIFT, JOHN and Jane Churchwell, bond 27 November 1800. John Weymoth (b).

THRIFT, JOHN and Nancy Douglass*, bond 19 September 1815. John Dougliss (b); Edward Dougliss, Jun. (w).

THRIFT, JOHN JR. and Sally White (spinster), bond 23 November 1808. John Bryant (b). John Thrift certifies to the court clerk that his son, John Thrift Jr., is of lawful age and that Sally White is 21 years of age "and lives in my family and that she has neither Father or Mother." Jeremiah Thrift (w).

THRIFT, RICHARD T. and Alice Ann Lewis, bond 14 October 1841. Consent by Jeremiah Lewis, father of the bride. Edward Douglass (b); John Douglass (w). MBB.,p.212

THRIFT, SAMUEL and Elizabeth Harris*, bond 10 November 1807. Robert Jeffries (b).

THRIFT, SAMUEL B. and Mary A.G. Webb*, bond 4 May 1844. William B. Hall (b); Griffin Headley (w) and William B. Hall (w). MBB.,p.249

THRIFT, WILLIAM and Jane Northen, bond 12 November 1818. Katharine G. Northen writes her consent for the marriage of her daughter. George Brooke (b); Sarah H. Cloughton (w).

THRIFT, WILLIAM and Nancy Joy*, bond 13 November 1845. William Bryant (b); William Thrift (w). Married 13 November 1845 by the Rev. Elijah L. Williams. MBB.,p.265

TIFFEY, JOHN B. (bachelor) and Ann Harvey (widow), bond 4 May 1829. Joseph S. Lyell (b). MBB.,p.54

TIGNOR, THOMAS and Sally Smith, bond 14 November 1791. Luke Jackson (b).

TILLERY, FORTUNATUS and Susanna Seabery*, bond 3 February 1789. Jery Nash (b).

TILLERY, HENRY and Mary Wascole, married 7 November 1675. NFPR.,p.171

TILLERY, JOB married by 1719 Mary Colwick, daughter of Hezekiah Colwick of Totusky Creek. In 1770 a suit in ejectment arose in Richmond County court in which it is recited that Hezekiah Colwick bought land of John Alloway on Totusky Creek; his only child Mary Colwick married Job Tillery and they lived and died on the land as did their son and heir, Job Tillery. The suit was brought by Job Tillery, son and heir of the last mentioned Job Tillery,

and grandson and heir-at-law of Mary (Colwick) Tillery. In 1770 Sarah
Saunders, aged 43, deposed that Job Tillery did not possess any land before he married Mary Colwick; this she says she learned from her mother
as the Colwick land lay "near a piece taken up by her father Edward Brumbelow." WB#5,p.156; ECD Papers, citing Tillery vs Lewis; see p.178.

TILLERY, JOAB married Elizabeth Mackgyer, 27 August 1730.   NFPR.,p.175
    [The bride was the sister of Mary Mackgyer (Mackgyar, MacGivier &c:) who
    married Phileman (Philemon) Bird (q.v.), p.18. DB#9,p.62,677; DB#10,p.138;
    references cited under Phileman Bird.]

TILLERY, THOMAS married by 13 August 1695 Priscilla Alloway, daughter of John
    Alloway of North Farnham Parish, all of whom were living 13 August 1695.
    DB#2,p.130.

TODD, CORNELIUS married Mary Jones, 17 December 1739.   NFPR.,p.175

TODD, HENRY [DOCTOR] (17??-1789) of King and Queen County, Virginia, and Burke
    County, Georgia, married by 12 April 1770, Apphia Bushrod Fauntleroy, dau-
    ghter of John Fauntleroy (1724-1761) and his wife first nee Judith Little-
    page. Journals of the House of Burgesses 1773-1776 [Volume #13,p.124],
    24 May 1774; Fauntleroy,p.802.

TODD, JOHN and Matilda Dodson, bond 23 December 1812. James B. Dodson (b).

TODD, PETER and Elizabeth B. Dodson, bond 15 December 1813. Oddly there is a
    consent signed by Raughley Dodson and Sharlet Dodson, his wife, but John
    Todd (b) certifies that Elizabeth B. Dodson "is the daughter of Rawleigh
    Dodson, dec.d and that she is upwards of 21 years of age." John Todd (b).

TODD, PETER and Frances Ann Pullen, bond 29 May 1816. John Todd (b).

TODD, WILLIAM [COLONEL] of King and Queen County married circa 1709, Martha
    Vicaris, daughter of Thomas Vicaris, Clerk, of Gloucester County, and
    Martha, his wife. In right of his wife, Colonel William Todd was possess-
    ed of a valuable tract of land near the falls of the Rappahannock River
    upon which the town of Falmouth was laid out in 1727. This property was
    in Richmond County when Colonel Todd and Martha Vicaris were married and
    fell into King George County in 1721 and finally into Stafford County in
    1777. The last will and Testament of Colonel William Todd was dated 12
    February 1736; it was recorded in a now lost King and Queen county record
    book but a portion of it is recited in Orange County DB#16,p.174. DB#7,p.
    116; King George County DB#3,p.268; Northern Neck Land Grant Book #1,p.1;
    Clayton Torrence, Winston of Virginia and Allied Families (Richmond, 1927),
    p.92 et seq.

TOMLIN, JOHN W. and Margaret W. Ball (spinster), bond 20 October 1804. Bartho-
    lomew McCarty (b). [Margaret Williamson Ball was the youngest daughter of
    Captain Williamson and Priscilla (Churchill) Ball (q.v.), p.9. John Walker
    Tomlin was the son of Colonel Walker Tomlin and his first wife nee Sarah
    Fauntleroy (q.v.), p.217. As the second wife of Colonel Walker Tomlin was

Priscilla Ball, the eldest daughter of Captain Williamson and Priscilla
(Churchill) Ball (q.v.), p.9, and his son by his first wife, John Walker
Tomlin, married the youngest daughter of Captain Williamson and Priscilla
(Churchill) Ball, it is seen that father and son married two sisters.
Major John Walker Tomlin (1778-1815) and his wife nee Margaret Williamson
Ball (circa 1782-1819) resided at Clifton in Hanover County; their issue
is in Hayden,p.127-128.]

TOMLIN, MOORE F. and Frances M. Levy, bond 23 April 1805. Ezekiel Levy (b);
John Edwards (w). [Moore Fauntleroy Tomlin was the son of Robert and
Susanna (Fauntleroy) Tomlin, (q.v.), p.217.]

TOMLIN, ROBERT (17??-1794) married circa 1770, Susanna Fauntleroy, daughter of
Colonel Moore and Elizabeth (Mitchell) Fauntleroy (q.v.), p.68. The groom
was the son of Robert Tomlin, Gentleman, (17??-1761), and his wife nee Winifred Webb, daughter of Giles and Elizabeth (Spann) Webb, and brother of Colonel Walker Tomlin (17??-1802) (q.v.), p.217. Robert Tomlin (17??-1761) was
the son of Captain Robert and Elizabeth Tomlin and grandson of Robert Tomlin,
Jr. and Hester Walker, his wife, who are mentioned next below. Robert and
Susanna (Fauntleroy) Tomlin had issue, viz: (a) Robert Tomlin (Jr.), d.s.p.,
1794; (b) Winifred Tomlin; (c) Moore Fauntleroy Tomlin (q.v.), p.217; (d)
Elizabeth Tomlin married 1788 Bartholomew McCarty (q.v.), p.122; (e) Catherine
Tomlin married 1803 Tarpley McCarty (q.v.), p.124; (f) Apphia Fauntleroy Tom-
lin married 1796 Charles Travers McCarty (q.v.), p.123; (g) Eleanor ("Nelly")
Tomlin, d.s.p., 1799; (h) Susanna Fauntleroy Tomlin married 1805 Alfred Beale
(q.v.), p.12. AB#2,p.293,309; WB#6,p.260; WB#9,p.11,19; Fauntleroy,p.664,825.

TOMLIN, ROBERT JR. (16??-1689) married 168? Esther [Hester] Walker, daughter of
Colonel John and Sarah Walker (q.v.); she married (2) John Peirce, Gentleman,
(q.v.), p.156. On 6 July 1698 Robert Tomlin, son of Robert Tomlin, deceased,
choose Captain George Tayler to be his guardian, and he is mentioned in the
records with his wife Elizabeth, circa 1720. Robert Tomlin, Gentleman, (17??-
1761) was the son of Captain Robert and Elizabeth Tomlin and the father of
Robert Tomlin (17??-1794), above, and Colonel Walker Tomlin (17??-1802), below. COB#1,p.31; COB#2,p.295,311; DB#1,p.85; Northern Neck Patent Book #3,p.
123; Fauntleroy, p.825.

TOMLIN, ROBERT G. and Eloisa T. McCarty, bond 26 September 1805. George Saunders
(b); Sydnor McCarty (w). [The groom was the son of Colonel Walker and Sarah
(Fauntleroy) Tomlin and the bride the first born of Bartholomew and Elizabeth
(Tomlin) McCarty (q.v.), p.122. Eloisa Tomlin McCarty was born in North Farnham Parish, 9 January 1789. Doctor Robert Giberne Tomlin died testate in Richmond County in 1812. WB#9,p.404; NFPR.,p.222.]

TOMLIN, WALKER and Sarah Fauntleroy, bond undated. LeRoy Peachey (b). [This
undated bond is filed with others in the 1796 bundle of marriage bonds; from
the phraseology it was written ante 1776. This was the first marriage of
Colonel Walker Tomlin (17??-1802); the recording cited under Doctor Henry
Todd (q.v.), p.216, in the Journals of the House of Burgesses 1773-1776
[Volume #13,p.124], dated 24 May 1774, makes it certain that the marriage
took place prior to this date and likely circa 1772. The groom was the son

of Robert and Winifred (Webb) Tomlin mentioned on the preceeding page. The
bride was the daughter of John Fauntleroy (1724-1761) and his first wife
nee Judith Littlepage, and widow of her first cousin Doctor George Heale
Fauntleroy (17??-1770) (q.v.), p.68. Colonel Walker Tomlin was a man of
affairs in Richmond County where he died intestate in 1802. AB#3,p.80,629,
635; WB#9,p.165; Fauntleroy,p.776-777; the records abound with genealogical
data.]

TOMLIN, WALKER and Priscilla Ball, bond 9 December 1788. Williamson Webb (b);
Robert Tomlin (w). [This was the second marriage of Colonel Walker Tomlin
(17??-1802), above mentioned; the bride was the eldest daughter of Captain
Williamson and Priscilla (Churchill) Ball (q.v.), p.9, and their issue is
outlined by Hayden, p.127. See references above.]

TOMLIN, WILLIAM married by 2 August 1694 Anne Hazlewood, administratrix of George
Hazlewood, deceased. COB#2,p.6,85.

TOMLIN, WILLIAMSON B. and Ann C. Carter, bond 5 May 1819. John Tayloe,Jr. (b).
[The Lunenburg Parish Register records the birth on 27 February 1792 of
Williamson Ball Tomlin, the son of Walker and Sylla (Priscilla) Tomlin.
See Hayden, p.127 for their issue, but the above citation will correct
said reference.]

TOONE   SEE : TUNE : TOONE PAGE 219

TOWLES, RAWLEIGH D. of the State of Kentucky and Fidelia A. Jeffries, bond 6 February 1816. Consent by John Belfield, guardian of the bride. George Saunders (b). [Rawleigh Downman Towles was the son of Major Stokeley and Elizabeth Porteus (Downman) Towles (q.v.), p. 218. In 1817 he deeded his interest
in certain Spotsylvania County real estate (DB "V",p.4). 8V428.]

TOWLES, STOKELEY [MAJOR] married 13 January 1773 in Goochland County, Elizabeth
Porteus Downman, born 21 February 1752, younger of the two daughters of
Captain Robert Downman (1720-1769) and Elizabeth Porteus, his wife, of Richmond County. Major Towles was the son of Stokeley Towles, Gentleman, (1711-
1765) and Elizabeth Martin, his wife, of Lancaster County. There is considerable record of Major Stokeley Towles and his family in the records of Richmond, Goochland, Spotsylvania &c: counties and the family has received attention by genealogical writers. Richmond County AB#2,p.4; DB#15,p.5; WB#7,p.
40,48; 8V320,428; The Towles Story by Mrs. Hester Towles Purcell, D.A.R. Library (1957); The Towles Family of Virginia by Ella Kirk France in the Daughters Of The American Revolution Magazine, Volume 89, p.427-430.

TRASEY, WILLIAM and Lucy Tucker*, bond 13 March 1834. William Gilbert (b);
Benjamin F. Tucker (w).   MBB.,p.116

TREVILIAN, ROSCOW C. and Elizabeth C. Clements*, bond 7 January 1846. James T.
Clements (b); Mary J. Oldham (w). Married 7 January 1846 by the Rev. Elijah
L. Williams.   MBB.,p.270

TUCKER, BENJAMIN and Harriet Thrift*, bond 21 December 1840. John D. Rock (b);
Samuel Wroe (w) and George R. Thrift (w). Married by Rev. Nathan Healy.
                                                              MBB.,p.201

TUCKER, THOMAS and Lucy Hammock*, bond 13 September 1815. The bride writes her own consent and this is also signed by Sarah Hammock. Thomas Bell (b); Fanny Hammock (w) and Lewis Hammock (w).

TUNE : TOONE

TOONE, ANTHONY and Dorcas Morris, bond 7 February 1749. No (b) and/or (w).

TUNE, ANTHONY and Nancy Sanders, bond 13 April 1787. Consent by George Sanders, father of the bride. John Sanders (b); Sarah Sanders (w) and Reuben Sanders (w).

TUNE, ANTHONY and Nancy Tune, bond 13 May 1793. Consent by Samuel Tune and Sarah Tune, parents of the bride. Thomas Tune (b).

TUNE, EDWARD K. and Leannah Dameron, bond 6 January 1823. Samuel Miskell (b). Peter J. Derieux made oath the bride was of lawful age.

TUNE, GEORGE D. and Elizabeth Hammack, bond 1 February 1808. Benedict Hammack (b).

TUNE, GEORGE D. and Patty F. Bryant*, bond 11 December 1815. Richard Smither (b).

TUNE, JAMES married Mary Jackman, 6 September 1680.   NFPR.,p.171

TUNE, JAMES and Mary Bailey (widow), bond 24 December 1796. Jilson B. Burch (b).

TUNE, JESSE and Elizabeth Davis*, bond 12 January 1798. Thomas Thomas (b). William Palmer writes the court clerk Betsy Davis has no guardian; he is uncertain of her age "but I believe she must be eighteen or more."

TUNE, THOMAS married Ann Harris, 24 July 1727.   NFPR.,174

TUNE, THOMAS and Winifred Dobyns, bond 29 January 1791. Consent by Annah Dobyns, mother of the bride. Christopher Chenault (b); Frederick Dobyns (w).

TUNE, THOMAS and Sarah P. Dozier, bond 30 December 1803. Richard Dozier (b).

TUNSTALL, ROBERT of King and Queen County and Ann Smith of Richmond County, bond 7 January 1795. John Smith writes his consent for the marriage of his daughter. David Williams (b); Fanny Smith (w), Patey Y. Richards (w) and Walter Burwell (w).

TURBERVILLE, EDWARD [GENTLEMAN] (16??-1750) of Richmond, King George and Orange counties, married (1) by 1 November 1704 Anne Size, widow of John Size (Sise), by whom he had an only child, Elizabeth Turberville who married Saint John Shropshire (ante 1697-1751); married (2) by 7 November 1735 Sarah (?) Willis Wood Hudson (16??-1761), by whom he had no issue. She was the widow of William Willis (16??-1716), Henry Wood (16??-1722) and Rush Hudson (16??-1735) and her will proved at Orange County court indicates she left issue by each of them. COB#4,p.3; King George County COB#2,p.36; Orange County WB#2, p.310-311; Lennoe S. Drew, The Shropshires and Allied Families, (1948, CS71: S5604), p.6.

TURNER, HEZEKIAH married Elizabeth Hugell, 8 June 1674.   NFPR.,p.171

TURNER, JOHN (16??-1742) of Northumberland County married by 20 January 1718
  Pheby Shippy, daughter of Richard Shippy [Shippie, Shippe &c:], Sr. of Richmond County who died testate in 1698. See references under Henry Metcalfe,
  p.131; also Northumberland County Record Book 1738-1743, p.171.

TURNER, THOMAS of Essex County and Martha Taliaferro, license August 1714.
                                                              DB#6,p.275
  [Thomas Turner is styled in the records "chyrurgeen," clerk of the court,
  gentleman and colonel. In 1726 as Thomas Turner of Hanover Parish, King
  George County, chyrurgeen (surgeon), he purchased 300 acres of land and in
  1729, joined by his wife Sarah, he disposed of this same land and signs the
  deed "T.Turner" in the same manner he records the said deed, being then the
  clerk of King George County court. As he served as clerk of King George
  County court 1723-1742, was a member of the House of Burgesses for many years
  and colonel of the militia, there is no evidence that he practiced his prof-
  ession. On 13 October 1756 as Thomas Turner, Gentleman, of King George County, aged 60 years and upwards, he made a deposition in Caroline County; this
  is the basis for the statement Colonel Thomas Turner was born 169?. Shortly
  after his first marriage, he began purchasing small parcels of land in what
  was soon to become King George County and this estate, immediately on the
  Rappahannock River opposite the town of Port Royal, he called Walsingham.
  He became very wealthy and acquired thousands of acres of land not only in
  King George County but in the adjoining counties in the Northern Neck of
  Virginia and across the Rappahannock River in Caroline and Spotsylvania coun-
  ties. He survived both of his wives and his three children who left issue
  and died testate in King George County in 1758. Colonel Thomas Turner (169?-
  1758) married (1) in August 1714, Martha Taliaferro, eldest child of Colonel
  Richard and Sarah Taliaferro (q.v.), p.203, by whom he had issue two sons,
  viz: (a) Major Harry Turner (171?-1751) who married (1) in 1743 Elizabeth
  Smith (172?-1750), daughter and heiress of Colonel Nicholas and Elizabeth
  Smith (q.v.), p.190-191, by whom he had an only child, Colonel Thomas Turner
  (circa 1745-1787). The handsome tombstone of Major Harry Turner and his
  first wife, bearing the Turner coat-of-arms, was moved some years ago from
  Smith's Mount to Emanuel Church at Port Conway. Unfortunately there is an
  error on the tombstone: the death date of Elizabeth (Smith) Turner is inscribed as 1752; she died in 1750 and by his will dated 14 November 1751
  Major Turner gave directions for this tombstone to be erected at Smith's
  Mount. Major Harry Turner married (2) circa 1751, Elizabeth Fauntleroy (1736-
  1792), daughter of Colonel William Fauntleroy (1713-1793) of Richmond County,
  by whom he had no issue; Major Turner mentions his second wife in his will and
  she married (2) by 7 May 1752, Bowler Cocke, Jr., Gentleman, (1727-1771) and
  promptly renounced the provisions made for her in Major Turner's will; she
  married (3) Thomas Adams and moved to Augusta County where he died testate
  in 1788. (b) Thomas Turner, Jr. (171?-1757), younger of the two sons of Col.
  Thomas and Martha (Taliaferro) Turner, married his cousin Mary Taliaferro,
  daughter of Charles and Sarah (Thornton) Taliaferro of Caroline County; he
  held property in Spotsylvania and Caroline counties and died intestate in
  Caroline County leaving issue. Colonel Thomas Turner (169?-1758) married (2)
  circa 1728 Sarah Taliaferro, sister of his first wife and youngest child of

Colonel Richard and Sarah Taliaferro (q.v.), p. 203; by her he had two
daughters, viz: (c) Mary Turner who d.s.p. after her father and (d) Sarah
Turner who married 9 July 1748, Captain Edward Dixon (circa 1702-1779),
merchant of Port Royal and man of affairs in Caroline County, and died
before her father leaving two sons. Richmond County DB#7,p.274,435; suit
in chancery, Dixon vs Turner, King George County COB#3,p.994-1012; King
George County DB#1,p.374,489; King George County COB#3,p.67,487; Caroline
County COB#4,p.249,409; 19T106-109; 20V438-439; Eubank,p.13-14; Fauntleroy,
p.526.]

TUTT, RICHARD (16??-1729) of Richmond and King George counties, married by 26 May
1703 Mary Underwood, daughter of Major William Underwood (1649-1717); she
married (2) circa 1745, John Fox of Spotsylvania County. Richmond County
MRB.,p.32 and WB#3,p.344; Westmoreland County W&D#3,p.148; 21T288-289.

TUXENT, STEWARD (bachelor) and Lucy Belfield (spinster), bond 8 October 1829.
Daniel Maiden (b). MBB.,p.57

U

UNDERWOOD, JOHN (16??-1723), eldest son of Major William Underwood (1649-1717),
married by 28 June 1719 Elizabeth Slaughter, daughter of Francis Slaughter
(circa 1658-1719) and Margaret, his first wife, (q.v.), p.189. DB#7,p.418;
King George County DB#2,p.476; see Underwood genealogy in 38V267 et seq.

UNDERWOOD, WILLIAM (16??-1726), son of Major William Underwood (1649-1717) of
Richmond County, married Jael Shippy, daughter of Richard and Ellen (Mott)
Shippy (q.v.), p.186. She married (2) Samuel Reeds (Reids) who died testate in King George County in 1749/50. Jael (Shippy) Underwood Reeds left
issue by both husbands and there is considerable record of these people on
the records of King George, Culpeper, and Fauquier counties. King George
County DB#3,p.130,345 and COB#2,p.652; see the Underwood genealogy in 38V
267 et seq.

V

VAN NESS, WILLIAM P. and Evelina Jane Montgomery, bond 5 January 1848. Consent
by Elizabeth T. Montgomery, mother of the bride. William Y. Sturman (b).
Married 6 January 1848 by the Rev. George Northam. MBB.,p.304

VASS, VINCENT and Judith Ball (widow), bond 27 November 1755. Samuel Rust (b).

VEENEY : VENEA : VENEY : VENIE

VENIE, EDWARD and Mary Thompson*, bond 8 September 1845. Henry Thompson (b);
Samuel B. Thrift (w). Married 11 September 1845 by the Rev. Elijah L.
Williams. MBB.,p.263

VEENEY, JAMES and Rachael Veeney, bond 14 July 1848. Joseph Veeney, Sr. (b).
MBB.,p.311

VENIE, JESSE and Anna Thompson*, bond 7 January 1819. Oddly the bride writes
her consent for the license to issue for her marriage to Travis Venea.
Hannamore Thompson gives her consent; no relationship stated. Henry Thompson (b); William Brickey, Senr (w) and William Brickey, Junr (w).

VENEY, MOSES and Judy Veney*, license 1 November 1851. Robert Jackson (w).
Married by the Rev. Elijah L. Williams.

VENEA, TRAVIS - See Jesse Venie, above.

VENEY, WASHINGTON and Mary Veney "free persons of colour," bond 8 January 1847.
Joe Veney, Sr. (b).   MBB.,p.286

VICKERS, THOMAS and Elizabeth Morris, bond 29 December 1847. Consent by John
Morris and Elizabeth Morris, parents of the bride. Robert Sanders (b);
Mary A. Sanders (w). Married 30 December 1847 by the Rev. John Pullen.
MBB.,p.304

W

WAIDE, ROBERT C. and Peggy Dennis, bond 12 September 1804. John Dennis (b).

WALE, TIMOTHY and Molly Alloway, bond 26 September 1792. Consent by Isaac Alloway, father of the bride. Jery Alderson (b).

WALKER, ALEXANDER and Penelope Beckwith, bond 17 April 1798. Clement Shackleford (b).

WALKER, EPPA: married Jane A. Dodson, 11 May 1847. No bond found. From a list
of marriages returned to the clerk of Richmond County by the Rev. Mr. Bartholomew Dodson on 3 February 1848.

WALKER, FRANCIS S. and Alice Jane Belfield*, bond 5 February 1849. William B.
Belfield (b).   MBB.,p.321

WALKER, FREEMAN (1734-1766) of Dinwiddie and Brunswick Counties, married between
1750-1757 Frances Belfield (born 22 March 1736), youngest child of Thomas
Wright and Mary (Meriwether) Belfield of Richmond County. She married (2)
Henry Broadnax and left issue by each marriage. AB#1,p.414; WB#5,p.652;
Garland Evans Hopkins, Freeman Forbears (1942),p.17,18; Judge L.H. Jones,
Captain Roger Jones of London and Virginia (Albany,N.Y.,1891),p.182-184;
21W(1)268; Brunswick County WB#3,p.454, will of Freeman Walker (1734-1766).

WALKER, JOHN [COLONEL] (16??-1668/9) married (1) unknown, by whom he had four
daughters, viz: (a) Anne Walker who married (1) circa 1668 John Payne, Jr.,
and married (2) 1670, John Daingerfield - detailed in Payne, p.53-56;

(b) Frances Walker; (c) Jane Walker married John Deane, Gentleman, (q.v.), p.53; (d) Elizabeth Walker; married (2) circa 1662 Sarah (?) Fleet, widow of Colonel Henry Fleet (c.1600-1660), by whom he had two daughters, viz: (e) Sarah Walker, born circa 1663, married Edwin Conway, Gentleman, (q.v.),p.43-44; (f) Hester [Esther] Walker, born circa 1665, married (1) Robert Tomlin, Jr. (q.v.),p.217 and (2) John Peirce, (q.v.),p.156. Sarah (?) Fleet Walker, widow, married (3) Colonel John Stone (q.v.), p.195; she must have been considerably the junior of her three husbands. On 15 October 1662, about the time of the marriage of Colonel John Walker and Mrs. Sarah Fleet, he executed a bond of record in Lancaster County COB#1, p.193, obligating himself "to pay unto Mary Burden the natural daughter of Mrs. Sara Fleete, £400 Current Money of England" when she is 16 years of age or upon her day of marriage and if she should die before then, the said payment to be made "unto the next heir or heirs of Mrs. Sara Fleete's body begotten by ye above said Colonel John Walker." It appears, from the various recordings, that after the death of Captain Henry Fleet his widow had a daughter dubbed "Mary Burden!" I have made reference above to Payne,p. 53-56, where Colonel Payne gives a sketch of the Walker family, however, this usually dependable source errs in stating the spouses of (f) Hester [Esther] Walker to such an extent it must be a typographical error. Richmond County DB#2,p.41; Sweeny,p.6-7,81-82,161-163; A.P.& P.,p.172.

WALKER, THOMAS of Northumberland County and Sarah Coleman, bond 27 April 1793. Thomas Coelman, father of the bride, gave his consent. Robert Coleman (b). [The bride was the daughter of Thomas and Betty Coelman (q.v.), p.41).]

WALKER, THOMAS and Mira Haynie, bond 27 December 1803. Wilalmira W. Haynie consents to the marriage of her daughter. Thomas T. Montague (b); Daniel L. McCarty (w). [The bride was the daughter of Captain Holland and Wilalmira (Webb) Haynie (q.v.), p.91.]

WALKER, THOMAS of Northumberland County and Milly Douglass, bond 23 December 1813. Eppa: Jones (b); J.G. White (w).

WALKER, THOMAS BELFIELD, son of Freeman and Frances (Belfield) Walker (q.v.), p. 222, married in 1803 his first cousin once removed, Elizabeth Smith, daughter of Colonel William and Mary (Belfield) Smith (q.v.),p.191. Garland Evans Hopkins, Freeman Forbears (1942),p.18.

WALKER, THOMAS W. and Juliet A. Weathers, bond 4 July 1832. Consent by Rebecca Weathers, mother of the bride. Ebenezer Jeffries (b); William R. Jeffires (w).   MBB.,p.90

WALKER, WILLIAM of Fayette County and Beckey Gill of Richmond County, bond 25 August 1788. Spencer Gill (b).

WALLACE, JOSEPH and Williann E. Garland*, bond 24 May 1843. Isaac S. Jeffries (b); Mary Garland (w) and William D. Garland (w).   MBB.,p.238

WALTER[S], THOMAS married by 11 November 1707 Rebecca Newton, widow of Gerrard Newton (16??-1706) (q.v.), p.146-147.

WARING, WILLIAM L. of Essex County and Elizabeth C. Hudnall, bond 1 May 1809.
Foushee G. Tebbs (b).

WARMOTH   SEE : WEYMOTH : WARMOTH PAGE

WARRICK, PHILIP and Bury Hazard*, bond 19 November 1839. Joseph T. Hanks (b).
                                                                MBB.,p.186

WARRING, THOMAS married Alice Underwood, 5 October 1673.   NFPR.,p.179

WARWICK, THOMAS S. of Lancaster County and Elizabeth B. Stott*, bond 29 March
1831. Richard Stott (b).   MBB.,p.76

WASHINGTON, SAMUEL and Maria Cook*, bond 28 November 1834. John Massey (b);
O.E.P. Hazard (w).   MBB.,p.127

WASHINGTON, THOMAS MUSE and Catharine Wheldon, bond 2 September 1799. Consent
by John and Amelia Wheldon, parents of the bride. John Wheldon (b); W.
Fergusson (w). [The Rev. Mr. Thomas Muse Washington (1772-1838) was a
Baptist Minister in Westmoreland County and environs; his wife was the
daughter of John and Amelia (Oldham) Wheldon (q.v.) of Richmond County.
The Rev. Mr. Thomas Muse Washington is identified 53V317, but this account
errs in spelling her maiden name. Rev. and Mrs. Washington left no issue
andhis will remains of record in Westmoreland County W&D#30,p.77. ECD Papers, Box 27, Yeatman Folder, contins the Bible record of the Rev. Mr. Thomas Muse Washington.]

WATSON, JOHN married Mary Huntly, 7 June 1730.   NFPR.,p.183

WATSON, JOHN and Mary McGinnis (widow), Bond 6 September 1790. Richard Clement
(b).

WATTS, JOHN married Mary Alverson, 9 January 1729/30.   NFPR.,p.183

WATTS, JOHN T. and Haney Hogans (widow)*, bond 19 February 1811. George Shearley (b).

WATTS, RICHARD and Anne McKay, bond 16 December 1767. John McKay (b).

WEADON, JAMES and Catherine Brown, license 13 July 1852. Richard Scates (w)
and Martin V. Bowen (w). Married 14 July 1852 by the Rev. William Balderson.

WEADON, SHELTON and Ann Ryals*, bond 22 December 1840. John McGuire (b). Married 22 December 1840 by the Rev. John M. Waddey.   MBB.,p.202

WEATHERS, EPPA: and Elizabeth Fleming, bond 6 October 1800. Consent by William
Fleming, father of the bride. Samuel Fleming (b); Abner Howe (w).

WEATHERS, GEORGE and Ma[r]y Sandy, bond 8 May 1790. Charles Travers McCarty
(b); Samuel Peachy (w). [George Weathers died in 1813; see WB#9,p.436.]

WEATHERS, JAMES and Hannah E. Harper*, bond 24 December 1844. James Crask (b);
    Richard S. Harper (w).   MBB.,p.252

WEATHERS, JAMES and Elizabeth Sutton*, bond 7 January 1846. James B. Moxley (b).
    Married 7 January 1846 by the Rev. Mr. Elijah L. Williams.   MBB.,p.270

WEATHERS, JOHN and Rebecca Beckwith Kelsick, bond 4 January 1790. M. Kelsick giv-
    es her consent for the license to be issued. George Thrift (b). [The bride
    was the daughter of Captain Younger and Mary (Barnes) Kelsick (q.v.), p.111.
    ECD Papers cite the Bible record of John Weathers (6 August 1763-27 July 1822)
    and Rebecca Beckwith Kelsick (10 January 1771-10 October 1836), his wife, who
    were married 4 January 1790 in Richmond County; they had issue, viz: (a) Will-
    iam Younger Weathers, born 16 September 1790 (q.v.) p.225; (b) Richard Kelsick
    Weathers, born 30 November 1793; (c) Elizabeth McKenny Weathers, born 12 Oct-
    ober 1795; (d) Richard Kelsick Weathers, born 1 October 1797; (e) Isabella
    Kelsick Weathers, born 30 October 1799; (f) Eleanor Weathers, born 30 July
    1802, died 10 April 1837, married 27 December 1818 William R. Jeffries (5
    April 1796-16 December 1833), son of Thomas and Ann Adams (Smith) Jeffries
    (q.v.),p.103; (g) Catherine Weathers, born 2 January 1805; (h) Addison Weath-
    ers, born 2 October 1807; (i) Malvina Weathers, born 2 March 1810; (j) Juliet
    Weathers, born 20 March 1813. AB#3,p.137,198; WB#9,p.5.]

WEATHERS, JOSEPH and Jane Brooks*, bond 20 March 1850. Samuel L. Beachman (b);
    Lemuel G. Bell (w). Married 20 March 1850 by the Rev. William N. Ward.
                                                                       MBB.,p.334

WEATHERS, SAMUEL (16??-1729) married circa 1718 Elizabeth Dune, daughter of Pat-
    rick Dune who died testate in 1719. WB#4,p.126; WB#5,p.136.

WEATHERS, VINCENT and Elizabeth Gill, bond 29 July 1799. Consent by George Gill,
    father of the bride. Griffin G. Garland (b).

WEATHERS, WILLIAM and Frances A. Hardwick (spinster), bond 9 February 1809. Con-
    sent by Aaron Hardwick, father of the bride. Daniel Harrison (b); James
    Harrison (w) and Daniel H. Hardwick (w).

WEATHERS, WILLIAM YOUNGER and Catherine W.H. Jackson, bond 27 June 1814. William
    G. Garland (b).

WEATHERS, WILLIAM Y. and Mary Leckie (widow)*, bond 16 January 1817. George Saund-
    ers (b); William R. Jeffries (w).

WEATHERS, WILLIAM Y. and Hannah R. Wright*, bond 27 July 1840. Richard O. Jeff-
    ries (b).   MBB.,p.196

WEBB, EWELL of Northumberland County and Jane Pullin (widow)*, bond 30 July 1808.
    William H. Davenport (b).

WEBB, EWELL of Northumberland County and Charity Ann Hall, bond 29 November 1827.
    William Forester of Lancaster County (b); Olive Stott (w).   MBB.,p.31
    Consent by Mary Stott, mother of the bride. WFMR dubbs the bride, Charity
    Ann Stott.

WEBB, HIEROME and Elizabeth Marmaduke*, bond 15 November 1833. William H. Hill
(b); Martha Hill (w).   MBB.,p.111

WEBB, HIRAM P. of Northumberland County and Mary Ann G. Headley*, bond 13 December 1837. Consent by Griffin Headley; no relationship stated. James
Elmore (b); Daniel M. Headley (w).   MBB.,p.162

WEBB, ISAAC married Mary Bedwell, 6 April 1678.   NFPR.,p.179

WEBB, ISAAC and Rebecca Suggitt (widow), license March 1715/16.   DB#6,p.275

WEBB, ISAAC (1709-1760) married Frances Barber (circa 1716-1782), youngest child
of Colonel Charles and Frances (Glascock) Barber (q.v.), p.9. The groom
was the son of Giles and Elizabeth (Spann) Webb and brother of John Spann
Webb (q.v.), p.226. [See references under the said John Spann Webb, below.]

WEBB, ISAAC and Elizabeth Kirk, bond 6 October 1800. Thomas T. Reynolds (b).

WEBB, JAMES and Fanny T. Reynolds, bond 2 February 1825. Consent by Benjamin
Reynolds, father of the bride. Benjamin Reynolds (b).   MBB.,p.8

WEBB, JEREMIAH and Apphia Northen*, bond 29 February 1808. William Webb (b).
AB#11,p.346; see notes, Thomas H. Jeffries, p.103.

WEBB, JOHN married Mary Samford, 14 July 1673.   NFPR.,p.179

WEBB, JOHN and Judith Ball (spinster), bond 17 September 1759. John Suggitt (b).

WEBB, JOHN and Polly How*, bond 2 April 1799. William Webb (b); Nancy How (w).

WEBB, JOHN and Mary Ann Newman, license 1851. Consent by John Hunter, guardian
of the bride. T.N. Balderson (w) and R. Saunders (w). Married 18 November
1851 by the Rev. John Pullen.

WEBB, JOHN SPANN (1705-1756), son of Giles Webb, Gentleman, (1677-1732) and his
wife nee Elizabeth Spann of Northumberland County, married circa 1740 Sarah
Alderson, only child of Jeloff Alderson, Jr. (16??-1719) and his wife nee
Rebecca Hatton. The only child of John Spann and Sarah (Alderson) Webb was
William Webb, Gentleman, (circa 1742-1765) (q.v.) p.226. AB#1,p.144; DB#12,
p.517,541,719; DB#13,p.206; WB#4,p.79,267; WB#5,p.174; WB#6,p.91; Northumberland County Record Book 1718-1726,p.287.

WEBB, RICHARD and Elizabeth Dale, bond 19 December 1795. Chichester Tapscott (b).
Charles Barnes [(?) Bane] certifies Elizabeth Dale, daughter of Joseph Dale,
deceased, is over twenty one years of age.

WEBB, WILLIAM and Winifred Griffin Tarpley, bond 16 December 1763. LeRoy Peachey
(b). [William Webb, Gentleman, (circa 1742-1765) was the only son of John
Spann and Sarah (Alderson) Webb (q.v.), p.226. Bond 4 February 1760 of John
Tarpley as guardian of William Webb, orphan of John Spann Webb, deceased. His
widow, Winifred Griffin (Tarpley) Webb married (2) 20 November 1771, Captain

James Montague (q.v.), p.135; she died testate in Richmond County in 1806.
William and Winifred Griffin (Tarpley) Webb had an only child, Wilalmira
Webb (1765-1822),who married Captain Holland Haynie (q.v.), p.91. Captain
James and Winifred Griffin (Tarpley) Montague had two children, viz: Harriot
Montague and Thomas Tarpley Montague. AB#1,p.567-569,691; AB#2,p.25; DB#9,
p.824; DB#13,p.206; WB#6,p.391; WB#7,p.8; WB#9,p.291; WB#10,p.8; suit in
chancery styled Montague vs Webb (1786).]

WEBB, WILLIAM and Fanny Reynolds*, bond 28 January 1797. James Webb (b).

WEBB, WILLIAM and Margaret M.C. Shepherd, bond 17 November 1825. Cyrus Simmonds
    (b).   MBB.,p.14

WEBB, WILLIAM and Nancy Reynolds*, bond 20 December 1842. Williamson Webb (b);
    James Reynolds (w). Married 21 December 1842 by the Rev. William N. Ward.
                                                               MBB.,p.229
    [The bride was the daughter of Richard and Sinah (Fowles) Reynolds, (q.v.),
    p.168. Richmond County, Petition to the Legislature, 22 January 1845.]

WEBB, WILLIAMSON and Sarah Askins*, bond 22 January 1822. John Gibbs (b).

WEBSTER, HENRY and Mary Ann Collins, married 15 September 1730.   NFPR.,p.183

WEBSTER, THOMAS and Katherine English, married 11 September 1739.   NFPR.,p.184

WEEDEN, THOMAS and Elizabeth Bowing, bond 4 June 1805. Consent by Joshua Bowing;
    no relationship stated. John Bowing (b); Joshua Bowing Jr. (w) and Molly
    Bowing (w).

WEIR, WILLIAM J. of Essex County and Harriet B. Mitchell, bond 18 September 1817.
    Consent by Priscilla Mitchell, mother of the bride. Robert B. Mitchell (b);
    J.L. Mitchell (w). [The marriage was announced in the Fredericksburg Vir-
    ginia Herald of 8 October 1817; this account states the groom was a merchant
    of Tappahannock and the bride the "daughter of Robert Mitchell, Esq., deceas-
    ed, of Grove Mount, Richmond County." They were married 18 September 1817 by
    the Rev. Mr. Templeman. William James Weir was the son of James Weir of Spot-
    sylvania County and his wife nee Lucy Marye, daughter of the Reverend Mr. James
    Marye (1731-1780), rector of Saint George's Church, and his first wife nee
    Sarah Vaulx. W.A. Crozier, Spotsylvania County Records (New York, 1905), p.
    35,508.]

WELCH, EDWARD and Hester Mills (widow), license January 1712/13.   DB#6,p.275

WELCH, JOHN and Hannah Collinsworth, bond not dated. The phraseology indicates
    the bond was executed prior to 1776 but it is filed in the 1796 marriage
    bond bundle. John Lysle (b).

WELDON   SEE : WHELDON PAGE 229

WELDON, DAVID and Elizabeth Davis, bond 14 April 1807. Consent by Edmund Davis,
    father of the bride. John Smith (b); James B. Burwell (w).

WELDON, SAMPLE and Sally Gaskins "Free persons of colour," bond 2 June 1828.
    George Henry (b).   MBB.,p.35

WELLDON, JOHN married Winifred Hobs, 7 July 1729.   NFPR.,p.183

WELLFORD, ARMISTEAD N. [DOCTOR] and Elizabeth L. Carter, daughter of Robert Worme-
    ley Carter, Esq., of Sabine Hall, license 30 December 1851. Married 30 Dec-
    ember 1851 by the Rev. Mr. John P. McGuire.

WELLFORD, HORACE [DOCTOR] and Elizabeth How, bond 24 July 1813. Consent by John
    How, father of the bride. Joseph Palmer (b); Clement Shackleford (w). [The
    death of Mrs. Betsy Howe Wellford, consort of Dr. Horace Wellford, near
    Richmond Court House, on 15 July 1820, was announced in the Fredericksburg
    Virginia Herald of 22 July 1820. Dr. Horace Wellford (1790-1828) married (2)
    on 29 September 1822, Rebecca Plater, second daughter of Thomas Plater, Esq.
    of Georgetown, D.C.; their marriage was announced in the Fredericksburg Vir-
    ginia Herald of 5 October 1822. The Fredericksburg Political Arena of 30
    May 1828 announced the death in Richmond County on 23 May 1828 of Doctor
    Horace Wellford, formerly of Fredericksburg. He was the son of Doctor Robert
    and Catherine (Yates) Wellford (q.v.), under Rowland Thornton, p.211-213.]

WELLING, CALEB (16??-1692) of Christ Church Parish, Middlesex County, married by
    1 June 1692 Elizabeth (Weekes) Vause, daughter of Abraham Weekes, Gentleman,
    and widow of John Vause, Gentleman, who died 9 September 1691. Caleb Welling
    [Whelling] died 3 September 1692 and his widow married (3) 14 December 1693,
    Thomas Spencer of King and Queen County. Richmond County COB#1,p.23; see the
    wills of Abraham Weekes (1692) and John Vause [Vaus] (1691) of record in Mid-
    dlesex County; CCPR.,p.39,53.

WELLS, BARNABAS [BARNSBY, BARNEBE &c:] married by 2 June 1731, Joyce Smith, only
    child of Thomas Smith, then deceased, who was the eldest son of William
    Smith, also deceased, who died testate in Richmond County. The Wellses were
    heirs of Francis Lucas (q.v.), p.121 and by 1741 they were residing in Amelia
    County, Virginia. DB#8,p.570; DB#10,p.28,266.

WELLS, STEPHEN married Alice Howard, 3 December 1677.   NFPR.,p.179

WELLS, STEPHEN (16??-1723) married 170? Elizabeth (Williams) Settle (16??-1725),
    widow of Francis Settle, Jr. (16??-1701/2) (q.v.), p.184 and daughter of Rice
    Williams (16??-1701); she left issue by each marriage. DB#1,p.165; DB#3,p.
    96; DB#8,p.169; DB#9,p.471; WB#2,p.37,45,125; WB#4,p.227,261.

WELLS, STEPHEN married Priscilla Redman, 21 August 1729.   NFPR.,p.183

WELSH, MICHAEL "of the Province of New England," and Ann Hendren (spinster), bond
    1 February 1771. William Hendren (b).

WEST, ROBERT of Richmond County and Margaret Buckles of Christ Church Parish, Lan-
    caster County, married 20 June 1735. Bondsman and witnesses: Hugh Brent,
    William Ball and Thomas Edwards.   LCMR#1,p.14
    [The bride was the daughter of John Buckles who died testate in Lancaster
    County in 1734; Lee,p.28.]

WEYMOTH : WARMOTH

WARMOTH, JOHN and Amey Churchwill*, bond 5 January 1791. Thomas Warmoth (b).

WEYMOTH, JOHN and Nancy Rice, bond 3 February 1804. Eppa: Jones (b).

WEYMOTH, THOMAS JR. and Judith Pritchett (widow), bond 4 July 1791. Charles T.
McCarty (b); Robert Tomlin, Jr. (w).

WHEELER, WILLIAM C. of Northumberland County and Elizabeth Pope (widow)*, bond
8 December 1817. Rawleigh Hazard (b); Richard Smither (w).

WHELDON   SEE WELDON PAGE 227

WHELDON, JOHN and Amelia Oldham, bond 8 December 1778. William Greenlaw (b).
[The bride was the daughter of William Oldham and granddaughter of William
and Priscilla (McLaughlin) Oldham (q.v.),p.150. Amelia (Oldham) Wheldon
died 28 January 1819, aged 56 years, in Richmond County; her obituary in
the Fredericksburg Virginia Herald of 13 February 1819 says "Her life was
exemplary as a wife, sister, mother and friend."]

WHELLING, CALEB   SEE CALEB WELLING PAGE 228

WHITE, ABRAHAM and Katy Morris (spinster)*, bond 3 July 1797. George Connolly
(b).

WHITE, BENJAMIN and Elizabeth Hoult [Holt], bond 7 February 1803. Abraham White
(b); John Hoult (w) and Griffin Finch (w).

WHITE, DANIEL [CAPTAIN] (16??-1748/9) and Ann Sterne, license February 1712/13.
DB#6,p.275
[The groom was the son of Thomas White (16??-1687) of Westmoreland County
and Jane, his wife, who married (4) Thomas Pace, Gentleman, (q.v.), p.152.
The bride was the daughter of David Sterne and Agatha, his second wife,
(q.v.), p.195. The land of Captain Daniel White and that of his brother,.
Captain George White (next below), fell into King George County in 1721
and in 1724 he received his commission in the militia and took the military
oath. Captain Daniel White died testate in King George County but his last
will and Testament was recorded in now lost WB#1 (1721-1752); however, the
inventory of his estate is of record in DB#6,p.41 and the remaining records
offer considerable genealogical data. MRB.,p.34A; King George County COB#1,
p.228; COB#2,p.608; DB#1,p.92; DB#2,p.501,510; DB#3,p.250; DB#6,p.41; Payne,
p.367-369.]

WHITE, GEORGE [CAPTAIN] (16??-1738), son of Thomas and Jane White (above mentioned), married by 13 September 1712 Elizabeth Birkett, one of the four daughters of John and Ann (Mills) Birkett (q.v.), p.18. Captain George White died
testate in King George County but his last will and Testament was recorded
in now lost WB#1 (1721-1752). In 1755 George White (Jr.), son and heir of
George and Elizabeth (Birkett) White, conveyed certain real estate in King
George County which he had inherited from his late mother. DB#6,p.72; WB#4,

p.138; King George County COB#1,p.228; COB#2,p.172; DB#1,p.51; DB#2,p.504; DB#4,p.191,240; Payne,p.367-369.

WHITE, GEORGE and Ann Wilson (spinster), bond 10 March 1754. John Tidwell (b).

WHITE, JAMES H. and Susan Hinson*, bond 20 January 1841. James M. Morris (b). Married 20 January 1841 by the Rev. John M. Waddey.   MBB.,p.205

WHITE, JOHN married by 1746 Ann Gower, only child of Francis Gower (1706-1727) and Rachel, his wife, to survive infancy. In 1737 John White was a resident of Richmond County and in 1746 he was living in King George County. By 1752 the Whites were residing in Orange County where her step-father and mother, John and Rachel Bramham (q.v.), p.23, were living, and joined in a deed to convey her interest in certain land in Richmond County which had descended to her as an heir of her great-great-great-grandfather, Thomas Mead(e), an early settler in that part of Rappahannock County which became Richmond County in 1692. AB#1,p.79, DB#7,p.13,14,60,492,545,547; DB#8,p. 55; DB#9,p.100,388,633; DB#10,p.40,366,368; DB#11,p.152,155.

WHITE, JOHN G. and Amelia A.T. Glascock*, bond 7 December 1816. Thomas L. Matthews (w); Manus Rowan (b).

WHITE, WILLIAM and Margaret Overton, license May 1712.   DB#6,p.275

WHITE, WILLIAM L. and Louisa J. Crewdson, bond 9 June 1825. John G. Crewdson (b).   MBB.,p.11

WHITING, WILLIAM married Martha Brown, daughter of Maxfield Brown (16??-1745) of Richmond and King George counties; by 5 November 1731 he absconded leaving her with several infant children. King George County COB#1,p.579.

WILCOX, JOHN married Ann Jenings, 2 March 1729/30.   NFPR.,p.183

WILCOX, JOHN and Nancy Goldsbary, bond 8 September 1821. Charles Everitt (b).

WILCOX, JOHN and Sally Joy*, bond 21 August 1835. Samuel W. Neasom (b); John R. Crutcher (w).   MBB.,p.135

WILCOX, WILLIAM and Frances Clark*, bond 13 February 1840. John D. Efford (b); Sydnor Efford (w).   MBB.,p.193

WILDEN [WILDY], WILLIAM married 176?, Sarah (Jesper) Williams, daughter of Thomas and Sarah (Taylor) Jesper (q.v.),p.106 and widow of John Williams (q.v.), p. 231. The births of the children of Sarah (Jesper) Williams Wilden (Wildy), by both husbands, are recorded in the North Farnham Parish Register. DB#12, p.643; WB#5,p.685,722.

WILDEN, WILLIAM married between 1769-1771, Anne Jones, daughter of Charles Jones who died testate in 1769. AB#1,p.590;WB#7,p.23.

WILLIAMS, ABRAHAM and Betty Jesper, bond 14 September 1764. Edward Oglesby (b). [The following two guardian bonds are in the unindexed loose paper files.

7 July 1760: Thomas Smith gave bond as guardian of Abraham Williams, orphan of Henry Williams, deceased. 7 February 1763: Edward Oglesby gave bond as guardian of Betty Jesper, orphan of Thomas Jesper, deceased.]

WILLIAMS, DANIEL and Ann Milner, bond 5 January 1761. Charles Taylor (b).

WILLIAMS, DAVID and Eleanor Ball Glascock, bond 6 May 1797. Joseph Tapscott (b).

WILLIAMS, FRANCIS married by 3 February 1704 Anne Jennings, relict and adminis-tratrix of John Jennings who died testate in 1698. COB#3,p.305.

WILLIAMS, FRANCIS and Alice Mathews, license October 1710.   DB#6,p.275

WILLIAMS, FRANCIS married Rachel Thornton, daughter of Thomas and Susanna (Smith) Thornton (q.v.), p.213-214. By 1762 Rachel (Thornton) Williams is deceased but her husband is yet living; their children were: (a) Susanna Williams married by 1762 William Brown of Westmoreland County; (b) Marina Williams, under age in 1762, was the wife of George Beard of Westmoreland County; and (c) Ann Williams, under age and unmarried in 1762. DB#12,p.361,422.

WILLIAMS, HENRY and Susanna Gower,married 22 December 1726.   NFPR.,p.183

WILLIAMS, HENRY and Priscilla Oldham, married 22 January 1729/30.   NFPR.,p.183
     [The bride was the widow of William Oldham (q.v.), p.150.]

WILLIAMS, HENRY and Ann Lightfoot, bond 18 September 1761. George Williams (b); Daniel Jesper (w) and Jesse Morris (w). [The bride was the daughter of Daniel and Alitia (Algar) Lightfoot (q.v.), p.119.]

WILLIAMS, JOHN and Eliz.^{a} Batten (widow), license July 1712.   DB#6,p.275
     [The bride was the widow of John Batten who died testate a few weeks before; his will was dated 3 May 1712 and was admitted to probate 3 September 1712. John Williams died intestate in 1715 and his widow married by 7 March 1716, William Stokes of Essex County (q.v.), p.195. DB#6,p.139; DB#7,p.100; WB#3, p.109,205.]

WILLIAMS, JOHN married by 7 February 1752 Sarah Jesper, daughter of Thomas and Sarah (Taylor) Jesper; she married (2) William Wilden (Wildy) (q.v.), p.230. See references cited under Thomas Jesper and also Thomas Freshwater, p.74, who married (2) Elizabeth Jesper (1712-1772), also daughter of Thomas Jesper. WB#5,p.685,722.

WILLIAMS, JOHN and Winefred Howard, bond 28 December 1781. LeRoy Howard (b).

WILLIAMS, LUKE and Katherine Barber, bond 8 May 1761. Thomas Barber (b).

WILLIAMS, MORGAN married in 1691 Catherine Stewart, widow, who next married Rich-ard White,who died in 1703. Morgan Williams d.s.p. and in 1705 Catherine White, widow, petitioned the office of the Proprietors of the Northern Neck of Virginia to grant to her son William Stewart 133 1/2 acres of land in Richmond County which had escheated to the Proprietors by the death of Morgan

Williams. On 25 January 1706 William Stewart received a grant for the aforementioned land and he died intestate in Richmond County in 1717.   DB#1,p.85;
WB#2,p.60; Northern Neck Patent Book #3,p.123.

WILLIAMS, ROGER married Ann Williams, 5 August 1728.   NFPR.,p.183
[The bride was the daughter of John Williams, Sr. who died testate in 1751.
WB#5,p.659.]

WILLIAMS, ROGER and Eliz.^{a} Serjant (widow), bond 10 February 1744. William North-
en (b).

WILLIAMS, SAMUEL and Betty Ann Hill, bond 12 October 1751. William Dew (b).

WILLIAMS, THADDEUS (17??-1799) married by 1787 Catherine Corrie, daughter of John
Corrie of Essex County. AB#3,p.222; WB#9,p.238; Essex County WB#14,p.74;
see notes under John Corrie Roy, p.174.

WILLIAMS, THOMAS and Katherine Hamon, license March 1712/13.   DB#6,p.275
[Katherine (Hammond) Williams married (2) Samuel Steele (q.v.), p.194.
Thomas Williams died in Richmond County in 1718. WB#4,p.39.]

WILLIAMS, THOMAS married Sarah Audley, 2 October 1726.   NFPR.,p.183

WILLIAMS, THOMAS married Winifred Pycraft, 8 June 1732.   NFPR.,p.183

WILLIAMS, WILLIAM of New Castle County,#Pennsylvania, married long before 8 June
1714 Anne Erwin, daughter of Thomas Erwin (circa 1629-1676) of Rappahannock
County. DB#6,p.249; Sweeny,p.32,40. [# Area in dispute; now Delaware.]

WILLIAMS, YOUELL and Sally Crabb, bond 2 May 1791. John Smaw (b).

WILLIS, JOHN SR. (16??-1715) married (1) unknown to me, and left issue; married
(2) per marriage contract dated 22 July 1693, Matilda Thacker, widow of
Henry Thacker who died testate in Richmond County in 1693, by whom he had
no issue. DB#1,p.84; WB#3,p.214. His eldest son is mentioned next below.

WILLIS, JOHN JR. (16??-1728) married by 1698 Mary Coghill (16??-1748), daughter
of James Coghill (16??-1685) of Rappahannock County and Mary, his wife, who
married (2) Henry Duckberry. Mary (?) Coghill Duckberry died testate
in Essex County in 1715. Mary (Coghill) Willis (16??-1748) married (2) John
Jennings (16??-1735) and both died in King George County during the period
(1721-52) covered by the now lost King George County WB#1; she had no issue
by either husband. DB#2,p.81; see also suit Willis vs Jennings (1732) in
King George County COB#1,p.607 et seq., and the two Coghill genealogies,
viz: James Henry Coghill, The Family of Coghill (Cambridge, Mass., 1879) and
The Family of Coghill Continued by William Hawes Coghill (Richmond, Va.,1956).

WILLIS, WILLIAM (16??-1716), second son of John Willis, Sr. and his unknown first
wife, married Sarah ___[?]___ (16??-1761) [see notes under Edward Turberville, her last husband, p.219] and their eldest son was John Willis (170?-
1762). He married in Saint Paul's Parish, Stafford County, 17 January 1734/5

Elizabeth Plunkett of Hanover Parish, King George County, and disposed of
his real estate in King George County and with his mother and her last husband moved to Orange County where he died testate in 1762. John and Elizabeth (Plunkett) Willis had a large family who gave rise to considerable progeny in Orange and adjacent counties. DB#3,p.68; King George County DB#2,p.
123-127; Orange County WB#2,p.323.

WILSON : WILLSON

WILSON, Abram P. of Essex County and Mary Jane Clarke, bond 30 December 1835.
    Atterson Clarke (b).   MBB.,p.139

WILLSON, ALLEN and Winifred Reynolds, bond 23 January 1826. Consent by James
    Reynolds; no relationship stated. George Thrift (b).   MBB.,p.18

WILLSON, DANIEL and Mary Marks, bond 19 January 1773. William Marks (b).

WILLSON, DANIEL and Nancy Hinson*, bond 1 June 1801. Daniel Marmaduke (b);
    Joseph Fones (w).

WILLSON, EDWARD and Mary Richardson, bond 7 November 1796. Daniel Willson (b).

WILLSON, ELIAS and Peggy Buckley*, bond 2 January 1798. James Marks (b).

WIL[L]SON, JAMES and Martha Craske, license January 1712/13.   DB#6,p.275
    [The bride was the daughter of Captain John and Elizabeth (Moss) Craske
    (q.v.), p.46. James Willson (16??-1738) and his wife nee Martha Craske
    (16??-1754) both died testate in Richmond County. AB#1,p.185; WB#2,p.120,
    126; WB#3,p.33; WB#5,p.329; WB#6,p.21.]

WILLSON, MORTON and Elizabeth Ford, bond 9 July 1753. James Mauldin (b).
    [Morton Willson died testate in Richmond County in 1799; see WB#9,p.117.]

WILLSON, THOMAS married long before 31 October 1774, Ann Brickey, daughter of
    John Brickey who died intestate in 1733. By 31 October 1774 Ann (Brickey)
    Willson is deceased leaving Richard Willson, then of legal age, her heir-
    at-law. DB#14,p.335; WB#5,p.189,208.[1774, Richard Willson of Bute Co.N.C.]

WILLSON, WILLIAM and Nancy Richardson, bond 6 November 1797. William Boring (b).
    Chilton [Shelton] Willson certifies Nancy Richardson is "eighteen years of
    age and over."

WINDER, MICHAEL married by 4 August 1720, Susanna (Stewart) Bruce, daughter of
    William Stewart [Steuart] and widow of Henry Bruce, Jr. (q.v.), p.27 of
    Richmond County. DB#7,p.264; DB#8,p.9,59; Westmoreland County W&D#3,p.299.

WINSTEAD, GEORGE and Nelly Feggett, bond 22 November 1813. Consent by W. Settle,
    guardian of the bride. Eppa: Headley (b).

WINSTEAD, GEORGE L. and Martha H.B. Headley, bond 8 November 1836. Consent by
    Griffin Headley, father of the bride. William B. Hale (b).   MBB.,p.150

WINSTEAD, JEREMIAH and Fanny Jenkins, bond 18 December 1792. Thomas Hogin (b);
   John How, Jr. (w).

WINSTEAD, JOHN H. and Diannah M. Lewis, license 22 October 1852. The groom was
   the minor son of Samuel Winstead and the bride the daughter of Sarah Lewis.
   Married 22 October 1852 by the Rev. William F. Barreck.

WINSTON, HOLLAND H. and Elizabeth Brown, bond 27 April 1831. James W. Brown
   (b).   MBB.,p.77

WOFFENDALE, JAMES married by 3 November 1698, Mary Clapman daughter of William
   and Mary (Thatcher) Clapman (q.v.), p.37. COB#2,p.121,167,350,474,500.

WOOD, JOHN and Maria Rich*, bond 21 November 1832. Bass Rich (b). MBB.,p.95

WOODBRIDGE, GEORGE (circa 1674-1706) had a concubine in Lancaster County called
   Mary Pincent; he is reputed to have married her before his death in Richmond County in 1706. Mary (Pincent) Woodbridge married (2) by 7 May 1707
   a Mr. Hall and moved to Lancaster County where she died intestate in 1718.
   George Woodbridge was the son of Paul and Bridget (FitzHerbert) Woodbridge,
   next below. George Woodbridge and Mary Pincent had two children, viz: (a)
   George Woodbridge who d.s.p., and (b) Elizabeth Woodbridge (circa 1706-1772)
   who married "a lame man," George Yerby (17??-1765) of Lancaster County, and
   left issue. COB#1,p.19; COB#2,p.40; COB#4,p.137,273; WB#2,p.117; suit in
   chancery Taff vs Yerby, VSL:AD #25391; Lee,p.103,236-239; Fairfax County
   Land Causes of Long Standing 1742-1770, p.342 et seq.

WOODBRIDGE, PAUL (1631-1691) of Rappahannock County married circa 1665 Bridget
   FitzHerbert and had issue, viz:(a) Major William Woodbridge (1668-1726),
   next below; (b) George Woodbridge (circa 1674-1706), next above; and (c)
   Elizabeth Woodbridge who married (1) Manus McLaughlin (q.v.), p.126 and
   (2) Peter Taff (q.v.), p.202. See references cited above under George
   Woodbridge; also Sweeny,p.50,151.

WOODBRIDGE, WILLIAM [MAJOR] (1668-1726), son of Paul and Bridget (FitzHerbert)
   Woodbridge, married (1) 1705 Sarah Keene, daughter of William Keene, Gentleman, (1642-1685) and his wife nee Elizabeth Rogers of Northumberland County; they had two children, viz: (a) Captain John Woodbridge (1706-1769) d.s.p
   in Richmond County and (b) Elizabeth Woodbridge (1709-17??) also d.s.p. befor
   her only brother. Robert Wormeley Carter, Esq: of Sabine Hall made the follc
   ing entry in his diary on 1 June 1769: "Went to the Burial of the late Captai
   John Woodbridge who it is imagined has died intestate altho he had many natur
   children." It appears Captain John Woodbridge (1706-1769) refused to make a
   will and stated that his handsome estate would descended by law to his maternal first cousin, Newton Keene, Gentleman, as his paternal first cousin, "Mrs
   Elizabeth Yerby came in at the back door;" see notes under George Woodbridge,
   above. WB#5,p.27; references above under George Woodbridge and Paul Woodbric
   Stafford County DB 1722-1728,p.217 from a copy first recorded in 1704 in Rick
   mond County DB#3,p.172. Major William Woodbridge (1668—1726) married (2)
   Sarah Brereton, widow of Captain Henry Brereton who died intestate in Richmor
   County in 1713; see the license next below.

WOODBRIDGE, WILLIAM and Sarah Brereton (widow), license July 1713. DB#6,p.275
[This was the second marriage of Major William Woodbridge (1668-1726) (q.v.),
p.234; his wife was the widow of Captain Henry Brereton who died intestate in
1713. COB#6,p.90,214; WB#3,p.142.]

WOODCOCK, WILLIAM (16??-1735) married ante 1718 Elizabeth Shearman, daughter of
Martin Shearman (1673—1727). This couple had a son John Shearman Woodcock,
born in North Farnham Parish, 24 January 1734; he married in Northumberland
County in 1759, Frances Rust, and removed to Frederick County where he was
named by his brother-in-law, Francis Humphrey Christian, as executor of his
estate (q.v.), p.36-37. COB#10,p.257; WB#5,p.59; 47V42; NFPR; WB#5,p.257.

WOODDY, ROBERT and Julia Plummer*, bond 14 September 1836. George N. Alderson
(b); Bartholomew Bell (w).   MBB.,p.148

WOODDY, ROBERT C.C. and Mary Ann Clarke, bond 2 October 1843. Consent by Nancy
Efford, mother of the bride. William H. Hill (b); Richard H. Beazley (w).
                                                             MBB.,p.241

WOODWARD, PHILEMON and Elizabeth [mutilated] (spinster), bond 5 July 1802. Richard Barnes (b). [ECD states the bride was Elizabeth R. Brockenbrough.]

WOOLLARD, AUSTIN R. and Betsy Reuick*, bond 27 November 1823. John Efford (b).

WOOLLARD, JOHN and Nancy Alloway, bond 4 January 1796. William Everett (b).

WOOLLARD, JOHN and Margaret Duff, bond 14 January 1799. Consent by Patsay
Duff, mother of the bride. William Everitt (b).

WOOLLARD, JOHN JR. and Mary Ann Hill*, widow, bond 5 March 1838. Richard Clarke
(b); Lucy D. Northen (w).   MBB.,p.170

WOOLLARD, JOSEPH JR. and Fanney Jesper*, bond 12 June 1811. Richard Jesper (b).

WOOLLARD, LEMUEL L. and Apphia T. Tune, bond 20 January 1824. Thomas Tune (b).

WOOLLARD, RICHARD and Betsy Warren*, bond 20 February 1818. George Saunders (b).

WOOLLARD, THOMAS W. and Mary Elizabeth Williams, bond 19 January 1847. Consent
by E.L. Williams, father of the bride. Robert Clarke (b); Griffin Williams
(w). Married 20 January 1847 by the Rev. Addison Hall.   MBB.,p.287

WOOLLARD, WILLIAM J. and Alice C. Garland (widow)*, bond 17 April 1813. Thomas
S. Davis (b); Samuel B. Kelsick (w).

WORNER, ROBERT and Mary Stoot, bond 17 January 1795. Roger Dameron (b). "This
is to certify that Mary Stoot, daughter of Robert Stoot and Elisabeth Stoot,
his wife, has bargain[d] and hath agreed to jone in wedlock with Robert Wornar
and Robert Stoot and Elisabeth, his wife, have agread to the same. Witness
our hands   Mary Stoot
Richard Claughton
Roger Dameron "

WREN, NICHOLAS of Loudoun County married by 11 January 1759 Elizabeth Jenkins, one of the daughters of John Jenkins late of Truro Parish, Prince William County, who was one of the children of William and Elizabeth (Skelderman) Jenkins (q.v.), p.104-105. In 1759 Lesha Jenkins, Elizabeth (Jenkins) Wren and Ann Jenkins, all of Loudoun County, were the sole heirs of their then deceased father, the aforementioned John Jenkins. DB#9,p.210,607,646; DB#12,p.142.

WRIGHT, ALEXANDER M. and Eliza M. Mothershead, bond 16 August 1845. Consent by Maranda P. [? B ?] Lathom, mother of the bride. Edwin C. Edwards (b); George W. Sydnor (w).   MBB.,p.262

WRIGHT, JOHN and Mary Thrift, bond 17 November 1783. LeRoy Peachey (b).

WRIGHT, JOHN and Ann Davis, bond 28 December 1797. Consent by John Davis, father of the bride; also by George Davis, guardian of the bride. Richard Stott (b); David Austin (w).

WRIGHT, JOHN M. and Elizabeth T. Dudley*, bond 28 December 1849. Samuel D. Mothershead (b).   MBB.,p.330

WRIGHT, MOTTROM M. and Malinda Lamkin, bond 6 April 1830. Charles L. Bell (b).
                                                                MBB.,p.62

WRIGHT, THOMAS and Betty Jacson, bond 21 June 1757. Edmund Bulger (b). [Edmund Bulger (q.v.),p.30, married by 2 August 1748 Jane Wright, widow of John Wright who died intestate in 1736. In 1748 Thomas Wright, son of John and Jane Wright, is said to be about fifteen years of age. COB#10,p.398; COB#12,p.158; DB#11,p.286,375; WB#5,p.285; WB#8,p.65.]

WRIGHT, WILLIAM of Westmoreland County and Lucy Pursell*, bond 11 November 1834. James L. Bell (b); Vin.t R. Pursell (w).   MBB.,p.126

WROE   SEE : ROE   PAGE 173

WROE, JOHN and Betsy B. Bryant*, bond 12 June 1813. Alexander Bryant (b).

WROE, PETER and Elizabeth Bearcraft*, bond 21 June 1788. James Robins (b).

WROE, PETER and Milly Powers*, bond 25 April 1807. James Brann (b).

WROE, PETER and Winifred Thornton (widow)*, bond 18 October 1809. Samuel Wroe (b).

WROE, NATHANIEL and Betsy Self*, bond 19 March 1833. John L. Clarke (b); William Briskey (w).   MBB.,p.104

WROE, SAMUEL and Frances Hammock*, bond 10 December 1823. John Wroe (b).

Y

YAGER, JAMES of Madison County and Sarah Woollard of Richmond County, bond 2 February 1796. Consent by Mary Ann Woollard, mother of the bride; she states Sarah Woollard is of lawful age. John Woollard (b).

YATES   SEE : YEATS PAGE 238

YEATMAN, HENRY A. of Westmoreland County and Nancy W. Reynolds*, bond 8 July 1833. Robert L. Montgomery (b).   MBB.,p.108

YEATMAN, JAMES and Nancy H. Wheldon, bond 7 January 1805. Consent by John Wheldon, father of the bride. John Yeatman, Jr. (b).

YEATMAN, JAMES E. and Mary S. Sanders*, license 1 September 1852. James M. Morriss (w), James Jones (w) and Samuel Marks (w). Married 2 September 1852 by the Rev. John Pullen.

YEATMAN, JOHN [GENTLEMAN] (circa 1685-1737) married Hannah Lewis, only child of Joseph Lewis who purchased land in Richmond County which descended to her. DB#11,p.192. Walter Clark Yeatman, The Yeatmans in America (Los Angeles, California, 1933), gives an excellent account of the Yeatman family in the Northern Neck of Virginia and some lines of descent are followed to other states. See also ECD Papers, Box #30; there are other Yeatman records widely scattered in other boxes in the ECD collection.

YEATMAN, JOHN JR. of Westmoreland County and Amelia Oldham Wheldon, bond 5 April 1802. John Wheldon (b).

YEATMAN, JOSEPH married by 1741 Martha Wilson, daughter of James and Martha (Craske) Wil(l)son (q.v.), p.233; the groom was the son of John and Hannah (Lewis) Yeatman (q.v.), p.237. AB#1,p.185; DB#10,p.476; WB#5,p.329.

YEATMAN, LEVI and Mary Beverton, bond 4 March 1850. Consent by Elizabeth Beverton, mother of the bride. Richard McGinnis (b); Henry Davis (w). Married 7 March 1850 by the Rev. George Northam.   MBB.,p.333

YEATMAN, MATHEW JR. and Elizabeth Figett*, bond 13 December 1826. James Yeatman (b); Levi Yeatman (b).   MBB.,p. 25

YEATMAN, MATTHEW M. and Mary Ann Yeatman*, bond 22 October 1838. Samuel Yeatman (b); Thomas Yeatman (w).   MBB.,p.175

YEATMAN, THOMAS and Elinor Thornton, bond 24 February 1746. Joseph Yeatman (b). [The bride was the daughter of Mathew and Eleanor (Craske) Thornton (q.v.), p.211; the groom was the son of John and Hannah (Lewis) Yeatman (q.v.), p. 237. Thomas Yeatman died in 1760 and his wife in 1766, both intestate; their three children, William, Sibella and Mary Yeatman, are mentioned in the wills of their maternal uncle, Crask(e) Thornton, 1771, and also their maternal grandmother, Eleanor (Craske) Thornton Mountjoy, 1776. WB#5,p.57; WB#6,p.194, 411; WB#7,p.79,220.]

YEATMAN, WILLIAM and Nancy Brown (widow)*, bond 3 September 1804. William Bragg
    (b). [The bride was nee Nancy Morris, widow of Thomas Brown (q.v.), p.26.]

YEATMAN, WILLIAM and Lucinda A. Guttridge*, bond 4 August 1834. Matthew V. Yeat-
    man (b).   MBB.,p.122

YEATS, ELIAS (16??-1693) married by 12 June 1679 Mary Hudson, daughter of Thomas
    Hudson (16??-1679). She had "many children" and survived her husband.
    Among her children were Francis Yeats, eldest son and heir-at-law, and Will-
    iam Yeats, both mentioned below. COB#1,p.85; Sweeny,p.80,81; 4 Hening 28;
    W.K. Winfree, Acts Not in Hening's Statutes at Large 1702-1732, November
    1711, page 118 [unpublished typescript, VSL:AD.]

YEATS, FRANCIS (16??-1724) married by 25 April 1707, Winifred Jacobus, daughter
    of Angell and Elizabeth (Clarke) Jacobus (q.v.), p.102. DB#4,p.124,155;
    DB#5,p.96; DB#6,p.21; DB#7,p.531; WB#4,p.244; 4 Hening 28, act of October
    1711 regarding the lands of Francis Yeats in Richmond County.

YEATS, WILLIAM married by 7 October 1708, Elizabeth Jacobus, daughter of Angell
    and Elizabeth (Clarke) Jacobus (q.v.), p.102. DB#4,p.155; DB#5,p.96.

YEARBY, ALBERT F. and Olivia B. McCarty*, license 2 July 1853. E.R. Pullen (w).
    Married 5 July 1853 by the Rev. William N. Ward.

YERBY, GEORGE (17??-1765) "a lame man" of Lancaster County, married Elizabeth
    Woodbridge (circa 1706-1772), daughter of George Woodbridge and Mary Pincent
    (q.v.), p.234. COB#1,p.19; COB#2,p.40; COB#4,p.137; suit in chancery styled
    Thomas Taff vs John Yerby, VSL:AD #25391; Fairfax County Land Causes of
    Long Standing 1742-1770,p.342 et seq.; Lee, p.236-239.

YERBY, GEORGE and Elizabeth Rust Garland, bond 11 May 1790. Consent by Griffin
    Garland, father of the bride. Thomas Williams (b); Griffin Garland, Jr. (w)
    and John Rust (w). [The bride was the daughter of Griffin and Mary (Rust)
    Garland; her ancestry is detailed in Rust of Virginia, p.55. This was the
    second marriage of George Yerby (17??-1793). By his first wife he had six
    children and on 23 May 1785 he executed his last will and Testament devising
    his estate to them, but in May 1790 he took a second wife and by her had two
    children and died without altering his aforementioned will which was proved
    3 June 1793 at Richmond County court and recorded in WB#8,p.157. His will
    was contested in the courts and there are notations in regard to this suit
    in 11W(2)120.]

YERBY, GEORGE and Eliz.^a U. Teackle, bond 11 October 1796. Charles Smith (b).

YERBY, JESSE of Lancaster County and Ellen Scurlock*, bond 1 February 1796.
    Daniel Scurlock (b); John K. Schofield (w) and George Scurlock (w).

YERBY, JOHN M. and Elizabeth D. McCarty, bond 17 June 1805. Consent by Judith G.
    McCarty, guardian of the bride. Bartholomew McCarty (b); Daniel L. McCarty
    (w).

YERBY, LEMUEL and Fanny M. Tomlin (widow), bond 19 January 1821. John Burke (b).

YERBY, THOMAS and Peggy Fauntleroy (spinster), bond 4 September 1786. Griffin
    Fauntleroy (b); Thaddeus Williams (w). [Captain Thomas Yerby (17??-1800)
    of Laural Grove, Richmond County, was the son of John Yerby (17??-1775)
    and grandson of George and Elizabeth (Woodbridge) Yerby (q.v.), p.238.
    Peggy (Fauntleroy) Yerby (circa 1771-1802) was the daughter of Griffin
    Murdock Fauntleroy (1747-1794) and his wife nee Anne Belfield (q.v.), p.
    68. A son of Thomas and Peggy (Fauntleroy) Yerby was Thomas Yerby, Esq.
    (1796-1868) of Belvoir, Spotsylvania County; he married 6 August 1818
    Harriet Pratt (1797-1887), daughter of John and Alice (Fitzhugh) Pratt of
    Camden, Caroline County, and were the ancestors of the Yerby family of
    Spotsylvania County.]

YERBY, WILLIAM G. and Fanny Pullin, bond 18 July 1815. William D. McCarty (b).

YOUNG, WILLIAM and Judith Stephens*, bond 18 March 1834. Henry Coats (b); John
    Roe (w).   MBB.,p.117

                                    Z

ZUCCARELLO, JOSEPH and Fanny Sisson, bond 13 November 1826. Miskell Saunders
    (b).   MBB.,p.24

"History is based on biography, and
biography is based on genealogy."

Dr. Amandus Johnson

GENEALOGICAL CHARTS[1]

ALEXANDER - HOOE	242	MILLS - STERNE - BIRKETT	256
BALL - CHINN - DOWNMAN	243	MOORE - BRONOUGH - NAYLOR	257
BARNES - BECKWITH	244	MOTT - DONIPHAN - SHIPPY	258
BELFIELD - WILSON - GLASS	245	PRATT	259
BILLINGTON - MC CARTY	246	ROBINSON	260
CAMMACK - THATCHER	247	SAMFORD	261
CONWAY - GIBSON	248	SETTLE	262
DAVIS - LAMPTON - JONES	249	STONE	263
DURHAM	250	STONE - PANNELL - KAY	264
FLEET - WALKER - CONWAY	251	STONE - METCALFE - BARROW	265
KENYON	252	TALIAFERRO - TURNER	266
LEWIS - FRESHWATER	253	TAYLOE	267
MEADE - HOBBS - GREEN	254	THATCHER - CAMMACK	268
MILLER	255	WASHINGTON - WILLIAMSON	269

1 - These genealogical charts, taken from my files, are an endeavor to bring into focus some members of the above mentioned families and those with whom they intermarried, however, lack of space oftentimes has prevented the tabulation of all members of a family and including other detail in the file.

* - The asterisk, placed before a name on the genealogical charts, indicates the party died testate, however, it does not necessarily mean that the last wills and Testaments of all these parties now remain of record. Many wills, although missing through the loss of the record book in which they were originally recorded, are recited in part in surviving deeds and court orders and oftentimes verbatim copies are found in chancery suit papers - sometimes in other counties as well as in district and federal courts.

*COLONEL JOHN[1] ALEXANDER (16??-1677)

He came to Virginia circa 1650, acquired large tracts of land in the Northern Neck of Virginia and died testate in Stafford County. By his wife Elizabeth, he had two sons who equally shared his estate, viz:

: :

*Colonel Robert[2] Alexander (16??-1704)
m. Frances, traditionally nee Ashton.
: Resided in St.Paul's Parish, Stafford Co.

*Major Robert[3] Alexander (1688-1735)
m. Anne Fowke (1692-1739), daughter of Colonel
: Gerard Fowke (1662-1734) of Charles Co.,Md.

: :

Ann[4] Alexander
m. 1726, Capt. John Hooe
: (1704-1766), son of Col.
: Rice and Frances (Town-
: shend) Hooe [A.P.& P.,
: p.213,336].

*Gerard[5] Hooe, Gentleman,
(1733-1785) of Barnesfield,
St.Paul's Parish, m. 1761,
Sarah Barnes (1742-1805),
daughter of Captain Richard
Barnes of Richmond County
(q.v.), P. 10,96.

*John[4] Alexander, Sr.,
Gentleman, (1711-1763)
m. 1734,Susanna Pearson
: (1717-1788), dau: of
: *Capt. Simon Pearson,
: Gent. (16??-1733).

John[5] Alexander, Gent.
(1739/40-post 1806)
m. 1761, Elizabeth
Barnes, daughter of
Captain Richard Barnes
of Richmond County, Va.
(q.v.), p.2,10.

Captain Philip[2] Alexander (16??-1705)
m. *Sarah Ashton (16??-1749); m(2) Thomas Clifton;
: m(3) *David McGill (16??-1725), Stafford County.

: :

*Philip[3] Alexander, Gentleman, (1704-1753) of Salis-
bury, St.Paul's Parish, where his tombstone now is.
m. Sarah Hooe (c.1708-1758), dau. of Col. Rice Hooe
: (c.1660-1726) and his wife nee Frances Townshend.

: :

*John[4] Alexander, Gentleman, (1735-1775) of Salis-
bury, St.Paul's Parish, now in King George County.
m. *Lucy Thornton (17??-1781), only child of *Will-
: iam Thornton, Gent. of King George County who died
: 1743/4 and his wife nee *Mary Taliaferro (17??-
: 1770) who m(2) *Colonel Samuel Donne (died 1764).

: :

*Philip Thornton[5] Alexander (1760-1783) of Salisbury,
a 1,500 acre estate at the time of his death in a
duel with Lawrence Washington (c.1760-1809) of Waterloo, King George County. He m(1) c. 1779, Jane Willis; m(2) 1782, Lucy Brockenbrough of Richmond County
(q.v.), P.2. Philip Thornton[5] Alexander had a son
by each of his aforementioned two wives, viz:

: :

*John Lewis[6] Alexander (1780-1803)
d.s.p. His death was caused by a
fall from his horse. He was very
wealthy and by the time he was 16
engaged in every form of dissipa-
tion known to mankind, say depon-
ents in the suit styled Alexander
vs Thornton, FDC#1. He bequeathed
his handsome estate to his only
half-brother, P.T.6 Alexander.

Philip Thornton[6] Alexander (1783-c.1817)
m. 1801, his first cousin, Lucy Brooke,
daughter of Dr. Laurence and Frances
(Alexander) Brooke of Smithfield, Spotsylvania County, Va. and left issue. His
handsome estate, Salisbury, which had descended to him from Colonel John[1] Alexander, was sold shortly after the death
of Philip Thornton[6] Alexander to satisfy
his creditors.

: :

[N.B. * Denotes these
parties died
testate.]

COLONEL WILLIAM¹ BALL (c.1615-1680) OF LANCASTER COUNTY, VIRGINIA
[Hayden,p.47-53; 30T80-86;259-27] :

*Mary Johnson 1707 -m(2)- *Col. Joseph² Ball -m(1)- Elizabeth   *Capt. William Ball -m- *Margaret Williamson
[widow] (16??- : (1649-1711) : Romney of   (1641-1694) of Lan- : (16??-1709), only child
1721); m(3) : Lancaster Co. Va. : England;   caster Co. [Hayden, : of James Williamson,Gent.
*Richard Hewes : [Hayden,p.56 et : by her he   p.53, errs: William : (16??-1656) of Rappahan-
(16??-1713/14), : seq.] By his second : had five   had only one wife; : nock Co. to leave issue;
Northumberland : wife Col. Joseph² : children.   she survived him.] : (q.v.)p.8. Will record-
Co.[15W(2)176] : Ball had an only child.   : ed Lancaster,#10, p.53.

*Mary³ Ball (1708-1789)   *Esther³ Ball 1703 -m- *Rawleigh Chinn,   -[X]-   *Margaret³ Ball -m- *Rawleigh Downman,
m.1731, *Capt.Augustine   (16??-1751) : Gent.(1684-1741),   See #   (16??-1759);her : Gent.(1680-1719);
Washington (1694-1743);   [18W(2)294-6] : Lancaster Co.Va.;   will proved in : will proved in Lan-
their eldest child was   Five children : son of John and   Richmond Co.Va., : caster Co. mention-
George Washington,Esq.   left issue. : Alice (?) Chinn.   [Hayden,p.72-74] : ed two children.

CHINN   DOWNMAN

*Joseph⁴ Chinn   Rawleigh   *Thomas⁴ Chinn   Chichester⁴   *Ann⁴Chinn   William⁴ Downman   *Rawleigh⁴Down-
(172?-1774),m.   (172?-1756)   (172?-1768), m.   (172?-1747)   (172?-1793)   (1717-1765),m.1747   man (1718/19-
1727, Elizabeth   m.Ann [2]   (1) 1735, Sarah   m.1739,Agatha   m.*Martin   Ellen⁴(Ball) Chich-   1781), m. 1750
Ball; he died   : d. 1756   Mitchell (1717-   Thornton, (q.   Shearman   ester, widow of   Frances⁴ Ball
testate, Lancas-   : by whom   1752); m(2) 1752   v.),p.35.   (172?-1771)   Richard Chichester,   (1720-1782), a
ter Co. [Hayden,   : he had   Ann (Conway) Ed-   of Lancast-   Gent. (172?-1743);   granddaughter
p.101, errs.]   : 2 daus.   monds who d.s.p.   er County.   left issue by each.   of Col. Joseph²
                                                                                    Ball;(above).

*John⁵ Chinn   Catherine⁵ Chinn   Anne⁵ Chinn   DOWNMAN
(c.1739-1791)   m.1756, Francis H.   m. 1758 Col.
m.1765, Sarah   Christian (172?-88);   Thaddeus Mc-   Rawleigh William⁵ Downman (1762-1838), widow, had three sons born out of wedlock in Richmond
Yates of   m(2) 1768, Ann⁵ Shear-   Carty (1739-   his cousin, Priscilla⁶ Chinn (1767-1812), daught-
Middlesex Co.   man (q.v.), P.36-37;   1787) (q.v.)   er of *John⁵ and Sarah (Yates) Chinn (see left);
[Hayden,p.120-   left issue by each.   p.124.   as his first wife, and had 16 children; among Dr.
121]   Joseph Henry⁶ Downman (1805-1830) m.1828, his
                                                    double cousin, Elizabeth Sophia⁷ Chinn (q.v.),p.
                                                    58, dau. Dr.John Yates⁶ and Sarah (Carter) Chinn.

Rawleigh Chinn, Gent, and Margaret³ (Ball) Downman, widow, had three sons born out of wedlock in Richmond
County, viz: *Charles Chinn, died in Fauquier County, 1788; *Christopher Chinn, died in Loudoun County,1770;
and *Elijah Chinn, died in Loudoun County, 1771. They are called "godsons" in the will of Rawleigh Chinn and
"sons" in the will of Margaret³ (Ball) Downman, but Richmond County COB#9,p.42,482,537,633 and #10,p.13,330
et passim confirms their parentage as does D.S. Freeman, George Washington, Volume I, p.530-534, 18W(2)294-6.
[* Denotes these parties died testate.]

244

B A R N E S

FRANCES INGO - - - married (1) - - - CAPTAIN RICHARD BARNES - - - married (2) - - - PENELOPE MANLY

FRANCES INGO - - - married (1)
daughter of James
and Frances (Moss)
Ingo of Richmond
County (q.v.), p.
101; they had an
only child, viz:

CAPTAIN RICHARD BARNES - - - married (2)
Born 169?
Died 30 September 1760
in Richmond County, Va.
Captain Richard and
Penelope (Manly) Barnes
died testate; their wills
were contested, (q.v.),
p. 10.

PENELOPE MANLY
Born 171?
Died 22 May 1768
She was the daughter
of William and Pene-
lope (Higgins) Manly
of Westmoreland Co.
She had six daughters
but no son.

Captain Richard and Penelope (Manly) : Barnes had six daughters, viz:

THOMAS BARNES, GENTLEMAN (c.1723-1767) (q.v.),p.10. m(1) 1745, Winifred Brock-enbrough; m(2) 1762, Mary ["Molly"] Beckwith Morton, daughter of Joseph and Margaret (Beckwith) Morton (q.v.),p.139; Thomas Barnes left issue by each spouse.

CATHERINE ["CATY"] BARNES Died c. 1750 [See #]

MARY BARNES m. c. 1752 Captain Younger Kel-sick (q.v.), p.111.

REBECCA BARNES m. 27 May 1753 Sir Jonathan Beckwith (1720-1796), (q.v.), p.13. They had six children, viz:

ELEANOR BARNES m.c.1752 John Morton Jordan,Esq. She d.s.p.

SARAH BARNES (1742-1805) m.9 Jan.1761 Gerard Hooe, Gent.(q.v.). p.96.

ELIZABETH BARNES, m. 1761, John Alexander, Gent; they moved to Loudoun Co. (q.v.),p.2.

Sir Jonathan and : Rebecca (Barnes) Beckwith had six children, viz;

SIR JENNINGS BECKWITH (1752-1835), m. 1787 Catherine Miskell, (q.v.),p.13. [See *]

REBECCA BECKWITH m. Marmaduke Brock-enbrough Beckwith

JONATHAN BECKWITH

RICHARD MARMADUKE BECKWITH, m. 1798 Elizabeth Scott Buchanan (c.1780-1834) (q.v.), p. 14.

BARNES BECKWITH

PENELOPE BECKWITH m. 1798, Alexand-er Walker (q.v.), p.222.

Catherine ["Caty"] Barnes is reputed to have been in love with Sir Jonathan Beckwith but her father violently opposed the marriage and she died of a broken heart. Sir Jonathan went to England in 1749 to transact business in regard to the estate of his uncle, Sir Roger Beckwith, Baronet, who died without issue and to whom his father, Marmaduke Beckwith, Gentleman, of Richmond County, was heir at law. Upon his return he married Rebecca Barnes, another daughter of Captain Richard and Penelope (Manly) Barnes.

*The interesting obituary of Sir Jennings Beckwith in the Richmond (Va.) Enquirer of 1 December 1835 is cited 14W(1)140 and his last will, dated 21 July 1835, is in Richmond County unrecorded will file. His family were favored by the will of Lawrence Butler, 1811, recorded in Frederick County WB#9, p.44. The chancery suit papers, Beckwith vs Bramham, FDC#27, are informative as to Sir Jonathan Beckwith's family.

Frances Wright -m(1)- *Dr. Joseph Belfield -m(2)- Elizabeth Dozier -m(3)- *James Wilson -m(3)- Jehu Glass

Frances Wright -m(1)-
(1686-c.1706),
dau: of *Mottrom
and Ruth (Griggs)
Wright of Lancas-
ter Co; she left
issue only child.

*Dr. Joseph Belfield -m(2)-
(1672-1738); he m(2)
1707, twice widowed
Mary (Lane) Mountjoy
Wilson by whom he had
no issue; (q.v.),p.15

Elizabeth Dozier -m(3)-
dau: of *Richard
Dozier who died
1751, Westmore-
land Co; she had
two children by
him, viz:

*James Wilson -m(3)-
(1722-1743) of
Richmond Co;
she had two
children by
him, viz:

Jehu Glass
In 1752 he
and wife,nee
E.Dozier, were
living in
Richmond Co.
[DB#11,p.131]

---

*Captain Thomas Wright Belfield
(1705-1743); m.1724, *Mary (Meriwether) Colston (1702-1750), widow of *William Colston, Gentleman,
(1672-1721), (q.v.),p.42. Capt. T.
W. Belfield had 8 children born in
Richmond Co; 4 attained maturity
and left issue, viz:

*Joseph Belfield
(c.1735-1770);he
d.s.p.,Culpeper
Co.,Va. 1752 Al-
vin Mountjoy was
guardian of Jos-
eph Belfield and
sister, Elizabeth.

Elizabeth Belfield
(c.1737-   ), m.
c.1754,   Benjamin
Cave of Orange Co;
they were the par-
ents of Colonel
Belfield Cave.

Richard   Sarah
[No attempt
has been made
to trace these
two children of
James and Eliza-
beth (Dozier)
Wilson.]

William Glass
b. c. 1749
m. c. 1774
Elizabeth
Christy; they
moved to
Scott Co.,Ky;
left issue.

---

*Captain John Belfield
(1725-1801); m. 1744,
Ruth Sydnor; (q.v.),p.14.
Their Bible record re-
cords births of 9 child-
ren of whom 6 attained
maturity and left issue
in the Richmond County
area, viz:

Joseph Belfield
(1727-1750)
m. Mary [?];
he left only
Nancy Belfield, m(1)
William Lane; d.1777;
m(2) 1778, Enoch Smith
(1750-1825); they mov-
ed to Kentucky.

Elizabeth Belfield
(1732-ante 1785), m.
as his second wife,
*Bolling Stark, Esq:
(1733-1788); he died
in city of Richmond
but his will of re-
cord in Henrico Co.,
WB#2,p.39.[21W(1)205]

Frances Belfield
(1736-18??), m(1)
*Freeman Walker (1734-
1766) of Brunswick Co.
m(2) Henry Broadnax,
widower; she left issue
by each spouse; (q.v.),
p.222.

Thomas Belfield
(1745-1804); m.
1780, Ann Harwar
Beale, (q.v.),p.
15. They had
eight children.

Elizabeth Belfield
(1747-17   ); m. 1764
*Robert Chinn (17??-
1784), (q.v.), p.36.
Resided in Lancaster
County, Virginia.
[Lee, p.51.]

Major John Belfield
(1751-1792); m.1785,
Mary Beckwith (q.v.),
p.14. Only child,
Alice Corbin Belfield
m.1806, Peter Rust
Garland (q.v.), p.75.

Mary Belfield
(1753-18   )
m.c.1771, *Col.
William Smith
of Essex Co.
(q.v.), p.191.

Anne Belfield
b.17 Nov.1754
m.c.1770,Grif-
fin Murdock
Fauntleroy;
(q.v.), p.68

***Sydnor Bel-
field** (1758-
1841),m.1782
Ann Young;
(q.v.), p.15.

The Richmond County court records abound with Belfield instruments. The Bible record of Captain Thomas Wright Belfield (1 January 1704/5-7 December 1743) is in Judge L.H.Jones, Captain Roger Jones of London and Virginia, p.182-184 (Albany, N.Y., 1891). It is a typographical error in giving the death date of Capt.John Belfield as 19 August 1805 as his will was dated 26 May 1801 and proved at Richmond County court 5 Oct.1801 [WB#9,p.158].

246

[Unknown first wife] - m(1) - LUKE BILLINGTON, GENTLEMAN, (16??-1672) - m(2) - BARBARA [?]
It is not definitely   of Rappahannock County by 1656; in 1661   (16??-1674). Her will,
stated Luke Billing-   wife Barbara joined him in a deed. He   and the wills of her
ton,Sr. had two wives,   died testate, 1672. [Hayden,p.84A-84B;   husband and son, indicate
but the records so in-   Sweeny,p.16-17.]   she was his second wife.
dicate.   [Sweeny,Pg.29.]

BILLINGTON

Mary Billington   Alicia [Elitia]   Luke,Jr.   Elizabeth Billing-   Jane Barbara Billington
m(1) Hugh Daniel;he died ante   Billington   d.s.p.   ton, m.Dennis Mc-   (16??-1727), m. Joseph
1672 about which time she m.   m.11 Sept. 1673 1687   Carty,Gent.(16??-   Tayloe,Gent.(16??-1716);
(2) Richard Hinds. Her son Wm. Dr.John Russell [Sweeny,   1694) (q.v.), p.   both died testate in Lan-
Daniel named in his grandfath- (q.v.), p. 175   p.127-8.]   123. They had   caster County. (q.v.),p.
er's will of 1671.   four children.   205. Three children.

MC CARTY

Captain Daniel McCarty -m(1),1698- Elizabeth (Pope)   Katherine   Ellen [Eleanor]   Elizabeth McCarty
(1679-1724), of West-   Payne (1667-1716)   (1678-1713)   m. in Nov. 1711   m. by 1706 John
moreland County. (q.v.),   m(2) Ann (Lee)   m.Timothy   Robert Bayliss   Sebree of North-
p.123. He held property   Fitzhugh (1683-1732); McDaniel   (1681-1725)   umberland County.
in several counties.   no surviving issue.   [McDonall]   (q.v.), p. 12.   [DB#4, p.41.]

m.Robert Baylis dsp.

MC CARTY

Anna Barbara McCarty   Billington McCarty,   Sarah   Winifred   Thaddeus   Major Dennis   Daniel,Gent;
m.by 5 December 1715   Gent. (1702-1745).   m.1728   m. 1728   (1713-31)   (17??-1743)   (17??-1744)
John Fitzhugh, Esq.   m. Anne Barber (1709-   Thomas   Robert   [Tombstone, m.1724, Sarah   m(1)Penelope
(1692-1733) of Mar-   1753) (q.v.), p. 122.   Beale   Massey   Hayden, p.   Ball. Will in   Higgins(1713-
mion. [OPR.,p.226]   They had issue four   d.s.p.   [SPR,p.93] 87.]   Fairfax Co.Va.   32) dsp;m(2)
                         sons, viz: (q.v.,p.12.   1735,Elizabeth,
                                                                                                        widow of Col.Nicholas Smith,
                                                                                                        (q.v.),p.190, had only son,
                                                                                                        Daniel McCarty,Gent.(1737-95)
                                                                                                        of Longwood,Westmoreland Co.
                                                                                                        m(1)1764,Mary Mercer (1740-64);
                                                                                                        m(2)1765,Winifred Thornton (c.
                                                                                                        1748-1791) by whom he had two
                                                                                                        children, viz:

MC CARTY

Daniel McCarty   Billington McCarty   Thaddeus McCarty   Charles Barber
(1733-1739)   (1736-1771), m.1756   (1739-1787), m.   McCarty (1741-
                    Elizabeth Downman,   1758, Anne Chinn,   1785) m.c.1760
                    (q.v.), P. 123.   (q.v.), p.124.   Winifred Tarp-
                                                                  ley.(q.v.)p.
                                                                  123.

[The records abound with genealogical data in regard
to the three sons of Billington McCarty, Gentleman.]

Elizabeth McCarty   1797   1802
m.1788,Burwell Bassett,Jr.   Daniel McCarty,Gent. -m.- Margaret Robinson -m(2)- Richard Stuart,Esq. (1770-
                             (1772-1801), last of   (1780-1808);left   1835) of Cedar Grove, King
                             Longwood.[SPR.,xxxiii]   issue by both.   George County, Virginia.

MC CARTY

WARWICK CAMMACK - married - *MARGARET [?]
(1636-c.1685) : (16??-1715)

He appears prominently on the Rappahannock County court records. By purchase and patent he acquired considerable land in the area which became Richmond County in 1692. It appears from the records he died circa 1685 as at this date Mrs. Margaret Cammack began appearing on the records in a manner he would not if she had been feme covert. The name has been rendered Cammack - Comack - Cammock - Comock &c.

She was the widow of *Sylvester Thatcher (16??-1667) by whom she had four children three of whom left issue. In 1709, when she wrote her will, she described herself as "very ancient;" this document makes it certain she had two daughters named Mary - one by each spouse. Naming all her living children, she bequeathed her estate to her three daughters by Warwick Cammack. [See Thatcher genealogical chart,p.268.]

John Cammack (c.1667-1717) In 1688 the court issued him a birth certificate, certifying he was the lawful son of Warwick and Margaret Cammack; d.s.p.

*Mary Cammack (16??-1743) m(1) *Francis Sterne (c.1638-1713) by whom she had two sons; m(2) *Isaac Truck [Trocq] (16??-1739) by whom she had no issue; they moved to Caroline County, with her three sons, where both died testate. Mary's eldest son was a bastard; he lived to be very old predeceasing several children who married into genteel family. (q.v.), p.195.

*Susanna Cammack (16??-1747) m(1) *John Foster (16??-1711) of Essex County and had an only child; m(2) *Gilbert Metcalfe (1682-1737) by whom she had no issue, (q.v.), p.131. There is considerable record of Susanna (Cammack) Foster Metcalfe and her spouses in Essex and Richmond counties. The only child of John and Susanna (Cammack) Foster was, viz:

*Margaret Cammack (16??-1740) m.*Dr. Paul Micou (1658-1736) of Essex Co. where they both died testate leaving a large family of children concerning whom considerable has been published. Perhpas their child concerning whom less had been written is their daughter, Mary Micou, next below:

(1) *William Cammack (c.1697-1783) of Caroline and Spotsylvania counties; he married and left a numerous progeny.

(2) *Francis Sterne (c.1700-1755) of Caroline County; he married and left progeny in Caroline and Stafford counties.

(3) David Sterne (1702-c.1748), m. by 1733 *Ann (Anderson) Evins [Evans] (17??-1775), widow of John Evins and daughter of Paulin Anderson; she moved to Amelia County where her will remains of record [WB#2,p.157].

(1)Ann Foster m(1) 1727 *Samuel Barber who died testate in 1736 leaving two sons; m(2) William Jordan, Gentleman; (q.v.), p.9.

(1) *Mary Micou (17??-1772) m(1) *Leonard Hill, Gent. (17??-1734) of Hill Park, Essex County; m(2) *Col. Joshua Fry (17??-1754). The wills of Col. and Mrs. Fry are of record in Albemarle County; she left issue by each spouse.

[N.B. * Denotes these parties died testate, however, all of their wills are not now of record.]

*Colonel John Walker (16??-1668/9) of Rappahannock County, Va. m(2) c.1662, Mrs. Sarah Fleet, (q.v.),p.222

Edwin Conway, Gentleman, (c.1610-1675), Lancaster County, Virginia. m. Martha Eltonhead [Hayden,p.221 et seq.]

*Major Francis Thornton (1651-1726) of Crows, King George County, Va. m(1) Alice Savage, dau:of Capt.Anthony Savage; (q.v.),p.210.

Sarah Walker (c.1663-ante 1695); two children, see p. 251. ─1680 m─

*Edwin Conway, Gentleman, (c.1643-1698) of Lancaster and Richmond counties; will verbatim, Hayden, p. 231; (q.v.), p.43-44. ─1695 m(2)─

*Elizabeth Thornton (1674-1732/3); she m(1) 21 May 1695 m(2) by 3 March 1698/9 ─1699 m(2)─

*Jonathan Gibson, Gentleman, (16??-1729) of Richmond and King George counties, (q.v.), p.77. They had issue, among others, 3 children below,viz:

*Francis Conway, Gentleman, (1696-1732) of Mt. Sion, Caroline County; m. 21 October 1717, *Rebecca Catlett (1702-1760), dau:*Col.John and Elizabeth (Gaines) Catlett; she m(2) *John Moore (16??-1759),widower, and both died testate at Port Conway, King George County. [Hayden,p.244 and Mt.Sion Bible] Issue, among others, viz:

Jonathan Gibson, Jr., (c.1700-1745) of Caroline and Orange cos; m. Margaret, dau:*Col. John and Elizabeth (Gaines) Catlett of Essex Co; left issue.

Alice Gibson (17??-1761) m.26 Sept.1727 *John Catlett (c.1705-1745) of Orange Co; left issue.

Rachel Gibson (1717-1761) m. *Col.George Taylor; he m(2) Sarah Taliaferro (1727 -84), see left. [Hayden, p.254, 673].

Francis Conway [Jr.], Gentleman, (1722-1761) of Mount Sion, Caroline County and Belle Grove, King George County, m.c.1744, Sarah Taliaferro (1727-1784), dau: of *Charles and Sarah (Thornton) Taliaferro; she m(2) 1764,*Col. George Taylor (1711-1792), widower of Rachel Gibson (see right above), of Orange County. [Hayden,p.254,673]

Eleanor Rose ["Nelly"] Conway (1731-1829), m. 13 Sept. 1749, Col. James Madison (1723-1801) of Montpellier, Orange Co. Their eldest child, Hon. James Madison (1751-1836), m. 15 Sept.1794 in Frederick Co., Dorothea (Payne) Todd; they had no issue. The second son of Colonel James and Eleanor Rose (Conway) Madison of Montpellier in Orange County is mentioned next below.

Captain Francis Conway (1749-1794) of Mt. Sion, m. 20 March 1770, Elizabeth Fitzhugh (1754-1823), dau: of John and Alice (Thornton) Fitzhugh of Bellaire, Stafford County; she m(2) Col. James Taylor of Orange County. Her portrait is at VHS. The eldest child of Captain Francis Conway was,

Major Ambrose Madison (1755-1794) of Orange County; m. Mary Willis Lee (1752-1798), dau: of Hancock and Mary (Willis) Lee and granddaughter of Col. Henry Willis (c.1690-1740) of Fredericksburg and his first wife nee Ann Alexander (16??-1726). The only child of Major Ambrose and Mary Willis (Lee) Madison was, viz:

Francis Fitzhugh Conway (1772-1803) who dueled with *William Thornton (1778-1803) (q.v.),p.213, over the affections of their cousin, Nelly Conway Madison (see right); both men were killed.

Nelly Conway Madison m. 12 Nov. 1804, her distant cousin, *Dr.John Willis (1774-1811) of Orange Co., son of Francis and Elizabeth (Perrin) Willis of White Hall, Gloucester County, Va; they had issue.

*JOSHUA DAVIS, GENTLEMAN, (16??-1710)

He was a prominent attorney at law in the Northern Neck of Virginia and frequently appears in the records of Rappahannock, Stafford, Westmoreland and Richmond counties but resided in Richmond County where he was a church warden in St.Mary's Parish, Stafford, and in which county his will remains of record. He married Katherine [?], who m(2) *James Butler (16??-1732) of Aquia Creek, Stafford County. Joshua Davis, Gentleman, had three children who were infants in 1703 when he made them a unique deed of gift "for their encouragement in learning their books," viz: (a) Joshua Davis, Jr., married Frances Harrison and died intestate in Stafford County in 1737; (b) *Samuel Davis married *Ann Butler; both died testate in Westmoreland County - he in 1750 and she in 1763; and (c) Hester [Esther] Davis (1692-circa 1762) who is mentioned next below, viz:

[Unknown -m(1)- first wife] :
She was the mother of 3 children

*William Lampton (16??-1723) m(2) 1715, *Mrs.Frances White, widow of Thomas White; she d.s. p.,1716. By purchase and patent he acquired land in Richmond Co. which fell into King George Co., 1721; (q.v.),p.114. He had an only child by his third wife.

1717 -m(3)-

Hester [Esther] Davis (1692-circa 1762). After being twice widowed she kept an ordinary at King George Courthouse. She was a woman of education and appears frequently on the court records.

1726 -m(2)-

*James Jones (17??-1744) of Hanover Parish, King George Co. By purchase and patent he acquired large land holdings in King George,Orange,Prince William, Culpeper and Fauquier cos. He had 3 children, viz:

William Lampton (c.1706-1760) m(1) Sarah [?] m(2) by 1749, Mary widow of *John Simpson who died 1744. He died intestate in c.1771 leaving a large family of Spotsylvania Co. Va. Wm. and Sarah Lampton had two known children, viz:

Ann Lampton m. by 1730 John Grigsby, Jr. He died intestate in Fauquier Co. in c.1771 leaving a large family of children.

Samuel Lampton d.s.p. ante 1730 in King George County.

Joshua Lampton (c.1719-post 1769) m.by 1749, Sarah - when of Prince Wm. Co. 1753 of Culpeper Co. and 1769 of Orange Co. Joshua Lampton left issue.

*Hon.Joseph Jones (1727-1805); m(1) c.1752, Mary Taliaferro (17??-77), d.s.p; m(2) Mary (Waugh) Dawson, widow of *Rev.Musgrove Dawson (17??-1764) of Caroline Co. [OPR. ,p.244]; she had 2 sons,viz:

Elizabeth Jones m.1752, *Spence Monroe, Gent. (1727-1774) of Westmoreland Co., nephew of Wm. Tyler, Gent.[see Tyler,Gent. right]. Their eldest son was, viz:

*Esther Jones (1732-78) m.by 1755 (as his 2d wife), Wm. Tyler, Gent. of Westmoreland Co.She had issue by him.

William Lampton (c.1733-1790), a soldier in the French and Indian War; m.1763, Martha ("Patsy") Schooler (17??-1811), dau: of John and Martha (Wharton) Schooler of Caroline and Spotsylvania counties; they moved to Clark Co. Ky. Ancestors of "Mark Twain."

Mary Lampton Born 30 June 1734 [SPR., p.81].

*Hon.John Dawson (1762-1814), member of Congress and intimate friend of President Monroe who called him "my relation.". He died unmarried.

Joseph Jones Jr. (1780-c.1808), d.s.p. Accompanied the Monroes to France, 1794. He is mentioned in the Monroe correspondence.

*President James Monroe (1758-1831); m. 1786, Elizabeth Kortright of New York City and had two only daughters both of whom married and left issue.

WHO WERE THE PARENTS OF THESE THREE SISTERS?

*William Smoot, Sr. (16??-1716); his will mentions wife, Jane; son-in-law, Thomas Durham, and three grand-children, viz: Margaret, Joseph and Sarah Durham. They are same as named in TD's will as his 3 eldest children.

-m- Jane [?] She died October 4, 1726. [NFPR]

*Thomas Durham (c.1660-1714); his will names his wife Doro-thy and the three children named below.

-m-

Dorothy [?] (c.1663-17??) m(2), 1715; *Jeremiah Green-ham (16??-1752) of Richmond Co. (q.v.), p.81.

*Alice [?] (16??-1701) m(1) *John Chinn (16??-1692); m(2)* John Stretch-ley, Gent. (c.1649-1698) [57V79;Hayden, 55-56]. Her daughter,viz:

Thomasin [?] m(1) *Abraham Marshall (16??-1709); m(2) *Will-iam Goodridge (16??-1713); all in Richmond Co.

D U R H A M

Elizabeth & Anne Smoot, twins, b.16 March 1698; North Farnham Parish; presumed to have died in infancy as they are not mentioned in their father's will of 1716.

Mary Smoot -m- c.1710-, b.7 April 1693 d.8 May 1750 [Dates, NFPR. It is possible her husband had two wives named Mary.]

*Thomas Durham, Jr. (1690-1734); his will mentions wife Mary; three eldest children by name and then "six small children." (q.v.), p.61.

John b.23 Nov.1698; NFPR.

*Mary Durham (1686-17??) m. c. 1701, *Thomas Dodson (1681-1740); see NFPR, (q.v.),p.57.

*Ann Chinn (1682-1729) m(1) *Capt. Wm.Fox (1674-1718); m(2) 1719, *Richard Chichester, Gent. (16??-1734); she d.s.p.,Lancaster Co. leaving an in-formative will.

Margaret Durham m. 2 Dec. 1729 Dominick Newgent (1709-17??), (q.v.), p. 145.

Joseph (171?-1742)

Sarah Durham m.26 Jan.1738 William Hanks, (q.v.),p.87.

Thomas (172?-1774)

John Durham b.14 Decem-ber 1725

Mary Durham b.24 August 1726

Susanna b.14 May 1728

Catherine b.18 March 1731

Millicent b.4 Aug. 1734

[These birth dates from North Farnham Parish Register]

By deed 2 August 1700, William Smoot,Sr., for love and affection for Dorothy Durham, wife of Thomas Durham, and her children, deeded 62 acres of land entailing it upon their eldest son Thomas Durham, Jr., their sec-ond son, John Durham and their eldest daughter, Mary Durham; he provides if all of these children d.s.p., the said land was to descend to the 4th, 5th and 6th children of the said Dorothy Durham [unnamed and ob-viously unborn] and if all the aforementioned children of Dorothy Durham d.s.p., said land to descend to Ann Fox, wife of William Fox, Gentleman, of Lancaster County. [Richmond County DB#3,p.57.]

In 1707 William Smoot deeded to Thomas Durham and Dorothy, his wife, an additional 50 acres of land and in 1707 Mary Gilbert, widow, deeded the same couple 50 acres of land adjoining the Smoot conveyance [DB#4,p. 109,111.] Reference is also made to WB#3,p.210,270; DB#10,p.474; H.W.Newman, The Smoots of Maryland and Virginia (Washington,1936),p.5-6; S.E.Lucas,Jr., Genealogy of the Dodson (Dotson), Lucas, Pyles, Rochester and Allied Families (Birmingham,1959),p.2 et seq.

[N.B. * Denotes these parties left wills of record in Lancaster or Richmond counties, Virginia.]

CAPTAIN HENRY FLEET - m- SARAH [2] -m(2)c.1662- COL.JOHN WALKER-m(1)c.1652- [?]
(circa 1600-1660) of : m(3) c.1670,Col.John Stone : (16??-1668/9) of : Four daughters;
Lancaster County,Va. : (1631-1698) (q.v.),p.195-6. : Rappahannock Co. : Frances and Eliza-
[A.P.& P.,p.172] : (q.v.),p.222-223,248. : beth of whom I
have no detail,
and two below.

FLEET | WALKER | WALKER

FLEET

Henry Fleet, Gentleman, (16??-1733) of Lancaster County. He was the ancestor of the Fleet family so long prominent in Virginia.

WALKER

Sarah Walker (c.1663-ante 1695) m. Edwin Conway, Gent.(c.1643-1698) as his first wife; (q.v.), p. 43-44. By her he had two children, viz:

Hester [Esther] Walker Born c.1663,m(1),168? Robert Tomlin,Jr.(q.v.), p.217; m(2) 1691, John Peirce, Gent.(16??-1698) (q.v.),p.156-157. By each husband she left one son, viz:

WALKER

Anne Walker Born c. 1654 m(1) c. 1668 John Payne,Jr. m(2)1670,John Daingerfield. [Payne,p.53-56.]

Jane Walker m. John Deane, Gent. (1648-1712) (q.v.), p.53; m(2) Elizabeth Thatcher.

CONWAY

Colonel Edwin Conway (1681-1763) of Lancaster County; m(1) 1704, Ann Ball;m(2) Ann Hack. [Hayden, p.234,238 et seq.]

TOMLIN

Captain Robert Tomlin (168?-17??),m.by 1720 Elizabeth [?] 6 July 1698 he choose Capt.George Tayler to be his guardian. They had an only known son, viz:

PEIRCE

William Peirce, Gentleman,(1697-1733) of Westmoreland Co. where his will is of record. He m.ante 1713, Sebellah [Sibella &c.];surname unknown; she predeceased him leaving four daughters [untraced] and two sons, viz:

TOMLIN

Robert Tomlin,Gent. -m- Winifred Webb (17??-1761);his will, : daughter of Richmond Co.WB#6,p. : Giles and 260, names two sons : Elizabeth only, viz: : (Spann) Webb

Robert Tomlin,Gent: (17??-1794),m.c.1770 Susanna Fauntleroy, (q.v.),p. 217.

Col.Walker Tomlin (17??-1802),m(1) c.1772,Sarah Fauntleroy; m(2) 1788, Priscilla Ball; (q.v.),p.217-218.

PEIRCE

William Peirce,Gent.(172?-1782) m(1)1753,Mary Mountjoy (q.v.),p. 157, and had three children;m(2) by 1769, Sarah [?] who survived him.

Joseph Peirce,Sr.,Gent.(c.1728-98) m.Sarah Elliott Ransdell (1737-85); dates from tombstones at Level Green, Westmoreland Co. His will names 5 daughters and an only son, viz:

Joseph,Jr. 1782 sold Richmond Co. land. [DB#15,p. 116.]

Eleanor m.by 1782 John Lawson; then of Culpeper Co. Va.

Mary m.by 1782 Churchill Gordon;in 1782 of Culpeper County,Va.

Ransdell Peirce (c.1770-1853) of Lancaster County where his will remains of record. He was twice married and there is record of himself and progeny in Lancaster County, Virginia.

*THE REVEREND MISTER ABRAHAM¹ KENYON (16??-c.1691) OF RAPPAHANNOCK COUNTY, VIRGINIA

He was a priest of the Protestant Episcopal Church and by patent and purchase acquired large land holdings on the north side of the Rappahannock River, which later fell into the counties of Richmond, King George and Stafford. His last will and Testament was recorded in a volume now lost, but Richmond County Deed Book #3, page 11, states his son and heir was John² Kenyon of Richmond County.

*John² Kenyon, Gentleman, (16??-1706) of Richmond County, Virginia
The name of his wife has not been ascertained. His last will and Testament remains of record in Richmond County Will Book #2, page 103; he had two sons, mentioned below.

*Abraham³ Kenyon, Gentleman, (16??-1750) of King George County; his will was recorded in now lost WB#1, however, the inventory of his estate is of record. He married Elizabeth Waddington, daughter of Francis and Margaret (Thomasin) Waddington of Stafford County, by whom he had no son but six daughters, below mentioned. [23T222-236]

*John³ Kenyon, Gentleman, (16??-1743) of King George County; his will was recorded in now lost WB#1, however, the inventory of his estate is of record and other surviving records impart considerable data. He married Jane [?] and probably had several children, but the name of only his son and heir has been discovered; he inherited his landed estate.

KENYON

Frances⁴ Kenyon m.Capt. Anthony Strother (1736-1787) of Albion, now Stafford Co., as his first wife and their son and heir was, viz:

Sarah⁴ Kenyon m.1741, *Capt. John Carter (1715/20-1783) of Spotsylvania County, as his first wife, and left issue.

Elizabeth⁴ Kenyon m.*Major William Newton (c.1720-89) of Little Falls in Stafford County, and left a large family of children.

Ann⁴ m.Wm.Clarke

Million⁴ m.*Richard Tutt, Jr.(17??-1767) of Spotsylvania Co.

Margaret⁴ m.*Capt. John Pollard (1728-1789) of Lambs Creek, King George County, Va.

*Capt.James⁴Kenyon (17??-1788); m.Ellen Bruce (17??-1790) dau.of Hensfield and Sarah Bruce of Richmond and King George counties; issue:

George⁵ Strother -m.cousin- *Sarah⁵ Kenyon (1772-1812) of Albion, now owned by Hunter R. Greenlaw.

1795 *Sarah⁵ Kenyon (17??-1825) No descendants living, 1963.

Jane⁵ Kenyon m. by 1788 Capt. James Went (1753-c.1830) of Wentsworth, King George Co.

Judith⁵ Kenyon (1772-1826) m. 1791, John Ficklin (1762-1804); to Mason Co. Ky.

Anne⁵ Kenyon m.1800,as his first wife, Charles Cary Bruce (1770-1845) of Springfield, Stafford Co.

Joseph⁵ Henry⁵ These two sons moved from Va. and probably settled in Mason Co. Kentucky.

[N.B. * Denotes these parties died testate; not all of their wills are now of record.]

EDWARD LEWIS OF NORTH FARNHAM PARISH, RAPPAHANNOCK COUNTY

He acquired land which fell into Richmond County upon its formation in 1692; this descended to his only son, John Lewis. John Lewis d.s.p. and intestate ante 1704/5 and this real estate in North Farnham Parish became the property of his five sisters all of whom had married prior to this date. They are named below, viz:

L E W I S

[1] Johanna Lewis -m- *William Linton (16??-1734) of Westmoreland Co. (q.v.), p.119
-m(2) 1730- Mary Hudson Died intestate Westmoreland Co. No issue

*Anthony Linton, eldest son and heir of his mother, died testate in Stafford County in 1738. [OPR., p.69]

*Thomas Freshwater, Sr. (16??-1726) of Richmond County, (q.v.), p.74.

[2] Mary Lewis -m- *Christopher Pridham (1672-1731) of Richmond Co. (q.v.), p. 162.

*Thomas Freshwater, Jr. (c.1700-1755) of Richmond County, (q.v.), p.74.
-m(1)- Ann Pridham (1705-173?)
-m(2)- *Elizabeth Jesper (1712-1772) [see below]

L E W I S

[4] Elizabeth Lewis (16??-1727)

[3] Ann Lewis -m. c. 1700- *Thomas Jesper (16??-1748) of Richmond County, (q.v.), p. 106.
*Thomas Jesper (16??-1748)

*Simon Taylor (16??-1729), (q.v.), p.206.

[5] Katherine Lewis m. Joseph Deeke (16??-1718) (q.v.), p.53.

*Thomas Jesper - m(2) in 1711 his wife's niece - Sarah Taylor Born 28 September 1692 in North Farnham Parish

*Elizabeth Jesper -m- *Thomas Freshwater, Jr. -m(1)- Ann Pridham (1705-173?), daughter of *Christopher and Mary (Lewis) Pridham [see above]
(1712-1772) (c.1700-1755); he left issue by both wives.

Sarah Freshwater -m. 1770- Henry Dobyns (q.v.), p.55.

Lack of space precludes naming all of the children of the above mentioned couples; the North Farnham Parish Register contains many entries in regard to them. The asterisk (*) denotes these parties died testate.

THOMAS MEAD[E] OF RAPPAHANNOCK COUNTY

In 1662 he held 700 acres of land which fell into Richmond County in 1692; this property descended to his only child and heir-at-law, viz:

Mary Mead(e)

She married Richard Hobbs (1644-1683) who died intestate in Rappahannock County, leaving an only child, viz:

Richard Green -m(1)- Ann Hobbs -m(2)- 1714 John Bramham
(1672-1705)   She died   He was living
(q.v.),p. 81   ante 1734.   in 1734; she
                                            had no issue
Three daughters of Richard and Ann   by him.
(Hobbs) Green survived infancy, viz:

G R E E N

Hester [Esther]-m-*John Gower : Eleanor Green-m-Benj:Rust : Edward Spencer-m(1)-Winifred 1714 -m(2)- *Stanley
Green   c.1705   (1702-1722) (1702-1754)   (q.v.), p. 193   Green   Gower; he
               (1672-1726)   Their only child d.s.p.;m(2) They had an only (1692-   d.s.p.,in
               m(2) Susanna   Sarah Metcalfe and left is-   child, viz: 1712?)   1718.(q.v.)
               [?]   sue. [Rust of Va., p. 49.]   p. 80.

Edward Spencer, Gentleman,
(1710-1753), of Orange County.
m. Elizabeth [?]
He died intestate in Orange
County; there is considerable
record there of his family.

*Francis Gower -m- Rachel [?] 1727 -m(2)- *John Bramham, Sr.
Born 2 Feb.1706   (1722-1761); they
Died 7 Jan.1727   moved to Orange Co.
Richmond County,   where he died test-
[See NFPR.]   ate. (q.v.), p. 23.

Ann Gower -m- John White : Francis Gower
(q.v.),p.230   (1726-1729)

N.B. Deed 6 November 1752, recorded in Richmond County DB#11, p.155, recites title to certain land and states Edward Spencer, a grandson, and Ann wife of John White, a great-granddaughter, are the only heirs of Ann Bramham, late of Richmond County, deceased. See also AB#1,p.79; COB#4,p.74; COB#6,p.258; DB#7,p.13,14,60,492,545, 547; DB#8,p.55, DB#9,p.100,388,633; DB#10,p.40,366,368; DB#11,p.152,155; MRB.,p.118; WB#2,p.87; WB#4,p.67; WB #5,p.20,29; Sweeny,p.84; C&P.,p.489; Silas Emmett Lucas, Jr., Genealogy of the Dodson (Dotson), Lucas, Pyles, Rochester, and Allied Families (Birmingham, 1959), p.226-229. *Denotes these persons died testate.

CAPTAIN SIMON MILLER (1642-1665?) of RAPPAHANNOCK COUNTY, VIRGINIA

He was an officer in the colonial militia and a man of affairs in the early settlement of Rappahannock County. His children were by an unknown first wife; his last wife was Margaret Prosser, widow of *John Prosser who died testate in 1677; she m(3) Hugh French and m(4) John Somerville (q.v.), p.192.

---

*Simon[2] Miller (16??-1720) of Richmond County. m. [unknown]; she m(2) William Smith. Simon[2] Miller had 3 children, viz:

: Eleanor[3] Miller m.1726, *Thomas Hord Gent.(1701-1766) of King George County. They left issue.

: Jane[3] Miller m. *Robert Ellison (17??-1785); Stafford County. They left issue.

Margaret[2] Miller (16??-1760) n.f.r.

*Isabella[2] Miller (16??-1760) m. *William Triplett of Caroline Co. (16??-1728) and left issue.

*William Miller (16??-1726); will in lost WB#1 of King George Co. m. [unknown] and left issue, among others, 2 sons, viz:

: *Simon[3] Miller (171?-1799) m(1) [unknown] m(2) 1740, Isabella[3] Miller [see,OPR,p.79]

: Benjamin[3] Miller (17??-44) Essex County.

Susanna[2] Miller (16??-1724) m. Henry Brice of Essex County; she d.s.p. [12T237-243]

*Captain John[2] Miller (16??-1743), styled "mariner," of Essex Co. m. Mary [?]; they had 8 children, among two sons named below.

: *Simon[3] Miller (17??-1770) of Fauquier Co. m. Anne O'Bannon. They left no male issue.

: *Capt.William[3] (17??-1767) of Spotsylvania Co. m. Jane Hord; they left two daughters.

: *Simon[3] Miller (17??-92) Sheriff, Essex Co., 1755;issue.

By (1) Simon[3] Miller had four children, viz.:

: *Simon[4] Miller (173?-1806) of Culpeper Co;eldest son. He m. Sarah [?] and left issue.

: Benjamin[4] Miller; he died ante 1783 with issue.

: Mary[4] Miller b.1737; m. 1755 her 1st cousin, *James Hord (1736-1803) of Culpeper Co; left issue.

: Alice[4] Miller b.c.1739; m.1763 *John Markham (1732-1804) of Stafford Co. as his first wife; left issue.

By (2) Simon[3] Miller had two children,viz:

: Eleanor[4] Miller b. 1742; m. ante 1768, Thomas Strother; to Bourbon Co.Ky. c.1802. They left issue.

: Eliza[4] Miller m. *Capt. William Richards (c. 1755-1817) of Culpeper Co; they had a large family of children.

The land of Simon[2] Miller and William[2] Miller fell into King George County upon its formation in 1721 and although the will of William[2] Miller is in lost WB#1 the terms of it are recited in various deeds remaining of record in King George County DB#1,p.188-191; DB#1-A,p.189; DB#2,p.481. The land of Captain John[2] Miller was in Essex County and those records hold considerable data in regard to his progeny. Simon[3] Miller (171?-1799) of Stafford and Culpeper counties lived to be very old; he left two wills which were contested in the courts. After the death of his second wife, who was the daughter of Captain John[2] Miller, the second will of Simon[3] Miller greatly favored Captain William Richards and his wife, their younger daughter, with whom they had made their home during their declining years. [N.B. * Denotes these parties died testate.]

WILLIAM MILLS (16??-1661) -married- JOANE [?]   m(2) James Yate(s);   STERNE

In 1654 he patented 400 acres of land on the north side of the Rappahannock River, later in Richmond County; he seated this plantation and it was occupied by some of his descendants for several generations. (q.v.), p. xvii

m(2) James Yate(s); he was called "father" in the will of his stepson, Peter Mills (16??-1677).

The two brothers mentioned below were headrights of Colonel Thomas Beale in 1666. (q.v.), p.195

---

*Peter Mills d.s.p., 1677 Rappahannock County; his will is of record there.

Ann Mills -m- *John Birkett (16??-1719,) Richmond Co. (q.v.), p.18. No male issue.
Ann Mills Died 16 Sept.1691 [Tombstone]:

Elizabeth Mills m. 1678

*David Sterne - m(2)- (1645-1692), Richmond Co. (q.v.), p.195 He left a daughter by each wife.

Agatha [?] m(2) *Col. Nicholas Smith (q.v.) p. 190.

*Francis Sterne (c.1638-1713), Richmond County m.*Mary Cammack (16??-1743) and had two sons. (q.v.), p. 195.

---

*Mary Birkett (16??-1745) m(1) N. Jones (q.v.), p.109; m(2) *T.Brock (q.v.), p. 24. She had issue by (1) only.

*Margaret Birkett (16??-1749), m(1) *John Pratt, Jr. (16??-1724)(q.v.), p.161; m(2) *Daniel French, Gent. (16??-1736) by whom she had no issue. Her only son to leave legitimate issue is mentioned next below.

*Ann Birkett (16??-1745) m.*Cornelius Edmonds (16??-1722) of Richmond and King George counties.

Elizabeth Birkett m. *Capt. Geo: White (16??-1738) (q.v.),p.229; left issue.

Frances Sterne m(1) *Wm. Pannell (d670-1716) and had 7 children; m(2) *Thomas Hughes (16??-1766) and had 3 children. (q.v.), p. 100, 154.

Ann Sterne m.1713, *Captain Daniel White (16??-1748/9) (q.v.), p. 229; left issue. He was a brother of Captain George White [see left].

---

*Thomas Pratt, Gentleman, (1721-1766) of Eden, Saint Paul's Parish, Stafford [now King George] County, m. c.1747, *Margaret Vivion (1724-1818), younger of the two daughters of Major Thomas Vivion (168?-1761) of Middlesex, King George and Westmoreland counties, and his first wife nee Frances Thacker (1696-1724), daughter of Henry and Elizabeth (Payne) Thacker and granddaughter of John and Ann (Walker) Payne. Thomas and Margaret (Vivion) Pratt had 8 children who married and left progeny.

[N.B. * Denotes these parties died testate, however, not all of their wills now remain of record due to the loss of various will books in several counties.]

M O O R E

Francis Moore (1660-1718) Merchant in Dublin, Ireland, and planter in Rappahannock River, Virginia; (q.v.), p.136. —m— 1707? *Ann [? Harbin ?] (167?-1744); moved to Orange Co. with her two sons. —m(2)— c.1719 # [See note] *John Naylor, Gentleman, (167?-1735) of Richmond and King George counties; (q.v.), p.143. —m(1)— 1712 Mary Rogers (167?-1717)

*Col.Francis Moore (1711-1796); moved to Orange Co.,1739. m. Elizabeth [?]: she predeceased him leaving a large family of children.

*Harbin Moore (1712-1802) of Culpeper Co. m. Anne Marks, dau.of *John Marks, d.1759.

A daughter m. Thomas Pattey, Jr. Moved from Orange to Lunenburg County, Va.

Martha Moore —m— *Capt.David Bronough (172?-1774); he m(3) Elizabeth Bruce, dau. of *Charles and Elizabeth (Pannell) Bruce of King George County. —m(1)— Hannah Naylor (1715-c.1737)

*Bernard Moore —m— (172?-1775) of Orange County; he left an only child, viz.

Catherine Price —m(2)— dau. of Arjalon and Joyce (Barber) Price of Richmond County; (q.v.), p.162.

* Capt.Reuben Moore (1754-1839) of Culpeper Co.Va. He m. (2) 1804, Elizabeth W. Stewart (1763- post 1853). [Revolutionary pension papers, W-8466.]

Ann Moore Bronough m. in June 1758 William Chadwell, Sr. (1728-1813) of King George County. [21T266]

Mary Bronough (c.1736-1799) m(1) Joseph Waugh m(2) Colonel Elijah Threlkeld, both of Stafford County, Va. [OPR.,p.236;21T265.]

Lucy Barbour Moore (1771-1837), m. *Captain Reuben Gaines (1765-1847); these dates from their tombstones at Locust Hill, Culpeper County, Va.

[N.B. * Denotes these parties died testate and their last wills and Testaments are now of record.]

It appears from the North Farnham Parish Register and the wills of John Naylor and Ann Naylor died in infancy.

This chart is designed to illustrate a few of the complex intermarriages of the above families; there were several others but the size of the paper precludes showing them on this diagram as well as all the issue of some of the above mentioned couples. We observe how these families, intermarried and associated in early Richmond County, continued their affinities as they moved up the Northern Neck of Virginia and into the Orange, Culpeper and Madison county area.

*GEORGE MOTT, GENTLEMAN, (162?-1674) -m- ELIZABETH [?] -m(2)- JAMES HARRISON (162?-1712)
With his bachelor brother, *Mr. John Mott,   1674   He died intestate in Essex
he patented extensive tracts of land in   County; they had an only
the Northern Neck which descended to his   daughter (q.v.), p.89.
four daughters, viz: (q.v.),p.57,71,79,186.

Margaret Mott -m- *Capt.Alexander Doniphan   Elizabeth Mott *Anne Mott   *Ellen Mott -m- Richard Shippy,
She was his   :   (c.1653-1717), (q.v.),p.   m. John Fossak- m.Capt.John   (c.1673-   :   Gent.(167?-1708)
second wife.   :   57; 26T275-285; 28T226-   er, (q.v.),p.71 Glendening,   1741)   :   of Richmond Co.
               :   238; 29T50-64.   (q.v.),p.79   :   (q.v.), p.186

*Mott Doniphan, -m- Rosanna Anderson,   Jael Shippy -m- *Wm.Underwood *Elizabeth-m-*James Hackley
Gent. (172?-c.   : dau.of Capt. George   m(2) *Samuel :   (167?-1726)   Shippy   : (c.1690-1748) of
1776)[OPR,p.218] : Anderson of Stafford   Reed(s)(1772- :   (q.v.),p.221   (1692-   : King George Co.
                  : County, Virginia.   1750), KGCo. :   1756)   :

*Capt.Alexander Doniphan -m- Magadaline Monteith,   *Lott Underwood -m- cousin- Mary Hackley
(172?-1761) of King George: dau.of Thomas Monteith, (172?-1773); to   :   She sold her land in
County   : Gent. (q.v.), p.136   Culpeper Co. Va. :   Culpeper Co., 1800

                          1774   Frances Underwood -married- William Pound
Elizabeth Doniphan -m- Richard Shipp, Sr.   She was mentioned in :   (1749-1823), of
(1759-c.1812);their : (1747-1828) of Caroline   her husband's will. :   Culpeper County; a
Bible record is pre-: County; moved to Ky.   :   Revolutionary sold-
served.   :   ier

                    1807   Capt. Richard Pound -m- *Ann Lyon (1783-1860)
Emma Grant Shipp - m- *William Truman   (172?-1812),Fairview :   m(2), 1814, George Chancellor,Esq.
Born in Va.,1787   : Born in Va.,1783   Spotsylvania County :   (1785-1836) of Chancellorsville,
Died in Ky.,1872   : Died in Shelby   :   Spotsylvania County, Virginia.
                   : Co., Ky., 1863

                    1846   1823
Anderson Shipp Truman -m- Mary Jane Holmes   *Frances Longwill Pound -m- *Major Sanford Chancellor
(1816-1887); moved   :   (1821-1879), dau.   (1803-1892); died at Oak :   (1791-1860) of Forest Hall,
from Shelby Co. Ky. :   Jesse and Ann   Grove, Spotsylvania Coun-:   Spotsylvania Co. Served in
to Jackson Co. Mo.   :   (Tyler) Holmes.   ty, Virginia.   :   War of 1812

                    1881   1893
John Anderson Truman - m- Martha E. Young   *Susan Margaret Chancellor -m- Capt.Vespacian Chancellor
(1851-1915)   :   (1853-1947)   (1847-1935), of Fredericks-: (1838-1908), grandson of
                     :   burg, Va. [71V259-277]   : George and Ann Chancellor

PRESIDENT HARRY SHIPP TRUMAN   [* Denotes these parties died testate.]

*JOHN¹ PRATT, SENIOR, GENTLEMAN, (16??-1714)

He is described as a merchant and a gentleman in the contemporary records. He acquired considerable property in Westmoreland, Richmond and Stafford counties and those records contain many references to him and his only known child, John² Pratt; the name of his wife is unknown to me.

*JOHN BIRKETT (16??-1719) of Richmond County (q.v.), p. 18.

m— ANN MILLS (16??-1691) daughter of William Mills

Elizabeth Jones daughter of *Mrs. Mary Jones (16??-1708) of Westmoreland County; she had an only child.

—married—

*John² Pratt, Junior, Gentleman, (16??-1724) —married (2)—

*Margaret Birkett (16??-1749); m(2) *Daniel French, Gent. (16??-1736) also of King George County by whom she had no issue.

Like this father he appears prominently on the court records. His will, probated in King George County, remains of record in COB 1766-1790, p.286 et seq., in the suit Hungerford vs Pratt. (q.v.), p.161. John² and Margaret (Birkett) Pratt had four children mentioned in family and court records.

Margaret³ Pratt m. William Tyler, Gent. (17??-1772) of Westmoreland Co. She d.s.p. and he m(2) *Esther [Hester] Jones (1732-1778) and left issue by her.

John³ Pratt (1710-1738) d.s.p. [The records state these two brothers died intestate and without issue in Stafford County,Virginia.]

Birkett³ Pratt (1713-1760) d.s.p.

Ann³ Pratt (1718-1800) m.c.1758,*Col. Thomas Hungerford (1712-1772) and left issue.

Thomas³ Pratt, Gent. (1721-1766) of Eden, Stafford [now King George] Co. m.c.1747, *Margaret Vivion (1724-1818), daughter of *Major Thomas and Frances (Thacker) Vivion. They had 6 daughters and 2 sons; all left issue, viz:

*Frances⁴ Pratt (1748-1830), m. *William Hooe, Sr. (1743-1808) of Pine Hill, King George County.

Margaret⁴ Pratt (1750-c.1828) m. 2 November 1771, *Captain Bernard Hooe (1739-1825) and resided at Hazel Plain, Prince William County, Va. where his tombstone is to be seen.

Ann⁴ Pratt (1752-178?) m. 28 August 1772, Capt.William Sthreshley (1749-1830) of Caroline Co. m(2) Elizabeth (Madison) Buckner (1760-1830).

*Elizabeth⁴ Pratt (1754-1829), m. *John Hipkins (17??-1804), merchant of Port Royal, Caroline County, Va.

Susanna⁴ Pratt (1756-   ) m. 13 November 1782 in St. Paul's Parish, William Hooe of Prince William County.

Mildred⁴ Pratt (1759-1853) m.12 March 1779 Capt.Henry Washington (1749-1825); moved to Alabama.

*John Birkett⁴ Pratt (1761-1843) of Camden, Caroline Co., m.4 Nov. 1784, Alice (Fitzhugh) Dixon (1759-1845); see OPR.,p.231.

Thomas⁴ Pratt (1765-1797) of Eden, King George Co. m. 23 June 1785, Jane Brockenbrough and had 4 daughters; she m(2) 1800, Francis Taliaferro of Epsom, Spotsylvania Co. Va.

[N.B. * Denotes these parties died testate.]

*COLONEL WILLIAM ROBINSON (162?-1742)

Traditionally a native of Yorkshire, England, he came to Rappahannock River in 1695 when he inherited a 1460 acre plantation in Richmond County from his uncle, *Maxmillian Robinson, Gentleman, (162?-1695); he had purchased it in 1686 while residing in Ware Parish, Gloucester County. This plantation at Southery Ferry, near Leedstown, was occupied by Colonel William[1] Robinson and his descendants for several generations; they called the estate Bunker Hill. Upon the formation of King George County in 1721 it fell into that county and upon a boundry alteration between King George and Westmoreland counties, after 1777 Bunker Hill was in Westmoreland County. Although a resident of King George County, Colonel William[1] Robinson served as King's Attorney for Richmond County from 1736 until his death on 20 September 1742. By 1699 he married Frances Blomfield [Bloomfield, Bromfield &c:] (q.v.),p.172 and they had an only child, viz:

[2 Alice ?] Thornton -married circa 1727- *Captain Maxmillian[2] Robinson -m(2) by 1759- *Hannah Fauntleroy daughter of *Col. William (1692-1776) of Bunker Hill, (1722-1778), daughter Thornton (1680-1742) of King George County. He owned of *Colonel William King George County. By her plantations in several count- Fauntleroy (1684-1757) he had two children, viz: ies. of Richmond County. [22V22-24]

Only child →

*William[3] Robinson, Gentleman, -m.circa 1750- Ann Watts, daughter of Richard Watts, Jr. who died intestate c. 1744, Westmoreland County. (172?-1777), also of Bunker Hill. In 1773 sold land in Fauquier County which had been bequeathed to him by his maternal grandfather, Col. William Thornton [Fauquier County DB#5,p.304]. William[3] and Ann (Watts) Robinson had two children, viz:

Frances[3] Robinson m. (as his first wife), Dr. William Flood (172?-1775) of Westmoreland Co; their only child, Alice[4] Flood, m. Hon. Walter Jones, M.D.,of Northumberland Co.Va.

*Henry [Harry][3] Robinson, d.s.p., 1778, Westmoreland Co. just prior to his mother; this event provoked a suit in chancery regarding their personal property.

*William[4] Robinson, Gentleman, -m.1777- *Margaret Williamson -m(2) 1783- *Colonel John Rose Alice[4] Robinson (1752-1782), also of Bunker Hill; (1755-1837), dau: of (172?-1802) of married will proved in Westmoreland Co.He Dr.Walter and Mildred Mount Rose in West- Butler Beckwith had three only children, viz: (Washington) William- moreland County,Va. [See SPR.,p.xxiii, 154] son; issue by each. [Eubank, p.36]

Anne Washington[5] Robinson *Daniel McCarty, 1797 Margaret[5] Robinson -m(2) 1802 *Richard Stuart, William Robin- (1778-182??), m.1795; *Dr. Gent.(172?-1801), -m- (1780-1808); she Esq. (1770-1835) son (1782- post Henry Rose (172?-1810) of of Longwood, in left issue by of Cedar Grove, 1850); see 22V Fairfax County, Virginia. Westmoreland Co. each spouse. King George Co. 24 for detail.

*JAMES1 SAMFORD (c.1624-1704) OF RICHMOND COUNTY

He appears on the records of Rappahannock County in 1664 with Mary Samford, his wife, and in this same year had a land patent on Totusky Creek now in Richmond County. It appears they had at least three daughters,viz: (1) Mary2 Samford m.1673, John Webb (q.v.),p.226; (2) [?] 2 Samford m. Edward Jones and had a son Samford Jones; (3) Catherine2 Samford m. Thomas Baylis (167?-1699) (q.v.),p.12. The only known son of James1 and Mary Samford is mentioned below. [C&P.,p.433,435,477,481,484,486,512,545; AB#1,p.38 et seq; WB#2,p.72; DB#8,p.49.]

*Samuel2 Samford (1662-1736) resided upon Totusky Creek, North Farnham Parish, (q.v.),p.177. He m(1) Elizabeth Keene (1669-c.1706), daughter of William and Elizabeth (Rogers) Keene of Northumberland County; she was the mother of all his children. He m(2) 21 November 1707 in Christ Church Parish, Middlesex County, *Isabel Langhee (167?-1725), widow. The wills of Samuel2 Samford and Isabel (?) Langhee Samford,also his mother-in-law, Elizabeth (Rogers) Keene Banks (167?-1720), are of prime genealogical import. Samuel2 and Elizabeth (Keene) Samford had seven children who reached maturity.

*Thomas3 Samford (1687/8-1762) m. Frances [?]; she died 1750. NFPR records their children's births. See Section A,below.

*James3 Samford (c.1690-1742) m.1728, Mary Barber; she m(2) 1753, Wm. Denton. NFPR records their children's births. See Section B, below.

*William3 Samford (1692-1763), m.c. 1713, step-sister Elizabeth Langhee; moved to Brunswick Co. NFPR records their child's births. See Section C, below.

*Giles3 Samford (1699-1727) d.s.p. [WB#5, p.56]

*John3 Samford (1702-1768) m. Sarah [?] His will names 2 children,viz: Giles4, b.1736; Ann4, b.1739. [WB#7,p.10]

Samuel3 Samford m.Margaret [?]. 1739 they sold land in Richmond Co. [DB#9,p.555]

Elizabeth3 m. 1727 *Bennett Boggess, d. 1745, Northumberland Co.

Section A: *Thomas3 Samford (1687/8-1762) [WB#5,p.315]; m. Frances [?] (172?-1750) and had six children, viz: (a) James4, b.1737 - he conveyed land to which he had right by descent from his great-grandfather, James1 Samford [DB#13,p.184; DB#15,p.263; DB#17,p.399]; (b) Mary4, b.1739, m. John Stewart Chilton (q.v.), p.35; (c) *Thomas4 (1741-1764), d.s.p. [WB#6,p.360]; (d) Elizabeth4, b.1743, m.1763 *John McCalley [McCaulley] (1740-1783); moved to Spotsylvania County (q.v.),p.122; (e) John Amis4 (1746-c.1797) m.1771, Betty Lightfoot (q.v.),p.177; (f) Frances4, b.1750; she is not mentioned in her father's will, 1762.

Section B: *James3 Samford (c.1690-1742) m.1728, Mary Barber who m(2) 1753, William Denton (q.v.),p.53,176. James3 inherited 200 acres of land from his paternal grandfather by will and some years after his death a chancery suit [Singleton vs Samford (1767)] say he died without male heir and mentions his daughters, their spouses and family connections, viz: (a) Ann4, b.1730, m.1749,Joshua Singleton (q.v.),p.187; (b) James4 (1733-1735); (c) Elizabeth4, b.1735, m.c.1755, William Miskell (q.v.),p.133; (d) Frances4, b.1737, m.1756, John Suggitt (q.v.),p.199; she d.s.p; (e) Winifred4, b.1739, m. Daniel Dobyns.

Section C: *William3 Samford (1692-1763) m.c.1713 his step-sister, Elizabeth Langhee; after the births of their children in North Farnham Parish they moved to Brunswick County. Their eldest son, *William Keene Samford (1722/3-1795), m.1742 Winney Dowden, (q.v.),p.177. [Brunswick County WB#4,p.317; WB#5,p.620]. See Ritchie and Wood, Garner-Keene Families of Northern Neck Virginia,(Charlottesville,Va.,1952), p.203 et seq.

*FRANCIS[1] SETTLE (16??-1707/8)

He died testate in North Farnham Parish, Richmond County. His will, recorded in WB#1,p.125, mentions that he is "well stricken in years." Several children are mentioned in his will as well as the two infant sons of his deceased son Henry[2] Settle (16??-1702), next below.

*Henry[2] Settle (16??-1702)

He died testate in North Farnham Parish; his will is recorded in WB#1,p.57. He married Mary Jackson; she is mentioned in the will of her father, Daniel Jackson (16??-1706), recorded in WB#1,p.106. They had two only sons, viz:

*Henry[3] Settle (20 September 1700-7 July 1772) —m— Anne Bailey (10 January 1698- of North Farnham Parish, Richmond County, Va. His will is of record in WB#7,p.117 and NFPR records the births of other children, but the Bible record records the birth of only the below mentioned son.

Anne Bailey (10 January 1698- 13 August 1773), daughter of John and Elizabeth Bailey. They were married circa 1721. The exact dates cited on this chart are from a Bible record.

*Francis[3] Settle (1702-1752) of King George County, Virginia. Will recorded in WB#2,p.17.

Lieutenant Bailey[4] Settle (26 January 1732/3-22 September 1813)

He was born in North Farnham Parish; he died intestate. He married Amy (surname not mentioned); she died 22 September 1813 an hour after her husband, relates the unique recording in their family Bible. Bailey Settle is mentioned as a lieutenant in the militia of Richmond County, 2 April 1759 [COB#14,p.281].

William[5] Settle (1772-12 November 1833)

The surviving pages of the Bible record fail to record the birth of himself and wife. He married on 9 August 1798 in Westmoreland County, Mary ("Polly") Greenlaw (1772-12 November 1845), daughter of William and Mary (Oldham) Greenlaw (q.v.),p.81. The Bible records the death of William Greenlaw on 29 January 1811 and that of his wife on 19 June 1825 and states they were the parents of Mary Settle. Omitting the four children whose births and deaths in infancy are recorded in the Bible, William and Mary (Greenlaw) Settle had issue as follows:

Anne Maria Bailey Settle[6] Born 27 November 1802; married 14 September 1820, Thomas Spence, Jr. of Westmoreland County (q.v.), p.193. They left issue.

Betsy Bailey[6] Settle Born 14 February 1806; married 20 February 1823, William G. Smith (q.v.), p.192.

Edwin Bailey[6] Settle, born 22 June 1813

John Alexander[6] Settle, born 22 July 1817

Frederick[5] Settle, born 17 November 1819

[N.B. * Denotes these parties died testate.]

*WILLIAM[1] STONE   - - married - -   *SARAH [?]
(16??-1704)   (16??-1717)

On April 3, 1680, while a resident of Gloucester County, William[1] Stone purchased 727 acres of land in Rappahannock County from Robert Bedwell; this property fell into Richmond County upon its formation in 1692. William[1] Stone and his wife Sarah Stone seated this plantation on Totusky Creek in North Farnham Parish and their progeny continued in the present Richmond County area for several generations. William[1] Stone also acquired land in Essex County from Richard Gregory but he disposed of it in 1699.

The terms of the last will and Testament of her husband caused his widow and executrix considerable concern and it appears it was only after considerable difficulty she succeeded in getting it admitted to record.

There are many recordings in the North Farnham Parish Register in regard to the issue of William[1] and Sarah Stone and their progeny.

Philip[2] Stone of Totusky Creek, North Farnham Parish, Richmond County, eldest son and heir-at-law of William[1] Stone. m. Sarah [?] ; issue, probably among others:

Joshua[2] Stone (16??-1719) m. Mary [?] ; issue, probably among others:

*William[2] Stone (16??-1749) favorite son of his parents; he moved to Amelia County, Virginia. m. Elizabeth [?]

Mary[2] m. Fan(n)

Elizabeth[2] m. William Dawson (q.v.), p. 52.

daughter[2] m. Glascock; their sons Gregory[3] and John[3] Glascock

William[3] Stone, styled Junior and of King George County in 1737 when he relinquished claim to land in Richmond Co. formerly the property of his grandfather, William[1] Stone, in exchange for land in Prince William County [DB#9, p.403].

*Joshua[3] Stone (1716-1774) m. 22 Nov. 1738 Wilmo(u)th Bryant (q.v.), p. 196. They left issue.

(1) Ann[3] Stone, b.1713, m. William Manire (q.v.), p. 127; he was William[2] Stone's executor.
(2) Margaret[3] Stone, born 1715, m. Mr. Hammond
(3) Philip[3] Stone, born 1716
(4) Elizabeth[3] Stone, born 1719, m. Mr. Taylor
(5) Henry[3] Stone, born 1726
(6) Katherine[3] Stone, born 1728
(7) Sarah[3] Stone, born 1734, m. Mr. Harper
(8) Lucy[3] Stone, born 17__, m. Mr. Green
These children are mentioned in the will of William[2] Stone dated 2 December 1748 and recorded 21 April 1749 in Amelia County WB#1,p.55 as recited in Richmond County DB#10,p.505.

William[1] Stone (16??-1704) and some of his progeny resided in North Farnham Parish, Richmond County, for several generations and there is considerable record of them there. His contemporary, Francis Stone (16??-1716), resided in the area which became King George County in 1721; I have observed no intimacy between the two families.
[N.B. * Denotes these person died testate.]

*Thomas Pannell -m- Katherine [?] -m(2)- *Thomas Swinburne
(162?-1677)   (162?-1697/8)
(q.v.), p. 153   (q.v.), p. 200

Elizabeth -m- Francis Stone (162?-1716) -m- c.1700 -m(2)- Mary Pannell — c.1687 -m(1)- James Kay [Key, Keys]

Elizabeth
[Although the legal proof is lacking, it appears the two men mentioned below were sons of Francis and Elizabeth Stone.]

-m- Francis Stone (162?-1716), of Rappahannock County, by 1672; died intestate, Richmond County, where his land was post 1692. In 1696 he was surveyor of the highways. He was a small planter and the records are scant.

-m- c.1700 -m(2)- Mary Pannell
She survived Francis Stone but disappears from the Richmond County records shortly afterwards.

No issue

c.1687 -m(1)- James Kay [Key, Keys] (162?-1698); he inherited considerable land near Dogue now in King George County from his father, James Kay. James and Mary (Pannell) Kay were survived by 3 children, viz.
[20T171-180;243-250]

.. Catherine Kay
   m. William Bland
   (q.v.), p. 19

.. Sarah Kay, m.1711,
   Mark Chilton, (q.v.)
   p.35

.. *James Kay [III]
   (1692-1794),m(1)
   by 1718, Mary [?],
   m(2)1763, Ann,
   widow of *James
   Pead (d. 1757).
   By (1) he had
   issue, among
   others, viz:

William Stone -m- Catherine Swinburne
(1679-c.1712)   (1682-post 1735);
Deposition in   she was a half-
1702 indicates   sister of her
residence near   husband's step-
Dogue now in   mother, Mary
King George Co.; (Pannell) Kay
near land of Mr. Stone.
James Kay.
STONE.

c.1713 -m(2)- John Plaile
He died intestate in King George County in 1734.

Francis Stone,Jr. (c.1681-1740); he moved to Prince William Co. where he had a land patent, 1711. He m. Esther [?] ,m(2) 1741, George Colvert.

PLAILE

Swinburne Thomas Richard John
[These four brothers appear infrequently on the records. In 1735 their mother made Richard and John Plaile a deed of gift for 100 acres; Richard Plaile sold it in 1753.]

John Kay m.Nov.1771, probably as his second wife, his stepsister, Catherine Pead. Their son, *James Kay (c.1772-1795), was mentioned in the will of his grandfather Kay; he d.s.p. [See King George Co.DB#8,p.565]

*Francis Stone (c.1702-1749) m.#Sarah Monroe (1722-1752);lived in King George County, Virginia. Issue:
(1) William Stone
(2) Francis Stone
(3) Sarah Stone
(4) Mary Stone
(5) A daughter m. by 1752, Lambert Rouse.

*William Stone (1709-1771) m.#Mary Monroe (1722-1776);lived in King George Co. Va. : Issue four children, viz:

Frances Stone m.first cousin, George Payne (1727-1790),son of John and #Jane (Monroe) Payne.

*Margaret Stone (1732-1784) m.John Ferguson She d.s.p. in Westmoreland County, Va.

Mary Stone (1739-1809) m. Samuel Major of Culpeper County, Va.

George Stone (1741-1771?, m.176?, Mary Scandrett, daughter of Isaac Scandrett (1722-1769) of Essex Co. They had two sons mentioned in the wills of *William Stone and *Margaret (Stone) Ferguson.

[# These three ladies were daughters of *William Monroe,Gent. (1666-1737) of Westmoreland County, Va.]

STONE - METCALFE - BARROW - RUST - LIGHTFOOT - RANSDELL

COLONEL JOHN STONE - married c.1670 - SARAH [2]

He appears prominently on the records of Rappahannock and Richmond counties and was first gentleman justice of Richmond County, 1692. His will was dated 27 April 1695; it was presented to court in 1698 by his son-in-law, Richard Metcalfe, Gentleman. Colonel John Stone (1631-1698) left an only child, Anne Stone; she was twice married and left issue by each spouse. (q.v.), p. 195

She m(1) Captain Henry Fleet (c.1600-1660)
She m(2) Colonel John Walker (1672-1668/9)
She m(3) Colonel John Stone (1631-1698)
She had issue by each as well as a daughter Mary, born circa 1662, while Widow Fleet; she is dubbed Mary Burden in the records! Colonel John Stone m(2) Mary [2] ; she died between the writing of his will, 1695, and its probate, 1698.

Elizabeth Fauntleroy 1685 -m- Richard Metcalfe, Gent. -m(2),c.1690- Anne Stone -m(2),c.1700- Edward Barrow,
daughter of Colonel : (1672-1699), (q.v.), p. : (c.1672- : Gent.(1672-1721)
Moore Fauntleroy : 131. [5W(1)10-13] : post 1728) : Richmond County

METCALFE ... METCALFE ... BARROW ...

Gilbert Metcalfe
Gent.(1687-1737)
m.Susanna (Cammack) Foster (1682-1747), widow of John Foster (1672-1711); they had no issue. (q.v.), p. 131.

Jane Anne Metcalfe
m. March 1714 Captain John Opie (q.v.), p. 151.
(spinster)

Mary Metcalfe
m(1) Austin Brockenbrough, (q.v.), p.24; m(2) John Spicer, Gent., (q.v.), p. 193. Issue by each.

BARROW

Elizabeth
m(1) 1725 Samuel Bayley (q.v.),p. 6; m(2) by 1741, William Bridges

John
d.s.p.,1728, testate.

Sarah
m. Benj: Rust (1702-1754) [#]

Edward Barrow (1702-1733)
m. Elizabeth Minor, (q.v.) p.11. Edward and Elizabeth (Minor) Barrow had 3 children,viz:

Margaret and Anne Barrow n.f.r.

BARROW

John Barrow (1729/30-1810)
m. Margaret Ball, daughter of Samuel and Anna Catherine (Tayloe) Ball; they resided in Culpeper County where they d.s.p. (q.v.), p.11.

Margaret Barrow
m.1744, Wharton Ransdell (q.v.), p.166.

Elizabeth Barrow
m.1747, William Lightfoot, (q.v.), p.119.

[# The children of Benjamin and Sarah (Metcalfe) Rust are detailed in Rust of Virginia, p.49-50.]

266

COLONEL RICHARD² TALIAFERRO (167?-1715) —m.169?— *SARAH [SURNAME UNCERTAIN] (167?-1718),
of Richmond County where he died intes-   only child of *Madam Martha Win(g)field
tate; they had four children (q.v.),p.203.   (167?-1709), a lady with wide interests.

*Richard³ Taliaferro,   Sarah³ Taliaferro -c.1728   1714:   Catherine³ Taliaferro
Gent. (1700-1721); he   She had two   -m- *Col. Thomas Turner -m- Martha³   (1706-1731), m. Col-
d.s.p., King George   daughters,   (2) (167?-1758) of Ess- (1) Taliaferro   one1 Rice Hooe, (q.v.),
County.   viz: ex, Richmond and   She had two   p.96.
                                                  King George counties. sons, viz:
                                                  (q.v.,p.220-221).

Mary⁴   Sarah⁴ Turner 1748   *Major Harry⁴ Turner (171?-1751)   Thomas⁴ Turner, Jr.,
Turner d. ante 1757 -m- *Capt. Edward Dixon   m(1) 1743 Elizabeth Smith (172?-   Gent., d. intestate
d.s.p. per her fath-   (c.1702-1779) of   1750); m(2) c.1751, Elizabeth   in Caroline County,
        er's will and   Port Royal, Caroline   Fauntleroy (1736-1792); (q.v.),   1757; m. his cousin,
        probably circa   County; he was a   p.190,220. Major Harry⁴ Turner   Mary Taliaferro.
        1751 in child-   wealthy merchant.   of Smith's Mount was survived   Their only child with
        bed.   by an only child, viz: issue was, viz:

*Turner⁵ Dixon   Harry⁵ Dixon   1779   *Major Harry⁴ Turner (171?-1751)   Sarah⁵ Turner
(c.1751-1785)   (c.1749—1783)   -m- Alice Fitzhugh -m(2)- *John Pratt,   -m- *Richard⁶ Turner
He d.s.p.;his   of Caroline Co. (1759-1845),   1784   Esq. (1761-   (1779-1829) of
will was con-   They had two   dau. of John   1843) of   Walsingham and
tested.   children, viz: Fitzhugh, Gent.,   Camden; m. 1819   Woodlawn, King
                                     of Bellaire,   Columbia Stanard   George County, Va.
                                     Stafford Co.,Va.   (1800-1822) of   left issue.
                                     [OPR.,p.231]   Orange County,
                                                                 no issue; see Hay-
                                                                 den, p. 673.

John Edward Henry Turner⁶   *Elizabeth⁶ Dixon   *John Pratt, Jr.   Alice Fitzhugh   *Col.Thomas⁵ Turner
Dixon (1780-1820) of Ver-   (1781-1840), m.   (1789-1855) of   Pratt (1785-   (c.1745-1787),m.
mont, Fauquier County; m.   1800, *George Con-   Camden; m. 1819   1862). Handsome m. * Colonel
1800, his cousin, Maria⁵   way Taylor (1769-   Columbia Stanard   tombstones of   Walker Talia-
Turner, daughter of Thomas⁴   1801) of Orange   (1800-1822) of   her parents, her ferro (1772-
and Jane (Fauntleroy) Turn-   County. They had   Roxbury, Spotsyl-   husband, herself, 1782) of Car-
er of King George County,Va.   no issue; see Hay-   vania County, and   and others are at oline County;
They left issue.   den, p. 673.   left issue.   Camden.   left issue.

*William Carter Pratt (1821-1891), son of John and Columbia (Stanard) Pratt, m.1860, his cousin, Eliza
Hooe⁸ Turner (1841-1927), daughter of *Richard H.⁷ and Margaretta S. (Hooe) Turner of Woodlawn and grand-
daughter of *Richard⁶ and Alice F. (Pratt) Turner; their son Richard Turner9 Pratt now owns Camden.
[N.B.*Denotes these parties died testate, however all of their wills are not now of record.]

TAYLOE IN GLOUCESTERSHIRE AND LONDON, ENGLAND

Anne Corbin -m(1)- Col. William Tayloe, -m(2)- Anne [?]   : *Joseph Tayloe, Gent.-m- *Barbara Billington
(1664/5-1694),   1685   Gentleman,(1645-1710);   m(2) 1716 : (16??-1716) of Lan-   (16??-1727), young-
daughter of   he died intestate in   *James Burne : caster County;   est daughter of
Hon. Henry   Richmond County, Va.   (16??-1721) of : (q.v.), p.205,246.   *Luke Billington,Sr.
Corbin. (q.v.),p.205.   (q.v.),p.205.   :Lancaster Co. :   (16??-1672).

Elizabeth   *Col.John Tayloe   *Col.William   Anna Catherine   Mary Tayloe   Anne   Joseph   Elizabeth
Tayloe   (1688-1747), m.   Tayloe (1694-   Tayloe,m.1717,   m(1) 1724;   d.s.p.   d.s.p.   Tayloe; m.
Born 1686   Elizabeth (Gwyn)   1770); m. ?;   *Samuel Ball,   John Lyell#;   c.1716   1724-   by 1726,
m.* Griffin   Lyde (1692-1745), they had an   Gent. (1686-   m(2) 1727/8,   1726.   John Thorn-
Fauntleroy,   widow of Stephen   only child   1751); moved to   *James Pendle-   bury (q.v.),
Gent. as his   Lyde, daughter of mentioned in   Culpeper Co.Va.   ton (1702-63);   p.209.
first wife.   Major David and   his will,viz: [Hayden, p.55]   he m(2) *Eliza-
                 Katherine (Grif-   beth Coleman
                 fin) Gwyn(n).   (17??-1769)##.

[There are several accounts of the family of Col.John Tayloe (1688-1747),founder of the Mount Airy estate in Richmond County. There are accounts in Colonial Families of the Southern States of America by Stella Pickett Hardy (New York,1911) and Genealogy of the Virginia Family of Lomax (Chicago,1913). The last mentioned records considerable data from records preserved in family of Col.John Tayloe (1721-1779).]

Anne Tayloe m. 10 January 1746 in Lancaster County, *John Wormeley, Gent. (1724-1785), son of *John Wormeley, Gent. (1689-1726/7) of Rosegill, Middlesex County, and his wife nee *Elizabeth Ring (1692-1761). *John Wormeley, Gent. (1724-1785) of Lancaster County was survived by his second wife, Frances [?] and an only child, named in her grandfather Tayloe's will, viz:

Elizabeth Wormeley m. William[6] Digges of Bellfield, York Co.Va.; a descendant of Governor Edward Digges (c.1620-1675), first of the name at Bellfield. [A.P.& P.,p.154-158 for Digges genealogy]

John Lyell died intestate in Lancaster County and on 8 February 1726/7 Jonathan Lyell was granted administration on his estate [Lancaster County WB#10,p.515]. On 1 March 1735 John Lyell of North Farnham Parish, Richmond County, with the consent of his uncle Jonathan Lyell, apprenticed himself to John Polly to learn the trade of a bricklayer; he was to be free when 21 years of age. [Richmond County, AB#1, p.92]

James and Mary (Tayloe) Pendleton had no children. His second wife, nee Elizabeth Coleman (17??-1769), was the daughter of *Thomas Coleman (16??-1748) of King and Queen County; they moved to Culpeper County,Va. where they both died testate. James Pendleton succeeded Captain Samuel Ball (1686-1751) as a vestryman in St.Mark's Parish and served in that capacity until his death in 1763 when he was succeeded by Captain William Ball, son of Captain Samuel and Anna Catherine (Tayloe) Ball. [Thomas Coleman's will #2817,VSL:AD]

*SYLVESTER THATCHER -married- *MARGARET [?] -married (2)- WARWICK CAMMACK
(1622-1667)   (1622-1715)   (1636-c.1685)

He patented land in Isle of Wight County in 1643; moved to Rappahan-nock County where he acquired a considerable landed estate by pur-chase and patent. His manor plan-tation fell into Richmond County in 1692. The surviving records mention his will, but it seems to have been recorded in a lost book. He had four surviving children,viz:

In 1709, when she wrote her will, she described herself as "very ancient;" this docu-ment makes it certain she had two daughters named Mary -one by each spouse. A bond dated 10 December 1692 offers excel-lent evidence Sylvester That-cher had "two only daughters," [Richmond County, DB#1, p.41.]

He appears prominently on the Rappahannock County court re-cords. By purchase and pat-ent he acquired considerable land in the area which became Richmond County in 1692. His only son, John Cammack (1667-1717), d.s.p. and his three daughters gave rise to a num-erous progeny. [See p.247.]

⋮

*Sylvester Thatcher, Jr. (1622-1718) of Richmond County; m. *Elizabeth Underwood (1622-1726) (q.v.), p.207 by whom he had 7 children; she m(2) *Francis Jett (1622-1724), widower, by whom she had no issue. The land of S. Thatcher and F. Jett fell into King George County in 1721.

Mathew Thatcher d.s.p.

*Mary Thatcher (1622-1727) m(1) *William Clapman [Clap-ham] (c.1654-1696) by whom she had 2 daughters; m(2) *Thomas Richardson (1622-1719) by whom she had a son named for her first husband. (q.v.,p.37,171.

Elizabeth Thatcher, m. ante 1693 *John Deane, Gentleman, (c.1648-1712), widower of Jane Walker (q.v.), p. 53. As his will indicates his three sons were under age in 1712, it appears they were by his second wife.

⋮

(1) *Sylvester Thatcher [III] (1622-1725), d.s.p., King George County.
(2) *Thomas Thatcher, died testate, 1751 in King George County; m. Catherine Pannell (q.v.), p.207; they left issue.
(3) John Thatcher, d.s.p., a minor.
(4) William Thatcher, d.s.p., 1742.
(5) Samuel Thatcher
(6) Margaret Thatcher
(7) Elizabeth Thatcher

(1) Mary Clapham m. James Woffendale, (q.v.),p.234
(2) *Elizabeth Clapham (1622-1722) m(1) George Green (q.v.,p.80; m(2) Richard West.
(3) *Clapham [Clapman] Rich-ardson, died testate in King George County, 1750; m. Elizabeth [?].

(1) *Charles Deane (c.1695-1748) m. Anne Jones (q.v.), p.53.
(2) *John Deane, died 1750 in King George County; m. Mary [?]
(3) *William Deane, died 1747, King George Co. m. Elizabeth [?].

Torrence, Virginia Wills and Administrations, 1632-1800 (Richmond, 1930), p.417, notes the will of Samuel Thatcher proved in Berkeley County [now West Virginia], 1776; this was doubtless the above mentioned Sam-uel Thatcher or his nephew, Samuel Thatcher (born c.1744), son of Thomas and Catherine (Pannell) Thatcher.

N.B. * Denotes these parties died testate, however, all of their wills do not now remain of record.

*CAPTAIN LAWRENCE1 WASHINGTON (1635-1677) OF RAPPAHANNOCK COUNTY

He came to Virginia in 1658 and settled on the Rappahannock River on the opposite side of the Northern Neck from his brother, Colonel John1 Washington (1632/3-1677), who settled on the Potomac River in Westmoreland County in 1656 and became the ancestor of General George4 Washington (1732-1799). Captain Lawrence1 Washington married (1) 26 January 1660 in England, Mary Jones, daughter of Edward Jones, Gent. of Luton; his wife died there and leaving their only child, Mary Washington, with her maternal grandparents, Captain Lawrence1 Washington returned to Virginia where he married (2) 1668/9 Joyce Jones, daughter of Captain William Jones (16??-1669) of Northampton County and widow successively of Anthony Hoskins, Gentleman, (16??-1665) and Captain Alexander Fleming (16??-1668) (q.v.),p.69,106,211; 49 V191-193; 33 Americana 1-31. Captain Lawrence1 and Joyce (Jones) Washington had an only child, viz:

John 2 Washington, Gentleman, (1671-1719) - married 15 March 1692 - Mary Townshend (1669-c.1727-1729), daughter of Chotank, Stafford County (now Waterloo, : of Colonel Robert Townshend (1640-1675) of King George County); he was sheriff of : Albion, St. Paul's Parish, Stafford County, Stafford County 1717-1719. He had 5 child- : and Mary Langhorne (1642-1685), his wife. ren; his second son was John3, next below. : [A.P.& P.,p.334-337; Eubank, p.27.]

*John 3 Washington, Gentleman, (1695-1742).-married in 1720 - Mary Massey (c.1702-post 1752), daughter of *Capt. He succeeded his father at Chotank and : Dade Massey (1679-1735) and his wife nee Elizabeth served Stafford County as sheriff and capt- : Ellis and granddaughter of Capt. Robert Massey and ain of the militia. He had 9 children. : his wife nee Mary Dade, all of Stafford County,Va.

*Langhorne Dade, Gentleman, (1718-1753) -m- Mildred4 Washington -m(2)- *Doctor Walter Williamson (17??-1772), of Albion, m. his cousin on 14 February : (1721-1784); died at : native of Scotland who settled in St. 1742/3 and their only son succeeded to : Bunker Hill, Westmore- : Paul's Parish, Stafford County, where that ancient family seat. [SPR.,p.34-35] : land County, Virginia. : they were married 1 March 1755.

*William Robinson, Gentleman, (1752-1782) -m- *Margaret5 Williamson -m(2)- *Colonel John Rose (17??-1802) of of Bunker Hill (q.v.), p.260; m. 20 Nov- : (1755-1837), only child : Mount Rose, Westmoreland County; ember 1777 in St.Paul's Parish and had 3 : of her parents to leave : they were m. in September 1783. children, the younger daughter being : issue. [SPR., p. xxiii, : Their only son, Charles Walter6 Margaret6 Robinson, next below. : 154.] : Rose, d.s.p.; their only daughter : is mentioned next below.

*Daniel McCarty, Gentleman, 1797 Margaret 6 Robinson 1802 Mildred Washington6 Rose (1772-1801) of Longwood, -m- (1780-1808); she had -m(2)- m. (as his first wife), 22 (q.v.),p.246; he had two two children by each *Richard Stuart, February 1810,*Capt. Alexan- daughters and was the last spouse. [SPR.,p.xxiii, Esqr. (1770-1835) der Fontaine Rose (17??-1831) of that distinguished name xxiv,xxxii; Eubank,p. of Cedar Grove, of Stafford County, sometime at that Westmoreland Coun- 43; family Bible.] King George Co. member of both houses of Va. ty seat. He had a son and General Assembly. a daughter by his only wife.

"Without genealogy, the study
of history is lifeless."

John Fiske

INDEX

Underlined are the pages referring to brides, bridegrooms, marriages by inference, important references to families and connubial alliances indicated on the genealogical charts.
Oftentimes the same name appears more than once on the same page.
When consulting the index, be mindful of the many interchanges in both Christian and surnames.

[Surname omitted], Delline   86

Abbay, Jonathan   112

Abshone, William   1, 194

Accomac[k] Co., Va.   106

Adams, James   1, 1, 124
    James J.   1
    Richard   1
    Thomas   220

Alabama, State of   101, 259

Albemarle Co., Va.   33, 74, 247

Albemarle, Earl of   xi

Albion, King George Co.,Va. 97, 269

Albion, Stafford Co., Va. 252, 269

Alborough, Westmoreland Co. Va. 45

Albreckt, Kasper   75

Alderson : Alverson
    Alice   118
    Ann   44, 130, 167
    Barbara B.   171
    Caty   100
    Eliza W.   99
    Elizabeth   207
    George N.   1, 170, 235
    James   1, 6, 70, 79, 148, 196
    Jane   148, 148, 189
    Jeliff   176
    Jeloff, Jr.   1, 150, 226

Jeremiah   1
Jery   1, 34, 222
John   1, 79, 153, 167, 189
Lucy F.   54
Margaret J.   180
Mary   34, 45, 224
Polly M.   70
Rachel   34
Rebecca (Hatton)   1, 150
Sally   101
Sarah   196, 226
Sarah Ann   1, 6, 148, 196
Teliff   1, 2
William   1, 2, 54, 98
    99, 118, 133

Alexander, family   242
    Ann   96, 242
    Elizabeth   242
    Euel   2
    Frances   242
    John   2, 2, 242, 244
    John Lewis   242
    Joseph   2, 52
    Lucy (Brockenbrough)   2, 242
    Philip   97, 242
    Philip Thornton   2, 242
    Robert   96, 242
    Thomas B.   2
    William   116, 212

Alexandria, Va.   42

Algar, Alitia   119, 119, 177, 231
    Mary   119
    Samuel   119
    Thomas   2, 20, 119

Allard, Henry   2

Allen : Allin
   Anne   46, 64
   Frank   2
   John   2
   Lucinda   113
   Rachel   113
   Thomas   2, 93
   Winney   2

Allerton, Frances   42, 98, 169
   Sarah   66

Allgood, Elizabeth   60, 187
   Sally S.   60
   William   3

Allison, Catharine   101
   Henry   3
   William   3

Alloway, Caty   1
   Elizabeth   65, 168
   Gabriel   3
   Henry   3
   Isaac   1, 3, 51, 222
   Jane   51
   John   3, 104, 215, 216
   Mary Ann   88
   Molly   222
   Nancy   235
   Priscilla   216
   Samuel   3, 3
   William   65

Alverson, see Alderson

Ambrose, Amelia   7
   Elijah   3, 7
   Mahala   7
   Molly   94,94
   Redman B. 3, 3, 40, 103, 178
   William   3, 94

Amelia County, Va.   8, 117, 127
         202, 228, 247, 263

Amory, Thomas C.   3, 103

Anderson, Ann   247
   Edward   3
   George   258

   James   156
   John   4
   Paulin   247
   Rosanna   258
   Samuel   44
   Walter   4, 214

Answorth, John   4

Anthony, James   4
   Thomas   4

Anton, John   4
   Robert   4, 125
   Samuel   197

Appleby, Lucy   121
   Richard   4, 121
   William W.   79

Appomattox Creek, Westmoreland
   County, Va.   154

Aquia Creek, Stafford Co., Va. 249

Armistead, Alice P.   167
   Elizabeth Burgess   42
   Francis   4, 175
   Henry   4, 34, 42, 156, 167
   John   4, 175
   Robert   4
   Sarah   4, 175
   Susanna   68

Arms, Roxy   164

Armstrong, Benjamin 4, 17, 87
                121, 184
   Lucy   87

Arnolds, Anne   4

Asbury, family   5, 61
   Ann(e)   172, 90, 193
   Bethiah   46, 180
   Eliz.^a   142
   Elizabeth   140, 167
   Frances   23
   Henry   5, 19, 180
   John G.   5
   Mary   19, 172

Nancy 19, 193
Richard 11
Thomas 5, 33

Ascough, Elizabeth (Ingo) 5, 59
Thomas 5, 59

Ashburn, Elizabeth 24
Elizabeth O. 186
Hannah 28
Melia 28
Milley 28
Milly 186
Polly 65
Rachel 186
Thomas 5, 28, 186

Ashton, Frances 242
Sarah 242

Askin : Askins
Alfred C. 148
Ann M. 194
Benjamin W. 5
Mary A. 126
Nancy 126
Sarah 227
Youell 5
Youell F.P. 146
William 5

Astin, Lawrence 5

Atchinson, Ellzey 103

Attorneys, Prosecuting of
Richmond County, Va. xv, 134

Atwell : Atwill
Daniel 25, 77, 140, 169
Thomas L. 5

Auburn, Spotsylvania County, Va. 42

Audley, Sarah 232

Augusta County, Va. 5, 35, 135, 220

Austin, Anne (Newman) Deen 25
Catherine 56
Chapman 5, 91, 106

David 236
Elizabeth 91
John 5

Avery, Yeo 6

Aylett, Mary 116
William 116

Ayres, Elizabeth 173

Ayrs, William 6

Baber, Lucy 165

Bagby, Susan Ann 91

Bailey : Baley : Bayley
Ann 114, 262
Charles 6, 101
Elizabeth 262
Elizabeth (Metcalfe) 265
Jeremiah Garland 6
John 6, 262
Joyce 9, 118, 162
Mary 219
Sally M. 134
Samuel 6, 9, 132, 265
Susan (Sydnor) 201
William 6
William H. 6
Barbara 55
Barbary 107

Baker, Betsy 197
Caty 107
Elizabeth 1, 6
John 1, 6, 55, 196
Nancy 145
Samuel 148, 149
Sarah Ann 149
William 6, 54

Balderson, David 7
Delila 7
E. 51
Edward T. 6
Elizabeth 14, 14, 33, 178
Frances 7, 14, 62, 79
Gilbert 14, 62, 79, 142, 166

Gilbert H.   7
Henry   7, 7
Hundley   xiv
James B.   7
James P.   7, 188
John   7
Lawienda   11
Leonard   7
Louisa W.   85
Lucy   51
Malborough B.   7
Mary   14
Nancy   14
Ransdel   7
Richard   7
Ruth (Peyton)   xiv
Salathiel G.   7
Sally Jarvis   166
Theoderick N.   7, 85, 94, 104
     107, 178, 179 , 226
Uriah   7
William   83, 178
William Jr.   7
William Sr.   7
William O.   7
William R.   3, 178

Bale, Sarah   87

Baley, see Bailey

Ball, family   243
Alice   8, 190
Ann   251
Burgess   4, 76
Carter   94
Chaney   8
Eliza B.   159
Elizabeth   9, 47, 243
Elizabeth (Burgess)   4
Elizabeth W.   50
Ellin [Ellen]   243
Esther   35, 78, 79, 243
Frances   243
George   8
Hannah   78, 134
Harrison   9, 30, 71, 144
James   82, 251
James K.   25
John B.   8
Joseph   243

Judith   9, 36, 68, 78
              82, 186, 221, 226
Lucy Harrison   9, 10
Margaret   8, 11, 243, 265
Margaret Williamson 9, 216, 217
Mary   94, 243
Mildred ["Milly"]   9, 201
Priscilla   8, 9, 90, 151, 217
                    218, 218, 251
Priscilla (Glascock)   8, 90
Richard   79
Samuel   11, 205, 265, 267
Sarah   87, 246
Thomas   8
Thomas P.   8
William   8, 8, 30, 31, 78
          134, 228, 243, 267
Williamson 8, 9, 10, 47, 78, 90
     186, 190, 201, 216, 217, 218

Baltimore, Maryland   147

Baltimore County, Maryland 209, 210

Bane [?], Charles   226

Banks, Elizabeth (Rogers) Keene 261

Barber, Ann(e)   118, 122, 123
              124, 176, 201, 246
Ann (Foster)   9, 110, 247
Charles   9, 53, 100
              123, 133, 176, 226
Elizabeth   100, 200
Frances   89, 135, 167, 226
James R.   9
Joyce   162, 257
Katherine   231
Mary 53, 133, 176, 187,199, 261
Samuel   9, 110,165, 247
Thomas   9, 23, 102,167, 231
William   x, 9, 118,162, 187

Barcroft, William   9

Barecraft, Elizabeth   17

Barker, Elias   10
Elizabeth   69
Lawrence   10, 10, 82
Mary (Skelderman)   10, 82

Barnes : Barns
    Barnes family   244
    Alice   215
    Catherine   35, 244
    Charles   10, 49, 226
    Edward   84
    Eleanor   244
    Elizabeth   2, 242, 244
    Ellen   2
    Fanny   141
    Mary 111, 115, 138, 210,225,244
    Molly   111
    Newman Brockenbrough   9, 10
    Penilopy   65
    Peter   10
    Peter M.   10
    Polley   49
    Rebecca   13, 14, 244
    Richard 2, 10, 13, 96, 111, 112
                 184, 235, 242, 244
    Samuel   10
    Sarah   96, 242, 244
    Thomas   10, 10, 96, 244
    Thomas R.   122
    Travers   10
    William F.   10

Barnesfield, King George County,
    Va.   96, 242

Baroh, Agnes   191

Barrett, Elizabeth   141
    James   141
    John   20
    Mary   141
    Sarah   20

Barrick, see Berrick

Barrot : Barrott
    James   11, 128
    Sarah   20

Barrow, family   265
    Ann (Stone) Metcalfe   196
    Anne   132, 196, 265
    Cicily [Cecely] 24,50, 110, 171
    Edward   11, 119, 132
                        132, 166, 265
    Elizabeth   265

    Honour   50, 171
    John   11, 24, 110, 171, 265
    Margaret   132, 166, 265, 265

Bartlett, Ann   84
    Catharine   163
    Elisha   11, 163
    Elisha Sr.   11, 11
    Isaac   11
    James   11
    Joel   179
    Johannah   179
    John   7, 11, 11, 84
    Joseph   11
    Louisa A.   181
    Lucy   139
    Matthew   104, 181
    Samuel   11, 181
    Thomas   140

Barton, Sarah   64

Bassett, Burwell Jr.   246

Bates, Edward   11

Bathurst, Essex County, Va.   189

Bathurst, Elizabeth   47
    Mary   16

Battaley, Moseley   129, 130
    Samuel   130

Batten, Elizabeth 11, 12, 195, 231
    John   11, 195, 231

Battletown, West Virginia   42

Bayley, see Bailey

Baylis : Bayliss
    family   12
    Amadine   86
    Frances   199
    Marcy   210
    Robert   12, 12, 246
    Thomas 12, 12, 86, 199, 210, 261

Baylor, Gregory   76
    Richard   76

Bayne, Elizabeth   27
    John   39

Beacham, Jane   113, 133
    John   13
    John, Jr.   83
    Samuel L.   13, 75, 225
    Thomas   133
    Thomas C.   45

Beages, William   13

Beah, Henry   111

Beale, Alfred   12, 139, 167, 217
    Alice   105
    Ann   8, 9, 85
    Ann (Gooch)   42
    Ann Harwar 15, 16, 21, 111, 245
    Anna   85
    Charles   xv, 77
    Eliza   154
    Elizabeth   23, 42
    Fanny   71, 72
    George   12
    Hannah   8, 78
    Jesse B.   85
    John   80, 86, 105
    Lucinda   124, 139
    Lucy   105
    Maria   85
    Mary   126
    Mary (Fauntleroy)   77
    Mildred   66
    Reuben   12, 15
    Richard   139
    Robert   12
    Samuel   85
    Sinah   85
    Thomas   8, 12, 42, 72
                    195, 246, 256
    William   12, 13, 154
    William Lee   36
    Winifred   33

Bean, John   167
    Levy   13

Bearcaff, John   13

Bearcraft, Elizabeth   236

Beard, George   13, 231

Beatty, Sophia   172

Beazley, Richard H.   235
    William   13

Beckwith, Barnes   111, 244
    Butler   260
    Jennings   13, 244
    Jonathan [Sir]   13, 14, 244
    Margaret   10, 139, 244
    Marmaduke [Sir] xvi, 10, 13, 13
                        31, 139, 158
    Marmaduke Brockenbrough   244
    Mary   14, 31, 75, 245
    Penelope   222, 244
    Rebecca   244
    Richard Marmaduke   14, 244
    Roger   13, 14, 31, 244

Bedder, Laurence   14

Beddoo, John   14
    John, Jr.   14
    Laurence   14, 40

Beddows, John   14

Beder, Juley   105

Bedford County, N.C.   175

Bedford County, Va.   80

Bedwell, Mary   226
    Robert   263

Been, Mathew   14

Belfield, family   245
    Alice C.   14, 75
    Alice Jane   222
    Ann H.   21, 75
    Anna Maria   15, 180
    Anne   68, 239, 245
    Anne C.B.   21
    Easter   146
    Elizabeth   14, 36, 202, 245
    Elizabeth (Dozier)   15, 245
    Elizabeth M.B.   48

Belfield, Frances   222, 223, 245
    Frances L.M.   122
    Frances M.   46
    Jane   146
    Jane C.   111
    John   14, 15, 36, 68, 75
                  191, 201, 218, 245
    John D.   14
    John W.   90, 122, 193, 209
    John W. Jr.   14, 48
    Joseph   15, 16, 19, 25, 46
                       140, 245, 245
    Lucy   221
    Maria   15, 180
    Mary   103, 191, 223, 245
    Nancy   25, 245
    Peggy   180
    R.A.   168
    Richard C.   14, 15, 171
    Susan Ann   102
    Sydnor   15, 36, 75, 180, 245
    Thomas 15, 16, 21,103, 111, 245
    Thomas Wright 14,16,141,222,245
    William B.   222
    William S.   103

Bell, Alice F.   134
    Bartholomew   1, 2, 17, 235
    Betsy   58
    Charles   16, 63, 75, 99, 118
    Charles L.   134, 236
    Eliza   58
    James L.   58, 236
    John   147
    Lemuel G.   16, 45, 179, 225
    Richard V.   16, 16
    Thomas   16, 47, 219
    William   16, 16

Bellaire, Stafford Co.Va. 248, 266

Belle Grove, King George Co.,Va.248

Belleisle, Lancaster Co., Va.   17

Belleview, Stafford Co., Va.116,117

Belle-ville, Richmond Co.,Va.   77

Bellfield, York Co., Va.   267

Belmount, Richmond Co., Va.   21

Belvoir, Spotsylvania Co., Va. 239

Benjamin, Dorothy   80

Benneham : Bennehan
    Ann   33
    Catherine   33
    Dominic   16, 16, 182
    Maria   180
    Mary S.   23
    Richard   8, 16, 29, 142
    Virginia A.   94
    Virginia Ann   28

Bennett, Charles   16

Benson, Robert   16

Berkeley County, West Virginia 268

Berkeley, Earl of   xi

Bernard, Beheathland   96

Berrick : Barrick
    Ann   101
    Caty   89
    Charles   16, 17, 91
    David   17, 24
    Elizabeth   63
    George   120
    George Jr.   17
    George B.   17
    Griffin   17
    Griffin G.   1, 5, 120
    James   17
    James V.   81, 188
    Mahala M.   89
    Mary   50, 86, 214
    Mary P.   173
    Newby   3, 17, 38, 108, 181
    Patty   60
    Reuben   17
    Thomas B.   5, 17, 29
    Thornton F.   17

Berry, family   17, 210
    Henry Jr.   17, 193
    John   210

Berry, Mary   210
    Sarah (Harper)   17, 193
    William   17

Berryman, Beheathland Gilson   213
    Elizabeth   147
    Gilson   213

Bertrand, John [Rev.]   17
    Marianne   81, 82
    Mary Ann   81, 82
    William   17, 81, 82

Betts, Royston   18

Beverley, family   18
    Byrd   18
    Robert   18
    Robert Jr.   18

Beverton, Elizabeth   237
    Henry   18
    Mary   237

Bevington, Francis   18

Bewdley, Lancaster Co., Va. 82, 251

Billens, Elizabeth   163
    Sarah   163

Billington, family   246
    Alicia   175, 246
    Barbara   123, 175, 205, 205
             209, 246, 246, 267
    Elizabeth   12, 123, 123, 246
    Jane   246
    Luke 123,175,205, 246, 246, 267
    Mary   246

Bird, Phileman [Philemon] 18,27,216
    Sarah   27
    William Jr.   174

Birkett, family   256
    Ann   62, 256
    Elizabeth   152, 229, 256
    John   xvii, 18, 24, 62, 109
             161, 229, 256, 259
    Margaret   xvii, 161, 256, 259
    Mary   24, 24, 53, 109, 256

Bispham, Ann   19, 22, 90
    Elizabeth Maria   193
    Margaret   19, 22
    Maria   19, 193
    Robert   19, 22, 90, 193
    William   19, 19, 84, 167

Blackerby, Thomas   19
    William   19

Blackley, George D.   19

Blackmore, George   19

Black River, Maryland   209

Bland, James   71
    William   19, 264

Blandfield, Essex Co., Va.   18

Bleak Hall, Westmoreland Co.,Va. 31

Blenheim, Albemarle Co., Va.   33

Blewford, George   19

Blomfield, Elizabeth (Jones) 19,172
                                  193
    Frances   19, 172, 260
    Samuel   19, 172, 193

Blueford, Robert G.   20

Bluford, George   20

Blum, Dr. and Mrs. William Sr.   12

Bodkin, Anne   80

Bogges, Bennett   20, 261

Boimard, Louis   186

Boing : Bowing, see Bowen
    Elizabeth   227
    James   20, 20
    John   20, 20, 181,227
    Jonathan W.   20
    Joseph   20
    Joshua   20, 227

Boing : Bowing, see Bowen
    Joshua Jr.   227
    Kelly H.   20
    Martha   20
    Mary   20
    Mary M.   178
    Molly   227
    Rebecca   20
    Richard   20
    Thomas   20
    William   20
    William H.   20

Bontz, Valentine   20

Booker, George   20
    George W.   168

Booth, Andrew J.   21
    Catharine M.   169
    Elizabeth   48
    James   21
    Martha L.   28
    Rodham   128, 203
    Walter N.   61
    William P.   169

Boothe, Kitty   197

Boring, William   233

Boston, Mass.   203

Boston, Robert   21

Boughton, Anderson   21
    Benjamin   21

Boulware, Andrew   144

Bourbon County, Kentucky   255

Bowcock, Edward   21
    Margaret   152
    Thomas   152
    Thomas, Jr.   152

Bowdoin, John   21
    Peter   21, 195
    Presson   21

Bowen, see Boing : Bowing
    Ann   127
    Frances   120
    Frederick   151
    James K.   21
    John   11, 21
    Jonathan W.   141
    Joseph   21, 140, 151
    Kelly H.   21
    Martin   127
    Martin V.   21, 128, 224
    Mary Ann   151
    Nancy   151
    Samuel   120
    William   18, 22
    William S.   151

Bowing, see Boing : Bowing and Bowen

Boyd's Hole, King George Co.,Va.   2

Boyle, John   22, 141

Bragg, Ann B.   40
    Benjamin   22
    Betsy   118
    Catherine   22
    Charles   22, 104
    Elizabeth   22
    Ishmael   22
    James   22, 181
    John   22, 22
    Joseph   22, 22
    Joseph Jr.   22, 22, 184, 187
    Keziah   77
    Mary   22, 85, 184
    Moore   22
    Newman   22
    Rebecca   27, 128
    Reuben   22
    Sally   104
    Sarah   111
    Thomas   22
    Thomas Moore   19, 22
    William   5, 22, 64, 111, 126
                          128, 140, 238
    William K.   22

Bramham : Branham : Brenham
    Alice   53
    Ann (Hobbs) Green   81

Bramham : Branham : Brenham
    Ann S.   206
    Benjamin   23, 53, 75, 98, 101
            151, 164, 189, 191
    Benjamin Jr.   23
    Eleanor Ann   103
    Elizabeth   141
    Frances   129, 206
    Frances E.   124
    John   23, 81, 193,   230, 254
    John B.   122, 124
    Lucy S.   144
    Margaret   185
    Mary   214
    Mary S.   16
    Vincent   21, 23, 50, 95, 185
    Vincent Jr.   23

Branan, Spencer   23

Brann, Andrew   23
    Betsy   182
    Corbin   23
    Edwin C.   167
    Elizabeth   39, 44
    Frances   13, 63
    James   236
    Jeremiah   39
    John C.   38
    Lucy   13
    Mary   45, 145, 182
    Nancy   39
    Reubin   39, 63
    Reuben G.   23
    Samuel   39
    Samuel G.   171
    Sarah   99, 145
    Sarah Jane   13
    Vincent   23, 184

Branson, Vincent T.   23

Brasser, Richard   23

Braxton, Carter   23
    George   129, 129
    Maria G. (Davis)   23, 24
    Thomas   23
    Thomas Corbin   23, 24, 127

Brent, George   24
    Hugh   24, 228
    William B.   24

Brereton, Henry   234
    Sarah   234, 235

Brett, William   24

Brewer, Martha   179
    Mary   179
    Mary Ann   179

Brian, see Bryan : Bryant
    Margaret   143

Brice, Henry   255

Brickey : Bricky
    Ann   101, 113, 233
    Betsy   39
    Betty   168
    Darcus   166
    Elener   137
    Elinor   137
    Elizabeth   184
    Jerard   24, 31
    John   142, 166, 168
              175, 208, 233
    Mary   208
    Polly Sidney   39
    Sarah   142, 175
    William   39, 137, 214, 236
    William Jr.   24, 222
    William Sr.   104, 113, 222

Bridger, Sarah   4

Bridges, Mary   102
    William   132, 265

Brinham, William   27

Brinhan, Catharine   155
    William   155

Brinnon, William P.   34

Briskey, William   236

Brissee, James   24

Bristol, England   165, 166

Brizendine, Ewen   24
    Lucy Ann   45

Broadnax, Henry   222, 245

Brock, Patience   50
    Thomas 24, 50, 109,110,171, 256

Brockenbrough Creek, Richmond Co.,
    Va.   xvii

Brockenbrough, Austin   24, 25, 68
                    131, 193,   265
    Benjamin W.   95
    Elizabeth   13, 31, 139
    Elizabeth R.   235
    Jane   259
    John   126
    John F.   25
    Littleton   25
    Lucy   2, 242
    Lucy R.   185
    Mary (Metcalfe)   24, 193,   265
    Mary (Newman)   25
    Moore Fauntleroy 19, 24, 25, 48
                    63, 94, 194
    Newman   10,   25
    Thomas   33
    William   13, 24, 25, 25, 111
    William A.   xvi, 50
    Winifred   244, 10

Bromley, Henry   184

Bronough, Ann Moore   143, 257
    David   137, 143, 143, 257
    Jeremiah Sr.   143
    Mary   143, 257

Broocke, Violett   109
    William   15, 25, 181
    William H.   25, 197

Brooke, Ann Pettit   157, 158
    George   25, 215
    Harriet   126
    Laurence   242
    Lucy   242
    Reuben   126

Robert   157, 158
Robin   157, 158
Samuel   25
Susan   12
Whitfield   25, 198
William   12, 126
William H.   197

Brooks, Ann   158
    Jane   225
    Richard   25

Broom, Thomas   81

Broomfield, see Blomfield

Brown : Browne
    Alice C.   29
    Ann   30
    Ann O.   113
    Betsy   99
    Catherine   65, 107, 224
    Charles Eden   25
    Christopher   25,   27
    Daniel 16, 25, 26, 89, 100, 194
    Edward 26, 50, 63, 86, 214, 215
    Edwin   19
    Eleanor   63, 100
    Elizabeth 30, 57, 92, 137, 167
            171, 193, 193, 206, 234
    Ellen   100
    Frances   33
    Frances (Moss)   27, 101
    George   26
    Hannah Lee   100
    Hanner   89
    Hudson   26, 26, 72
    James W.   43, 234
    Jeremiah   74, 110, 172
    Johanna   135
    John   26, 27, 64, 137, 171
    John R.   26
    Judith   104
    Lucy   10
    Martha   230
    Mary Ann   1
    Mary F.   181, 181
    Maxfield   27, 137, 230
    Nancy   38, 86, 238
    Nancy H.   103
    Newman   26

Brown, Patty   28
    Polly   64
    Richard   60
    Sally   85,167
    Simon   26,182
    Solomon J.S.   26
    Thomas   26, 26, 72, 85, 107
                  134, 150, 185, 238
    Vincent   149
    William   25, 26, 27, 63, 101
                  137, 193, 206, 231
        William M.   27
        William S.   26
        William W.H.   27

Brownlee, William R.   xv

Bruce, Andrew   27
    Benjamin   27
    Charles   143, 257
    Charles Cary   252
    Elizabeth   143, 257
    Elizabeth (Bragg)   22
    Ellen   252
    George   27, 27
    Hensfield   252
    Henry   27, 137
    Henry Jr.   27, 233
    Joseph   27
    Margaret   47
    Reuben   27
    Sarah   212, 252
    Susanna (Stewart)   27,233
    Thomas   27

Brumbelow, Edward   178, 216
    Sarah   178, 216

Brunswick Co.,Va. 177, 222,245, 261

Bryan : Bryant, see Brian
    Alexander   28, 29, 54, 70, 71
                  133, 182, 236
        Alicia   71
        Almorein   50
        Ann   104
        Ann E.   71
        Ann S.   61
        Betsy B.   236
        Catherine   29, 56, 65
        Charles   28

Daniel   27, 194
Edward   28
Elizabeth   29, 59, 83, 88, 95
Elizabeth H.   148
Fanny   119
Fanny L.   54
Fedelia D.   29
Frances   29, 71
Hannah   133
Henry   28, 29
James W.   29
Jesse   28, 104
Jesse G.   28, 43, 90, 104
John   28, 28, 58, 83, 215
Jonathan   28, 58, 83
Joseph   25, 28, 28, 57
                  79, 84, 119
Joseph W.   4, 56, 60
Judah   58
Lettice   57
Lucinda   29
Lucy   38
Lucy T.   160
Lydia   83
Mary   48, 86
Patty F.   219
Peggy   83
Priscilla   215
Rachel   29, 58
Rawleigh   29, 95
Rawleigh D.   28, 29
Reuben   28, 29, 84
Richard P.   29, 29
Robert   29
Sally   189
Sally A.   79
Samuel   29
Sarah   61
Thaddeus   29
Thaddus   29
Thomas   2, 29, 29, 51
                  71, 160, 177, 196
Thomas F.   29
Thomas L.   29
Thomas W.   27, 29, 38, 56
                  58, 65, 118, 174
Violet   25
William   16, 29, 29, 32, 215
William C.   29
William E.   29
Wilmoth   196, 263

Bryan : Bryant, see Brian
    Winifred   57

Bryer, Bridgett   162, 170
    George   162, 170

Buchanan, Andrew   14
    Elizabeth Scott   14, 244

Buckles, John   228
    Margaret   228

Buckley, Mary   73
    Peggy   233
    Reuben   29
    Sarah   127

Buckner, Elias Edmonds   2, 25, 30
    Elizabeth (Madison)   259
    Richard   30

Bulger, Edmund   30, 236, 236
    John   30
    John Jr.   30
    William   30
    William S.   30

Bunbury, William   130

Bunker Hill, Westmoreland Co.,
    Va.   172, 260, 269

Bunyan, Catherine   8

Burch, Gilson B.   30, 65
    Jane M.   28
    Jilson B.   30, 219
    Lucy   101
    Lucy S.   43
    Susan S.   43

Burden, Mary   223, 265

Burditt, Henry   4, 108, 213

Burgar, Ann   82

Burgess, Elizabeth   4
    James H.   30
    Molly   142
    William   22, 84, 85

Burke County, Georgia   216

Burke, John   30, 239

Burkett, see Birkett

Burn : Burne
    Anne (?) Tayloe   206
    Christopher   30
    James   205, 206, 206, 267
    Joseph   30

Burras, Benjamin   22

Burrell, Thomas   30, 31

Burt, David   31

Burton, Elias S.   7
    George W.   52
    Thomas   31

Burwell, George   31, 170
    James   40
    James B.   227
    Nathaniel   31
    Thomas   30, 31
    Walter   219

Bush, Urbane   31

Bushrod, Ann   47
    Apphia   47, 157
    Elizabeth   23

Bushy Park, Middlesex Co., Va.   9

Bustle, Hannor   52
    Nancy   52

Bute County, North Carolina 175,233

Butler, Ann   249
    Beckwith   31
    Catharine P.   84
    Frances T.   31, 181
    Isaac O.   31, 41
    James   249
    Lawrence   31, 31, 244
    Mary   40
    Peggy   31

Butler, Roberta W.   181
    Samuel C.F.   31
    Thomas   23

Buxston, John   31

Byrd, Ann   84
    William   84

Cadeen, Fanny   106

Cain, Margaret Walker   38

Call, Elizabeth   77

Callahan, James   32

Callehan, John   71

Callis, Robert   32, 144

Cambell, Alexander   32

Cambrom: Cambron : Cambrum
    Allen   6, 32
    Mary   209

Camden, Caroline Co.,Va.239,259,266

Camel, Katherine   88

Cammack, family   247
    John   247, 268
    Margaret   68, 131, 182
                     195, 207, 247
    Mary   195, 247, 256
    Susanna(h)   9, 131, 247, 265
    Warwick   131, 182, 195
                     207, 247, 268
    William   195, 247

Cammell, George   32

Campbell, Alexander   xv, 32
    Archibald   32, 32
    John   xv, 32
    T. Elliott   44
    Wily   174

Camron, Dennis   32

Canes, Anne   129

Cannada, see Kennedy
    John   116, 113

Cannaday, see Kennedy
    John   47

Cannan, see Kennan
    Sally   100
    William   32

Cannon, Betsy L.   163

Canterbery, Margaret   190

Carill, Daniel   33

Carlton, Stafford Co., Va.   186

Carlton, Frances T.   90

Caroline County, Va. 4, 30, 41, 55
    63, 80, 161, 176, 192, 195, 213
    220,221,239,247-249,258,259,266

Carpenter, Ann   178
    Eli C.   33
    Frances   79
    John   33, 79
    Overton   33
    William   33

Carr, Mr.   117

Carter, Alice   94
    Ann   128
    Ann Beale   33
    Ann C.   218
    Carolianna   84
    Charles   33, 33, 84
    Charles B.   33
    Charles C.   141, 185
    Charles Landon   213
    Daniel [Jr. & Sr.] 11, 33,   33
                     85, 94, 109, 179
    Edward   33
    Elizabeth   34, 120, 211
    Elizabeth L.   228
    Elizabeth S.   185
    Fanny   116, 117

Carter, Fanny A.   60
    Fenner   33, 181
    Frances Anne-   25
    George   33, 34, 38
    James R.   6, 33, 85, 178, 179
    John   33, 120, 252
    John Champe   33
    John S.   11, 34, 151, 187
    Joseph   34
    Landon   18, 33, 34, 34, 42, 60
               64, 68, 111, 169, 211
    Lucy   42, 42, 84
    Lucy Ann   109
    M.A.   33
    Mahala   11
    Maria   18
    Maria L.   166
    Martha   104
    Mary   33, 33
    Mary L.   64
    Mary Walker   33
    Rebecca   109
    Robert   71, 117
    Robert W. Jr.   94
    Robert Wormeley 18, 33, 34, 112
               116, 144, 148, 151
               208, 211, 228, 234
    Sally   211
    Sarah Fairfax   127, 243
    Sophia   151
    Susan   85
    William   3, 7, 33, 34, 109, 188

Cary, Mary   102

Cash, John   34, 34
    Rose Ann   139
    William   34, 72, 139

Casson, Sarah   212
    Thomas   212, 212

Cat Point Creek, Richmond Co. xvii

Catlett, John   248, 248
    Margaret   248
    Rebecca   44, 248

Cauthorn, John   52
    Pearson   102, 180

Cave, Belfield   245
    Benjamin   245

Cearron, William   34

Cedar Grove, King George County,
    Va.   246, 260, 269

Celsed, see Selsad : Selsed

Chadwell, William   143, 143, 257

Chamberlain, John   34
    John L.   34, 86, 130, 214

Chamberlane, Sarah   188

Champe, John   130, 161
    Mary   34

Chancellor, George   258
    Sanford   258
    Susan M.   258
    Vespacian   258

Chancellorsville, Spotsylvania
    County, Virginia   258

Chandler, Francis   34

Chanler, John   34

Chapman, Joseph   35, 40
    Philip P.   35

Charles' Beaver Dam, Richmond
    County, Virginia   xvii

Charles County, Maryland   96, 242

Charlestown, West Virginia   76

Charlotte County, Virginia   163

Chattin, Sarah   142

Cheazum, William   35

Chenault, Christopher   35, 219

Chestnut Hill, Richmond Co., Va. 12
                             66, 126

Chichester, Ellen   171
    Ellen (Ball)   243
    Hannah   78
    Richard   243, 250

Chilton, Ann C.   156
    Cyrus   48
    John Stewart   35, 122, 261
    Mark   35, 264
    Ralph H.   35
    Thomas   12

Chinault, Christopher   35, 219

Chingateaque Creek, King George
    County, Virginia   27

Chinn, Alice   243
    Ann(e)   36, 37, 124, 124
                    243, 243, 250
    Ann M.   203
    Bartholomew C.   8, 35
    Catherine   36, 37, 243
    Charles   243
    Chichester   35, 36, 243
    Christopher   243
    Elijah   243
    Elizabeth   103
    Elizabeth Sophia   58, 243
    Gertrude G.   95
    J.W., Jr.   xv
    John   93, 243, 243, 250
    John L.   134
    John Yates   30, 78, 127, 243
    Joseph   36, 82, 135, 243
    Joseph W.   36
    Marianna   95
    Mary Eliza   135
    Priscilla   92, 243
    Rawleigh 35, 36, 124, 204, 243
    Robert   36, 202, 245
    Sally   202
    Sally E.   134
    Sarah F.   92, 127
    T.C.   xv
    Thomas   36, 36, 243

Chissell, Ann   93

Chotank, Stafford County, Va. 269

Chowning, William   157, 158

Chrimse, Thomas   182

Christian, Francis Humphrey 36, 37
                           235, 243
    Nancy   34

Christie, Robert   37

Christopher, George   37
    Mary   192
    William 37, 49, 56, 60, 91, 121

Christy, Elizabeth   245

Churchill, Armistead   9
    Lucy   200
    Priscilla   9, 10, 186
                    216, 217, 218
    Samuel   37

Churchwell : Churchwill
    Amey   229
    Ann   52
    Elizabeth   57
    Elizabeth C.   56
    James   52
    Jane   215
    Samuel   37
    Sarah   188
    Simon   37
    Susan   175

Clapham : Clapman
    Elizabeth   80, 268
    Mary   234, 268
    Mary (Thatcher)   37, 171, 268
    William   37, 80, 152
                    171, 234, 268

Clark County, Kentucky   249

Clark : Clarke
    Alice   38
    Ann   43
    Atterson   37, 125, 233
    Benjamin   142
    Catey   73
    Charles   37

Clark : Clarke
  Cyrus 56
  David 37, 39
  Edward 37
  Eliza 45
  Elizabeth 16, 51, 59, 102, 110
    112, 114, 151, 238
  Elizabeth B. 38
  Eppa: 39
  Frances 65, 73, 114, 214, 230
  Hannah 109
  Hannah S. 91
  Henry 102
  Hiram 38
  James 38, 43
  Joan 102
  John 38, 38
  John H. 38
  John L. 39, 87, 91, 121, 184
    197, 202, 214, 236
  John R. 38
  Joseph 3, 17, 108
  Judy 201
  Juliet 51
  Lucy 28, 86, 118
  Mary 93
  Mary Ann 235
  Mary Jane 233
  Meshack 38, 114, 190
  Nancy 38, 63, 107, 136
  Patsy 190
  Presley 38, 39, 118
  Presley S. 38
  Randall 38, 114
  Rebecca M. 43
  Reuben 38, 39
  Richard 16, 26, 28, 39, 192, 235
  Richard Jr. 39
  Richard Sr. 21
  Robert 45, 67, 124, 151, 235
  Rodham 87, 211
  Samuel 39
  Sarah M. 22
  Septimus M. 33, 55
  Shadrach [Shadrack] 38, 39, 39
    73, 87, 131, 160
  Susan N. 39
  Susanna 118
  Thomas 39
  Thornton 39
  Vincent 38, 39, 73, 109, 118, 136

  Walker 39
  Wilalmira 104
  William 22, 39, 73, 114, 201, 252
  William Jr. 39
  Winneyfrit 87

Clarkson, Maria F. 28
  Richard H. 39

Clatworth, Roger 199

Claughton, see Cloughton
  Fanny 125
  Hiram 120
  John 39
  Richard 40, 108, 235
  Sally Lewis 108

Clayton, Thomas 40

Claytor, Ann B. 111
  Richard 40

Clear View, Stafford Co., Va. 14

Cleave(s), Emanuel 40, 173

Clemens, Samuel L. ["Mark Twain"]
  114, 249

Clement, Richard 224

Clements, Elizabeth C. 218
  James T. 218
  John W. 169
  William 40

Cleve, King George County, Va., 33
  34, 84, 211

Clifton, Hanover County, Va. 217

Clifton, Thomas 242

Clotworthy, Elizabeth 199
  Roger 199

Cloudis, A. 57

Cloughton, see Claughton
  Sarah H. 215

Coats, Charles L.   40
    Henry   40, 40, 239
    James   33, 40
    James Jr.   156
    Miskell   40
    Rebecca   156
    Susan   33
    Thomas   40, 182
    Thomas B.   34, 40, 40
    Zachariah   40

Coburn, John   40

Cocke, family   40, 41
    Alice Thornton   40, 41, 41
    Bowler, Jr.   220
    Catesby   40, 41
    Catherine   40, 41, 41
    Elizabeth 40, 41, 41, 161, 162
    Elizabeth (Fauntleroy) Turner
                              220
    John Catesby   40, 41, 211
    Lucy   41
    Peter T.   41
    Presley Thornton   40, 41
    William   161

Coear, Jane   46

Coghill, James   232
    Mary   232, 232

Coleman : Coalman : Coelman
    Ann   33, 41
    Betty   41, 67, 197, 223
    Elizabeth   205, 267
    James   41
    Lucy   41, 67
    Mary ["Molly"]   41, 197
    Richard   41
    Robert   41, 223
    Sarah   41, 223
    Thaddeus   41
    Thomas   28, 41, 41, 48, 67
                197, 205, 223, 267
    Wilson   41

Coles, Mary M.   141

Collee, Thomas   41

Collidge, Hezechia   45
    Mary   45

Collier, Mary   163

Collins, Drusilla   42
    John W.   31, 41, 154, 155
    Mary Ann   227
    Richard   42
    Thomas   42, 118

Collinsworth, Edmund   42
    Hannah   227
    John   42

Colonial Virginia Abstracts   xiii

Colston, Charles   42, 42
    Elizabeth Griffin   147, 156
    Elizabeth L.C.   42, 84
    Frances   42, 98, 139
    Mary   42, 190
    Mary (Meriwether)   16, 42, 139
                          190, 245
    Susan(na)   42
    Travers   156
    William   x, xvi, 16, 16, 42, 42
                   84, 139, 190, 245
    William Travers   42, 42, 84

Columbia County, Georgia   158

Colvert, George   264

Colwick, Hezekiah   215, 216
    Mary   215, 216

Conaway, Felcy   203

Cone Place, Northumberland County,
    Virginia   134

Conkling, Elizabeth   135

Connell, Davis   42
    Michael   43

Connellee : Connelly : Conoly
    Autumn   41, 43

Connellee : Connelly : Conoly
  Betty   108
  Daniel 20, 32- 43, 43, 69, 127
  David   43
  Elizabeth   182
  Frances E.   13
  George   43, 62, 108, 229
  George K.   43
  James S.   43, 56, 90
  John   43
  Lucinda   90
  Margaret   56, 171
  Mary F.   54
  Milly   139
  Nancy   179
  Patrick   43
  Peggy   84
  Richard H.   43
  Washington T.   43, 54
  William   43
  William H.   43, 170, 182

Conor, Margaret   3

Conserve, Emanuel   43

Conway, family   248, 251
  Ann   243
  Edwin 43, 44, 77, 223, 248, 251
  Eleanor Rose ["Nelly"]   44, 248
  Elizabeth (Thornton) 43,77, 248
  Francis   44, 248
  Francis Fitzhugh   213, 248
  Mary   251
  Sarah (Taliaferro)   248

Cook, Anthony   43
  Maria   224

Cooke, Elizabeth P.   75

Cookman, Ann   108
  Ezekiel   51, 188
  Hannah   105
  Jeremiah   90
  Polly Sydnor   108

Corbin, Anne   205, 267
  Elizabeth Tayloe   24
  Gawin   44
  Henry   205, 267

John R.F.   207
Richard   44

Cordere, Henry   44

Corey, Matilda   65

Cork, Ireland   165

Cornish, William   44, 57

Cornwell, Ann C.   44
  Artemisa G.   44
  John   44
  John B.   44
  Louisa V.   44
  Mary (Garland)   44
  William G.   44

Corotoman, Lancaster Co., Va.   71

Corrie, Ann   174
  Catherine   115, 174, 174, 232
  Hannah (Rust) Rust   175
  John   174, 175, 232

Corson, Alfred   44

Coton, Loudoun County, Va.   116

Courtney, Catharine S.   160
  Henry   44
  Jeremiah   44
  John   45
  Leonard [Lennord]   45, 160
  Maria   153
  Nancy   153
  William   44, 45, 45

Coushee, Margaret   77

Covert, Morris   45

Coward, James   45
  Margaret   83

Cox, Carlos   28, 162
  Elizabeth Ann   162
  James   75
  John   45
  John H.   99, 114

Cox, Mary W.   189
    Presley   45
    Sarah Ann   132
    Thomas M.   45
    William P.   45, 164, 198

Crabb, Benedict M.   45
    Jane   45
    Nancy   111
    Sally   232
    Sarah L.L.   165
    William M.M.   45

Craine, Chloe [Cloway]   19
    James   45
    Sarah   73

Cralle, Darius G.   38, 45, 45, 67
    K.R.   20
    Kenner   46, 91
    Samuel   32, 34, 51
    Samuel Jr.   46, 146

Crane, see Craine

Cranston, Andrew   46

Crask : Craske
    Ann   85
    Elizabeth (Moss)   46
    Ellin [Ellen, Eleanor] 11, 140
                       157, 211, 237
    George   46
    James   46, 225
    Jesse   46
    John 11, 46, 46,120,140,211,233
    Joseph M.   103, 179
    Martha   233, 237
    Richard   85
    Sarah   46
    Selina   103
    Vincent   46
    William   46, 211
    Winifred   11

Crawford, Elizabeth   47

Crawley, Ann   80
    Nancy   80
    William   46

Creel, William   46

Creswell, Frances   154
    William   46

Crewdson, Emily C.   54
    Henry   46
    John G.   230
    Louisa J.   230
    William   47

Cribin, Elizabeth   193

Critcher, Amanda   61
    Thomas   172

Crittenden, George W.   xv

Croder, Lucy   75

Crolorir, Thomas   47

Crondall, Richmond County, Va. xvii

Crookhorn, Thomas   47

Croswell, Gilbert   47

Crow, William   47

Crowder, Susan   188

Crow's, King George Co.,Va. 212,248

Croxton, J.   93
    Peggy   15

Crump, John J.   129
    Susanna   14

Crutcher, George   47, 92
    John R.   230

Culpeper County, Va. 11, 12, 41, 47
    68, 114, 129, 131, 136, 186, 189
    198,205, 221, 245, 249, 251, 255
                    257, 258, 264, 267

Cumberland, England   111

Cumberland County, Va.   4

Cummings, Gidion   62

Cundiff, Benjamin   160

Currell, Isaac   47

Curren, Dennis   47

Currie, Alice   82, 159
    David   82, 159
    Ellyson   xv

Curtis, Agatha   35
    Henry C.   47, 55
    John   47

Dabney, James   47

Dade, Francis   96
    Francis Jr.   97
    Horatio   130
    Langhorne   269
    Mary   96,97, 269
    Mildred (Washington)   269
    Townshend   9, 47, 82, 146

Dagod, see Doggett
    Margaret   56

Daingerfield, Elizabeth   189
    John   251, 222
    William   47, 47, 48

Dale, Ann   149
    Elizabeth   226
    Elizabeth W.   197
    Frances   21
    Joseph   48, 133, 165, 170, 226
    Nancy   121
    Polly   165
    Thomas   184
    William   48

Dalton, John   25, 121, 133, 194
    Mary   6, 194
    Winifred   56, 133

Damerl, Robert   48

Dameron, Ann   67

Christopher   197
Elizabeth   109, 118
Frances   191
George   16, 48
Hannah   7
John C.   48, 52
John C. Jr.   48
Leannah   219
Nancy   133
Rebecca B.   89
Richard   48
Robert H.   48
Roger   13, 48, 48, 133, 235
Samuel L.   48
Sarah   52
William Jr.   48, 48, 133

Dammurell, Ann   34

Daniel, Beverley   48, 204
    George   48
    Hugh   246
    Sally   38
    William   246

Darby, John   38, 174
    Lucy B.   1
    Thomas L.   1, 39, 103
    William B.   48

Darracott, Richard T.   48
    William P.   48

Darrell, Anne Fowke (Mason)   69

Dasey, William   48

Daughity, James   48

Daughters of the American Revo-
    lution Magazine   xii

Davenport, Ann H.   120
    Betty Hale   56
    Catherine D.   37
    Elizabeth H.   19
    Elizabeth P.   49
    Fanny T.   61
    Fortunatus   197
    George   49, 49, 90, 183
    George W.   49

Davenport, Joseph   49, 160, 197
     Joseph H.   49, 197
     Joseph P.   49, 66
     L.   149
     Linsey O.   19, 49
     Lucy   49
     Lucy T.   37
     Nancy Opie   67
     Opie   49
     Thomas D.   49
     Rachel   1
     Rachel M.   90
     Sally S.   19
     Sarah   197
     Susanna   66
     William   37,   49
     William E.   49
     William H.   49, 90, 187, 225
     William T.   61

Davis, family   249
     Alfred   49
     Alice   168, 202
     Alice G.   85
     Ann   147, 236
     Bartley   49
     Betsy   169, 219
     Catharine   99, 168
     Charles   49
     Edmund   227
     Edward   49, 51
     Elizabeth 50, 51, 79, 86, 90
        169, 208, 214, 214, 219, 227
     Esther   114, 161, 249
     Faney   48
     Fanny L.   185
     G.   185
     George   50, 54, 236
     Grace   2
     Hannah S.   25
     Henry   237
     Hester   114, 161
     Humphrey   49
     Jane   166
     Jesse   50
     John   17, 50, 63, 69, 73, 117
                  168, 172, 182, 236
     John L.   50
     John S.   50
     Joseph   50
     Joshua   114, 249

     Julia   159
     Juliet A.   172
     Katherine   249
     Lucius   50
     Lucy Ann   168
     Luke W.   50
     Maria G.   23, 24
     Maria S.   49
     Mary B.   183
     Mary (Berrick)   50
     Mary W.   20
     Peter   92
     Rebecah D.   17
     Reuben   50
     Richard   50, 51, 214
     Richard W.   50
     Robert 51, 51, 59, 86, 102, 166
     Robert H.   49, 51, 159, 173
     Rodham   51
     Sally   100
     Samuel   249
     Sarah   55
     Sarah A.   149
     Staige   24
     Susanna   56, 59
     Sydnor   50, 51
     Thomas   51, 188, 208
     Thomas S. 1, 7, 45, 51, 89, 235
     Walter   51
     William 50, 51,51, 52, 214, 214
     William F.   52, 69, 171
     Wilson   52
     Winifred   91, 102

Dawkins, John   52

Dawson, Ann   67
     Epaphaditus   52
     Fanny   48
     George L.   52, 189
     Jeremiah   52
     John   2, 249
     Lindsey O.   52
     Lindsey T.   52
     Mary (Waugh)   249
     Richard   52, 119
     Sarah   137
     William   52, 263

Day, Jane   37

Deacon, Elizabeth   28
   Nancy   28

Dean : Deane
   Agatha   70
   Aseneath   70
   Charles   53, 109, 268
   Clare   179
   Elizabeth   70, 145, 268
   Jane   70, 145
   John   x, 53, 70, 145
                      223, 251, 268
   Mary   268
   Susanna   70
   William   268

Deathey, Christopher   95
   Sally   95

Deately : Deatley
   Charlotte P.   85
   Julia H.   54
   Mary B.   141
   Nancy   105
   William   53, 54

Deatney, Betty   37

Deeke, Joseph   53, 253

Degge : Degges
   Ann   75
   Isaac   xiii, 53
   Mary   53
   Robert   53

de Jolie, Charlotte   17

Delano, Augustine   53
   Elizabeth   137
   Ellis Carter   v, xii, xiv
   George   100
   Gertrude (Payne) Sanford   xiv
   Joseph   53
   Joseph P.   99

Delaware, State of   232

Demeritt, Benjamin   53
   Elenor   100

   John   53
   Luke   53
   Molly   86
   Winefred   86

Demervill, John   214

Denby, John   53

Denham, Ann   156

Dennis, John   222
   Peggy   222

Denton, William   53, 176, 261

Derieux, Peter J.   219

Deschamp : Deschamps
   Cordelia G.   187
   Delia   G.   182
   Joseph   53, 90
   Mary S.   55
   Virginia W.   182, 187

Deshields, Joseph   53, 54

Dew, Elizabeth 14,134, 200, 201,204
   Flora   88
   Mary   115
   Samuel   23, 54
   Thomas   200
   William   232

Dewbre, John   54
   Josephine   121

Dickenson, Elizabeth (Brocken-
      brough)   13
   Thomas   13

Dickson, James   54

Didier, Henry   54

Digges, Edward   267
   William   267

Dinwiddie County, Virginia 121, 222

Diskin, John   54

Ditchley, Northumberland Co.,Va.
                              66, 155

Dixon, Alice (Fitzhugh)   259, 266
    Edward   221, 266
    Elizabeth   266
    Elizabeth (Clotworthy)   199
    Harry   266
    John   199
    John E.H.T.   266
    Turner   266

Dobbins : Dobbyns : Dobyns
    Abner 49, 54, 56, 147, 181, 190
    Abner Jr.   54
    Alice   55, 60, 61
    Ammy [Amney]   55, 140
    Ann   6, 101
    Annah   219
    Augustine W.   54
    Betsy P.   55
    Betty   153, 196
    Betty Hale   153
    Brunetta W.   200
    Catherine [Katharine]   86, 121
                            190, 203
    Charles   6, 54, 55, 56
                        78, 159, 191
    Chichester   54
    Christopher L.   55, 60, 148
    Daniel   49, 54, 55, 153
                  176, 190, 214, 261
    Daniel Jr.   54, 153
    Edward   54
    Edwin   55
    Elizabeth   191
    Elizabeth S.   203
    Fanny   148
    Frances   49
    Frances L.   32
    Frederick   54, 55, 219
    George H.   145
    Henry   55, 196, 253
    Henry M.   55, 56, 112, 153
    Jesse   55
    John Lawson   55, 55
    Joseph A.   55
    Juliet Ann   112
    Katharine, see Catherine
    Leroy   54, 55, 56, 60
                        148, 185, 191

    Leroy, Jr.   54, 55
    Lucy   26
    Margaret F.   32
    Margaret N.   106
    Maria L.   159
    Mary   53
    Mary S.   47
    Matilda C.   55
    Mildred   49
    Nancy   150, 153, 155
    Parthenia   111
    Peggy   197
    Rawleigh W.   61
    Rebecca   54, 55, 101
    Rebecca M.   37, 55, 148, 149
    Rebecca Sisson   54
    Samuel   71
    Sarah   86, 148
    Sarah L.   54, 55, 78, 191
    Suckey   160
    Sydnor L.R.   55
    Tabitha   140
    Thomas   49, 55, 55, 56, 86, 88
       150,153,155,190,200, 203, 214
    Thomas Thornton   54
    Thomas W.   56
    Washington   56
    William   50, 54, 55, 56
                        86, 101, 127
    William Forrester   56
    Winifred   145, 219

Dodson, Ailcey   26
    Alexander   85,10, 26, 56
    Alfred   56, 84
    Alice   46, 84
    Bartholomew   112, 186
    Catherine   58, 65
    Charles   44, 56, 56, 57
                        64, 172, 173
    Charlotte   64,216
    Edward L.   56
    Edwin L.   87
    Elizabeth   163, 172
    Elizabeth B.   216
    Elizabeth D.   27
    Elizabeth N.   186
    Fanny   29, 29
    Fortunatus   56
    Frances   29, 29
    George   56

Dodson, James B.   29, _57_, 169, 216
  James Booth   197
  Jane A.   222
  Letty   92
  Louisa   85
  Lucinda   56
  Mary   75
  Matilda   216
  Nancy   92
  Raughley   216
  Rawleigh   _57_, 216
  Rawleigh, Jr.   57
  Reuben B.   57
  Richard   57
  Ruth   44
  Sally   169
  Sarah   174
  Sharlet   216
  Susan   56
  Susannah   26
  Thomas   46, _57_, 250
  William   _57_, 57
  Winney   26

Doggett : Dog(g)ed, see Dagod
  Coleman   57
  Isaac   57
  John   57
  John W.   38,   52
  Lucy Ann   58
  Milly   48
  William   23

Dogue, King George Co., Va.   264

Dolphin, Katherine   126

Donahoe, Edmund   57
  Edward   57

Donaway, see Dunaway

Doniphan, family   258
  Alexander   x, _57_, 258
  Anderson   136
  Elizabeth   258
  Mott   258

Donnahan, Richard H.   57
  William H.   191

Donne, Samuel   242

Doon, Elizabeth   158

Doren, John   102

Doughty, Enoch   17
  Margaret   17

Douglas : Douglass : Douglis(s)
  Alice   64
  Ann   58
  Edward   _58_, 87, 183, 186, 215
  Edward Jr.   215
  Elizabeth   103, 183
  James   58
  John   _58_, 58, 83, 215
  John C.   58
  John Wesley   29
  Lucy   29
  Malindy   58
  Mary   52
  Milly   223
  Nancy   215
  Samuel H.   58
  Susanna   186
  Thomas   13, _58_, 58, 108, 186
  Thomas H.   _58_, 84
  Thomas H.L.   58
  William   58
  William G.   58

Dowden, Winny   177, 261

Dowle, Jane   166
  Joanna   166

Downey, John   160

Downing Bridge at Tappahannock xvii

Downing, George   58
  Robert E.   58

Downman, Ann M.   78
  Elizabeth   5, _78_, 123, 159
  Elizabeth Ann   127
  Elizabeth Porteus   218,218
  Ellen B.   160
  Frances E.   134
  Frances R.   5

Downman, Frances S.   39
    James   58, 200
    Joseph Henry   58, 59, 243
    Judith P.   86
    Margaret (Ball)   243
    Mildred   8
    Priscilla   50
    Rawleigh 8, 59, 78,191, 203,243
    Rawleigh William   243
    Richard   59, 59
    Robert   8, 59, 218
    Robert Porteus   59
    William   59, 59, 78, 160, 243

Doyle, James   74
    John   74
    Mary   74

Dozier, Conoway   39, 59
    Elizabeth   15, 113, 245
    Frances   77
    James   59
    James M.   59
    John   51, 59
    Leonard   59, 59
    Leonard Jr.   5
    Martin P.   59
    Mary   101
    P atcy   39
    Rebecca   39
    Richard   15, 59, 101, 219, 245
    Sarah P.   219
    Thomas   208

Drake, Corbin   60
    Fidelia Ann   18
    Henry   60
    Jane   70
    John J.   60
    Martha   170

Draper, Caty   21
    Elizabeth   77
    Leannah   21
    Mary Ann   153
    Richard   60

Dublin, Ireland   136, 257

Dublin Merchant [ship]   136

Duckberry, Henry   232
    Mary   232

Dudley, Alexander   60
    Elizabeth T.   236
    Frances   211
    Griffin   60
    Griffin G.   55, 60
    John   5, 60, 60
    John W.   xiv
    Thomas   60

Duff, Margaret   235
    Patsay   235
    Patty   175
    Peter   60
    Peter T.   115, 176

Dugliss, Thomas   13

Dulany, Henry R.   60

Dunaway, Alice   17
    Charles   60
    Elizabeth   105
    John   60, 196
    John G.   60
    John J.   61
    Malachi   61
    Presley   61
    Rawleigh W.   61
    Samuel   1, 105
    Thomas   61
    Thomas S.   49
    William   61

Duncan, see Dunkan and Dunkin
    Coleman   61, 61
    Henry   61, 61
    Robert   61

Dune, Elizabeth   225
    Patrick   225

Dunkan, Charity   113

Dunkin, Ann   137

Dunmore County, Virginia   166, 189

Durham, family   250

Durham, Catherine   250
   Dorothy   57, 61, 81, 250
   John   61, 250
   Joseph   250
   Margaret   145, 250
   Mary   46, 57, 61, 81, 250, 250
   Millicent   250
   Sarah   87, 250
   Susanna   250
   Thomas   57, 61, 61, 81
                   87, 145, 250
   Thomas Jr.   61, 61, 250

Durrett, Ann C.T.   56
   Richard   56

Dye, Anne   111
   Avery Jr.   146
   Avery Sr.   62
   Catherine   146
   Fauntleroy   111
   Hannah Ann   167
   Mary   111
   Nancy   22

Eagle's Nest, King George County, Virginia   123

Easton : Eaton
   Ann   129
   Heathy   129

Eden, King George County, Va. 161
                256, 259, 266

Edgcomb, John   199
   Sarah   12, 199, 199

Edge Hill, Prince William Co.Va.66

Edison : Eidson
   James   62
   John   22, 110, 145, 176, 179
   Joseph   176
   Susanna   111
   Winifred   111

Edmonds, Ann (Conway)   243
   Cornelius   62, 256
   Elias   30, 41

Judith   30
Vincent   62

Edmondson, James   62, 99
   James, Jr.   62

Edwards, Benjamin xix, 62, 62, 63
   Edwin C.   65, 139, 236
   Elizabeth O.   49
   Fanny   22
   Haden   62
   Jane Gray   62
   John   217
   Mary   194
   Mary Smith   62
   Richard   63
   Samuel   63
   Sarah   62, 62, 153
   Thomas   78, 81, 228
   William   62, 63
   William Lee   63

Edwars, Maliady   38

Efford, Alice   131
   Elizabeth H.   117
   Frances   174
   Frances D.   23
   George   W.   63, 173
   Hannah   29
   Jane   164
   John   63, 235
   John D.   63, 230
   Lucindy   170
   Lucy   70
   Martha   168
   Mary   39
   Mary Ann   127
   Matildy   141
   Nancy   35, 235
   Richard   63, 66, 148, 159
   Richard M.   4
   Samuel   163
   Samuel A.   23, 63, 99
   Sarah   110
   Sydnor   230
   William   63
   Williamson   63
   Zachariah   64, 131

Eidson, see Edison : Eidson

Elder, Elizabeth   78
    Lucy   54

Elgin, Joseph   66

Eliason, William Alexander   64

Eliff,   see Oliff(e) : Olliff(e)
    George   64, 126

Elkins, Amy   175
    Benjamin   136
    James   64, 175
    Richard   64, 175

Ellis, Elizabeth   269

Elliston, Robert Sr.   64,255

Elmore, Charles   64, 65
    Elizabeth   34, 65
    Francis   64
    George W.   64, 65
    Henry   57, 64
    James   65, 226
    John   65
    John W.   65
    Joseph   65, 65
    Kitty   110
    Lucy   57
    Mary   17
    Mary Ann   17
    Nancy   28
    Olivia N.   29
    Rawleigh   65
    Richard   65
    Susan J.   85
    Thaddeus   65
    Thomas   17, 65, 65, 86
    William   58, 64, 65

Eltonhead, Alice   205
    Martha   248

Emanuel Church, King George
    County, Virginia   220

England   x, xi, 13, 19, 82,   106
        107, 111, 116, 132, 162, 165
    166, 205, 209, 210, 244, 260, 267

English, Barbara   6
    Betsy   51
    Catharine B.   10
    Caty   51
    James   65
    John   65
    Katherine   227
    Lucy   133
    Samuel W.   53
    Susan   88
    Thomas   10, 65
    William   6, 10, 13, 65,133

Ennis, Nancy   74

Enquirer, Richmond, Va.   154, 244

Epsom, Spotsylvania Co.,Va. 202,259

Ersking : Ersbien
    Penelope   71
    William   65, 71

Erwin, Anne   232
    Elizabeth   73
    Thomas   73, 232

Eskridge, George   xv
    Hannah   32

Essex, Earl of   x

Essex County, Virginia   ix, x, xv
    xvi, 9, 12, 15, 17, 18, 23, 24
    25, 40, 47, 52, 57, 62, 66, 68
    70, 74, 76, 80, 89, 96, 99, 100
    103, 108, 109, 129, 131, 136,
    139, 144, 156, 157, 158, 159,
    174, 175, 182, 189, 190, 191,
    193, 195, 198, 199, 202, 207,
    212, 219, 224, 227, 231-233,245
    247, 248, 255, 258, 263,264,266

Etmon, Margaret   6

Eubank, Henry Ragland   xiv

Eustace, John   65, 66
    William   65, 66

Evans, see Evins

Evans, Elizabeth 7, 76
  Elizabeth T. 39
  Francis 66
  John T. 66
  Kemp 66
  Solomon 66
  William 66,115

Evelyn, John xi

Everett : Everitt
  Charles 66, 230
  Thomas 66, 66, 188
  William 69,175, 235

Evins, Ann (Anderson) 247
  John 247
  Richard 167

Ewell, Jesse 12, 66
  Solomon 78

Eyre, Littleton 21

Fairfax County, Virginia 246, 260

Fairfax, Thomas Lord xvii, 89

Fairview, Spotsylvania Co.,Va. 258

Fall Hill, Spotsylvania Co.,Va. 213

Fallen, Catharine 43
  Joseph H. 43
  Samuel E. 43

Fallin, Dennis 67
  Jeremiah 67
  Samuel E. 67
  Thomas 67, 215

Falmouth, Va. 14, 112, 186, 216

Fann, Mr. 263
  Anne 41
  William 67
  Winifred 85

Farmer's Hall, Essex Co.,Va. 76

Farrell, Edward L. 67
  John W. 67

Faulkner, Jesse 67

Faulks, William 41, 67

Fauntleroy, family 67, 68
  Ann 32, 157, 158, 208, 208
  Apphia 33, 47
  Apphia Bushrod 216
  B. 32
  Catherine 32, 47, 76, 128, 144
  Elizabeth 68, 109, 131, 131
    151, 220, 265, 266
  Ellen 202,202
  George Heale 68, 218
  Griffin 47, 68, 205, 239, 267
  Griffin Murdock 68,203,239, 245
  Hannah 260
  Henry 88
  Jane 266
  John 36, 68, 68, 82, 216, 218
  Joseph 32, 68, 109
  Judith 27, 207
  Julia 67
  Juliet 67, 144
  Katherine 137
  Lettice Lee 24, 68
  Louisa 68, 207
  Mary 77, 157
  Moore xvii, 2, 67, 68, 68
    77, 128, 131, 144, 217, 265
  Moore Jr. 68
  Peggy 239
  Polly 32, 208
  Robert B. 88
  Sally 68
  Sally Anne 88
  Sarah 68, 216, 217, 218, 251
  Susanna 122, 123, 124
    217, 217, 251
  William 33, 47, 68, 97
    97, 157, 220, 260
  William Henry 68

Fauquier County, Va. x, 30, 69, 76
  89, 100, 114, 155, 175, 221
  243, 249, 255, 260, 266

Faver, John 68

Faver, William   68

Favor, Eliz.[a]   158

Fawcett, Grace   77
    John   11, 19, 109, 138, 181
    Samuel   68

Fayette County, Kentucky   223

Feagans : Feagins
    Hannah   52
    William   28, 68

Ferry Farm, Stafford Co., Va.   89

Feggett, Nelly   233

Fenton, Samuel   68

Ferguson : Fergusson
    Jane   120
    John   37, 264
    Nancy   69
    Robert   60, 68, 69
    W.   69, 113, 224
    William   69
    William R.   69

Ficklin, Christopher   69
    Christopher D.   69, 69, 150
    Eleanor   52, 69
    Elizabeth   69
    Ellen   52, 69
    Famous   52, 53, 69
    John   252
    John D.   69, 69
    LeRoy D.   69
    Mary A.F.   140
    Nancy   69
    Sally   69
    Virginia   150
    William W.   69

Field, Daniel Jr.   74, 91
    Mary   91

Figett, Elizabeth   237

Figit, Ann   22

Finch, Enoch   22
    Griffin   69, 229

Findley, John   69

Finley, Sarah   5

Finnall, Jonathan   136

Fisher, John   69, 182
    Mary   182
    Peggy   163

Fiske, John   270

FitzHerbert, Bridget   234, 234

FitzHugh : Fitzhugh
    Alice   239, 259, 266
    Ann (Lee)   123, 246
    Barbara   32, 125
    Elizabeth   248
    John   125, 246, 248, 266
    Thomas   69
    William   41, 123

Flanagan, Catherine   74

Fleet, family   251, 265
    Henry   69, 156, 195
                             223, 251, 265
    Sarah   156, 195, 196
                        223, 248, 251, 265

Fleming County, Kentucky   118

Fleming, Alexander   69, 70, 70, 152
                             211,   212, 269
    Alexia   152
    Elizabeth   108, 152
                             211, 212, 224
    Joyce (Jones)   106, 211
    Margaret   191
    Samuel   137, 224
    William   224

Flinn Daniel   13, 70, 99, 105, 183
    Elizabeth   105
    Lucy   127
    Polly S.   183
    William   65

Flood, Alice   260
   Elizabeth (Peachey)   122
   Katherine   122
   Nicholas   122
   William   260

Florida, State of   59

Flowers, Eleanor   30

Flynt, Richard   184

Fogg, Lewis B.   70
   Maria L.   158

Fones, Catherine   26, 34, 72
                             105, 128
   Elizabeth   84
   James B.   156, 166
   John   22
   John H.   70
   Joseph   25, 70, 70, 233
   Joseph S.   70
   Mary   40
   Rachel   22
   Richard   1, 70
   Richard J.   166
   Richard P.   200
   Robert A.   33
   Sarah   84
   Thomas B.   1, 70
   William T.   70, 70

Forbes, William   70

Ford, Elizabeth   35, 173, 233
   George   35
   Jane   35, 70
   John   35, 40, 70, 173
   Mathew Thornton   35
   Patience   40, 173
   Thomas   35
   William   35, 141

Forest Hall, Spotsylvania Co. 258

Forrest, William Sr.   202

Forester : Forrester : Forrister
   Alice   53, 75, 118
   Amony   54

   Bridgett   71, 100
   Eliza Ann   100
   Eliza G.   53
   Fanny   100
   Nancy   49
   Richard P.   53, 100
   Robert   60, 71, 100, 118
   Thaddeus   35
   William xii,53, 67, 71, 71, 225
   William W.   71, 100, 208

Fossaker, Elizabeth   71, 198
   John   71, 79, 198, 258
   Richard   71, 198

Fossett, Livinia   142

Foster, Ann   9, 110, 247
   Edward B.   71
   Ezekiel   71
   John   9, 131, 247, 265
   Katherine   183
   Nancy   16
   Susannah (Cammack) 131,247, 265

Foulis, Richmond Co., Va. 134, 189

Fouls, see Fowles

Foushee, Elizabeth   72
   Francis   71, 72
   James   17, 72
   John   72
   Susanna   17, 82

Fowke, Anne   242
   Gerard   242

Fowler, Elizabeth   29
   Sarah   182
   Timothy   72

Fowles, George   72, 168
   Nancy   168
   Sinah   72, 168, 227

Fox, Ann (Chinn)   250
   John   221
   Nathaniel   147, 212, 213
   William   207, 250

302   MARRIAGES OF RICHMOND COUNTY

Foxhall, Thomas   72   Frederick County, Virginia 36, 37
                                               42, 79, 112, 131, 157, 235, 244
Frack, see Freake
                                             Frederick County, Maryland   159
France, in Europe   x, xi, 249
                                             Fredericksburg, Virginia ix, 2, 4
France, Bathsheba   72   12, 13, 14, 18, 21, 24, 25, 33,
  Betsy   72, 105   34, 41, 49, 60, 64, 76, 84, 90
  Elizabeth   73   116, 122, 126, 142, 144, 151, 155
  Fanny   72, 128   171, 186, 213, 227-229, 248, 258
  Felishehe   34, 72, 139
  Hugh   103   Fredericksburg Ledger   97
  John   26, 34, 72, 73, 73
           105, 107, 128, 178, 181   French, Alice   108
  John Jr.   21, 72, 73   Daniel   161, 256, 259
  John T.   73   Hugh   74, 91, 192, 255
  Joseph   73   James   74
  Kitty   26, 72   John   xix,62,74
  Mary   128   Margaret   192
  Nancy   72   Sarah Ann   58
  Polly   26, 72   Vincent   201
  Rodham   73
  Sally   26, 72   Freshwater, John   74
  Samuel   73   Mary (Hudson)   74, 119, 253
  Sarah   74   Sarah   55, 253
  Susan   128   Thomas   6, 55, 74, 74
  Thomas   73   119, 231, 253

Frances, John   73   Frier, Samuel   74

Francis, John   see John Francis   Fristow   74
                John France
                                             Fry, Joshua   247
Franklin, Elizabeth G.   133
  Elizabeth (Rock)   74   Fryer, John   180
  James   73
  John   73   Fulks, Ann   173
  Louisa   69   John   173
  Polly   153   William   41, 67
  Samuel R.   73
  Steward   73   Fuller, Mary   94
  Thomas   73, 113, 116, 188   Thomas   94
  William A.   73, 74, 172

Frary, James   46   Gaines, Bernard   74
  Peggy   46   Daniel   74
                                              Elizabeth   248
Freake, Ann   92   Reuben   257
  Martha   92
  William   92   Galbrath, Robert   75

Galligo, James   75

Gallop, Ann   61
  Elinor   24, 152
  Mary   64
  Phillis   136
  Robert   24, 61, 64, 136, 152
  Telis   136

Gardener, John   xv

Gardner, Elizabeth Macon   24
  John   24
  Richard   75

Garland, Alice C.   235
  Ann   44, 76
  Anna Maria   90, 92
  Benjamin N.   60, 73
  Betsy   16, 75
  Daniel   39, 54, 75, 142, 185
  Elizabeth   63, 66, 75, 159
  Elizabeth B.   8
  Elizabeth Rust   238
  Felicia Ann   122
  George   75, 76, 115, 153
  George T.   55, 75, 75
  Griffin   60, 75, 75, 87
            88, 185, 238
  Griffin G.   225
  Henrietta   75
  James V.   75, 103, 122
  Jeremiah   8
  Jesse   75
  John   7, 66, 75, 108, 115, 158
  John B.   66
  John D.   xv
  Mary   44, 75, 115, 223
  Mary Griffin   60
  Melia   153
  Moore F.   66, 75
  Nancy   137
  Peter R.   14, 36, 75
  Sophia   75
  Sophia Carter   46
  Vincent   46, 75
  Vincent Jr.   122
  William   16, 44, 66, 68
        75, 118, 137, 144
  William D.   75, 223
  William E.   75

William G.   76, 225
Williann E.   223

Garner, Jesse   76
  Richard   76

Garnett, Anne Tilden   76
  Henry   76, 144
  John   76
  Margaret (Miskell)   76
  Thomas   76, 76

Garrett, Margaret M.   116

Garton, John   154
  Katherine   154
  Martha   154
  Mathew   154
  Richard   154
  Ruth   154

Gaskins, David   77, 111, 176
  Dinah Moore   111
  Sally   228

Gathings, Cobham   77

Gatly, Jane   166
  Joanna   166

Gault, Mr.   118

Gawen, Hannah   22

Gaythings, Ann   189
  John   189

George, Amey P.   116
  Martin   77
  William   81

Georgetown, D.C.   228

Georgia, State of   158, 216

Gervase, Margaret   74

Gethings, Ann   189
  John   189

Gibbins, Patrick   77

Gibbs, Elizabeth   126
    John   194, 227
    John C.   77

Giberne, Isaac William   77

Gibson, see Gipson, Gipton,
            Gupten, Gupton
    Alice   248
    Betsey Suggit   197
    John   77
    Jonathan   43, 44, 77, 248
    Mary   184
    Mary (Washington)   106
    Rachel   2, 248
    Robert   77
    William   123

Gilbert, D.P.   164
    John   77
    Mary   250
    Samuel   42, 77, 190
    William   43, 77, 89, 218

Gill, Beckey   223
    Edward   77
    Elizabeth   225
    George   111, 225
    Lucy   59
    Patty   111
    Spencer   223

Gipson, Betsey Suggit   197

Gipton, Elizabeth   166

Glascock : Glasscock
    A.A.   154
    A.W.   159
    Aldea   78, 154
    Amelia A.T.   230
    Ann(e)   9, 87, 95, 116
            123, 171, 201, 204, 204
    Ann T.   100
    Catherine   192
    Eleanor Ball   231
    Eliza   130
    Elizabeth   59
    Emma D.   33, 71, 86
    Evelina S.   100
    Frances   9, 53, 100, 123
            132, 133, 176, 226

    Frances F.   63
    George   78, 87, 156, 192
    George Jr.   100
    Gregory   71, 78, 133, 192, 263
    Jean   116
    Jane   116
    John   78, 192, 263
    John D.   5, 43, 78, 134, 149
    Joseph   130
    Judith   36, 93, 100
    Mary   95, 156
    Melissa   116
    Million   155, 156, 192
    Milly   87
    Milton   59
    Milton Syms   78, 116
    Peter   78
    Polly   145
    Priscilla   8, 56, 90, 190
    Rawleigh D.   78
    Richard   8, 78
    Richard M.   35
    Sarah   93, 192
    Susan   F.C.   35
    Thomas x, 9, 71,95,116, 201, 204
    Thomas M. 78, 116, 134, 149,160
    Washington   78, 100, 134
    William   8, 9, 59, 78, 79, 79
            87, 90, 93, 123, 124,
                    155, 156, 171, 201
    Winifred Ball   59

Glasgow, Scotland   136

Glass, Belfield   245
    Jehu   15, 245, 245
    William   245

Glendening, John   79, 258

Glew, John   18

Gloucester County, Va.   3, 4, 35
        108, 115, 134, 138, 161, 187
        192, 212, 213, 216, 260, 263

Gloucestershire, England   205, 267

Goad, Ellis   56

Goddard, Mr.   118

Godfrey, Alice B.   81

Goldsbary, Nancy   230

Goldsborough, David   94

Goldsby, Ann   87, 88, 195
     David   79, 88, 94
                     168, 169, 195
     Edward   79, 87, 88
     George W.   41, 79
     Jane   60, 88
     John   79, 88

Gooch, Ann   42

Goochland County, Va. 50, 115, 218

Goodlett, Adam   79

Goodridge, William   250

Goosby, see Goldsby

Gordon, Churchill   251
     Elizabeth   120
     Elizabeth M.   55
     Frances A.   45, 188
     James   79
     John   79, 109
     Kitty S.J.   99
     Lucy   130
     Maria G.   45
     Susan   130
     Susannah   120

Goulding, Mary   110

Gouldman, Phebe   188

Gower, family   78,80
     Ann   230, 254
     Elizabeth   107, 206
     Frances   188
     Francis   23, 230, 254
     John   254
     Peirce   79
     Rachel   23, 230, 254
     Stanley 3, 80, 116, 193,206,254
     Susanna   231

Graham, John   151
     John Jr.   52

Grant, Daniel   80
     Elizabeth   80
     James   129
     William   80, 80

Granville County, N.C.   172

Gray, Jean   xix, 62
     Samuel   62, 80, 213
     Thomas   80

Green, Mr.   263
     Ann   23, 80, 81
     Daniel   80
     Eleanor   254
     Elizabeth   80, 80
     Esther   254
     George   80, 80, 268
     Grace   80
     Hester   254
     Isaac   80
     John   57, 80, 80
     Joseph   80
     Mary   94
     Nancy   202
     Nathaniel   81
     Richard   23, 80, 81, 193, 254
     Robert   80
     Samuel   80
     Thomas   80
     William   80
     Winifred   80, 193, 253

Green Bank Farm, Stafford Co.,Va.176

Greenfield, Essex County, Va.   47

Greenham, Jeremiah   61, 81, 250

Greenlaw, Anders G.   81
     Ann   118
     David   81, 81
     Donald   81
     John Oliver   81
     Hunter R.   252
     Lucy Ann   81
     Mary   192, 193, 262
     Mary Agnes   81

Greenlaw, William   81, 81
                    192, 229, 262
     William Bowden   81

Green Spring, James City, Co.   117

Greenwich pensioner   171

Gregory, James   81, 125
     Richard   263

Gresham, George   81
     Richard T.A.   15, 91, 182
     William   24

Griffin, Alice Corbin   156
     Anne Corbin   82, 159
     Cyrus   82
     Elizabeth   1, 36, 82, 82
     Jane   136
     Judith   68, 82
     Judith (Ball)   68, 82
     Katherine   267
     LeRoy   36, 68, 81, 82, 82, 159
     Thomas   82, 155
     William   82, 82
     Winifred   66, 131, 155, 155

Griggs, Ruth   15, 245

Grigrye, Ann   94

Grigsby, John, Jr.   114, 249
     Thomas   82, 82, 146

Grimes, Sarah   168

Grimstone, Mary   82
     Sarah   82
     Thomas   10, 82

Grove Mount, Richmond County,
     Virginia   6, 70, 227

Grymes, Charles   116
     Lucy   116

Gui[l]bert, Mathew   82, 146

Guilliams, Lucy   101

Gupten, Nancy   17

Gupton, Haney   106
     Stephen   71, 83

Gutridge : Guttridge
     Apphia C.   3
     Elizabeth   3, 34
     Henry R.   83
     John   166
     Joseph R.   94
     Lucinda   132
     Lucinda A.   238
     Mahalah   40
     Newton   83
     Rebecca   46
     Reuben   3, 34, 84
     Richard C.   166
     Susanna   84
     William   94
     William A.   33, 94

Gwien, Alice   30

Gwyn, David   267
     Elizabeth   205, 267
     Sarah   190

Habron, Benjamin   83
     Charles   83
     Lucy   3
     Margaret   196
     Mary   77
     Nancy   158, 163
     Nancy Lambert   196
     William   83

Hack, Ann   251

Hackley, James   258
     Mary   258

Hackney, Benjamin   159
     Eliz.[a]   159

Hading, Elizabeth   151

Hadon, Elizabeth   73
     Sally   47

Hail : Haile, see Hale &c: below

Hais, Anne 31

Hale : Hail : Haile
Benjamin 28
Benjamin Jr. 83
Fedelia B. 200
Frances 95
James 54
John 83, 83
Mary 73
Moses 83
Peggy 54
Richard 83
Samuel 83
Sarah J. 54
Thomas 73, 83, 85, 215
Thomas R. 54, 84, 148
Thomas W. 84
William 83, 99
William B. 38, 65, 149, 233
William S. 84, 112

Halifax County, Va. 96, 202

Hall, Mr. 234
Ann 104
Benjamin Harrison 42, 84
Bladen 84, 104
Blaton 40
Charity Ann 225
Charlotte T. 171
Dewanah 162
Elisha 84
Elizabeth 40, 70, 73, 157
Griffin D. 84
Isaac 64, 84
James 11, 84
John 84
Joseph 84
Julia 128
Lucy Jane 48
Maria 179
Mary 73, 108, 178
Mary A. 179
Mary Ann 85
Mary (Blount) 67
Mary Elizabeth 72, 73
Molley 128
Newman 84

Reuben 84
Richard 84, 105
Richard L. 85
Robert xvi, 171, 188, 200
Robert Sandy 85
Sally 88, 103, 103
Sarah 215
Stephen 85
Thomas 85
William 85
William B. 215
Williamson 70, 84, 85, 85

Halloway, see Alloway

Hames, William 85

Hamilton, Ann 63
Gilbert 85
William B. 12, 85

Hammack : Hammock
Augustine M. 171
Benedict 83, 85, 219
Benjamin Jr. 85
Catherine M. 92
Charles 83, 85
Elizabeth 137, 219
Fanny 219
Frances 117, 236
Jane 117, 183
John 73, 85, 86
100, 101, 105, 158
John W. 86
Lewis 86, 118, 219
Lucy 87, 219
Maria 87
Mary 64, 107
Mary P. 17
Molly 83
Nancy 63
R.C. 65
Robert 86
Rodham 86, 92, 168
Sally 5, 100
Sarah 219
Sophia 173
William 5, 39, 63, 85, 86, 107
Winnef: S. 171

Hammond : Hammon : Hamon

Hammond : Hammon : Hamon
  Mr.   263
  Betty   93, 162
  Catherine   6, 194
  Elizabeth 86, 102, 106, 138, 160
  Jane   93, 168
  Job Jr.   86
  John   42, 60, 86, 133
  Joyce   118
  Katherine   113, 194, 232
  Leroy   79
  Lucy   86
  Mary Ann   3, 211
  Nancy   175
  Raney   177
  Rebecca Sisson (Lawson)
    Thornton   55, 86
  Suckey   42
  Susannah   50
  Thomas   55, 86, 214
  William   86, 175

Hammontree, Ann   98

Hampsfield, England   209

Hampshire County, W.Va.   213

Hamwell, O.J. Company   xv

Hand, Lawrence   86

Hanes, Ann   153

Hanks, Elinor   10
  Elizabeth   87
  Ewell   10, 86
  Fayall   121
  Hannah   197
  John   87, 142
  John E.   87
  Joseph T.   87, 224
  Judith P.   87
  Luke   10, 48, 87
  Luke S.   87
  Sally   10
  Sarah   87
  Susanna   93
  Turner   87
  William   87, 87, 250

Hanover County, Va.   151, 217

Harbin, Ann   136, 137, 257
  Elizabeth   6
  George   160
  Hannah   160

Harburn, David   87

Harding, Cyrus   134
  James   87
  William   87

Hardwick, Aaron   87, 88, 225
  Daniel   31, 89, 141
  Daniel H.   225
  Elizabeth C.   45
  Felicia   46
  Frances A.   225
  Hannah Elizabeth   187
  Jane Redman   45
  John   45, 46, 172, 187, 190
  John Jr.   172
  Juliet   172
  Polly P.   190
  Samuel R.   88, 114
  Sarah Ann   172
  William   87, 88

Harford, Alice   182
  Betty B.   105
  Edith   168
  Fanny   66
  Henry   22, 66, 88, 211
  Henry, Jr.   22
  John   105, 153
  Martha   176, 188
  Mary   153, 176
  Mary L.   22
  William   66, 88, 182
  Winifred   79

Harnsberger, Stephen M.   88

Harper, Mr.   263
  Abraham   88
  Benedict   88
  Downing   88
  Emmaline Susan   104
  Hannah   58
  Hannah E.   225

Harper, John   88
  John C.   88
  Richard   88
  Richard S.   225
  Sarah   17, 193
  William   17, 48, 193
  William P.   1, 88

Harrington, John   88

Harris, Ann   219
  Elender   56
  Elizabeth   215
  Fanny   112
  Franky   64
  George   115
  Henry M.   88, 130
  Hugh   88, 99, 150, 183,201
  James M.   88
  Jane   84
  John   44, 45, 89, 191
  Mary   115
  Nancy   99, 117, 201
  Peggy   67
  R. M.   88
  Robert   130
  Sally   183
  Sarah Ann   88
  Sarah B.   130
  Susanna   85
  W. N.   168
  William   14, 26, 70, 89, 117

Harrison, Abigail   113
  Alice   151
  Alice Griffin   32
  Ann   25, 196
  Betty George   32
  Betty Linton   32
  Daniel   89, 90, 121, 162, 225
  Daniel C.   45
  Elizabeth   43, 185
  Frances   249
  George   32, 131
  Hannah   4, 9, 113
  Izabel   207
  Jael   89
  James   x, 89, 162, 225,258
  Jane   121
  Jeremiah   89, 196
  John   43, 58, 118

  Lucinda S.   121
  Malinda B.   162
  Mary   25, 89
  Mathew   25, 43, 89, 118
  Nancy S.   132
  Polly C.   121
  Richard   125
  Richard H.   89,99,118
  Robert   89,198
  Samuel   89, 90, 132,196
  Tabitha   96
  Thomas   90
  William   4, 25, 43, 90, 104

Harrow, Mary   202

Hart, Elizabeth   22
  Fielding   90
  John   90

Haruear, Harwear   12

Harvey, Ann   215
  Jane   210
  Jane (?) Bowcock White   152
  John   210
  Joseph F.   127
  Marcius C.   90, 193
  Margaret   163
  Mungo   8, 90
  Thomas   152

Harwar, Ann   12, 21

Harwood, Louisa R.   91
  Mary Frances   15
  Richard H.   15, 91

Haseard, see Hazard : Hazzard
  Elizabeth   181
  Joseph   181

Hastie, William   90

Hatch, Joseph   90

Hathaway, Elizabeth   60
  Lawson   47
  William   49, 61, 90, 190

Hatton, Rebecca   1, 26, 150, 226

Hause, see Hawes

Haw, John   120

Hawes, Henry   90, 90

Hawkins, Mr.   118

Hawksford, John   92

Hay, Elizabeth   203
    John   203

Haybered, see Heaberd

Haydon, George   28
    John   28, 91
    Margaret   83
    Winny B.   28

Haymarket, Prince William Co.,   33

Haynes, Austin B.   91
    John R.   91
    William C.   20, 46, 91, 206

Haynie, Ann   31
    Delia Griffin   53
    Elizabeth   194
    Holland   53, 91, 223, 227
    Joseph   31
    Maxmillion   100
    Mira   223
    Polly   187
    Wilalmira (Webb)   53, 223
    William   187
    Yarret   31

Haywood, John   61

Hazard : Hazzard, see Haseard
    Bury   224
    Elias   121
    Elinor   208
    Henry   18, 91
    Henry H.   132
    James   91
    John   91
    Joseph   91, 112, 208
    Mahala   112, 121
    Mahalah   112

Mary   194
Nancy   64
O.E.P.   224
Polly   194
Rawleigh   91, 100, 160, 229
Thomas   69, 91, 194
William   91, 112

Hazell, John   91

Hazel Plain, Prince William Co. 259

Hazlewood, Ann   218
    George   218

Heaberd, John   92
    William   92

Head, Alexander Spence   92
    Henry   92

Headley, Daniel M.   226
    Eppa: 233
    Ezekiel   108
    Griffin 65, 148, 215, 226, 233
    Henry   5, 92, 163
    Henry W.   92
    Henry Wiatt   92
    James   148
    John T.   92
    Lindsey   38, 54, 149
    Lucy   208
    Maria Louisa   70
    Martha H.   65
    Martha H.B.   233
    Mary   194
    Mary Ann G.   226
    Patsey   99
    Paul   92
    Rachel   5
    Randall   92
    Ransdall   173
    Ransdall P.   92, 92, 172
    Ransdell P.   92,   92
    Robert P.   92, 92, 159
    Sarah L.   159
    Susan S.   65
    Thomas H.   92,   92
    William   48, 92, 194
    Winney   148, 148

Heale, Ann   68
    Catherine   112
    Elizabeth   49, 201
    George   112, 151
    Joseph   68
    Sarah   25, 151

Heall, Elizabeth   201

Heath, John   93

He[i]fford, see Efford

Helford, Zacharias   93

Henderson, Elizabeth   206, 206
    George   91
    James   93
    John   93
    Mary   46, 91
    William   93

Hendley, Elizabeth   67
    Hannah   67

Hendorson, Elizabeth   206

Hendren, Ann   184, 228
    Mary   78
    Rosey   91
    William   78, 93, 184, 228

Hening, Robert   143, 147

Henrico County, Va.   147, 245

Henry, Frederick   93
    George   77, 228
    Harry   93
    James   93

Hewes, Richard   243

Hewitt, James   14

Hiden, Martha W.   xvii

Higgins, Augustine   191
    Penelope 10, 190, 191, 244, 246

Hightower, Charnel   93

William   93

Hill, Betty Ann   232
    Eleanor   47
    Elizabeth   52
    George   93, 97
    John   54, 93, 162
    John Jr.   162
    Katey   162
    Leonard   247
    Mary (Micou)   247
    Martha   226
    Martin   93
    Mary (Micou)   247
    Mary Ann   235
    Sarah   157
    Susan Ann   182
    Thomas Suggitt   176
    Virginia Ann   65
    William   93, 94
    William E.   20, 94, 188
    William H.   65, 94, 226, 235

Hill Park, Essex Co., Va.   247

Hillman, Richard   94

Hillyer, Elizabeth Peachy   44
    Esabella   193
    Isabella   193
    James   60, 94

Hinds, Benjamin   94
    Betty   78, 78
    Charles   94
    Elizabeth   3, 78
    James   78, 94, 119
    John   78
    Judith   3, 200
    Mary   28, 78, 119
    Richard   3, 200, 246
    Sarah   96
    Thomas   94

Hinkley, Edward   94
    Elizabeth   94

Hinson, Andrew J.   94
    Ann   97
    Anna   105
    Catherine   94

Hinson, Carter   179
   Daniel   94, 178
   Elizabeth   3
   Frances   127, 128
   George W.   94
   Haney [Haynie]   3, 4
   Henry   181
   James   3, 94, 181
   Jane   128
   John   40
   Jonas   3
   Julia Ann   30
   Madrith   94
   Mahaly   94
   Mary   97,128
   Meredith   128
   Nancy   178, 233
   Patty   181
   Reuben   31
   Salathiel S.   94
   Sarah   105
   Sarah Ann   40
   Sophia   146
   Susan   230
   William   94, 105, 127, 146
   William Jr.   95
   William Sr.   94
   William W.   95

Hipkins, James W.   132
   John   95, 295
   Mary W.   45
   Rebecca H.   21
   Richard   32
   Robert S.   45, 66, 95, 189
   Samuel W.   95
   Samuel William   95
   Sarah E.   186

Historic Northern Neck of Virginia   xiv

Hix, Mary   118

Hobbs, Ann   23, 80, 81, 193, 254
   John G.   95
   Richard   81, 254

Hobs, Winifred   228

Hodgson,   see Hudson

Hogan : Hogans : Hogin : Hogins
   Alice   118, 118
   Ann   95
   Christopher D.   95
   Elizabeth   84
   Fanny   133
   Frances   148
   Haney   224
   Hannah B.   58, 103
   James   95
   Jeduthan   95, 95, 108, 118
   Milly   108
   Nancy   58, 99, 103, 118
   Polly L.   95
   R.G.   165
   Richard   118
   Richard H.   95
   Thomas   58, 68, 95, 95
                  99, 103, 118, 234
   Traverse [Travis] 95, 95, 118

Holland, Margaret   185
   Thomas   96

Holmes, Jesse   258
   Mary Jane   258
   William Wilson   96, 96

Holt, Elizabeth   229
   John   229
   Simon   96

Holtzclaw, B.C.   5

Hooe, family   96, 97, 242
   Anne   14
   Apphia Bushrod   97
   Bernard   259
   Elizabeth   97
   Gerard   96, 242, 244
   Harris   14
   Howson   97
   John   96, 97, 242
   Margaretta S.   266
   Rice 96, 96, 97, 203, 242, 266
   Robert Howson   97, 128
   Sarah   97, 242
   William   259

Hooper, Thomas   97

Hopkins, Elizabeth   46, 211
  Frances   6, 97
  George   6, 62, 97
  John   97
  Robert   211

Hopper, Katherine   13

Hopwood, Moses   94, 97

Hord, James   255
  Jane   255
  Thomas   255

Hore, Elias   98

Horgin, James   98

Hornby, Daniel   12, 98, 143

Hoskins, Anthony   106, 269
  Elizabeth   106, 107, 207

Hoult, see Holt

How Justice Grew   xvii

How^r [?], Elizabeth   23

How : Howe
  Abner   52, 162, 224
  Dozier   98
  Elizabeth   23, 228
  Fanny   26
  George   98
  Hannah   132
  James   98, 142, 187
  John   149, 164, 191, 228
  John Jr. 5,73,92, 98, 140, 234
  Matilda   115
  Nancy   149, 150, 226
  Polly   226
  Thomas   98,179, 187
  William   164
  William T.   98

Howard, Alice   228
  James   98, 98
  Jereboam   98, 197
  LeRoy   48, 98, 231
  Winefred   231

Howarth, John H.   98

Howe, see How : Howe

Howell, Diana   24
  George   24

Howend, James   98

Howson, Anne   97
  Robert   97

Hubard, James   98, 139
  Eppa: 62, 99

Hudnall, Elizabeth C.   224

Hudson : Hutson
  Alice   20
  Ann   26, 65, 83, 189
  Bryan   59, 74, 183
  Charolous   99
  Eliza   90
  Elizabeth   59, 69
  Frinefrid   69
  Hudson, Henry O. 38, 83, 99
                   99, 117, 174
  Jane Wroe   206
  John   38, 99
  Martha   99
  Mary 59, 74, 119, 183, 238, 253
  Meridith 38, 99, 101, 117, 202
  Nancy   174
  Presley   52, 99
  Rawleigh   99
  Richard   125
  Robert   89
  Robert H.   99
  Rush   219
  Samuel   99, 125
  Sarah (?) Willis Wood 219
  Susan   125
  Thomas   238
  William   63, 99
  William R.   99

Hugell, Elizabeth   220

Hughes, Anna   154, 160
  Anne   154, 160
  Elizabeth   100

Hughes, Hannah   154, 160
    John   100, 113, 154, 160
    Thomas 100, 100, 154, 195, 256

Huguenots,   17

Humphries : Humphris
    Elias   100
    Fanny   49
    William   49
    Winney   48
    Winneyfred   49

Hundley, Elizabeth G.   43
    John   100, 153
    Patsy   164
    William L.   100

Hungerford, Thomas xvii, 161, 259

Hunt, Elizabeth   28
    Frances C.   149
    George   100, 211
    John   28

Hunter, John   100,226
    Taliaferro   204
    Thomas Lomax   26

Huntly, Mary   224

Hunton, Alexander   77
    Betty   145
    Elizabeth W.   124
    James   100
    Ludwell A.   100
    Nancy   40, 77, 145
    Robert   77, 100
    Salley   77
    Susanna(h)   144, 183
    Thomas   145
    William W.   100

Hutson, see Hudson : Hutson

Hutt, Ann   101
    Eliza Ann   151
    Gerard   100
    Myrenda   103
    Richard B.   6, 100
    Steptoe D.   101

S.S.   103, 151
    Thomas   198

Indians   ix, xvii, 97, 174

Ingo, Elizabeth   5, 59
    Frances   10, 96, 244
    James   10, 27, 96, 101, 244
    John Sr.   5, 59, 101
    Mary   96, 101

Ingram, William   44, 45, 188

Innis, Elizabeth   72
    James   72, 175
    Sarah   175

Ireland in Europe xi, 136, 165,257

Isaacs, Elijah   17

Isle of Wight County, Va.   269

Isles, Absolom   101

Islington, Richmond County, Va. 81

Ives, William   101

Jackman, Mary   219

Jackson County, Missouri   258

Jackson, Betsy   75
    Betty   236
    Catharine   95
    Catherine S.   99
    Catherine W.H.   225
    Christopher   28
    Daniel   13, 59, 72, 99
                101, 111, 119, 262
    Elizabeth   28, 95, 95
    Jane E.   52
    Joanna   50
    Luke   26, 40, 50, 75, 99
                101, 193, 206, 215
    Mary   262
    Nathaniel   101
    Robert   222

Jackson, Sophia 119
Thaddeus 28, 99
Vincent 101
William 47, 81, 101
Winnefred 65

Jacobs, John 102
William 102

Jacobus, Angell 51, 59, 77
102, 110, 238
Ann 110
Elizabeth 238
Susanna 51, 59, 86, 102, 166
Winifred 238

Jacson, Betty 236

James City Co.,Va. 21,116,117, 139

James River, Virginia 97

James, Francis 102, 173
John 102
Margaret 102, 106, 173
Thomas 102

Jarrett, Shevell 102

Jarvis, Margaret 74

Jasper, see Jesper

Jefferson County, Kentucky 119

Jefferson County, W.Va. 76

Jefferson, Thomas 76

Jeffrey, Margaret 28

Jeffries, Ann A. 102
Betsy R. 186
Clementina (Webb) 103, 198, 199
Ebenezer 23, 102, 102, 223
Edmund R. 10, 56, 103, 103, 186
Edward 29
Edward R. 9, 58
Elinor 110
Elizabeth 29
Fidelia A. 218

Griffin 103, 163
Isaac S. xvi, 8, 25, 41, 75
88, 180, 198, 223
John F.B. xvi, 10, 39
69, 150, 173, 180
Joseph R.xvi, 45, 103, 165, 187
Margaret 29, 196
Maria F. 39
Mary Ann 29
Mary B. 173
Nancy 103
Nancy H. 186
Richard Orlando 23, 103
130, 148, 225
Robert 103, 215
Robert G. 103
Thomas 103, 191, 225
Thomas H. 103, 198, 199, 226
William R. 21, 42, 76, 103, 153
164, 170, 214, 223, 225, 225

Jenifer, James C. 103

Jenings, Ann 230
Edmund xvi
Elizabeth 13

Jenkins : Jinkins
Ann 104, 236
Bladen 103, 104
Daniel 105
Eliza 105
Elizabeth 3, 104, 236
Fanny 26, 234
Frances 178
George 103
Hannah 26
Henry 103, 104
James 3, 103, 104, 145
James H. 40, 104
Joel R. 104
John 3, 104, 112, 236
John W. 104
Lesha 236
Mansfield 51
Maria 105
Martha 51, 104, 145
Marthy 26
Matthew 104
Matthew Jr. 104

Jenkins : Jinkins
    Molly   89
    Nancy   4
    Nelly   3
    Peter   104
    Reuben   4
    Richard   104
    Robert   104
    Robert A.   104, 168
    Susanna   145
    Tascoe C.   104
    Thomas   104
    Thomas A.   104
    William 51,89,104,105,105,   236
    William J.   28, 50

Jennings, see Jenings
    Anne   231
    James   72, 105, 109, 180
    John   105, 231, 232
    John Melville   xiv
    Sarah   180

Jesper : Jasper
    Ann   63
    Betty   230, 231
    Catharine   28, 101
    Daniel   231
    Eleanor   194
    Eliza   22
    Elizabeth 55, 74, 106, 231, 253
    Fanney   235
    George   26, 101, 104, 187, 215
    Harriet   148
    Joanna   69
    Margaret N.   33, 141
    Mary   43, 93
    Mary Ann   194
    Nancy   174
    Peggey   148, 149
    Richard   63, 105, 235
    Richard Taylor   142
    Robert   105
    Samuel B.   105
    Sarah   101, 230, 231
    Thomas   43, 74, 101
                    106, 230, 231, 253
    Thomas Jr.   17
    Thomas H.   106
    William   28, 106, 109, 194

Jesse, John   106
    Polly Greenwood   106
    Richard   106
    Thomas   106

Jett, Francis   207, 268
    J.B.   107
    Martha   106
    Mary   106
    Peter   106, 106
    William   106, 106, 207
    William N.   107

Jinkins, see Jenkins : Jinkins

Jobson, William   107, 121

Johnson, Dr. Amandus   240
    Frances   155
    James   73
    John   107
    Joyce   96
    Mary   243
    Richard   89, 132

Johnston, Betsey   24

Jones, Alicia   155
    Ann(e)   22, 53, 109
                     137, 194, 230, 268
    Barbary   9, 25
    Benjamin   107, 163
    Benjamin F.   74
    Betsy   207
    Caty   179
    Charles   29, 63, 107, 194, 230
    Clinton   6, 73, 107
    David   107
    Edward   9, 25, 107,148,157, 261
    Edward Jr.   107
    Eleanor [Ellianor]   172
    Elizabeth   9, 11, 19, 25, 92
                     115, 157, 161, 180
                183, 188, 212, 249, 259
    Elizabeth Travers   109
    Epaphroditus 108, 125, 223, 229
    Esther   115, 161, 249, 259
    Frances W.   65
    Francis D.   108
    George   95, 108, 147
    George Lewis   108

Jones, Griffin 108
  Hanner 92
  Hester, see Esther
  Hiram M. 121
  Isaac 9, 25, 107, 148
  James 3, 6, 42, 44, 104, 108
    114, 121, 161, 237, 249
  Jane 15, 134, 135, 189
  Jeremiah Nash 108
  Jesse 108
  John 53, 92, 108, 109, 141
    165, 211, 212, 212
  John Jr. 92
  John W. 113
  Joseph 114-115, 249
  Joseph N. 108, 108
  Joyce 106, 211, 269
  Leanah 48
  Lodowick 108, 204
  Louisa 6
  Lucy 25, 40
  Lucy E. 121
  Margaret 54, 148, 149
  Margaret Ann 3
  Maria 178
  Martha 165
  Mary 73, 161, 216, 259
  Mary Ann M. 44
  Mary (Birkett) 24, 53, 109
  Mary M. 42
  Matilda 131
  Milly 48
  Molly 163, 165
  Nancy 59, 92
  Nebuchadnezzar 24, 53, 109, 256
  Owin 109
  Patty 176
  Peggy 181
  Polly 214
  Priscilla L. 108
  Rebecca [Rebecah] 117, 131, 141
  Richard 109
  Richard H. 109
  Robert 109
  Sally 125
  Samford 85, 101, 109
    110, 174, 261
  Sanford 109
  Sarah 120
  Sarah Ann 149
  Susanna(h) 179, 181

  Thomas 15, 19, 108
    109, 134, 162, 193
  Thomas Jr. xv, 109
  Thomas ap C. 2, 109
  Thomas D. 65, 109
  Viley 149
  Vincent 51, 109, 110, 181
  Violet 65
  W.A. xv
  Walter 260
  William 110, 269
  William L. 183
  Williamson P. 110
  Willis 108

Joneses Falls, Maryland 209

Jordan, Eliz.[a] 53
  John Morton 110, 139, 157, 244
  Richard 110
  Robert 110
  William 9, 110, 139, 247

Joy, Joseph 110
  Nancy 215
  Sally 230

Kane, William 207

Kay, Catherine 19, 264
  James 19, 35, 110
    153, 195, 264, 264
  John 264
  Levinia 188
  Mary (Pannell) 153, 195, 264
  Sarah 35, 264

Keene, Elizabeth 176, 177, 177, 261
  Newton 234
  Sarah 234
  William 177, 234, 261

Keiser : Keasar, see Keyser
  Ann 201
  John 57, 101
  Millian 57

Keith, Elizabeth (Snead) 139

Kelly, Alexander 110

Kelly, Beckham   111
    Edward   110
    Elizabeth   105, 151
    James   5, 110, 111, 111, 155
    James Jr.   111, 111
    John   5, 22, 59, 138, 155
    John Jr.   111
    Mahala   138
    Molly   5
    Reuben   111, 138
    Richard H.   111
    Sally Maulden   5
    Susannah   155
    Thaddeus   111
    Vincent   111, 111
    William   111
    Winnefred   111

Kelsick, Ann Younger   126
    Eleanor Barnes   210
    Isabella Barber   138, 115
    Joseph   209
    Joseph B.   106, 111
    Mary   31, 126, 225
    Mary Ann   209
    Rebecca Beckwith   225
    Richard   111
    Samuel   31, 111, 115
    Samuel B.   1, 111, 209, 235
    Younger   46, 53, 111, 111, 115
                   138, 210, 225, 244

Kem, William T.   112

Ken, Joanna   160

Kendal[l], Westmoreland, England
                                        209

Kendall, George   195
    William   11

Kenmore, Fredericksburg, Va.   186

Kennan, see Cannan
    John   112
    Lefever   112, 156
    Mahalah B.   50
    Sally   148, 149
    William   95, 112, 188

Kennedy, Alitia   2, 119
    Kennedy, Isabel   116
    John   2, 20, 70, 112, 113, 116
    Mary   20
    Sarah   70
    Thomas Allen   112, 160
    William   70

Kenney, Isabel   116
    John   116

Kenner, Rodham Griffin   112
    William   112

Kennon, see Kennan and Cannan
    Lefevre   112, 156

Kent County, Maryland   76

Kent, Lucy   202
    Martha Ann   113
    Sarah   38

Kentucky   42, 48, 118, 119
              134, 135, 149, 218, 223
              245, 249, 252, 255, 258

Kenyon, family   252
    Abraham   252
    Ann   252
    Elizabeth   147, 252
    Frances   252
    James   252
    Jane   252, 252
    John   252
    Joseph   252
    Judith   252
    Henry   252
    Margaret   252
    Million   252
    Sarah   252

Keser, James   112, 170

Key, Henry G.S.   112

Key : Keys, see Kay

Keyser see, Keiser : Keasar
    John   91
    Mary   125

Keyser   see,   Keiser : Keasar
    Polly   91
    Sally   79
    Walter   112

Killingham, Mr.   204
    Nancy (Tarpley)   204

Killingsby, Elizabeth   43

Kilpatrick, Samuel   112

King Charles I of England   xi

King Charles II of England   x, xi

King James II of England   xi

King Louis XIV of France   x, xi

King William III of England   ix
                                x, xi

King George County, Virginia   x
    xvii, 2, 4, 14, 16, 17, 18, 19
    24, 26, 27, 32, 34, 35, 37, 39
    44, 50, 53, 57, 62, 64, 71, 72
    77, 79, 80, 84, 92, 96, 97, 98
    99, 100, 102, 110, 113,114,120
    125, 127, 128, 130, 132, 136-9
    143, 146, 151,152,162,172, 175
    176, 182, 186,187,190,193, 196
    197, 200, 203,207,210,211, 212
    216, 219, 220,221,229,230, 232
    233, 242, 246,248,249,252, 255
    256, 257, 259, 260, 262, 263
    264, 266, 268, 269

King and Queen County, Virginia 24
    66, 76, 129, 130,   174
    205, 216, 219, 228, 267

King William County, Virginia   189
                                207

King, Alice   47
    Benedict B.   83
    Furdelia Bisky   84
    Henry P.F.   84, 112, 200
    Hiram S.   100, 113
    James   113, 113

Jane   65
John   38, 112, 113, 113
Richard   113
Sally R.   113
Samuel   65, 113
William   38, 113, 113, 194

Kircum, James   113
    William   113

Kirk, Elizabeth   226
    John   69, 88, 113
    Randall R.   113
    Sarah   69
    Sarah R.   88
    Thomas   146, 113
    William   113

Kirkham, Grace   102
    James   113
    William   113

Kirkmire, Frederick   113, 199

Kirtley, Polly   89
    Polley N.   89

Kneller, Sir Godfrey   ii, xi

Knight, John   114

Knott, Richard   52, 73
    Rutha   106

Kortright, Elizabeth   249

Lake, Philip   80

Lambard, William   22

Lambeart, Elizabeth   37

Lambert, James   114, 196, 201
    Mildred   85
    William   114, 184

Lamb's Creek, King George Co., Va.
        130, 143, 161, 252

Lamkin, James L.   109

Lamkin, Malinda   236

Lampton, family   114-115, 249
    Ann   114, 249
    Esther (Davis)   114, 249
    Joshua   114, 249
    Mary   249
    Samuel   114, 249
    Sarah   249
    William   97, 114, 114, 115, 249

Lancashire, England   209

Lancaster County, Virginia   xii
    xiii, 1, 8, 9, 15, 17, 24, 27
    33, 36, 36, 37, 47, 49, 54, 57
    59, 60, 61, 67, 68, 69, 71, 78
    81, 82, 90, 93, 97, 112,115,116
    120, 124, 129, 130, 134,135,145
    148, 151, 152, 153, 155,158,159
    163, 167, 171, 185, 197,201-206
    208, 209, 218, 224, 225,228,234
    238,243,245,246,248,250,251,267

Lancaster Creek, Virginia   xvii

Landman, John   185
    Margaret   181, 185
    Peggy   185
    Vincent   115
    William   163

Landon, George H.   115
    George W.   192

Landrum, John   115
    Elizabeth   115

Lane, Mary   15, 139, 140, 245
    William   15, 115, 140, 245

Langhee, Elizabeth   177, 177, 261
    Isabella   177, 177, 261
    Patrick   177

Langhorne, Mary   97, 269

Lankford, Henry L.   115

Lansdowne Plantation, Richmond
    County, Virginia   93

Lase, Ann   33

Latham Lucy A.   188
    Robert W.   115

Lathom, Emily C.   65
    H.   65, 139
    Maranda   236
    Martha Ann   139

Laural Grove, Richmond Co., Va. 239

Laurence, William   115

Lawson, Bathsheby   3
    Belinda   164
    Betsy   56
    Betty   53
    Catherine   66
    Christopher   143
    Daniel   101, 214
    Daniel Jr.   115
    Daniel Sr.   56
    Elizabeth   142, 193
    Epaphroditus   117, 152
    Isabella Barber (Kelsick)   138
    Joanna   185
    John   115, 142, 251
    Joshua   164
    Lucy   55, 60, 143, 148, 191
    Mary   167
    Rebecca Sisson   54, 55, 86, 214
    Richard   115, 136, 138
    Rowland   116
    Thomas   167
    William   116

Laycock, Pinkston   67

Leacock, Daniel   116

Leader, Elizabeth   86
    Richard   116

Leckie, Mary   76, 76, 225

Lee, Ann   66, 123, 246
    Frances Lightfoot 18, 21, 116
    Hancock   66, 248
    Henry   116
    Judith (Steptoe)   155

Lee, Lettice   82
    Mary Willis   248
    Philip Ludwell   116
    Richard   71, 123, 155
    Richard C.   116
    Thomas Ludwell   116, 116, 117
    William   116, 117
    William L.   45, 104,160

Leedstown, Va. xvii,18,172,190,260

Leesburg, Va.   62

Leland, Samuel A.M.   58, 63

Lemoine, F.   88
    Feriol Jr.   21, 46, 117
    Morean   60

Lemon, Mary   14

Letman, William   120

Levaine, Judith A.   83
    William   83

Level Green, Westmoreland County
    Virginia   251

Levy, Ezekiel   30, 105, 117
                     192, 201, 217
    Frances M.   217
    Matilda F.   30

Lewce, William   169

Lewis, family   253
    Affire   108
    Alice   118
    Alice Ann   215
    Ann(e)   38, 43, 106, 253
    Apphia [Aphier]   108, 148
    Betsy   52, 75
    Betty   54
    Bridgett Lovelace   118
    Charles Nelms   118
    Deborah   160
    Diannah M.   234
    Edward   17, 53, 106
                    119, 162, 206, 253
    Elizabeth   17, 88, 93, 106
                    118, 183, 206, 253

Elizabeth F.   58, 99
Fanny   99
Fleet W.   58, 112
Frances   118
George   39, 175
George Jr.   117
George H.   117
Griffin   117
Haney   95
Hannah   52, 118, 237, 237
Hannah Lane   39
Henry   117
Hiram B.   117
Isaac   39, 118
James   75,118, 118
James Jr.   118, 162
Jeremiah   23, 52, 89
                    95, 118, 183, 215
Jeremiah S.   99
Johanna   119, 253
John   21, 118, 253
John Jr.   118
John Banks   135
Joseph   237
Joseph B.   118
Katherine   53, 253
Martha A.G.   29
Mary   23, 74, 94
                    121, 162, 253
Nancy   58, 99
Peter   118
Peter B.   118
Rebecca   52
Richard   118
Robert   118, 148
Robert G.   51, 108, 117, 118
Rubin [Reuben]   39
Sarah   234
Susanna   90
Thomas   3, 23, 118, 160
Thomas O.   38
Thomas P.   7, 38, 67, 99, 118
Valentine   29
William   92, 118, 119
William D.   118

Lexington, Kentucky   135

Lightfoot, Ann   119, 189, 231
    Betty   119, 177, 261
    Daniel   119, 177, 231
    Daniel Jr.   119

Lightfoot, Elizabeth G.   177
    Frances D.   52
    Goodrich   119
    Samuel   119
    Thomas   48, 119, 119, 177
    William   119, 119, 189, 265

Lilley, John   152
    Mary   152

Lillis, Mary   147

Linton, Anthony   119, 253
    William   74, 119, 253

Lisle, John   119

Little Falls Plantation, Stafford
    Co.,Va. 82, 146, 147, 213, 252

Littlepage, Judith   68, 216, 218

Littman, William   120

Littrall : Littrell : Littrill
             Luttrell : Luttrill
    Alfred   120
    Elizabeth   116
    Elizabeth P.   171
    Fanny   130
    Frances G.   16
    Hannah   31
    James   186
    John 17, 65, 74, 116, 120, 188
    John M.   142
    John P.   16, 120, 171, 173
    Leroy   31, 48, 120
    Mary   173
    Richard   84, 113, 120
    Sally   188
    William   120, 180

Ljungstedt, Mrs. Milnor   xiv

Lloyd, Edward   120
    John   120

Lockhart, Elizabeth (Moss) 46, 120
    James   46, 120

Locust Hill, Culpeper Co.,Va.   257

Lomax, Presley Thornton   xv

London, England 116, 132, 205, 267

Longwith, see Longworth
    Burgess   120, 164
    Nancy   164
    William   120

Longwood, Westmoreland Co., Va. 190
                    246, 260, 269

Longworth, see Longwith
    Burges [Burgis] 121, 162, 164
    Jemima   211
    John   121
    Katharine   162
    Millicent [Millisent] 210, 211
    William   210, 211

Lord Bellasis   xi

Lord Brundenell   xi

Lort, Mary   205
    Richard   205

Loudoun County, Va. 2, 4, 36, 62
                63, 116, 184, 212
              213, 236, 243, 244

Louis, Frances   77

Louisiana, State of   97

Loury, Courtney   29
    Martha   76

Lovelace, Charles   121

Lowery, Jane   87
    Orange   119
    Stokley D.   121

Loyd, Elizabeth   158, 159
    Joan   158, 159
    Lewis   158, 159

Lucas, Francis   121, 228

Luckam, Joseph   121, 194

Luckham, John   121
    Martha   184
    Mary A.   112
    William   121,   184

Luckum, Joseph   121,   194

Luggitt, family   xiii

Luin, Mary   169

Lunenburg County, Va.   136,   257

Lunn, Alicia   107
    Mary   107
    Roger   107
    William   107

Lusby, Margaret B.   141

Luttrell : Luttrill, see Littrall
    Littrell : Littrill :
    Luttrell : Luttrill , p. 322

Lyde, Elizabeth (Gwyn)   205,   267
    Stephen   267

Lyell, Henry   121,   140
    John   121,   122,   128
                            205,   206,   267
    John A.   5
    Jonathan   121,   194,   267
    Joseph   121,   165
    Joseph S.   59,   215
    Juliet F.J.   75
    Lucinda   128
    Mary (Tayloe)   205
    Peggy S.   98
    Richard H.   28,   50,   75
                            122,   140,   149
    Robert   122
    Samuel   98
    Samuel M.   75,   122
    Sarah   S.   164
    William M.   122

Lyells, Richmond County, Va.   112

Lyne, Ann   5,   138
    James   5
    Jane   5

Mary   5, 61, 61,   184
Susannah   138,   184
Thomas   5,   61,   184

Lyon, Ann   258

Lysle, John   227

McCall, Archibald   122
    Elizabeth   122
    Katherine Flood   122

McCalley, Ann   122
    Charles   122
    John   122,   261

McCan, John   122

McCance, Eliza   127

McCarty, family   246
    Albert G.   5,   92
    Alice B.   167
    Anna Barbara   125,   246
    Bartholomew xvi, 5, 23, 30,   32
        42, 48, 50, 54, 56, 60,78,79
        87, 101, 110, 122, 123,   124
        147, 180, 189, 198, 202, 203
        204, 207, 216, 217, 217, 238
    Billington   xiii, 122, 123
                            123,   124,   246
    Charles   36,   45,   54
    Charles Barber   123,   122,   204
    Charles Travers   63,   123,   123
                            129,   147,   217
                                   224,   229
    Chrain   123
    Cordelia B.   35
    Daniel   xv, 12, 40, 41,   122
                    123, 123, 125,   190
            190,   191, 246, 260,   269
    Daniel L.   123,   125,   223,   238
    Dennis xv,12, 78, 123, 123,   246
    Ellen [Ellin,Eleanor]   12,   246
    Elizabeth   45,   144,   246
    Elizabeth D.   238
    Eloisa Tomlin   217
    Fanny P.   124,   174
    Frances E.   136
    Frances R.   124,   134

McCarty, George B.   180
  George B. A.   124
  George Y.   124
  James B.   134
  John   124, 124
  Judith G.   124, 167, 207, 238
  Julia E. Y.   8
  Juliet Ann   144
  Katherine   246
  Lavinia A.   134
  Louisa H.   58
  Lucinda (Beale) Moss   124
  Lucy P.   155
  Madison P.   43, 124
  Margaret (Robinson) 246,260,269
  Nancy Y.   207
  Olivia B.   238
  Robert W.   124
  Sarah   12, 246
  Sydnor   124, 217
  Tarpley   124, 217
  Thaddeus 45, 124, 243, 246, 246
  Virginia A.   124
  William   124, 139, 155, 207
  William B.   49, 124
  William D.   25, 124, 125, 239
  Winifred   246
  Winifred T.   189

McClanahan, Augusta Marmaduke   125
  Caroline (Webb)   37
  Elizabeth   129
  Meredith Miles   125
  Nancy D.   65
  Peter   125
  Vincent M.   37, 125

McDaniel, Timothy   246

McCaulin, see McLaughlin

McDonall, Timothy   246

McCaulley, see McCalley

McGawley, William   126

McGill, David   242

McGinnis, Mary   224
  Richard 11, 30, 84,95, 181, 237

Samuel   105
Susanna   111

McGlathlin, see McLaughlin

McGuier, John   30
  William   125

McGuire, John   30,   224
  Mary   120
  William   125

McIndree, James   125, 133

McKay, see Maccay and Mackay
  Anne   224
  John   224
  William   32, 125

McKenney : McKenny
  Baldwin Bell   126
  Benjamin   125
  Catherine P.   126
  Cornelius   125
  Elizabeth   214
  Fanny   182
  Frances S.   140
  Gerrard   18, 23, 33
  Ger(r)ard A.   164
  James   125
  Julia   20
  Lucetta W.   169
  Mary E.   164
  Meley   20
  Milly   20
  Presley   126
  Rebecca   177
  Samuel   140
  Susanna   25
  Vincent B.   125
  William M.   126
  William R.   126

McKie, Elizabeth   209

McKildoe, James   41
  Mary S.   41
  Robert   126
  Robert D.   126

McKindree, see McIndree

McKindree, James   133, 125

McKnight, James A.   188

McLane, James S.   126

McLaughlin, Bridgett   107, 121
   Elizabeth (Woodbridge) 126, 202
   Manus 107,121, 126,150,202, 234
   Priscilla 16,81,92,93,98,150,229

McLynch, Edmund   108
   Elizabeth   108
   Jane   108

McMillion, Charity   6
   Frances   6, 62,97
   John   6, 62,97
   Katherine   62

McNamara, John   126

McNeil, Hugh   126

McPherson, James   126
   Mary   142
   Samuel   121

McTier : McTyre
   Elizabeth G.   100
   Frances   160
   Judith   134
   William C.   126

Maccay, Henry   126

MacGivier, see Mackgyar

Mackay, see Maccay and McKay
   Hannah   32, 32
   John   34
   William   32, 125

Mackgyar, Elizabeth   18, 216
   Mary   18, 27, 216

MackMillion, see McMillion

Mactear : Mactier
   see McTier : McTyre
   Elizabeth G.   100

Judith   134
Judith B.   122

Maden, see Maiden

Madestard, Elizabeth   152

Madison County, Va.   12, 237

Madison, Ambrose   248
   Elizabeth   259
   James   44, 248
   Nelly Conway   213, 248

Maiden, Daniel   221
   Elizabeth   126
   George   68
   John   126
   Joseph   126
   Levina   68
   Maria   126

Maith, Ellin   203

Major, Catherine   2
   Samuel   264

Maley, see Mealey : Mealy
   John   52
   Lunsford   127
   Richard   64
   Sally   52

Malone, John   127
   John Whitfield   127

Man, Elizabeth   60

Manire, William   127, 196, 263

Manly, Penelope 2, 10,13,96,111,244
   William   10,244

Marcey, see Marsy
   John   77
   Mary   77

Marders, James   127
   Lovell   127

Mariner, Mary A.   79
   Richard N.   19

Mark Twain   114, 249

Markham, Elizabeth   128
   James   128
   John   255
   Lewis   128

Marks : Markes
   Ann(e)   145, 257
   Betsy   181
   Edward   29, 43, 46, 127
   Frances   103
   Hannah   43
   Jackson   178
   James   3, 26, 94, 127
                     143, 178, 233
   John   257
   Lemuel   127
   Lucy   178
   Mary   143, 233
   Peggey   94
   Reuben   68,   72, 128
   Samuel 128, 128, 139, 178, 237
   Thornton   128, 178
   Vincent   128
   William   128, 233
   William B.   128

Marlton, Duley   60

Marmaduke, Daniel   11, 22, 27
                          128, 233
   Elizabeth   226
   James B.   88, 128
   Rebecca   88

Marmion, King George County,
   Virginia   125, 246

Marriages of slaves, Negroes,
   mulattoes, people of color
   &c: see, Negro Marriages

Mars Hill, Richmond Co.,Va. 32,208

Marsh, Robert M.   128

Marshall, Abraham   32, 250
   Ann   128
   Catherine (Fauntleroy) 97, 128
   George   97, 128

Hugh   187
John   99, 128, 128, 129, 187
Mary   32
Richard   90, 129
Sarah A.   20
Thomas   129
Thomasin   32, 250
William   129

Marsy, see Marcey
   John   129

Martin, Alice   24
   Caty   23
   Elizabeth   218
   Hannah   23
   John   129
   Nicholas   129
   William   129

Mary Jane, a Negro   208

Marye, James   227
   Lucy   227

Maryland, State of 11, 20, 75,76,82
   96, 112, 120, 147, 159, 209, 242

Maslin, William   129

Mason County, Kentucky   252

Mason, Anne Fowke   69
   Elias   129
   George Carrington   xiv

Massachusetts, State of   203

Massassaponax Creek, Spotsylvania
   County, Virginia   202, 203

Massey, Benjamin   97
   Dade   97, 269
   John   224
   Leroy   129
   Mary   269
   Robert   97, 246, 269
   Thomas   97

Mathews : Matthews
   Alice   208, 231

Mathews : Matthews
  Baldwin   130
  Edward   144
  Elizabeth   129, 130
  Francis   130
  Giles   27
  John   130
  John R.   36
  Margaret   130
  Mary   27, 129
  Prissey   129
  Richard E.   130
  Samuel   129, 130
  Syntha   129
  Thomas L.   230
  William   208

Mauldin, James   233

Maxwell, Herbert   130

Mayo, John   38, 65, 186, 189

Mazuro, Juliann   43
  Louis   43

Meade, Mary   81, 254
  Thomas   81, 230, 254
  William [Bishop]   xiii

Meads, Susanna   68

Mealey : Mealy, see Maley
  Frances   88
  Jesse   130
  John   130
  Richard B.   131
  Samuel   88, 95, 131

Mecklenburg County, Va.   81

Meeks, Ann   187, 187, 125, 133
  Judith   143
  Mary   125, 133
  Richard   125, 133, 187

Menokin, Richmond Co., Va. 21, 116

Menzies, Adam   122, 131, 131
  Samuel Peachey   76, 131, 131

Mercer, Mary   246

Meriwether, Francis   16
  Mary   14, 16, 42
              139, 190, 222, 245

Messer, Hannah   38
  Mary Stephens   38

Messick, William J.   131

Metcalfe, family   265
  Ann(e) 131, 151, 151, 196, 265
  Anne (Stone) 11, 131, 132, 265
  Elizabeth   6, 132, 265
  Gilbert   9, 131, 247, 265
  Henry   131, 220
  Jane   131, 265
  John   132, 265
  Mary   24, 131, 132, 193, 265
  Richard   6, 11, 24, 131, 131
              132, 151, 196, 265
  Sarah   132, 254

Mezingo, Hannah   47
  John   47

Mickelborough, Richard S.   132

Micou, Elizabeth   182
  James Roy   95
  Margaret   68, 77
  Mary   247
  Paul   68, 182, 247

Middlesex County, Va. 24, 35, 36, 48
    79, 91, 95, 102, 108, 109, 115
    135, 136, 154, 177, 205, 228
              243, 256, 261, 267

Middleton, Benjamin S.   132
  Jeremiah   13, 132
  Mary C.   23
  Robert R.   132
  William   132
  William P.   23, 113

Milden Hall, Richmond County
  Virginia   147, 155, 156

Miles, George   132

Millenbeck, Lancaster Co., Va.   8

Miller, family   255
  Alice   255
  Benjamin   255, 255
  Eleanor   64, 255
  Elizabeth   145
  Isabella   98, 255
  Jane   255
  John   255
  Margaret   255
  Mary   255, 255
  Patience   88
  Richard   132
  Simon   64, 132, 132, 192, 255
  Susanna   255
  William   144, 255

Milner : Millner
  Ann   231
  Benjamin   132, 133
  Benjamin Jr.   133
  John   133
  Judith   77
  Luke   125, 133
  Mary (Meeks)   125, 133

Mills, family   256
  Ann   xvii, 18, 24, 62, 109
            161, 229, 256, 259
  Elizabeth   154, 195, 256
  Esther   87
  Hester   227
  Joane   18, 195, 256
  Mary   48
  Peter   256
  William xvii, 18, 195, 256, 259

Milner, see Millner : Milner

Minor, Elizabeth 11, 119, 166, 265
  James F.   91, 202
  John   60, 64
  Nicholas   11

Minter, John   63, 133, 206
  Rose   206

Miskell : Maskill : Meskill
  Addaline   182
  Ann   141

Ann E.   133
Bartholomew   55
Bartholomew M.   133
Catherine   13, 181, 244
Catharine A.   47
Daniel   133
Elizabeth   112, 151, 198
Elizabeth M.   57
Frances   131
George   28, 56, 93, 106
          112, 133, 160, 181, 198
George H.   133
Henry   6, 56, 133
Jane   204
Jane H.   37
John Austin   133
Lilly A.   182
Lucy   127, 188
Magdalene   93, 180
Margaret   76
Mary   182
Million   119
Milly   119
Newman   105, 133
Peggy   76
Polly S.   55
Rachel   55
Rebecca   56
Samuel   112, 133, 219
Sarah   75
Thomas A.   133
William   13, 76, 131, 133
                138, 151, 176, 261
William D. 55,127, 133, 133, 188
William H. 37, 78, 87, 134, 164
Winifred   14, 75

Missouri, State of   30, 88, 258

Mitchell, Ann (Sydnor)   204
  Charity   61
  Edmond   105, 176, 177
  Elizabeth   68, 128, 160, 217
  Frances   113, 201
  Frances T.   70
  Harriet B.   227
  J.L.   227
  James   134
  John C.   45, 134
  Julia L.   6
  Judith   78

Mitchell, Littleton Downman   134
    Mary   21
    Olivia Ann   124
    Priscilla   227
    R.   70
    Richard   36, 134, 201
    Robert   36, 68, 78, 134
                     134, 201, 202, 227
    Robert B.   124, 227
    Sarah   36, 243
    Sophia F.   45
    Susanna   78
    Thomas   134
    Virginia J.   107
    William B.   78
    William C.   134
    William D.   134

Monroe, family   135
    Andrew   135
    Catherine   135
    James   76, 115, 152, 249
    Jane   264
    Jane Jones   135
    John   xv, 134, 134, 135, 189
    Joseph Jones   44
    Lucy   135
    Mary   264
    Sally Skelton   135, 189
    Sarah   264
    Spence   115, 249
    Thomas J.C.   135
    William   152, 264

Montague, Edward   135
    Elizabeth   135, 136, 149
    Frances   28
    Harriet S.   149
    Harriott   53, 227
    Henry Albert   39, 135
    James   91, 135, 136, 227
    John   28
    Nancy   28
    Peter   135
    Thomas   135
    Thomas Tarpley   135, 136
                         149, 223, 226

Monteith, Elizabeth   136
    James   136
    John   136

    Magdaline   136, 258
    Phillis (Gallop)   136
    Thomas   136, 258

Montgomery, Elizabeth T.   221
    Evelina Jane   221
    Robert G.   136
    Robert L. 5, 126, 136, 168, 237

Montpellier, Orange Co., Va.   248

Moody, William   136

Moore : More
    family   257
    Ann   90, 90, 136, 137
                     143, 143, 257
    Ann C.   203
    Bernard   257
    Catherine (Price)   257
    Elijah   73, 136
    Elizabeth   257
    Francis   136, 136, 143, 257
    Garland   207
    Harbin   136, 257
    James G.   39, 89, 90, 137
    Jane   89
    John   248
    Joseph   45, 104, 137
    Joseph G.   45, 88, 137
    Lucy Barbour   257
    Martha   137, 143, 257
    Mary   115
    Nancy   45
    Patsey   200
    Peter   16, 24, 137
    Reuben [Reubin]   137, 257
    Sampson   137
    Sarah Scandrett   23
    Thomas   73, 89, 90, 137
    Thomas H.   89, 90
    Walker   137
    William   136

Morattico Creek   xvii

Morattico Hall,.Richmond County
    Virginia   21, 30

Morgan, Andrew   137
    Anthony   137, 137

Morgan, Benjamin   30, 137
    David   137, 138
    Elizabeth   5, 84, 206
    Evan   137, 193, 206
    Fanny   138
    John   137
    Josiah   138
    Lamberth   38
    Lucy   30
    Nancy   138
    Patty   57
    Peter   138
    Peter N.   182
    Sarah   68
    Thomas   138,154
    William   39, 138, 138, 164
    Winifred   30

Morris : Morriss
    Ann   16, 26, 34, 86
    Caty   13, 229
    Covert   45
    Dorcas   219
    Edward   138
    Elizabeth   155, 222, 222
    Fereen [?]   166
    Frances   84, 166
    Hudson   138
    James M. 7,128, 138,178,230,237
    Jesse   231
    John   79, 84, 111, 138, 138
              155, 164, 178, 179, 222
    John F. 3, 7, 20, 103, 143, 187
    Julia Ann   21
    Katy   13, 229
    Lucy   101
    Margaret   179
    Martha   194
    Mary   62, 110, 140
    Mary A.   178
    Mary Ann   26
    Mary Jane   166
    Molly   62
    Nanc(e)y   26,238
    Sally   43,140
    Samuel   108, 165
    Simon   138
    William   26, 43, 62
              104, 111, 138, 138
    William H. 30, 104, 105, 140

Morrison, Elizabeth M.   94
    Hannah   138
    Joseph   138
    William   138
    William Sr.   138

Morrow, Andrew   138, 164
    see , Murrah : Murray
          Morrow : Murrow
          Purcell, Tobias

Morse, Ann   72
    Nancy   72
    Sinah   72,168
    Thomas   72, 72, 139

Morson, Arthur   147

Morton, family   139
    Andrew   27
    Frances   98, 139
    James   139
    John   110, 139, 139, 140
    Joseph   10, 42, 98, 139, 244
    Mary   27
    Mary Beckwith   10, 244
    Mary (Mountjoy)   110, 139
    Molly Beckwith   10,244
Moseley, Edward   139

Moss, Mr.   62
    Elizabeth 46, 120, 140,211, 233
    Frances   10, 27, 96, 101, 244
    Harriet A.   94
    Jane Gray (Edwards)   62
    John A.   124, 139
    Lucinda (Beall)   124, 139
    William 27, 46, 101, 120,   139

Mothershead, Alice   108, 138
    Ann   140
    Ann L.   165
    Apphia R.   60
    Eliza M.   236
    Elizabeth   11
    Elizabeth T.   60
    George   9, 26, 27, 122, 139
              169, 179, 182, 183, 200
    George M.   139
    Henry   183
    James S.   139, 194

Mothershead, James T. 60
  John 11, 139, 176
  Lucy 192
  Martha Elizabeth 200
  Mary 9, 180
  Mary Ann 194
  Nathaniel 138
  Richard 59, 140
  Richard H. 9, 98, 140
  Samuel 139, 140
  Samuel D. 140, 236
  William 21, 73, 140
  William H. 140
  William R. 140
  Sally 176

Mott, family 258
  Ann(e) 79, 258
  Elizabeth 71, 89, 198, 258
  Ellen 186, 221, 258
  George 57, 71, 79, 89
    186, 212, 258
  James 140
  John 71, 212, 258
  Joseph 87, 140
  Margaret 57, 258
  Nancy 54
  Sally 54

Mount Airy, Richmond County,
  Virginia xvii, 18, 21, 93
    112, 116, 120, 205, 267

Mount Atlas, Prince William County, Virginia 33

Mountjoy, Alvin 15, 139, 140
  140, 157, 211
  Eleanor (Craske) Thornton 237
  John 108, 140, 141
  Mary 110, 139, 140, 157, 251
  Mary (Lane) 15, 140, 245
  Sarah 108, 141
  Sebella [Sibella] 140, 157
  Thomas 140

Mount Rose, Westmoreland County
  Virginia 260, 269

Mount Scion, Caroline County
  Virginia 213, 248

Moxley, Betsy Muse 157
  Daniel 23
  James B. 141, 225
  Jemima Sanford 23
  Joseph 23
  Nancy N. 101
  Richard Jr. 141
  Sally 5
  Thomas 141

Mozingo, Alfred S. 141
  Barnes B. 70, 141
  Christopher B. 141
  Edward 141
  Eleanor 199
  Elizabeth 141, 199
  James F. 141
  John 47, 199, 208
  Jonathan 141
  Joseph 141
  Margaret 34
  Mary 18, 123, 167
  Miskell 141
  Nancy 208
  Peirce 141
  Sarah 34
  Thomas 77
  Thomas C. 141
  William 141
    see, Menzingo

Muddy Creek, boundry Stafford and
  King George cos., Va. 71, 212, 213

Mullins, Benjamin 106
  James 142
  John 142
  Thomas 106, 142

Munday, Henry 142

Murdock, Margaret 33, 68

Murphey, Ann 179

Murphy, Eliza Ferguson 32

Murrah : Murray : Morrow : Murrow, see also Morrow and Purcell
  John Purcell 164
  Lucy Purcell 164

Murrah : Murray : Morrow : Mur-
row, see also Morrow and Purcell
Mary Ann   137, 164, 185
Tobias Purcell   164
Winifred Pursell   137, 164

Murren : Murrin
William T.   129, 142

Murrow, see Murrah &c: 331, 332

Muse, family   142
Betty   141
Daniel   141, 142
Elizabeth   60
Hudson   40
Jane   60
John   28, 60
Nicholas   142
Reubin   142
Thomas   142

Nanzatico Indians   174

Nash, Agathy   54
Ann   9, 30
Betsey   120
Catherine   31, 86
Elizabeth A.   70
George   29, 142, 208
George M.   129
Hannah   142, 160
James   142, 145
Jerry   215
John   10, 87, 165, 192
Lucinda   31
Lucy   30
Lucy A.   129, 160
Mary   120
Milley   57
Molly   10, 57
Newman   142
Richard   57, 142, 183, 196
Sally   138
Sarah   145
Susannah   176
Thomas   143
William   86, 143
Winder   129
Winnefred   183

Zachariah   143

Naylor, Anne   143
Avery   40
Elizabeth   143
Hannah   143, 257
John   137, 143, 257
Joyce   143
Patience   40

Naylor's Hole, Richmond Co. xvii,33

Neale, Ann (   ) Reynolds   144
Augustine   xv, 124, 144, 192
Elizabeth   32, 144
Hannah Shapleigh   144
Judith   80, 144
Margaret   76, 144
Mary L.   169
Mary S.   15, 180
Richard   32, 76, 79, 144, 144
Susanna   144
William   144

Neasom : Neasome : Neasum, see
Newsom : Newsome   333
Catharine   160
Caty L.   56
Eppª L.   145
Frances   122, 203
Jane   214
Nancy W.   148
Robert   55, 145
Robert B.   50
Samuel W.   145, 160, 197, 230
William   145
William J.   145

Negro Marriages 2, 30, 31, 37, 77
89, 104, 111, 126, 146,169, 170
204, 208, 209,222, 228

Neives, Sarah   169

Nell, Elizabeth   61

Nelms, Hannah   118
Joshua   145

Nelson, Alexander   145

New Aberdeen, York River, Va. 162

New, Sarah   185

Newby, Cyrus   145
    Oswald   145
    William   145

New Castle County, Pennsylvania
    [now Delaware]   232

Newcomb : Newcombs
    Catherine   129
    Edward   145
    Julia Ann   129
    Margaret   183
    Susan   182

New England   203, 228

Newgent, Dominick   145, 250
    Frances   142
    George   145, 160
    George C.   91, 197
    Judah   48
    Margaret C.   17
    Mary   208
    Peggy   197
    Rawleigh   48, 197
    Sarah   160

Newington, King and Queen Coun-
    ty, Virginia   129

Newman, family   145-146
    Alexander   146, 204
    Alice   208
    Anne   25
    Elizabeth   31, 165, 204
    Frederick   2, 145, 208
    George   145, 165
    Hannah   208
    Henry   145
    Jane   2, 43, 208
    John   2, 70, 145, 208
    John Jr.   146
    Joseph   50, 138, 145, 146
    Josiah   7
    Lucy   67
    Mary 13, 24, 25, 121, 133, 194
    Mary Ann   226

    Parmela   138
    Patty   90
    Samuel M.   138, 146
    Sephens   146
    Sophia   94
    Thomas   146, 146

News of Fredericksburg, Va.   24

Newsom : Newsome, see also
    Neasom : Neasome : Neasum
    Elizabeth A.   50
    Mary F.   188
    Robert   197
    William   146
    William J.   188

Newton, Elizabeth   82, 146, 147
    Gerard   82, 146, 223
    Isaac   147
    John   146, 179, 213
    Mary E.   156
    Millicent   146
    Rebecca   146, 146, 223
    Rose   82, 146
    Sarah   147, 212, 213
    Thomas   147
    William   146, 147, 213, 252
    William Jr.   147

New York   172

Nichals, William   147

Nichols, Charles   147
    John   147
    Mary   166

Nicholson, John   147, 156

Nickerson, Nancy   112

Nickins, Sally   205

Nomony Hall, Westmoreland Coun-
    ty, Virginia   117

Norris, Epaphroditus ["Eppy"] 148
                              197
    James   190
    Nancy O   49

Norris, Polly   190
     William   148

Northampton County, Va.,   21, 192
                               195, 269

North Carolina, State of   35, 74
                          149, 172, 175, 233

Northen : Northern
     Aldwin   109
     Alfred G.   148
     Apphia   37, 103, 125, 198, 226
     Barbara B.   1
     Catharine M.   148
     Edmund   28, 55, 130, 148
     Edmund N.   55, 148, 149, 185
     Edward J.   1, 13, 28, 39, 50
          55, 65, 71, 111, 138, 148
     Edward J. Jr.   111, 148
     Elias   25, 148, 149
     Elizabeth   21
     Frances   83
     George   25, 54, 67, 148, 149
     James   148, 148, 153
     Jane   149, 185, 215
     Jeremiah   149
     Katharine G.   215
     Levinia C.   188
     Lucy D.   28, 214, 235
     Lucy S.   186
     Margaret   109
     Margaret J.   28, 159
     Mary   30, 186
     Nancy   71
     Peter   148, 148, 149, 167
     Peter Smith   47, 50, 135
                       148, 149, 170
     Polly   55
     Richard G.   30
     Robert F.   65, 149
     Samuel   149
     Sarah   39, 145
     Sarah Ann   148, 167
     Susan S.   30
     Thomas H.   186
     Thomas S.   120
     William   149, 149, 232
     William S.   49, 93, 149
     Winifred   54

Northern Neck of Virginia and
     the Proprietors thereof   ix
     xvii, xviii, 42, 57, 72,89, 98
     123, 140, 156, 157, 161, 174
     231, 237, 249, 258

Northumberland County, Va. 1, 2, 5
     9, 10, 16, 18, 19, 27, 28, 29
     39, 40, 41, 45, 46, 47, 48, 52
     53, 58, 63, 65, 66, 67, 72, 74
     83, 85, 92, 93, 99, 100,108,110
     113, 118, 119, 125, 128,131,134
     138, 139, 140, 144, 148,150,151
     155, 162, 165, 167, 169,171,172
     173, 174, 177, 183, 185,186,192
     197, 198, 203, 207, 208,220,223
     226, 229, 234, 235, 243,246,260

Norwood, Ann   99
     Charles   149
     Hannah   99
     John Sr.   149

Oakeley, John   194

Oak Grove, Spotsylvania Co.,Va. 258

O'Bannon, Anne   255

Obear, William   149

Ockely, John   194

Oglesby, Edward   230, 231

O'Harrow, Elizabeth   22
     Thomas   149

Old Churches and Families of
     Virginia   xiii

Oldham, Amelia   224, 229
     Ann   98, 121, 150
     Betsy   150
     Catharine   16, 26, 150
     Edward   150
     Elizabeth   35, 153
     Fanny   150
     George B.   162
     James   149, 150, 150, 184

Oldham, Jinny   150
   John   150
   Katherine, see Catharine
   Leannah   150
   Margaret   43
   Mary   81, 81, 121, 192, 262
   Mary J.   218
   Nancy   150
   Nancy (Dobyns)   150, 155
   Peter   1,   26,150
   Priscilla   93, 231
   Priscilla (McLaughlin) 150, 231
   Richard T.   132
   Sally   150
   Samuel   134, 150
   Samuel Butler   150
   Sarah   92
   Susan C.   182
   Susannah Sydnor   150
   Tabitha   150
   Thomas   16, 39, 55, 60, 85
        103, 131, 135, 150, 177
   William 16, 81, 92, 93, 98, 149
        150, 150, 155, 229, 231
   William C.   69, 150
   William Howe   150

Oliff(e)   :   Olliff(e), see Eliff
   Elizabeth M.   7
   Mariah Ann   94
   Susannah D.   7
   Thomas   151
   Wesley B.   151
   William Jr.   151
   William B.   151
   William D.   7, 151, 151
   William S.   7

Oliver, Benjamin Jr.   151
   David   151
   Ellen   98
   Thomas   151

Omohundro, William H.   151

O'Neal, Daniel   151

Opelousas, Louisiana   97

Opie, family   151
   John   131, 151, 151, 265

Lindsay   68, 151

Orange County, Va.   23, 81, 90, 100
   114, 119, 136, 137, 154, 162
   184, 193, 198, 211, 213, 216
   219, 230, 233, 245, 248, 249
        254, 257, 266

Orenbaum : Orinbaun : Ornbaun
   Lewis   151, 152

Orleans, Duke of   xi

Orr, John   157

Osborne, Thomas   152

Oswald, Henry   174

Overton, Margaret   230

Owens, John   152

Pace, Mary (?) Lilley   152
   Thomas   152, 229

Packet   :   Packett
   Anne   154
   Anne (Scrimger)   152, 154
   Elizabeth   22
   Henry   152, 153, 154
   James L.   153
   John   45, 153
   Judah   35
   Nancy [see Anne, above]   98
   Richard   153
   William   59, 120, 138
        152, 153, 153
   William A.   66, 88
   William H.   44, 153, 154, 194

Page, Judith F.   122
   Thomas T.   122

Paise : Pasie see, Pace, above

Palmer, Ann   160
   Armistead J.   153
   Betty   101
   Caty   54

Palmer, Charles   106
    Chloe   48
    Elizabeth   56
    Fanny   145
    Frances A.   49
    George G.   95, 127, 132, 153
    Henrietta   60, 132
    Janey   19
    John   148
    Joseph   159, 228
    Mary G.   132
    Mary M.   49, 95
    Nancy   160
    Parmenus   153
    Rawleigh   153
    Robert   148, 153
    Sally   153
    Truman   153
    William   54, 132, 153
                    153, 160, 219
    William Jr.   75, 153, 160

Pannell, family   264
    Catherine, see Katherine
    Elizabeth   154, 257
    Frances (Sterne)   100, 154
    Isabella   114,153, 158
    Katherine   153, 154, 158
                200, 207, 264, 268
    Mary   19, 35, 80
                110, 153, 195, 264
    Sarah   138, 154
    Thomas   110, 138, 153, 153
                154, 158, 200, 264
    Thomas Jr.   153, 153
    William   80, 100, 143, 153
                154, 195, 207, 256

Paradise, Essex County, Va.   207

Pare, Harriet Ann   77
    Henry   139

Parker, Augustine G.   154
    Horace W.   188
    Richard   xv, 136, 154
    Thomas   164

Parr, James   154
    Virginia   153

Partridge, Elizabeth Bathan   106
    John   154
    Matthew   106

Pasquitt, Lucy   76

Patapsco River, Maryland   209

Paterson, William   199

Patty, see Petty : Pettey
    Thomas   154
    Thomas Jr.   136, 257

Paullin, Miss   129
    Elizabeth   130
    Thomas   130

Pavey, Walter   94, 154
    Webley   154

Paxen, Mary   49

Payne, Dorothea   248
    Elizabeth (Pope)   123, 123
                    125, 190, 246
    George   124, 152, 154, 264
    James H.   155
    John   222, 251, 256, 264
    Judith   8
    Merriman   150, 155
    Richard   155
    Richard A.   155
    Thomas E.   155
    William   123, 155

Payton, see Peyton
    Catharine   164
    Charles W.   155
    Elizabeth   14, 15
    John A.   110, 125, 151
                    155, 178, 179
    Mary E.   14

Peace, Mary   63

Peachey, Alice Corbin   65, 66
    Catherine   66
    Eliza G.   16
    Elizabeth   66, 122

Peachy, LeRoy   xvi, 42, 54, 75, 94
        106, 107, 113, 116, 131, 146
        155, 180, 204, 217, 226, 236
    Phebe   131
    Samuel   66, 131, 155
                            155, 156, 224
    Susanna   147
    William 4, 147, 155, 155, 156
    William Travers   15, 16, 204
    Winifred   4, 42, 156, 167

Peacock, Richard   156

Pead, Ann   264
    Catherine   264
    James   264

Pearce,   see Peirce : Pierce
    Elizabeth   119

Pearson, Catherine J.   186
    Jesse   156
    Lawson T.   156
    Simon   242
    Susanna   2, 242

Peart, Griffin   54

Peck, Ann T.   45
    Elizabeth H.   50
    H.   50
    Harriot   108
    Jane   11
    Lucy Jones   108
    Martha   80
    Walter J.   127

Pecurara, William   156

Peebles, Isabella   94

Peed, John   40, 156

Peers, Hannah   27, 194
    Susanna   27, 194

Peg, James   168

Peirce : Pierce,   see Pearce
    family   156, 157, 251
    Eleanor   251

John   156, 157, 157
                        217, 223, 251
Joseph   157, 251, 251
Lovell   157
Mary   174
Ransdell   251
Sarah   87, 157, 251
Sebellah   251
William   140, 156, 157
                        157, 174, 251

Pendergrass, see Spendergrass

Pendle, Mary   186

Pendleton, Francis W.   xvi,   58
    Henry   205
    James   66, 205, 267
    R.C.   88

Penley, Thomas   157

Pennsylvania, State of   97, 232

Penny, John   157

Peorey, Hannah   27, 194
    Susanna   27, 194

Pepeticker Creek, Richmond Co. xvii

Perpetoc Creek, Richmond Co.   xvii

Peters, Otho   157

Pettit, John   157, 158
    Lydia Bushrod   157, 158

Petty : Pettey, see Patty : Pattey
    Frances   129
    Prudence   145
    Thomas   158

Pew,   see Pugh
    Frances A.   192
    Frances Ann   192
    Martin   99, 158, 163, 192
    Martin Lewis   158, 163
    Mary   99

Peyton, see Payton

Peyton, see Payton
  Townshend D.   12

Philips : Phillips
  Ann   29
  Bryant   100, 158
  Catherine   114
  Elizabeth   196
  George   158, 158, 200
  James   114, 153, 158, 158
  Jeremiah   158
  John W.   158
  Katherine   114, 208
  Leonard   158
  Milley   192
  Sally   197
  Sarah   158
  William   158, 159

Philpott, Benjamin   159

Piarse, Mary   113

Pierce, see Peirce : Pierce

Pincent, Mary   234, 234, 238

Pine Hill, King George Co.,Va. 259

Pinkard, Elizabeth   155
  Thomas   82, 159

Pitman, Molley   18

Pittman, Fanny H.   18

Pitts, Fanny L.   121
  Reuben L.   121, 159

Place, Francis   161
  Mary   161

Plaile, John   200, 264
  Richard   264
  Swinburne   264
  Thomas   264

Plater, Rebecca   18, 116, 228
  Thomas   228

Pleasant Hill, Richmond Co.,Va. 109

Pleasantville, New Jersey   xv

Plummer, Albert G.   60, 85, 149
  Ann   23
  Augusta W.   66
  Elizabeth   66
  Fleet B.   66, 159
  John   159, 159, 191
  Julia   235
  Mary   6, 23
  Mary E.   122
  Rebecca Willoughby   92
  Richard B.   92, 159
  Sarah   75
  Thomas   53, 75, 132, 159

Plunkett, Elizabeth   233

Political Arena of Fredericksburg, Virginia   228

Polk, Ann M.   85
  Charles Peale   160
  Ellen B.   85

Pollard, Mrs. James Claiborne   67
  John   252

Polley : Polly
  Frances   63
  Jane   46
  John   267
  Joseph   160

Polling, Simon   160

Pooley, William   160

Pope, family   165-166
  Alice   126
  Betsy H.   40, 120
  Charles   165
  Elizabeth   7, 12, 123, 123, 125
           166, 190, 229, 246
  Fortunatus   160
  George   160
  George D.   126
  Humphrey   76
  Jane   166
  Joanna   166
  John   33, 61, 120

Pope, Joseph 206
  LeRoy 4, 17, 145, 160
  Lucy A. 187
  Martha A. 56
  Mary 4, 51, 165, 166
  Nathaniel 166
  Natuy 160
  Penelope 5
  Sarah 17
  Sarah Ann 33
  Susan 24
  Susana(h) 29, 171
  Thaddeus 1, 40, 61, 160
  Thomas 165, 166
  Wesley 160

Pope's Creek, Westmoreland County, Virginia 165

Port Conway, King George County,
  Va. 44, 210, 220, 248

Port Royal, Caroline County,Va. 41
  220, 221, 259, 266

Port, Margaret 93
  Robert 154, 160

Porter, Eliz.ᵃ 104
  Hannah H. 149
  Samson 160
  William 149

Porteus, Elizabeth 8, 59, 218

Portland, Earl of x

Portsmouth, Duchess of x, xi, xii

Potter, Eliza A. 45
  James 160
  John 113

Pound, Frances L. 258
  John 160
  Richard 258
  William 258

Poutridge Creek, King George
  County, Virginia 92

Powell, Honorias 161
  John 93, 161
  Mary Smith (Edwards) 62
  Place 161
  Thomas 161
  William 62

Powers, John 173
  Milly 236

Pratt, family 161, 259, 266
  Alice Fitzhugh 266
  Ann xvii, 161, 259
  Birkett 161, 259
  Caroline 3
  Elizabeth 259
  Elizabeth (Cocke) 161,162
  Frances 259
  Harriet 239
  Jane (Brockenbrough) 259
  John [of York River] 161, 162
  John 162, 239, 259, 259, 266
  John Jr.xvii, 161, 256, 259, 266
  John Sr. 161, 259
  John Birkett 259, 266
  Margaret 161, 259
  Mary 138
  Mildred 259
  Richard Turner 266
  Susanna 259
  Thomas 161, 161, 256, 259, 266
  William 161
  William Carter 266

Preseon, Ann 32

Pression, Elizabeth 4

Pretty, Polly 176

Price, Arjalon 162, 257
  Catherine 257
  John 129
  John Hill 162
  Mary 162
  Meriday 182
  Richard 162
  Sarah 97

Priddy, Ann H. 95
  Ann J. 24, 95, 153, 195

Priddy, Mary   153

Pridham, Ann   74, 253
   Bridgett (Bryer)   162, 170
   Catherine   121
   Christopher Jr.   74, 162
                           162, 253
   Christopher Sr.   74, 94, 121
                      162, 162, 170
   Edward   137
   Elizabeth   74, 94
   John   162
   Mary Anne   137
   Mary M.   132
   William R.   45

Prince, John   176
   John alias Rymer, see Rymer

Prince William II of Orange   xi

Prince William County, Va. 19, 22
   33, 36, 41, 44, 62, 66, 68, 89
   114, 121, 175, 184, 236, 249
                      259, 263, 264

Pritchett, George F.   162
   Judith   229
   Nancy   192
   Rodham   74, 109, 115
                162, 163, 192, 215
   Samuel   57
   Samuel C.   163
   Thomas   116, 171

Proctor, Abraham   151
   Alice   190
   Fanny   37
   Lezebeth   162
   William   37

Prosecuting Attorneys of Richmond County, Virginia   xv, 134

Prosser, John   192, 255
   Margaret   255

Prou, Cyprian   4, 16, 176
   Frances   16
   Margaret   176
   Susanna   4

Pugh, see Pew
   family   163
   Ann(e)   163, 163
   David   107, 163
   Elizabeth   107, 163
   Henry   163
   John   163
   Lewis   107, 158, 162, 163
   Lydia   162
   Martin Lewis   158, 163
   Nancy   24
   Willoughby   163

Pullen : Pullin
   Catherine   20, 179
   Elizabeth   13, 179
   Ellen   140
   Evarard   163, 163
   Everett R.   20, 207, 238
   Fanny   239
   Frances Ann   216
   Henretta   140
   James   13, 31, 108, 207
   Jane   197, 225
   Jeduthan [Jeduthun, Jeduthum]
            91, 140, 163, 164, 165
   Jesse   84, 85, 163
   John   20, 104, 140, 163, 179
   Jonathan   91, 163, 164, 165
   Katherine   20
   Moses   140
   Rebecca   140
   Sally   91

Pully, Patty   138

Purcell : Pursell, see Pursley
   and Murrah : Murray : Morrow &c
   Alice   2
   Benedict R.   164
   Benjamin   32, 71, 163
   Catharine   128
   David   164, 164
   Edward Minty   164
   Elizabeth   3
   Elizabeth R.   91
   Frances   47, 164
   Frances R.   160
   George   16, 112
   George R.   52
   H.M.   132

Purcell : Pursell, see Pursley
   and Murrah : Murray : Morrow &c
   John R.   164
   Joseph R.   164
   Letty R.   52
   LeRoy   112
   LeRoy C.   164
   Lewis   164
   Lucy   236
   Margaret   3, 164
   Molly   175
   Nancy   45
   Reuben   164
   Samuel   2, 164
   Sarah   16, 45, 112
   Sarah Davis   112
   Sarah S.   19
   Stephen D.   164, 192
   Tobias   3, 128, 137
                        164, 164, 175, 185
   V. R.   2, 236
   William R.   165
   Winifred   137

Purkins, Gabriel   165
   Thomas   165

Pursell, see Purcell : Pursell

Pursley, see Purcell : Pursell
   Elizabeth M.   133
   John   165

Purty, Polly   176

Pycraft, Winifred   232

Quarles, Ann Howell   207
   Ann (West)   207
   Henry   207
   William P.   2

Quay, Amanda J.   88

Queen Anne of England   xi

Queen Catherine of England   x

Queen Mary of England   ix, x, xi

Quesenberry : Quesenbury
   Lewis W.   165
   Nicholas   20, 165
   William C.   67, 165

Rains, Alfred J.   165
   J. B.   xvi
   William   165

Rallings, Rebecca   32

Ramey, see Reamy : Ramey

Ramze, Isabell   189

Randall, Anne   93
   Francis   93, 165
   Mary   59, 167
   Samuel Jr.   165
   Thomas   166

Ransdell, Edward   210
   Millicent [Millisent]   210, 211
   Sarah Elliott   251
   Wharton   166, 265

Rappahannock County, Va., ix, x, xv
      xvi, xvii, 2, 8, 10, 17, 18, 19
      27, 47, 57, 69, 70, 73, 75, 82
      89, 90, 92, 93, 101,102,105,110
      120, 123, 126, 127, 129,131,132
      136, 137, 152, 153, 158,169,170
      171, 172, 173, 182, 183,186,192
      195, 199, 202, 203, 205,206,212
      230, 232, 234, 243, 246,247,248
      249, 251, 252, 253, 254,255,256
      263, 264, 265, 261, 268, 269

Rappahannock Creek, Richmond Coun-
      ty, Virginia   xvii, 146

Rappahannock River ix, x, xvii, 41
      72, 76, 81, 89, 130, 136
      140, 216, 220, 257, 260

Raven, William   166

Rawlin(g)s, Thomas   166

Raynolds, see Reynolds : Raynolds &c

Read, Ann   5
  Hannah   204
  Mary   31

Reade, Robert   169

Reamy : Ramey
  Adeline   132
  Berryman [Beriman]   166, 166
  Daniel   166
  Hannah   200
  Hannah Ann   165
  James   95, 166
  James O.   166
  Joshua   11, 33, 83, 95, 125
      155, 164, 165, 166, 166
  Maria F.   125
  Mary   43
  Robert G.   85, 166
  Robert N.   166
  Samuel   165, 167
  Samuel T.   139, 166, 170
  Susanna   33
  William Daingerfield   166
  William J.   7

Redman, Alice B.   58
  Elizabeth   185
  Frances   185
  Hannah   101, 164
  John   22, 123, 164, 167
  John Jr.   167
  John Sr.   115, 167
  Joseph   105, 164, 197
  Joseph Jr.   149, 167
  Letty   164
  Maria C.   132
  Mary Lawson   184
  Priscilla   228
  Rebecca   164
  Richard L.   167
  Sally   190, 197, 197
  Solomon   167
  Vincent   126, 184

Reed, Ely   167

Reed(s), Samuel   258

Reeves, Margaret   173

Reid, Joseph B.   167
  Simon   89

Reids, Samuel   221, 258

Religious Herald   127

Rennolds, see Reynolds : Raynolds
        Rennolds, below

Republican Citizen   116

Reuick, see Ruick &c:

Reveer : Revere : Riveer
  James   167
  William   167

Reynolds : Raynolds : Rennolds
  Ann   65, 79, 126, 144, 169
  Ann Webb   168, 237
  Benjamin   20, 81, 170, 226
  Benjamin Jr.   170
  Betsy   168, 195
  Betsy Thornton   168, 169, 195
  Cleopatra   26
  Edward   168
  Edwin J.   22, 141, 167
  Eliza   30
  Elizabeth   170, 171
  Elizabeth T.   136
  Fanny   171, 227
  Fanny T.   226
  Frances   30
  George   53, 144, 167
  Haney   52
  James   27, 125, 167, 168
      168, 188, 227, 233
  Jane   149
  Jane P.   168
  Jesse D.   70, 168
  John   144, 168, 169
  John J.   168
  Mariah   170
  Mary   27
  Nancy   168, 227, 237
  Richard   72, 168, 188, 227
  Robert   149

Reynolds : Raynolds : Rennolds
  Sally   168, 171
  Sally E.   26
  Sally E. G.   81
  Sally T.   100
  Sarah   52
  Thomas   79, 168, 168
  Thomas Thornton 2, 51, 136
                  168, 169, 226
  Vincent   168, 169
  William   79, 168, 168
                  169, 169, 195
  William Henry   169
  Winifred   233

Rian, Dennis   169

Rice, Anney   63
  Charles   63, 118, 169
  Frances A.   43
  James   100, 169
  John   169, 196
  Nancy   118, 229
  Peter W.   43
  Richard   169
  Richard Jr.   63
  Richard Sr.   63
  Samuel S.   169
  Steptoe T.   101
  William   169

Rich, Ann   93
  Bass   170, 204, 234
  Beverly   169
  Charles   169
  David   170
  Elizabeth   170, 204
  George   170
  Griffin   170
  Lin(d)sey 2, 169, 170, 170, 205
  Maria   234
  Nancy   170
  Polly   170
  Richard   169
  Robert   31, 170, 170
  Robert Jr.   170

Richards, Alice   98
  Austin N.   170, 187
  Bridgett (Bryer) Pridham
                      162, 170

Eliza   104
Elizabeth   41, 99, 163
Fanny   24
John   170, 170
Lewis   162, 170
Nancy   70, 158, 163
Patey Y.   219
Reuben S.   41, 170
Richard   76
Robert   130
Susanna   70
Wade   170
Ward   50
William 34, 51, 70,76, 170, 255
William S.   168, 170

Richardson, Ann G.   16
  Clapham   268
  Elizabeth   268
  Elizabeth P.   16
  George S.   16, 112, 170
  Honour (Barrow)   50
  John   60
  Mary   60, 233
  Nancy   233
  Thomas   37, 171, 268
  Thomas A.   171
  William   171
  William T.   155

Richmond City, Va.   42, 90, 154
                     141, 244, 245

Richmond County, Virginia
  Prosecuting Attorneys   xv, 134
  Clerks   xvi, 13

Richmond, Duke of   ii, x, xi, xii

Rimer, see Rymer
  Rebecca   38

Ring, Elizabeth   267

Ringo, Catherine   118
  John   118

Ripping, Edward   204
  Elizabeth   204
  Mary   204

Riveer, see Reveer : Revere : Riveer

Roberson, Ann   90

Roberts, Jane   131
    John   131
    Margaret   64
    Thomas   64

Robertson, Andrew   171
    Elizabeth   69
    Jonathan P.   171
    Sally   50

Robins : Robbins
    Ellen   47
    Isabel   115
    James   112, 236
    John   35, 47, 171
    Lucy   112
    William   3, 47, 115, 171, 214

Robinson, family   260
    Alice   260
    Ann   203
    Anne Washington   260
    Brown   171
    Epaphroditus   171
    Frances   12, 260
    Harry   260
    Henry   260
    James   171
    John   171
    Jonathan P.   171, 180
    Joyce   9
    Margaret   246, 260, 269
    Maxmillian   171, 260, 260
    Morgan P.   xvii
    William   xv, 19, 172, 260, 269

Rocherson, John   106

Rochester, New York   172

Rochester, Elener   137
    Hannah (Thrift)   172
    John   172
    Nathaniel   172
    Nicholas   172
    William   172, 172

Rock, Alexander   173
    Elizabeth   73,   74
    Francis   173
    Griffin   73, 172
    James   172
    John   74, 172, 173
    John D.   173, 218
    Thomas   173
    Thomas C.   173
    Wesley   173
    William   173
    Winnefred   9

Rockbridge County, Va.   151

Rockwell, Augillia   171
    Emily   103
    Mary B.   69
    Seth   39, 103, 193
    William   173

Roe, see Rowe   and   Wroe
    Jane   198
    John   55, 99, 239
    Samuel B.   40, 173

Rogers, Catharine J.   127
    Elizabeth   177, 234, 261
    Grigsby   173
    John   164
    Mary   143,257
    Nicholas   173

Roles, Tillize   51

Rolls, William   173

Romney, Elizabeth   243

Rootes, John N.   191

Rose, Alexander F.   269
    Charles Walter   269
    Emily S.   183
    Henry   260
    James   173, 183
    John   260, 269
    Mary   200
    Mildred Washington   269

Rosegill, Middlesex Co., Va.   267

Rosser : Rossier
    David   102, 173, 173
    Margaret   173

Rouse, Lambert   264

Rout : Routt
    Mr.   41
    Ann   16
    John   174
    Lucy   134

Rowan, Manus   174, 230

Rowe, see Roe   and   Wroe
    Sarah   113

Rowley, John   97, 174

Rowzee, Edward   174
    Mary (Peirce)   174

Roxbury, Spotsylvania Co.,Va.   266

Roy, Beverley   174, 174
    Elizabeth Corrie (Williams)
                                     66,174
    John Corrie   174, 232
    Kitty T.   174

Ruelk, Daniel   109

Ruic : Ruick : Reuick &c:
    Alice   63
    Ann Beale   86
    Catherine   179
    Betsy   235
    Daniel   109,174
    James   174
    John   174
    Mary   180
    Nancy   26, 63
    William   64, 85, 99, 174

Ruix, John   174

Rush, Benjamin   175

Russell, Ann   191
    John   175, 246
    Joseph Jr.   4, 175

Thomas   175

Rust, family   175
    Ann Harrison   116
    Alice   3
    Benjamin   132, 254, 265
    Benjamin D.   9, 23, 128
    Elizabeth   81
    Frances   235
    George   175
    Hannah   175
    James B.   175
    James H.   63, 113, 175
    John   175, 238
    Martha   147
    Mary   75, 238
    Peter   147, 175
    Samuel   175, 175, 221
    Susan   197
    William   175

Ryals, Ann   224
    Samuel   176
    William   176

Ryland, Charles Hill   66
    Josiah   66

Rymer, see Rimer
    Katherine   176
    John   176
    Margaret (Prou)   176
    Mark Jr.   176
    Mark Sr.   176
    Richard   176

Sabine Hall, Richmond Co., Va.   18
        33, 34, 64, 116, 117
        144, 208, 211, 228, 234

Sacra, Charles C.   11, 22, 176
    Sarah Ann   11

Sadler, Patsey   28
    William   101, 176

St. Landry, Louisiana   97

St. Mary's County, Maryland 75, 112

Salisbury, King George Co. 2,97,242

Sallard, Ann   79
    Charles   195
    Elizabeth   187
    George   176
    Jane   95
    Mary   195
    Polly   5
    William   176

Samford, see Sandford and Sanford
    family   261
    Alicia   67
    Ann   62, 176, 187, 261, 261
    Catherine 12, 86, 199, 210, 261
    Elizabeth 13, 20, 39, 76, 122
              131, 133, 151, 176, 261
    Frances   35, 122, 176
                     177, 199, 261
    Giles   261
    James   12, 53, 122, 133, 176
        177, 187, 197, 199, 261, 261
    John   261
    John Amis   107, 119, 177, 261
    Keene   177
    Margaret   261
    Mary 35, 53, 177, 226, 261, 261
    Mary (Barber)   53, 176, 261
    Polly   64
    Rany   83
    Samuel   176, 177, 177, 261
    Sarah   261
    Thomas   35, 122, 177, 261
    William   177, 177, 180, 261
    William Keene   177, 261
    Winifred   176, 261

Sampson, George   61, 177

Samuel, Harriet   188
    Martha A.   188

Sanders, see Saunders
    Alexander   178, 179
    Almon   26, 209
    Amanda Ann   188
    Ann   14, 21
    Carter   179
    Elizabeth   7, 7, 111
    Frances A.   7
    George   177, 178, 194, 219
    George W.   4, 21, 178

Griffin   151, 178
Henry   178
Henry V.   7, 178, 178, 181
James   127, 178
James A.B.   103, 104
                105, 178, 178
James C.   4, 21, 178, 178
James L.   128
James S.   4
John 21, 72, 104, 178, 178, 219
John Sr.   104
Joseph F.   103, 178, 178
Julia Ann   7
Lucy   181
Maria   7
Mariah A.   178
Martha   21
Mary   20, 104, 151, 194
Mary A.   222
Mary C.   194
Mary S.   237
Nancy   219
Pattey   20
Rebecca [Rebeckah]   33, 110
Reuben   219
Robert   7, 34, 84, 178
                178, 194, 222
Sarah   178, 216, 219
Susan   146, 178, 181
Thomas   7, 51, 151, 179
William 110, 128, 178, 179, 179
William A.H.   179
William O.   179
Zachariah   21, 111, 151

Sandford   see, Samford & Sanford
    Albert   179
    Edward   179
    Elizabeth   103
    Fanny R.   179
    John   179
    Robert   179
    Sally M.   179
    Susan W.   179

Sands, Maria   180
    Mary Catharine   180
    O.H.   180

Sandy, Ann M.   98
    E.M.   180

Sandy, Elizabeth   173, _191_, 191
    Fanny   182
    Henry   7
    John   98, _179_, 179, 180, 191
    John E.   141
    Lemuel G.   98, _179_, 179, 200
    Mary   _188_, 191, _224_
    Mary Ann   7
    Mary Jane   180
    Mason [Mayson]   173, 188, _200_
    Nanny Murfey   98
    Samuel   _179_
    Thomas   98
    Uriah   _179_
    William   _179_
    Winney   _173_

Sanford, see Samford & Sandford
    family   180
    Augustine   173
    Barbara   180
    Bethiah (Asbury)   _46_, 180
    Daniel   85, _104_, _179_
    George   180
    Harriet   _179_
    James   _177_
    Jemima   180
    John E.   1
    Lucy Y.   179
    Rany   83
    Richard   _46_, _180_
    Robert   _147_, 169
    William   _180_, 180
    William H.   180

Saunders, see Sanders
    Ailsey   _166_
    Alice M.   _156_
    Allen   180
    Ann Maria   117
    Augustine N.   144, _180_, 185
    Billy   180
    Catherine   182
    Catharine R.   _156_
    Daniel   _180_
    Edward   1, 145, _180_
    Edward Jr.   _180_
    Edward Sydnor   _15_, 25, _180_
    George   xvi, _15_, 16, 23, 28, 35
             39, 55, 56, 58, 63, 71, 77
             92, 93, 117, 123,124, 133

              136, 144, 148, 167, _180_
              181, 185, 186, 209, _217_
                     218, 225, 235
    Henry S.   180
    Hundley   _182_
    James   180
    James C.   _127_
    John   48, 73
    Joseph   181
    Julia   _104_
    Juliet Ann   _185_
    Miskell   38, 86, 92, _112_
                 180, _181_, 185, 239
    Peggy Shackelford   181
    Richard   156, 180, 182, 226
    Richard S.   181
    Sally   _104_
    Sarah   _55_, _133_, 178, 216
    Thomas   _7_, 37, _181_

Savage, Alice   43, 77, 202
                     _210_, 213, _248_
    Anthony   210

Scandrett, Isaac   264
    Mary   _264_

Scates, Bartlet   95, _181_
    Charlotte   _178_
    Deliley   _20_
    Elijah   _181_, 181
    Elijah Jr.   111
    Elizabeth   178
    Harriet   _83_
    James   40, _181_
    John B.   103, 178, _181_
    Joseph   11, 30, 95
                 105, 109, _181_, 181
    Leah   _11_
    Maria   _95_
    Patty   _73_
    Rachel   _109_
    Richard   121, 139, _181_, _224_
    Sally   _109_
    Sarah   11, _109_
    Susan   20
    Thomas   _181_
    Washington   _168_

Schofield, John Kent   _181_, 238

Schooler, John   249
    Martha   249

Schrimsher, see Scrimiger &c:

Scotland, North Britian   x, 82
                          90, 136, 269

Scott County, Ky.   134, 135, 245

Scott,   see   Scutt
    Ann   181
    Elizabeth (Micou)   182
    George   181
    Henry   121
    James   x, 182
    James T.   182
    John   181, 182, 182
    Matilda A.   182
    Milly   39
    Molly   85
    Robert 35, 53, 65,133, 181, 182
    Thomas   181, 182
    Thomas Jr.   22

Scrimiger : Scrimger : Schrimsher
    Scrimsher &c:
    Catharine   98
    Elizabeth   1
    Frances R.   40
    George B.   182
    James   34, 40, 120
                    152, 182, 182, 187
    James W.   182
    Mary   214
    Mary Ann   34
    Mary J.   183
    Nancy   152
    Thomas   17, 182
    Thomas J.   127, 182, 183, 183
    William   88
    William G.   183

Scurlock,   see Sherlock
    Ann   199
    Catherine   1
    Daniel   91, 113, 238
    Ellen   238
    George   32, 49, 197, 238
    George Jr.   183
    Margaret   138

Mary   98, 197
Thomas   183

Scutt,   see   Scott
    Charles   125
    Frances   125
    James   183
    John   182, 183
    Thomas   182
    Zachariah   183

Seabery, Susanna   215

Seabry, Warner   183

Seagar, Henry   183

Seamons, John   183

Sebery, John   183
    William   183

Sebra : Sebree, see Seabry-Sebery
    Gilbert   112
    John   246
    Lucinda   112
    Martha A.   60
    William   183

Selden, John   79

Self, Betsy   236
    Elizabeth   99
    George   183
    Hannah   4
    Hannah L.   39
    Jane   202
    John   183
    Jeremiah   38
    Lucinda   53
    Moses   49, 53, 99, 183
    Rebecca B.   109
    Sally B.   49
    Samuel A.   38, 184
    Samuel Z.   184, 197
    Stephen   184
    Walter   45, 162
    Winifred   38

Selsad : Selsed : Celsed in
    Baltimore County, Md.   209, 210

Selsad, Westmoreland, England 209

Serjant, Eliz.[a] 232

Settle   see, Suttle
  family 262
  Amy 262
  Anne 192
  Anne Maria Bailey 193, 262
  Bailey 192, 262
  Betsey Bailey 192, 193, 262
  Edwin Bailey 262
  Elizabeth (Williams) 184, 228
  Francis Jr. 184, 228, 262
  Francis Sr. 184, 262
  Frederick 262
  Ga(y)ton 22, 184
  Henry 262
  John Alexander 262
  Reuben 184
  William   46, 70, 81, 146, 184
        192, 193, 207, 233, 262
  William Henry 142

Shackelford : Shackleford
  Alice 142
  Clement 75, 184, 222, 228
  Eliza M. 48
  Elizabeth 126
  Elizabeth F. 135
  Frances A. 75
  Lucy C. 25
  Lyne 54, 66, 94
        121, 124, 185, 206
  Peggy 181
  Richard 164, 185, 181, 185, 185
  Richard L. 72, 75, 149, 185
  Sally 72
  Sally A. 49
  Vincent 145, 185
  William 184, 185
  William R. 185

Shapleigh, Judith 144

Sharp, Thomas 185

Shaw, Christian 19
  William 185

Shearley : Shearly : Sherley
  see also Shirley : Shurley
  Elizabeth 58
  George   118, 119, 169, 194, 224
  John 186
  Peter 13, 186
  Polly 52

Shearman, see Sherman
  Ann 37, 243
  Elizabeth 36, 235
  James 36
  Jane 74
  Joseph W. 132, 186
  Joseph W.B. 186
  Martin 36, 37, 235, 243
  T. W. M. 23

Shehan, John 52

Shelby County, Missouri 88, 258

Shelly, Esther 48

Shenandoah County, Va. 189

Shepherd, James 33, 186
  Margaret M.C. 227

Sherlock, see Scurlock
  Deborah 138, 164
  George 49
  James xvi, 13
  John 138

Sherman, see Shearman
  James 36
  Jane 74

Sherwood, Anne 47
  Martha 129
  Mary 102, 173
  Philip 47, 102, 129, 173
  Sarah 173

Shipp, Emma Grant 258
  Richard 258

Shippy, Elizabeth 258

Shippy, Jael   221, 258
 Pheby   220
 Precilla   131
 Richard   186, 221, 258
 Richard Sr. 131, 186, 220

Shirley, Charles City Co., Va. 33
   see
Shirley,/ Shearley &c; also Shurley
 James   186
 Jane   115
 John   186
 Thaddeus   186

Short, Ann   191
 Clark   186
 Eleanor   52, 214
 Elizabeth   89
 John   9, 186
 Milly   184

Shropshire, Saint John 219

Shurley, see Shearley & Shirley
 Jeremiah   187

Silby, William   187

Simmonds, Cyrus   227
 Lucy   49

Simpson, Elizabeth   187
 John   143, 187, 249
 Joseph   187, 187
 Mary   249
 Thomas   187

Singleton, Ann 94, 175, 187
 Ann McCarty   62, 99
 James   79
 Joshua 62, 99, 175, 176
     187, 187, 199, 261
 Robert   62, 187, 192
 Susanna   192

Sipes, Alexander   187

Sisson, Ann   72
 Archibald 141, 148, 187
 David   187
 Elburton H.   73, 187

 Elizabeth S.   167
 Fanny   239
 George 51, 137, 187, 211
 Hannah   137
 Henry   22, 34, 167
     187, 188, 188, 214
 Hierome   188
 Hiram   188
 James   1, 188
 Jemima   142
 John B.   188, 188
 John M.   167, 188
 John T.   73
 Martin 3, 25, 53, 67, 148, 188
 Mary   1, 20, 51
 Mary A.   214
 Mary B.   190
 Moley   72
 Nancy   72
 Patty   3, 51
 Randall   188
 Richard   20, 188
 Robert   188
 Solomon   188
 Susan   1, 88
 Susan S.   73
 Susan W.   190
 William   188
 William H.   30, 73, 84
      181, 188, 190
 William Henry   188
 Winnefried   167, 211

Size, Anne   219
 John   219

Skelderman, Ann   90
 Elizabeth 51, 104, 105, 236
 Herman 10, 51, 82, 90, 105
 Mary   10, 82

Skelton, Sally   134

Skinker, Mary   187
 Samuel   187

Skrine, Anne   130
 Elizabeth   130
 William   96, 130

Slaughter, Elizabeth 221

Slaughter, Francis   26, 189
                    189, 206, 221
    John   189
    Margaret   206, 221
    Martha   26
    Mary   206
    Phoebe   155
    Robert   189
    William B.   135

Slave Marriages,.see Negro Marriages

Small, Oliver   189

Smart, William   113

Smaw, John   232

Smith, Agatha   190
    Alice   23, 149, 191
    Ann   121, 141, 142, 145, 219
    Ann Adams   103, 191, 225
    Benjamin   189, 192
    Betsy (Sydnor)   201
    Catherine   30, 36, 50, 144
    Catharine Gwinn   148
    Charles   124, 192, 208, 238
    Charles W.   124, 189
    Colston   189
    David   189
    Edwin Bathurst   135, 189
    Elies   192
    Eliza T.   144
    Elizabeth   15, 31, 104, 159
             190, 191, 191, 195, 198
             220, 220, 223, 246, 266
    Elizabeth B.   185
    Enoch   245
    Fanny   219
    Frances   28, 152
    Frances Ann   124
    Francis   191
    George H.   189
    George W.   191
    Gracie   77
    Hannah Bushrod   23
    Henryretta   191
    Isaac   21, 189, 195
    James   30, 190
    James L.   192
    James S.   24, 30, 190

    Jane   60
    Jane Ann   124
    John   ix, 8, 31, 40, 42
             75, 101, 112, 141, 159
             189, 190, 219, 227
    John Ogle   192
    Joseph   190
    Joseph Woollard   190
    Joyce   228
    Katherine   110
    Lucy   40
    Margaret   21, 104
    Margaret A.   191
    Maria   191
    Maria C.   167
    Maria Henrietta   30
    Marianna   36
    Martha C.   125
    Mary   42, 111, 189
    Mary B.   78
    Mary Colston   75
    Mary E.   191
    Mary W.   132
    Meriwether   189
    Molly   40
    Nancy   50, 183
    Nicholas 190, 195,220, 246, 256
    Peter   191
    Philip   23
    Polley   24
    Robert   191, 192
    Sally   38, 215
    Sally T.   192
    Sarah   25, 159, 195, 202
    Sarah S.   39
    Sarah L. (Dobyns)   55, 191
    Susanna   4, 13, 27, 30, 62
             80, 171, 213, 214, 231
    Thomas   6, 14, 178
             202, 214, 228, 231
    Thomas P.   39, 57, 191
    William   30, 75, 80, 84
             103, 119, 125, 132, 159
             167, 168, 191, 191, 192
             213, 223, 228, 245, 255
    William Jr.   191
    William C.   39, 148, 185
    William G.   192, 193, 262
    Winefred [Winnefred] 125, 142
                        187, 187
    Winifred T.   124

Smith's Mount, Westmoreland County, Virginia   190, 220, 266

Smither, Betsy   53
   Dewanna   2
   Gabriel   134
   Judith   49
   Lancelot   192
   Lancelot [Launce] L.   2, 37
   Nancy   37
   Richard   49, 91, 192, 219, 229
   Thomas   192
   Winter B.   192

Smithfield, Spotsylvania Co.   242

Smoot, Anne   250
   Benjamin F.   192
   Elizabeth   250
   Jane   61, 250
   John   192
   Mary   61, 87, 145, 250
   William   61, 250

Snead, Charles   139, 192
   Charles   Jr.   205
   Charles   Sr.   205
   Elizabeth   139, 205
   James Allanelia   192
   Sarah T.   30, 144

Sommevell [Sommerville], John   192
                                 255

Sorrell, Thomas   192
   Thomas   A.   57, 193

Southampton County, Va.   245

South Carolina, State of   147

Southery Ferry, Westmoreland
   County, Virginia   260

Spann, Elizabeth   217, 226, 251
   Priscilla (Churchill)   9
   Richard   9

Spark(s), Alexander   193

Spence, Alexander   92, 193, 206

Dorcas   193
Elizabeth M.A.   59
Frances   92
Henry   193
John   90,111,193
Patrick   193,204
Thomas Jr.   193, 262

Spencer, Edward   80, 81
                193, 193,   254
   Elizabeth   254
   Thomas   228
   Winifred (Green) 80, 193, 254

Spendergrass, John   193

Spicer, Arthur   19, 24, 193
   John   24, 132, 193, 265

Spiller, John   17, 193

Spilman : Spillman
   George T.   22
   James   K.   178, 194
   Mary   A.   115

Spooner, Eliza Pitman   60

Spotsylvania Co., Va.   42, 77, 89
   92, 96, 129, 130, 203, 218, 220
   221, 239, 242, 247, 249, 252
                     255, 259, 261

Spragg, John   194

Springfield, Stafford Co., Va.   252

Springwood, Loudoun Co., Va.   4

Stafford Co., Va.   x, 2, 4, 14,.19
   64, 71, 72, 76, 80, 82, 92, 96
   97, 106, 112, 114, 116, 119,125
   128, 130, 136, 143, 146, 147,152
   161, 166, 175, 176, 186, 210,212
   213, 216, 232, 242, 247, 248,249
   252, 253, 255, 256-259, 266, 269

Stanard, Columbia   266
   Dr. William G.   212

Standley, Thomas   194

Stanfield, Betty   6
  Mary (Dalton)   121, 194
  Thomas   6, 121, 194

Stark : Starke
  Bolling   245
  Francis   203
  Martha   203

Starks, Darcus   37
  Eleanor   2
  Eleanor (Todd)   1, 1,194
  James   1, 2, 37, 194
  Jane   1

Steavens, Judy   3

Steel, Lewis P.   194

Steele, Samuel   27, 177, 194, 232

Stephen, Daniel   194

Stephens, Ann   50
  Elias   194
  Elizabeth   109, 115
  Ellen   215
  Jefferson   5, 61, 194
  Jeremiah   52, 194
  John H.   194
  Judith   239
  Mark   194
  Mary   38
  Nancy   197
  Sally   3
  Thomas   194

Steptoe, John   155
  John Jr.   195
  Judith   155

Sterling, Joseph   169, 195

Sterne, family   256
  Agatha   190, 195, 229, 256
  Ann   152, 195, 229, 256
  David   154, 190, 195
                195, 229, 247, 256
  Frances   80, 100, 143
                154, 195, 207, 256
  Francis   195, 195, 247, 256

Mary (Cammack)   195, 256

Stevens, Mark   25, 194

Stewart, Catherine   73, 231
  Elizabeth W.   257
  Katherine   73, 231
  Mary   167
  Susanna   27, 233
  William   27, 73, 157
                167, 231, 232, 233

Sthreshley, William   259

Stiff, Cornelia A.   31
  James M.   31, 41, 154, 155
  Louisa James   155
  Mary Sophia   41
  Sarah E.   154

Stith, Griffin Jr.   195
  William   195

Stokes, William   12, 195, 231

Stone, family   251, 263, 264, 265
  Ann(e)   6, 11, 24, 127, 131
             132, 196, 263, 265
  Catherine (Swinburne)   200
  Elizabeth   52, 127, 195
             200, 263, 263, 264
  Esther   264
  Frances   264
  Francis   110, 153, 195, 196
             200, 263, 264, 264
  George   264
  Henry   263
  John   ix, x, 11, 131, 195
             196, 223, 251, 265
  Joshua   47, 196, 263
  Katherine   263
  Margaret   263, 264
  Mary   196, 263
             263, 264, 264, 265
  Philip   263, 263
  Sarah   52, 127, 157, 196, 196
       263, 263, 264, 264, 265
  Sarah [Sary] Ann (Alderson)   6
                                 196
  Thomas   6,94,196
  William   52, 127, 196, 196
             200, 263, 264, 264

Ston(e)ham,   see Stonum

Stonum, Betty   32
  Elizabeth   105
  Elizabeth C.   1
  Ellen   91
  Fanny   142
  George   105
  George B.   149
  George N.   196
  Hiram   1, 124
  Jane   79
  Nancy   158
  Richard   197
  Sally   113
  Sarah   71
  Susan   124, 177
  William   1, 71, 91, 105
                            142,158,197

Stoot, Elizabeth   235
  Mary   235
  Robert   235

Stott, Caty   138
  Charity Ann   225
  Elizabeth   3, 10, 197
  Elizabeth B.   224
  Ellen   98
  Epp.^a   29, 86, 197
  J. C.   58
  James   197
  Joel   197
  John   10, 87, 197
  John Oliver   58, 65, 197
  LeRoy   10, 23, 87, 197, 197
  Levina   87
  Louisa M.   118
  Mary   86, 225
  Mary C.   108
  Oliver   41, 197, 197, 225
  Olivia   91
  Richard   197, 224, 236
  Sally   29
  Sally C.   86
  Thadd(e)us C.   49, 86, 197
  Thomas   48
  Thomas H.   197
  Vincent   197

Stowers, Ann   41

Lettice   33
Nicholas   139
Samuel   41
Thomas   22, 180

Stratford, Westmoreland Co.,Va. 116

Straughan, Betsy S.   113
  James   197
  Jane L.   113
  John C.   113, 197
  Mary J.   170
  Peter P.C.   45
  Richard   198
  Sally   170
  Thomas N.   183

Street, Catharine   91
  Elizabeth   46, 91, 193, 206
  Frances H.   206
  Jane   113
  Maria   91
  Polly   148
  Richard   133, 148, 198
  Susan M.   46

Stretchley, John   250

Strother Plantation, Stafford
  County, Virginia   89

Strother, family   198, 252
  Anthony   252
  Benjamin   198
  Dorothy   198
  Francis   71, 198
  George   252
  Thomas   255
  William   198

Stuart,   see Stewart
  Charles   x
  Christina   82
  John   82
  Richard   246, 260, 269

Stuckey : Stukky
  Elizabeth   119
  Hannah   169
  Mary Beachum   119
  William   119

Sturman, family   198-199
   Elliott   198, 199
   Mary (Young)   198
   William Young xv, 45, 89, 103
                 103, 198, 199, 221

Suffolk County, Mass.   203

Suggett : Suggitt
   family   xiii
   Edg(e)comb   117, 189, 199
   Elizabeth   93, 189
   Hannah   107
   James   199
   Jennie   189
   John   12, 68, 117, 176
              189, 199, 199, 226, 261
   Lucy   117
   Rebecca   226
   Sarah   94
   Sarah (Edgcomb)   12, 199
   Thomas   199

Sullinger, Eliza   199
   Peter   199

Sullivan, John   199

Sullivant, Daniel   1

Sussex County, Virginia   245

Suttle,   see Settle
   Mary   22
   Strother   199

Sutton, Edward   199
   Elizabeth   225
   Fanny   200
   George   200
   John   200
   Mary   208
   Sally   27
   Thomas   200
   William   200, 200

Swain, William   200

Swan, Alexander   x, 3, 200

Sweeny, Lenora (Higginbotham)69,70

Swinburne, Catherine   200, 264
   Martha   158, 200
   Thomas   153, 158, 200, 264
   William   200

Swope, Elijah   200
   Joseph   200

Sydnor, A. Judson   169
   Ann   134, 201, 204
   Anthony   14, 134, 200
                          200, 201, 204
   Anthony Jr.   59
   Anthony Sr.   134
   Betsy   201
   Betty   123, 155, 200, 204
   Dewanna(h)   5, 200, 201
   Elizabeth   54, 59
   Epaphroditus   9, 59, 67, 186
              189, 200, 201, 201, 202
   Fanny   59, 201
   Frances   117, 201
   George W.   15, 236
   Giles   201
   Harrison   201
   James   53, 75
   Johannah   115
   John   6, 16, 59, 117
                189, 200, 201, 201
   John Jr.   86, 117, 202
   Judith   86
   Lucy   58, 113, 200
   Mary   189, 202
   Mary S.   165
   Nancy   83, 179, 188
   Richard   69, 202
   Robert   38, 113, 201, 202
   Robert B.   171, 185
   Ruth   14, 15, 36, 68
                        191, 201, 245
   Samuel   201
   Susannah   6, 150
   Thomas   17, 36, 122, 202
   Thomas   Jr.   194
   Thomas   S.   134
   William   83, 90, 202, 202
   William Jr.   202
   William Sr.   202
   William F.   202
   Winifred   174, 200, 200, 201

Taff : Taft : Toff
    John   202
    Peter   126, 202, 234
    Rawleigh   183
    Thomas   79, 126, 202, 238

Taite, Thomas   38

Talburt, Elizabeth   214

Taliaferro, family   202-203, 266
    Catherine   96, 203, 266
    Charles   220, 248
    Francis   202, 203, 259
    John   202
    Laurence   202
    Martha   203, 220, 266
    Mary   220, 242, 249, 266
    Richard   96, 203, 203
                 220, 221, 266, 266
    Robert   129, 203
    Sarah   96, 203, 203, 220
             220, 221, 248, 266, 266
    Walker   266

Tallahassee, Florida   59

Talley, Moses   203

Tappahannock, Va. xvii,25,122, 227

Tapscott, Ann M   1
    Chichester   122, 203, 226
    Elin   47
    Elizabeth   121
    Elizabeth S.   5
    Elizabeth T.   122
    Frances Catherine   25
    James   160
    Joseph   140, 203, 231
    Samuel C.   203
    Warner L.   29, 55, 124, 203

Tarkington, John   203

Tarpley, Betty   155, 204
    Charlotte P.   53
    Edward Ripping   204
    Eliza   90
    Fanny   36, 204
    Frances A.   177

Frances Ann   53
James   204
John 1, 131, 146, 204, 204, 226
John Jr.   xv, 204
Lucy   36, 48, 108, 194, 204
Milley   48, 204
Nancy   204
Tertius Quintus   204
Thomas   90
Thomas G.   204
Travers xix,14, 36, 48, 58, 108
        123, 155, 200, 204, 204
Winifred   122, 123, 204
Winifred Griffin   91, 135
                    136, 226, 227

Tate, Eliza   170
    Elizabeth   204
    Ellen   169
    Hester   204
    James   204
    Jane   204
    Joseph   204
    Joseph T.   204
    Tasker   205
    William   204

Taverner, John   42
    Rebecca (Travers)   42

Tayler, George   74, 217, 251
    Francis   205
    Martha   74

Tayloe, family   267
    Ann(e) 205, 206, 206, 267, 267
    Anna C.   11, 205, 265, 267
    Betty   44
    Catherine   34
    Elizabeth   120, 205, 209, 267
    Henrietta H.   112
    Jane   18
    John   xvii, 18, 40, 44, 69, 93
            112, 116, 120, 149
            205, 206, 218, 267
    Joseph   xvi, 205, 205
            206, 209, 246, 267
    Joseph Jr.   205, 267
    Louisa R.   103
    Mary   205, 206, 267
    Rebecca Plater   116

Tayloe, William   205, 205, 267

Taylor, Mr.   263
  Bridgett   40
  Charles   25, 231
  Elizabeth   199
  George   x, 248
  George Conway   266
  Hannah   160
  James   193, 206, 248
  Jane   145
  John   206
  Joseph H.   94, 206
  Joshua   44
  Katherine   27
  Mary   205
  Mary Bramham   169
  Moses   206
  Samuel G.   129, 206
  Sarah   74, 106, 230, 231, 253
  Simon   106, 206, 253
  William   199, 206

Teackle, Eliz.ᵃ U.   238

Teague, Jenny   183
  Jonathan   206
  Newman B.   206
  Susanna   23

Tebbs, Daniel   95, 206
  Elizabeth   207
  Foushee G.   xv, 22, 145
              149, 207, 207, 224
  Henry William   207
  Samuel   207
  William F.   121, 124, 180

Tellis, J. C.   108
  Rodham   207

Temple, Peter   46, 70, 207

Tennison, Joshua   41

Texas, State of   50

Thacker, Mr.   xvi
  Frances   152, 161, 256, 259
  Henry   232, 256
  Matilda   232

Thatcher, family   247, 268
  Catherine (Pannell)   207
  Elizabeth   53, 251, 268, 268
  Elizabeth (Underwood) 207, 268
  John   268
  Margaret   207, 247, 268, 268
  Mary   37, 80, 171, 234, 268
  Mathew   268
  Samuel   268
  Sylvester   37, 53, 171
              207, 247, 268, 268
  Sylvester Jr.   207, 207, 268
  Thomas   207, 268
  William   208, 268

The County Court Note Book   xiv

The Falls, Spotsylvania Co.,Va. 213

The Reporter of Lexington, Ky. 135

The Virginia Magazine of History
    and Biography   xiv, xvii

Thom [a Negro]   208

Thomas, Ann   94
  Austin   64
  Beckham   208
  Daniel J.   208
  Frances   142
  Griffin E.   208
  James   208
  Job   19, 208
  Joseph   208
  Mary   19
  Royston   64
  Thomas   91, 129, 219
  William   77, 120, 141, 208

Thomasin, Margaret   252

Thompson, Anna   222
  Charles R.   15, 208
  Daniel   208, 208, 209
  Darcas   209
  George   208
  Hannamore   104, 222
  Henry   104, 208, 221, 222
  James F.   209
  John   35

Thompson, John Jr.   209
    John Sr.   209
    Mary   221
    Moses   209
    Peggy   209
    Rebecca   104
    Robert   145
    William F.   35

Thomson, Alexander   129
    Richard   209

Thornberry :· Thornburg : Thorn-
    bury : Thornburgh &c.
    family   209-210
    Francis   209, 210
    John   205, 209, 267
    Mary   210
    Rowland   209, 210, 210

Thornley, Aaron   210, 210
    John   210
    Mary (Berry)   210

Thornton, families   210
    Mr.   210
    Agatha   35, 36, 243
    Alice   248, 260
    Ann   4, 108, 140, 141,168, 169
           169, 195, 210,213, 214
    Anthony   114, 213
    Benjamin Berryman   213
    Catherine (Yates)   213
    Charlotte [Sharlott]   211
    Crask   211, 237
    Eleanor, see Ellen
    Eleanor Barnes (Kilsick)   210
    Elizabeth   34, 43, 44, 77
                     211, 214, 248
    Elizabeth (Carter)   34, 211
    Elizabeth (Fleming)   108, 211
                           212, 212
    Ellen [Ellin, Elinor, Eleanor]
                        47, 115, 140
              171, 211, 214, 237
    Esabell   17
    Frances (Dudley)   88, 211
    Frances Sisson   54, 214
    Francis   40, 43, 44, 77, 114
              202, 210, 212, 213, 248
    Hannah   188

Hopkins   211
Isabell   17
John   40, 211, 212, 213
Lucy   2, 242
Luke   140, 141, 210, 213
Margaret   21
Mary Randolph   213
Mathew   46, 140, 211, 211, 237
Nancy   74
Peter Presley   34, 40, 41, 211
Presley   40, 41, 211
Rachel   13, 27, 214, 231
Rebecca   46, 211
Rebecca Sisson (Lawson) 86, 214
Robert   50, 88, 211
Rowland   70, 108, 152, 209
           211, 212, 212, 213, 228
Sarah   202, 220, 248
Sarah (Bruce)   212
Sarah (Newton)   212, 213
Susannah (Smith) 80, 213, 214
Thomas   4, 13, 27, 35, 50, 51
           54, 55, 79, 80, 86, 169
           171, 213, 214, 214, 231
William   40, 87, 211, 212, 212
           213, 214, 242, 248, 260
Winifred 40, 41, 211, 236, 246

Threlkeld, Eleanor (Short) 52, 214
    Elijah   143, 257
    George   214
    Henry   52, 214
    William   214

Thrift, Absalom   214
    Amaniah   160
    Ann   28
    Ann D.   173
    Annaniah   160
    Catherine M.   92
    Elizabeth   50, 51, 51, 95, 159
    Elizabeth C.   41, 170
    Elizabeth W.   63
    George   214, 225, 233
    George R.   3, 5, 17, 29
                63, 108, 131, 218
    George W.   214
    Hamilton   41
    Hannah   172
    Harriet   218
    Jane   120, 170

Thrift, Jeremiah   83, 215
  Jery   215
  Jesse   215
  Jessey   84
  John 28, 48, 63, 131, 215, 215
  John Jr.   215
  Keterah   118
  Louisa   83
  Lucy   5
  Maria   17
  Mary   29, 236
  Massey   131
  Nancy   71, 116
  Nathaniel   95
  Richard T.   215
  Samuel   215
  Samuel B. 63,118, 173, 215, 221
  Sarah J.   48
  William   172, 215, 215
  Winney   95

Thurston, Caty   163
  Mary   66, 163

Tidwell, John   230

Tiffey, John B.   79, 142, 215

Tignor, Caty S.   197
  Thomas   206, 215

Tilden, Miss   76
  Charles   76

Tillery, Charlotte   57
  Fortunatus   215
  Henry   215
  Job   18, 215, 215, 216, 216
  Mary   175
  Thomas   216

Tippett, Abigail   57, 80
  Ann   57
  Thomas   57, 80
  William   57

Todd, Cornelius   216
  Dorothea (Payne)   248
  Eleanor   1, 2, 37, 194
  Hannah   38
  Henry   1, 194, 216

  Henry P.   13
  Jane   1, 194
  John   13, 216, 216
  Nancy   147
  Peter   216
  William   216

Toff, see Taff : Taft : Toff

Tomlin, family   216-218, 251
  Ann   89
  Apphia Fauntleroy   123, 217
  Catharine   124, 217
  Eleanor   217
  Elizabeth   122, 217, 217, 251
  Fanny M.   239
  John Walker   9, 216, 217
  Lucy Harrison   151
  Judith L.   110
  Moore Fauntleroy 179, 217, 217
  Nelly   217
  Robert   68, 122, 123, 124
       128, 217, 217, 218, 251
  Robert Jr.   156, 229
         217, 223, 251
  Robert Giberne   217
  Susanna Fauntleroy   12, 217
  Walker 9, 68, 80, 110, 137, 151
     216, 217, 217, 218, 251
  William   218
  Williamson Ball   218
  Winifred   217

Toone, see Tune : Toone

Totusky, Richmond County, Va. 126

Totusky Creek, Richmond Co.,Va. 178
          215, 261, 263

Towles, Rawleigh Downman   218
  Stokley   xv, 218, 218
  William S.   40

Townshend, Frances   96, 242
  Mary   269
  Robert   96, 269

Traquair, Ninth Earl of   82

Trasce : Trasey
  William   77, 202, 218

Traveller's Rest, Stafford County
    Virginia   4, 76

Travers, Rawleigh   169
    Rebecca   42, 169
    Samuel   42, 98, 169, 196
    William   169
    Winifred   98

Trent, Anne   102
    James   102

Trevilian, Roscow C.   218

Triplett, family   98
    Francis   106, 120
    Isabell(a)   98
    William   98, 255

Trosee, William   77

Truck [Trocq], Isaac 195, 247

Truman, Anderson Shipp   258
    Harry Shipp   136, 258
    John Anderson   258
    Sarah   191
    William   258

Tucker, Benjamin 5, 17, 29, 38, 77
    83, 84, 190, 201, 202, 218
    Benjamin F.   218
    Harriet   83
    Lucy   218
    Thomas   219

Tune : Toone
    Ann   196
    Anthony   219
    Apphia T.   235
    Carter   79
    Caster   79
    Catherine   181
    Edward K.   109, 219
    Elizabeth   50, 79
    Elizabeth D.   192
    George   192
    George D.   219
    James   10, 219
    Jesse   219
    Lewis   196

    Lucy   7
    Mary   181
    Nancy   219
    Sally   98
    Samuel   219
    Sarah   219
    Thomas   39, 77, 219, 219, 235
    Winifred   10

Tunstall, family   130
    Edmund   130
    Katherine   130
    Robert   219

Turberville, Edward   219, 232
    Elizabeth   219
    John   45
    Martha Filecia   12

Turner, family   266
    Eliza Hooe   266
    Elizabeth (Fauntleroy) 220
    Elizabeth (Smith)   220
    Harry   190, 220, 266
    Hezechia [Hezekiah] 93,161, 220
    James   42
    John   220
    Maria   266
    Mary   221, 266
    Michall [Michell]   161
    Richard   266
    Richard H.   266
    Sarah   221, 266
    Thomas 203, 203, 220, 220, 266
    Thomas Jr.   220, 266

Tutt, Margaret (Miskell) Garnett 76
    Mary (Underwood)   221
    Richard   221
    Richard Jr.   252
    Richard J.   76

Tuxent, Steward   221

Tyler, Ann   258
    Dr. Lyon G.   xiii
    William 115, 161, 249, 259

Underwood, Alice   224
    Elizabeth   207, 207, 268

Underwood, Frances 258
  Jael (Shippy) 221, 258
  John 221
  Lott 258
  Mary 221
  Sarah 77
  William x, 77, 207, 221, 258

Upshaw, Caleb B. 192

Vallott, Ann 102
  Claud 102

Vance, Mr. 135

Vanlandingham, Nancy 95, 95

Van Ness, William P. 221

Vass, Vincent 221

Vaulx, Sarah 227

Vause, Elizabeth (Weekes) 228
  John 228

Venie : Venea ; Veney : Veeney &c
  Darky 170
  Edward 221
  James 222
  Jerrie 170
  Jesse 170, 222
  Joseph 222
  Judy 170, 222
  Mary 222
  Moses 222
  Rachel 222
  Travis 222
  Washington 222

Vermont, Fauquier Co., Va. 266

Vicaris, Martha 216, 216
  Thomas 216

Vickers, Thomas 84, 222

Virginia Counties, Bulletin of
  the Virginia State Library xvii

Virginia Gazette of Williamsburg, Va. 89, 120, 213

Virginia Herald of Fredericksburg, Va. 12, 13, 14, 18,25,33
  41, 45, 46, 49, 59, 60, 64, 71
  76, 77, 90, 99, 110, 116, 122
  126, 134, 142, 144, 155,171,227
  228,229

Virginia Historical Index xiii

Virginia Historical Society xii, 34

Virginia State Library xiii, xvii,5

Vivion, Margaret 161, 256, 259
  Thomas 152, 161, 256, 259

Waddington, Elizabeth 252
  Francis 252

Wade, Jean 160

Wafel, Amelia 11
  Mariah 11

Waide, Matilda B. 53
  Robert C. 222

Wale, Timothy 222

Wales, Great Britain 107, 163

Walker, family 251
  Alexander 222, 244
  Almira L. 38
  Ann(e) 68, 222, 251, 256
  Edmund 153
  Elizabeth 223
  Elizabeth Ann 66
  Eppa 222
  Esther 156, 217, 217, 223, 251
  Frances 223
  Frances (Belfield) 222, 245
  Francis S. 222
  Freeman 222, 223, 245
  Hannah 117
  Hester 156, 157, 217, 223, 251
  Jane 53, 79, 223, 251, 268

Walker, John 43, 53, 156, 157, 195
              217, 222, 223, 248, 265
    Mary F.B.   153
    Polly   109
    Sarah   43, 156, 195, 196, 217
             223, 223, 248, 251, 265
    Thomas   41, 223
    Thomas Belfield   191, 223
    Thomas W. [T.W.]   70, 153, 223
    Wilalmina L.   177
    William   57, 223
    William G.   59
    William M.   142

Wall, Betsy   84
    Edward   169
    Elizabeth   84
    James   52, 92
    Nancy   169
    Peggy   105

Wallace, Joseph   223

Waller, Edwin   100

Walmoth, Judah   95

Walsingham, King George Co.220,266

Walters, Thomas   146, 223

Waphul, Hannah   21

Waple, Haney   95

Ward, D.F.   151
    William N.   57

Waring, William L.   224

Warmoth, see Weymoth : Warmoth

Warner, see Worner
    L.D.   xvi
    Lucy   38
    Sarah   94
    Susanna   79

Warren, Betsy   235

War(r)ick, see Warwick

Warring, Thomas   224

Warsaw, Richmond Co.,Va.xiv,xvii,66

Warwick : War(r)ick
    Frances W.   197
    Philip   224
    Thomas S.   197, 224

Wascole, Mary   215

Washington, D.C.   160

Washington, family   269
    Augustine   89, 243
    George   89, 243, 269
    Henry   47, 259
    John   106, 107, 269, 269
    Lawrence   2, 106, 211, 242, 269
    Mary   106
    Mildred   260, 269
    Samuel   224
    Thomas Muse   224

Waterloo, King George Co. 2,242,269

Watson, John   224

Watts, Ann   67, 260
    Clarkey   10
    Fanny   58
    John   224
    John T.   224
    Richard   224, 260
    Spencer   58
    William   67

Waugh, Joseph   143, 257
    Mary   249

Waughope, Catherine   134

Waverley, King George Co., Va.   26

Way, Thomas   203
    William   203

Weadon, James   128, 224
    Mary   128
    S.   7, 128
    Shelton   73, 224

Weatherburn, Henry 21

Weathers, Addison 225
  Ann 5
  Catherine 198, 199, 225
  Eleanor 103, 225
  Elizabeth 88
  Elizabeth McKenny 225
  Ellen 137
  Eppa: 35, 137, 145, 149, 224
  Fanny 137
  George 191, 224
  Isabella K. 3, 225
  James 225
  John 3, 103, 198, 209, 225
  Joseph 137, 225
  Juliet 225
  Juliet A. 223
  Malvina 138, 225
  Mary W. 191
  Peggy A. 191
  Polly 90
  Rebecca 138, 223
  Richard Kelsick 225
  Samuel 225
  Vincent 225
  William 17, 225
  William Younger 225, 225
  Winifred B. 146

Weathersbee, Jane 68

Weaver, Hopeful 81
  Lorinday 81

Webb, Ann 2, 62, 168
  Caroline 37, 125
  Catharine Ann 87
  Clementina 103, 198, 199
  Eliza 93
  Elizabeth 89, 165, 170
  Elizabeth K. 126
  Ewell 48, 87, 197, 225
  Fanny Ellen 170
  Francis T. 170
  Giles 217, 226, 251
  Hierome 226
  Hiram P. 226
  Isaac 2, 89, 135, 226
  James 79,89, 168, 170, 226, 227
  Jeremiah 37,98,103,125,198, 226

  John 89, 168, 170, 226, 261
  John Spann 135, 226, 226
  Maria 168
  Mary 168, 170
  Mary A.G. 215
  Nancy 168
  Richard 121, 226
  Sarah 66
  W. 75
  Wilalmira 53, 91, 223, 227
  William 50, 54, 91, 135, 163
  168, 169, 226, 227, 227
  Williamson 136, 218, 227, 227
  Winifred 217, 218, 251
  Winifred Griffin (Tarpley) 91
  135, 136, 226, 227

Webley, Mary 154
  Richard 154

Webster, Henry 227
  Thomas 227
  William 47, 88, 153, 168

Weeden : Weedon, see Weadon
  Elizabeth 108
  Patsy 108
  Thomas 108, 227

Weekes, Abraham 228
  Elizabeth 228

Weekly Recorder of Fredericksburg, Virginia 24

Weir, James 227
  Robert 25
  William James 227

Weire, Elizabeth 75
  John 75

Welch, Ann 38
  Edward 227
  John 227
  Reuben 96

Weldon, see Wheldon
  David 227
  George 89
  Judah 30

Weldon, Judy   89
    Rebeckah   89
    Sample   228
    Sampson   30

Welldon, John   228

Wellford, Armistead N.   228
    Horace   67, 100, 132, 159, 228
    Robert   213, 228

Welling, Caleb   228
    Elizabeth (Weeks) Vause   228

Wells, Barnabas   228
    Juda   170
    Mary   31
    Stephen   184, 184, 228

Welsh, Michael   228

Went, James   252

Wentsworth, King George Co.,Va. 252

West, Ann   207
    Francis   207
    Richard   80, 268
    Robert   228
    Susanna (Littlepage)   207

Westcomb, James   204

Westfalia, Rappahannock Co.,Va. 70

West Indies   203

Westmoreland, England   209, 210

Westmoreland County, Virginia   x
    xii, xvii, 4, 5, 6, 10, 11, 13
    15, 18, 22, 23, 27, 30, 31, 32
    33, 38, 40, 45, 46, 52, 59, 62
    63, 72, 73, 74, 77, 79, 80, 81
    82, 83, 84, 89, 90, 91,100-103
    106, 113, 115, 116, 117,   119
    121, 123, 125 - 129,132,134-36
    140, 142, 146, 149, 152 — 157
    160, 161, 164 - 169, 172, 174
    175, 180, 182, 183, 190, 191
    193, 197, 198, 199 , 204, 206

    210, 214, 224, 229, 231, 236-37
    244-246, 249, 251, 253,256, 259
    260, 262, 264, 269

Westover, Charles City Co., Va. 84

West Virginia, State of   42, 76
                              213, 268

Weymoth : Warmoth
    Catharine   56
    Elizabeth   109
    Frances   57
    John   56, 215, 229
    Sally   37
    Thomas   37, 44, 229
    Thomas   Jr.   229

Whaley, Eliz.^{a} 69

Wharton, Martha   249

Whealey [? Wheatley ?], William 100

Wheeler, William C.   160, 229

Wheldon ; See   Weldon
    Amelia   186, 224
    Amelia Oldham   237
    Betsey W.   186
    Catharine   224
    John   92, 186, 224, 229, 237
    Nancy H.   237

Whelling, Caleb   See Welling

Wherret, Mr.   11

White Hall, Gloucester Co., Va. 248

White, Abraham   73, 229, 229
    Amelia A.T.   154
    Ann   81
    Ann C.   70
    Benjamin   229
    Catherine   231
    Daniel   152, 195, 229, 256
    Elizabeth   69
    Erretto A.   92
    Frances   114, 249
    Frances A.   187

White, George   31, 40, 152
                229, 229, 230, 256
    George   Jr.   229
    Hannah   42
    J. G.   221
    James H.   230
    Jane   152, 154, 154, 229
    John   69, 81, 230, 254
    John G.   159, 230
    Lovell   127
    Margaret   107
    Mary   29
    Mary S.   177
    Mildred   127
    Molly   31
    Polly   68
    Richard   87, 231
    Sally   215
    Thomas 114,136,152,154,229, 249
    William   230
    William L.   230
    Zechariah   29, 69, 90, 179

Whitehaven, England   111

White Plains, King George Co.   210

Whiting, Mary   76
    William   230

Wiatt, James C.   3

Widdilow, Mary   43

Wilcox, Hannah   169
    John   230
    William   230

Wilden, William   230, 231

Wildey, Elizabeth   69
    Jane   69
    William   69

Wildy, see Wilden and Wildey

Wilkerson, Jane   109

Wilkins, Jane   84
    Mary Ann   184

Williams, Abraham   230, 231
    Ann   133, 194, 202, 231, 232
    Barbara   146
    Betsy   203
    Catherine   66, 115, 115
                174, 174, 177, 194
    Catherine (Hammond)   177
                          194, 232
    Christian   64
    Daniel   231
    David   16, 53, 219, 231
    E. L.   235
    Elizabeth   12, 48, 72,184, 228
    Elizabeth (?) Batten   195
                                231
    Elizabeth Corrie   174
    Evan   64
    Francis   13, 27, 93, 214, 231
    George   231
    Griffin   235
    Hannah   198
    Henry   102, 150, 202, 231, 231
    Hugh   174
    Jael (Harrison)   89
    James   89
    Jane   107, 198
    John   12, 107, 133
                195, 230, 231, 232
    Judith   202
    Katherine, see Catherine (2)
    Luke   231
    Mary   64, 175, 177, 184
    Mary Elizabeth   235
    Mellinor   93
    Millinder   93
    Marina   13, 231
    Morgan   231, 232
    Moriah   104
    Rice   184, 228
    Roger   232
    Sally   198
    Samuel   78, 96, 232
    Sarah (Jesper)   230
    Susannah   27, 231
    Thaddeus   48, 115, 119, 168
                174, 174, 232, 239
    Thomas   81, 177, 184, 194
                198, 232, 232, 238
    William   89, 146, 232
    Winifred   72
    Youell   232

Williamsburg, Virginia   23, 71
                          120, 161, 204

Williamson, James   8, 243
    Margaret   8, 8, 243, 260, 269
    Walter   260, 269

Willis Hill, Fredericksburg,Va. 34

Willis, Francis   248
    Henry   248
    Jane   2, 242
    John   232, 233, 248
    John Jr.   232
    John Sr.   102, 232
    Lewis   2, 34
    Mary   102, 248
    Mary (Coghill)   232
    Mildred   34
    Sarah   219, 232
    William   219, 232

Wilson : Willson
    Abram P.   233
    Allen   233
    Ann   115, 230
    Bridgett   146
    Chilton   233
    Daniel   46, 233, 233
    Edward   233
    Elias 15, 127,139, 140,146, 233
    Elizabeth   110, 139
    Frances   97
    Henry   110
    Isabella   188
    James 15, 113,194, 233,237, 245
    John   115
    Joseph   46, 137
    Martha   137, 137, 237
    Mary   20
    Mary (Lane) Mountjoy   15, 245
    Morton   233
    Richard   233,245
    Sarah   245
    Sarah M.   46
    Shelton   233
    Susan(nah)   110, 155
    Thomas   233
    William   233

Win, Judith   53

Winder, Michael   27, 233

Windsor, Elizabeth   149

Win(g)field, Martha   203, 266

Win(n), Judith   53

Winstead, George   233
    George L.   48, 233
    Jane   68
    Jeremiah   234
    John H.   234
    Nancy   117
    Samuel   234
    Willia L.   119

Winston, Holland H.   234
    William   96

Withers, John   97, 132

Woffendale [Woffendall], Adam   89
                          198, 210
    Ann   210
    Elizabeth   89
    Francis   210
    James   234, 268
    Mary   198

Wood, Cornelius   106
    Elizabeth (Hoskins)   106, 107
    Henry   219
    John   234
    Mary Ann   208
    Thomas   208
    William   97, 174

Woodbridge, Elizabeth 107, 121, 126
             150, 202, 234, 234, 238, 239
    George   234, 234, 238
    John   202, 234
    Mary (Pincent)   234
    Paul   126, 202, 234, 234
    William   234, 234, 235

Woodcock, John Shearman   235
    William   235

Wooddy, Julia   173
    Martha A.R.   98

Wooddy, Robert   3, 65, 98, 235
 Robert C.C.   235

Woodford County, Kentucky   48

Woodford, Richmond County, Va. 155

Woodford, John   190

Woodlawn, King George Co., Va. 266

Woodward, Philemon   235

Woollard, Alice   108
 Ann   47
 Austin R.   235
 Catharine   67
 Caty   133
 Drucilla R.   37
 Eleanor   61
 Elizabeth   5, 40, 50, 190
 Elizabeth R.   40
 Hannah   138
 John   34, 47, 51, 61
  131, 175, 235, 237
 John Jr.   235
 John W. 5, 40, 43, 50, 67, 173
 Joseph Jr.   235
 Lemima   118
 Lemuel L.   37, 235
 Mary   40, 51, 118, 138
 Mary Ann   47, 61, 73, 188, 237
 Matilda   118
 Priscilla   105
 Richard   5, 40, 53, 206, 235
 Samuel   78, 190
 Sarah   237
 Thomas W.   235
 William J.   235
 Winnefred   173

Wormeley, Elizabeth   267
 Frances   267
 John   205, 267, 267

Worner, Robert   235

Wren, Nicholas   236

Wright, Alexander M. 145, 150, 236
 Edward   5

Eliza   202
Elizabeth   50
Elizabeth M.   92
Emily M.   145
Frances   15, 16, 140, 245
George M.   92, 202, 204
Hannah R.   225
Jane   30, 236
John 30, 100, 141,199, 236, 236
John M.   236
Mary   75
Mary A.F.   69
Mottrom   15, 245
Mottrom M.   236
Thomas   30, 236
William   236

Wroe,   see   Roe   and   Rowe
 Betsy   13
 Catherine   87
 Elizabeth (Pope)   166
 Jane   29,198
 John 39, 40, 100, 120, 236,236
 Nathaniel   236
 Peter   236
 Samuel   83, 95, 218, 236, 236
 Sary Rus   113
 Thomas   129
 Winney   38

Yager, James   237

Yarrington, Catherine E.   187
 Landon   187

Yates,   see   Yeates   and   Yeats
 Catherine   213, 228
 James   256
 Richard   200
 Robert   213
 Sarah   243
 William   46

Yearby, see Yerby
 Albert F.   238

Yeatman,   family   237-238
 Adeline   141
 Alice   208
 Elijah V.   73

Yeatman, Eliza A.   84
    Ellender T.   113
    Henry Austin   168, 237
    James   237, 237
    James E.   237
    John   26, 237, 237
    John Jr.   237, 237
    John H.   83
    Joseph   237, 237
    Levi   113, 237, 237
    Lucinda   83
    Lucy Robinson   149
    Martha H.   27
    Mary   237
    Mary Ann   237
    Mathew Jr.   237
    Matthew M.   22, 237
    Matthew V.   22, 238
    Polly   34
    R. W.   59
    Robert   20
    Samuel   208, 237
    Sarah   120
    Sibella   237
    Thomas   27, 193, 211, 237, 237
    William   157, 176, 237, 238

Yeates, Judith   86

Yeats, Elias   238
    Francis   238, 238
    William   238, 238

Yerby, Albert F.   238
    Ann B.   123
    Apphia F.   124
    Elizabeth Woodbridge   123
    George   234, 238, 239
    Jesse   238
    John   79, 123, 126, 238, 239
    John M.   167, 238
    Judith   124
    Lemuel   239
    Margaret F.   125
    Nancy   207
    Sally Meredith   78
    Thomas   78, 239, 239
    William G.   239

York County, Va.   31, 204, 267

York River, Virginia   161, 162

Yorktown, Virginia   161, 212

Yorkshire, England   13, 260

Young, Ann   15, 180, 245
    Martha E.   258
    Mary   198, 199
    Sarah   79
    William   15, 198, 239

Younger, Eleanor   111

Zuccarello, Joseph   239

Zwelling, David   207

COLOPHON

WITHOUT HESITANCY I admit this volume is not a scholarly publication; some may consider it a grand hodgepodge. In the first place, the title is not explicit. I have used the preposition "of" in the title because compilers of other like volumes have, but perhaps a more applicable appellation would be MARRIAGES IN RICHMOND COUNTY, VIRGINIA. But this title would also have been a bit deceptive as there are references to many marriages solemnized <u>ante</u> 1692 before Richmond County was formed. Many of these marriages took place within the territory which became Richmond County in 1692, while others were solemnized across the Rappahannock River in the area which became Essex County in 1692, and others elsewhere, but are reflected in the cited records. In order not to aggravate library cataloguers and indexers, as well as those who may wish to cite this volume as a reference, I have dispared of a long descriptive subtitle.

The inferred marriages, supplemental data, genealogical charts and comments may well have been omitted and by so doing a neater format produced. However, feeling this material may be of interest to some persons, I have included it.

The supplemental data is miserably unbalanced - much concerning some persons and families - nothing concerning others! This came about by my having at hand as this volumes was typed for lithoprinting, large files on some families and little or nothing on others. Some material at hand, concerning persons and families mentioned herein, has not been included for varying reasons and the twenty eight genealogical charts are but a sampling of the many in my files. Furthermore, while I dislike to be discouraging, it is an indisputable fact that many parties mentioned in this volume do not appear elsewhere in the Richmond County court records.

I trust the KEY TO ABBREVIATIONS OF TITLES AND SYMBOLS will not be confusing. Some do not follow the strictest editoral dictums, yet, for instance, to underline the names of authors of frequently cited and well-known printed reference books will, most often, immediately inform the reader of the cited source in a brief manner.

I feel this arrangement fully covers the marriage bonds and licenses av' l- able for Richmond County; the marriages recorded in the North Farnham Paris.. Register 1668-1800; the marriages pertaining to Richmond County persons in the marriage register kept by the Rev. Mr. William Forrester 1802-1842, and the marriages pertaining to Richmond County persons <u>ante</u> 1800 as noted in Lancaster County Marriage Register No.1. The present volume very inadequately covers the many inferred marriages in the various record books of Richmond County; this I have emphatically mentioned in the PREFACE. I never expect to see published a complete coverage of the inferred marriages in the Richmond County records. I hope to publish an arrangement of the North Farnham Parish Register 1668-1800 and the Lunenburg Parish Register 1790-1800 and this will greatly supplement the genealogical material in the present volume. When this is accomplished, it will be all the more evident that the original recordings abound with many inconsistences, errors and flagrant disregard to the manner many names are rendered.

Geo: H.H. King